SOVIET UNION

FODOR'S MODERN GUIDES

are compiled, researched and edited by an international team of travel writers,
field correspondents, and editors. The series, which now almost covers the globe,
was founded by Eugene Fodor.

OFFICES
New York & London

Editorial Staff for SOVIET UNION 1981

Area Editor: HILARY STERNBERG

Executive Editor: RICHARD MOORE

Editorial Contributors: JOHN FINCHLEY, LUCY HANNA, ANN HODGSON,
FRANCES HOWELL, XENIA NORALL, RICHARD PARIS, GEORGE
SCHÖPFLIN, HEDRICK SMITH, RICHARD TAYLOR, DAVID TENNANT,
GABRIELLE TOWNSEND, GRAHAM WEBB

Photographs: P. E. ROBINSON, THOMSON HOLIDAYS, DAVID TENNANT

Drawings: BRIAN DENYER

Maps: MAPS PRODUCTIONS, LTD. BRYAN WOODFIELD

FODOR'S®

SOVIET UNION 1981

FODOR'S MODERN GUIDES, INC.

Distributed by
DAVID McKAY COMPANY, INC.
New York

The following Fodor Travel Books (English language) are current.

CURRENT FODOR'S COUNTRY AND AREA TITLES:

AUSTRALIA, NEW ZEALAND
  AND SOUTH PACIFIC
AUSTRIA
BELGIUM AND
  LUXEMBOURG
BERMUDA
BRAZIL
CANADA
CARIBBEAN AND
  BAHAMAS
CENTRAL AMERICA
EASTERN EUROPE
EGYPT
EUROPE
FRANCE
GERMANY
GREAT BRITAIN
GREECE
HOLLAND

INDIA
IRELAND
ISRAEL
ITALY
JAPAN AND KOREA
JORDAN AND HOLY LAND
MEXICO
NORTH AFRICA
PEOPLE'S REPUBLIC
  OF CHINA
PORTUGAL
SCANDINAVIA
SOUTH AMERICA
SOUTHEAST ASIA
SOVIET UNION
SPAIN
SWITZERLAND
TURKEY
YUGOSLAVIA

CITY GUIDES:

LONDON   PARIS   ROME

FODOR'S BUDGET SERIES:

BUDGET EUROPE
BUDGET TRAVEL IN AMERICA
BUDGET CARIBBEAN
BUDGET BRITAIN
BUDGET FRANCE

BUDGET GERMANY
BUDGET ITALY
BUDGET MEXICO
BUDGET SPAIN
BUDGET JAPAN

USA GUIDES:

USA (in one volume)
CALIFORNIA
HAWAII
FAR WEST*
ALASKA*
SOUTHWEST*
SOUTH*

NEW YORK
NEW ENGLAND*
FLORIDA
MIDWEST*
OUTDOORS AMERICA*
SUNBELT LEISURE
  GUIDE*

SPECIAL INTEREST SERIES:

WORLDWIDE ADVENTURE GUIDE*   CIVIL WAR SITES*

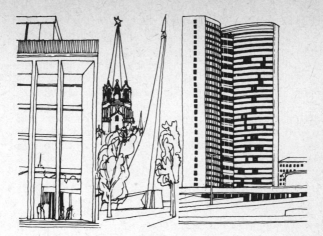

FOREWORD

As we go to press with this edition of our Guide to the Soviet Union, international confusion brought about by the 1980 Olympics is at its height. This situation has made it difficult for us to present information with any feeling of certainty. We trust that our readers—benefitting from knowledge which we, currently, cannot have—will understand our difficulties and forgive us if, from time to time, we make a point that has been rendered obsolete by subsequent events.

Most visitors to the USSR anticipate a trip for the very earnest reasons of political, social and cultural curiosity. Certainly no one goes to the Soviet Union to find the kind of relaxed fun that you would expect from a holiday in the West. Almost everyone is aware that a visit to Russia has little to do with creature comforts—sun, sand and *après ski,* or any of the other frivolous pursuits associated with having a good time. The reason for going is, pure and simple, curiosity—curiosity about a completely different way of life.

For this reason we have adopted a somewhat different format for this book from the others in our series. In order to satisfy the visitor's need for background information, we have given preponderant treatment to the political, social and cultural aspects of the Soviet Union, as well as covering many parts of the country that the normal tourist is not likely to see.

We believe that it is essential for those of us engaged in encouraging tourism to support all sincere attempts by People-to-People contact, no matter where or with whom, and specifically without regard to political differences between nations. We hope that the current tensions will lessen and conditions return in which such immediate contact can once more flourish.

We hope that our policy of editorial moderation, of refraining from emphatic critical commentary on economic or political matters, will not lead our readers to believe that we are glossing over the many undesirable practices and failings of the monopolistic organization that is in charge of receiving and caring for every visitor arriving in the country. The reception practices of Intourist can be rudimentary, unpolished and sometimes even hostile. Its clumsiness can leave a bad taste in your mouth and might even spoil your trip. Many Soviet officals with sufficient experience in international tourism are the first to admit that complaints about inept treatment are justified, and some of the best of them are trying very hard to improve and correct the situation. Indeed, the massive preparations for the Olympics included a program of training of guides and others who would deal directly with visitors, and this training has had very noticeable effects in the improvement of standards.

The complex world of the USSR is fascinating beyond belief: your encounters with individual Russians, Latvians, Mongolians or Georgians (to name but a few) can be a heartwarming experience; the Soviet social order, so different from ours, will provoke the imagination if you are politically aware; the fine arts, in the form of museums, theater, dance or music, will impress you by the sheer volume of participants. On a more mundane level, you may enjoy the skill of Soviet athletics, which has more than ten million registered active participant enthusiasts, and the excitement of the very best in competition. And, despite the frequent bad service in restaurants, you will probably enjoy the various regional food and drink specialties of the country.

Special advice for a special situation

You will find throughout this book the theme: "Visiting the Soviet Union is like nothing you've ever done before." Because this is so, we'd like to offer some special advice for visiting a very special country.

We're not trying to make the ordinary problems of logistics seem worse than they are, but our experience, and that of many other travelers, indicates that the following hints may help to prepare you for your adventure into another way of life:

1. The Soviet Union welcomes visitors, but isn't begging for them, and wants you to consider your trip as an educational experience, not just a holiday.

2. Go to the USSR on a group tour if you can possibly do so, especially if it's your first visit, or if you don't speak Russian. Group tourists get priority over individual tourists, even if the latter do pay more than the former.

3. Be careful not to break any laws, and if you're not sure, follow this rule: if you aren't certain something is allowed, it is safer to assume it is definitely forbidden. Sticking to your pre-arranged itinerary, not photographing any rail stations, installations, buildings, etc. which might be regarded as "sensitive", not selling your blue jeans, or not offering a dollar bill or pound note for a tip, all these are covered by some law or other and, for ignoring things like these, visitors have run into trouble and some have even been expelled from the country.

4. If you are traveling individually and expect to spend more than a day or two in the USSR, register with your embassy in Moscow, preferably in person, but at least by mail or telephone, giving your full name,

passport number, date and place of birth, occupation, hotel and room number, purpose and dates of visit, home address, and (if applicable) names and addresses of any relatives to be visited in the USSR.

5. Carry your passport with you at all times, even when going to pick up mail in your hotel. Keep it in a *safe place* on your person—not in hip pocket where it can easily be stolen. There is a black market in British and US passports, which change hands, if reports are to be believed, for very large sums.

6. Plan well ahead, meaning that *everything* you want to do in the Soviet Union, and especially all the cities you want to visit or special interests you want to pursue, is arranged before you leave your home for the airport.

A note on spelling and reading Russian

Although we have tried to be consistent about the spelling of Russian names in this book, we find the Soviet authorities themselves are not consistent about transliteration of the Cyrillic alphabet into our familiar Latin letters. In Moscow, for example, Intourist spells a street name "Chaikovsky", but in Leningrad it's "Tchaikovsky". We've tried to stick to internationally recognized British and U.S. systems of transliteration, but don't be surprised if you occasionally come across differences like Chekhov and Tchekov, Tolstoy and Tolstoi, Baykal and Baikal, Tartar and Tatar, rouble and ruble.

Hints on reading Russian signs and on pronunciation, as well as an English-Russian tourist vocabulary, can be found at the end of the book.

Reading street names is important, of course. To help you, a word or two about how they work in Russian. Many Russian streets and squares are named after *people,* but the people's names may appear in different spellings—often they are made into adjectives. Suppose we have a street called Pushkin street, after the poet. The word street, ULITSA in Russian, is feminine (all Russian nouns have a gender). So you will see the street name as *Pushkinskaya ulitsa,* a feminine form of Pushkin. Pushkin Avenue would be *Pushkinsky Prospekt* in Russian (the word for avenue is masculine). Pushkin Chaussée would be *Pushkinskoye Shosse* (Chaussée is neuter). Don't be worried if you see one of these signs when our guide tells you you are on *Pushkin* street, avenue, etc.—it's the same thing! Almost every Soviet town has its *Leninsky Prospekt*—Lenin Avenue. As a general rule, once you have deciphered the first few letters, you will recognize the name—forget about the ending!

Another common way of naming streets is to say, for example, "Street of Pushkin", "Avenue of Lenin" etc.— *Ulitsa Pushkina, Prospekt Lenina* and so on. Here again, the *name* is easy to spot—its ending is not a spelling mistake, just a genitive case form of Pushkin, Lenin, etcetera. If you do get lost, most passers-by will understand if you ask for a street by its English name.

For the Tables of the Russian alphabet, which appear at the end of the book, we owe a deep debt of gratitude to the *Government Affairs Institute,* Washington, D.C., for their permission to reproduce them. We think they are the most helpful guide to the Cyrillic alphabet we have seen.

We would like to thank our many friends who have helped in the preparation of this edition, but most especially Hilary Sternberg, for putting her knowledge and advice so generously at our disposal.

The reader will, we sincerely hope, be aware of the difficulties inherent in the collection and verification of material for such a book as this. We are always grateful for letters from our readers telling us of their experiences and bringing points to our notice from their own visits to countries covered by our Guides. This is especially true of the Soviet Union, where every visitor may have quite different and useful hints that can be passed on to other travelers.

Send your letters to one of the following addresses:

In the US: Fodor's Modern Guides, 2 Park Avenue, New York, NY 10016;

In Britain: Fodor's Modern Guides, 1–11 John Adam Street, London, WC2 England.

CONTENTS

CONTENTS

**FACTS
AT YOUR
FINGERTIPS**

FACTS AT YOUR FINGERTIPS

See also Practical Information in the Regional chapters

FACTS AT YOUR FINGERTIPS

 PLANNING YOUR TRIP. If you are thinking of going to the Soviet Union on the spur of the moment, our advice is: don't. Even if you could get a visa quickly, you might find that there is an All-Union Congress of Tractor Engineers in Moscow or a meeting of international agronomists in Leningrad and accommodations are impossible to obtain. Give yourself time for planning, consider your own likes and dislikes, your special hobbies and interests. In this vast country of which you will be able to explore only a small section, there is so much to see it is essential to make a choice and then make plans accordingly.

Are you allergic to cold? Stay out of the areas of frost and snow and go in summer. Does the heat bother you? Avoid July and August, when Moscow can sizzle like New York and be as humid as London. Above all remember that improvisation following sudden fancies and urges, is rarely possible in the USSR. The individual traveler isn't really welcome, only tolerated, and even if you want to travel only with your family or a small group, it is better to pick a tour that suits your purpose best. If you should decide that you would like to extend or vary it after arrival this is possible, though not without problems, and much pushing on your part.

 TOURS. These fall into two main categories: individual and group. There are also "special interest" tours, which we'll describe later.

For the individual tours, any *Intourist* itinerary can be chosen. According to the latest information at press time, the following places are open to tourists and have Intourist hotels and services available: Abakan, Alma-Ata, Ashkhabad, Baku, Batumi, Beltsi, Bratsk, Brest, Bukhara, Chernovtsy, Cherkassy, Dombaiskaya Polyana, Donetsk, Druskininkai, Dushanbe, Essentuki, Erevan, Fergana, Frunze, Gelendzhik, Gori, Irkutsk, Ivanovo, Kalinin, Kazbegi, Khabarovsk, Kharkov, Kherson, Kiev, Kislovodsk, Kishinev, Krasnodar, Kursk, Leningrad, Listvyanka, Lvov, Minsk, Moscow, Murmansk, Nalchik, Novgorod, Novosibirsk, Odessa, Ordzhonikidze, Orel, Pasanauri, Petrozavodsk, Pitsunda, Poltava, Prielbrusye, Pskov, Pyarnu, Pyatigorsk, Repino, Riga, Rostov-on-Don, Rovno, Samarkand, Simferopol, Smolensk, Sochi, Stavropol, Sukhumi, Suzdal, Tallinn, Tashkent, Tbilisi, Telavi, Ternopol, Tiraspol, Tskhaltubo, Ulyanovsk, Urgench, Uzhgorod, Viliandi, Vilnius, Vinnitsa, Volgograd, Yalta, Yaroslavl, Zaporozhye, Zheleznovodsk.

In addition, day sightseeings (no overnight stops) are available from: Baku to Kobystan, Shemakha, Sumgait; Batumi to Kobuleti, Kutaisi, Tsikhisdziri; Cherkassy to Kamenka, Korsun-Schevchenkovski; Donetsk to Slavianogorsk; Dushanbe to Nurek, Kurgan-Tube; Erevan to Dilizhan, Echmiadzin, Kirovakan, Tsakhkadzor; Ivanovo to Palekh; Kalinin to Klin; Kherson to Novaya Kakhovka; Kiev to Chernigov, Kanev; Kislovodsk to Teberda; Kishinev to Bendery; Krasnodar to Novorossiisk; Kursk to Zheleznogorsk; Leningrad to Pavlovsk, Petrodvorets, Pushkin; Moscow to Klin, Pereslavl-Zalesskii, Podolsk, Rostov, Vladimir; Odessa to Belgorod-Dnestrovski; Petrozavodsk to Kizhi; Pyatigorsk to Teberda; Riga to Sigulda, Yurmala; Rostov-on-Don to Azov, Novocherkassk, Taganrog; Samarkand to Pendzhikent; Simferopol to Bakhchisarai; Sochi to Gagra; Sukhumi to Gagra, Novy Afon; Suzdal to Vladimir; Tallinn to Paide, Tartu; Tashkent to Angren, Chirchik; Tbilisi to Bakuriani, Borzhomi, Kazbegi Mtskheta; Tskhaltubo to Kutaisi; Urgench to Khiva; Vilnius to Kaunas, Trakai; Yalta to Bakhchisarai; Yaroslavl to Pereslavl-Zalesskii, Rostov.

Note These lists are constantly being revised. Check with Intourist for the most recent, last-minute changes.

Tourist travel is normally limited to standard itineraries. All travel, hotel accommodations, meals, etc., should be arranged and paid for in advance. By working through Intourist or an accredited US or UK travel agent, "special interest" tours can sometimes be arranged encompassing visits to areas of professional interest to the traveler and appointments with Soviet specialists in the traveler's field. However, some travelers recently have expressed dissatisfaction with Intourist arrangements, noting especially the difficulty in obtaining refunds for travel and services which they paid for in advance but never received. There is substantial evidence that Intourist has in the past been offering travel and hotel facilities, particularly in the higher priced range, to more travelers than it has the capacity to accommodate. Because arrangements between traveler and Intourist are based on private contract, the traveler who is dissatisfied with services provided or seeks refund for unused travel coupons must make a claim to Intourist or through his travel agent as provided for in the contract. If the claim for refund cannot be resolved directly the traveler may institute legal action in the city or state where the contract was entered into. Intourist regulations permit refunds for full unused days of Intourist services only if the traveler obtains a certificate *(spravka)* from Intourist while in the USSR stating that the services were not used. See below under Currency Regulations for the use of charge cards.

There are **three classes** of tourist accommodation: (Prices are given in roubles; during 1980 the exchange rate was 64.35 roubles to US $100. This rate is fixed by the Soviet government and is subject to change without notice)

Deluxe Class. Accommodations in hotel rooms with private baths, superior category (3-, 4-, or 5-room suites are also available from 126 roubles per person per day in Moscow/Leningrad, 86–107 roubles elsewhere, depending on season). Breakfast included. Three-hour excursions per day by car with chauffeur, the services of a guide-interpreter for three hours per day (six hours if deluxe suite class), all transfers upon arrival and departure to include two pieces of hand luggage at each stop. (If deluxe rooms are not available, first-class accommodations will be offered.) The price *per person* per day is approx. 64 roubles single, 33 roubles double in Moscow and Leningrad, 44–54 roubles single, 22–28 roubles double elsewhere, depending on season. Lunch and dinner are available at about 6 roubles extra per person.

First Class. Available in most Intourist itineraries. The rooms have baths or showers, breakfast with a first-class menu, one guided 3-hour excursion by car or bus in each city, transfers as in deluxe class. Lunch and dinner available at about 4 roubles extra per day per person. The prices *per person,* 36 roubles single, 20 roubles double in Moscow and Leningrad, more in top hotels; elsewhere 24–30 roubles single and 14–17 roubles double according to season.

Tourist Class. This is limited to certain cities; check with Intourist agent when booking. It is usually not available in Moscow, Leningrad and Kiev from April to September. Accommodations: hotel room with wash basin, with bath or shower available on same floor. Breakfast with first-class menu, one 3-hour guided excursion by car or bus in each city, transfers as in deluxe class. Lunch and dinner are available at about 4 roubles extra per day per person. Price *per person,* 24 roubles single, 14 roubles double in Moscow/Leningrad, elsewhere 16–20 roubles single and 10–12 roubles double according to season.

The **off season** lasts from January 1 through March 31 and from October 1 through December 31, **ordinary season:** April through September except in Moscow and Leningrad where high season special rates apply all year round. The high season in Caucasus and Black Sea coastal resorts is from June 1 through September 30; in mountain resorts from June 1 through October 20 and January 15 through March 31 (skiing).

Cars and guides are usually available only from 9 A.M. to 6 P.M.; they must be ordered one day in advance. Entrance fees to museums, etc. are included in the cost of the tour. Twin-bedded rooms are available only for double reservations. Check-out time is noon.

Group Tours have fixed starting dates but it is possible to join a group upon arrival in Moscow; Intourist then organizes the groups. Accommodations are available only in the first-class category; they include hotel room with bath or shower, full board (three meals a day), excursions by bus, entrance fees, transfers upon arrival and departure, transportation while within the USSR and porterage for two pieces of hand luggage. The cost is dependent upon the itinerary chosen.

Group tours are offered by American and British travel agents by arrangement with Intourist. Some 250 different tours, each with a number of departure dates, are available, and you can combine the USSR with other countries if you want to. Cost naturally depends on type of accommodations, length of stay, method of transportation and the itinerary.

The group tours usually comprise 20 to 25 people. Fixed-date tours are offered to tourists who speak English, French or Italian. From October 1 through April 30, package services are available at a 15–25% discount, depending on the class of the service.

For somewhat cheaper group tours for students, see below under Special Interest Travel.

 SPECIAL INTEREST TRAVEL. Intourist and its associates cater for special interest groups and link their tours to the seasonal events. For the *Moscow Stars Theater Festival* (12 days, from about May 4), a tour is arranged which spends the first 7 days in Moscow, then moves to Leningrad for 4 days. There are sightseeing tours with optional excursions and (for extra payment) 6 visits to theaters, including transport. Return to London is on the 12th day.

The *White Nights Festival* (leaving mid-June) also takes in both Moscow and Leningrad. On your outward trip the first stop is Moscow, where you spend 2 nights (with a day's sightseeing and an optional theater visit). On the morning of the 3rd day you fly to Leningrad. The 3rd to the 11th days are spent in Leningrad for the White Nights Festival, including sightseeing tours, optional excursions and theater visits. You return to Moscow at midnight on the 11th day by sleeper train, where you spend the last 3 days of your holiday. Again there are sightseeing tours and optional theater visits. You return home on the 15th day.

The *Song Festival Tour* to Riga usually departs around July 18, in time for the festival, which is held between July 20 and 24.

The *Golden Autumn Festival* is held at Sochi between September 6 and 20 and *The Georgian Arts Festival* at Tbilisi between September 21 and 26. Of course, it is possible to visit both on one trip.

The *Ukrainian Arts Festival* is at Kiev, between October 1 and 10.

The *Russian Winter Festival* in Moscow lasts from December 25 to January 5. *(All the above tours leave from Britain.)*

Although most Western travel to the USSR is handled by Intourist, youth and student travel is arranged by *Sputnik,* which offers group tours for students through the Scandinavian Student Travel Service. In the US, write to the *Council on International Educational Exchange,* 205 E. 42 St., New York, N.Y. 10017; in Canada apply through the *Association of Student Councils,* 44 St. George St., Toronto, Ontario. Ask for the booklet entitled, *SSTS Student Tours to the USSR.* Although Sputnik's tours are cheaper, the number of itineraries available is much more limited than those available through Intourist. Sputnik's address is, International Youth Tourist Bureau, Lebiazhy 4, Moscow G 19. Independent study in the USSR can be arranged through the *International Research and Exchanges Board,* 655 Third Ave., New York, N.Y. 10017. For summer programs only, see *Summer Study Abroad,* published by the Institute of International Education, address below.

There are special services available for *business travel* to representatives of industrial, commercial, financial and other organizations who want to visit Soviet cities for business negotiations with corresponding Soviet organizations or to participate in trade fairs and exhibitions.

 HOW TO GO. It obviously depends on the length of your vacation and your special inclinations whether you will fly, take a train from some point in Europe or a ship from one of the ports with a regular service to the Soviet Union. You may wish to take your own car or travel by bus from an adjoining country. It will also depend on the season; motoring in the dead of winter or during the heavy autumn rains may not be very pleasant. Considering the vastness of the country, you may want to travel by air from one place to another.

Travel agents. Travel agents are experts in the increasingly complicated business of tourism. They have contacts with carriers and tourist offices all over the world; they know about sudden changes in schedules and fares, they keep a check on cancellations at times of the year when planes and ships are booked to capacity, and their racks and files are bulging with information on the latest tour and excursion possibilities. A good travel agent can save you time and money through his knowledge of details which you could not be expected to know about. In the all-important phase of planning your trip, even if you wish to travel independently, it is wise to take advantage of the services of these specialists.

As we have indicated, except for Sputnik (the travel bureau which organizes youth travel on an exchange basis) and the trade unions (reciprocal tours for union functionaries only), *Intourist* is the only organization that deals with tourists inside the Soviet Union; and all arrangements made outside the USSR must eventually go through Intourist anyway. Since Intourist has only one office in each Western country, there are fortunately a number of regular agencies that have experience in dealing with Intourist and advising on travel in the USSR, and we have listed some of them below.

Whether you select *American Express, Thomas Cook, Maupintour,* or a smaller organization, is a matter of preference. They all have branch offices or correspondents in Moscow. But there are good reasons why you should engage a reliable agent.

If you wish him merely to arrange a steamship or airline ticket or to book you on a package tour, his services should cost you nothing. Most carriers and tour operators grant him a fixed commission for saving them the expense of having to open individual offices in every town and city.

If, on the other hand, you wish him to plan for you an individual itinerary and make all arrangements down to hotel reservations and transfers to and from rail and air terminals, you are drawing upon his skill and knowledge of travel as well as asking him to shoulder a great mass of details. His commissions from carriers

(5% to 7½%) won't come close to covering his expenses. Accordingly he will make a service charge on top of the actual cost of your trip. The amount of this charge varies with the agent, the complexity of your tour, the number of changes you have made in your itinerary, etc.

If you cannot locate a travel agent near your home, write, if in America, to the *American Society of Travel Agents,* 711 Fifth Ave., New York, N.Y. 10022; or ASTA Canada, 130 Albert St., Suite 1207, Ottawa, Ont. In Britain, to the *Association of British Travel Agents,* 50–57 Newman St., London W1P 4AH. Any agency affiliated with these organizations is almost sure to be thoroughly reliable.

The following are the offices of Intourist in the USA, Britain and some main European countries:

U.S.A.: Suite 868, 630 Fifth Avenue, New York, N.Y. 10020.

Britain: 292 Regent Street, London W.1.

West Germany: 1 Berlin 15, Olivaez Platz 8.

Sweden: Sergelgaten 21, Stockholm.

Austria: Schwedenplatz 3–4, 1010 Vienna.

France: 7 Boulevard des Capucines, Paris 2e.

Denmark: Vester Farimagsgade 6, 1606 Copenhagen V.

Offices also in: Amsterdam, Brussels, Frankfurt, Helsinki, Mexico City, Montreal, Oslo, Rome, Tokyo, Zurich, all Eastern European capitals, Delhi, Beirut, Cairo, and Kabul.

Soviet Embassies, consulates and trade delegations will also provide travel information, but they are not noted for their helpfulness.

There are about 50 travel agencies in the United States linked with Intourist; more than a dozen in Britain.

SOME U.S. AGENTS PROMOTING TRAVEL TO THE USSR

Afton Tours, Inc., 1776 Broadway, New York, N.Y. 10019.

Allied Travel, Inc., 530 Fifth Avenue, New York, N.Y. 10036.

American Express Co., American Express Plaza, New York, N.Y. 10004 and all branch offices).

American Travel Abroad, Inc., 250 West 57th Street, New York, N.Y. 10019.

Anniversary Tours, Inc., 250 W.57 St., Suite 1428, New York, N.Y. 10019.

Bennett Tours, Inc., 270 Madison Avenue, New York, N.Y. 10016 (and branch offices in San Francisco and Chicago).

Cartan Travel Bureau, Inc., One Crossroads of Commerce, Rolling Meadows, Illinois 60008.

Thos. Cook & Son, Inc., 587 Fifth Avenue, New York, N.Y. 10017 (and all branch offices).

Cosmos Travel, Inc., 488 Madison Avenue, New York, N.Y. 10022.

Eurotop Tours, Inc., 50 Clinton St., Hempstead, N.Y. 11550.

Extra Value Travel, 5 World Trade Center, New York, N.Y. 10048.

Four Winds Travel, 175 Fifth Avenue, New York, N.Y. 10010.

Garber Travel Service, Inc., 1406 Beacon Street, Brookline, Mass. 02146.

General Tours, Inc., 2 West 45 Street, New York, N.Y. 10036.

Globus Gateway, 105–14 Gerrard Place, Forest Hills, N.Y. 11375.

Gordon Travel Service, Inc., Prudential Plaza, Chicago, Illinois 60601.

Harvard Travel Service, Inc., 1356 Massachusetts Ave., Cambridge, Mass. 01238.

Hemphill Harris Travel Corp., 10100 Santa Monica Blvd., Suite 2060, Los Angeles, Calif. 90067.

Lindblad Travel, Inc., 133 East 55th Street, New York, N.Y. 10022.

Maupintour, Inc., 900 Massachusetts Street, Lawrence, Kansas 66044; 408 E 50 St., New York, N.Y. 10021.

Music City Tours, 1501 North Vine St., Hollywood, Calif. 90028.

One World Travel Service, 447 Sutter St., Rm. 707, San Francisco, California 94108.

Citizen Exchange Corps, a New York-based cultural exchange firm, is offering a tour through the USSR via the 6000-mile Trans Siberian Railway. Leaving New York on Finnair, the 23-day trip includes Moscow, Leningrad, Novosibirsk, Irkutsk, Khabarovsk and Lake Baikal. Return from Khabarovsk will be by air to Leningrad, then via Helsinki to New York. Price includes transportation, first-class hotel accommodation, sleeper berth, meals, tips and sightseeing. Contact: Citizen Exchange Corps, 18 E.41st St., New York, N.Y. 10017, tel. 212/889-7960.

Orbis Polish Travel, 500 Fifth Avenue, New York, N.Y. 10036.

Percival Tours, Inc., 5820 Wilshire Blvd., Los Angeles, Calif. 90036; 48 E 43 St., New York, N.Y. 10017; other regional offices.

Russian Travel Bureau, Inc., 20 East 46th Street, New York, N.Y. 10017.

Travcoa Travel Corp., 875 North Michigan Avenue, Chicago, Ill. 60611.

Travel-Go-Round, 516 Fifth Ave., New York, N.Y. 10036.

University Travel Co., 44 Brattle Street, Cambridge, Mass. 02138.

MAJOR UK TOUR OPERATORS

American Express Co., Inc., 6 Haymarket, London, S.W.1.

Thos. Cook & Son Ltd., 45 Berkeley Street, London, W.1.

Intourist Moscow Ltd., 292 Regent St., London W.1.

Rankin Kuhn & Co. Ltd., 19 Queen Anne St., London, W.1.

Sovereign Holidays (British Airways), PO Box 410, West London Air Terminal, Cromwell Road, London, S.W.7.

W. F. & R. K. Swan (Hellenic) Ltd., 237 Tottenham Court Road, London, W.1.

Thomson Holidays, Greater London House, Hampstead Road, London, N.W.1.

SOME CANADIAN TOUR OPERATORS

Thos. Cook and Son, 344 Seventh Avenue, S.W., Calgary, Alberta.

World Tours Ltd., 425 Howe Street, Suite 12, Vancouver, B.C. V6C2A9.

Globe Tours, 615 Selkirk Avenue, Winnipeg, Manitoba, R2W2N2.

Voyages Claude Michel, Inc., 2 Place Quebec, Quebec 4, Quebec, G1R2B5.

Samples of tours from the USA include;

Russian Travel Bureau's 8-, 10-, 15-, or 22-day guided tours have year round departures from New York or Washington. Charter flights are available; regular flights offer stopovers. Prices from $689 up to $1549, first-class, or deluxe.

General Tours offers a variety of 9-, 14-, and 21-day packages taking in all the major cities of Russia itself, plus the Ukraine, Central Asia, Scandinavia, Siberia, Mongolia, and Eastern Europe. Rates anywhere from $1000 to $2600, fully escorted, via Pan Am, Aeroflot, SAS and JAT. General Tours also arrange independent tours in the Soviet Union; land arrangements for 16 days, first class, from about $350, plus transportation. A 9-day package to Moscow and Leningrad (with side trips to Vladimir and Suzdal) costs from $969 to $1,122.

Russian Travel Bureau offers a 10-day tour of Russia for from $850 to $930; a 15-day tour of Moscow, Leningrad, Kiev, and Odessa for about $1230; and a

22-day tour that takes in Siberia and Central Asia for about $1610. Air fare included in all of these.

Pan American's "Spotlight on Russia" tour: 16-day tour (plus extra day off-season) New York-Moscow-Kiev-Yalta-Leningrad-Moscow-New York. First-class hotels, all meals (including four at famous restaurants), three theater performances, sightseeing, all transportation, farewell dinner. $760. (Pan Am also has 8-day tours, theater tours, etc.)

Anniversary Tours offers 15-days in Russia, the Ukraine and the Black Sea for about $1100; 22 days in Russia, Siberia, and Central Asia for about $1600; 22 days in Russia, and Siberia for about $1600.

American Travel Abroad offers 8-, 10-, and 15-day escorted tours to Moscow, Leningrad, the Ukraine, and Poland. Including air fare, costs are from $975 to $1495.

Travel Go Round has one-week and two-week trips to Moscow, Leningrad, Kiev and Odessa, with side trips. Low price range is about $695 to $945; high range is $945 to $1197.

Air France have deluxe 15-day programs of escorted tours through Russia in high style; including Vienna, the trip will cost from $1,186.

Bergen Line, 505 Fifth Avenue, New York, also run a fly/cruise scheme: by air to Helsinki, then a 4-day cruise to Leningrad and back (no Soviet visa necessary); May through September. Sightseeing and entertainment on shore included. Also 2-day cruises Helsinki-Tallinn. Fares, excluding air fare from U.S.A.: Leningrad cruise from $155; Tallinn cruise from $66.

From U.K.:

Swan's Art Treasures Tours, excellent operators of art-oriented tours, guided by expert guest lecturers, have a 15-day Moscow-Leningrad trip for £576. Even more interesting is their 17-day (£650) tour of Central Asia and Transcausasia.

Intourist to Baltic: London-Moscow-Vilnius-Riga-Tallinn-Leningrad-London. 15-day escorted tour, all travel by air. All rooms with private bath or shower. All meals included. Cost: from £290. Intourist departure also from Manchester.

Sovereign's "Golden Road to Samarkand" is a 14-night escorted tour which takes in Moscow, Leningrad, Kiev, Tashkent and Samarkand for from £450.

Thomson Holidays have several trips lasting 3, 4 or 7 nights. They have special Moscow and Leningrad 2-center holidays from £197. They have a tour of Siberia and Outer Mongolia, 7 nights from around £350; x nights in Central Asia for around £350; and 14 nights in the Black Sea area for around £260. Thomson experts in the field, arrange about 70% of UK/USSR package tours, all of which are excellent value for money. They also have a 7-nights Moscow and Baltic package.

The head-office of *Intourist* in Moscow is at 16 Prospekt Marxa. For general enquiries and help in contacting other tourists, call 203-69-62. The American Department's telephone number is 292-86-70; the British Department's 292-26-97. The Excursion Department (MEO) has offices in the following Moscow hotels:

Bucharest: tel. 232-00-29, ext. 149.

National: tel. 229-62-24.

Rossiya: tel. 298-54-37 and 298-55-33.

Ukraine: 243-26-90.

Metropole (Excursion Hall): 225-69-70/71/72.

ROUGHING IT. There *are* ways to travel cheaply in the Soviet Union, but you are still subject to Intourist arrangements. Hitch-hiking is practically impossible. There are not enough cars on the roads and long-distance trucks are strictly forbidden to pick anybody up. Nor will you find the native motorist inclined to do so (except for unofficial local taxi services).

Camping, however, has a fairly long tradition, and because of the growing interest in it, Intourist has expanded its facilities for foreign campers. But the number of camping sites is still rather limited (24 as of mid-1980) and special arrangements must be made for each group (more difficult for individual campers to do). You have to follow a pre-fixed itinerary, day by day. Intourist will supply latest information on itineraries and campsites.

One British organization which arranges camping tours by minibus is *Jet-Trek,* 25 Battersea Bridge Road, London SW11, tel. (01)-223-2244. Another is *Contiki Travel Limited,* 7 Rathbone Place, London W1, tel. (01)-637-2121, whose tours run from 4 to 11 weeks. Intourist itself also offers low-cost camping tours for motorists who travel by bus or private car, *on the Intourist motor trip routes.* It is *not* advisable to wander off these routes, which are discussed in the section on travelling by car within the USSR.

All campsites are pleasantly located in green belt areas near main cities. They open on June 1, except the Butovo (Moscow) site which opens July 1. Most close on October 1, some in mid-September. Butovo closes on September 1.

They offer three kinds of services: (1) a parking site only; (2) a parking site and bed; and (3) a parking site and bungalow, costing 3.50, 4.50 and 6.00 roubles per person per day respectively (prices at presstime). These rates include (according to Intourist) the rental of bedding, kitchen utensils, tableware, use of electricity, showers, laundry, cooking facilities, etc., plus one sightseeing tour in each city on the tourist's itinerary, either in the tourist's own car (a guide joins you) or by Intourist bus. But take whatever basics you can with you, just in case.

While there are food shops in or near the camping areas, you are advised to bring as much food as you can carry with you—coffee and packet soups are two items practically unobtainable. Detergents are also useful.

 WHEN TO GO. In a country as vast as the Soviet Union, it is possible to enjoy a holiday at almost any time of the year. Some experts consider August and September the best months. This is the high season, so you must reserve well ahead to avoid disappointment. In the central part of the Soviet Union, June and July are fairly hot and on the Black Sea coast it is even hotter. But on the Black Sea May is a particularly attractive month and you can bathe from the beginning of that month through October. If you choose June or July, pick the Baltic countries and Leningrad, which will be just pleasantly warm. Central Asia is best visited in March-April or September-October as you will find the climate in summer almost tropical yet dry and dusty.

Winter in Moscow can be fierce in January and early February but the rest of the year is tolerable. There is, of course, plenty of snow and in the dry cold the city looks very attractive under its white cover. Some people find the cold most exhilarating, and Russian interiors are always well-heated.

Here are the average temperature ranges of the five main tourist centers (lowest monthly *average* and highest *average*):

Leningrad: 18.5°F. to 63.5°F. (−7.7°C. to 17.5°C.).
Moscow: 12.6°F. to 65.3°F. (−10.8°C. to 18.5°C.).
Odessa: 25.7°F. to 71.6°F. (−3.7°C. to 22.1°C.).
Sochi: 60.0°F. to 73.4°F. (16.0°C. to 23.0°C.).
Yalta: 38.3°F. to 75.2°F. (3.7°C. to 24.2°C.).

In the off season, October through April, deluxe tours are 15% less expensive and the first- and tourist-class tours 25% less, outside Moscow and Leningrad. This is the best time to see the country and have the pick of the full theater and concert season. You can enjoy skiing, skating, troika rides and tobogganing in these months. You'll also sample the best cooking: the hearty winter dishes that Russia is famous for are in season then. In summer, light clothing will be sufficient, but you should take at least one warm suit or pullover. A raincoat and rubber overshoes or boots will also be useful. Evening dress or formal clothes are not necessary for the theaters or restaurants. Do not wear shorts or beach wraps in towns—you may not be allowed into museums or cafés. Women in trousers now accepted.

 SEASONAL EVENTS. These include the May Day celebrations, the anniversary of VE Day (May 9) and the military parades of the Great October Revolution (actually commemorated on November 7 each year). The parades are followed by mass pageants and sports displays in Moscow's Red Square and the centers of other large cities.

The Russian Winter Festival lasts 12 days from December 25 to January 5. Carnivals take place in the immense Luzhniki Stadium in Moscow and elsewhere there are circuses and special theatrical performances. The Russian New Year is usually celebrated in restaurants and cafés.

There are the Festival of Moscow Stars (May 5–13), the Leningrad White Nights (June 21–29), various art festivals and the Riga Song Festival (August 1–9), all of which offer a rich fare of ballet, opera and drama. The Moscow International Film Festival is held every odd-numbered year in July, with entries from all over the world.

Sporting highlights include national and international ice-hockey and soccer (football) matches, skating and skiing championships, athletic meets, boxing competitions and many other events.

The November 7 celebrations are particularly brilliant in Moscow, with the whole city decked out in bunting, gaily-colored streamers and flags. The Soviet leaders take the salute on top of the Lenin Mausoleum while the long military parade rolls past to the strains of a large brass band. (The exact position of the leaders is supposed to be an indication of their actual standing in the hierarchy of the Party.) Then follows a spectacular gymnastic display after which folklore groups from all over the country perform. The march-past of workers, many carrying their children on their shoulders, can last three or four hours. In the evening, the buildings are illuminated, fireworks light up the sky, and there is dancing and entertainment in the central squares and streets (which are closed to traffic). In Leningrad, the Soviet Baltic Fleet sails up the Neva and drops anchor opposite the Winter Palace. Illuminated at night, the warships draw great crowds to the embankments.

In Moscow, Leningrad, Kiev and other towns the theatrical season usually starts in October.

 MEDICAL SERVICES. It is also possible to visit the Soviet Union for whatever ails you. There are two types of facilities: *complete* and *out-patient.* The first is for *resident patients* and is available at the health resorts of Sochi, Tskhaltubo, Kislovodsk, Essentuki, Pyatigorsk and Zheleznovodsk (all in the Caucasus); and Repino (near Leningrad). In these places the off season runs from January 1 through May 31 and November 1 through December 31, the ordinary season from June 1 through October 31. The rates (available from Intourist offices) cover full medical treatment for 24 days in Kislovodsk, Sochi, Essentuki, Pyatigorsk, Repino and Zheleznovodsk and for 20 days in Tskhaltubo. The classes of services range from deluxe to first class and tourist. The cost includes accommodations at a sanatorium for the duration of the treatment, medical treatment under a doctor's care, medical examinations and analyses, X-rays and therapy, transfer for therapy and other treatments, services of an interpreter-guide during examinations and treatments, all meals (as prescribed by the dietician), transfers upon arrival and departure (except in certain cities), and porterage.

Out-patient medical treatment is available in Sochi and Pyatigorsk, where first- and tourist-class services are available. The cost is about 16–26 roubles daily in ordinary season, 12–21 off season; the fee covers doctor's care, medical examinations, laboratory analyses, X-rays and therapy, transfers to the medical center and the services of an interpreter during examinations and treatments. This is available during the off season and the ordinary season. The rates also cover hotel accommodations, three meals daily within the first-class price limit, and transportation on arrival and departure.

Tourists coming to the Soviet Union for medical treatment should bring an up-to-date medical history from their physicians. In some cases, these may be obtained after a thorough examination in the Soviet Union at an authorized clinic for an an additional fee of 50 roubles per person. Medical treatment is not usually available to children. Unused days of the treatment are not refundable. Sightseeing, excursions and any extra services can be purchased through Intourist offices.

SPORTS. Mountain climbing and skiing facilities are available in the Elbrus and Dombai areas of the Caucasus at the Hotel Itkol and Hotel Dombai respectively (skiing only at Dombai). (Only tourist-class accommodations can be reserved.) The rates are, generally speaking, the same as at the vacation resorts. The *skiing* season is January to March, *climbing,* June to August. The off season is April 1 to May 31 and November 1 to December 31, and the ordinary season is January 1 to March 31 and June 1 to October 31.

Horse-riding classes are available through Intourist at Pyatigorsk for individuals and groups. Pack your own clothes.

Hunting and fishing vacations are offered in the Northern Caucasus at the Krasny Les and Krasnaya Polyana hunting preserves, which are, respectively, 50 and 70 km. from Krasnodar. You can hunt deer, bear and boar here and also at the North Ossetian hunting preserve in the Caucasus, about 20 to 45 km. from Ordzhonikidze. Here the hunting is for deer, roe-deer, aurochs (ibex), chamois, boar and bear; trout fishing is also available. At the Rostov hunting and fishing preserve, 125 km. from Rostov-on-Don, game bird shooting and freshwater fishing are offered. In Siberia, there is the Baikal hunting preserve, about 150 km. from Irkutsk, where you can hunt for Manchurian deer and bear. Finally, in Azerbaijan, at the Kubinsk hunting preserve (260 km. from Baku), the Caucasian aurochs (ibex) is hunted.

Extra services are provided: transfers by car to and from the hunting areas (the cost depending on the distance); transportation within the preserve either by car or by horse at a daily rate; services of a huntsman or huntsmen, depending on the type of game; rental of a hunting rifle (with units of ten cartridges); accommodations in hunting lodges or tents (if hotel accommodations have not been reserved in advance) with full board.

You can bring your own hunting gun into the Soviet Union, provided that you carry a voucher issued by an Intourist office or an accredited travel agent to the effect that you intend to hunt on Soviet territory. All sporting rifles must be presented for customs inspection and the serial numbers declared in the customs form. Sporting rifles brought into the USSR must be taken out when the hunter leaves the country.

STUDYING IN THE USSR. Scholarships can be arranged (though the procedure is usually long and complicated) through the various friendship societies and cultural exchange organizations in your own country, such as, in Britain: *The British Council,* Davies Street, London W1; *The British Soviet Friendship Society,* 36 St. John's Square, London EC1; *The Great-Britain-*

USSR Association, 14 Grosvernor Place, London SW1; *Russo-British Chamber of Commerce,* 2 Lowndes Street, London SW1.

Similar organizations are active throughout the United States and Canada.

The Institute of International Education (IIE) and the *Council on International Educational Exchange* (CIEE) have information on scholarships and study in the Soviet Union.

IIE deals only with graduate study abroad. They maintain an extensive library of foreign college catalogues and related reference material at their office at 809 United Nations Plaza, New York, N.Y. 10017. The IIE also has regional offices in Chicago, Denver, Atlanta, Houston, Washington D.C., Los Angeles and San Francisco.

The CIEE (205 East 42 St., New York, N.Y. 10017) arranges college-level studies and scholarships at Leningrad State University.

The International Research and Exchange Board arranges Doctoral scholarships to the Soviet Union but also has information on undergraduate scholarships and study. They are at 655 Third Ave., New York, N.Y. 10017.

The *American Association for the Advancement of Slavic Studies,* 190 West 19th Avenue, Ohio State University, Columbus, Ohio 43210, is the central source of information on study about or in the Soviet Union, and publishes two complete directories of resources and programs in this field.

From the U.S.A. the *Citizen Exchange Corps* offer visits combining tourism with meeting Soviet people and attending lectures and seminars by Soviet experts. They also handle special-interest groups, reciprocal cultural exchanges (art exhibitions, music tours, etc.). Their address is Citizen Exchange Corps, 18 East 41 St., New York, N.Y. 10017. Tel: (212) 889-7960.

In the Soviet Union, the headquarters of these societies is at 14 Pr. Kalinina, Moscow; the Western Europe department can be reached here as can the Institute of Soviet-American Relations, housed in the same building.

Other important addresses (all in Moscow) for would-be students are:

USSR Academy of Sciences, 14 Leninsky Prospekt.

Moscow State University, Leninsky Gory.

Moscow State University, 18 Prospekt Marxa.

Lumumba Friendship University, 7, 5th Donskoy Proyezd.

Moscow Tchaikovsky Conservatory, 13 Ul. Gertsena.

All-Union Cinematography Institute, 3rd Selskokhozyaistvennaya 3.

Maurice Thorez Foreign Languages Pedagogical Institute, 38 Metrostroyevskaya Ul.

The *Bolshoi* and its attached ballet school are on the Ploshchad Sverdlova.

Russian-language seminars are available for independent and group tours. Intourist, in cooperation with the Ministry of Education, organizes these seminars every year for foreigners who wish to study Russian. All arrangements must be made through travel agents. Your college or university will advise you; or contact the *Association of Teachers of Russian* (ATR) in Britain. *Progressive Tours Ltd.* at 12 Porchester Place, Marble Arch, London W2, (tel. (01) 262 1676) have Easter, summer and autumn courses in Leningrad, Kiev, Moscow, Krasnodar and Yalta. The cost includes accommodations in two- or four-bedded rooms, full board, tuition, transportation, and transfer on arrival and departure. There is a registration fee.

 SOVIET CITIZENSHIP. Foreign governments cannot determine whether a naturalized American or British citizen or resident alien who was once a resident of Imperial Russia, the Soviet Union, or territory now under Soviet control may be considered by the Soviet Government to be a citizen of the USSR. The possibility cannot be excluded that such a person may be detained in the Soviet Union on the claim that he is also a Soviet citizen. Naturalized citizens or resident aliens who may be regarded by the Soviet Government as still possessing Soviet citizenship can clarify their status before leaving the US or UK by renouncing Soviet citizenship through expatriation application to the USSR Embassy in Washington or London.

A decision as to whether a former resident of the USSR or territories now under Soviet administration should travel there can only be made by the individual himself in the light of his background and all other pertinent factors. Former Soviet citizens with a record of what Soviet authorities construed as "anti-Soviet activity" on USSR territory have on occasion been harassed or expelled, or imprisoned.

VISITING RELATIVES IN THE USSR. Requires *Visitor's Visa*, which can take up to 6 months to obtain. It costs nothing if you do it yourself. You must also obtain a letter of invitation from your Russian relatives. You may spend as little or as much money as you like; there is no set amount.

In order to avoid delay or refusal of a visitor's visa, tourists have sometimes taken an Intourist tour to the USSR and arranged on their own to meet relatives at a Soviet city near the place where the relative resides. This has not always worked out, for the Soviet authorities have sometimes prevented the Soviet citizens from traveling to meet their relatives. In such cases Intourist assumes no responsibility for any failure to meet relatives. The traveler hoping to visit relatives should mention them in his visa application.

Occasionally, some tourists visiting relatives in the USSR have been subjected to harassment by local officials or over-zealous Party agitators. This harassment, which at times was directed against the Soviet relatives themselves, has included press articles attacking the visitor.

 CRUISES on the Black Sea and the Baltic are available in Soviet and foreign ships, calling at Batumi, Odessa, Leningrad, Sochi, Sukhumi, Yalta, Riga, Tallinn and other ports. A 15-day Black Sea cruise has stops of one to three days at the major ports. The cost depends on the class of travel; there are single and double cabins with or without private showers and cabins for four to six passengers. River trips in Soviet ships down the Danube start in May and end in October. Sailings are from Vienna, stopping at Bratislava, Budapest, Belgrade, Turnu-Severin, Lom-Ruse-Djurdjñ, Galaz and Ismail. At the last port, tourists change to a sea-going motorship for Yalta, where a day is spent sightseeing and bathing. You can return by the same route or by air via Kiev and Moscow. In addition, 11-day cruises on the Volga and 10-day cruises on the Dnieper rivers are available in both directions from early summer to early fall.

> **Note:** the following costs are correct for 1980 as we go to press. For latest prices check with your travel agent while planning your trip.

 WHAT WILL IT COST? We have already given some figures for the various types of accommodations and travel available; and the prices which we are quoting here are naturally *subject to alteration*, just as exchange rates may rise or fall. As of 1980 the official exchange rate stood at around 1 rouble = £ 0.70 pence; 64.35 roubles to US $100, or 1 rouble to $1.51; and although a rouble does sell for 38¢ in New York, importation of roubles into the USSR is strictly forbidden and severely penalized.

Individual travel is possible in three (sometimes four) different classes. In the *deluxe class,* in the high season, it varies from 54–64 roubles per person per day for a single room and 28–33 roubles per person for a double room. Included are accommodations, three *à la carte* meals daily, daily excursions with an interpreter-guide and use of a car up to three hours a day; transfers on arrival and departure, including porterage. In the *tourist class* the first-class accommodations (with bath) cost 30–36 roubles single and 17–20 roubles double per person; a room with a washstand only but with a bath, or shower on the same floor, costs slightly less. Tourist-class clients are not accepted in July and August.

Holiday-makers on the Black Sea coast of the Crimea and Caucasus in the high season pay 23 roubles single and 14 roubles each, double, for a room with bath; without a bath the price is 13.50 single and 8.50 (without bath) each, double. Apart from the room, the prices include three meals daily, one excursion by bus with a guide every three days and beach facilities. These prices are also effective for groups which are provided with transfers by bus on arrival and departure (except in Yalta where, arriving in Simferopol, there is an extra charge for transportation Simferopol–Yalta–Simferopol.

Group tours fall into the first class category. At press-time 1981 summer prices were not available, so check with either your nearest branch of Intourist or a travel agent. The prices will include room, three meals daily, two excursions per day by bus with a guide-interpreter (lasting up to six hours), and transfers by bus on arrival and departure at each point. The number of single rooms available is always limited.

Bus tours are also divided by cost according to the number of people in the group and the type of accommodations. (The buses bring the passengers to the Soviet Union from the point of departure or, in any case, from outside the country.) The costs vary for these according to the numbers in the groups and the type of accommodations selected. On a daily basis the price runs between 10 and 20 roubles per day per person. The prices include hotel accommodations in the appropriate class of service, three meals daily, two 3-hour excursions daily with a guide-interpreter (using the tourists' bus); porterage on arrival and departure at the hotel, two technical servicings of the bus with washing and parking.

For bus groups wishing to **camp,** the price is about 1 rouble a day per person which includes space for a tent and parking with one 3-hour excursion every day of the tour in the tourists' coach with a guide-interpreter.

Children over ten pay the full rate; those between two and ten are granted a 50% discount.

There are **price lists** for separate services including guides and interpreters, transportation for business calls and theaters, theater tickets, meal coupons, gasoline (petrol) coupons, transfers on arrival and departure. These are subject to change and should be checked with your travel agent.

Discounts are available from October 1 through April 30 (with the exception of transport between cities and separate services) and these range upwards from 15% on medical treatment courses and 25% on group tours (except for bus tours which get only 15%). As some cities will have only modest hotel accommodations, those on deluxe tours get a discount if they have to stay in a lower category room. Tourists arriving for medical treatment are given a 45% discount on the domestic tariffs for travel to and from the place of treatment.

 WHAT TO TAKE. While shortages may be local, certain items are rarely or never available and you might find it useful to stock up with a modest amount of the following: adhesive (Scotch) tape, ballpoint pens and refills, insect repellent, films, spare radio batteries, laxatives, indigestion tablets, aspirins, and any medicine you take regularly. Also take cigarettes, a spare pair of glasses or contact lenses, sunglasses, stick-on heels and soles, detergent, clothes pegs, toothpaste, soap, cosmetics, shampoos, a sewing kit, safety pins, buttons, chewing gum (a welcome gift), candy (ditto), a tin of instant coffee (which now costs over £20 ($46) a 1 lb jar in Russia), kleenex, sanitary napkins, lighter fuel and flints. A flat, wide suction-type bath plug might also come in very handy in some hotels and a roll of electrical tape for fixing faucets, etc. Other items that can make welcome gifts in lieu of tipping are: felt pens, cigarettes, pantyhose, cosmetics—especially eye make-up. Guides are officially not allowed to receive tips, but books—British and American classics in paperback—are appreciated.

For most tourist destinations, airline baggage now goes by size rather than weight, and the free baggage allowance is now: First class, 2 pieces up to 62 inches overall measure each piece; Economy class, 2 pieces, neither one over 62 inches, both together no more than 106 inches; carry-on baggage up to 45 inches. If you go to the USSR by *Pan Am,* your baggage will be carried on this basis, with added proviso that no piece weigh over 77 pounds. *Aeroflot,* however, still goes by the weight rules: 44 pounds for Economy class, 66 for First class.

Packing. Travel light. This is the advice of most seasoned travelers who have learned not to take along the things that *might* be needed, only those that *will* be.

Unless you are going on a package tour with baggage handling inclusive, you will save time, money and frustration by sticking to what you can carry yourself without strain. For most people this means one suitcase with a total weight of 30 pounds or less, or two weighing 20 pounds apiece or less. A shoulder bag should weigh not more than 10 pounds.

Canvas suitcases with rigid frames are very durable and lightweight, although they are not waterproof and offer little protection for fragile items. Molded-plastic luggage is not much heavier and fairly rainproof, but cannot be stretched to accommodate extras as a canvas bag can. Some suitcases are made with hangers and pockets so that they can be hung up in your hotel room without unpacking. This type weighs more, however.

Shoulder bags should have outside pockets for convenience and a foam shoulder pad to distribute weight and keep the bag from slipping off.

Keep in mind that some package tour operators will only accept conventional hard luggage or framed soft bags. Duffle bags and the like are considered harder to fit on a tour bus.

It's a good idea to keep important papers, a camera, guidebooks, a change of underwear, your passport and shot card, other personal items, and perhaps a folding raincoat and hat in your shoulderbag. Women may wish to keep a small handbag in it as well.

Carry the shoulderbag with you at all times. Get in the habit of draping the strap around your knee whenever you sit down and you will not lose it.

What to wear. Starting from the bottom up, a good pair of shoes with thick soles and firm arch supports is your best protection against traveler's limp. Make sure the shoes are well broken-in and also well-heeled. You may have trouble getting repairs done on the spot in the USSR. Clothes should be light in the summer—cotton rather than synthetic; shirts and underwear drip-dry; laundry service is slow and cleaning facilities are limited. There are virtually no self-service launderettes except in a few new housing-estates, out of the tourist's reach. A raincoat, a cardigan or pullover (even in summer) are musts. In winter you will need a heavy overcoat plus woolen underwear, fur- or fleece-lined boots and gloves. (Fur hats—*shapka*—can be bought in the country but are now fairly expensive.)

If you're a woman, put together your travel wardrobe by selecting one or two basic colors and coordinating other colors with them. For example, choose a comfortable dress or suit, add a raincoat which goes with it and select accessories to harmonize. Separates (skirts, sweaters, etc.) allow you to mix and match outfits more freely and to get the most mileage out of the least amount of clothes. Plan ahead to have the right clothes for the occasion whether it is sports, evening or whatever. A few scarves and some nice jewelry can vary the look of a basic outfit. Trouser suits are generally acceptable nowadays. "Smart informality" is the key. Beware of *over-dressing,* even for the Bolshoi Ballet. Your Intourist hotel is probably the only place where you might prefer to look really sophisticated.

Both men and women will want casual clothes such as jeans and a tank top or turtleneck for real relaxing. Never wear a bikini away from the beach or shorts in a city restaurant.

With today's fabrics you can take a travel wardrobe that requires little care as you go. Crease-resistant double knits and wash-and-wear are the modern way to go. Do your laundry at night in the bathroom sink and have it fresh in the morning. Use non-flammable spot remover to save dry cleaning and avoid the harsh solvents used in some countries. These can damage sensitive fabrics.

For cooler weather, try the layer system. Instead of dragging along a heavy coat, wear a lighter one with a sweater, insulated underwear, and extra layers of clothing. It is a more flexible system and will keep you warmer. In *really* cold weather wear woolen tights, *never nylon*—it can freeze on your knees! Winter boots should be waterproof, not fashion.

Light indoor clothes are a must for winter. Russian central heating is efficient and you will *swelter* at night in a woollen nightgown.

 TRAVEL DOCUMENTS. US citizens: Apply several months in advance of your expected departure date. US residents must apply in person to the US Passport Agency in Boston, Chicago, Detroit, Honolulu, Houston, Los Angeles, Miami, New Orleans, New York, Philadelphia, San Francisco, Seattle, Stamford (Conn.), or Washington D.C., or to their local County Courthouse. In some areas selected post offices are also equipped to handle passport applications. If you still have a previous passport issued within the past eight years you may use this to apply by mail. Otherwise, take with you: a birth certificate or certified copy thereof or other proof of citizenship; two identical photographs, 2 inches square, full face, black and white or color, on nonglossy paper, and taken within the past six months; $14 ($10 if you apply by mail); proof of identity such as a driver's license, previous passport or any governmental ID card. (Social Security and credit cards are *not* acceptable.) If you expect to travel extensively, request a 48- or 96-page passport rather than the usual 24-page one. There is no extra charge. US passports are valid for 5 years. If your passport is lost or stolen, immediately notify either the nearest American Consul, or the Passport Office, Department of State, Washington, D.C. 20524. Record your passport's number and date and place of issue in a separate, secure place.

If a non-citizen, you need a Treasury Sailing Permit, Form 1040C, certifying that Federal taxes have been paid; apply to your District Director of Internal Revenue for this. You will have to present various documents: blue or green Alien Registration card; passport; travel tickets; most recently filed Form 1040; W-2 forms for the most recent full year; most recent current payroll stubs or letter; you'd be advised to check that this is all that's needed! To return to the United States you need a reentry permit if you intend to remain abroad longer than 1 year. Apply for it in person at least six weeks before departure at the nearest office of the Immigration and Naturalization Service, or by mail to the Immigration and Naturalization Service Washington, D.C.

Permanent Resident Aliens in US: *Requirements for Departure and Reentry.* A permanent resident alien contemplating travel to the Soviet Union, as well as to most Eastern European countries, is required to apply to the Immigration and Naturalization Service for a reentry permit. Although an Alien Registration Receipt Card (Form I-151) is valid as a reentry document after travel to most countries, it is *not* valid as a reentry document after travel to the Soviet Union and certain other countries.

Additionally, a reentry permit is not valid as a reentry document after travel to most Eastern European and certain other countries unless appropriately endorsed to show waiver of that restriction, or unless presented with a letter granting such waiver from the Department of State or the Immigration and Naturalization Service, depending on the itinerary of the traveler.

A permanent resident alien having doubt as to the validity of Form I-151 for reentry because of the contemplated itinerary abroad, should consult with the nearest Immigration and Naturalization Service office prior to commencing travel.

Permanent resident aliens of the United States, including stateless persons, who plan to visit the USSR, are cautioned that the Soviet Government does not recognize that the U.S. Government may have a valid interest in their welfare while they are in the Soviet Union. Permanent resident aliens planning to visit the USSR should therefore bear in mind that the U.S. Government will be unable to assist them if they should be arrested or detained in the USSR for acts allegedly committed during their sojourn or while they were residents of the USSR in the past. The Soviet Government is most severe in punishing those whom it considers to have committed "war crimes" against the USSR.

British subjects must apply for passports on special forms obtainable from the Passport Office or a travel agent. The application should be sent to the Passport Office according to residential area (as indicated on the guidance form). Apply at least 4 weeks before the passport is required. The regional Passport Offices are located in London, Liverpool, Peterborough, Glasgow, Newport (Mon.) and Belfast. The application must be countersigned by your bank manager or by a solicitor, barrister, doctor, clergyman or justice of the peace who knows you personally. You will need two photos. The fee is £11 for a 32-page passport, £22 for a 90-page one; valid for 10 years.

Visas. To enter the Soviet Union you need a visa. For the tourist, the necessary application form will be supplied by Intourist or your travel agent. Three passport photographs must be enclosed. You should make your application either directly or through the travel agent not less than six weeks before you wish to enter the USSR. There is no charge for visas but if you obtain yours through Intourist, they levy a small charge for the service. In the US there is a charge of $7.00 per visa to cover "postage and telegraphic expenses."

Should you wish to make your application for a visa in person, you can do so at the Soviet Consulate, 1609 Decatur St. N.W., in Washington, D.C. 20011, or the USSR. Consulate General, 2790 Green St., San Francisco, California 94123; or in London, at the Soviet Consular Department, 5 Kensington Palace Gardens, W.8. You must enclose a letter from a travel agent confirming your hotel reservation, or you won't get a visa at all.

Transit visas are issued to those wishing to travel through the USSR on their way to another country. Visitors applying for such a visa should make sure that their passport carries an entry visa (where required) to the next country to be entered from the Soviet Union and that a confirmed ticket for travel through the USSR is submitted in addition to three photographs, a completed form and a confirmation of hotel reservation for any stopovers. Visas for business trips are the same as tourist visas.

Visas for private journeys are granted to people who visit relatives and friends in the USSR and therefore do not require hotel reservations. Application should be made to the Consular Department in Washington, DC or London in person. (See previous section, "Visiting Relatives," also.)

No visas are required for passengers changing planes at a Soviet airport in transit to another country, provided they do not leave the airport and hold a valid air ticket to the country of destination with a clearly-stated time of departure not more than 24 hours after their arrival.

Passengers on cruises calling at Soviet ports *do not* require visas for a stay of up to 48 hours at each port, provided that they arrive and leave by the same ship and do not travel to any other city in the USSR and that they use the ship as their hotel and purchase Intourist shore services. Round-trip passengers on regular scheduled sailings, however, must obtain visas in the usual way, supported by a letter from an accredited Intourist travel agent or the shipping agency. Groups of school children under 18 years of age, traveling on educational cruise ships, are allowed to enter ports of call and visit cities in the Soviet Union *without visas.* They must carry either passports or identity cards to be presented to the authorities at the ports of call.

 HEALTH REGULATIONS. Visitors to the USSR coming from Africa, South America and Asia must have an international certificate of smallpox vaccination and those arriving from India and Bangladesh also require a certificate of vaccination against cholera. Tourists from other countries do not need to present any health certificates and there will be no medical examination. However, Soviet public health officers may ask for additional proof of health from tourists arriving from countries known to have an epidemic at the time of arrival. Medical service in the USSR is free of charge and is available in any city or town. If a tourist is indisposed he is asked immediately to call in a doctor through his interpreter or through the hotel administration. First aid treatment and doctors' visits are gratis. If hospitalization is necessary a charge of 16 roubles daily is levied; this may be waived against unused prepaid travel services.

The American Embassy in Moscow recommends that US tourists planning to travel to southern areas of the USSR—the Ukraine, the Caucasus, Moldavia, Soviet Central Asia, and the Black Sea Coast—have up-to-date cholera vaccinations. This saves much delay and inconvenience.

Your Health. Don't let us scare you by mentioning the word "health." Unless you have a special problem, such as being allergic to caviar, you are just as safe in the USSR as you are in the US or Britain.

Water is usually safe. If you have any doubts you can stick to the ever-present bottled or mineral water or coffee, tea and beer. The USSR Health Ministry is now, however, advising even native Leningraders to boil their drinking water owing to local outbreaks of parasitic infections.

Food is as safe as it looks or as you see it handled. Greasy-spoon restaurants are a hazard anywhere in the world, so be certain that dairy products—including cheese and ice cream—have been carefully processed and handled, that fresh-vegetable salads are clean, and so on. Generally speaking, only independent travelers going off into the remoter, non-European parts of Russia—Central Asia, for instance—need worry about the food. You should, however, be warned that some visitors to Russia, especially to Leningrad, have returned home with a form of diarrhea called *giardiasis* caused by an intestinal parasite. It can be effectively treated, but needs slightly different drugs from the normal ones for diarrhea. If you find yourself suffering from such an illness after you return home, then consult your physician.

If you wear *glasses,* carry along an extra pair. Also, have your optician fill in the optical prescription on your yellow vaccination card.

Those with *diabetes*, people who are allergic to *penicillin* or other common drugs, those with a rare blood type, should wear a tag or bracelet or carry a wallet card indicating this.

Prescription medicines can be obtained with your home prescription only rarely. If you take a prescription medicine regularly, bring enough to last. If you are travelling in the winter or spring, take cough and cold remedies, especially for the northern USSR.

$P£ **INSURANCE.** We suggest that you be fully covered with theft, loss, and disability policies prior to your arrival in the USSR. This does not mean that thefts are more prevalent here than elsewhere but you will be covering a lot of territory and we advise it for precaution's sake.

Generally speaking, you can insure: yourself and your family, your baggage, and your travel expenses. For personal accident insurance, "family" usually means a spouse and dependent children 14–21 years old. Benefits are paid for loss of life, hands, feet, eyesight, for total disability, and for some medical expenses.

Baggage and personal possessions can be insured against loss or damage. Usually covered are clothing, luggage, jewelry, cameras and sports equipment. Loss due to governmental seizure is *not* covered.

Trip cancellation insurance covers the non-refundable parts of your transportation and hotel expenses that you may lose from having to cancel because of death, illness, injury or pregnancy.

Liability coverage carried by local transportation, including taxis, is either non-existent or so low that you should take out your own coverage at home before leaving. If your local agent won't cover you for a trip to the Soviet Union for some reason, you may be able to obtain insurance for baggage loss, etc. from *Ingosstrakh*, a Russian firm, which has representatives at some airports and border crossings.

Getting to the Soviet Union

 BY AIR. From the US: As we go to press, relations between the USSR and the US have deteriorated to the point where the Russian carrier, *Aeroflot*, is operating only one flight a week from New York to Moscow (10 hours non-stop); there is no service by an American airline and the link between Washington DC and Moscow has been terminated. Diplomats have indicated to us that this meager direct air service is likely to continue through 1981. It is possible, however, that if the demand warrants it, PanAm or some other US carrier may resume a weekly service.

The Soviet Union can be reached from more than a dozen US cities by making a connection in London, Paris, Brussels, Amsterdam, Copenhagen, Frankfurt, Zurich and other Continental cities, as Aeroflot and the reciprocal carriers of most European countries have frequent services to Moscow. Leningrad can be reached only by Aeroflot; Kiev from Vienna, Zurich and all Eastern European capitals.

It is also worth noting that you can get to Vilnius from Warsaw, to Minsk from East Berling, to Tashkent from Bangkok, Calcutta, Karachi or Copenhagen; and to Khabarovsk from Tokyo if you want to enter the USSR by one of its side doors.

Aeroflot is the world's largest airline in terms of route mileage and possibly passenger traffic as well as number of aircraft—though it does not publish such statistics—and has extended its wings to five continents. Most of the major airlines of the world, the US excluded, have direct flights to Moscow.

Fares: Apart from first-class and tourist-class fares, there are also group excursion rates. Recently the regulations governing charter flights have been greatly liberalized, so tour operators now offer a variety of possible formulas and advantageous fares. These are part of the package rates, so if you are going to the USSR as part of a tour group, ask what the basis of your airfare is and what are the alternatives, because rates vary greatly. Sample New York-Moscow round trip fares are: $1,954 first class, $974 to $1,166 economy. Some excursions such as the APEX start as low as $520 but these generally do not permit stopovers.

From Britain: *Aeroflot* has daily flights, both non-stop and via Copenhagen, to Moscow. *British Airways* has a daily non-stop service by three-engine Tridents as well as several Boeing 707 which continue on to Tokyo on the trans-Siberian route.

Return fares from London to Moscow are: First class £763; Economy £513; 10-30-day excursion £267. Stopovers in Europe and Scandinavia are permitted on full fares only. The cost of air travel can be greatly reduced by taking an inclusive tour with Intourist.

From the Continent: With a few exceptions, all the major capitals in Western Europe have direct flights to Moscow, while an increasing number have several weekly services to Leningrad, too. You usually have choice between Aeroflot and the national carriers of the country you are departing from. Flying time from Central Europe to Moscow is about 3 hours, less from Iron Curtain countries.

 BY SHIP. From North America: There is a summer service from both New York and Montreal to Leningrad; calling at London (Tilbury), Le Havre and Bremerhaven, by the *MS Alexandr Pushkin* and the *MS Mikhail Lermontov*. Both ships are 20,000 tons, single class. One-way fare is around $485–$1340. Bookings can be made through Intourist offices or through *March Shipping Passengers Services,* One World Trade Center, 52nd Floor, New York, N.Y. 10048; or the *CTC Lines,* 1/3 Lower Regent Street, London SW1.

From Britain: The Baltic State Steamship Line runs comfortable ships from London to Leningrad. A weekly service is maintained by the modern motor vessels *Estonia, Krupskaya, Kalinin* and *Ulyanov,* each about 5,000 tons and carrying 330 passengers. There is also the *Baltika* of 8,500 tons (430 passengers) and the *Ivan Franko* of nearly 19,000 tons.

The London-Leningrad trip usually takes five days each way. The ships sail from Tilbury and call at Copenhagen, Stockholm and Helsinki. There are first- and second-class accommodations; two-, four- and six-berth cabins are available, on the outside. Single-berth cabins are only available on the *Baltika,* but they cannot be guaranteed. Except for the cabins, there is no difference in the services and amenities available. The service and the food are of a good European standard.

From elsewhere: You can also sail to Leningrad direct from Le Havre. The boats have a 4- to 6-hour stop at Copenhagen, Stockholm, Helsinki, Rostok and Riga. During the summer there are ship connections between Stockholm and Leningrad and Helsinki and Leningrad. From East Asia there is a regular service to Nakhodka from both Hong Kong and Yokohama. All these services are by the latest Soviet ships of the *Estonia* type, carrying 330 passengers. From Le Havre to Leningrad, the trip takes six days.

BY TRAIN. From Britain: Direct services carrying a Soviet sleeper-coach are available throughout the year from London in conjunction with Harwich-Hook of Holland or Dover-Ostend boats. They offer a comfortable two-day journey through Central and Eastern Europe with no need to change compartments or trains. Soviet sleeper-coaches are designed for long-distance travel—as we shall see when discussing travel within the USSR—and the compartments normally have two berths (first class) or four berths (second class). There are washstands in first class compartments. In winter, a minimum inside temperature of 64°F. (18°C.) is maintained. Each coach has its own conductor. On most sections of the route, a restaurant car is attached. Tea, coffee and biscuits are served by the conductor, but many travelers on long hauls buy food in stations. Dining cars belonging to various railway systems are attached to these trains. In Western Europe there is no problem. After crossing into East Germany (The German Democratic Republic) problems can arise. Payment is usually accepted only in western currency from Western travelers. And the change, if you do not have the right amount, is likely to be in kind, e.g. chocolate or a bottle of beer. In the USSR roubles only are accepted in the dining car. Try if possible to change some of your currency at the Brest station (Polish/USSR frontier) into roubles to pay for your meals.

During the summer, the through train departs daily from London's Liverpool Street Station, at 9.40 A.M., and goes via the Hook of Holland. In winter it runs on Mondays, Wednesdays, Fridays and Sundays. It arrives at the Byelorussky Station in Moscow at 2.30 P.M. two days later. Trains via Ostend run from London's Victoria Station, leaving at 9.44 A.M., daily all the year round. The schedule includes stops at Berlin and Warsaw.

Moscow and many other Soviet cities have direct rail connections with Helsinki, Berlin, Hook of Holland, Paris, Rome, Prague, Vienna, Budapest, Belgrade, Bucharest, Sofia, Berne, Athens, Venice, Brussels.

From Finland: A pleasant way to visit the USSR is to enter from Helsinki by train. There are three through trains from Helsinki: the first (operating May to September only) leaves the Finnish capital at midday, arriving in Leningrad at 8 P.M. The second to Leningrad, leaving Helsinki at 10.30 P.M. and arriving at 9.40 A.M.; the third direct Helsinki to Moscow (depart 3.30 P.M. and arriving at Moscow at 8.55 A.M. with no stop at Leningrad).

BY CAR. You can enter the USSR by car at the following border points: From **Finland:** Torfyanovka and Brusnichnoye. From **Poland:** Brest and Shaginya. From **Czechoslovakia and Hungary:** Chop. From **Romania:** Porubnoye and Leusheny. It is obligatory to plan your trip in advance and notify Intourist of your route and then keep to it.

It is possible to take your car by boat to Leningrad or ship it to the Soviet Black Sea ports.

Automobile travel along certain specified routes is presently permitted, with or without Intourist guides. Only mature and experienced drivers should consider unaccompanied motor trips. Driving conditions are far more rugged than in Western Europe; service stations are rare. Soviet driving regulations are complex and very strictly enforced. Foreign drivers who violate them are subject to the full severity of Soviet law (including trial and extended imprisonment).

Automobile travelers should be fully insured under policies valid for the USSR. Such insurance may be placed with a number of Western firms or with Ingosstrakh, the Soviet organization which insures foreigners. (See "Motoring in the USSR", later in this section).

Upon entering the Soviet Union, all auto tourists are required to sign an obligation guaranteeing the re-export of their automobiles; this guarantee also applies to damaged vehicles. Tourists have been required to pay quite large sums to ship their damaged automobiles out of the Soviet Union to neighboring countries for repair because necessary repairs could not be made in the USSR.

 BY BUS. In 1979 a UK tour operating company, *Wallace Arnold*, started a through bus service from London to Moscow during the summer running weekly from April through to September. They plan to run this again in 1981 but it could not be confirmed as we went to press. The route goes from London via Dover, Belgium, West Germany, Berlin, Warsaw, Minsk and Smolensk, taking four days (three nights) in all to reach Moscow. One night is spent traveling; one night is in Warsaw and another in Minsk. A fascinating but tiring journey as many roads in the USSR are somewhat rough. The 1981 rates were not available as we went to press but are likely to be around £65 single, £115 return, with reductions for both students and children; and there are reduced rates for groups of 15 or more. Cost includes overnights, but food must be paid for locally. Check all details with operator Wallace Arnold Ltd., 8 Park Lane, Croydon CR9 1DN, England.

Arriving in the Soviet Union

 CUSTOMS. A customs declaration form must be filled out on arrival which should be retained until departure from the country. This allows you to import free of duty and without any special license all articles intended for personal use, clothing, food (except fresh vegetables and fruits, which must be presented for examination), tobacco and cigarettes, alcoholic drinks, perfume, sports equipment, camera, cine-camera—all of this in reasonable quantities for personal consumption or use. It is illegal to sell personal possessions in the Soviet Union. It is prohibited to import weapons and ammunition; opium, hashish and pipes for smoking them; pornographic articles and pictures; printed matter, printing blocks, negatives, exposed film, photos, phonograph records, tape recordings, motion picture films, manuscripts, designs and drawings "harmful to the USSR politically or economically". This includes religious literature. You are allowed to import *one* Bible, in your native language, for your own use, but you are expected to take it out again with you when you leave.

You can export the following articles bought in the USSR for foreign currency exchanged for roubles at the USSR Foreign Trade Bank and the USSR State Bank: fur coats, muffs, boas, etc. (one each), pocket or wrist-watches (two), dinner-, tea-, or coffee-sets (one of a kind). You can also take out souvenirs, in reasonable amounts. Of items made of precious metals, you may take out one wrist-watch or bracelet or a pocket-watch without a chain, one wedding ring, one ring with precious stones, one gold-framed pair of spectacles, one pair of earrings with precious stones (only women tourists) and articles made of silver not heavier than 400 grams (less than half a pound). Recent reports suggest that no amber can be exported, even if purchased in a Beryozka (foreign currency) shop. But check with Intourist. Other goods bought for foreign currency in the specialized Beryozka shops at the airfields, hotels, railway stations and ports (including cameras, phonograph records, handicraft articles, caviar and musical instruments) can also be taken out upon presentation of the appropriate shop receipts. Books published before 1945, technically need an export permit—Intourist will advise you.

Never try to smuggle out ikons (see page 82) or antique items. On entering the Soviet Union, drivers must sign a declaration that they will re-export their car at the end of their tour. No taxes or customs duties are payable for a temporary import.

CURRENCY REGULATIONS. You must *not* import or export roubles, Soviet State loan bonds or Soviet lottery tickets. All foreign currency in travelers checks and banknotes which tourists bring with them must be declared upon entry. There is no limit as to the amount you can import and, in fact, Russia is one country where it is more useful to have a fair supply of small denomination foreign cash handy than travelers checks—especially for use in foreign-currency stores and bars. Roubles cannot be obtained outside the country. Foreign currency can be converted at the exchange office *(bureau de change)* of the Soviet State Bank at all border points, at the official rate of exchange, now about £1 per 1.40 roubles, $1 per 64.35 kopeks. These offices can be found in the hotels, at the international air and sea ports of the Soviet Union, but hours of operation are often irregular, so travelers should plan ahead. Each transaction will be recorded on a receipt which you must preserve. On leaving the country, you can change back the remaining roubles into foreign currency. It is illegal to carry out any transactions in foreign currency except through the USSR State Bank or Intourist or other authorized State Organization. You would be well advised not to change too much of your currency at a time, the more so as the re-exchange rate when you leave the country is less than the exchange rate was when you entered it, so you lose some as you convert back. You will not need, by and large, to use a great deal of Russian money, and changing it back when you leave can be tedious. (There is a black market, but unless you are *very* foolhardy, you will not have any dealings with it.)

Credit cards. At the moment, both *American Express* and *Diners Club* credit cards are accepted in a limited number of Intourist offices in the Soviet Union for additional tours booked on the spot, some restaurant reservations, theater tickets, etc. You can be sure they will be recognized in Moscow and Leningrad, and Intourist reports that 21 other major destinations now accept them as well. *Bankamericard, Mastercharge, Carte Blanche* and *Eurocard* are now widely accepted also.

Staying in the Soviet Union

HOTELS AND OTHER ACCOMMODATIONS. Detailed information about hotels, etc., will be found in the chapters dealing with the different cities and regions, later in this book. You can state your preferred hotel from the list supplied by Intourist but you cannot pick one *not* on this list. You will find, more often than not, that you do not get your first choice. Nor can you normally alter your booking once you have made it.

Many of the Intourist hotels are modern and reasonably comfortable, though their ratings differ according to individual experiences. Only the deluxe class can be considered to be near the highest American and British standards and even in these you will find that the elevator, perhaps, cannot be used for going down less than three stories and that you have to hand over your key every time you leave your room to the rather severe lady sitting at the stairhead. Room service is neither regular nor enthusiastic. Beds can be uncomfortable—and *short!* The water supply may be interrupted and you may find that while you can have milk in your coffee in the coffeeshop, you have to drink it black in the restaurant, a hundred yards away. Dining-room service can range from fairly good to unbelievably bad.

For American and most British travelers, Intourist recommends deluxe class, in which all reservations and services are included. In first class and tourist class, the traveler is not always guaranteed a guide and car for additional sightseeing. Rates, as we have indicated before, vary according to season. The top hotels, according to the latest ratings by travel agents and various tourist experts, are the *Leningrad, Yevropeiskaya* and *Astoriya* in Leningrad, and the *Cosmos, Intourist, Rossiya* and *National* in Moscow. This does not mean that there are not others in which you will be well-lodged and reasonably well-fed; and the ratings, of course, are neither permanent nor necessarily up-to-date. We will provide further details about hotels in each geographical section.

 RESTAURANTS. For eating in the Soviet Union you need, above all, patience, especially in hotels. It is quite useless to rebel against the system that decrees a minimum two hours for lunch or dinner though it may be three or even more. On the other hand, when you reserve a table at a restaurant through your Intourist bureau, you go to the head of the line and get priority over Soviet citizens! On often elaborate menus, ignore all the items where no prices are marked, since they are not available anyway. Except for some of the regional restaurants, the food is likely to be hearty and ample rather than *cordon bleu.* Although service is glacially slow, you can sometimes speed it up somewhat (relatively speaking!) by asking the waitress what she *suggests* and going along with her suggestions. Placing a packet of cigarettes on the table has been known to work—you imply that the waiter/waitress will get it if the service is good.

It is very difficult to get a late meal in the Soviet Union. Cafés usually close at 10 or 11 P.M. and restaurants at 11 or 11.30 P.M. but diners are *not* admitted during the half-hour before closing time. The best restaurants usually accept Intourist meal coupons. The smaller ones have no foreign language menus, but you can always point and hope!

By the standards of most Western capitals, restaurants in the Soviet Union are modestly priced and quality is equally modest. Except when otherwise indicated in our listings, the normal dinner for two will cost between 6 and 10 roubles. This usually includes *zakuski* (hors d'oeuvres, often the highlight of the meal as they are in Russian homes), a main meat course, dessert and coffee. The same food at lunch costs a bit less. With Russian vodka and caviar, or Soviet champagne or cognac, the meal prices can mount rapidly.

At least once during your visit try a snack in a good café outside your hotel, in one of the open-air cafés in the culture parks that are the pride of every Russian city, in a cafeteria, or in one of the many places specializing in shishkebab, pancakes, doughnuts, or ice cream.

Most Intourist package tours come with meals included. Tourists are issued books of coupons to pay for meals in their hotels. The coupons are valid in the restaurants of other Intourist hotels as well, but not in outside restaurants. Reservations at the latter are a must; otherwise, you may be turned away by the doorman. Go early. Wave your foreign passport quite shamelessly. Russian dinner hours are earlier than those in Western Europe and in season, the crowds gather early. Please remember that quality of service and food vary from time to time at each restaurant in spite of recommendations given.

Intourist will provide all your meals unless you are camping or on a business trip. The meal coupons have a definite value in roubles which varies according to deluxe, first- or tourist-class reservations. Mineral water is included in the cost of all meals. You might also like to try the national dishes which we will describe in the various geographical chapters.

Drinks are ordered by grams (100 or 200) or by the bottle. A normal bottle will hold about ¾ of a liter. Soviet regulations forbid the serving of more than 100 gr. of vodka per person per meal. There are several varieties: *starka* ("old" vodka); *khorilka s pertsem* (Ukranian, with hot peppers in it); *tminaya* (caraway flavored) or *yubileinaya* (jubilee); *pshenichnaya* (made from wheat) and *krepkaya* (at 110 proof, the strongest!). The Crimean and Caucasian wines are excellent, though some people will find them rather sweet. Good also is Armenian brandy. Azerbaijani cognac is even better, but expensive. Port, madeira and vermouth have their Russian approximations if not equivalents.

NIGHTLIFE. By and large, there is no such thing in the Soviet Union, no nightclubs or bars, though there is often singing while you eat in restaurants and hotels, and a couple of Moscow and Leningrad hotels have late-night bars (open till 2 A.M.). There are *clubs* in great profusion, attached to various organizations and enterprises and also for writers, artists, etc. Some have restaurants which are not open to the public, though you might find a Russian friend who can take you there. But as factory and office work starts early, generally—except in their own homes or the country cottages (the *dachas*) of the privileged—people go to bed well before midnight and restaurants, bars, theatres, clubs and just about everything else closes by 11.30 P.M. In the summer resorts there is some relaxation of the rule, but even there, with many seeking rest or medical treatment, night-birds are not encouraged. But things are slowly improving, especially in Moscow, Leningrad and Tallinn, where there are now bars on the western model. In some places, they even serve western drinks for roubles, but entry charges are expensive. Not worth it unless you are homesick.

CULTURAL ACTIVITIES. You cannot fail to be impressed with the fact that culture is taken very seriously in the Soviet Union, and by all levels of the population, from the sophistication and elegance of the great opera and ballet theaters to the more "popular" but large, well equipped and well-kept Culture Parks.

The theater, ballet and cinema are very popular and the number of seats available for tourists is limited, though many of the *best* are reserved for them. You should apply to the Service Bureau at your hotel as soon as possible—don't count on getting in at the last moment. In provincial cities it may be easier to buy tickets on the spur of the moment than in the major cities. By the same token, the programs may be less impressive, though interesting in unexpected ways. Most performances start at 6.30 or 7 P.M. and few end later than 11 P.M. On Sundays there are matinees, usually at 11 A.M. Even if you do ask for your tickets well in advance, you will probably find out only on the actual day whether you have got them—so planning your evening entertainment is not always easy. Tickets are priced from about 2 to 5 roubles and can be bought, apart from Intourist, from kiosks inside the Metro stations or in the street (if you speak Russian!).

The ballet seasons in Moscow and Leningrad last until the end of May and start again early in September. But many of the leading artists perform during the long summer recess in other towns, sometimes at open-air shows. Synopses are available in English at the Intourist service offices.

The Moscow Stars and the Leningrad White Nights festivals (the first in May, the second in June) are very popular and reservations for these events must be made well ahead of time.

The Obraztsov Central Puppet Theater in Moscow is a sheer delight; if some of its plays are rather heavily weighted with propaganda, the puppets are magnificent and the wit is sparkling. The Romany Gipsy Theater at 26 Pushkin Street, Moscow, is quite spectacular. You must deposit your overcoat in the cloakrooms and you might want to hire a pair of binoculars for about 50 kopeks at the same time. This will enable you to get at the head of the usually long queue at the end of the performance (persons returning binoculars get priority).

Foreign-language films are always dubbed in Russia—no subtitles. Performances are not continuous and your ticket only entitles you to a certain showing, after which the movie house is emptied. The same theater might show different films during the same day. Smoking is not allowed.

There are chamber and larger concert halls in all major cities, many of them attached to special organizations—such as the House of Trade Unions, the Army, the Art Workers, etc.

Circus performances are given both indoors and (during the summer), outdoors in parks. There are evening performances, with matinees on Sundays and holidays.

If your schedule permits, be sure to spend an afternoon in the nearest Culture Park. These are a combination of public garden, performing arts center and amusement park or fun fair; and they are green, attractive, well kept, and well attended. You can eat, stroll, listen to music, contemplate monumental statuary, or ride the merry-go-round; and the openness and spontaneous enjoyment of the ordinary Soviet people around you is very catching. They are fun in winter, too!

 PHOTOGRAPHY. Bring your own film and have it developed after you return home. You can photograph most things, but use your common sense: don't photograph anything that is clearly a "sensitive" installation—airports, factories, military installations or personnel, prisons, railway junctions or stations, telephone exchanges, etc. If in doubt, ask your guide. Photography is *un*restricted in most tourist locations, but it is wiser *not* to take pictures from airplanes or trains, etc. If you intend taking close-ups of people, *ask them,* even if only by gestures . . . this isn't security, just politeness.

 TIPPING. Officially, there is no tipping in the Soviet Union except in some hotels in Moscow and other large cities, where a 5–15% service charge may be added to your bill. Unofficially, you will find that no one is insulted by it—especially taxi-drivers, barbers, delivery men and shoeshine boys (20 kopeks for all of them). Sometimes a small gift of a stick of chewing gum or a lipstick or cigarettes will be even more welcome. Be careful about giving foreign coins or notes (even as a gift for collectors)—it is technically illegal. Felt pens, cigarettes and books (non-political!) make welcome gifts in lieu of tips. In fact the liberal gifts of chewing gum gave the Russians such a taste for the stuff that they have now built a factory to satisfy local demand. If you want to offer a tip, do—but don't press it on a reluctant recipient, though reluctance is fast disappearing. Suggested for waiters: 5 percent, porters about 30 kopeks each bag.

 CLOSING DAYS AND HOURS. Banks, state offices and some shops and service establishments are closed on January 1–2, March 8 (International Women's Day), May 1–2 (May Day), May 9 (Victory Day), November 7–8 (Day of the Revolution) and December 5 (Constitution Day). There are no additional regional holidays.

Banks and government offices are open from 9 or 10 A.M. until 5 or 6 P.M., with an hour's break for lunch. Groceries, bakeries and dairies open from 8 or 9 A.M. till 8 or 11 P.M., with a lunch break from 1 to 2 P.M. Other stores are usually open from 11 A.M. to 7 P.M., with a break from 2 to 3 P.M. Big department stores are open from 9 A.M. without a break. All shops, except a few food stores, now close on Sundays.

Restaurants are usually open from 11 A.M. till 11.30 P.M., cafés from 8 A.M. to 8 P.M., though some open and close later. Movie shows start at different times during the day but mostly run from 9 A.M. until 10.45 P.M. A few Intourist hotels have foreign currency bars that stay open until 2 A.M. Museums have varying hours; on the day *before* their closing day, visiting hours end two hours earlier than usual. The subway (Metro) runs from 6 A.M. until 12.30 A.M. except on holidays when it closes later. Public transportation runs from about 5 A.M. until almost 1 A.M. Taxis are available 24 hours a day, but you may have a long wait after 1 A.M.

LAUNDRY AND DRY CLEANING. Available in Intourist hotels, but service is generally slow and not always punctual. Make arrangements with your chambermaid for laundry, as room service is available only in very few hotels. Try the porter for dry cleaning. Launderettes are few and far between in Moscow and Leningrad, virtually non-existent elsewhere. If you do use one, you have to remove all buttons from your clothes first . . .

MEASUREMENTS. The Soviet Union uses the metric system. Useful conversion tables: 1 pint = about ½ liter; 1 liter = about 2 pints; 1 gallon equals about 4 liters. 1 kilogram is 2 lb. 2 oz.; 1 kilometer = ⅝ mile; one mile equals 1.6 kilometers; 10 miles = 16; 50 = 80.5; 100 = 160.9. One meter = 39¼ inches; 1 hectare = 2½ acres.

Temperatures are measured in degrees Centigrade. To convert Centigrade to Fahrenheit, multiply by 9, divide by 5 and add 32. To turn Fahrenheit into Centigrade, subtract 32, multiply by 5 and divide by 9.

Air pressure for tires is measured in kilograms per square centimeter, instead of pound per square inch.

14 lb.—1.00 kg.	18 lb.—1.26 kg.
22 lb.—1.54 kg.	28 lb.—1.96 kg.
32 lb.—2.25 kg.	36 lb.—2.53 kg.

Moscow Time is 7 or 8 hours (depending on time of year) ahead of New York and 2 or 3 hours ahead of London, Kiev, Kharkov, Leningrad, Lvov, Minsk, Odessa, Riga, Simferopol, Sochi, Sukhumi, Vilnius, Yalta are on the same time. Aeroflot time tables are all based on Moscow Time, to which also the whole of the Trans Siberian rail link is kept.

ELECTRICITY. Sometimes this is 127V, sometimes 220V, and usually it is AC. Better enquire before plugging in anywhere.

GUIDE SERVICES. Guides and interpreters are provided by Intourist both for regular and special tourists. These, of course, vary in efficiency and intelligence, but all are carefully vetted by their employers. Many of them are students or language teachers earning extra money during their vacations or between jobs. Within certain limits, you will find that they identify themselves with your needs, interests and tastes; do not embarrass them by discussing politics or making unfavorable comparisons between the Soviet Union and your own country or vice versa.

If you require a guide for business visits or to the theater outside the regular arrangements of Intourist, you can hire one for 8 roubles for up to 3 hours (12 roubles for business negotiations); for each extra hour another 2 roubles are payable (3 roubles for business). Guides for large groups of tourists cost 1 rouble per person for a period up to 3 hours; thereafter 30 kopeks per person for each extra hour become payable.

SHOPPING. You will probably buy most items in the foreign-currency *Beryozka* shops. Other Russian shops may prove interesting, educating, and cheaper. They are generally crowded, and in most of them you will find that you have to line up three times—first to pick out what you want to buy and collect a ticket, then at the cashier's desk to pay and get the ticket stamped, and finally to collect your purchase. But at least you will be able to look at the people and see them in action—fighting to obtain some goods in short supply or arguing over this or that piece of merchandise.

In Moscow, *GUM,* on Red Square and *TSUM,* near the Bolshoi Theater, are the largest department stores and very characteristic of Soviet daily life. In other major cities, there is at least one such store. All of these have special souvenir departments. The larger shops have information desks whose staff speak foreign languages.

In the self-service shops, you are expected to give up whatever bag or case you are carrying in exchange for one supplied by the shop and then transfer your purchases after you have paid. In some ordinary shops, you can pay over the counter without having to stand in line again and again. There is no delivery to the hotels (except food from certain shops) nor will any shop mail presents abroad.

Some of the best presents include black caviar (sold in small sealed jars or large tins), Ukrainian hand-embroidered skirts or blouses, phonograph records, books, traditional silver-gilt and enamel ware, and wood, alabaster or pottery articles. The caviar is, in fact, in such short supply that it is likely to be found only in the special foreign-currency food shops in Moscow. Other good buys are balalaikas, guitars, samovars, fur hats, painted and lacquered boxes, the traditional Russian wooden nest of dolls *(matryoshkas),* clay figurines from Kymkovo, brightly painted bone carvings from Northern Russia; semi-precious ornaments from the Urals, and malachite, jasper and amber from the Baltic republics (we have had reports that amber can no longer be exported—check with Intourist); Daghestan and Turkoman carpets, Vologda handmade lace, cameras, chocolates, gift boxes of wine and vodka.

You might like to visit one of the big markets, which you should do as early in the day as possible. Usually you will find good-quality fresh fruit, which the hotels rarely serve, but prices are high. Honey, fresh eggs, dairy products and local handiwork are also available. The markets usually close at 5 P.M.

MAIL. Any mail addressed to Moscow, Leningrad or other major cities can be sent either "Poste Restante" or care of Intourist. The addresses in Moscow are: K-600, Poste Restante, 1 Gorky Street; or to the Intourist bureau at Hotel Intourist, 3–5 Gorky Street, Moscow, USSR (next door to the Poste Restante). It is advisable, if mail is sent in advance, to give the date of your arrival at your destination. Intourist will keep letters for you to collect. In Leningrad, the Poste Restante is: C-400, Nevsky Prospekt 6, Leningrad. Mail from European countries takes 3–10 days, from the U.S.A. and Canada a week or more. The address must be legible. The Post Office in Moscow is open daily from 8 A.M. to 10 P.M., at 1 Gorky Street (National Office). Post offices also handle the sales of stamps, registered mail and coupons for long-distance calls. Airmail letters abroad cost 32 kopeks up to ¼ of an ounce, postcards, 18 kopeks. Telegrams, ordinary rate, cost 23 kopeks per word to Great Britain, 30 kopeks to all cities in the U.S.A. Express telegrams are charged at double the regular rate.

Parcels are not delivered to hotels but the addressee is notified of their arrival and told where to collect them.

To dispatch parcels, you should not pack their contents but rather purchase a standard wooden or cardboard box at the nearest post office. It will be packed for you by post office personnel. The maximum weight, including packing, is 22 lb. or 10 kg.

 TELEPHONES. Most Intourist hotels have dial telephones in each room. Usually, you dial "8" before the town number needed, except in Moscow where it should be "2". With non-dialing telephones, ask the operator for *"go-rod"* (outside) and wait for a dialing tone. If you are unable to speak Russian, use English or, for general assistance or in case of emergency, ask the operator for "Service Bureau" or "administrator". In public booths, drop a 2-kopek coin or two 1-kopek coins in the slot, lift the receiver, wait for dialing tone and then dial. There is a limit of 3 minutes if there is a line of people outside but no extra charge for overtime. If the line is busy, hang up and the coin is returned. For service, dial 05, for telegraph and cables 06, for long-distance 07, for information 09.

Long-distance calls (including international) made from the hotel must be booked through the Service Bureau. Otherwise, go to a long-distance telephone office (called *peregovorny punkt*) where you will be asked to pay in advance. Telephone calls cost about 6 roubles for three minutes to Great Britain; 15 roubles to the United States. Calls during holiday season (e.g. on New Year's Eve) should be booked well ahead. Urgent calls can sometimes be arranged with much less delay at double the normal charge.

Traveling in the Soviet Union

 BY AIR. The Soviet Union claims to have the world's longest air routes. The big cities are all linked by air. The main airport of Moscow is Sheremetyevo, which is modern and very well equipped. Domodedovo and Vnukovo are used mostly for domestic flights. Transportation to and from the airports is supplied by Intourist and is likely to be included in the cost of your booking. Baggage delivery and customs inspection can be very slow at Sheremetyevo. Foreigners are assigned to a special *Intourist* lounge—make sure your bus or taxi sets you down at the right building for departure.

Three types of planes are used on the Soviet airlines—the Ilyushin, the Tupolev and the Antonov, all named after their designers and identified by the first two letters of their names. The airlines have both jets and turbo-prop planes. The IL–86, a two-deck, 350-seater airbus, the first Soviet plane equipped to show in-flight films, will shortly be introduced.

While their sound-proofing is not always perfect and you might be disturbed by the noise of the engines, the seats are comfortable, meals are satisfactory, service fair. Soviet air hostesses, as an American traveler remarked, are hired more for sturdiness than looks. Anyhow, you don't often hear of a Soviet plane being hi-jacked to Havana or Tripoli! Most of the tours within the Soviet Union include air travel—either exclusively or in combination with other forms of transportation. Your average luggage allowance is 44 lb. Sometimes they weigh hand-luggage, too.

In late autumn and winter, bad weather often causes considerable delays in air travel in the USSR. Overbooking on domestic flights can also be a problem; double check your booking!

BY TRAIN. All Soviet trains start exactly on time (if they are not mysteriously canceled altogether); there is a broadcast warning five minutes before departure but no whistle or "all aboard!" call, so you must be careful not to be left behind. There are four classes, of which the *deluxe* offers soft seats and private washrooms; the other classes have washrooms at the end of the cars. The *first-class* service is called "soft seat", with spring-cushioned berths; there are two or four berths in each compartment. There is no segregation of the sexes and you might find yourself sharing a two-berth compartment with someone of the opposite sex. The *second* or "hard-seat" class has a cushion on wooden berths, available in two-, three- and four-berth compartments. The *third class*—wooden berths without compartments—is used mostly in local service and rarely sold to foreigners. Most compartments have a small table, limited room for baggage (including under the seats) and usually a loudspeaker which can be cut off other than for arrival announcements on the rare occasions when these are made. In soft class there is also a table lamp.

The Moscow-Leningrad route is the USSR's prime railway service with new very fast trains doing the 410 miles in about 4½ hours, slower trains taking an hour or so longer. The leading overnight train with sleeping cars in both soft and hard cars is the *Red Arrow* which leaves each city at about midnight arriving at 8 A.M. the next day. The longest route is that of the Trans-Siberian Railway, with a mystique all of its own. During the time it takes to get from Moscow to Irkutsk, for example, you'll find yourself plunged into a different world. People wear pyjamas or dressing-gowns, there is much tea-drinking and talk—and you are likely to find someone speaking some Western language with whom to strike up a friendship. The dining cars are well equipped, the meals have generous portions and tea and snacks are available almost constantly. In every car, the conductor keeps a samovar on the go night and day and serves you refreshing hot lemon tea in tall glasses. It is not always easy to get a meal just when you want it on a Russian train. You won't starve but lunch could be at midday one day and three in the afternoon the next. Likewise with dinner. You are always handed an impressive menu—but are more than likely to find that most of the dishes are "off".

Railway tickets are called coupons and are sold in a stapled cover without which they are not valid—so you must make sure that the conductor removes only the appropriate section. The baggage allowance is 77 lb. in the compartment; any excess must be placed in the baggage car. Soviet trains are either electrically or diesel hauled although steam is still used in places for freight haulage and local services. (But many lines are electrified.) Soviet trains use broad-gauge tracks and their running is smooth and there is more space than in the European cars. The passenger trains are divided into three types: fast, express and long-distance trains of sleeping coaches alone. There are local commuter trains into all major cities.

 BY CAR. These are the *official rules* for foreign motorists touring the USSR:

(1) In the streets of towns, populated areas and on highways, traffic keeps to the right.

(2) Touring motorists must follow *only* Intourist routes, according to whichever tour they have chosen.

(3) Tourists driving in the USSR must have the following papers: a passport that has been stamped at the hotel, motel or camping site at the first stop-over point after their entry; an international driver's license or a national license *with an insert in Russian* (available at the first Intourist service bureau en route for 50 kopeks), an international certificate of registration of the motor car in the country of departure; a voucher for Intourist service coupons; a "Motoring Tourist's Memo" indicating the tourist's name, citizenship, car license number, itinerary,

dates and stop-over points. This is obtainable on arrival in the country. You also need a certificate of obligation promising to take the car out of the USSR, to be registered with the customs at the point of entry. On arrival in the USSR you also have to pay a 10 rouble road tax.

(4) Such a "Memo" is not issued to groups traveling in a bus. Such groups must be accompanied by an interpreter-guide and must have a program of visits to towns on the itinerary with indication of their arrival and departure dates from each town, camping site or motel.

(5) The car must have a national license plate as well as an international sign indicating its country of origin, conforming to the rules established by international convention.

(6) Motoring tourists must observe the traffic regulations in force in the USSR "as well as the rules maintaining law and order". Any change in their chosen itinerary must be authorized by a written permit registered at the nearest Intourist branch office on the highway.

(7) For any breach of law and order, traffic regulations and rules of travel through Soviet territory, tourists are answerable under Soviet law.

(8) Motoring tourists must keep their cars in good technical condition and abstain from driving if their cars endanger traffic safety.

(9) In all cases, motorists must be observant of traffic safety. They should *avoid night driving,* drive at a safe speed (particularly after rain, in fog and in poor visibility): in towns and populated areas they should not exceed the speed limit of 60 kph (37 mph), though it might be pointed out here that on the wide streets of Moscow few people observe this rule. The official regulations warn you to be careful when passing other vehicles in motion; to dip your headlights at night at least 150 yards from the oncoming traffic; to switch on parking lights in the evening and night when in towns; refrain from halting in forbidden areas or where only transit passage is permitted.

(10) The use of the horn is permitted only on highways out of towns or in cases where an accident or collision can only be prevented by sounding it.

(11) Tourists must give right of way to special-purpose vehicles—such as fire-engines and ambulances—on hearing their sirens. In some big cities a special lane is reserved for "official" cars which speed along apparently in defiance of the 60 kph limit. They are usually local Party dignitaries, etc. Be prepared.

(12) At traffic lights you can only proceed when the light is green—and this includes left and right turns. You must wait for a signal—an arrow—permitting the turn.

(13) Drunken driving carries *very heavy penalties.*

(14) Foreign tourists may travel on Intourist itineraries in their own cars or in cars hired from Intourist, which can be hired with or without drivers. Buses are not rented without drivers.

(15) As many foreign insurance companies are unwilling to insure cars touring in the Soviet Union or will charge very high premiums, you may wish to insure with *Ingosstrakh* against traffic accidents and damage, as well as against civil liability for damage caused to third persons within the Soviet Union as a result of using the car. Ingosstrakh also insures against other types of claims. Its Moscow address is Moscow–12, 11/10 Kuibyshev Street. (Cables: Moscow, Ingosstrakh.) Insurance may be arranged in any currency; the premium is paid in the appropriate one and claims will be settled accordingly. Insurance can be obtained at the point of entry into the USSR, as well as in Moscow. Cars hired in the Soviet Union carry accident insurance and tourist drivers are covered against civil liability arising from the use of the car; the premiums are included in the rental.

Note: In many cases, Ingosstrakh insists on its coverage, even if this duplicates foreign insurance.

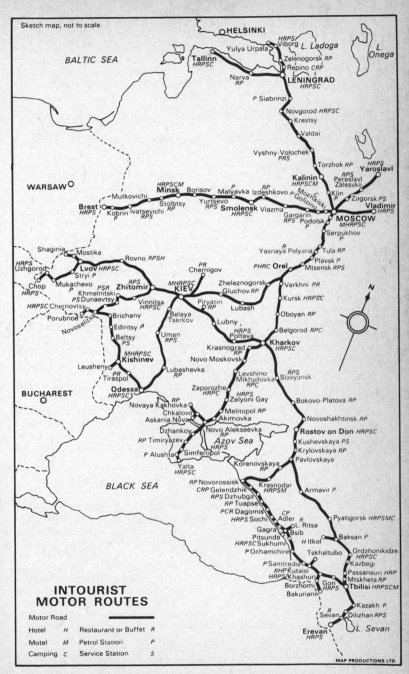

Sketch map, not to scale

BALTIC SEA

HELSINKI

L. Ladoga
L. Onega

Viborg *HRPS*
Yulya Urpala
Zelenogorsk *RP*
Repino *CRP*
Tallinn *HRPSC*
Narva *RP*
LENINGRAD *HRPSC*
P Siabrinzi
Novgorod *HRPSC*
Krestsy
Valdai
Vyshny-Volochek *PRS*
Torzhok *RP*
Yaroslavl *HRPS*
WARSAW
Kalinin *HRPSCM*
Pereslavl *RPS* Zalesskii
Mutkovichi
Minsk *HRPSCM* Borisov
Klin
Zagorsk *PS*
Malyavka Izdeshkovo *RP* Mozhaisk *P*
Vladimir *HRPS*
Brest *HRPS* Stolbtsy Yurtsevo *RP* Goldino
Kobrin Ivatsevichi *RP* Smolensk *HRPSC*
MOSCOW *MHRPSC*
Shaginia
Mostika
Rovno *RPSH*
Viazma
Gargarin *RPS* Podolsk
Serpukhov
Uzhgorod *HRPS*
Lvov *HRPSC*
Stryi *P*
Chernigov
Yasnaya Polyana *R*
Tula *RP*
Chop *HRPS*
Mukachevo
Khmelnitskii *PS* Dunaevtsy
Zhitomir *RPS*
KIEV *MHRPSC*
Zheleznogorsk *R*
Orel *PHRC*
Plavsk *P*
Mtsensk *RPS*
Chernovtsy *HRPSC*
Vinnitsa
Piryatin
Gluchov *RP*
Verkhni *PR*
Porubnoe
Belaya Tserkov *HRPS*
Lubash
Kursk *HRPSC*
Novoselitsa
Brichany
Edintsy *P*
Uman *RPS*
Lubny
Lubny *RP*
Poltava *HRPS*
Oboyan *RP*
Belgorod *RPC*
Beltsy *PS*
Kishinev *MHRPSC*
Lubashevka *RP*
Krasnograd *RPC*
Kharkov *HRPSC*
Leusheny
Novo Moskovsk
Tiraspol *PR*
Odessa *HRPSC*
Zaporozhe *HRPC*
Levshino
Mikhailovka *RPC*
Slavyansk *RPS*
BUCHAREST
Novaya Kakhovka *RP*
Chkalovo
Zelyoni Gay *HRPS*
Bokovo-Platova *RP*
Askania Nova *PSR*
Melitopol *RP*
Akimovka
Novoshakhtinsk *RP*
Dzhankoy
Novo Alekseevka *RP*
Azov Sea
Rostov on Don *HRPSC*
RP Timiryazev
Simferopol *HRPS*
Kushevskaya *PS*
P Alushta
Krylovskaya *RP*
Pavlovskaya
Yalta *HRPSC*
Korenovskaya *RP*
BLACK SEA
Novorossisk *RP*
Gelendzhik *CRP*
Krasnodar *HRPSM*
Armavir *P*
Dzhubga *RPS*
Tuapse *RP*
Dagomis *PCR*
Adler *CP*
Pyatigorsk *HRPSMC*
Sochi *HRPS*
L. Ritsa
Gagra *R*
Baksan *P*
Pitsunda
Bsib
H Itkol
Sukhumi *HRPSC*
Tskhaltubo
Ordzhonikidze *HRPSC*
P Ochamchire
Kazbegi
Samtredia *P*
Passanauri *HRP*
Kutaisi *RHP*
Khashuri *HRPS*
Mtskheta *RP*
Borzhomi *HRPS*
Gori *HRPS*
Tbilisi *HRPSCM*
Bakuriani
Kazakh *R*
Sevan
Dilizhan *RPS*
Erevan *HRPS*
L. Sevan

INTOURIST MOTOR ROUTES

Motor Road ——

Hotel	*H*	Restaurant or Buffet	*R*
Motel	*M*	Petrol Station	*P*
Camping	*C*	Service Station	*S*

MAP PRODUCTIONS LTD.

Police. Traffic control on Soviet highways is exercised by traffic inspectors who are stationed at permanent posts, patrol in cars and on motorcycles. Information can be obtained from them on rules and specific conditions of travel by car on their itinerary; they will supply directions to hotels, motels, camping sites, restaurants, cafés, telephones, first-aid stations, filling and service stations. In case of any damage to the car, they will help in towing the damaged car to a service station. A tourist involved in a traffic accident must immediately report it to an inspector.

Filling up. Be sure to refill your tank whenever possible, as service stations are few and far between.

When starting, it is much better to leave large towns early in the morning to avoid traffic jams. Use your horn very sparingly.

In some narrow Moscow and Leningrad streets it is forbidden to park or overtake but in general you can park anywhere without looking for a parking sign (though you must not park facing oncoming traffic). Night driving is discouraged and, in any case, not pleasant; few cars are equipped with dipping headlights and trucks are often parked along the road without parking lights. Russian pedestrians are not a very disciplined lot—they are likely to cross any time, even with the lights against them, so watch out. Hitch-hiking is discouraged. Keep your car clean—we have heard of people being fined for having a dirty car.

Driving might be a very enjoyable and instructive way of seeing the USSR but it is also apt to produce adventures and frustrations. One reason why you must keep to the Intourist-chosen roads is the poor quality of the lesser roads.

Some other useful points. According to the latest information (subject to change), Intourist offers itineraries to motorists (with certain stopovers and local excursions); these are covered by the routes shown on the map on page 79. Contact Intourist for the latest details; ask for their brochure *Motor Tours of the Soviet Union*. It is possible to camp in the Soviet Union along the Intourist approved routes. See *Roughing It* earlier.

The British AA has issued a route map and guide for motorists traveling to Moscow from the West.

Gasoline coupons should be bought in advance; if you stay for a certain length of time you are entitled to a free voucher for 100 liters. The rental arrangements are of three kinds: self-drive cars for a definite rental period; self-drive cars with unlimited mileage; and chauffeur-driven cars. Details from Intourist or allied travel agent offices.

Rental cars without drivers are hard to find.

Intourist generally insists you take a driver with the car, especially for out-of-town trips.

Deviation from Approved Itinerary. Most of the Soviet Union is off limits to foreigners. About one quarter of the USSR is officially closed to foreigners and a greater area is in effect barred because Intourist declines to arrange travel there. Any deviation from a scheduled itinerary will draw immediate and strong reaction from Soviet authorities.

Finally, motorists are advised to bring a complete set of tools, a towing cable, a pressure gauge, a pump, a spare wheel, a repair outfit for tubeless tires, a good jack and one or two tire-levers, gasoline petrol can, a spare fan-belt, spare windscreen wiper blades and spark plugs. Have also a set of lamp bulbs and fuses, a set of contact-breaker points for the ignition distributor, a spare condenser, a box of tire valve interiors and a roll of insulating tape.

Leaving the Soviet Union

 CUSTOMS ON RETURNING HOME. If you propose to take on your holiday any *foreign-made* articles, such as cameras, binoculars, expensive time-pieces and the like, it is wise to put with your travel documents the receipt from the retailer or some other evidence that the item was bought in your home country. If you bought the article on a previous holiday abroad and have already paid duty on it, carry with you the receipt for this. Otherwise, on returning home, you may be charged duty again (for British residents, V.A.T. as well). In other words, unless you can prove prior possession, foreign-made articles are dutiable *every time* they enter your own country.

Soviet regulations. You cannot take out of the Soviet Union works of art such as paintings, sculptures or carpets. Antiques (including ikons, old coins, books published before 1945, furniture, or musical instructions) may only be taken with a permit from the Ministry of Culture and after paying 100% *duty* on the item.

US customs. At this writing, Americans who are out of the United States at least 48 hours and have claimed no exemption during the previous 31 days are entitled to bring in duty-free up to $300 worth of bona fide gifts or items for their personal use. The value of each item is determined by the price actually paid (so have your receipts). Every member of a family is entitled to this same exemption, regardless of age, and the family allowance can be pooled. Infants and children do not get the exemption on alcohol and tobacco. Purchases intended for your duty-free quota can no longer be sent home separately—they must accompany your personal baggage. Do not think that *already used* will exempt an item. If, for example, you buy clothing abroad and wear it during your travels it will nonetheless be dutiable when you reenter the US.

Not more than 100 cigars and 200 cigarettes may be imported duty-free per person, nor more than a quart of wine or liquor (none at all if your passport indicates you are from a "dry" state, or if you are under 21 years of age). Only one bottle of perfume that is trademarked in the United States may be brought in, plus a reasonable quantity of other brands.

Small gifts may be mailed to friends, but not more than one package to one address and none to your own home. Notation on the package should be "Gift, value less than $25." Tobacco, liquor and perfume are not permitted.

Do not bring home foreign meats, fruits, plants, soil, or other agricultural items when you return to the United States. To do so will delay you at the port of entry. It is illegal to bring in foreign agricultural items without permission, because they can spread destructive plant or animal pests and diseases. For more information, read the pamphlet "Customs Hints," or write to: Animal and Plant Health Inspection Service, US Department of Agriculture, Washington D.C.20250.

British residents. There is now a two-tier allowance for duty-free goods brought into the UK, due to Britain's Common Market membership. *Note:* It is not advisable to mix the two allowances.

If you return from an EEC country (Belgium, Denmark, France, W. Germany, Holland, Eire, Italy, Luxembourg) and goods were bought in one of those countries, duty-free allowances are: 300 cigarettes (or 150 cigarillos, or 75 cigars, or 400g. tobacco); 1.5 liters of strong spirits (or 3 liters of other spirits or fortified wines), plus 3 liters of still table wine; 75g. perfume and .375 liter toilet water; other articles up to £120 value.

If you return from a country outside the EEC, such as the USSR, *or if the goods were bought in a duty-free shop on ship, plane or airport,* the allowances are *less:* 200 cigarettes (or 100 cigarillos, or 50 cigars or 250g. tobacco); 1 liter of strong spirits (or 2 liters of other spirits or fortified wines) plus 2 liters of still table wine; 50g. perfume or .25 liter toilet water; other articles up to £28 value.

Canada. In addition to personal effects, the following articles may be brought into Canada duty-free: a maximum of 50 cigars, 200 cigarettes, 2 pounds of tobacco and 40 ounces of liquor, provided these are declared to customs on arrival. The exemption for purchases is $150, and gift parcels may be worth $15.

**THE
SOVIET
SCENE**

BY WAY OF BACKGROUND

Some facts and figures

Geography

The Union of Soviet Socialist Republics—or, to give the Russian appellation, the *Soyuz Sovietskikh Sotsialisticheskikh Respublik, abbreviated CCCP* in Cyrillic characters—is the largest country in the world. Sprawling over the continents of Europe and Asia, spreading from the Baltic to the Black Sea, from the Carpathians to the Pacific, from the Arctic to Southwestern Asia, it is almost 7,000 miles from west to east and 2,500 miles from north to south. Of its vast territory 2,110,-000 square miles are in Europe and 6,537,172 square miles in Asia. Its total surface is larger than the face of the moon we see from the earth. An express train needs a week to cover the distance from Moscow to Vladivostok. There are 11 time zones in the union; people on the Pacific coast are eating their suppers when the citizens of Moscow are having lunch. It is the only major power in the world that has kept its territory substantially intact for centuries and in fact, in the last forty-odd years, made substantial additions to it.

Its boundaries are over 40,000 miles long. The northernmost point of the continental Soviet Union is Cape Chelyuskin, at 77° 44′ N latitude; its southernmost lies in the city of Kushka, 35° 18′ N latitude, on the frontier of Afghanistan. The western tip of the USSR is Mamonovo, on the Baltic, 19° 59′ E longitude. The most easterly point is Cape Dezhnev on the Bering Strait, 169° 40′ E of Greenwich. The Union is bordered by Norway, Finland, the Baltic Sea, Poland, Czechoslovakia, Hungary and Romania on the west; the Black Sea, Turkey, Iran, the Caspian Sea, Afghanistan, China (Sinkiang and Manchuria) Mongolia, the Amur and Ussuri rivers, and Korea on the south; the Arctic Ocean on the north; the Bering Strait, the Bering Sea, the Sea of Okhotsk and the Sea of Japan on the east. Off the northern coast there are four island groups: Novaya Zemlya (New Land), Franz Josef Land, Severnaya Zemlya (North Land) and the Novosibirskiye (New Siberian) Islands. Off the eastern coast lie the islands of Sakhalin and the Kuriles.

The basic outline of the USSR is very simple: it is an immense plain framed by mountains. In some places there are impressive plateaus. The complex of mountain chains which form the two great mountain ranges (called knots) of the Pamir and of Armenia are extended and arranged in great arcs, concentric with the so-called Siberian shield. The Siberian mountains, sometimes covered by glaciers, include the Kamchatka, Anadyr, Kolima, Sayan, Stanovoy, Verkhoyansk and Yablonovy mountains. Some are quite ancient while others are newer with rugged outlines, and there are several active volcanoes, especially in the Kamchatka Peninsula. The peaks of the Altay Mountains rise to 15,157 feet on Mount Belukha. Southwest of these, the colossal Tien-Shan (Pobeda Peak, 24,-406 feet) and the Hindu Kush have huge glaciers feeding the rivers of the Turan Lowlands in Soviet Central Asia. West of the Pamir knot, though a considerable distance away, is the barrier range of the Elburz Mountains, forming the southern end of the Caspian basin and the northern frontier of Iran. These extend to the Armenian knot. The lofty massifs are south of the Transcaucasian valley, flanked in the north by the great bastion of the Greater Caucasus Mountains, with few passes. 15 of the peaks are higher than Mont Blanc.

The Ural Mountains are generally considered to be the boundary between Europe and Asia. They are a low range, little above 6,000 feet, with a general elevation of about 2,000 feet. In the center section, the range is divided into individual ranges.

The great rivers of the USSR, among the largest in the world, are of vital importance as transportation arteries, though both in European Russia and Siberia they are frozen during the winter. In European Russia, the most important rivers rise in the Valday Uplands and the Smolensk-Moscow Hills, flowing outward to the surrounding seas; the Dnieper and Don to the Black Sea, the Western Dvina to the Baltic, and Volga to the Caspian. The chief rivers of Central Asia, the Amu Darya and Syr Darya, water the alluvial oases of the foothills and the extensively irrigated deserts of the Central Asian deserts. The largest rivers east of the Urals, the Ob, the Yenisei and the Lena, follow the dip of the land north to the Arctic. Their lower reaches remain frozen after their upper lengths have thawed and, as a result, vast areas are flooded every spring (especially in the case of the Ob), creating immense areas of permanent and impassable marshes. In the far east, the only important river is the Amur, which flows into the Pacific. Of the great lakes, the Aral Sea and Lake Baikal are the most important; Lake Ladoga and Lake Onega in the northwest are the two largest in Europe.

Climate

The climate of the Soviet Union is largely determined by its geographical situation. It is open to the north, while to the south there is a barrier of high mountain ranges. The cold arctic masses of air sweep across from the Arctic Sea, while the tall southern ranges prevent the warmer currents of air from prevailing.

Over the greater part of the USSR's territory, the western winds from the Atlantic predominate. These cause a good deal of precipitation and, as they move eastward, though their effect gradually decreases, they still have a considerable influence on the climate as far as the Central Siberian uplands. The currents of the Pacific are stopped by the coastal mountain ranges and it is only along a narrow coastal strip, and in the valley of the Amur, that a weakened effect of the monsoon becomes noticeable. The regions far from the oceans have a continental climate, with great differences in temperature between summer and winter. Above Asia, during the winter, the air cools off considerably in the uplands and long periods of high pressure develop, which means that under the cloudless, clear skies, the cold is intense for months on end. From this central area masses of cold air spread out in every direction. During the summer, high barometric pressures disappear in this region. The southern parts of Asia become warmer and a low-pressure area develops over Iran and northwest India. Currents start from the west and northwest and these bring the most rain to the Soviet Union.

Naturally, the higher elevations also play their part in shaping the climate by influencing the movement of air masses. The Caucasus and the Crimean mountains protect the sea coast from the intrusion of northern cold currents. In the Soviet Far East, the mountains also impede the monsoon. The descending currents at the foot of the Central Asian mountains, which are dry and hot, have had an important role in the evolution of the desert regions.

By and large, the climate of the Soviet Union is extremely severe and its effect on agriculture and transportation is fundamental. In January, almost the whole of the country has a mean monthly temperature below 32° F; only the southern Crimea, the lowlands of the Transcaucasus and the southern parts of the Turan Lowlands are above freezing point. All the areas to the north and east are covered by snow for at least some weeks each winter. Of course, this also has some advantages—crops are protected and later, with the spring thaw, watered. The Russians have developed great skill in keeping transport moving over snow and on the frozen lakes and rivers. The Russian winter becomes more intense from south to north and west to east in proportion to the distance from the milder influences of the Baltic, the Black and the Caspian seas. At Batumi, on the Black Sea coast, the mean winter temperature is 43° F; in the same latitude, Tashkent is only 31° F; Leningrad, on the Baltic, with a January mean temperature of 15° F, is three degrees warmer than Moscow, further south. The Leningrad winter, however, begins earlier and lasts longer than Moscow's.

In summer, temperatures are much more even than in winter. The highest occur in some parts of the Turan Lowlands, far from the oceans' cooling effect. July mean temperatures reach 86° F. The lowest temperatures are along the Arctic Ocean, but even here, long hours of sunshine raise the temperature to 45–50° F.

Spring and fall are short. During the spring *rasputitsa* (thaw season), rivers and roads are often impassable; the annual floods are often disastrous, especially on the north-flowing rivers. The end of the fall is a period of alternating frost and thaw, which again makes travel difficult.

The most abundant rainfall is on the Black Sea coast of Transcaucasia, with Batumi recording nearly 100 inches. From the Baltic Coast to Moscow there is a zone that gets more than 24 inches, but as you move east and beyond the Urals, the rainfall lessens. Most of the rain falls in spring and summer. In winter there are heavy falls in many parts of European Russia brought by moist westerly air streams.

The climate of Asiatic Soviet Russia is also severe. In January, the coldest month, most places register mean temperatures below freezing. The coldest area is northeast Siberia, where Verkhoyansk has a mean January temperature of −59° F, and −94.4° F has been recorded here and at Oimyakon, the lowest temperatures ever found outside Antarctica.

But the Siberian winter is tempered by the dryness of the air and the comparative lightness of winds. Areas to the south and east often have much worse weather conditions with cold, piercing winds from the interior. Parts of the Pacific coast are cold for their latitude. The growing season ranges from 200 days in southern Turkmenistan (Central Asia) to only 80 days in the Siberian Arctic. Rainfall and snowfall are both fairly low; only a narrow central belt between the Urals and the Tien-Shan gets more than eight inches. Along the Pacific coast, this increases southwards; southern Kamchatka and the area southeast of the Amur receive more than 24 inches. Most of the rain falls in late spring and summer. In Siberia, there is a permanently frozen subsoil everywhere, except along the coast, southeast of the Amur, in Kamchatka and in the Kuriles.

Population

The most recent estimate of the Soviet Union's population is 262 million in 1980. The growth is uninterrupted, and it was a woman from the Moscow area who produced the greatest number of children ever recorded. In 27 confinements one Madame Vassilet gave birth to 16 pairs of twins, seven sets of triplets and four sets of quadruplets—69 in all. She lived in the 19th century however, and has had no recent challengers.

The most important group of people are the East Slavs: Russians, Ukrainians and Byelorussians, representing more than three-fourths of the total population. The Russians number about 130 million, mainly in the Russian Soviet Federated Socialist Republic, the vast area that stretches as far as the Pacific. But they also represent an important proportion of the population in all the other republics of the Union. The Ukrainians number some 40 million, the majority living in the Ukrainian Republic, but there are other sizeable colonies of them, some in the Far East. The Byelorussians (over 10 million) live mostly in their own Union Republic.

The second largest group, numbering about 40 million, are the nationalities of Turkic origin, living mainly in Central Asia. They include the Tartars (or Tatars) largely concentrated near Kazan on the Volga River, east of Moscow; the Kazakhs; the Uzbeks of the southern oases of Central Asia (at 12 million, the third largest group after the Russians and Ukrainians); and the Azers with their Persian-influenced culture.

The Caucasus is an even more complex mixture of nationalities than Macedonia. Its mountain and valleys have been a haven for countless refugees and exiles. The Armenians (nearly three million), and the Georgians (about the same), provide the main elements in this melting pot.

The Finno-Ugrians were forced out of their Altai home some 1,100 years ago by the nomads of the steppe and driven north and west. The largest groups of these peoples are the Mordvinians and Udmurts of the Volga-Urals area and the Estonians, Finns and Karelians in the northwest of European Russia. Farther south, the Latvians and the Lithuanians are descended from Slav communities who settled along the Baltic after the Finno-Ugrians but before the Russians. Although their languages are *distantly* related to the Slavonic group, the Latvians and Lithuanians regard themselves as primarily non-Slav peoples, while their strongest historical links are with what is now Western Europe, Poland and Scandinavia. The Estonians, Latvians and Lithuanians had their brief independence between the two world wars. The Moldavians, numbering about two and a half million today, are closely related to their Romanian neighbors. Although of very mixed origins, they claim to be descendants of the Roman legionnaires once stationed on the fringes of the Black Sea.

About two million Jews are scattered throughout the Soviet Union, and many of them are now being allowed to emigrate to Israel. They are mainly concentrated in European Russia (especially in the cities), and in a small autonomous province near the Pacific coast. The Volga Germans (descendants of settlers brought to Russia by Catherine the Great and others) were deported to Siberia during the last war and only a fraction of them have returned to their old homes. The same applies to the Kalmyks, who lived west of the Volga delta; accused of collaboration with the Germans, they were shipped to beyond the Urals, but in 1958 their Autonomous Soviet Socialist Republic was restored. They are Mongols, like the Buryats of the Baikal area. The Crimean Tatars, who shared the same wartime fate as the Kalmyks, have been less fortunate; they are still campaigning to be allowed to return to their old homeland, the Crimea, and many suffer for their efforts.

Asian Russia, apart from Russians, Ukrainians, Kazakhs and Uzbeks, includes the semi-nomadic Kirghiz people and the more-or-less stationary Turkmen. These are now settled in the autonomous republics of the southwest, between the Caspian and Sinkiang. Scattered throughout eastern Siberia are a number of pre-Turkic and pre-Russian tribes, including the Evenki of the Lena valley (possibly related to the American Indians) and the Tadzhiks, on the borders of Afghanistan, of Iranian origin. A few other minorities, known collectively as "Old Asiatics" and related to the Eskimos, live along the Bering Strait. In the Soviet Far East, there are still several aboriginal communities, including the Ainus of Sakhalin.

Cities and Villages

As in practically all countries, there is a general movement from the countryside into the cities. This flow is being balanced in the Soviet Union by government action, and permits are needed for a change of domicile or even for travel within the country. The housing shortage, which despite constant efforts still continues, is another deterrent. In spite of this, the cities are growing. Moscow is the fifth largest city in the world, with some eight million people living in the metropolitan area, an increase of over 25% in the last 20 years. Leningrad follows with almost four and a half million. The other great cities (all with populations over one million) include Kiev, Taskent, Baku, Kharkov, Gorky, Novosibirsk, Kuibyshez, Sverdlosk, Minsk, Odessa and Tbilisi. Other cities which are pushing the one million mark are Donetsk (the former Stalino), Chelyabinsk, Kazan, Dnepropetrovsk, Perm, Omsk, Volgograd (previously Stalingrad), Rostov-on-Don, Ufa, Yerevan, Saratov, Riga, Alma-Ata, Voronezh, Zaporozhye, Krasnoyarsk, Krivoi Rog, Lvov, Karaganda, Yaroslavl, Novokuznetsk, Krasnodar and Tula. The Soviet policy of settling certain regions either by compulsory transfer or by holding out particular incentives is shown in the spectacular population increases of such places as Togliatti (Stavropol) with 247%, Petropavlovsk-Kamchatsky (259%) or Balakovo (181%). There are over 60 cities with more than 200,000 inhabitants, and the list of those with more than 100,000 would run to several pages.

The main ports of the Soviet Union are divided between the most important stretches of coast line. On the Black Sea, Batumi and Odessa are the principal ones, followed by Nikolayev, Novorossisk, Rostov-on-Don and Zhdanov (formerly Maryupol). On the Caspian, Astrakhan and Baku are the most significant ports; on the Baltic, Leningrad and Riga rate tops with Kaliningrad, Liepaya, Tallinn and Ventspils following. On the Arctic Sea, the most important are Archangel and Murmansk, and on the Pacific, Vladivostok.

How irresistible the lure of the city has been is shown by the simple statistic that out of the over 262 million people of the Soviet Union, 56% now live in urban areas and, despite the vital claims of agriculture, only 44% live in the country.

It is now over 45 years since the collectivization of agricultural land in Russia (by 1936 more than 90% of peasant households and almost all of the country's arable land had been organized into collectives). This, of course, completely changed the typical Russian village. Living conditions, still primitive in certain respects, have been greatly improved; electricity has now reached all but the most remote areas.

The villages are now either in the center or on the borders of collective farms, of which there are two main types, the *kolkhozes* and the *sovkhozes*. The former are cooperatives in which the peasant's land, machinery and most of his animals are the collective property of the farm's members. The *sovkhozes* or state farms, much larger than *kolkhozes*, are financed by the State and their workers are state employees with fixed wages. There have been many policy changes and much reorganization in the last 30 years. The number of *kolkhozes* dropped from 252,000 in 1950 to only 36,200 in 1967, with an average area of 2,800 hectares (about 7,000 acres) of land, whereas the number of state farms rose to more than double, and their average arable area was more than twice as large. In 1967 an experiment was started to end state subsidies to *sovkhozes* by making more of them fully responsible for their own profits and losses.

The many thousands of villages are mostly tied to agricultural production, though some might shelter hunters or fishermen, especially in the Soviet Far East. Much folk art and folklore has survived here. But the tourist is not likely to see much of the villages, except for some show places. With a few modern improvements, the Russian villager follows the same way of life, has the same joys and sorrows as his forefathers, and if he is young, he is likely to strive hard to escape to the city.

The State

At present, the USSR is divided into 15 Soviet Socialist Republics, sometimes called Union Republics, on the basis of nationalities. They represent the most populous and culturally most advanced groups of peoples. In administrative respects, they show certain parallels with the 50 states of the USA.

The 15 republics are:

The *Armenian Republic,* with an area of 11,502 square miles and a population of 2,728,000. Its capital is Yerevan.

The *Azerbaijan Republic,* population 5,514,000; capital: Baku. Area: 33,436 square miles.

The *Byelorussian Republic,* population 10,500,000; capital: Minsk. Area: 80,154 square miles.

The *Estonian Republic,* population 1,418,000; capital: Tallinn. Area: 17,413 square miles.

The *Georgian Republic,* population 4,878,000; capital: Tbilisi. Area: 26,911 square miles.

The *Kazakh Republic,* population 13,928,000; capital: Alma-Ata. Area: 1,064,092 square miles.

The *Kirghiz Republic,* population 3,219,000; capital: Frunze, Area: 76,642 square miles.

The *Latvian Republic,* population 2,454,000; capital: Riga. Area: 24,-695 square miles.

The *Lithuanian Republic,* population 3,262,000; capital: Vilnius. Area: 25,173 square miles.

The *Moldavian Republic,* population 3,764,000; capital: Kishinev. Area: 13,012 square miles.

The *Russian Republic,* population 132,913,000; capital: Moscow. Area: 6,593,391 square miles.

The *Tadzhik Republic,* population 3,283,000; capital: Dushanbe. Area: 55,019 square miles.

The *Turkmen Republic,* population 2,430,000; capital: Ashkhabad. Area: 188,417 square miles.

The *Ukrainian Republic,* population 48,136,000; capital: Kiev. Area: 232,046 square miles.

The *Uzbek Republic,* population 13,289,000; capital: Tashkent. Area: 158,069 square miles.

These figures show that the Russian Soviet Federated Socialist Republic is by far the largest in both area and population, representing more than half of the total. Within the Russian Federation, the major nationalities (other than Russian), are subdivided into 16 Autonomous Soviet Socialist Republics. These include the Yakut, Bashkir, Buryat, Dagestan, Kabardino-Balkar, Kalmyk, Karelian, Komi, Mari, Mordovian, North-Ossetian, Tatar, Tuvinian, Udmurt, Chechen-Ingush and Chuvash Autonomous Republics. The Union Republics, except some smaller ones, are divided into *oblasts, krays* and Autonomous Republics. All these are on an appropriate level of jurisdiction and are directly responsible to their respective Union Republics. The *oblast* is a purely administrative subdivision without any important nationality group other than the one after which the Union Republic is named and of which it is a part. The Autonomous Republics administratively have the same function as the *oblasts,* but their boundaries serve to give political recognition to some important minority nationality group. The *kray* is like a combination of the first two. Its lesser policies are based on nationality groups, autonomous *oblasts* or national *okrugs*. *Oblasts* are regions and *krays* are territories, and these are further divided into districts *(rayons)*, cities and rural communities.

How does this rather complex system work? At the very top of the state stands the Supreme Soviet of the USSR, roughly equivalent to a parliament. This is divided into two "houses", the Soviet of the Union and the Soviet of the Nationalities. Both have their standing committees. The Soviet of the Union has a Credentials Committee, a Legislative Proposals Committee, a Budget Committee and a Foreign Affairs Committee. In the House of the Union, one representative is chosen for every 300,000 people; it corresponds roughly to the House of Representatives in the United States or the House of Commons in Britain. In the House of Nationalities (resembling the US Senate), each Soviet Socialist Republic has 32 representatives, each Autonomous Republic 11, each autonomous *oblast* five and each national *okrug* one. The House of Nationalities has the same committees as the House of the Union, with the addition of an economic committee.

The next authority, at least in theory, is the presidium of the Supreme Soviet, with the Supreme Court and the Procurator General of the Soviet Union almost its equal, all three being under the two legislative chambers. The Council of Ministers of the USSR supervises the committees and agencies which are above the All-Union Ministries and the Union Republican Ministries. The number and names of these committees and agencies are subject to change at irregular intervals, but there is a board of some kind to regulate almost every facet of life from labor and wages, through television and aviation to foreign economic relations and mineral fertilizers. Under these agencies and committees we find the All-Union Ministries, those of Foreign Trade, the Merchant Marine, Railroads, the Medium Machine Building Industry, Power Station Construction and Transport Construction. The Republican Ministries are those of Higher and Secondary Specialized Education, Geological Surveys, Public Health, Foreign Affairs, Culture, Defense, Communications, Architecture and Finance.

The Party

It is a unique feature of the Soviet Union and one which has been copied by all Communist countries in Europe that the state is controlled by one political party, the Communist Party of the Soviet Union. Through it, the dictatorship of the proletariat is exercised. Its guiding principle is Marxism-Leninism. All the high officials of the state are recruited from the top ranks of the party. Party membership is theoretically open to any working person "if he does not exploit the labor of others, if he accepts the party program and rules, if he actively takes part in the execution of the Party program and if he works in a Party organization and carries out all party decisions". According to recent figures, out of 262 million Soviet citizens about 10% of the population are members or candidates for membership. The Party has about 200,000 full-time paid officials, the *apparatchiks*.

The Party hierarchy is a complex one. It is headed by the General Secretary who, while the title of his office might be a modest one, is far more important than the All-Union President, usually a figurehead (though the present Party Secretary, Leonid Brezhnev, recently invested himself with the title of President as well, in place of ex-President Podgorny), or the prime minister of even the largest Republic. Below him is the Politburo and the Secretariat (on a somewhat lower level), and *below* those, the Central Committee. Then follows the All-Union Party Congress, and on the next level, the Congresses of the 14 Republics, the Republic Central Committees and the Secretariats. The next echelon is represented by the Provincial Conferences and the Provincial Committees and Secretariats. One rung lower are the District Conferences, Committees and Secretariats. And at the bottom of the ladder we find the cells, bureaus and local secretariats.

At almost every level, the official state organization is paralleled by a Party organization; it is only at the top that the state and Party pyramids merge. The cells are usually established in factories, farms, villages, army and navy units, educational centers and similar places. The smallest cell or primary unit must have at least three members, but there can be several thousand, as in a large factory or a ministry. Above the primary level, the party units run more or less parallel with the administrative subdivisions of the state. Each city, district, region, territory and Union Republic has a separate Party organization—except the Russian Soviet Federated Socialist Republic, which is run by the central Party organs.

The basic principle, as proclaimed by Lenin, is "democratic centralism", which, in effect, means that the proletariat cannot determine policy but has to be led. This leadership is effectively provided by the Politburo, a select group whose size has varied throughout the years. The Party Congress meets at least once every four years, though it has frequently convened more often. It is supposed to "determine the tactical line of the Party on major questions of current policy", something which it does very rarely. The Central Committee, which carries on in the intervals, is elected by the Congresses. The Central Committee is supposed to meet at least once every six months. It supervises every sphere of the nation's life, and maintains controlling departments for the army, for heavy and light industry, for foreign policy, the arts, propaganda, finances, youth, and, most importantly, for personnel. The last department handles the promotion, demotion or transfer of all top Party officials. The various sections are directed by members of the Central Secretariat of the Party, which meets daily to deal with current political and administrative problems and reports directly to the Party leadership.

How do the State and Party relate? Quite simply: the Party determines policy; the State administers it. The task of government officials is to put into effect the policies originated by the Party, that is by the Politburo and the Central Committee. This has certain advantages: the policymakers, unlike those in Western democracies, are relieved of routine tasks. The executive of the State is the Council of Ministers and its chairman is the Premier, the formal head of the Soviet national government. While the late Nikita Khrushchev combined the roles of General (or First) Party Secretary and Premier, this was an exceptional situation; today Leonid Brezhnev holds the supreme Party role and Aleksei Kosygin is Chairman of the Council of Ministers although Brezhnev is clearly the leader in this duumvirate.

The Economy

The Soviet Union is the world's leading producer of, among many things, wheat, butter, iron ore, manganese, books and, surprisingly, cigars.

But the figures and "visible" facts, the statistics and the five-year plans tell only part of the story, if they tell it at all. Genuine economic reform has been sometimes blocked by the Party because it would have given too much power to industrial managers, experts, trading concerns and local authorities. It could be argued that the Party's very existence depends to a great extent on the comparative inefficiency of the economy; its main task is to exhort, flatter, and shame people into working harder. As a British analyst pointed out, there are really *two* economies in the Soviet Union. Of these, the inefficient one is the visible one "the shambling giant which ploughs the fields, mines the coal and weaves the textiles". The West knows a good deal about this economy as its faults and irrationalities are quite freely discussed in the press. The main difficulty is the lack of incentives. It is, obviously, difficult to feed people for a long period with mere promises of a better life.

But there is another aspect of the economy, well-hidden from prying eyes. This is the sector which manufactures arms and spacecraft, handles the USSR's international finances, provides the material base for the police and intelligence services and creates the funds for political action outside the country. No statistics are available about it; in the budget it appears under general and very broad terms. It recruits the most brilliant people and often gives them material rewards which the average Soviet citizen does not even dream about. By all indications, this part of the economy functions more efficiently, perhaps, than the equivalent sectors in any Western country.

Certainly, during the 64 years of Soviet rule immense progress has been made. Czarist Russia was a predominantly agricultural land with few and feeble industries. The First World War and the subsequent civil war disrupted and destroyed the nation's economic life; the difficulties were almost insurmountable. After the period of NEP (a mixed, partly private enterprise economy), it took the USSR until 1927 to regain its pre-1914 level of production. The first *pyatiletka* (five-year plan) began on October 1, 1928. The Second World War prevented the completion of the third five-year plan since industry had to switch to armaments. During the war, hundreds of industrial plants were transferred beyond the Urals and these remained in their new locations. The long conflict caused damage and loss costing more than 700,000,000,000 roubles. Much of the rebuilding was done within three years after the end of the war.

The following five-year plans demanded tremendous efforts. Industrial production, mostly in capital goods, was multiplied. Until fairly recently, the concentration on heavy industry was aimed to support the country's large military program and to establish a firm base for further economic growth. Today the emphasis has shifted somewhat in the direction of consumer production. The standard of living has risen, though perhaps less quickly than expected; science and technology have accelerated their expansion and Soviet military power has, in many respects, overtaken the West. Apart from the products we have mentioned, new industries are being developed in plastics and pharmaceutical products and computers.

Much emphasis has been placed on building up the industries in the eastern and far eastern territories, which are rich in natural resources. In late 1978 President Brezhnev announced in a speech to the Party Central Committee that these industrial complexes "accounted for the entire increment in oil production, for nearly the entire increment of gas production, and for a considerable part of the increase in power generation, coal and iron ore and the production of trucks and tractors" over the past 3 years.

Energy Production

Coal is still the most important source; according to recent estimates, the Soviet Union has more than 8.6 billion tons in reserves. Most of these sources are in Asian Russia. Their value is increased by the fact that the mines produce a good deal of hard coal with a high calorie content. The 1978 production figure was 727 million tons. Of this, over a quarter is used for coke-production in which the Soviet Union leads the world. About a quarter of the coal is obtained by surface mining.

The most important mining districts are in the Donets Basin, the Kuznetsk Basin, the Karaganda Coal Basin (which is semi-desert) and the Pechora Coal Basin, where intensive exploitation began during the Second World War. There is brown coal in the Moscow district and the Urals yield raw materials for the chemical industry from the Kizel and Chelyabinsk mines. In Eastern Siberia, the Irkutsk Coal Basin, centered around Cheremkhovo, is one of the most important. Coal mining in the Soviet Far East is also developing quickly.

The Soviet Union is also one of the leading oil-producing countries of the world. New areas are continually being surveyed and developed and the forecast for 1980 was 620 million tons. In former times it was Baku that provided the major portion of oil; today some 66% comes from the "second Baku", situated between the Volga and the Urals. This immense oil field stretches into the Tatar Republic and Bashkiria with deposits around Kuibyshev, Saratov and Volgograd. Long-distance pipelines deliver the oil to important foreign industrial countries, such as Czechoslovakia, Hungary, Poland and the German Democratic Republic. Another pipeline leads to eastern Siberia.

The oil fields of Baku have been known for centuries. Hundreds of wells have been drilled off the Apsheron Peninsula, tapping the deposits lying under the Caspian Sea. A pipeline connects Baku with Batumi, the Black Sea port. At the northern foot of the Caucasus, Grozny, Maykop and Neftegorsk are the main centers. The fields along the eastern and northern shore of the Caspian, those in the Nebit-Dag area of the Turkmen Republic, and the Emba fields in the North Caspian Lowland remain important; their reserves are comparable to those of Baskhiria. In the Far East, the oil production of Sakhalin has grown considerably. Local needs are filled by the wells of the Fergana Valley and of the Ukraine and Central Asia. Crude oil is refined partly locally and partly at the terminal points of the pipelines. In oil transportation, the Volga oil tanker fleet plays an important part and thus every major Volga port has large oil refineries.

Natural gas is found partly in the oil-bearing areas, though in many places it is exploited independently. In 1977 the total production was some 340 billion cubic meters. It is used partly as a source of energy and partly as raw material for the chemical industry. The most important fields are at Saratov (the Volga district), Central Asia (Gazli), the Northern Caucasus (Stavropol), the northern slopes of the Carpathians (Dashava), Transcaucasia, Western Siberia, the Fergana Valley, Turkmenia and many other places. The gas is transported in pipelines from the most important fields to the primary industrial centers. It is piped into Moscow, Kiev, Rostov, Voronezh, Kharkov, Leningrad, Tbilisi, Yerevan, Chelyabinsk, Sverdlovsk and other cities. The mining of oil shale still continues in Estonia in the adjacent parts of the Russian Republic, in the Middle Volga, in the northeastern Siberian plateau west of the Lena River, and in Kazakhstan, east and northeast of Lake Balkhash.

The Soviet Union, with several of the world's greatest rivers and high mountain regions, has resources of hydroelectricity which have been calculated at 420 million kilowatts, or 11% of the total world potential. More than four-fifths of this is provided by the great rivers of Asian Russia, though the potentials of the Amur and Lena are not yet fully utilized. The principal hydroelectric stations in Siberia are on the Angara, an outlet of Lake Baikal, at Bratsk and Irkutsk. Other large stations are at Krasnoyarsk, on the River Yenisei, at Novosibirsk on the River Ob and at Kamensk, near the mouth of the same river. In the republics of Central Asia, the many rapid mountain rivers of the Tien-Shan, Pamirs and other mountain ranges have huge potentialities though the power stations so far built are small. The main plants are on the Chirchik near Tashkent, the Farkhadskaya River, the Kayrak-Kumskaya station in the Fergana Valley, the Alma-Ata station on a tributary of the River Ili and the Nurek station on the River Vakhsh near Dushanbe. There is a "cascade" of seven stations on the Volga, with others under construction. About 25 hydroelectric power stations have been built on rivers flowing from the Greater and Lesser Caucasus, of which the largest is at Mingechaur in Azerbaijan. There are other groups in Armenia, in the Karelian Republic and on the Kola Peninsula. By the end of 1978, the total output of electricity was estimated at 1,207,000 million kilowatts.

The Russians were the first in the world to complete an experimental nuclear-power station for public use; it opened in 1954 at Obninsk, southwest of Moscow. The first large atomic-power plant went into operation in 1958, "somewhere in Siberia", to provide electrical power for the production of plutonium for military purposes. The first major civilian installation began to operate in 1964 at Beloyarka in the Urals. The largest atomic plant of all is the Novovoronezhsky on the River Don with a capacity of 1.5 million kilowatts. The latest plan provides for a 21 percent increase in nuclear power generation.

Heavy Industry and its Raw Materials

The iron ore resources of the Soviet Union are the largest in the world. Large-scale mining continues in more than 100 localities. The more important centers are at Krivoi Rog (where the proximity of the Donets Basin makes quick smelting possible), on the Kerch Peninsula, in the Urals (Magnitogorsk, Chelyabinsk, Zlatoust, Nizhny-Tagul, the Kuznetsk Basin and Karaganda), in the Central Black Earth Region (Tula and other places), in Siberia (adjacent to the Kuznetsk Basin in the Soria Mountains, in the Angara district and the valley of the Amur). After the

Second World War, valuable iron ore deposits were opened up in Kazakhstan, in the Kustanai Oblast.

The development and raw material supply of the iron and steel industries have been assured by the amplitude of different metals needed in refining. The Soviet Union produces 40% of the world's manganese (at Chiatura in the Colchis Lowland of Georgia, the Nikopol Basin, the Urals, Kazakhstan and Western Siberia). Chromium is found in the Urals, Kazakhstan and Eastern Siberia. The deposits of nickel, wolfram, molybdenum, vanadium and titanium are also significant.

In 1975 the USSR produced 98.6 million tons of pig iron and 141 million tons of steel, the second-largest output in the world. The 1980 target for steel production was 165 million tons.

In the Ukraine, this production is based on the coal of the Donets Basin, on hydroelectricity, the oil of the Caucasus, the iron ore of Krivoi Rog and Kerch, and the manganese of Nikopol. The foundries have been built partly in the vicinity of the coal mines and partly close to the iron ore deposits, and a "shuttle system" has been developed between the deposits and the sources of energy. The important cities of heavy industry are Donetsk, Makeyevka, Dnepropetrovsk, Zaporozhye, and Kramatorsk. The Ural's center is the Ural-Kuznetsk *kombinat* (iron and coal cooperative); it was developed mainly during the last war. The centers of iron and steel production coincide with those of iron ore mining. The Central Industrial District (Moscow, Lipetsk and Tula) exploits partly the local iron ore and partly scrap-iron. It plays an important part in the production of refined steel for the machine industry. Some new centers have developed recently: the Cherepovets Combine refines the iron ore of the Kola Peninsula, using the coal of Vorkuta. A similar more recent center is that of Karaganda, using the iron ore of Kustanai. In Transcaucasia, Eastern Siberia and the Soviet Far East, the iron and steel industry is also making considerable strides.

Nonferrous metallurgy is also highly developed. There are large deposits in Kazakhstan (Kounrad, Dzhezkazgan), in Armenia and the Urals. Considerable quantities of copper are exported. Lead and zinc are found primarily in the Altay Region, in Kazakhstan, the Caucasus, Siberia and the Far East. The centers of mercury smelting are Chelyabinsk in the Urals, Ust-Kamenogorsk in Kazakhstan, Ordzhonikidze in the Caucasus, and some of the cities of the Donets and Kuznetsk basins. Lead is processed mainly at Leninogorsk and Chimkent in Kazakhstan and Ordzhonikidze in the Caucasus.

Aluminum production is based on several ores; the production, being a two-stage process, requires large amounts of electricity and is done mostly near large and cheap sources of current. The bauxite of Tikhvin is processed around Volkhov. The raw material of the important bauxite deposits of the Urals is smelted partly at Zaporozhye, partly locally. The nephelite of the Kola Peninsula also serves to supply Zaporozhye, though the Kandalaksha and Nadvoitsy plants also use it. Recently alumite deposits have been opened up at Zaglik, south of Kirovabad in the Kura River Valley of Transcaucasia. The raw materials are transformed into aluminum at Yerevan and Sumgait. The increase in the capacity to provide energy in the Eastern territories has intensified the development of Siberian aluminum smelting; the most important units are at Novokuznetsk, Krasnoyarsk and Bratsk.

After South Africa, the Soviet Union is probably the world's largest producer of gold. Main production at present occurs in Eastern Siberia and the Far East, but older mines still function in the Urals and other mountain areas. Newly discovered lodes have become important in Kazakhstan. Platinum is plentiful in the Urals and the diamond mines of Yakutia are very rich.

The machine industry has been given priority in the Soviet economy. In 50 years, its capacity has been increased by 500% and it is now the second largest in the world. Huge and specialized centers have been developed; the largest are near Moscow and Leningrad, followed by the Urals, the Ukraine and the Volga district. But much progress has been made in the Caucasus and in Western and Eastern Siberia as well.

In the power industry, Moscow, Leningrad, Kharkov, Kiev, Riga, Sverdlovsk and Kuibyshev represent the most important centers providing the equipment for power stations, transportation, etc. The large-scale projects of electrification and the introduction of diesel engines have brought considerable change in transportation. Since 1956, no steam locomotives have been manufactured, and the old ones have been gradually replaced. The Soviet Union is a leading manufacturer of tractors and trucks. While the manufacture of automobiles has lagged behind, Russia has built up a considerable industry, partly with the help of Fiat of Italy, who have built a plant in the USSR. Production is said to have quadrupled between 1975 and 1980. Agricultural machinery is being manufactured throughout the Union, frequently in specialized form according to local needs. Thus grain-harvesters are made in Rostov, Taganrog and Saratov, in the Black Earth belt; Tashkent produces cotton pickers and, in Zaporozhye, corn pickers are manufactured.

Complex precision instruments and machinery are concentrated most in the plants of Leningrad, Moscow and the Baltic Republics.

Since the end of the war, household equipment—refrigerators, vacuum cleaners, television sets, washing machines—have also found place in the manufacturing program.

The chemical industry had to be created afresh and during the last decade or so, the greatest increase in capital investment was in this field. No detailed statistics are available, but the major categories of finished products are mineral fertilizers, synthetic rubber, artificial and synthetic fibers, plastics, paints and dyes, soaps and detergents, insecticides and weed killers, pharmaceuticals and various products for use in industry, such as chemicals required in oil refining and metallurgy. Superphosphates are manufactured in the Ukraine, the Carpathians, the Baltic Republics, the Urals, Kazakhstan, the Kola Peninsula and elsewhere. The production of sulphuric acid, hydrochloric acid, ammonia and caustic soda has increased almost fourfold since 1950.

Like most large industrial countries, the Soviet Union is still struggling with the housing shortage caused by the war and by the planning priorities that gave comparatively little attention to "living space". Though the manufacture of concrete, fireproof bricks, glass and pre-fabricated units has substantially increased, space is still severely rationed and (especially for young couples) an independent, self-contained home often remains an impossible dream. There is ample material for industrial and public building, including granite, basalt, volcanic tufa and other substances and Soviet statistics put the number of houses built annually at 11 million.

Timber and Paper Industry

Though the timber reserves are largely in Siberia, lumbering, wood-working and paper-milling remained until recently more highly developed in European Russia. Intensive development has now raised the participation of the Eastern territories to about 80% and this is still increasing. The majority of the forests consist of pine. The timber is mostly processed locally, much of it having been transported by rafts to the factories. Four million tons of paper are produced yearly, which seems to cover basic needs. Considerable quantities are recycled. However, books, until recently very inexpensive, are becoming less so as paper costs rise.

Light Industries

The most important of these is the textile industry, and within it the cotton mills, using almost entirely local raw material. Fine wool fabrics are produced mainly in Moscow, Ivanovo and Yaroslavl. Cotton is grown in Central Asia and Transcaucasia. Hemp is an old crop in Russia, while jute is a newcomer. The largest hemp/jute industry used to be concentrated in ports, but smaller mills have now been built in many localities. The traditional centers of the silk industry are in Central Asia and Transcaucasia, where silk worms are grown, feeding on the mulberry trees planted along irrigation canals. Linen is produced primarily in the Central Industrial Region and the northwest, where the flax is grown. The shoe industry is being developed rapidly.

Food Industries

These are mainly concentrated in the farm districts. Sugar is one of the most important branches and about 10 million tons are produced annually. The flour-milling industry is centered in the big grain-growing areas, the meat-packing industry in the cattle-raising territories and also in the consumer centers. The dairy industry is most highly developed in the Baltic Republics, in the southern zone of the West Siberian Lowlands and around the big cities. The Soviet Union is the biggest producer of butter; though even so, in 1977, she was happy to purchase a large quantity of cut-price EEC surplus. The canning industry has a very important role in supplying the northern industrial districts which are underdeveloped agriculturally. Fish plays a substantial role in feeding the population. Almost seven million tons of seafood, fresh and processed, annually serve this purpose. Vegetable oils are also essential and several million tons are produced each year. Sunflower oil is the leading product, but in Tashkent, vegetable oil production has established a large industry linked to cotton milling. Breweries and tobacco factories have also been developed considerably in recent years.

Agriculture

In spite of almost superhuman efforts, agriculture has remained the Achilles' heel of the Soviet economy. The charlatanism of Lysenko, a geneticist whose theories flew in the face of common sense but were enthusiastically endorsed by Stalin, caused setbacks that hindered sensible and rational development for years. Nor did Khrushchev's pet scheme for the Virgin Lands fulfil expectations. In recent years the USSR has had to import grain almost every year, and much of its gold reserves and exports have gone to pay for this. Outsiders, as the noted American observer Charles W. Thayer has pointed out, seldom see collective farms, except a few show places. While the farms each have about 10,000 acres to cultivate, individual farmers are allowed to have "private plots", varying in size from half an acre to two-and-a-half acres (depending on the fertility of the plot) where they grow vegetables for their families, fodder for their strictly limited livestock and some produce to sell at the nearest town market. Human nature has been changed little, even by the Soviet system, and peasants give priority to their own plots over the collective tasks; nor is it possible to enforce the kind of discipline which prevails in factories and offices. The Soviet Union, in addition, is poorly provided with good soil; even where it is excellent, as in the famous Black Earth areas in the Ukraine and parts of Siberia, the rainfall is often uncertain. Recurrent shortages, bad harvests and inefficient working methods all contribute to the difficulties. Khrushchev's largely irrational schemes had failed and his successors are still struggling with the same problems that have bedeviled Russia's leaders for over 60 years. The 1970s saw a series of disastrously poor harvests and the USSR has been importing grain on a vaster scale than ever before—by all accounts causing tremendous problems of transport congestion at seaports and on the railroads.

According to the official statistics, only 23.6% of the Soviet Union's territory is arable land, of which less than half represents orchards, kitchen-gardens and grain-bearing areas; the rest is meadow and grazing land. Wheat is the main grain product—the USSR claims 30% of the world's total production. Earlier it was the Ukraine, Moldavia, the Northern Caucasus and the Volga district that supplied most of it; now Kazakhstan and Western Siberia contribute about 40%. Official Soviet statistics also claim that the USSR leads in growing rye, barley and oats. In the last decade, corn production has expanded, with sweet and field corn equally important. Rice is grown in the Southern Ukraine, in the Northern Caucasus, in Kazakhstan, some irrigated parts of Central Asia and in the Soviet Far East. Sugar beet, cotton and sunflower seeds are other important agricultural products; so is flax (in the Baltic Republics, the Moscow Basin and Byelorussia); jute is grown mainly in the Northern Ukraine and the Volga district's rainier parts. More than 75% of the world's production of sunflower seeds is provided by the Soviet Union. Potatoes, perhaps the most important part of the Soviet diet, are grown throughout the country, but mainly in the northern zone of the steppes. Vegetables are concentrated in the supply districts of the industrial center; but the Ukraine, Moldavia, the Caucasus and the Volga district supply most of the raw materials for canned vegetables. The sub-tropical tea plantations and tropical fruit orchards are long-established. Grapes are grown in Moldavia, the Crimea and the Southern Ukraine and the best wine is that of the Caucasus.

Cattle-breeding still lags behind, but has recently been encouraged by increased investment for animal husbandry. However, cattle were slaughtered on a large scale during a recent winter because of lack of fodder following on a disastrous year for agriculture. The Ukraine and the Baltic Republics lead in dairy products. The Ukraine, too, is the center of pig-breeding but this is also concentrated in the areas growing corn, potatoes and sugar beet. Sheep are bred both for their wool and their meat; the centers are in the Ukraine, the Caucasus, the republics of Central Asia and Kazakhstan. The famous karakul sheep provide astrakhan fur. Reindeer, camels and horses are all bred in various areas.

The Soviet Union's economic and industrial progress has suffered because many of their discoveries are said to have been made already outside the Union, but have remained unknown in the USSR through censorship of foreign publications.

Social Services

About as many doctors graduate annually in the Soviet Union as there were at any one time in the whole of the Czarist empire. Four out of every five Soviet doctors are women. In the 1970s there were 700,000 physicians, one to every 375 people, while in England and Wales there is something like one to every 900. However, the ratio of doctors to inhabitants in rural areas is only one-third that of the urban average.

All medical care is free of charge, except for the purchase of medicines. The Soviet press frequently reports about shortages, especially in the provinces. Doctors can carry on a private practice after their hours at the hospitals and clinics and their charges can be quite high. There are also several private cooperative clinics with some 48 hospitals where patients have to pay—and get much better service. The level of dentistry in the USSR seems to be lower than in the West; Soviet tourists to Britain frequently include a visit to the dentist among their activities.

Old-age pensions were not introduced until 1956, though previously a very low pension was paid to invalids and the disabled, or granted for special merit. A 1926 law states clearly that children must provide for the needs of their disabled parents. The pensionable age is 60 for working men and 55 for women. The size of the pension depends on the last basic salary scale of the pension it represents, that is, 100% of a wage or salary not exceeding 35 roubles, gradually descending to 50% of the last pay scale if the salary has been more than 100 roubles. "Personal pensions" are granted for "heroes of labor", "people's artists", Party and state officials and important scholars. These have no upper limit. State pensions for collective farmers were not introduced until 1965; the pensionable age for farming men is now 65, for women 60. In 1968 the minimum annual holiday was extended to 15 working days; income tax was reduced and the temporarily disabled, if they had worked for eight or more years, now receive 100% of their pay. However, non-union members get only 50% of the regular sickness benefits.

There have been no unemployment figures published in the Soviet Union since 1930. Unemployment benefits were abolished at the same time. In 1960, 78% of able-bodied citizens of working age were employed; in 1965 this rose to 87%, but these figures do not take into account seasonal unemployment and the fact that in 1967 State Committees on the Use of Labor Resources were established with the same functions as Western employment offices (labor exchanges). The essential difference is that they do not pay any benefits but merely help the unemployed to find work. In 1970, there were 1,170.7 females to every 1,000 males in the Soviet Union (the highest recorded imbalance in the world), and most women work outside their homes. Technological unemployment is believed to be considerable; even for the trained industrial worker, it takes 20 to 30 days to find employment, yet he is given only two weeks' pay when he is released from his previous job.

Religion

Before the 1917 Revolution, the Russian Orthodox Church was the established church of the Russian Empire, and most of the Great Russian, Ukrainian, Byelorussian and Georgian people belonged to it. The Czar was also head of the church. The Soviet Government disestablished the Church, confiscated its property and launched a large-scale anti-religious campaign.

Article 124 of the Constitution states that "the church in the USSR is separate from the State," and that "freedom of worship is recognized for all citizens." However, the same article also guarantees "freedom of anti-religious propaganda," and this is what appears to prevail in practice. After the Revolution all churches were closed and all religions were persecuted, but during World War II, Stalin, hoping to stimulate nationalism, relaxed these policies and this tolerance has been continued by his successors. All citizens can engage in worship (though it is mostly the elderly and women who do), and some new churches have been built since the war. But there are severe restrictions on evangelical activities, and the religious instruction of children is illegal. The nine main branches of Christianity are represented, as well as Islam, Judaism, Buddhism and smaller communities.

The Russian Orthodox Church, headed by the Patriarch of Moscow and All Russia (assisted by the Holy Synod), is still the largest. Before the revolution it had over 77,000 churches. Until 1959 it had 20,000. Now, only about 6,500 function, though there are still millions of adherents, including the Russians, Ukrainians, Byelorussians and most of the Finno-Ugrians. The Holy Synod is composed of the Metropolitans of Moscow, Leningrad, Kiev, Tallinn and Tula, and three bishops from the regions that make up the Patriarchate of Moscow. There are also many Old Believers, the conservative sect which separated from the Orthodox Church in the 17th century. The Church of Georgia also has a separate organization and 40 open churches.

The Armenian Apostolic (or Gregorian) Church has more than a million adherents in the Armenian Soviet Socialist Republic. About 40 million Moslems live in Central Asia, European Russia and Siberia, Ciscaucasia and Transcaucasia. Protestantism is represented mainly by Lutherans (in Estonia and Latvia) and the Union of Evangelical Baptists, both with well over a million members.

Roman Catholics are most numerous in Lithuania and the Western Ukraine. Their highest ranking prelates are four bishops. The Buddhists live in the autonomous republic of the Buryat-Mongols, in the Kalmyk and Tuva autonomous regions and around Chita and Irkutsk. They are organized under a Lama.

In spite of the Nazi extermination camps and the post-war emigration (now apparently gathering a little more speed), there are still almost two million Jews in the Soviet Union. Anti-Semitism, seldom far from the surface even in Czarist times, was an integral part of Stalinism, and his successors seem to have followed in his footsteps. Though Jews have occasionally held high Party and state posts, they have always been insecure. There are only a dozen rabbis in the whole country.

There are two main atheist organizations in the USSR, the Society of the Militant Godless and the All-Union Society for the Dissemination of Political and Scientific knowledge.

Education

Before 1917, almost three-fourths of the population were illiterate; by 1950, illiteracy had been almost eliminated. Schooling is universal, compulsory and free from the ages of 8 to 15 (in some cases to 17). There are ample facilities for the care and education of pre-school infants. According to a recent estimate, nearly a third of the entire population is engaged in full or part-time training.

In nursery school, parents must pay one-fifth of the cost. Primary and secondary grades are usually taught in the same school. Until the early 1960's, students attended either four-, seven-, or ten-year schools. The first of these were common mainly in rural areas. The majority of children attended either a seven-year (incomplete secondary) or a ten-year (complete secondary) school. Only a small group of the former went on to higher education. Students in both categories could, however, enter or transfer to a *technikum* (ages 15–19), where various vocational skills were taught. The present system calls for all students to attend an eight-year school (ages 7–15). At the end of Eighth Grade, examinations determine what type of secondary education the child can pursue. There are three types of schools. First a general labor polytechnical school consisting basically of ten classes, though in non-Russian areas (where Russian is taught as a foreign language), an eleventh is added. Graduates receive a school-leaving certificate, needed to pursue higher education. There are four sub-types of part-time general schools: the schools of Working or Rural Youth, Schools for Adults and Correspondence Schools.

Secondly and thirdly are the vocational and the middle-grade specialist schools, of which there are almost 5,000. Training brigades are added to the vocational schools directly at the place of work. In the 3,800 middle-grade special educational institutions, a two- to four-year course is offered for middle-grade specialists. Finally there are the universities and institutes. The universities (of which there are 42), offer training in a wide variety of specialties. The institutes, usually much smaller establishments, are limited to a few closely allied faculties. At present, about one in every five or six of tenth-year school leavers can expect to get a place in a full time institution. Most institutions offer four- to six-year courses in about 350 officially approved specialties; art subjects take about four years, engineering and science five, medicine six. Higher education is free, and some 70% of the full-time students receive modest maintenance grants, depending on their family circumstances.

The Press

Like all the other means of communication, newspapers, magazines and all periodicals are state-owned. Newspapers are published in 70 languages. *Pravda* (Truth) is published every morning in 23 cities; *Izvestia* (News) is the next largest daily. All political publications are controlled directly by the government; but censorship is usually exercised by the editors, who are chosen carefully and can be removed at the slightest deviation from the party line. *Krokodil,* a satirical weekly, is allowed to criticize lower and middle-level bureaucrats and human failings (such as alcoholism or absenteeism), but must not touch any important *apparatchik* or policy problem. The Soviet Union set the trend in the Communist world for the so-called "fat" magazines, monthly or quarterly journals either literary, critical or scientific, in whose pages (often of monumental tedium) many important ideological battles are carried on. *Novy Mir,* the most liberal of these, had its ups and downs, and since the death of its editor, Tvardovsky, has once again become a bastion of orthodoxy. The Soviet Movie Workers' Association has a monopoly of fan magazines and movie stills and does very well out of it. There are, of course, thousands of specialized magazines.

Foreign newspapers are very hard to obtain in the USSR—even the New York *Daily World,* the London *Morning Star,* the Paris *Humanité* or the Italian *Unità* can be found only in the big hotels. East European papers are, however, available at street stalls, though by no means always. A select number of Intourist hotels sell limited copies of *The Times,* again, irregularly, depending on the political sensitivity of the contents. They are normally available only to Western tourists. There is *Moscow News,* a Soviet English-language weekly which publishes a small amount of carefully-chosen news and a large number of officially-approved photographs about Soviet achievements. You must be prepared, therefore, while in the Soviet Union, to be cut off almost completely from the world press; nor will radio or television help you in this respect. And it is not likely that you will be within reach of the products of *samizdat,* the underground network of typed or mimeographed publications. For one thing, those who produce them must be extremely careful, as even the unauthorized possession of a duplicating machine is a criminal offence; for another, these are all in Russian or other languages of the USSR. *The Chronicle of Current Events,* the most important of them, has appeared regularly every two months or so since 1968. In 1973 it ceased to be published after large-scale arrests had taken place of members of its editorial and information network. But it later resurfaced with presumably new—still anonymous—editors, who are evidently prepared to risk imprisonment, and was still going strong in 1980.

Russians and the Foreigner

Though the Soviet Union has been at peace for over 35 years, the so-called siege mentality, the distrust of the foreigner (especially the Westerner), and spy-mania have not quite been eradicated. The USSR was born out of a civil war and foreign invasion; people still remember how the former allies of the Czarist state landed in Archangel and how the Japanese held on to Vladivostok until 1922. To the Soviet citizen, the Munich Pact was as much a betrayal as the "containment policy" of the cold war years. Yet the attitudes are highly ambivalent. On one hand, the long years of conditioning have created fear and suspicion; on the other hand, the foreign visitor is an object of great curiosity and attraction. Very few Russians have traveled abroad—about 8,000 Russians visited Britain in 1979—(except on official missions), and when they go, they move in groups, as individual foreign travel is all but impossible.

The behavior of the average Soviet citizen to the foreign visitor is also guided to some degree by fear of the authorities.

You must remember all this in your dealing with the Russians. Their pride in their undoubted achievements is great, but it is combined with a strong inferiority complex, for which some of them are apt to over-compensate by boasting, aggressiveness and hostility. Yet basically they are friendly, warm-hearted and generous, if given the chance.

There are a few simple rules, some "do's" and "don'ts", to guide your own behavior in your relationship with Russians:

1. Don't deal with the black market, whether it involves currency or clothing, cameras or tape recorders. Do bring with you postage stamps, postcards and any other politically innocuous gifts; chewing-gum never fails to please.

2. Be careful about taking pictures from planes or trains or of important junctions or bridges and don't photograph people before asking their permission.

3. Do learn a few words of Russian, and carry a phrase book.

4. Don't lose your patience and do avoid arguments. Do give praise where praise is due.

5. Don't compare Western standards with Russian ones. Do seek points of common interest and understanding.

6. Beware of *agents provocateurs*. Avoid sexual entanglements.

7. Don't wear shorts or bathing suits in the streets. Always remove your coat in restaurants, theaters, libraries etc. Keeping it on is considered the height of rudeness. There is always a cloakroom at these places—use it!

8. Be careful about tipping. In some cases it may be quite acceptable, in others it may be considered an insult. If in doubt, offer the money with a look of "is it all right for me to give you this?" plainly stamped on your face.

Languages

The dominant language of the Soviet Union is Russian, which is officially promoted as a "second native tongue" and, since 1938, has been a compulsory subject in all non-Russian-speaking general and secondary schools. The Indo-European languages are by far the most important; apart from the Slavonic and Baltic tongues, these include the Indo-Iranian tongues. Russian, Ukrainian and Byelorussian all belong to the eastern sub-group of the Slavonic branch of the Balto-Slavic tongues. The Cyrillic alphabet (named for St. Cyril, the apostle of the Slavs who devised it for the translation of the Bible and the liturgy in the ninth century) is in use throughout the Union with the exception of Armenia, Georgia and the Baltic Republics, where it co-exists for official purposes with the Latin or native alphabets. Encouragement has helped the development of national cultures, such as to the Turkic peoples and Old Asiatics who, in Czarist times, had no written languages, but were given these under the Communist regime, based on the Latin alphabet. The Georgians and Armenians have kept their old Japhetic alphabets (derived from Aramaic and Greek script), while the Latvians, Lithuanians, Estonians and Karelians have retained Latin script. The Mari and the Yakut have established national literatures; the Kazakhs and the Kirghiz have crystallized local cultures which previously were fragmented. Russian, however, serves as a *lingua franca* among the 70-odd languages of the Union. The younger generation of non-Russian nationalities is accepting that bilingualism is a necessity for personal advancement even though the national languages survive.

Many Russians study Western languages. After many years of neglect, English appears to be the favorite. Because of the still prevalent isolation of the country, the results appear to be somewhat uneven; but the English language instruction in some secondary schools is excellent in main cities, and, in addition, large numbers of people regularly listen to the BBC and Voice of America in English, both stations now being officially tolerated, and virtually free of jamming.

THE SOVIET WAY OF LIFE

Completely Different but All too Human

With the instant communications of the 20th century, constant world travel, broadening trade and above all, East-West detente, tourists tend nowadays to assume that the world is becoming homogenized. It seems almost axiomatic that if leaders East and West get along better and ordinary people fly similar jets, land at similar airports, ride cars, don suits and ties (or pants suits and jeans), launch spacecraft, turn over their problems to computers, erect atomic power stations, and find their young people keeping time to a common rock-beat, that the ways of life in East and West must have become much the same.

In the Soviet Union, the superficial similarities are likely to reinforce such impressions among tourists who stay close to international hotels and their tour guides, and who devote more attention to buildings and monuments than to people. Those who set out for Moscow or Leningrad in hopes of the adventure of something really new and different may be disappointed by surface resemblances. But let them be reassured that in the less visible ways in which societies work, in life-style and in people, the Soviet Union is a thing apart from what they have seen before.

Two Cautionary Notes

First, some words of caution about two problems: The first is that the USSR is not just one nation, but a continent of peoples living together. The uninitiated usually equate "Russian" with "Soviet" and vice-versa, but Russians comprise only about half the total population of 262 million. By official count, there are 104 nationalities, speaking 120 different (recognized) languages, living in 53 nationality republics, autonomous regions or other nationality areas. Americans, asked their nationality, immediately call themselves American. But ask a Soviet citizen, and he will say Russian, Armenian, Uzbek, Latvian, Ukrainian, or some such. There is no such thing as a Soviet national.

American visitors may mistake this as roughly equivalent to their own penchant for immediately announcing their home state to new acquaintances. But Britons, with centuries of thinking of themselves as Scottish, Welsh, Irish or English, will understand that this is something that goes much deeper. It is a more fundamental form of identity that reveals deep-seated traditions and values, and tells much about contemporary attitudes, attachments, manners and morals.

The life style of each nationality has distinctive character. Tall, blonde-haired Estonians and Lithuanians look like kin to the Scandinavians across the Baltic Sea and have much in common with Scandinavian tastes and outlook; they are the most westernized of Soviet peoples. The short, dark-haired, swarthy Georgians are as Mediterranean and as temperamental as Basques or Sicilians and have similar social codes. The wiry, Persian-looking peoples of Uzbekistan, Turkmenia, Tadzhikistan and Azerbaijan quietly perpetuate traditional Moslem marriages and funerals and the clannish loyalties and other holdovers of centuries of Islamic rule. Lithuanians look to Catholicism and Armenians to their own Orthodox Church as expressions of national identity. Far to the north, in what were once regarded as the Siberian wastes, the narrow-eyed, high-cheeked people of Yakutia resemble American Eskimos not only in looks but in their flair for hunting, trapping, reindeer-herding and ice-fishing, as well as in their adaptation to modern life. Riga, the capital of Latvia, still bears the flavor of its Hanseatic League days and a closeness to German culture. So important are such differences to the Soviet peoples that Soviet passports acknowledge their tremendous diversity by providing a blank for "nationality," along with name, sex and date of birth.

More than a half-century of Soviet rule has, of course, brought these peoples closer together and provided a common overlay. Many of the republic capitals and other big cities have a numbing architectural uniformity, but beneath the veneer, diversity persists. And these differences are compounded by the vast gap between city life and rural life in the Soviet Union.

In this chapter, one must, for simplicity's sake, concentrate mainly on the Russians as such, and on city-dwellers. But it behooves the traveler to go beyond the Russian metropolises of Moscow and Leningrad to savor some of the human and cultural richness in other parts of this vast land, for Moscow is probably less representative of the USSR than New York of the United States.

The second problem about which we want to caution you is that Soviet life, on a personal level, is often difficult to observe. The language, of course, is a formidable barrier. (Without training, it is hard to read or speak, and it does not readily lend itself, as do some other tongues, to a traveler's pidgin language, though Russians are marvelously tolerant of foreigners' mistakes in their tongue.) Furthermore, there is the legacy of the political tensions that have made many middle-aged and older people wary of more than fleeting contact with foreigners, unless job or circumstances allow them more lingering attachment. Finally, there is a subdued, almost expressionless quality to the man-made landscape, the scenery in general, and people *en masse,* that leaves the visitor sensing a way of life that is strange and foreign, and yet somehow not quite strange or exotic enough to be quickly recognized.

Neither the massive blocks of apartment buildings nor the passive throngs of patient shoppers offer anything picturesque to arrest the eye immediately or to convey the essential flavor of the Russian spirit or of Soviet life. What eludes the traveler is a quick trademark like the sidewalk cafés and lively bistros of Paris. Moscow's Kremlin and St. Basil's Cathedral are fairytale wonders, and the gilded onion domes of Russian churches are peaceful ornaments of the past. But they seem suspended in time, disconnected from today's ordinary public life, which has a more stolid, more passive, and less communicative feel.

Politics Unlimited

Yet a closer look almost anywhere reveals signs of the special politicization of public life that is a hallmark of the Soviet Union. Russians themselves have come to take it so much for granted, they barely notice. Commercial advertisements, as westerners know them, have only lately taken toehold, but political advertising is ubiquitous.

Everywhere political slogans gaze down with silent reminders: "The Party and the People are United," "Long Live the Soviet People, Builders of Communism," or simply, "Glory to Work." The visitor, asking directions, will come across such landmarks as Karl Marx Prospekt, Lenin Prospekt, Fiftieth Anniversary of the Revolution Square, Prospekt Mira (Peace Avenue). Along sidewalks, he will notice Communist Party and government newspapers posted in glass-encased bulletin boards for easy, stand-up reading. Loudspeakers in public parks often provide strollers with martial music or radio broadcasts of speeches and news reports. Travelers on overnight trains may be awakened with similar selections.

Another fixture of public life is heroic statuary. In Moscow, the central shrine is the red marble tomb of Lenin on Red Square. In any other city, the central square is presided over by a statue of Lenin, in a wind-furled overcoat, confidently striding towards a brighter future, or, hand-raised and eyes agleam, exhorting the proletariat to unite. The energetic civic consciousness of socialist realism is strikingly conveyed in the towering World War II monument in Volgograd, a 93m-tall woman on a hillcrest, symbolizing Mother Russia with sword raised against the foe, her dead prayerfully buried around her, or in the dynamic stainless steel Figures of Communist Construction in Moscow—a muscular young worker, one fist clenched around a hammer and another arm locked with a young collective farm girl wielding a sickle. The latter stands outside the Exhibition of the Achievements of the People's Economy. Nearby, a dramatic upswept rocket, with a tail of exhaust that is many stories high, shoots skyward in monumental commemoration of Soviet space exploits.

The Olympian scale of these monuments is an important clue to their public appeal and an insight into the Soviet spirit. People here like awesome structures, impressively broad avenues, sweeping vistas, and images of titanic exploits. They have a Texan's love for exaggerated bigness that seems to outdo even the American love of bigness. With the spirit of Paul Bunyan, Russians take pride in the sheer magnitude of the great hydroelectric dams they have thrown across the broad rivers of Siberia. They revel in the size of their rockets, steel plants or heavy trucks, and marvel at the mass of the mock-Gothic sandcastle skyscrapers erected in their capital city by Stalin. Moscow's Rossiya and Kosmos Hotels lay claim to be the largest in the world; apartment blocks have an oaklike solidity with the mass of ocean-liners, often more imposing at a distance than close up. "In Russia," a visitor from Eastern Europe once remarked, "even a barbershop is a block long."

In much the same spirit, the Soviet life-style makes a fetish of huge exhibitions and mass public spectacles that would arouse the envy of a Cecil B. de Mille. The permanent economic exhibition in Moscow sprawls across more than 550 acres, occupying more than 100 pavilions, drawing crowds from the Soviet hinterlands who come to gaze in wonder at displays of Soviet achievements from sputniks to ship engines or farm equipment. Each major Soviet city has a more modest exhibition of the same kind. And for rituals of national solidarity and loyalty, few events in the world rival the massive parades on November 7 (Revolution Day) or May Day. Red Square literally becomes a giant outdoor television studio for displaying disciplined, goose-stepping military units and awesome weaponry (though the military side of these displays is nowadays deliberately played down and is sometimes entirely absent), or colorful phalanxes of marching, flag-waving strong-armed youths and the lithe-limbed girl gymnasts doing field figures on a scale that dwarfs the half-time shows of big-time American football games.

Kollektiv-consciousness

On a less exalted plane, probably the most important distinguishing characteristic of the Soviet life-style for the ordinary Ivan Ivanovich Ivanov is the *kollektiv,* the Soviet counterweight to the individualism of the West. Though the *kollektiv* has many forms, the work *kollektiv* assumes the greatest importance for Ivan. Whether he—or his wife Nadya—works in a factory or a collective farm, he becomes an element of a brigade—"an essential link in a chain," the press is fond of saying. Even management and white-collar workers, salesgirls and waiters are inculcated with the spirit of the *kollektiv.* Our average Ivan has both his individual and his group work-norms. Farm brigades vie with other farm brigades, assembly lines with other assembly lines, shifts with other shifts on a collective basis in what is known as "socialist competition".

If our Ivan lives in a city, his labors and those of his fellow office, factory or university colleagues will be collectively volunteered at least one Sunday in the autumn to go to the countryside to help bring in the potato harvest or loads of cabbages. In the spring, the *kollektivs* of urban and rural workers will participate automatically in the nationwide *sub-*

botnik, the working Saturday that Ivan and all other Soviet citizens donate free to the welfare of their country.

The work *kollektiv* is infused with more than Communist mystique, hailed in the Party press and glorified in factory dramas on stage. It has practical importance for everyday life. For most ordinary Ivans, the factory or state farm is a paternalistic provider of many services, and works much like the old company town in the West. The factory is not only a place of work but the source of housing, the site of day-care centers for children, neighborhood schools and medical clinics, where services are provided free of charge. Many younger workers live five or six together in communal dormitories. Some communal apartments for families persist, but the majority have been replaced by individual flats. Even these are small by Western standards, though Russians do not seem to feel the same claustrophobia that Americans or Britons would experience from such confining conditions.

The work *kollektiv* also influences leisure time. It provides a community House of Culture, which sponsors a variety of clubs and guided activities. Many farms, factories, institutes, publishing houses or other public enterprises have their own vacation facilities that can handle part of their work force, and Pioneer camps for the children in summer months. If our Ivan is among the more fortunate, more productive and more civic-minded employees, he will probably qualify for a *putyovka*—a subsidized, cut-rate, 26-day vacation pass to a sanitarium rest house or group excursion arranged by his trade union. His factory may also give him an occasional chance to go to the theater by buying out the house for a performance. Or his *kollektiv* shift in the factory may decide to rent a bus from the front office to go off in the countryside fishing or for an autumn weekend of mushroom-picking (a popular pastime among Russians).

The paternalism of the *kollektiv* (and ultimately the State) with its free education, free health care and subsidized vacations, is immensely important to most Russians, whatever drawbacks they may experience in practice. To most Soviet citizens, the unemployment, open inflation, high costs of university education and medical care in the West sound very frightening. The free unpredictability of Western life unsettles them. Even at the cost of freedoms, the vast majority of Soviet citizens seem to prefer sheltered communalism to what they regard as unbridled individualism of the West which they do not understand.

Today's Links with the Past

The temptation for many a Soviet apologist is to present the *kollektiv* and other facets of modern Soviet life as a complete break with the past and something entirely new for Russia. But along with new elements, there is much that links the Russia of today with the Russia of centuries past. The spirit of the *kollektiv* has roots in the *mir,* or communal assembly of peasant villages under the czars and landlord nobles, or in the strong communal orientation of the Russian Orthodox Church. The collective farmers' markets of today, where individual peasants can sell what they have grown on their small private plots, had their precedent in the right of serfs under the czars to do much the same. The massive parades in Red Square, in which pictures of Communist Party leaders are carried aloft, are reminiscent of religious processions through the same square in which church icons were born aloft by worshippers on special holy days. The most widely appreciated ballet, literature and drama today are from 19th-century Russia. Even the nervousness which many Russians exhibit toward picture-taking by foreigners has roots in the czarist past. (When the great writer, Leo Tolstoy, died in a provincial town, for instance, Russian photographers were forbidden to take photographs of his body lying in the local railroad station until permission had been sought from and granted by government officials in St. Petersburg.)

Running through Soviet public life, there is a law-and-order kind of conservatism that can be startling to western visitors. Soviet crowds betray none of the restlessness or kinetic unpredictability that visitors encounter on the streets of New York, Tokyo or Beirut. The bright, informal and sometimes outlandish plumage of the sidewalks of western cities gives way here to a dark, cloth-coat utilitarian respectability. Red Square is the very picture of stolid serenity, with its orderly queue of Russians, their voices hushed by the vast expanse. They are waiting—as Russians seem endlessly to wait in lines wherever they go—for a glimpse of their entombed leader, Lenin.

Not only Red Square, but main streets in most big Soviet cities, are remarkably well-swept. The metros (subways or undergrounds) are immaculate by comparison with the graffiti-pocked subways of New York (and, in Moscow, worth a ride or two if only to enjoy the ornate decorations and statuary). Somehow, along with all this tidiness, there is a curious undercurrent of unruliness, sublimated in deliberate jaywalking, an unkemptness on side streets and an unwashed look to much of the countryside, the sudden dissolution of bus lines in one mass lurch for the back door when the vehicle appears after a long wait, or a tendency to lie down on the job and "let George do it".

But in most spheres of life, a rather Puritan public morality prevails. The sprinkling of jeans and other Western styles of dress and behavior do not really reflect a challenging counter-culture or qualify Moscow and Leningrad as swinging cities like London or New York. Night life is not a Soviet strong point. Some bars shut down as early as 9 P.M. but most public places close by midnight and stop taking guests much earlier (except in international hotels). Entertainment, by western standards, is clean-cut and wholesome, with a solid Victorian bias toward classical ballet and 19th-century symphonic music, the high art of the central Moscow Puppet Theater, or snappy, brightly-costumed traditional folk dances by the Moiseyev or Beryozka dance troupes. Instead of bitterly modern Western plays, leggy reviews, or spicy shows, the Soviet scene offers some of the best trapeze artists and animal trainers in the world. Theaters begin early, let out early and, with no nightclubs for the theatergoers to visit afterward, the streets are abandoned at an early hour to red arm-banded *druzhinniki,* voluntary brigades of civilians who enthusiastically help the uniformed militia keep order.

Everyone is Big Brother's Keeper

Soviet people, moreover, consider themselves their brother's keepers more than people in most other countries. Not only will a lost stranger be given directions, but on a crowded bus, Russians will helpfully make change and buy each other's bus tickets because conductors are rarely used. They will also publicly admonish each other's behavior when they think someone has stepped out of line and done something *nekulturny* (uncultured), such as wearing his coat in a theater or trying to jump a queue. Busybodies will stop a stranger to advise him to bundle up more warmly, or tell him not to sit on stone steps for fear he will catch cold.

As a people, Russians have won a legendary reputation for their virtues of endurance, resilience, hardiness, patience and stoicism that enabled them to persevere and eventually wear down the armies of Napoleon and Hitler. Sometimes these qualities come across in public as indifference, a passive acceptance of authority, or a lack of polish and civility among crowds or in shops. But this external toughness springs quite naturally from the rigors that Russians have endured. "Think of it," a middle-aged writer said to me once, "I know people who have lived through the Bolshevik Revolution, the Civil War, the time of Stalin—industrialization, collectivization and worse—and then World War II. They have lived through hunger such as you have never known. They have endured this cold. Think of it, in one lifetime, to have lost a father, then a brother, and to have had to struggle to hold on to life itself."

Twenty million Russians died in World War II alone, and hardly a family today in European Russia, the Ukraine or Byelorussia was untouched. Large areas were devastated by the bitter conflict. Millions more perished in earlier phases of establishing, building and protecting the Soviet state under Stalin. None of this is forgotten today. The war especially is a constant memory, binding the Russian people together.

Much as life has improved in the postwar years, with people beginning to enjoy more consumer goods, even today it is not an easy lot for many people. Unthinkingly, Russians refer to life as a struggle, a word that is often used. The chill monotony of the long wintry season, from November into April, is exhausting and all-consuming. Yet hardy peasant women, with two buckets on a shoulder yoke, trudge a couple of times a day in the icy cold from their log-cabin *izbas* to the nearest village well to fetch water. With better urban transportation, very few people in cities now walk miles to work as they once did, but it is not uncommon for them to endure an hour or an hour and a half on crammed buses or streetcars getting to their jobs, just as in New York or London. Shopping is such an ordeal that Soviet publications have estimated each person spends an average of two hours a day in line. Inefficiency, shortages and red tape compound the problems. As they have inured themselves to such monumental waiting and nuisances, ordinary Russians have taken on the self-protective shell of public passivity and fatalism.

The Russians at Play

But this public face is only half of the Russian personality. Meet Russians relaxing, at play or at home, and you find their brusqueness melts away. They are among the warmest, emotional and overwhelmingly hospitable people on earth. They can be as sentimental as the Irish, as straightforward as Americans, as garrulous as Italians. The reverse side of their public fatalism is an almost childish optimism that may account for their doting so on children. Russian families are small, largely out of economic necessity (though big families are common among Caucasian and Central Asian peoples), but on their one child, or sometimes two children, Russians lavish affection and the best clothes, toys and whatever else they can buy. In public, children may be sternly disciplined; but at home, they are a spoiled, privileged class. Normally, the spoiling is done most by the *babushka,* the grandmother, who lives at home as a built-in baby-sitter and permanent member of the family.

Russians love a party and seize upon most holidays and even on the unexpected arrival of a stranger as a pretext. Frugality and planning ahead do not come naturally to them; they live for the moment. So when the occasion arises, they will throw an entire bonus or a huge chunk of pay—more than they can sensibly afford—into a single evening's hospitality and emotional Slavic self-indulgence. They may go out on the town with friends to a restaurant with a loud dance band and fling themselves into bouncy foxtrots, mazurkas, polkas and athletic mutations of the twist, the monkey or some rock-beat numbers, returning periodically to a table well fortified with vodka, cognac or sweet Soviet champagne to keep their party mood afloat. Or they may, as most seem to prefer, contribute ten or fifteen roubles a couple for a grand holiday feast, often around the kitchen table, which still maintains a place of central importance in Russian family life.

On such occasions, Russians abandon themselves to the orgy of feasting and drinking with a gusto that echoes the memory of times when food was not so plentiful. With advance warning, the women work for days preparing *zakuski,* the Russian *hors d'oeuvres* that are properly the most celebrated part of a Russian meal. *Zakuski* are never consumed without a string of good-natured and often long-winded toasts, each punctuated by everyone's gulping down a shot-glass of chilled vodka in one go. At such a feast anything and everything is washed down with vodka.

Even without numbing quantities of alcohol, a visitor can suddenly find himself included within a trusted circle of friends and warmed by roaring Russian hospitality. In cities like Paris or Rome, a foreigner could live for years without penetrating the full intimacy of a French or Italian home, but if luck creates the right circumstances, it can happen within hours in Russia.

When that occurs, the foreigner gains a glimpse of the great importance of friendships to the Russian, in whose life so much is governed by public authority and so little left to personal taste. It is perhaps understandable that Russians both give without moderation and expect others to respond in the same way. There is an intensity in their personal relationships that Westerners find both exhilarating and exhausting. For Russians, when they finally open up, are looking for soul mates, not mere conversational partners. They may feel offended at the circumspection of Westerners, especially intellectuals given to careful reasoning and qualification, and make plain that what they long for is a personal commitment from friends that Westerners rarely accord to more than a very few people in life. With Russians, it is quite possible to enter into that intense intimacy and involvement even on the first meeting if the Russian feels he has found a soul brother, especially if there is vodka to cement the bond (though the morning-after often spawns emotional misgivings as well as physical hangovers).

It is this directness in the Russian character, this tendency to startling and direct openness that makes many Americans and some Britons feel that Russians are more like them in some essential way than are sophisticated continental Europeans, restrained Teutonic Germans or temperamental Latins. Russians call this trait of openness their broad spirit *(shirokaya dusha)* and count as one of the glories of life talking *dusha-dushe*—heart-to-heart, or literally, soul-to-soul.

Meet the Russians

The traveler need not actually visit a Soviet home to rub shoulders with Russians and gain personal exposure to them. Almost any big Soviet city has a collective farmers' market where housewives go to haggle over such staples of Russian life as potatoes, cabbages and pickled cucumbers, or to buy more exotic items flown by the suitcase-load to northern cities by canny, individualistic peasants from southern regions who know they can clear a handsome profit by traveling on low-cost jets to regions where fresh fruits and vegetables are in short supply. In winter, prices on tomatoes or fresh fruits in Moscow can go as high as on room service at the Ritz.

Another good place to mingle with Russians is at restaurants, especially on weekends and if there is a dance band. Unless Intourist puts you in a special banquet room or at a reserved table segregated from Soviet guests, local restaurants follow the European practice of using every available seat and putting strangers together at tables. In that situation, any Russian who is asked to pass the salt and understands even a few words of a foreign language will start to open up, and if you get to showing them pictures of your children, *they* will probably produce a snapshot of theirs for *you*.

Few public places rival Soviet trains for meeting strangers and getting an immediate feel of Russian life. Although Russians normally contain their emotions in public, they are greatly moved by farewells. Their railway stations thus become great scenes of hugging, sobbing, parting advice, and promises to write, that are so intense and personal that onlookers are simply ignored. Once aboard a long-distance or overnight train—quite a comfortable and pleasant way to travel in the USSR—Russians fall naturally into a communal feeling, especially among those who go second class. (Foreigners usually travel first class, two to a compartment, in accommodations used mostly by government or public enterprise officials or educated people, segregated from the great mass but also more likely to know a foreign language.) In second class, four to a cabin, the more ordinary folk doff their street clothes and the men immediately don blue warm-up suits that they use for train pyjamas and general wear.

On a long trip, Russians will arrive with a great quantity of luggage and odd-shaped bundles, at least one of which contains food. In no time at all, they break out sausage, cheese, cucumbers and the dark bread for which Russia is justly famous. To drink, they normally have watery Soviet beer or overly-sweet, carbonated, fruit-flavored soft drinks. The foreign visitor who has had the forethought to provision himself with a bit of food, beer, or better yet, a small bottle of vodka from his hotel, will have an instant introduction that will make him quick friends. Much the same occurs in the dining car over *borshch* (beet soup) or *shchi* (cabbage soup) or *solyanka* (meat or fish soup) served in metal, cafeteria-style bowls, if one shares his beer or wine. The offer to share food and break bread together is almost certain to lead to a conversational exchange.

Under most circumstances, both similarities and differences will emerge. Like Americans and Britons, Russians are great sports fans, probably even more nationalistically enthusiastic about their teams than most Westerners. The Soviets play to win, and hate to lose. Russians generally love the outdoors, especially their birch woods and pine forests, largely as a relief from cramped housing in overcrowded cities. From train windows or from a car driving through big cities, the traveler can see the Russians in summer playing an impromptu game of volleyball, browsing for mushrooms in the woods in autumn, or darting off on cross-country skis among the sun-dappled birches on a bright day in January.

Patriotism and Work

The combination of the national sports craze and the shared ordeal of World War II help to reinforce the very deep-seated patriotism that Russians feel. Anglo-Saxons, as probably the most individualistic and mobile of all races, have trouble comprehending the strong pull of nationhood on Russians. The latter are rooted to the land in a way that restless and rootless people like Americans would not readily believe. Words like *rodina* (motherland) and *narod* (folk, or people) have tremendous emotional significance for Russians, in the way that words like freedom and democracy affect Anglo-Saxons. For *rodina* and *narod,* Russians are prepared to make great sacrifices.

Another difference that may quickly strike a Western traveler is in the approach to work. The vast majority of Russians are not as conscientious about it as Westerners are, except under great pressure. Time has less significance; deadlines can slip and slip. Those Russians who have close exposure to Westerners, especially Americans, think they work like fanatics and do not understand why. With job security guaranteed and career perspectives often limited, the great mass of Russians take a comparatively indifferent attitude toward their jobs.

The Soviet Woman

In many ways, Russian women seem to work much harder than men—and this is often one of the first striking visual impressions on foreign visitors. Let a traveler fall ill, and a woman doctor, a pleasant mother in her 40s, will probably attend to his needs. The vast majority of doctors in the Soviet Union are women, as are the teachers. In terms of access to jobs, women in the Soviet Union are definitely liberated. They are a vital part of the labor force, and the government provides an extensive network of child care centers and kindergartens to care for their children all day so that mothers can stay on the job.

More than 80 percent of working-age women have jobs, many of them rugged. In winter, burly women in *valenkis* (traditional peasant black-felt boots) and dressed in layers of clothing like cabbage leaves, chip ice on sidewalks and shovel snow. In summer, they sweep the streets with long-handled twig-brooms. At construction sites, they carry bricks; at stations on the Trans-Siberian Railroad, they shovel coal; on road gangs, they load cracked concrete onto dump trucks; on farms, they do much of the backbreaking labor of preparing the fields and picking the crops. Women are engineers, physicists, economists, tractor operators, government officials, heads of institutes, even deputies of the Supreme Soviet, or parliament, which holds brief meetings twice a year. Almost any

Intourist guide can rattle off the percentage of women delegates in her area as evidence of the feminine role in public affairs (though almost none can supply the same figures for female membership in the Communist Party Central Committee or Local Committee, where the real power lies).

As in the West, much of Soviet life remains quite patriarchal. In peasant homes, the father is still considered the head of the family, and in many urban families as well. Not only women themselves but Soviet newspapers such as the Writer's Union weekly, *Literary Gazette,* have printed studies showing that for all the importance of women in the labor force, men hold down most of the choice executive posts or the higher-paying jobs in heavy industry. Moreover, women carry a double load: a regular job plus a second shift of daily shopping, housework and minding the children, and they have only a few modern appliances to ease their work at home.

But men or women, Russians share a common characteristic with many travelers: they are immensely curious about the outside world. Young men will bombard foreigners with questions about cars, rock groups, guitars or hi-fi equipment. Perhaps more shyly at first, young women will inquire about fashions, home life, movies or books. Engineers or factory workers will ask about salaries and the cost of living. Working mothers will want to know how non-working Western women can endure the boredom of being without a job, and also, how their husbands can support a family on one salary. In the process, some Russians will exhibit a surprising acquaintance with one facet or another of Western life, though little overall comprehension of it, and they will assume that any foreigner is a walking encyclopedia on his own country.

The curiosity is immense, especially among younger people who have a great suppressed hunger to travel abroad. It is more intense about America than about any other country because Russians regard it as the one really worthy rival, the one real national yardstick for themselves. Sometimes ordinary people will react incredulously to a traveler's revelations. A few will be agog; others will come back defensively, "we have everything, too!" But most often, they will declare at some point that they really want peace between the Soviet Union and the United States—and they will say it in such a way that you believe them.

THE PEOPLES OF THE SOVIET UNION

Unity and Variety

BY
GEORGE SCHÖPFLIN

When is a Russian not a Russian? The answer to this improvised conundrum has in it the essence of the variety of nations that make up the Soviet Union. It might go something like this: a Russian isn't a Russian when he is a Ukrainian or a Georgian or a Central Asian Moslem or a member of any of the hundred or so nationalities that make up nearly half the population of the country. Non-Russians are very insistent on their separate identity.

For most foreigners, ignorant or otherwise, Russia is the same as the Soviet Union. Yet at the last published census in 1979, the Russians had only a bare majority of the then 262 million population—about 52 percent. Demographers are predicting that the margin will be even closer when the results of the next census are published later in the 1980s.— indeed, the non-Russians may even have moved into the majority because of their higher birthrate. By the year 2000 they are expected to have dropped to 44 percent of the population. But even then the Russians will be far and away the largest single national group. In 1979, there were 137 million Russians to 40 million Ukrainians, the next largest national group, and the third largest, the Central Asian Uzbeks, were 12.5 million and growing. At the opposite end of the spectrum, Soviet enumerators took account of some very small national groups indeed—the 600 Yukagir, for instance, a Siberian group light years from the 20th century.

Official government policy fully reckons with this ethnic diversity in the Soviet Union. A glance at publications like *Soviet Weekly,* a paper intended for readers in the English-speaking world, will show that Soviet officialdom takes great pride in the continued existence of small, picturesque ethnic groups and insists that this is what Soviet policy is all about, to provide conditions in which their traditions can be maintained. This will probably come as a surprise to many readers, but, in fact, Soviet policy on nationalities goes back to Lenin (but then, *every* Soviet policy goes back to Lenin), who asserted that in the Soviet Union policy towards individual national groups was "national in form and socialist in content". What this was supposed to mean was that Lenin had nothing against the preservation of national languages and national cultures, provided that these were socialist, that they accepted and perpetuated his Communist vision of the world.

Lenin and After

Furthermore, at the time of the Russian Revolution in 1917 and after, Lenin saw the political value of promising full national devolution to the non-Russians, who even then formed a very high proportion of the population. The anti-Bolshevik Whites who opposed him were reluctant to consider autonomy for the non-Russians, so that Lenin's promise of national freedom ensured the Communists the support of many non-Russians, who did, indeed, fight for the Revolution (though, as may be guessed, not necessarily from revolutionary convictions).

In the early years after the Revolution, policy towards the non-Russians followed Lenin's precepts closely. The Soviet Union was established as a federation in 1922, with a complex hierarchical system of union republics, autonomous republics, autonomous *oblasts* or provinces and national *okrugs* or areas. All these administrative subdivisions enjoy different kinds of legal rights and, according to the Constitution, union republics are in theory entitled to leave the Soviet Union and set up on their own. What guarantees the cohesiveness of this apparently loose structure is the disciplined rule of the Communist Party.

At first, in the 1920's, Soviet policy-makers were genuinely concerned to make up for decades of neglect, oppression and Russification under the Czars. The emphasis, in the first place, was to create the bases for national cultures. Languages which had had no literatures (or, in many cases, were not written at all) were encouraged to grow, and institutions were set up to foster national traditions among the non-Russians. The Moslems, who had come under Russian rule through centuries of conquest, were supported in their attempts to give up the Arabic alphabet, which is extremely unsuitable for the Turkic languages that most of them spoke. They chose to write their languages in a Latin alphabet.

Gradually, however, as Stalin consolidated his power, he began to abandon the policy of toleration towards national diversity and pursued an ever more rigid centralization in which there was no room for any divergence from the norm on the part of non-Russians. Many talented non-Russian cultural personalities lost their lives in the purges of the 1930's and, a highly symbolic step, at the end of that decade, the various Latin alphabets introduced earlier were scrapped and replaced with Cyrillic, the alphabet used by the Russians. What this meant in practice was that an educated Moslem, say, born in 1900, would have written his mother tongue in three alphabets by the time he was 40—in the Arabic script, then in the Latin alphabet and finally in Cyrillic characters.

Building the "Soviet Man"

The principal theoretical aim of nationalities policy today is that the peoples of the Soviet Union are entering upon a process of "drawing together", which will lead ultimately to their "merger" into the "Soviet man". This is seen to be a gradual process, and it is emphasized that the basis on which the "Soviet man" will order his life will be socialism. However, some non-Russians are quick to point out that it looks rather as if this "Soviet man" will be Russian-speaking, and they ask what will happen in the process to their own languages and cultures.

Certainly, enormous emphasis is placed by the Soviet educational system on the learning of Russian. Throughout the Soviet Union, Russian is a compulsory language even for schools in which the language of instruction is *not* Russian, and there is a widespread network of schools, including many in non-Russian areas, where the schooling *is* in Russian. The authorities argue that Russian serves as the means of communication among non-Russians, that it is a window on the wider world, and that advancement can come only on the basis of a sound knowledge of Russian, which is "not just a world language, but even a language of outer space". The non-Russians would like to be able to live a national life with their own national languages and cultures, without having Russian forced down their throats at every turn.

In a word, many non-Russians have the impression that official Soviet policy, Lenin's principles and all, is at times not much more than a gloss on traditional Russian attitudes of regarding the non-Russians within the country as "younger brothers" who should be grateful for the tutelage of the Russian "elder brother". It is well to remember that not every grumble by a non-Russian is automatically evidence of Russian intolerance, and further, that national friction in the Soviet Union is not necessarily a dispute between Russian and non-Russian. In Transcaucasia, for instance (of which more later), relations between the Moslem Azerbaijanis and Christian Armenians have traditionally been tense, and intercommunal quarrels are not uncommon.

Equally, Soviet policy contributed materially to the strengthening of weak national cultures, by providing written languages and encouraging literatures. On the economic side, too, Soviet investment policy has tended to favor the development of poorer areas inhabited by non-Russians, and the latter have benefited from this. Being part of the Soviet Union is, further, undoubted protection for certain non-Russians against outside powers. The small Moslem nations of Central Asia probably prefer rule from Moscow to Chinese overlordship—though it is hard to be dogmatic about this for lack of evidence. And the Armenians, with their tragic history of massacres at the hands of the Turks, have traditionally looked towards Christian Russia for protection.

This said, non-Russians might argue that while they welcome the benefits of membership of the Soviet Union and are fully committed to Communism, they find it irksome that in practice so much of the Soviet system means having to do things the Russian way. Many of them have venerable cultural traditions of their own and see nothing deplorable in favoring their own national ways, not least in an era when small states in Africa and Asia can claim all the advantages of national independence and sovereignty.

The Pattern of Peoples

The various peoples who live in the Soviet Union may be classified into certain broad categories, by language, by religion or by other distinguishing characteristics. By far the largest category is the Slavs—the Russians, the Ukrainians and the Byelorussians. They are almost all Orthodox Christians—it should be understood that religious adherence is in all cases nominal and does not automatically mean that every member of a national group practices his religion—and they speak closely-related Slavonic languages. These are related in turn to the Slavonic languages of Eastern Europe (Polish, Czech, Serbo-Croat, Bulgarian and others). They write their languages in the Cyrillic alphabet, which is, in fact, well adapted to reproducing certain sounds found in the Slavonic languages. So whereas the Cyrillic script can convey the sound *shch* (as in Khru*shch* ev) with one character, Polish, which uses the Latin script, is forced to employ the ugly cluster of letters *szcz.* The Slavs of the Soviet Union originally inhabited the vast plains north of the Black Sea and west of the Ural mountains. Today, they are found everywhere in the Soviet Union. Indeed, northern Kazakhstan, which was once inhabited by nomadic Kazakh tribesmen only, is now a region of Russian settlement and some Russians claim that it should be transferred to the Russian republic. It is worth noting, too, that outside European Russia and the Ukraine, particularly in Central Asia, the friction that sometimes exists between Russians and Ukrainians disappears in the face of the more alien Central Asians, for whom there is little to distinguish a Russian from a Ukrainian anyway. (This may be seen as a neat example by those who believe in the "common enemy" theory.)

The next largest group is the Moslems, of whom those of Central Asia have already been mentioned. Although they are now almost completely settled, there is still a certain difference in outlook between the former nomads—the Kazakh, the Kirghiz and the Turkmen—and the long-settled Uzbeks and Tadzhiks, with centuries of cultivation behind them. Converted to Islam in the early Middle Ages, the Central Asians look back to the empires of Genghis Khan and Tamerlane, whose tomb is still shown at Samarkand. The Azerbaijanis or Azeris, whose capital is the oil city of Baku on the Caspian Sea, are of the Shiite sect of Islam (as distinct from the great majority of Sunni Moslems), and have looked towards Persia rather than the Arab world and Turkey, despite the fact that the Azeri language is virtually identical with that of Turkey. Further to the north, in the central Volga Valley, the Tatars of Kazan and the Bashkirs have had a far longer association with the Russians, and consequently are more open to European influences. The Tatars have been in the forefront of Islamic modernization and were the principal champions of the reform movement known as *jadidism* at the turn of the century. Other Moslem groups are to be found in the northern Caucasus. The Crimean Tatars, who were deported to Central Asia *en masse* during the war, are still lobbying for permission to return to their ancestral homelands in the Crimean Peninsula.

The great majority of Soviet Moslems speak Turkic languages, and as a general rule they all understand one another without too much difficulty. But not all the Turkic peoples are Moslem (the Chuvash of the Volga are Christian) and not all Moslems speak Turkic languages (the Tadzhiks speak a language which is hardly more than a dialect of Persian, though written in Cyrillic). Equally, in the northern Caucasus, Moslem peoples like the Avars speak what are known as Paleo-Caucasian languages, thought to be among the most fearsomely difficult in the world. Another of them, Kabardinian, has four ways of pronouncing the sound *f*, for example, which must make life difficult for a Kabardinian with a lisp!

If one were to ask a Central Asian what he regarded himself as, and he were to reply openly, he might well say, "I am a Moslem first, an Uzbek (or Kazakh or whatever) second and a Soviet citizen third."

Caucasians, Balts, Finns and Others

The next group, although they are in no way related linguistically or ethnically, is formed by the two great Christian nations of Transcaucasia, the Georgians and the Armenians. They were both absorbed by the Czars into their empire, having sought the protection of the largest Christian power in the region against Oriental encroachments. The Georgians speak a Paleo-Caucasian language, while Armenian is Indo-European—hence distantly related to English (*very* distantly).

The Estonians, Latvians and Lithuanians of the Baltic were part of the Czar's empire until the Revolution, after which they clung on to a precarious independence for two decades, and finally were absorbed into the Soviet Union. The Baltic states were long under German and Scandinavian influence; they are undoubtedly part of the mainstream of the Central European tradition which also includes the Poles, Czechs and Hungarians.

The various Finnic peoples of the Soviet Union are small in number and have long been in contact with the Russians, who have been the main influence on them. They are Orthodox Christians (except the Lutheran Estonians) and accept the Russian way of life in most respects. Their various languages are more or less distantly related to Finnish (and even more distantly to Hungarian), and they are quite unable to understand one another. They tend to work in agriculture and forestry, though since the Revolution, urban settlements have arisen in their homelands, which are in various parts of European Russia. The bulk of the population of these towns, as in so many non-Russian areas, tends to be Russian.

In addition to these general groups, there are other peoples who do not fit readily into any of the above categories. Here one might mention those nationalities which are splinters of groups which have a nation-state of their own outside the Soviet Union. These include the Poles (in the western marches of the Soviet Union), the approximately two million Germans (moved to Central Asia and Siberia during the war), Greeks (remnants of the old Greek colonies on the Black Sea, again removed to Central Asia), Koreans (from the Soviet Far East, but removed to Central Asia), Bulgarians in the Ukraine, Hungarians on the Soviet-Hungarian frontier, Finns (mostly in the Karelian Isthmus ceded by Finland in 1944), and a few Czechs and Slovaks. The Moldavians speak a language that is for all practical purposes the same as Romanian, except that (unlike Romanian) it is written in Cyrillic, and that the authorities go to great lengths in insisting that Moldavian is a quite distinct language.

There are also some 175,000 gypsies, mostly in European Russia and the Ukraine. The Kalmyks of the lower Volga, removed during the war but allowed to return later, have the distinction of being the only Buddhist people within geographical Europe.

Finally, there is what is best described as the ethnographic museum—the small groups of peoples of the North, Siberia and the Far East, who are regularly cited by official Soviet sources as examples of the success of Soviet nationalities policy. They range from the Uralic Samoyeds—whose languages are remote cousins of the Finno-Ugrian group—on either side of the Ural mountains along the North Sea, to the Chukchi in the extreme northeast of Siberia, not all that far from Alaska. The 1970 census returned only 151,000 of these small peoples put together. Many of them have barely left the Stone Age and continue their age-old occupations of hunting, trapping and fishing. Those who leave assimilate rapidly.

The Russians

The Russians are sometimes known as the Great Russians. This is not a title of honor, but a means of distinguishing them from the Little Russians (now universally called the Ukrainians). The Russians are without a doubt one of the most talented and intriguing peoples of the world, let alone of the Soviet Union. They have the ability to arouse directly contradictory opinions among those who encounter them. Some people find them open, helpful, hospitable and generous; others find them sullen, suspicious, underhand and servile. The truth, for once, is not somewhere between these two extremes, but rather that they both represent aspects of the Russian stereotype, for both kinds of behavior are met with in different contexts.

It is well to bear in mind that these are just stereotypes and that far from every individual Russian will conform to them. But with this proviso, it is probably fair to say that the official Russian—the customs man, the hotel porter, the state functionary—is more likely to exhibit the second, "unpleasant", face of Russia, while the individual met by chance in the street at a person-to-person level will show the "pleasant" face.

Then again, one must distinguish between the Russian intellectual and the great mass of non-intellectuals, a distinction that is far more relevant in the Russian context than in the West. The intellectual stereotype is likely to be someone deeply, even desperately, concerned about whatever he happens to be concerned about, and profoundly committed to gaining his objective.

The Russian intelligentsia is curiously isolated from the great mass of the people. Yet because Russia is a land of paradoxes, the intellectual is looked up to and poets, say, are revered in a way that is most commonly associated with pop stars in the West.

It would be foolish to be dogmatic about this, but it is more than likely that the role of the Russian Orthodox Church and the very deep imprint it has left on Russian society have contributed materially to this state of affairs, as well as to a whole host of other Russian attitudes. Because literacy was traditionally associated with the Church (until the 18th and 19th centuries) and because the Church was looked up to by the great mass of uneducated Russian peasants as the only source of guidance in a wicked world, it is arguable that some of the reverence formerly rendered unto the Church has passed to the intelligentsia.

The Russian attitude of suspicion and contempt, touched with a trace of illicit curiosity, towards everything associated with the outside world —for all practical purposes this meant the West until very recently—can also be traced back to the Church, if only in part. The Orthodox Church regarded itself as the Third Rome, the center of Christianity (after Rome and Byzantium) and as the true and only repository of Christianity, not defiled in some way or another as, in its view, both Roman Catholicism and Protestantism are. This has led to what can only be called a kind of messianism, a belief that the Russians are a chosen people, singled out for a special destiny to bring salvation to an otherwise benighted and sinful world. Translated on to a secular plane, this sense of mission spilled over into much of the 19th-century Russian intelligentsia and ultimately it came to infect the Communists too—although they would deny it very strongly. (To be sure, it is next to impossible to give the scientific proof to suggestions of this kind that would satisfy a professional sceptic).

But if one does accept that the Russian Orthodox Church has played a social role along these lines—and a global view of Russian history points in that direction—then, evidently, its influence can be seen in other areas of life as well. A strong candidate is the almost superstitious awe in which all manifestations of authority are held. The individual Russian (and let it be stressed again that this is a stereotype) is far readier to accept administrative abuse and arrogance than his Western counterpart. It has also been suggested that the readiness to put up with inconvenience, and even suffering, which might almost be called fatalistic, can be traced back to the long period of Tatar conquest and Moslem overlordship of Russia. The duality of Russian culture, looking East as well as West, and especially the love-hate attitude towards both, is an undoubted fact of Russian life.

The Climate

Yet another factor which has had an unmistakable impact on the Russian way of life (though, as before, it is impossible to assess just how far and in what way) is the climate. It is no secret that Russia suffers terrifyingly cold winters and hot summers. This is certainly true of the areas of European Russia and Siberia which have a predominantly Russian population, even if Central Asia and Transcaucasia enjoy a milder climate. True Russia, then, is the land of Generals January and February, who defeated Napoleon and helped to do likewise to Hitler 150 years later.

At the most superficial level, Russians, together with Scandinavians and other inhabitants of northern latitudes, are heavy spirit drinkers and probably every traveler to Moscow has his story of cheerless drunks staggering around the streets, just as in another northern city—Glasgow. The problems of alcoholism and persistent drunkenness have become serious enough for the authorities to mount huge campaigns against them.

If it is difficult to sum up the character of an individual in a few, brief paragraphs, how much more daunting to attempt to describe the genius of an entire nation in the same space. The truth is, of course, that any comments, like those above, on the Russians (or any other nation for that matter) can only be a broad canvas, showing a few, blurred outlines. The details must be filled in by the visitor to the Soviet Union, who has the extra challenge of knowing that he can never complete the picture.

The Ukrainians

Much of what has been said about the Russians applies to the Ukrainians, too. There is a great deal in common, at least to the complete stranger, between the two most numerous Slavonic nations, whose similarities seem more important than their differences. Perhaps there is a perceptible difference in that there is a certain quickness among the Ukrainians, a great readiness to consider the outside world. There is a good historical reason for this. The Ukrainian nation has never been anything like as isolated as the Russian, having been under Polish, Ottoman, Tatar and other influences. And Galicia, the so-called Western Ukraine, with its capital at Lvov (L'viv in Ukrainian, Lwów in Polish, Lemberg in German—travelers who know Europe east of the Rhine will be aware that most larger towns are known by different names in different languages) was part of Austria-Hungary until 1918.

It is hard to say just how Ukrainians and Russians differ, but the difference is deeply felt by those Ukrainians who are conscious of themselves as Ukrainian. There are not a few Ukrainians, who feel that the difference is no more than a sentimental one, and who are, therefore, ready to accept the Russian language and eventually regard themselves as Russian.

Where a definite difference can be detected between Ukrainians and Russians is that the Ukrainians lack the abounding self-confidence that characterizes the Russian attitude towards the rest of the world. The Russians, when faced with non-Russians, seem to know that they are born to rule; the Ukrainians are much less sure.

It is true that a number of major "Russian" cultural figures have been Ukrainian by birth—the writer Nikolai Gogol is an example. However they have made their names through Russian, and much of the Ukrainian political establishment today is more Russian in culture than Ukrainian. It is easy for a Ukrainian to adopt Russian ways. Not only does the Soviet educational system encourage this, but the environment of many Ukrainian cities tends to be Russian rather than Ukrainian. There is a very substantial Russian minority in the Ukraine, some nine million people, and its two best-known representatives are Nikita Khrushchev and Leonid Brezhnev, the former and present party leaders. One of the few things that may remain to remind an assimilated Ukrainian of his origins could be the characteristic Ukrainian name endings in -enko or -chuk. In other respects, he will be a good Russian.

The Byelorussians

A lot of the above, about the Ukrainians, applies to the Byelorussians, too, except that in the case of the latter, it is only *more* so! They are closer to the Russians in just about every possible way. The Byelorussians are far fewer in number than the Ukrainians (less than 11 million in 1976); they have failed to develop an intense national identity, they remain mostly on the land and speak their language at home. In public, in the towns at least, they accept Russian. A fair comparison may be made here with German-speaking Switzerland, whose inhabitants speak Swytzer-dütsch at home and High German in public.

In general, the modesty of the Byelorussian national effort is summed up by the slogan of the first Byelorussian publishing house, set up in 1906: "In our windows, too, the sun shall shine." Even their name, which means "White Russian", indicates that the Byelorussians are barely more than a branch of the Russians themselves. The Byelorussians appear to have accepted the fact that access to the wider world must be via Russian. The great bulk of education in the republic is carried out in Russian—the two languages are fairly alike—even while the Byelorussian Soviet Socialist Republic enjoys full membership of the United Nations (as does, incidentally, the Ukraine). More is published by the republic's presses in Russian than in Byelorussian. The streets of Minsk, the republican capital, resound to the sounds of Russian rather than Byelorussian, and the Byelorussian Academy of Sciences prefers to issue its scholarly output in Russian.

In many ways, it can be argued that the Byelorussians are the greatest success story of Soviet nationalities policy: the Byelorussian nation exists and it has accepted that its existence is expressed through what is the language of "the Soviet man", Russian.

The Baltic States

It is a very different story, though, among the Estonians, Latvians and Lithuanians. There, national self-assertiveness and attachment to national language remain strong, as do pride in local national traditions and achievements. The Balts will go a long way to stress that they have always belonged to Europe—unlike, they may say, the Russians—and that their contacts with the outside world are direct, especially with the Germans and Swedes who ruled the area over the centuries. For less than a generation, the Baltic states enjoyed a precarious independence. They had been part of the Czar's empire, then proclaimed their independence and ultimately found themselves ruled from Moscow after the carve-up of Eastern Europe between Hitler and Stalin in 1939–40. (The Balts fell to the latter.)

The European influence on which the Balts rely is apparent even to the casual tourist. The architecture of towns like Riga, Tallinn (which originally meant "Danes' Town") and Tartu proves that these settlements have had long contact with cultures well to the west of the Baltic lands. They are readily recognizable as stylistic first cousins of German towns like Lübeck and Swedish towns like Lund or Visby.

This difference between Baltic towns and genuine Russian settlements is understood by Russians, too, many of whom have come to live in what they regard as Europe. So many have come that Riga now has more Russians living in it than Latvians. (How the Latvians feel about this can only be guessed at.) In fact, the pace of Russian immigration into the Baltic states is the fastest into Latvia.

The Estonians and Latvians are readily recognizable as Scandinavians of a kind. They prefer the same sort of light and airy style, the clean-cut lines, the feel for simplicity that are so characteristic of the Finns and Swedes. Like the Scandinavians, the Estonians and a large proportion of the Latvians are Protestant. The Lithuanians, on the other hand, are devoutly Catholic. For many Lithuanians, the Church has become identified with their nation and much resentment arises from the anti-religious aspects of Soviet atheism. The Lithuanians differ somewhat from the other two Baltic peoples in another respect as well: they look back on a spectacular historical past in association with Poland, to the Polish-Lithuanian Commonwealth, which lasted until the end of the 18th century, when Poland was partitioned.

Latvian and Lithuanian are the only surviving members of the Baltic group of languages. Both these languages, written in the Latin alphabet, are distantly related to the Slavonic group and thus to Russian. Estonian, by contrast, is a Finno-Ugrian language, close enough to Finnish for Finns and Estonians to be able to understand one another. Indeed, many Finns are now able to take weekend trips to Tallinn, the Estonian capital, so reinforcing old links.

A Westerner's impressions of the Baltic states will certainly be conditioned by where he has just come from. If he goes to Tallinn or Riga directly from the West, he will be convinced that he is in the middle of the Russian East, with all that that implies. But if, as is more likely, he goes there after having absorbed the atmosphere of Moscow and Kiev, he will react at the familiarity of what is distinctively European.

Transcaucasia

If the Baltic states form a kind of transition between Europe and Russia, Transcaucasia is very clearly an intermediary between Europe, the Middle East and Western Asia. The Transcaucasians, the three most numerous peoples of which are the Georgians, the Armenians and the Azerbaijanis or Azeris, see themselves consciously in this role, albeit firmly on the European side of the divide. In this sense, there is good reason for regarding Transcaucasia as the Soviet Middle East, the place where East meets West.

The two Christian peoples of the region, the Armenians and the Georgians, have traditionally looked towards Russia as the source of protection against the Moslems of the south, from whom both have suffered during their long history. The Azeris, on the other hand, have been more influenced by the attitudes of their fellow Shia Moslems in Iran. Indeed, there is still a substantial number of Azeri Turks in northern Iran.

Because of the long history of friendly contact between Georgians and Armenians with Russians, these two peoples have a somewhat special position in Soviet politics. Until very recently, they were allowed considerable latitude in the running of their own affairs in their own way, and it took the eruption of a major scandal first in Georgia and then, more recently, in Armenia before tighter control was imposed. The Azeris have always been subject to closer attention, not only because they are Moslem, but also because of the existence on their territory of the earliest substantial oilfield in the Soviet Union. Moscow has understandably regarded this oil as a vital strategic resource and has ensured that it would not be abused. The city of Baku, the Azeri capital and the Soviet Union's equivalent of Houston, has for a long time housed a very large number of Russians involved in the oil industry. On top of this, there is a sizeable Armenian community there as well.

Possibly because of the presence of Baku as an alien center in their midst, the Azeris have been in the forefront of Soviet Moslems in adopting Western ideas, together with the Volga Tatars. They were the first to give up writing their language in the highly unsuitable Arabic script and to use Latin letters instead. (The Arabic script is unsuited to the writing of Turkic languages because it makes virtually no provision for the expression of vowels, whereas the Turkic languages have a complex and essential vowel system.) In the 19th century many Azeris eagerly adopted Western ways, which they had learned through the medium of Russian. Some rose high in the Czar's service. After the collapse of his empire, the Azeris formed part of the short-lived Transcaucasian Federation, and then enjoyed a very brief period of independence before being absorbed into the Soviet Union.

The Armenians

The Armenians, the second of the three great Transcaucasian peoples, have never had much fondness for the Azeris, understandably, since their entire history has been one of persecution by Moslem Turks. The Armenian massacres of the early years of the century were only the culmination of a very long and tragic process. It is not by chance that an Armenian poet has written that his country's history has been marked by a sorrow that was like a shoreless sea.

This has had a number of important results. Armenians have, as already mentioned, looked towards the Russians for protection, and conversely, they have enjoyed a greater trust in the eyes of the Russians than other non-Russians. Secondly, the scattering of the Armenian population has led to an enormous diaspora that can only be compared with that of the Jews. There are substantial Armenian communities all over the Middle East and in North America. Thirdly, the Soviet authorities have encouraged all Armenians to regard Soviet Armenia as their homeland and the Armenian repatriation law is very similar to the Israeli law of Ingathering. It offers full rights and economic assistance to any Armenian who moves to Soviet Armenia. A fair number of expatriates have taken advantage of this and many have settled down to enjoy the benefits of Soviet rule. A few decided that the move was a mistake and have re-emigrated where they could.

Within the Soviet Union, the Armenians have a reputation of being the fixers, the people who get round the system, who operate around the edges of bureaucratic rigidity. They form an internal diaspora within the country, not least because Soviet Armenia is too small to permit all of them to exploit their undoubted talents and high level of education.

Armenians are famed for their entrepreneurial talents, their liveliness and for producing a brandy that is rivalled in the Soviet Union only by the output of Georgian distilleries. Armenians are easily recognized by the fact that virtually every Armenian name ends in -yan or -ian. Their culture is a very ancient one; their script is far older than Cyrillic and the Armenian Church, a focus of loyalty for every Armenian wherever he may be, is tolerated up to a point. In common with other peoples which have suffered long persecution, the Armenians are extremely conscious of their national identity and most of them accept that for want of anything better, the Soviet framework offers them their best chance of survival.

Georgians

The Georgians, too, have a strong self-awareness. They take great pride in being different from everyone else in the Soviet Union. They are ebullient and are inclined to live life larger than it is. If, for example, Georgia is racked by financial and political scandals—as was the case in 1972-3—then these will be the most spectacular the country has ever seen, even including a local "Godfather" who ran a vast network of illegal factories and dispensed patronage with a free hand. The Georgians also claim to have produced the largest concentration of centenarians in the world. It is certainly not unusual to find people over 120 years of age. They attribute this great age to the clean, healthy mountain air which they breathe, the vast quantities of yoghurt they eat and the beneficial effects of the local brandy (vastly superior to the stuff brewed down the way in Armenia).

The Georgians have also given the world another product who preferred to do things on a spectacular scale—in the person of Joseph Vissarionovich Dzhugashvili, better known as Stalin. Another Georgian, Lavrenty Beria, ran the Soviet secret police until his sudden demise in 1953, a few months after the death of Stalin. Stalin's memory is still honored in Georgia; his birthplace at Gori serves as a shrine.

Again, like the Armenians (for whom there is little love in Georgia), the Georgians are heirs to a very ancient cultural tradition. Georgia is supposedly the place where the Argonauts of Greek mythology sailed to find the Golden Fleece. The curlicued Georgian script is centuries older than Cyrillic and suits their complex language, reputedly impossible for an outsider to master, very well. Georgian names are likewise fairly easy to spot, as most of them end in -vili or -dze.

The capital Tbilisi (Tiflis in the 19th century), which derives its name from the warm, sulphurous springs found there, bears out the Georgian preference for being different. It is a pleasant relaxed town, rather Mediterranean in atmosphere, not least because the Georgians are wine drinkers (as distinct from the Russians, who drink the ubiquitous vodka). It is evident that the Georgians enjoy a level of prosperity frequently above that of European Russia.

The Central Asians

Traditionally, Central Asia was the area bounded by the Kazakh steppes in the north, the Caspian Sea in the west and the mountains and the Oxus River to the east and south. Today, the expression normally includes Kazakhstan as well. The natives of the region, which used to be known as Turkestan, are undoubtedly marked by a certain cultural unity, in that they are all Moslem, that they mostly speak Turkic languages with a high degree of mutual comprehensibility (many of the Iranian Tadzhiks also understand Uzbek), and that they came under European rule in the 19th century. They are conscious of being the heirs of an ancient and glorious civilization, linked with the names of Genghis Khan and Tamerlane, and of having produced a flowering of Islamic culture in the Middle Ages. This had seriously degenerated by the last century and Russian rule has unquestionably raised their educational, social and medical levels. A European going to Tashkent or Alma Ata might find them shabby and somewhat dilapidated; an Asian will see that the people are well-fed and clothed, that there are no beggars, and that even the swarms of flies seem less aggressive than further south.

Today, the population of Central Asia is very mixed. There has been an enormous influx of Europeans—Russians and Ukrainians for the most part—to the extent that of its total population of 32 million, some 10 million are Europeans. From the Soviet point of view, Central Asia is a strategically sensitive area, having a frontier with two fairly small states, Afghanistan and Iran (with India and Pakistan beyond), and with China. The Central Asians themselves are not insensible to the presence of the Chinese across the border in Sinkiang, and they are aware that the Turkic population of Chinese Turkestan is often worse off than they are.

This said, the Central Asians are a good instance of how non-European peoples can adopt European ways and go through the process of modernization in the space of two or three generations. Quite apart from the externals of modernization—houses, roads, schools, hospitals—the local languages and cultures have been provided with all the encouragement needed to sustain vigorous standards. Whereas before the Revolution, illiteracy was virtually universal among Central Asians (in 1920 there were only 25 Turkmen women able to read), today literacy is universal and a substantial proportion of the population has been through higher education as well.

Much of this effort has been successful, and the Central Asian nations have increased in self-confidence. They are fully conscious of their separate Islamic traditions and, it would seem, carefully cultivate these. An Uzbek noted on one occasion, "it cannot be considered normal when an educated Uzbek feels that he does not have to know the Uzbek language well." Educated Central Asians accept the need for learning Russian as their means of communication with the outside world (from which they would otherwise be cut off), but insist increasingly on the value of their own native languages, too. It is certainly instructive that in a recent census nearly all the Central Asians said that their native languages were their mother tongues (and not Russian, as is the case with one or two nationalities), and that only an average of about 20 percent of them admitted to speaking Russian at all. Russian, of course, is taught in the schools, and this knowledge is reinforced during service in the armed forces. But once back in Central Asia, it would seem, the Moslems prefer to keep to themselves and to restrict their contacts with European settlers to their place of work or when dealing with officials. In the countryside, it is easier to keep up ancient Moslem customs, but even in towns Central Asians will try to have at least one room in the house furnished in the traditional style. Again, while women are not veiled (as demanded by Islamic law), it is still rare for Central Asian girls to pursue careers.

More and More Moslems

Central Asian attitudes among women are also suggested by the staggeringly high birthrate among the Moslems. This is partly the direct result of better medical facilities and the consequent decline in infant mortality, together with factors like better nutrition and health care; but it is also attributable to the survival of the tradition of large families. Despite the probability that the high Central Asian birthrate will level off eventually, the substantial growth in their absolute number cannot fail to exert an important influence in the years ahead.

The Central Asians seek to point up their national identities in many ways. Central Asian scholars have done a great deal of work on the history of the area, and much of the great literary output of the medieval period has been reissued. National monuments are now better looked after than used to be the case, though this is partly at least the result of a keener awareness of the tourist trade. Mosques and other shrines, including the tomb of Tamerlane in Samarkand, are now kept in a reasonable state of repair and are shown off with a good deal of pride as being the creations of the Central Asians themselves.

Both nationally and culturally, the Central Asians are something of an enigma. They are Europeanized Asians, having adopted European ways to a far greater degree than any other non-European people except the Japanese. At the same time, while accepting modernization on European terms, the Central Asians today are clearly anxious to preserve as much of their traditional culture as is compatible with Europeanization, and perhaps more. But it is impossible to assess with any pretence at accuracy which element in the mix is the dominant, the European or the Asian.

The non-Russians of the Volga

The non-Russians of the central Volga Valley are far from being a single cohesive group of nationalities, except in one respect—they have all been in very long contact with the Russians and have adopted many of their ways, while retaining their own individuality to a greater or lesser extent. There are six nationalities involved: the Moslem Tatars and Bashkirs, the Finnic Mari, Mordvins and Udmurts, who are all nominally Christian, and the Turkic Chuvash, who are also Christian. They live in a vast area which stretches almost to the River Don in the west and up to the Urals in the east, thinly scattered and often mixed with Russian settlements. The towns of the area, particularly, tend to be predominantly Russian.

The most remarkable and most distinctive, as well as the most numerous, of these nationalities are the Tatars. The descendants of the Tatar conquerors of Russia in the Middle Ages, they had begun to develop a strong middle class two generations before the 1917 Revolution. This middle class, the pillar of a sense of national identity in any community, was based on the merchants of Kazan and the growing number of educated Tatars in the late 19th century, who for a period made Kazan the third most important center of Islamic thought (after Cairo and Constantinople). Indeed, around the turn of the century, the Tatars were actively engaged in converting neighboring peoples, like the Mari and the Chuvash, to Islam, in direct competition with the Russian Orthodox Church.

After the Revolution, the Kazan Tatars pressed for the creation of a separate Tatar republic, which would possibly have included the Bashkirs as well, but Moscow was not prepared to contemplate this. Instead, a Tatar Autonomous Republic (abbreviated to Tatar ASSR) was set up, where the Tatars now form just under half the population; in addition, there are substantial numbers of Tatars in Bashkiria and elsewhere in the Soviet Union; indeed, there is hardly a major town in the country without a Tatar community. With this kind of a history, it would be surprising if the Tatars were not strongly conscious of their national traditions and identity.

The Bashkirs, a closely related Turkic nationality (which the Tatars in effect attempted to assimilate), were much less advanced culturally at the time of the Revolution. They were still seminomadic in the early years of this century. Since then, they have been encouraged in their efforts to build up an autonomous cultural tradition of their own. Because the Bashkir people are so widely scattered, they form only about a quarter of the population of the Bashkir ASSR, which also contains large numbers of Russians (and Tatars).

Of the Volga Valley's three Finnic peoples (whose languages, incidentally, are only distantly related to Finnish itself), the most numerous are the Mordvins. Once much feared as cruel and pitiless fighters, the Mordvins are now engaged in more peaceful pursuits. About one-third of them live within the Mordovian ASSR and the rest are scattered over a wide area. There is considerable evidence that the Mordvins have accepted Russian ways for their future and have done so with equanimity.

The Mari are far fewer in number—600,000 as against the 1.2 million Mordvins—but they are conspicuously more attached to their national traditions. They have had a distinctive history, in that they have been in long and intimate contact with the Tatars and Bashkirs, as well as having an extensive record of peasant uprisings against Russian rule. The conversion of the Mari to Christianity is a relatively recent event—some of them are Moslem—and pagan practices among them certainly survived into this century.

The Udmurts live in a fairly compact area to the north of Kazan, around the River Kama, and make up about half the population of the Udmurt ASSR. The rest are urban Russians and some Tatars. The Udmurts are less advanced culturally than the other Finnic peoples of the Volga and their ancient clan system remained in being up to the present century, as did traces of their pagan forms of worship.

The Chuvash are in an unusual position in that they speak a Turkic language, but one very distant from the speech of all the other Turkic peoples of the Soviet Union. There is no question of a Chuvash being able to understand a Tatar, whereas a Tatar and, say, an Uzbek, can make one another out. Secondly, the Chuvash are Christian, and thus more intimately linked with the Russians than with the Moslems. Thirdly, the Chuvash, who are over a million-and-a-half strong, look back to the Bolghar Empire of the 10th and 11th centuries, which ruled over vast tracts of what is now European Russia.

The Northern Caucasus

If the central Volga Valley has a nationally mixed population, northern Caucasia and Daghestan contain a veritable confusion of peoples—one authority cites 32 different nationalities living in a comparatively restricted area. It is interesting that the Daghestan ASSR is the only one which takes its name from a region rather than from a people or a nationality. Although the Caucasians and Daghestanis are mostly Moslem, they speak a bewildering number of languages—some are Paleo-Caucasian, some Turkic, some Iranian—and until the Revolution, Turkic and Arabic, the holy language of Islam, served as the means of communication. Since then, these have been largely replaced by Russian.

Despite the great linguistic and national diversity, the people of the northern Caucasus did unite in the middle of the last century under their great military leader Shamil against the troops of the Russian Czar. Shamil, who is venerated as a hero, fought off the Russians for 25 years. Nowadays, the northern Caucasians and Daghestanis remain attached to their Islamic ways and to their traditional egalitarianism.

The Jews

Many people might question whether the Jews are a nationality at all. The Soviet authorities certainly classify them as such—1.8 million people gave their nationality as Jewish in the 1979 census, as opposed to 2.1 million in 1970—and without a doubt many Soviet Jews regard themselves as culturally different, even when their mother tongue is Russian or Ukrainian. Only 17 percent of the Jews gave their mother tongue as Yiddish. The Soviet authorities even established a Jewish autonomous province in Siberia, in Birobidzhan on the River Amur, which was to serve as a center of Soviet Jewish life. Less than 10 percent of its small population is Jewish.

Within the Soviet Union, the Jewish communities fall into separate categories. The overwhelming majority are Ashkenazim, who moved eastwards from Central Europe in the Middle Ages and were constrained to remain in the Pale of Settlement in Western Russia under the Czars. Smaller communities were long established in Georgia, in the Caucasian mountains (where they speak an Iranian dialect) and in Central Asia.

Although many Jews accept that their future lies with the Soviet state, some of them have been anxious to emigrate to Israel, where they feel they will have better opportunities, not least to practice the tenets of Judaism which can be difficult in an officially atheistic country. In the last decade, the Soviet authorities, while simultaneously campaigning energetically against Zionism, have let about 250,000 Jews leave, clearly as a contribution to the widely proclaimed spirit of international detente.

A MINI-HISTORY OF RUSSIA

From Rurik to Romanovs

Reigning Monarch	Dates	Important Events
	830	Varangians (Vikings) begin to leave Scandinavia.
Rurik	862–79	Great Novgorod, one of most important Slav towns, falls to Rurik, Varangian chieftain, and he is called on to rule over town.

Kievan Russia

Reigning Monarch	Dates	Important Events
Oleg	879–912	Oleg makes Kiev his capital in 880.
Igor	912–45	Treaty with Constantinople.
Olga (widow of Igor)	945–62	Olga baptized a Christian in Constantinople in 957.
Svyatoslav (murdered)	962–72	Svyatoslav defeats the Bulgarians in 968.
Yaropolk (murdered)	973–8	Betrayed by an adviser.
Vladimir	978–1015	In 988 Vladimir accepts Byzantine Christianity; in 977 Novgorod gains self-government from Kiev.
Yaroslav the Wise	1015–19	
	1019–54	12 sons of Vladimir struggle for succession. Peaceful reign. Kiev becomes first center of Orthodox Church in Russia.

Church law imported from Constantinople.

1054–1113 Sons of Yaroslav and heirs feuding.

Vladimir
Monomakh   1113–25   Brief period of unity.

1125–1220 Land divided again and in conflict until Mongol invasion.

Mongol Invasions and Rule

1220	First Mongol-Tatar attack in Caucasus.
1223	First Mongol invasion: Russians and Polovtsy are defeated.
1235–40	Conquest of Caucasus by Tatar-Mongols; capture of Kiev.
1240	Alexander Nevsky, Prince of Novgorod, defeats Swedes on Neva.
1242	Alexander Nevsky defeats Knights of Teutonic Order on the ice of Lake Peipus. Tatar headquarters established on lower Volga. Tatar domination for next 250 years, holding 9 principalities in their power. Principalities gradually fell between 1261 and 1533 under control of Moscow.

The Rise of Moscow

	1301–3	First territorial acquisitions of Muscovy.
	1310	Moscow becomes the See of Orthodox Church.
Ivan I	1325–40	Nicknamed "Kalita" (Moneybags) because of economic hold of Moscow over other principalities.
Ivan II	1353–9	
Dmitriy Donskoy	1359–89	Kremlin of Moscow begun (1367); Moscow defeats Tatars (1378).
Vasiliy I	1389–1425	Nizhny-Novgorod absorbed by Moscow (1393).
Vasiliy II	1425–62	1439 Council of Florence reunites Eastern and Western Churches; Church of Moscow independent (1448).
Ivan III [the Great]	1462–1505	Many cities incorporated into Moscow (1463–1489); Building of new Kremlin (1485–1516); War with Sweden (1496–7); Destruction of Golden Horde by Crimean Tatars in 1502 (conquered by Turks in 1475).
Vasiliy III	1505–33	Crimean raids on southeastern Russia (1507)
Ivan IV (the Terrible)	1533–84	First Russian sovereign to be crowned czar (in 1547 in Uspensky Cathedral, in Kremlin); Marriage to girl with Romanov connections; Fire of Moscow (1547); War with Sweden (1555–7); Livonian war (1558–83); Crimean Tatars

		burn Moscow (1571); Beginning of conquest of Siberia (1581); Truce with Poland (1582); Truce with Sweden (1583).
Fyodor I	1584–98	Boris Godunov as Regent (1587–98); War with Sweden (1590–3).
Boris Godunov	1598–1605	Boris elected Czar by the Zemsky Sobor; Time of Troubles; civil wars (1604–13).
Fyodor Godunov	1605	Czar for few weeks before army goes over to Dmitriy. Fyodor murdered by pretender's agents.
False Dmitriy I	1605–6	
Vasiliy Shuisky	1606–10	First peasant war in Russian history: uprising led by Ivan Bolotnikov.
False Dmitriy II	1607–10	Polish invasion: occupation of Moscow (1610); Novgorod occupied by the Swedes (1611); National uprising led by Minin and Pozharsky: Poles burn Moscow before retreating (1611–12).

The Romanovs

Mikhail	1613–45	Elected by Zemsky Sobor. Peace with Sweden: Moscow loses Baltic outlet (1618); Truce with Poland; War with Poland again (1632–4).
Aleksey	1645–76	Last Zemsky Sobor summoned to vote on the incorporation of the Ukraine (1653); Beginning of the Schism—Old Believers (1654); Russo-Polish war: truce of Andrusovo cedes Smolensk, Kiev and Ukraine to Moscow (1654–7); War with Sweden (1656–8); Stenka Razin's revolt (1670–1).
Fyodor III	1676–82	War with Turkey and Crimea (1676–80).
Peter (the Great)	1682–1725	First outward-looking reign in Russian history. Peter opened window on Western ideas; techniques flooded into Russia. "Permanent peace" with Poland (1686); Reform of calendar; beginning of Great Northern War against Sweden, settled by 21 years later (1700); Foundation of Saint Petersburg (later Petrograd and now Leningrad) (1701–3); Conquest of Livonia, Estonia and Vyborg (1710); War with Turkey; loss of Azov (1711); Conquest of Finland (1713–14); Acquisition of Livonia, Estonia, Ingria and Karelia; Peter adopts title of Emperor (1721); War with Persia; acquisition of western and southern shores of Caspian (1722).
Catherine I	1725–7	Peter's widow, utterly incapable.
Peter II	1727–30	Succeeded at 11, died of smallpox.
Anna	1730–40	Daughter of Ivan V, niece of Peter the

		Great. War with Turkey (1735–9).
Ivan VI	1740–41	Various contesting regents. War with Sweden.
Elizaveta	1741–61	Daughter of Peter the Great and Catherine I.
Peter III	1761–2	Alliance with Frederick II.
Catherine II (the Great)	1762–96	Wife of Peter III. War with Turkey: gets Black Sea steppes (1768–74); First partition of Poland (1772–3); Revolt led by Pugachev (1773–4); Ukraine absorbed completely into Russian Empire (1781–6); Annexation of the Crimea; Sevastopol founded (1783); Russian protectorship over eastern Georgia (1783); Settlement in Alaska (1784); Wars with Turkey and Sweden (1787–91); Second and third partitions of Poland; Koscziuszko's rebellion (1793–5); War with Persia; campaigns in Da gestan and Azerbaijan (1796).
Paul I (murdered)	1796–1801	Enacted new law on succession based on male primogeniture, which gave Russia a series of five more emperors and freedom from dynastic upheavals that had been a feature of previous centuries. The Russian-American Company (formed in 1797 as the United American Company) (1799); Suvorov's campaigns in northern Italy and Switzerland (1799); Alliance with Napoleon (1800).
Alexander I	1801–25	Involved in his father's murder, Alexander sought to repair the ill Paul had done. He rehabilitated over 12,000 people who had been banished or dismissed from their posts by his father, abolished Paul's secret police, abolished censorship, lifted the ban on foreign books and travel and seemed at one time to want to free the serfs and relax the autocratic rule. Diplomatic relations restored with England; Peace treaty with France; Eastern Georgia annexed; Conquest of Transcaucasia begun (1801); War with Persia; Russian sovereignty of Georgia; Russia annexes northern Azerbaijan (1803–13); War with Turkey, Bessarabia annexed (1806–12); Treaty of Tilsit (1807); War with Sweden, annexation of Finland (1808–9); Napoleon and Battle of Borodino, burning of Moscow, pursuit of retreating Napoleon into France (1812); Pushkin active (1820–37); Revolt, sometimes called the first Russian revolution, in December (1825).

Nicholas I	1825–55	A reactionary Czar; organization of political police force, war with Persia, annexation of Armenia (1826); war with Turkey (1827); Polish rebellion; Uprising of Novgorod military colonies (1830–1); Alexander Herzen active (1831–70); First Russian railway opened between St. Petersburg and Tsarskoye Selo; Pushkin dies in a duel (1837); Lermontov, poet, dies in a duel (1841); Publication of Gogol's *Dead Souls* (1842); Dostoyevsky active (1846–81); Turgenev active (1847–83); Russia intervenes in Hungary (1849); Tolstoy active (1852–1910); Crimean War (1853–6).
Alexander II (assassinated)	1855–81	"The Czar Liberator," a reforming czar. Annexation of Amur and Maritime Provinces (1858); Complete conquest of Caucasus (1859); Expansion of railways (1860–73); Emancipation of serfs (1861); Russian-American Company liquidated (1862); Polish rebellion (1863); Sale of Alaska to United States (1867); First Russian translation of Karl Marx's *Das Kapital;* Agreement with England on partition of Central Asia into spheres of influence (1873); Organization of Land and Freedom Party (*Zemlya i Volya*) (1876); War with Turkey (1877–8); Attempted assassination of Alexander (1879); Attempt to blow up Winter Palace and assassinate Alexander (1880).
Alexander III	1881–94	Conservative and nationalist like grandfather Nicholas I. Organization of the revolutionary group; Emancipation of Labor (Osvobozhdeniye Truda) by Russian émigrés in Geneva (1883); Assassination attempt on Alexander by Alexander Ulyanov (Lenin's brother) (1887); Trans-Siberian railway begun (1891).
Nicholas II (assassinated)	1894–1917	The last Russian czar. Marked dislike of elected politicians and intellectuals. Married Queen Victoria's granddaughter, Princess Alix of Hessen-Darmstadt. Chinese-Russian defensive alliance against Japan (1896); Founding of Russian Social Democratic Labor Party in Minsk, Chinese-Russian treaty grants Russia lease of Port Arthur and Liaotung Peninsula (1898); Boxer Revolt, Russia occupies Manchuria (1900); Social Revolutionary Party formed (1901); Chinese-Russian agree-

ment on evacuation of Russian troops
from Manchuria; Social Revolutionary
Party member assassinates Minister
of the Interior (1902); Kishinev pogrom
(1903); Japan attacks Russia at Port
Arthur without declaring war; Battle of
Tsushima; Treaty of Portsmouth; Assas-
sination of new Minister of Interior,
Plehve, by another Social Revolutionary
Party member (1904);

General strike in St. Petersburg; Bloody
Sunday. Assassination of Grand Duke
Sergei by Social Revolutionary Party
member; First Soviet formed in Ivanovo-
Voznesensk; General National Strike;
Convention of Constitutional Demo-
cratic Party (Cadets), formation of St.
Petersburg Soviet, Nicholas' Manifesto
(October) summoning Duma (legislative
assembly), extending suffrage rights,
freedom of speech, press and assembly.
Formation of Moscow Soviet, formation
of Octobrists and Union of the Russian
People, arrest of members of St.
Petersburg Soviet, general political
strike in Moscow, Moscow uprising
(December 1905).

HISTORY OF THE SOVIET UNION

A New Force in the World

BY

GRAHAM WEBB

> **Note:** for a brief outline of pre-revolutionary Russian history, see our "Mini History of Russia" chapter, immediately preceding this history of the Soviet Union.

Few events have changed the course of modern history more decisively than the Russian Revolution. Like many dramatic events, it had its dress rehearsal, which was held on the ninth of January 1905, a day which came to be called "Bloody Sunday". As one eye-witness, the novelist Maxim Gorky, put it, "everything was cut short and smashed on that accursed but instructive day. I believe," he wrote to a friend on the evening of Bloody Sunday, "that this is the beginning of the end of the bloodthirsty Czar." The end, though, was not to come for another 12 years, for it was not until February 1917 that the czarist autocracy that had ruled Russia for over 300 years collapsed. After the abdication of Nicholas II, a provisional government was set up which survived until the fateful night of October 24–25, 1917, when the Bolshevik faction of the Social Democrat Party, led by Vladimir Ilyich Lenin, seized power in Petrograd and established a government which was to build the world's first socialist state—the Union of Soviet Socialist Republics.*

---

* The Julian calendar used in Russia until February 1918 was 13 days behind the Gregorian calendar used in western Europe, so the Great October Socialist Revolution is commemorated in the USSR on November 6 and 7.

There was, however, one event which preceded the "revolution" of 1905 and which was to be of vital importance in this final overthrow of the autocracy. This was the Second Congress of the Russian Social Democratic Labor Party, held in Brussels in July 1903. It was after this congress that the party split into two factions, led by Lenin and Julius Martov; Lenin's faction called themselves the "majoritarians", or Bolsheviks, and dubbed the other faction "minoritarians", or Mensheviks. The split was caused ostensibly by Lenin's attempts to remove three of his colleagues from the editorial board of the party's underground paper *Iskra* (Spark), but was really due to the fact that Lenin had a much stricter idea of the party as a highly disciplined, tight-knit group of wholly dedicated professional revolutionaries than any of his five colleagues on the *Iskra* board. Two years later the Bolsheviks and Mensheviks were holding separate congresses.

Within Russia by 1905 trouble was brewing. A decade of famines, agricultural stagnation and the punitive tax system had brought the peasantry—still the overwhelming majority of the population—to a new peak of discontent which had erupted in two major uprisings in 1902 in Poltava and Kharkov provinces. This discontent was being fanned by the propaganda of the new Socialist Revolutionary Party, which called for nationalization and redistribution of the land and also undertook a campaign of terror and assassination. By the end of 1904 even the liberals who led the *zemstva*—the organs of local self-government set up in 1864—were demanding the abolition of the autocracy, the establishment of a parliament, universal suffrage, equality before the law, freedom of the press and of assembly and personal and civil liberties. In the war with Japan, morale in the Russian army and navy had fallen very low following a series of defeats, and when Port Arthur fell, strikes broke out in St. Petersburg, the workers signing a petition calling for basic liberties, a constituent assembly and an eight-hour day. The petition was carried to the Winter Palace by a peaceful procession of about 150,000 workers, led by Father Gapon, an Orthodox priest who was also a trade union leader. On its arrival in the square outside the Winter Palace, the procession, which was bearing icons and portraits of the Czar and which was singing hymns, was fired on and a thousand workers were killed and thousands more wounded. It was, indeed, a Bloody Sunday.

Revolt flared up, and by the end of the month almost 500,000 workers were on strike; they were joined by professional classes who formed themselves into unions to demand political concessions from the government. Peasants attacked landowners, nationalities claimed home rule and the reign of terror began again with the assassination of the Czar's uncle, Sergei. In June the crew of the battleship *Potemkin* mutinied in Odessa, providing Sergei Eisenstein with the subject of one of his finest films, and, a month before, the Baltic Fleet had been routed by the Japanese at the Battle of Tsushima.

The First Duma

In this revolutionary year of 1905 neither the Social Democrats nor the Socialist Revolutionaries were able to shape the discontent into a movement and provide it with leadership, although revolutionary soviets —or councils—were set up in the major cities. With the whole country paralyzed by September with strikes, peasant violence and mutinies (which had taken the revolutionaries by surprise), the Czar was advised by Count Witte, his Finance Minister, to issue his October Manifesto, promising full civil freedoms and a State Duma, or Parliament, to be elected on a fairly wide (but still very unequal) suffrage.

With this first constitution, the Russian autocracy was transformed—in theory—into a constitutional monarchy. Yet in their attitudes to the Duma, there was no compromise from any of the parties. Lenin, who was still abroad, wanted nothing to do with it, and for the next six years the Bolsheviks drew further and further away from the Mensheviks. The Mensheviks felt that the revolution could be made if the workers were trained and taught how to defend their rights within the constitutional structure that now existed. The Bolsheviks, however, stressed leadership, discipline and unity, and were determined at all costs to avoid compromise. Lenin's most original contribution to Marxism—contained in his pamphlet of 1901, *What is to be Done?*—was the view that, of their own accord, workers are capable only of developing what he called "trade union consciousness". Unless the truth of Marxism was brought to them by intellectuals and unless they were led by professional revolutionaries, the workers would be concerned only to secure for themselves better wages and better working conditions and not at all to change the basis of their society.

Yet in spite of Lenin's contempt for the First Duma, it did contain both Bolsheviks and Mensheviks. When it opened in May 1906 it immediately became the scene of violent demands for the government's resignation, for a political amnesty, for a democratic electoral system and for the right to strike. By July the Czar had had enough and dissolved it, saying it had exceeded its competence. The Second Duma met in February 1907 and lasted three months before being dissolved when a Social Democratic deputy was falsely accused of plotting Nicholas's assassination and encouraging mutiny in the armed forces. The Third Duma ran its course, albeit with an even more limited suffrage, and the Fourth Duma lasted until February 1917 and the advent of the Provisional Government.

Between 1906 and 1911 the Czar's new Prime Minister, P.A. Stolypin, tried to desensitize the peasants to the infection of revolution by enabling them to buy their own land. Lenin saw the purpose and, to him, the danger of this measure, saying: "If this goes on for very long we may well be forced to abandon completely any revolutionary agrarian program . . . Agriculture will become capitalistic and no revolutionary solution of the agrarian problem will be possible under capitalism." Lenin's fears were over in September 1911, when Stolypin was murdered, for the dynamism went out of the scheme.

When Russia entered the First World War, on the Allied side, unprepared and in a chaotic internal condition, there was a general feeling that this was the time for all Russians good and true to come to the aid of their country. However, Lenin, in exile in Poland with his close circle of supporters, was alone in seeing the war as the chance for revolution: the cry was "Turn the imperialist war into civil war." But as the war dragged on, Lenin came round to the view that his generation would probably not live to see the revolution that was inevitably to come.

The Imperial Collapse

When the autocracy collapsed in February 1917, the spontaneity of the uprising took the government and the revolutionaries equally by surprise. The Bolshevik and Menshevik underground committees played hardly any part in the disturbances which broke out in St. Petersburg on February 23, for they had suffered much through arrests and repression during the war. After nine days of rioting and strikes, the Czar dismissed his Interior Minister and ordered the dissolution of the Fourth Duma. The Duma refused to withdraw and by February 27, czarism was dead. Four days after the almost-bloodless overthrow of the autocracy, the new Provisional Government was announced to the country; headed by Prince Lvov, it contained only one socialist, Alexander Kerensky, the Minister of Justice, who later became Prime Minister.

The Provisional Government saw the revolution as an opportunity to bring the war to a victorious conclusion; the soviets, which had been springing up all over Russia, saw it as a hope for peace and as a chance for the peasant in uniform to get his own land. For Lenin, the February Revolution was the bourgeois revolution which Marxism said had to precede the proletarian revolution, and when he arrived in the renamed capital of Petrograd on April 3, he had decided that the advent of the proletarian revolution could be hastened. His cries of "Fraternization at the front," "No support for the Provisional Government" and—most famous of all—"All power to the soviets" soon brought into the Bolshevik ranks the brilliant revolutionary, Lev Trotsky, who had been arguing for the previous 12 years that the bourgeois and proletarian revolutions could be telescoped into one "permanent revolution."

The failure of an insurrection by the new Commander-in-Chief, General Kornilov, whose forces had been opposed by Bolsheviks, Mensheviks and Socialist Revolutionaries, led to a growth of Bolshevik influence in the soviets and in the countryside. With the tide running his way, Lenin, still in Finland, said: "History will not forgive us if we do not seize power now." The decision was taken on October 10; Lenin came out of hiding and the vote went ten to two (Zinoviev and Kamenev) in favor of armed uprising. Six days later the Petrograd Soviet, whose chairman was Trotsky, set up a military-revolutionary committee, which by a week later had fixed a date for the rising. On the morning of October 24, the Bolsheviks' Central Committee—with the exception of Lenin, Stalin and Zinoviev—met to make the final plans. The coup, directed by Trotsky, went according to these plans and was bloodless.

Lenin's first decree proposed an immediate armistice of at least three months and called on all the belligerents to open negotiations for an "honest democratic peace;" finally, he appealed as a good proletarian internationalist for the working classes in Britain, France and Germany to support the Soviets' peace policy. His second decree nationalized all private, ecclesiastical and czarist land without compensation: this decree sanctioned the seizure of the land by the peasants which had been going on for some months.

On November 12, elections were held to the Constituent Assembly. This was something the Bolsheviks had called for throughout the period of the Provisional Government, but the results of the elections confirmed that the Bolsheviks had been unable to win the peasants over from their traditional allegiance to the Socialist Revolutionaries; they polled only a quarter of the votes and the Socialist Revolutionaries took 370 of the 707 seats, an overall majority. When the Constituent Assembly met in January 1918 and refused to accept the Bolsheviks' program, they and the Left Socialist Revolutionaries withdrew and the Bolshevik Red Guards broke up the meeting and prevented it from reassembling. Lenin justified his action by saying that it was too soon—three weeks—after the revolution for the elections to be meaningful and that in any case no election that took place before the workers were fully in control of the state could be valid.

War's End

The Treaty of Brest-Litovsk was signed on March 16, 1918 and the Russians had to give up Estonia, Latvia, Lithuania and Russian Poland; they had to recognize the independence of the Ukraine, Georgia and Finland; to leave Kars, Ardahan and Batumi; and had to pay reparations of 6,000,000,000 marks. However, the Bolsheviks set about consolidating the gains of their revolution; they introduced press censorship, nationalized big industry, outlawed strikes, nationalized the banks, built up a police force (the Cheka) and the Red Army, and organized the requisitioning of grain for the army and the urban population. But for the next two and a half years the Bolsheviks were also engaged in a civil war with the White armies of the Right; although the Reds, led by Trotsky, won, the emergency measures introduced under the title of "War Communism," which included seizure of the peasants' produce, had led to peasant risings by mid-1920, strikes and demonstrations in the capital by the end of the year and open revolt by the sailors of the Kronstadt garrison in March 1921.

The Kronstadt revolt took place a few days before the Tenth Party Congress and, following expressions of extreme peasant discontent with the catastrophic effect on agriculture of the war and the government's requisition policy, and the demoralization of the urban workers with the collapse of industry (which was forcing people to leave the towns for the country), the congress forced Lenin to scrap War Communism in favor of a New Economic Policy (NEP). He recognized, as he told the Tenth Congress, that "the poverty of the working class was never so vast and so acute as in the period of its dictatorship. The enfeeblement of the workers and peasants," he told delegates, "is close to the point of complete incapacitation for work." So it was a question of saving the revolution. Since there had been no socialist revolution in the advanced countries, there would have to be compromise between the proletariat and the peasantry. Requisitioning was virtually stopped and the peasants were given freedom in cultivating their land and marketing its produce; there was a tax on a proportion of the surplus produce left over after the peasant's family had been fed. So the peasant was encouraged by the NEP to produce more, in order that his share of the surplus would be more—and this he was allowed to sell on the market. Under the NEP the state still controlled industry, foreign trade, banking and transport, while agricultural production was controlled by the peasants. This mixed economy—what Lenin called "state capitalism"—lasted until 1928.

Apart from introducing the New Economic Policy to Russia, the Tenth Party Congress (March 1921) took one other decision which was to mark it as a watershed in the country's history; it voted to prohibit the formation of groups or factions within the Party, to limit criticism, to improve the organization of the Party, and to carry out a purge which by the beginning of 1922 had resulted in the expulsion of one-fifth of the membership. At the same time, Socialist Revolutionaries who had been arrested were put on trial; the Mensheviks had already ceased to be a force to reckon seriously with now that their leader, Martov, was in exile. The about-turn in economic policy, the ban on dissent and the elimination of opposition marked the beginning of the notion that the Party could never be wrong, or at least could never admit to being wrong; it was the party of the working people and their party could not be wrong, by definition.

After Lenin

Under Lenin's successor (the founder of the state died in 1924) the distinction between dissent and opposition became blurred as the new leader strove to secure his own position within the party and within the country. For the man who was to be undisputed ruler of the USSR for the next 30 years, Joseph Stalin, had begun to consolidate his power base even before Lenin's death. In 1922 he was appointed General Secretary of the Party's Central Committee and with this appointment the balance of power within the party shifted from the policy-making Politburo to the policy-executing Secretariat. Stalin's growing power was a cause of some anxiety for Lenin in his last months and he even proposed that he be removed from office; such was Stalin's power that the proposal was suppressed. The succession struggle had begun before Lenin's death and intensified after it. First Stalin allied himself with Kamenev and Zinoviev against Trotsky, forcing the last to resign as Commissar for War. Then Kamenev and Zinoviev broke with Stalin and formed an alliance with Trotsky; this led to the three of them being removed from the Politburo and finally from the Party itself, along with 75 followers. Just over a year later, in early 1929, Trotsky was deported from the country. With the defeat of this "Left Opposition," which had never accepted NEP fully— seeing it as a retreat from socialism—and which advocated more rapid industrialization and harsher methods of extracting capital from the peasantry, Stalin found himself in alliance with Rightist leaders, and it was now necessary for him to eliminate this "Right Opposition" which had emerged in the Politburo. Within a year this had been done—the leaders (Bukharin, Tomsky and Rykov) were all removed from the Politburo, giving Stalin control of this topmost Party body. Stalin now set about securing rapid industrialization and the enforced collectivization of the peasantry in his attempt to build "socialism in one country," leaving the international revolution for the moment to take care of itself.

No plan of rapid industrialization could be envisaged without including agriculture, so in order to increase agricultural exports to pay for the import of capital equipment needed for industrialization, it was necessary, Stalin argued, to collectivize the 25,000,000 peasant households into larger and more economically viable groupings and to "smash the kulaks"—to eliminate these wealthier peasants, who were charging excessively high prices for their greater surpluses, "as a class." A kind of civil war came to the countryside. There was immense loss of life; millions of kulaks and their families were deported to forced labor camps and to new industrial areas and famine was caused by the disorganization of agriculture. The kulaks retaliated against the government's policy by killing their cattle, burning crops and destroying their homes; doing anything rather than allow their property to be taken by the state. In the five years between 1928 and 1933, the number of cattle and horses more than halved and the number of pigs, sheep and goats dropped by two-thirds. Collectivization was undertaken by Stalin at enormous cost.

The First Five-Year Plan

The other side of the coin was the first Five-Year Plan, which went into operation on October 1, 1928 and was to treble production of coal, iron, steel and oil as well as treble engineering output, double the production of consumer goods, raise the production of electricity by 600 percent and raise overall output in the entire economy two and one-third times. The workers' sense of patriotism was tapped and encouraged by the full force of government propaganda, for hardly any foreign governments were prepared to provide capital. From the end of 1929 industrialization and the Plan took precedence in the government's mind over collectivization, and, worried by the way agriculture was becoming disorganized, it temporarily halted the campaign; however, such was the flight from the collective farms that they were recollectivized. On the industrial front the call was "Fulfil and overfulfil the Plan!". Workers were rewarded according to their productivity and some became model workers, like the coal miner Stakhanov, in the race to set new records.

Life was tough for the Soviet citizen in the 1930's, even if he did not become personally entangled in the Great Terror, the mass purges which swept like some crazed prehistoric beast into every corner of the Union, trampling down and brutalizing every living thing as it took on a momentum and frenzy of its own. The Great Terror began for all practical purposes with the murder of the Party chief in Leningrad, Sergei Kirov, at the end of 1934. In his secret speech denouncing Stalin at the 20th Communist Party Congress in 1956, Nikita Khrushchev virtually admitted that the crime was initiated by Stalin to rid himself of one of his toughest and most valued supporters who was building a power base and beginning to get ideas of his own. To start with, Stalin liquidated the Leningrad Party apparatus and tried to pin the murder on Kamenev and Zinoviev, but then he must have realized the enormous potential his crime had as an opportunity to settle scores all round. He launched a reign of terror which was to plunge the Soviet Union into a nightmare which lasted until 1938 and affected all strata of society from the Party Central Committee—three-quarters of whose members were either executed or sent to labor camps—and the Red Army—whose High Command was smashed—down to ordinary men and women who found themselves denounced on trumped-up charges by people they had trusted. Two years passed before the No. 1 Enemy, Lev Trotsky, fell victim to a Stalinist ice-axe in Mexico in August 1940. At this point, Stalin was unassailable.

By 1940 the Soviet Union was a major industrial power. The average annual rate of growth of industry in the period 1928–40 was nine percent, and this at a time of depression in the West and political purges and a disorganized agriculture at home. However, the human cost was enormously high; it has been estimated by one Western scholar that if the collectivization casualties and the labor camp deaths are added together, a figure of 20,000,000 is reached, which is approximately the total of the Soviet Union's military and civilian losses in the Second World War.

The Second World War

The Soviet Union's catastrophic involvement in the Second World War—catastrophic, that is, in terms of casualties, not of foreign political advantages—began with a 10-year non-aggression pact signed in Moscow in August 1939 between Molotov and Ribbentrop. There was a secret codicil to the pact, laying down the division of Poland and the allocation of Estonia, Latvia and Bessarabia to the USSR and of Lithuania to Germany. Stalin later—after his country had been invaded—explained why the Soviet government had signed this pact with "so deceitful a nation, with such criminals as Hitler and Ribbentrop." It was, he said, to gain 18 months' peace in order to make military preparations; he made no mention of the territorial gains involved in this marriage of convenience. (In fact the Soviet Union's expansionist interests at the time exceeded those contained in the secret codicil; there was, for example, great interest in the Balkans beyond Bessarabia.)

By biding his time while the capitalist states were at each other's necks, Stalin could but gain advantage, but on June 22, 1941 German troops suddenly invaded the Soviet Union. The Germans made rapid advances and Stalin called on the people to wage guerrilla warfare. The Great Patriotic War was on and the Soviet people's achievement in defeating Hitler was truly colossal; although Stalin was to blame for an opportunistic policy which left the country unprepared for the war, he did provide great nationalist leadership during it. It was 1812 all over again, as Marshal Zhukov led the counter-offensive that saved Moscow. The successful defense of Stalingrad in November 1942 was a major turning-point in the war, as was the three-year siege of Leningrad.

As the Soviet forces swung back westward pushing the retreating Germans home, Stalin's self-confidence returned and he began to think farther ahead than his immediate wartime alliance. He at last responded to Polish communist requests for support and his relations with the London-based, Polish government worsened. Churchill's acknowledgement of Soviet interests in Eastern Europe, expressed in Moscow in October 1944, was taken by Stalin to signal Western agreement to his having a free hand in his sphere of influence. So communist governments came to power in Eastern Europe with the help of the Soviet occupation forces, but it was not until the communist government was established in Prague in February 1948 that the West fully realized what was happening.

Later in 1948, however, Tito's Yugoslavia broke away from the Soviet sphere of influence, and seeing this as "nationalist deviation," Stalin sought to ensure that it would not be repeated. He instituted a purge in Eastern Europe as he had in the Soviet Union in the 1930's. The Czechoslovak leaders Rudolf Slansky and Vlado Clementis, the Hungarian Laszlo Rajk and the Bulgarian Traicho Kostov were killed, and the Pole Wladyslaw Gomulka was imprisoned. Back home, Stalin closed the door after the war and went about restoring life to what it had been before the Germans invaded, happy in the knowledge that he had political and economic friends on his western and southern flanks.

The hatches were clamped down particularly firmly in matters of culture, for this was the period of Andrei Zhdanov, the Politburo member whose chauvinistic decrees reimposed socialist realism as the touchstone of the arts. Soviet culture was supreme; non-*Russian* culture was rejected. By 1949 the Zhdanov campaign—which had survived its author, who had died the year before—took an anti-Jewish turn and reached a climax in January 1953 when a group of Jewish doctors were accused of having killed Zhdanov and of having planned to undermine the health of Soviet leaders on behalf of an American-Jewish organization. Stalin's anti-semitism was probably exacerbated by the creation in 1948 of the state of Israel and the desire of a good many Soviet Jews to leave for the new country. The "doctors' plot" looked very much as if it might turn out to be another Kirov affair with a massive purge, but in the nick of time—on March 5, 1953—Stalin succumbed to a brain hemorrhage and died. An era in Soviet and world history which had lasted almost 30 years was at an end.

After Stalin, Khrushchev

It was difficult for most people in 1953 to envisage the Soviet Union without the man whose name had been synonymous with it for a generation. Feelings were sometimes curiously ambiguous. As Stalin's ultimate successor, Nikita Khrushchev, put it in a conversation with the American diplomat Averell Harriman: "I wept. After all, we were his pupils and owed him everything. Like Peter the Great, Stalin fought barbarism with barbarism, but he was a great man." Although dazed, Khrushchev must have seen that with Stalin gone, his long-standing rivalry with Georgiy Malenkov, Stalin's close associate, would come out into the open. Indeed at first it looked as if Malenkov was the new leader, for two days after Stalin's death it was announced that he was to be Prime Minister and the senior member of the Communist Party Presidium. For a week the press gave him a Stalin-like personality build-up, but then the Central Committee "granted his request" to stand down from his party post; by September the title of First Secretary was Khrushchev's. The Party machine grew in importance during the two years of collective leadership and after Malenkov's fall became dominant, for his successor, Nikolai Bulganin, was a man whom Khrushchev had no difficulty in manipulating. From 1955 to the middle of 1957, Khrushchev was conducting a struggle against what became known as the "anti-Party" group, top leaders who disagreed with Khrushchev's policies and who were driven from office and into obscurity.

Within little more than three months of Stalin's death, the new collective leadership faced a major challenge in the form of a workers' uprising in East Berlin, capital of the German Democratic Republic. The revolt was put down with the help of Soviet troops and tanks, a combination which was to have its uses in similar situations later. The uprising of June 17, 1953 was followed by the arrest and shooting of Lavrenty Beria, the secret police chief, who had been developing a power base and had apparently been saying that the German Democratic Republic should be sacrificed as too great a liability. With the fall of Beria, Khrushchev had removed support from Malenkov and was able to bring the secret police to heel, separating it finally from the Ministry of Internal Affairs and putting it under an inter-departmental committee.

The second major step in breaking with Stalinism took place at the 20th Congress of the Communist Party of the Soviet Union, which met in Moscow between February 14 and 25, 1956. At this Congress, Khrushchev made a secret speech denouncing Stalin. Stalin's mistakes and his terrible abuse of power had been the results of defects in his character; all would have been well had there not developed a cult of Stalin's personality, Khrushchev said. By this emphasis, Khrushchev was seeking to break with the past without endangering the Soviet system and the authority of the party of Lenin or, of course, of himself. The effect of this secret speech on the Soviet Union's allies in Eastern Europe was enormous.

Within four months there were riots in the streets of Poznan and the Polish Party leaders only just managed to keep the situation under control; Khrushchev was clearly very worried by developments in Poland and made a hurried visit to Warsaw in October, when he learned that the Poles were planning to appoint as First Secretary Wladyslaw Gomulka, the nationalist communist whom Stalin had imprisoned in the 1950's. Khrushchev utterly misunderstood what was happening, but if he over-reacted to the changes in Warsaw, he was soon to be faced with a much more real threat to the Soviet bloc's unity—in Hungary. For on October 23, 1956 a revolution broke out in Budapest which was of far more serious proportions, and this time Khrushchev underreacted—at first. However, once the "rebel" Hungarian government of Imre Nagy had announced early in November that Hungary was leaving the Warsaw Pact—the Soviet bloc's counterpart to NATO—the Soviet leader was convinced of the need for force and the revolution was put down with the aid of Soviet troops and tanks.

In March 1958, having thwarted the challenge from the "anti-party group", Khrushchev took over the Premiership from Bulganin and he was now predominant until his fall in October 1964. He is remembered for his disavowal of Stalin's terror, for a short-lived reform of industry and for reforms in the organization of the Party. During his period of office the USSR launched the first artificial earth satellite and the first man into space and signed the nuclear test ban treaty; it also stepped back from the brink of war over the installation of missiles in Cuba and saw its ideological dispute with the Chinese communists develop into a seemingly unbridgeable gulf which made a mockery of the doctrine of the unity and infallibility of Marxism-Leninism. The Khrushchev years were exciting years and as the world saw this rough peasant stomping amiably around the world, something of the fear which had been felt towards Stalin's Kremlin dissolved. His prestige, however, was always higher abroad than it was among his colleagues, for he had by his policies undermined their authority in many ways. Foreign and domestic affairs had become very separate departments of policy. While Khrushchev's personal style of diplomacy was advancing the idea of peaceful coexistence with capitalism, he was more cautious at home. The decentralization of industrial planning was an attempt to increase economic efficiency, but there was a constant awareness at the center of the danger of local interests gaining precedence over national ones. Khrushchev's great campaign to cultivate the "virgin lands" of Kazakhstan was a dismal failure and was held up by his successors as an example of his "adventurism." Policy towards the creative arts was unpredictable—while Vladimir Dudintsev's *Not by Bread Alone* and Alexander Solzhenitsyn's *One Day in the Life of Ivan Denisovich* were published (the latter on Khrushchev's personal word, as he thought it would help in his de-Stalinization campaign), books less obviously provocative were often severely censored or even banned.

After Khrushchev, the Pragmatists?

By the autumn of 1964 a majority of his colleagues seem to have come to the conclusion that Khrushchev had to go, and go he did—into retirement, and in a quite new manner. There was little of the press denunciation that might have been expected and no attempt to make him an "unperson". His style had become anachronistic; his unpredictable, voluntarist way of implementing policies and a tendency to interfere and take decisions off the top of his head had become too much for his colleagues, many of whom considered him an embarrassment and a liability.

On his fall, Khrushchev's dual functions were separated: Leonid Ilyich Brezhnev became Party First Secretary (the title was later changed back to that used by Stalin, General Secretary) and Alexei Nikolayevich Kosygin became Prime Minister. Collective leadership had been restored and—to the surprise of many observers—it has survived, although by the early 1970's there were unmistakable signs of Brezhnev's emergence as undisputed *primus inter pares.*

Since 1964 a tough policy has been pursued at home towards all expressions of dissent and opposition, involving arrests and trials on a very large scale, while abroad progress has been made in securing Western acknowledgement of the post-war *status quo* in Europe and in gaining access for Soviet industry to advanced Western technology. Much praise is given in the Soviet and East European press to Brezhnev's personal contribution in bringing about this era of detente and peaceful coexistence. There is, however, considerable unrest in the Soviet Union's East European satellite countries; the development of democratic socialism in Czechoslovakia was suppressed by the Russians in 1968, though a cautious liberalization is being tolerated in Hungary and Poland. The Soviet intervention in Afghanistan in December 1979 shook the West and brought the process of detente to a halt, reawakening longstanding mistrust of the USSR's intentions on the international front.

The Brezhnev-Kosygin leadership has not been a particularly activist one and the political stability of the Soviet Union today makes it unlikely that there will be any dramatic changes in the foreseeable future, even if, as rumor continually predicts, Brezhnev's resignation—and the retirement of other ageing leaders—is imminent. With the gradual sweeping-away of revolutionary ardor, the Soviet Union has become survivalist, conservative and pragmatic. Many of its problems must have a *déjà-vu* feel about them—the need to modernize industry and provide more consumer goods and the need to secure the agricultural base—and the temptations must be great to seek the easiest rather than the best way to solve them. Each time the Soviet Union turns to the West, there is the increased danger of cooperation leading to *ideological* coexistence and creeping bourgeoisification, and that could mean that dissent would be strengthened. Enormous arbitrary power is still exercised by the Communist Party and the Soviet State, unrestrained by an independent judiciary, uncriticized by a free press and unanswerable to an electorate. There are many magnificent achievements of which the Soviet citizen is justly proud, but he is likely to go on pressing his Party and his Government to allow him the freedoms his Constitution grants him and the rights the Helsinki Agreement apparently requires his country to concede to him.

RUSSIAN ART AND ARCHITECTURE

Icons and Onion Domes

BY
JOHN FINCHLEY

Russian civilization derives from Byzantium, as that of Western Europe derives from Rome. As the English, the Germans, the Scandinavians and the Magyars have taken their written history to begin from the date of their conversion to Christianity by missionaries owing their allegiance to Rome, so the beginning of Russian history is conveniently dated from the acceptance of Christianity from Constantinople by Vladimir, Grand-prince of Kiev, himself married to the sister of the Byzantine emperor, in 988.

The close links with Byzantium, and the adherence to the Eastern arm of Christendom, thus established, were to endure. Though there were signs during the twelfth century that Western might displace Byzantine influence, these links were reinforced during the period of the Mongol invasion and domination, from the mid-thirteenth to the later-fifteenth century, when, for the greater part of Russia, contact with the West all but ceased, and Byzantium retained the prestige of the citadel of civilization. The relationship was simply reversed after the fall of Constantinople in 1453, and the re-emergence of a united and independent Russia, based on Moscow, under Ivan III (1462–1505). Ivan III saw the new Muscovy as the heir to Constantinople, as the "Third Rome." Married to the niece of the last Byzantine emperor, he took the latter's title of "caesar" (czar). It was not until the reign of Peter the Great (1682–1725) that Western Europe replaced Byzantium, and the traditions of Muscovy itself, as the major source of cultural and spiritual inspiration, and Russia began to consider herself as part of the civilization, and of the international political system, of the West.

This fact was to have momentous consequences: for literature and thought; for religion and the Church; for ideas of government and the concept of kingship. Not least is it evident in the development of art and architecture. The forms of Byzantium, the Roman arch, the cruciform domed church and, in painting, the icon, were to remain dominant in Russia until the 16th and 17th centuries. The history of Russian art and architecture over this long period is the history of the evolution of these essentially Byzantine themes.

Influence of Kiev and Novgorod

The oldest surviving building in Russia, which amazingly escaped destruction both during the sack of Kiev by the Mongols in 1240, and during the Second World War, was the finest of the Kievan period of Russian history. St. Sophia, named after Constantinople's cathedral of the same name, was built from 1036 to 1046 by Vladimir's son, Yaroslav the Wise. Its exterior has been disguised by 18th-century additions. But its interior remains substantially unaltered, a magnificent example of the Byzantine style, revealing Kiev as a major center of that cosmopolitan Eastern Mediterranean culture, stretching from Russia to Venice, which had lasted down the centuries since Justinian built Constantinople's St. Sophia and the churches of Ravenna in the sixth century. Now, in the 11th, it produced Kiev's St. Sophia and St. Mark's in Venice: monuments quite outshining anything which contemporary Western or Northern Europe had to offer. The mosaics and frescos of St. Sophia, purely Byzantine in their two-dimensional serenity, laid the foundation for the Russian school of painting.

As this architectural style penetrated northwards it gathered original and specifically Russian characteristics. Yaroslav built a second St. Sophia in Russia's second city, Novgorod, in 1045–52. Built on the same cruciform plan as its forerunner in Kiev, it is clearly adapted, with its steeper roofs and narrower windows, to the demands of a harsher climate. Its greater external austerity is matched by a similar restraint within—in particular by an absence of mosaics—and already stands in some contrast to the exuberance of contemporary Byzantium.

These tendencies became even more marked in the Church of St. George at the Yuriev Monastery in Novgorod, built at the beginning of the following century. The latter is the first example of the practice, which was to become distinctive, of dividing the outer faces of the north, south and west walls of churches into three vertical sections by means of raised bands of stone or brickwork, matching the three convex protrusions of the main and two side apses at the east end. These three churches also represent the evolution of the dome from the low, rounded Byzantine cupola of Kiev's St. Sophia to the more pointed dome of Novgorod, set in a steadily lengthening drum. From the latter, which was more suitable for the snowfalls of the north, the onion dome was to evolve.

Vladimir

From the 12th century on, the Crusades and the increasing activity of Italian merchants in the Mediterranean—culminating in the sack of Constantinople by the Venetians in 1204—undermined the commercial importance of Kiev as a route between Western Europe and the Near East. The rulers of Russia began to find it more convenient to make their base in the more central and more easily defensible forest area to the east of modern Moscow. Andrei Bogoliubsky, great-great-grandson of Yaroslav the Wise, having sacked Kiev in the course of a struggle for succession, transferred his capital to Vladimir in 1169. It was here, in the area between the Oka and Volga rivers, that the classic phase in Russian architecture opened.

The essential square, cruciform ground plan of Vladimir's churches, and the engineering of arches and domes, remained Byzantine. By taking these elements and moulding them in their own way, the (anonymous) Russian architects of the period produced a series of churches in white stone, of modest size and of subtle but disciplined proportions, which were single works of art in themselves. It was as if the grandeur and vulgarity of Rome had given way to the confident simplicity, good taste and human scale of Greece.

As is to be expected of one of the first examples of a new genre, the Church of the Savior at Pereslavl-Zalessky seems at first sight crude and excessively unpolished. But, on second view, the interrelation of the side and main apses, and the perfect balance between the weight of the dome and the body of the church become evident. Vladimir-Suzdal architecture reached its zenith with the Church of the Intercession of the Virgin at Bogoliubovo (1165) and the Cathedral of St. Dmitri at Vladimir (1197). Both show an austerity and a rigorous harmony of proportion which were not to be recaptured in Russian architecture. Though their evolution from the Russian-Byzantine style is undisguised, both display elements of decoration, especially in their porches, and in the carved relief sculptures on the outer walls, which betray the influence of the Western Romanesque.

Such was the young, vigorous and distinctive civilization that went down before the Mongol invasion in 1240. Only Novgorod resisted occupation, and then only at the price of heavy tribute. Cultural, and even national, continuity survived largely thanks to the continued independence of Novgorod, and to the efforts of the Church, and particularly of the monasteries which sprang up in large numbers, especially in the forest land of the northeast. The great monasteries acted as fortresses against attack, as preservers of the new written language and of icons and manuscripts from the past; and, through exchanges with Constantinople and Mount Athos, as links with the outside world. Virtually the only stone buildings to be erected for over 200 years are in Novgorod (or neighboring Pskov) or in monastic foundations. The rest of the country reverted to building exclusively in wood, though no examples of wooden churches, palaces or other structures from the period survive.

Icons

For this newly introverted, impoverished and deeply religious society, the icon acquired a special importance. Small enough to be preserved from the invader; produced, in its simplest form, in sufficient quantities to become, as it remained down to the twentieth century, the possession of each household, the icon became the symbol of the strength, extent and survival of Russian Christianity and Russian culture. The earliest "Russian" icons—including, for example, the majestic *Virgin of Vladimir,* dating from the mid-twelfth century and now in the Tretyakov Gallery in Moscow—had been commissioned in Byzantium or, somewhat later, from Byzantine masters living in Russia. Only from the twelfth century on did icons or wall frescos of real merit appear which had been produced by native Russian artists. In the Kievan period the figures retained the cold and stiff remoteness, and glazed expressions, of Byzantine art. But, as the center of gravity of the new civilization moved to the Vladimir-Suzdal region, a new, more informal, spirit was revealed. This tendency became increasingly marked after the Mongol invasions, which, by limiting her contacts with the outside world, forced Russia to build upon her artistic and spiritual heritage largely on her own. The subjects of icon paintings, the saints, the prophets, the Madonna with Child, and the absence of perspective and movement, remained the same. But a new warmth and humanity was evident: colors became warmer, faces more life-like and more expressive of feeling and character. Byzantine classicism had given way to a more popular and more spontaneous inspiration.

The political fragmentation of the country during the Mongol period led to the development of distinct schools of icon painting in each major region of Russia, often most easily to be identified by the predominant colors of their works. Novgorod used a characteristic bright red; Tver a light blue; Pskov a distinctive gold highlighting.

It was in independent Novgorod, the wealthiest city of Russia, that, through the re-establishment of artistic links with Byzantium, icon painting reached a new level of technical and artistic distinction and entered its golden age. Theophanes the Greek, as he has been known ever since, came to Novgorod from Constantinople in about 1370. He brought to the native Russian love of color, and concern with human character and emotion, a new confidence of technique and discipline of form. The re-uniting of the two traditions is very evident in the work of Theophanes's Moscow pupil, Andrei Rublyev (c. 1380–1430), and the latter's life-long collaborator, Daniel Chorny. Rublyev is perhaps the only Russian painter of world stature to emerge until the close of the nineteenth century.

His work is distinguished by a boldness of stroke and economy of line, and a harmony of shape and color, which set him in a class apart. His figures have all the serenity of the subjects of Byzantine painting, but none of their coldness or stiffness. Indeed, his devout religious faith is very clear in the humane, sympathetic treatment of his subjects. His reputation was enormous, both in his lifetime and beyond. His *Old Testament Trinity* (now in the Tretyakov Gallery), in particular, was to be endlessly copied.

After Rublyev, Russian icon painting lost something of its inspiration. Moscow, increasingly unchallenged as the political capital of the country, remained its artistic center. The well-known painter Dionysius (c. 1450–1505) whose elongated and exaggerated figures and more lavish colors represent something of a descent into monumentalism, had a large and productive workshop. Thereafter, there are no names that are worth recording. Rublyev had taken the Russian tradition to its high point of perfection; there was little more that could be done in that direction. But official church and government policy, re-emphasized by the Council of the Hundred Chapters in 1551 and enforced with particular rigor under the patriarchate of Nikon (1652–67) forbade innovation, or the adoption of Western secularism and realism. The result was sterile, and often naive, imitation of traditional themes and techniques. The originality indispensable to artistic achievement was lost, and the distinction between the work of major artists and folk-art became blurred. The visitor to Russia is easily disoriented by the icons and wall frescos of the sixteenth and seventeenth centuries: to Western eyes they frequently appear to date from no later than the fourteenth century.

The Kremlin Churches

But this period was a most productive one for architecture. Ivan III determined to celebrate his final renunciation of the Mongol overlordship (1480), and his annexation of Novgorod and Tver, by launching a major building program, the greatest fruits of which were the churches of the Moscow Kremlin. The art of construction in stone had so declined during the Mongol centuries that architects suitable to the task had to be imported from Pskov (in the Novgorod region, which had escaped occupation by the Mongols) and from distant Renaissance Italy. But Ivan III determined to build in the style of the period before the Mongol invasions, thus affirming the continuity of his newly united realm with the Russia of the eleventh and twelfth centuries. While the engineering skills and craftsmanship of the Pskov and of the Italian architects (most notably Marco Ruffo, Pietro Solario and Rodolfo Fioravanti) were indispensable, and though the latter left the imprint of the Italian Renaissance on many decorative motifs and in the style of the windows of the Palace of Facets in the Kremlin, the general design of the Kremlin churches represents a deliberate reassertion of the traditions of the Vladimir-Suzdal period.

This was not because architecture had failed to evolve in Russia during the interval. But, except in Novgorod and in Pskov, building had been confined to wood. As a result, the old themes of arches and domes had been transformed. From being a half sphere, the dome had developed into an almost complete sphere on a thin neck: the onion dome that was to remain characteristic. Three other features distinctive to Russian architecture also emerged, all of them owing their origin, in part at least, to the exigencies of the climate: steeply roofed "tent-shaped" churches; the "trapeza", or gallery with open sides, giving shelter outside the western door of the church; and the "Kokoshnik" gable (so named after the curved and winged headdress worn by peasant women), perfectly adapted to heavy snowfalls. Once the need to perpetuate self-consciously the architectural style of the preconquest era had been fulfilled, it was natural that these forms should begin to be reproduced in stone. The Church of the Ascension at Kolomenskoye near Moscow (1533) was one of the first, and finest, stone churches to be built on the "tent-shaped" pattern and to incorporate a "trapeza".

But the most remarkable construction of all was St. Basil's in Moscow. It was built from 1555–60 at the order of Ivan IV ("The Terrible") to celebrate his capture of the Mongol capital of Kazan (1552). Its two architects, Postnik and Barma, are reported to have been blinded by the Czar after its completion "in order that they should never produce anything better." St. Basil's is not easy to appreciate by applying conventional criteria; it is a riot of exuberant color and contrasting patterns. To Western contemporaries it must have seemed exotic, compelling but utterly barbarian. It is the result of the flowering, in a new age of confidence and prosperity, of a style nurtured in isolation from the rest of the world, and of techniques mastered when wood was the only material in which it was feasible—or prudent—to build.

Few churches or other monumental buildings were constructed during the "Time of Troubles" (consisting of civil war and foreign invasion) which followed the death of Ivan IV. When building was resumed in the mid-seventeenth century it was under the conservative and anti-Western regime which culminated in the patriarchate of Nikon.

The ecclesiastical, and indeed the secular architecture of the time represents a deliberate attempt to produce a purely Russian style synthesizing all the major past tendencies in Russian architecture: the onion dome and the "trapeza" now serving decorative rather than functional purposes. The "revolution in color", translated into the stone architecture during the previous century, retained its force: there was no return to the unbroken wall surfaces of the classical period. On the contrary, polychromy became the rule and exteriors were frequently decorated with glazed tiles, carved stone ornamentation and brick patterns; roofs of churches were often blue and the onion domes above gold. But the elements were interpreted in a surprisingly harmonious way, and the churches built by Nikon in particular are distinguished not only by a greater severity, by an insistence on the use of the arch and the dome and the complete rejection of the "tent-shaped" method of construction, but by the subtle mutual balance of the proportions of the tower, the domes and the long rectangular body of the church. Good examples of the style can be seen in the Church of the Twelve Apostles in the Moscow Kremlin, in the church of Our Lady of Kazan at Kolomenskoye, in the Refectory at Zagorsk and in several churches in Yaroslavl.

The fall of Nikon in 1667 removed the last major obstacle which stood in the way, after such a long interval, of the return of Western intellectual, esthetic and social influences. The next 40 years were a watershed between two ages: in art and architecture neither a xenophobic adherence to native traditions, nor a ruthless Westernization, was enforced: the two influences were allowed to merge and to fertilize each other, almost spontaneously. The result was an architectural style which combines many of the forms of Russian architecture with the spirit of the European Baroque. Of the examples which survive, the most striking is the Church of the Intercession at Fili (now a suburb of Moscow). It is undoubtedly one of the finest gems of Russian architecture.

Peter's New Priorities

The reign of Peter the Great brought this process to an end. Russian styles in architecture and painting (the latter already, it must be admitted, in a state of sterility) were rejected as symbolic of the backwardness of the country. Western models were insisted upon in their place. A decree of 1710 banned all new building in stone except in the new capital of St. Petersburg, where it was especially easy for the government to ensure that, in all new building, the new canons of taste and style were being followed.

Peter's priorities in his new capital were secular. He built only one church. This and other decrees therefore had the additional consequence of bringing the construction of stone churches in Russia to an almost complete, if temporary, halt. The masterpiece of wooden ecclesiastical architecture, the monastery at Kizhi, dates from this time; it represents the final flowering of a tradition began during the Mongol period. Nevertheless, from Peter's reign onwards the emphasis in architecture shifts permanently to palaces, public buildings and even private houses. Hitherto such buildings had been strictly utilitarian, though there were rare exceptions (such as the Palace of Facets in the Moscow Kremlin). Both during the 18th century and subsequently, few churches of any architectural note were built, except for the St. Petersburg cathedrals.

The new capital was intended to be a purely Western city. It contained elements of Florence, of Venice, of Versailles (then at its zenith under Louis XIV) and of contemporary Holland. The leading architect Peter employed was an Italian, Domenico Tressini. Nevertheless, for all Peter's determination to avoid any but authentic Western styles, these varied influences could not be brought together in a new nothern environment without taking on a distinctive character of their own. Such was the Russian Rococo style, which reached its climax in mid-century with the construction of the Winter Palace and of the Catherine Palace at Tsarskoye Selo (now Pushkin), both built by Bartolomeo Rastrelli. The two buildings are particularly successful and pleasing in the way in which enormous horizontal expanses of outer wall are broken up by vertical lines and the alternate variation and repetition of lintels, pediments, porches and other decorative elements. Rastrelli's two best-known churches, the Smolny Cathedral in St. Petersburg and St. Andrew's Church in Kiev, incorporate in their fluid Rococo designs the Russian onion dome—the first reappearance of this indigenous motif since the reign of Peter the Great.

Holding to her Westernized course, Russia now followed Western classical. The Grand Palace at Pavlovsk, built by the Scottish architect Charles Cameron between 1782 and 1796, is one of the first examples of the latter style in existence. The St. Petersburg Stock Exchange (1804–10) by Thomas de Thomon and the Cathedral of Our Lady of Kazan (1801–11) by Voronikhin are in the same spirit. As in the West, however, neo-classicism lost its early gracefulness and Greek sense of proportion and evolved towards the heavier, more monumental, imperial style. This tendency is well illustrated by the work of C. I. Rossi (1775–1849), who built, or re-built, much of central St. Petersburg during the 1830's and 1840's. His buildings include the War Office (opposite the Winter Palace), the Michael Palace (now the Russian Museum) and Theater (now Rossi) Street.

From mid-century on, Russia underwent the same urge to imitate the medieval that afflicted the rest of Europe in the "Victorian" period. The results can best be seen in the gaudy and tasteless interior of St. Isaac's Cathedral (completed in 1858), in the incongruous St. Savior's Church, also in Leningrad, built between 1883 and 1907 to commemorate the spot on which Czar Alexander II was assassinated in 1881, and in St. Vladimir's Cathedral and the refectory of the Pecherskaya Monastery in Kiev, completed in 1882 and 1900 respectively, both in pseudo-Byzantine style.

Russian Painters

In the reign of Peter the Great, artists began equally abruptly—and perhaps still more slavishly—to imitate Western models. In order to enforce the "right" Western standards, Peter set up a school of drawing in St. Petersburg which was later elevated by Catherine the Great to the Academy of Fine Arts. The success of this Westernizing policy was complete—excessively so. In the late eighteenth century, Russia did produce a number of talented portraitists in the Gainsborough manner—an example is Dimitri Levitski (1735–1822)—and in the 19th a school of artists in the mould of the French and German Romantics (most notably Karl Bryullov (1799–1852) and Orest Kiprensky (1782–1836). But unlike the architects, Russian artists failed to put their own stamp on the foreign styles they had imported or to make a distinctive contribution to the development of these styles.

In 1863 a number of talented painters broke away from the Academy as a reaction against its deadening influence. Inspired by the idea—fostered chiefly by the critic Chernyshevsky (see chapter on literature)—that art should serve a social purpose, they determined to represent the life and sufferings of the common people with the utmost realism. They organized a series of traveling exhibitions throughout the country—hence the name they adopted: the Wanderers. As with their Pre-Raphaelite contemporaries in England, their art was literary. It was designed to convey a social message or to inspire moral feelings rather than simply to be enjoyed esthetically. Their favorite subjects, alongside scenes evoking the cruelties and abuses of contemporary life, were drawn from the Russian past. In this way, too, they represented a reaction against the Westernism of the Academy.

The supreme artist among this group was Ilya Repin (1844–1930), whose *The Volga Bargemen* and *They Were Not Expecting Him* have remained to this day perhaps the most widely-loved and reproduced of Russian paintings. Their popularity in the Soviet period has been matched only by the historical canvases of V. Surikov (1848–1916)—in particular *The Boyarinya Morozova*—and V. Vasnetsov (1848–1926).

But the Wanderers had a historical importance beyond the value of their own works. By breaking with the Academy, they re-established an authentic Russian school of art. They reintroduced into painting the sense of color that had distinguished early Russian icons from their Byzantine models. Above all, by taking realism and social content to their logical extremes and thus demonstrating the limitations of both, they cleared the way for the remarkable achievements that were to follow.

In particular, three young artists emerged who, though they owed much in their early training to the Wanderers and to the colony of artists brought together by the wealthy Mamontov family at their estate at Abramtsevo near Moscow, would eclipse all their elders, except possibly Repin himself. These three were Mikhail Vrubel (1856–1910), Isaac Levitan (1860–1900) and Valentin Serov (1865–1911). They all displayed in their paintings a bold brushwork, a flair for essentials and a sense of form that contrasted sharply with the obsession with detail and heavy-handed narrative style of the Wanderers.

Levitan is the greatest of Russian landscape painters. His canvases are evocative and perhaps even nostalgic—no one who knows and loves the endless perspectives, the broad rivers and wide skies of Russia can fail to be moved by them. But his effects were achieved, like Cézanne's, through an analysis of the essential shapes, colors and textures of his landscapes.

Serov adopted a similar approach to portraiture. Few artists have ever brought their subjects to life more effectively. Though his study of Nicholas II will probably remain his most famous work, one of his masterpieces was painted when he was only twenty-two. This was *Girl with Peaches,* a portrait of Vera Savishna Mamontova that still hangs in Abramtsevo.

Vrubel was the most original of the three. The metaphysical side of his work is most evident in his series of illustrations for Lermontov's poem, *The Demon.* But it is also revealed in his tortured, dissecting, many-angled studies of still-life and flowers. Though he lacked the cool intellectualism of the Cubists, he foreshadowed them in his tireless investigation, from every viewpoint, of the visual potentialities of his subjects.

"The World of Art"

These artists of the 1890's, nurtured in the circle of Abramtsevo, would have regarded themselves more as the heirs of the Wanderers than as their over-throwers. The first deliberate and full-blooded reaction against the latter came with the new century. It can be dated from the foundation of the magazine *The World of Art* in 1898, or from the first exhibition organized by the group of the same name in the following year. The aim of this group, of which the leading members were Alexander Benois (1870–1960) and Sergei Diaghilev (see section on ballet), was to proclaim the doctrine of Art for Art's Sake and to introduce into Russia the works of the French Impressionists and Post-Impressionists, whose works were first shown in the country at successive "World of Art" exhibitions. They thus intended to displace the influence of the Wanderers, who no doubt appeared insufferably provincial to the international culture of St. Petersburg to which Benois and his circle belonged.

The "World of Art" group brought together artists and avantgarde poets who were simultaneously introducing into Russia the latest French literary ideas. The two movements were characterized by the term Symbolism. Both disdained banal portrayals of reality and sought to create a higher world of beauty and harmony. The canvases of Victor Borissov-Mussatov (1870–1905) and Pavel Kuznetsov depict human figures and themes drawn from nature, but the colors are ethereal, the vision is distant, dreamlike and pantheistic, revealing a still, silent and timeless world.

While St. Petersburg was dominated by Symbolism, a group of young painters in Moscow, most notable of whom were Mikhail Larionov (1881–1964) and his life-long companion Natalia Goncharova (1881–1962), had begun to rediscover the Russian icon and to paint in a primitivist style inspired by it. It was the confluence of Symbolism, of the primitivist insistence on line and pure form, of the experiments of Vrubel and of the influx of new Western styles (French Fauvism and Cubism and Italian Futurism) that produced, in the second decade of the century, a revolution in art no less momentous in its field than the coincident turmoils in politics and society.

The "Rayonnist" paintings of Larionov and Goncharova (which date from 1911–13) represented the first breakthrough into modernism. The Rayonnists' optical experimentalism was inspired, in part at least, by the Cubism of Picasso and Braque, while the intensity of surface working in their paintings and their dramatic representation of movement paralleled the Futurism of Marinetti, Carrà and Severini. A similar kinetic quality is evident in the "Cubo-Futurist" works (so called after the French and Italian influence apparent in them) of Kasimir Malevich (1878–1935) and his followers of the period: but here the aim was no longer, as in Rayonnism, to examine the effects of the crossing of the reflected rays from objects, but to break down figures and background into elemental blocks of color. The massive and rhythmic use of color in Cubo-Futurist paintings derived directly from Russian primitivism.

Primitivism, Rayonnism and Cubo-Futurism were all authentically Russian movements, though they were but one aspect of the contemporary ferment in the arts throughout the Western world—a world of which, in culture as in economic and political life, Russia had never been so fully a part as in the generation before the October Revolution. But for all the talent, technical innovation and achievement of Russian artists, they had not up to this time given any decisive new impetus to the development of Western art as a whole. In the four vital years 1913–17, all this was to change. From having been the precocious pupil of the West, Russia then, if only briefly, took the lead.

In 1913 Malevich began to devise his system of "Suprematism." His earliest paintings in the new style were single geometric forms (squares, circles, crosses and triangles) on contrasting backgrounds, originally black on white. From there he moved on to assemble, in one composition, various geometric elements seemingly revolving on invisible axes, flawlessly balanced. His last paintings, executed in 1917–18, his famous "White on White" series, represented the ultimate rejection of objects drawn from, or relating to, the human or visible world. Meanwhile, Vassily Kandinsky (1866–1944), who returned from Munich to Russia at the onset of war in 1914, had already begun to paint his 'free' improvised compositions, containing no geometric or defined shapes at all but only lines, and areas of contrasting color. If Cubism had still been concerned with the traditional analysis of perceived objects. Malevich and Kandinsky, in their different ways, had launched out on a new course altogether: the creation of pure form without reference to visible things. Together with the Dutchman Mondrian, they stand as the founders of abstract painting.

Two further—and quite diverse—trends were to emerge from this fertile period. Marc Chagall (b. 1877), whose early work is Symbolist, evolved his own, deeply personal style. Though he has the instinctive sense of form of all great painters, his primary concern is psychological, even psychoanalytical: his use of fantasy, unreal colors and dream images inaugurated the Surrealist movement.

The Constructivists and the Revolution

Nor did art fail to suffer the politicization experienced by other aspects of Russian life in the period immediately following the 1917 Revolutions. Suprematism, with its dynamic interrelation of abstract geometric forms, gave birth to three-dimensional models and to the design of real machines and useful objects, from workers' outfits to furniture and buildings. The artist had become the artist-engineer. Constructivism was born. A great controversy ensued between those who, like Malevich, continued to insist that art was essentially a spiritual activity to be pursued for its own sake, and the Constructivists, led by Vladimir Tatlin (1885–1953) and by two former Suprematists, Alexander Rodchenko (1891–1956) and El Lissitzky (1890–1941), who insisted that art must serve a useful purpose and remain close to life. It followed that art should not pursue its own course in the creation of the esthetically pleasing, but that it should obey the laws and requirements of the real world. Technique replaced style. Easel painting was all but abandoned, while Constructivist design and architecture became distinguished by an uncompromising functionalism.

It was indeed in architecture that the contrast with the immediately preceding period was most marked and the achievements of Constructivism most notable and lasting. Though in St. Petersburg throughout the Czarist period architecture had continued to imitate the latest Western fashions, the new plutocracy which emerged in Moscow from the 1870's to 1914 (years of great economic advance) increasingly built themselves, in the "Art Nouveau" style, houses whose asymmetry and fantasy reveal direct affinities with contemporary Symbolist esthetic ideas. Moscow, for example, retains the finest collection of Art Nouveau architecture in Europe. The interested visitor should see the former house of Maxim Gorky on Vorovsky Street; the Ryabushinski House on Tolstoy Street; the Australian Embassy on Kropotkin Pereulok, the Tretyakov Gallery and the Yaroslavl railway station, all dating from the first decade of the century.

When building resumed after World War I and the Civil War, it was evident that an architectural revolution had taken place. The predominantly Constructivist style, its austerity no doubt reflecting the economic stringency of the times as much as esthetic theory, made no concessions either to the imagination or to conventional ideas of comfort or finish. Stark outlines, unrelieved expanses of wall or window, and harsh angular lines became the rule. Among the best examples of the style—which so impressed contemporary visitors as the reflection of a new, iconoclastic, and compellingly single-minded society—are the Izvestia building, built by G. Barkhin in 1926; the Zuyev Club by Ilya Golosov, which dates from the same year; the Ministry of Agriculture building designed by Aleksei Shchusev and erected from 1928–33; and the Central House of Cinema Actors, built by the brothers Vesnin in 1931–4, all of them in Moscow.

Constructivist painters, too, regarding themselves as the natural exponents and inspirers of the new age, put their talents at the service of the Bolshevik regime. El Lissitzky and Rodchenko both spent much of their time producing political posters, often in the Suprematist style of their early paintings. Tatlin labored long and hard on a futuristic design for a grandiose *Monument to the Third International.* Constructivist artists and typographers co-operated with Futurist and "Constructivist" poets and writers in founding in 1923 the magazine *LEF,* which was to herald the art of the future (see chapter on literature). But with the enforcement of the doctrine of "socialist realism" from 1932 onwards, the activities of Constructivist artists and architects came to as abrupt an end as those of their counterparts in literature.

Socialist Realism

In art the period since the 1930's has seen an officially-induced return to the programmatic and illustrative painting of the Wanderers, with the difference that the conscious aim is no longer to depict the suffering of humanity, but rather the happiness, confidence and optimism of Soviet society. Such are the works of T. N. Yablonskaya (b. 1917). Many of her best-known canvases of contented workers and overflowing grain harvests were executed at the worst moments of the Purges and material privations of the Stalin period. This is not to say that socialist realism has not, if untypically, produced works of real inspiration. There is no denying, for instance, the enormous, pristine force of the sculptured stainless steel group, *Worker and Collective Farm Woman* (1937), by Vera Mukhina (1889–1954).

In architecture, as in art, "socialist realism" demands in theory that works be both easily comprehensible and inspiring to the masses. In practice they must also conform to the—instinctively philistine—tastes of the Party. The architecture of the 1935–55 period reflects both these requirements. Symmetry and monumentalism became the order of the day. Though these features are common to almost every construction, the buildings of the time display a curious amalgam of stylistic influences: the nineteenth-century Petersburg of Rossi with its classical themes and columns; a Florentine style (though without any Renaissance sense of proportion) evident, for example, in Moscow's Gorky Street and Prospekt Mira; and, more especially after World War II, the "modern" style of the 1930's West, with its emphasis on scale, and use of external fluting, massive pediments and lintels and other Egyptian motifs. The Manhattan of the 1930's is particularly recalled by the seven prominent skyscrapers erected in Moscow after World War II, though their crenelated turrets and fussy external decoration are all their own. These enormous constructions, together with the stations of the Moscow Metro —subterranean temples of marble—remain, as they were intended, permanent and evocative monuments of Stalin's rule.

Since 1955, quantity has replaced quality, solidity or style as the overriding aim. The rectangular, barrack-like apartment blocks in grey or yellow brick of the late 1950's and early 1960's—a feature of every Soviet town—have been succeeded by the more elongated, but no less severely utilitarian, blocks in prefabricated concrete sections which characterize the building program of the last few years. There have been several interesting and imaginative advances in design and in town planning, for example in Moscow's Kalinin Prospekt and the New Arbat district, as well as in some of the capital's newer suburbs, though the results are too often marred by bad workmanship or the use of inferior materials—not failings of the Stalin years. Few Soviet buildings can stand comparison with the achievements of contemporary architecture in the West. One notable exception is the SEV (Council for Mutual Economic Assistance) headquarters in Moscow, built by S. Egorov and Y. Semyonov in 1967.

In art, the imposition of "socialist realism" was totally effective, at least until the mid-1950's. The creativeness and experimentalism of the first decades of the century were brought to an abrupt end. Those artists who had been associated with the great age of Russian painting but who did not go abroad (Larionov and Goncharova had left at the time of the

Bolshevik Revolution, and Kandinsky and Chagall were to emigrate in the 1920's)—virtually ceased to paint. Even the ardent Communists Tatlin and Rodchenko were forced into an intimidated inactivity, their works denounced as "non-objectivist" and "formalist". The latter's family destroyed a large number of his canvases in panic during the Purges. The Union of Artists, at once mutual benefit society and self-regulating guild, on the whole succeeded in maintaining the required conformism without the need for the spectacular repression of individual dissidents that has marked Party regulation of literature.

In the more relaxed atmosphere that followed the Twentieth Party Congress in 1956, a body of "unofficial" artists (not members of the Union) began cautiously to emerge. Such was the spirit of the times that an exhibition of their work was even held in the Manège Gallery in Moscow. But a savage denunciation by Khrushchev himself made it clear that "formalism" was, after all, not to be tolerated. Moreover, the 40 years of close Party control and isolation from the artistic life of the rest of the world had done their work.

Beneath the official surface of "socialist realism" there indeed lurk a number of original talents—even some outstanding ones. It is not possible to speak of "movements." The work of unofficial artists in the Soviet Union varies from the tense and tortured drawings and sculptured figures of Ernst Neizvestny (who finally emigrated to Israel in early 1976) to the dark and pessimistic paintings of Oscar Rabin, with their telling use of Russian imagery, to the cool abstraction of the canvases of Lydia Masterkova and her former husband Nemukhin. There has been some recent revival of Western interest in contemporary Russian art, and some "unofficial" artists' paintings bought by foreigners and brought to the West or brought out by emigrating Russians have been displayed in exhibitions large and small in Europe and the USA.

There are occasional signs that the Soviet government is relaxing its attitude towards some of these "unofficial" artists. Groups are sometimes allowed to hold exhibitions although they are also sometimes squashed, literally, with the help of bulldozers and police.

But there is still a long road ahead if Russia is to regain the ground she has lost and return to the mainstream of international developments in art. So far, contrary to the expectations of so many artists in 1917, political revolution has proved incompatible with creative revolution.

**The Spassky Tower, the tallest
of the Kremlin's nineteen towers**

Two Moscow scenes: shopping in the
GUM Department Store; inside one
of the palatial Metro stations

The Space Museum in Moscow's
Park of Economic Achievements

Part of the ornate façade of
the Winter Palace in Leningrad

RUSSIAN AND SOVIET LITERATURE

Giants of Conformity and Dissent

Few would deny that the Russians have produced the greatest of European literatures, at least in the fields of poetry and the novel. But this achievement, like so much in their country, has been based on a very late start. As late as the year of Pushkin's birth, 1799, it would scarcely have been possible for contemporaries to have foreseen the creation of a modern national literature in Russia. There had been no serious drama or social comedy; nor even any lyrical poetry to speak of. Russia had remained virtually untouched by the literary achievements of the European Renaissance and its aftermath, and had nothing of her own to set against the works of Petrarch, Ronsard, Shakespeare, Molière, Racine and their successors in the West.

This state of affairs is not hard to explain. From the time of its conversion to Christianity in the tenth century, to the beginning of the Mongol invasions in the 13th, Russia had been a full part of a cosmopolitan Christian civilization, in contact alike with Scandinavia, with Western Europe and with Byzantium. The chronicles which have come down to us from this period, written in the old Church Slavonic, are not unlike their contemporary counterparts in Scandinavia and in England. In the generation before the first Mongol invasions, Kievan Russia produced its greatest literary masterpiece, the epic poem *The Lay of Igor's Campaign.* There followed 250 years of Mongol domination, of intermittent resistance to the invader followed by further repression at his hands, of political fragmentation into small princedoms, of the frequent destruction of cities and the interruption of economic life. Russia was effectively cut off from outside influences and ceased to share in the economic and cultural development of the West. If she survived at all as a cultural and political entity, that was the achievement of the Church and of the monarchy, both, from the 14th century on, based in Moscow. No other institution came through. Together they enjoyed a monopoly of the written word until the late 17th century, 200 years after Russia's release from the "Mongol yoke".

Throughout all this period, in sharp contrast to the versatility and innovative brilliance of the contemporary West, "Russian literature" (still written in Church Slavonic) consists of little more than sermons, lives of saints and similar religious pieces; and ballads and other works glorifying the exploits of kings. As the balance of power in the state shifted from Church to monarchy, so the proportion of total literary output devoted to the latter's cause increased. It is interesting that the first work to break out of this mould, and also the first to be written in modern colloquial Russian (as opposed to Church Slavonic), *The Life of the Archpriest Avvakum* by himself (1672–3), was composed by the leader of the "Old Believers" movement, which represented the first serious challenge to the authority of the centralized monarchy and of the established Church.

Avvakum devoted his life to opposing the encroachment of Western influences in Church and State. But modern Russian literature traces its beginnings to the success of the trends which Avvakum and the Old Believers had attempted to resist. The westernizing reforms of Peter the Great (1682–1725) and the construction of the new capital of St. Petersburg as a "window on the West" opened a new era. By the reign of Catherine the Great (1762–96), herself a child of the European Enlightenment and a correspondent of Voltaire, Diderot and other philosophers, the westernization of the Russian upper classes, at least in Petersburg, was complete. The widespread circulation, for the first time in Russia, in the original and in translation, of works of contemporary French, English and German literature was a natural part of this process, as was the emergence of a native literature strongly influenced by them.

M. V. Lomonosov (1711–65) is often regarded as the father of modern Russian literature. He set out, self-consciously, to establish a language suitable for the imitation of the literary achievements of France and England, distinguishing between the old Church Slavonic for elevated prose, a colloquial Russian to be used for fables and comedy, and an intermediate style for general literary use. Lomonosov also published the first Russian grammar. His own verse, written in a formal and philosophical style, for the most part in rhyming couplets, owes something to the influence of Boileau and of Alexander Pope.

N. M. Karamzin (1766–1826) wrote the first novel in the Russian language, *Poor Liza*, a sentimental story strongly influenced by Richardson's *Pamela*. In the same year, 1790, appeared two interesting, and ultimately influential, prose works; Karamzin's *Letter of a Russian Traveler* and A. N. Radishchev's *Journey from Petersburg to Moscow*. Both are clearly influenced by Sterne's *Sentimental Journey*. But both employ a literary device, the journey through Russia revealing contrasts of human type and social condition on the way, which was to be used to good effect by future writers. And the Radishchev book, with its subtle criticism of serfdom (which caused Catherine II to exile the author to Siberia) inaugurated the tradition of Russian social satire. One further writer of the period deserves mention. G. R. Derzhavin (1743–1816) is the most important poet before Pushkin, and the first Russian poet to enjoy a major reputation both in his own country and in the West.

Pushkin and Lermontov

Aleksandr Sergeyevich Pushkin (1799–1837) occupies in Russian literature the position enjoyed by Shakespeare and Goethe in the Literatures of England and Germany; all his immediate successors, and the greatest writers of the remainder of the 19th century, acknowledged their debt to him, and his reputation remains unchallenged today. His works include lyrical and narrative poems, short stories (including *The Queen of Spades* and *The Captain's Daughter*), the verse play *Boris Godunov* and the verse novel *Eugene Onegin*. The latter, a tale of frustrated romantic love which introduced into Russian literature Onegin, the type of the "superfluous man," has remained his most popular work in Russia. Pushkin's characters are neither villains nor positive heroes; they are depicted as a combination of many qualities, and are seen more as the victims than as the arbiters of their own fates. In this respect, Pushkin broke with the conventions and stereotypes of the past and cleared the way for the achievements of Tolstoy and Chekhov.

This human sympathy in Pushkin is no doubt due to his own lack of pre-conceived ideas or fixed credos, to his openness before the experiences of life combined with disillusionment at its reverses and scepticism as to its overall meaning. His own emotional and sexual life, which he lived to the full in true Byronic fashion, is reflected in some of the finest love lyrics, and erotic poems, which exist in any language; though a sense of despair at the superfluity of existence is all pervasive.

Pushkin inspired a generation of poets, including E. A. Baratynski (1800–44), F. I. Tyutchev (1803–1873) and A. A. Fet (1820–92), all of whom wrote intense, lyrical poetry of the highest quality, evoking the emotions of love and the sights and sounds of nature in clear, mellifluous language. But the greatest literary figure after Pushkin is that of M. Yu. Lermontov (1814–41). His flights of imagination and his images are more strikingly unexpected than those of his contemporaries, his language more rhetorical and more effortless. These qualities are well illustrated in his poem, *The Demon,* which was to inspire Vrubel's paintings as well as to influence future poets. Of his prose works, the only one to enjoy lasting attention has been his short novel, *A Hero of Our Time,* a work of remarkable modernity, based as it is on the exploits of an anti-hero, Pechorin, bored with life, unable to respond to human affections, aimless and amoral ("alienated" as we would now say). He reminds the mid-twentieth century reader of no one so much as the "hero" of Camus' *The Stranger.* Indeed, precociousness, and precocious disillusion, are the hallmarks of Lermontov's career. At the age of 27 he was killed, like Pushkin, in a senseless duel.

The brilliance of Pushkin, Lermontov and their circle, as a result of which Russia was brought for the first time into the forefront of European literature, had its origin in the impact of the Western Romantic movement on a young, vigorous and aristocratic culture. The Napoleonic wars, which brought Russian troops to Paris and ensured the full integration of the Russian Empire into the European political system, and the liberal policies of Alexander I (1801–25) permitted the intensification of these contacts. Both victory in war and relative liberalism at home inspired a new confidence in the future; an assumption that Russia's destiny lay in imitating the political institutions of the West; and, in literature, the neglect of specifically national subjects in favor of more universal themes and the cultivation of individual sensibility.

Poetry is the typical literary mode of expression of the age. The reign of Nicholas I (1825–55) opened with the Decembrists' Rising, which the young monarch attributed to the disrupting effect of foreign ideas, and to which he reacted with a fierce repression, and with the rejection of Western political, industrial and cultural influences. All contact, even personal travel, was made more difficult (Pushkin was himself refused permission to go abroad); and thinking Russians became increasingly aware of their country's isolation, its political backwardness, and its failure to take part in the unprecedented economic expansion then taking place in Western Europe. The great intellectual debate of the reign was between the "Westerners" and the "Slavophiles", i.e. those who believed that Russia had a distinct Slav historical mission of her own. In literature, this mood produced a new national introversion, and a concern with social themes. Its typical form of expression is the novel.

Gogol and Turgenev

The great age of the Russian novel begins with the publication, in 1842, of *Dead Souls* by N.V. Gogol (1809–52). The story of Chichikov, an amiable rogue, who hits upon the idea of making a fortune by buying up the title deeds to dead serfs and proceeds to visit a series of provincial landowners, reveals a whole gallery of human types. Gogol is less widely read in the West than Turgenev, Tolstoy and Dostoyevsky, perhaps because his characters are difficult to appreciate fully outside a Russian context. But in his ability to paint living and memorable—if caricatured —social types, he has rightly been compared with Dickens; and in his sharp eye for human weakness, petty vices, and folly, with Molière. His secret is perhaps his talent for combining humor and pathos. He is the first of the great Russian humorists, and in his attacks on officialdom in his play, *The Inspector General,* adopts what is to be one of their favorite butts. But he also shows a darker side, most especially in his stories, *Nevsky Prospekt, Memoirs of a Madman* and *The Overcoat,* an exploration of human despair which foreshadows Dostoyevsky.

The works of I. A. Goncharov (1812–91) and of I. S. Turgenev (1818–83), though their appeal is universal, also illustrate, in their various ways, peculiarly Russian themes. In *Oblomov,* Goncharov created, in the hero of that name, the archetypal "superfluous", Hamlet-like character of Russian literature. A man paralyzed by his own weakness, indecision and inertia, who for long periods cannot even bring himself to get out of bed, Oblomov fails to take advantage of any of the opportunities, personal or romantic, with which life presents him, and dies after an existence which appears to have been without purpose or meaning. He remains, in Russia, one of the best-loved of all literary creations.

In his technique, Turgenev is the most Western of the great Russian novelists; like the leading nineteenth-century realist writers of France and England, he is content to describe his characters, and the physical world around them, from the outside; he lacks the philosophical dimension of Tolstoy, or the psychological penetration of Dostoyevsky. But his subjects are entirely Russian. *Notes of a Hunter* depicts, with great sympathy and affection, the Russian countryside and the Russian peasant; it was considerably influential at the time as an indictment of serfdom. A *Nest of the Gentry,* a moving tale of thwarted romantic love, describes the atmosphere of life among the old provincial gentry, as does his play, *A Month in the Country. Fathers and Sons,* inspired by the contemporary conflict of generations in Russia, is the story of Bazarov, the new type of "nihilist" who rejects all religious values and Russian traditions, in the name of a ruthless materialism.

Tolstoy and Dostoyevsky

There is no need to make out a case for the greatness of Count Lev Nikolayevich Tolstoy (1828–1910). *War and Peace* (1865–69) is perhaps the most ambitious novel ever undertaken anywhere: a vast tapestry of Russian life during the period of the Napoleonic Wars, it embraces the whole range of human experience, from love to death in war, and integrates the story of its individual characters with the flow of the impersonal currents of history. In this respect it was to be followed by the great novels of the 20th century, Sholokhov's *And Quiet Flows the Don* and Pasternak's *Dr. Zhivago.* In *Anna Karenina,* the heroine, by following the impulses of her own heart, transgresses the conventions of society, and is inevitably destroyed. The novel is at once high tragedy in the Greek sense, a horrendous indictment of contemporary social hypocrisy and the "double standard" applied to men and women, and, above all, one of the finest examples of that sympathetic treatment of human suffering which is so characteristic of Russian literature. *The Death of Ivan Ilyich* and *Resurrection* (1886 and 1899, respectively) were written after Tolstoy's conversion to his own brand of Christianity, and strongly reflect his new religious perception of life; the first is a study in depth of death, the second of the redeeming power of love. Tolstoy also composed in these years his *Confession,* a number of religious and political works, and a series of childlike allegorical stories intended to illustrate his religious and moral convictions. Some have seen in these stories the simplicity of genius; others a regrettable, if deliberate, descent into naïveté.

F. M. Dostoyevsky (1821–81) is the originator, and the master, of the psychological novel. His works, of which *Crime and Punishment, The Idiot, The Possessed* and *The Brothers Karamazov* are justly the most famous, exercised a considerable influence on Freud, and on other psychologists and writers of the 20th century. Arrested as a young man on political charges, Dostoyevsky was condemned to death and suffered a mock execution before being exiled to Siberia. Like Solzhenitsyn, therefore, he had himself experienced the moral dilemmas and sufferings of which he writes. Dostoyevsky belongs to the tradition of Russian realism; but it is a realism that is directed, above all, to describing the internal dramas of the soul.

Russian prose in the period between the death of Dostoyevsky (in 1881) and 1917 is dominated, apart from the aged Tolstoy, who continued to write until his death in 1910, by three figures: A. P. Chekhov (1860–1904), Maxim Gorky (pen-name of A. M. Peshkov, 1868–1936) and I. A. Bunin (1870–1953).

Though all can loosely be called realists, Chekhov is quite distinct. His medium is the play and short story rather than the novel; his style impressionistic rather than exhaustively descriptive: indeed, no writer has been better able, with a few brief strokes, to conjure up a complete character or convey a situation or a mood. Chekhov's most evident qualities are his acute powers of observation of people, and his great sympathy for them: perhaps both characteristics derive from his early training and experience as a doctor. Chekhov's view of life is stoically pessimistic: he is always conscious of the gulf between ideals and personal aspirations, and reality. Many of the characters of his best short stories (*The Kiss, Lady with the Little Dog*) and his plays (*The Seagull, The Three Sisters, Uncle Vanya, The Cherry Orchard*) are suddenly made aware of the futility of their current existence but have ultimately to resign themselves to the abandonment of their romantic illusions and to a banal and mindless future.

Gorky and Bunin are firmly in the realist tradition. Gorky's *Former People* and *Mother,* his autobiographical *Childhood,* and Bunin's *The Village* paint unforgettable pictures of the misery, squalor, drunkenness and violence of life among the poor at the turn of the century. Bunin's later writing (*The Gentlemen from San Francisco*) is more metaphysical. A poet as well as a writer of prose, Bunin left Russia after the Revolution and lived the rest of his life in France. He was awarded the Nobel Prize in 1933. Gorky also left Russia after 1917, but subsequently returned. He was retrospectively acclaimed as the founder of "socialist" realism in literature, and in 1934 made Chairman of the new Union of Soviet Writers. He died in mysterious circumstances in 1936, during the Purges.

Poetry after Lermontov

Poetry during the half century from the death of Lermontov to the 1890's was largely eclipsed by the novel. Three names alone stand out, none of them to be compared with their forerunners or successors: Tyutchev, Fet and N. A. Nekrasov (1821–77). The latter, with his narrative style and his concern with the themes of the Russian countryside and the Russian peasant, is in some ways the equivalent of Turgenev in prose: in the Soviet Union, he is accorded a higher stature than any nineteenth century poet after Pushkin. But realism and social content—which had reached a high point during the 1850's and '60's, when some critics and writers had argued that literature should serve a strictly utilitarian social purpose—provoked a reaction similar to that which set in against the "Wanderers" in art. Moreover, the headlong course of industrialization and Westernization on which the Russian Empire was embarked, with increasing momentum, from the 1860's until the Bolshevik Revolution, had its impact on literature as on painting: the rich seeds of Western, and especially French, modernism were implanted in the fertile but relatively unsown soil of Russia.

In literature, these two trends combined to produce the Russian Symbolist movement—memorable for its achievements in poetry rather than in prose. The movement begins in the early 1890's with the first works of K. D. Balmont (1867–1943) and V. Y. Bryusov (1873–1924) whose poetry is nearest to French symbolism. It reaches its climax in the period 1900–17 with the work of Andrei Bely (pen-name of B. N. Bugaev, 1880–1934) and of A. A. Blok (1880–1921). Like their French counterparts, the Russian symbolists were uniquely concerned with the personal vision of the poet, breaking with the Romantics in insisting that this vision could not be adequately conveyed by literal description, by the choice of the "right" word, but only by the use of symbols.

Symbolism gave way to two movements, both of them entirely Russian in origin, which together were to dominate the poetic scene until the 1950's. Acmeism was an artistic reaction against Symbolism and in favor of a restoration of clear images and precision in the use of language. It produced three great poets: N. S. Gumilyov (1886–1921), O. E. Mandelstam (1892–1940?) and A. A. Akhmatova (pen-name of A. A. Gorenko, 1888–1966), whose first husband was Gumilyov. Their fates provide good illustrations of the period through which they lived: Gumilyov was shot by the Bolsheviks in 1921; Mandelstam, arrested in 1938, died in a camp perhaps in 1940; Akhmatova, though she lost both her second husband and her son by Gumilyov in the 1936 purges and was herself savagely denounced in the 1940's, survived to be generally recognized by many Russians, by her death in 1966, as their greatest living poet.

Of the three, Mandelstam's poems are the most classical and polished; their serenity and perfection are in sharp contrast to the turmoil and suffering in which the poet was to end his life. Akhmatova's poetry is more direct and personal; much of it deals with love both in its romantic and its sensual aspects. But the ordeals of her tragic life come through in a series of poems which have been published in the West, under the title *Requiem*. They are the most moving poetic document of the Purges.

Futurism

Futurism was another reaction against Symbolism, both technical and philosophical. In place of the mysticism of the Symbolists, their concern with the "other world" of beauty and art, the Futurists reasserted the material world and delighted in its technology and its politics. Not for nothing was the manifesto of the movement, issued in 1912—over the signatures, among others, of the two major Futurist poets, V. V. Khlebnikov (1885–1922) and V. V. Mayakovsky (1893–1930)—called *A Slap in the Face of Public Taste*. Their defiance of the rules of grammar and syntax, their stunningly unexpected metaphors and imagery, their exhibitionist behavior and outlandish clothes were all deliberately designed to shock.

Behind the histrionics and the self-advertisement was a serious purpose: to solve the perennial problem of poetry that a feeling once expressed is distorted by the limitations and extraneous associations of the words used. The sound of a word, and its appearance on the printed page, thus acquire a new importance of their own, and the Futurists set great store by their public declamations of their poems, and by their typographical experiments, both of which contributed to their remarkable notoriety in Russia on the eve of the Great War.

The Futurists were intimately linked with the *avant garde* movements in art in their day (Mayakovsky and Kruchonykh were both professional artists; D. D. Burlyuk, [b. 1882], was even better known as a painter than as a Futurist poet) and their poetry can often be best read as an attempt to use language to build up contrasts and patterns in new and suggestive ways, rather than to convey a literal message, in the manner of contemporary Cubist and Rayonnist paintings.

No country in Europe, in the years before 1914, displayed greater vitality and variety in the arts, greater or more fruitful interaction between them, or greater passion in the controversies between the various movements and cliques within them. It is wrong to see this process as having come to an end with the Revolutions of 1917. Many writers—perhaps initially the majority—welcomed the new order. The Futurists instinctively identified themselves with it and Mayakovsky and others founded in 1923 a new journal, *LEF* ("Left Front"), with the aim of proclaiming the art of the future.

But Futurism, like all experimentalism in the arts, fell into increasing official disfavor, as being both insufficiently suseptible to Party control, and too highbrow to serve the Party's needs (Lenin, whose tastes were nothing if not bourgeois, had already denounced Futurism as "literary hooliganism"). But official censorship and control were at first exercised with a light hand, and the decade saw a lively controversy between, on the one hand, Futurism, and its successor movement, Constructivism (which emphasized the tendency in Futurism towards the creation of a close-to-life, technological literature), and, on the other, the Association of Proletarian Writers, whose attempts to create a popular, realistic and immediately comprehensible literature produced little worthwhile poetry, though a number of important works in prose. Both movements believed with equal passion that they represented the wave of the future. But it was the latter that finally triumphed. Mayakovsky, shortly before his suicide in 1930, was himself forced to join the Proletarians. In 1934, all remnants of heterodoxy were abolished when all literary groups were compulsorily merged in the new "Union of Soviet Writers."

The great events in poetry in the 1920's were publication of the first major collections of poems of Boris Pasternak (1890–1960), and of the works of Sergei Esenin (1895–1925). The latter described himself as "the last poet of wooden Russia." The description is apt: his personalized, homely and always melodious lyrics, sometimes on political and patriotic themes, but more often recalling the seasons of love, bear little relation to the work of the myriad movements of the time (though those who insist on labels refer to him as an "Imagist"). Born of peasant stock, Esenin welcomed the October Revolution; though his suicide, like that of Mayakovsky five years later, has sometimes been attributed, at least partially, to political frustration and disillusionment. He has remained perhaps the most popular of twentieth-century poets.

Pasternak, on the other hand, together with Blok and Akhmatova, with whom he shares a world stature, has always been the favourite of Russian intellectuals. His poems published in the '20's show the influence of the Futurists, a movement with which he is often identified and with which he undoubtedly had close personal contacts. But his poetry displays a musical quality, a rhythmical regularity, concision and discipline of form, and above all, a hint, of the metaphysical. His poems written after the Second World War—and particularly the *Zhivago* poems—with their greater simplicity of language and their religious themes, have become well known in the West.

The Soviet Novel

But, as in other periods in Russian history when political and social themes have come to the fore, the most notable literary achievements of the Soviet period have been in the field of the novel. As in poetry, the 1920's wei~ a period of enormous range and variety. I. E. Babel (1894–

1941?) brought realistic description to a new point in his *Red Cavalry* (1926), with its vivid and horrifying verbal pictures of the violence and brutality of the Civil War. *Cities and Years* by K. A. Fedin (b. 1892) is a thoughtful account of a Russian intellectual, brought up in the humanistic values of the old order, who returns to Russia after a long absence and attempts to come to terms with the new situation.

Both these themes are among those reflected in the greatest Russian novel of the first half of the century, *And Quiet Flows the Don,* by M. A. Sholokhov (b. 1905), a panoramic picture of the lives of the inhabitants of a Cossack village from the pre-1914 period through the vast upheavals of the First World War and Civil War. Though the novel has always been accorded high official acclaim in the Soviet Union, its power and originality, its magnanimous sense of the complexities, contradictions and poignancies of life, owe nothing to dogma. Its sympathetically depicted hero fights for the Whites, while there can be few more unpleasant characters anywhere in literature than the Red, Misha Koshevoi.

But classical realism by no means held the field in the post-revolutionary period. There was also a revival of the tradition of humor and social satire which had lain almost dormant since Gogol. The satirical, and often brilliantly funny, works of M. M. Zoshchenko (1895–1958) and of Il'f and Petrov (pen names of I. A. Fainzilberg, 1897–1937, and Y. P. Kataev, 1903–42) won great popularity in the 1920's and have recently enjoyed a mild revival. They do not of course ridicule the Soviet system as such, though their most frequent targets are the absurdities of officialdom.

The surrealistic works of E. I. Zamyatin (1884–1937) and of M. A. Bulgakov (1891–1940) represent, in their different ways, a more profound reaction to the events of the time, and in particular to the growing suppression of dissent and individual freedom and to official insistence on the emergence of a New Communist Man with new standards of morality of his own. Zamyatin's *We* (1924), which has never been published in the Soviet Union, anticipates Huxley's *Brave New World* and Orwell's *1984* in its nightmarish description of the totalitarian state of the future. Still largely known in the Soviet Union as a writer of orthodox plays (and one not quite so orthodox, *The Days of the Turbins,* in which the heroes are White officers), Bulgakov's chief claim to fame lies in his novels *The Heart of a Dog* (written in 1925) and *The Master and Margarita* (written some ten years later, but only discovered in 1967, when it was published in the West, and, in a severely-censored version, in Russia). Mixtures of the fantastic and the allegorical, with frequent satirical allusions to contemporary Soviet themes, both novels can be read as Aesopian attacks on the moral assumptions of the Bolshevik regime.

Threatening ultimately to displace all other trends was the Proletarian movement with its attempts to produce a new Communist literature. Gorky's *Mother* (1907) was subsequently claimed as marking the beginning of the new era in literature. But its real pioneers were F. V. Gladkov (1883–1958) and A. A. Fadeev (1901–1956). Gladkov's *Cement,* published in 1925, and Fadeev's *The Rout,* which appeared a year later, introduced the new type of revolutionary hero: the leader of the proletariat, acting "in tune with history," purposeful, resolute, ruthlessly dedicated to the cause of the Party, and utterly contemptuous of "bourgeois" humane values. Though part of the drama of *The Rout* is provided by the hero's momentary loss of resolution, such heroes normally display little internal conflict or even private emotional life; their opponents, counter-revolutionaries or relics of the past order, doomed by history, appear in equally monochrome tones.

Socialist Realism

It was natural that this style should be adopted as the norm as Party control over the arts was extended and intensified during the period of the First Five Year Plan (1928–33). The Party of the Stalin period had little use for fantasy, allegory or satire. Nor was classical realism an approach to be encouraged. Soviet literature should present positive heroes who would serve as models for the reader. It should be inspiring and optimistic. Socialist realism therefore demanded not that life should be depicted as it is (with all its imperfections), but as it should (and ultimately would) be—in short, it is in *no* way to be confused with realism!

Official direction and control of this kind was a new phenomenon in Russia: Czarist censorship, haphazard and rarely onerous, had been purely negative; it had never attempted to enforce particular subjects, aims or styles upon literature or art. The consequence of the enforcement of socialist realism was certainly not any diminution in the number of works produced. On the contrary, vast numbers of novels appeared, all of them characterized by their didactic and moralizing tone, their idealized "positive" heroes and a remarkable similarity of situation and plot.

Among the most famous examples of the genre are Sholokhov's *Virgin Soil Upturned,* a description of the process of collectivization as seen from the official point of view; *Courage* by V. K. Ketlinskaya (b. 1906), which recounts the story of the building of Komsomolsk-on-Amur; *The Second Day* by I. G. Ehrenburg (1891–1967), which deals with the construction of a Siberian steel plant; *Tanker Derbent* by Yu. Krymov (pen-name of Yu. S. Beklemishev, 1908–41), which has been praised as "a skilful study of socialist construction in the transportation industry"; and *How the Steel was Tempered* by N. A. Ostrovski (1904–36), which tells the story of a young Bolshevik from a poor background who joins the revolutionary cause and succeeds, under the new regime, in realizing his ambition to be a writer.

With the Second World War, the war itself replaced industrialization as the most favored theme in Soviet literature. The subject was only too natural in the aftermath of the war itself. But its political attractiveness, its scope for creating inspiring "positive" heroes, and, especially, for identifying patriotism and the defense of the Russian homeland with the cause of the Party, have ensured that it would remain, into the 1970's, a dominant motif in officially approved and published writing. The most celebrated of the early war novels were Fadeev's *The Young Guard* and B. Polevoi's *The Story of a Real Man.* The subject has been the basis of the careers of K. M. Simonov (b. 1915), Yu V. Bondarev (b. 1924) and innumerable others.

The requirement that literature should serve the Party's ends (and should display *partinost,* or party spirit) and the contention that only the style of "socialist realism" can satisfy this requirement have remained, and are likely to continue to remain, the foundations of official policy. Only the narrowness with which these principles have been interpreted, and the rigor with which they have been enforced, have varied. The death of Stalin in 1953, and the publication the following year of Ehrenburg's novel *The Thaw* (which actually dares to mention the Purges of the 1930's) appeared to herald a new era of literary freedom; the denunciation of Stalin at the Twentieth Party Congress in 1956 seemed to indicate that there could be no reversion to the tight control of the past. And, indeed, Khrushchev, in his attempts to outmaneuver and discredit his Praesidium rivals, Malenkov, Molotov and Kaganovich, who had been much more implicated in Stalin's crimes than he, found it very useful to permit the publication of literary works exposing those crimes. By far the most notable of these was *One Day in the Life of Ivan Denisovich,* by A. I. Solzhenitsyn (b. 1918) published in the periodical *Novy Mir* in 1962.

That Party control over literature was not to be relaxed except for particular Party purposes was well demonstrated by the storm of abuse which greeted the award of the Nobel Prize to Pasternak in 1958 for his novel, *Dr. Zhivago,* which had been published in the West. A work entirely in the tradition of *War and Peace* and *And Quiet Flows the Don* in its synthesis of individual with great historical themes, it is nonetheless very much a poet's novel, more remarkable for its insight into the human mind, and its sense of the scale and significance of life, than for the structure of its plot. Its great faults in official eyes are its refusal to adopt the simple orthodox view of the great events of the Revolutionary period, and the introverted, complex and often ambiguous reaction to them of the hero, Zhivago.

Not all writers are in trouble with the authorities. Many good writers steer clear of political disputes entirely, turning out new versions of the "Grand Russian Novel" from time to time. Among the best are K. Paustovsky (b. 1892), with his many-volumed *Story of a Life,* Yuri Kazakov (b. 1927), and Vladimir Tendryakov (b. 1923), author of *Three, Seven, Ace.*

Victor Nekrasov (b. 1910), whose most famous work is *Front Line Stalingrad,* eventually became involved in political dissent and emigrated to France in 1974. Vladimir Maximov, another talented and imaginative prose writer, also recently emigrated to France and is now editor of a literary-political journal, *Kontinent,* published in the West since 1974.

Khrushchev and After

Notwithstanding the persecution of Pasternak, and of other, lesser, writers and artists, the Khrushchev era, with its illusion of a new literary emancipation, and its relaxation of police controls throughout society, saw a new flowering of literature. The poets E. A. Evtushenko (b. 1933) and A. A. Voznesensky (b. 1934), who have strong affinities with the Futurists, declaimed in public to large audiences. Prose writers, on the whole, were less fortunate: those who were most original were rarely published. The period saw a remarkable revival of the tradition of satire, coupled often with surrealism, as in the work of V. Tarsis (b. 1906), A. Sinyavsky (b. 1925) and Yu. Daniel (b. 1925) (the latter two publishing in the West under the names of Terz and Arzhak). Yet this revival ended badly: Tarsis was confined in a mental hospital and Sinyavsky and Daniel, at a celebrated trial in 1966, were sentenced to long terms in labor camps. (Tarsis and, more recently, Sinyavsky came to settle in the West, while Daniel, after his release, still lives near Moscow.)

But by far the greatest figure has been fully in the tradition of Russian realism. None of Solzhenitsyn's major works, after *One Day . . .*, has been published in the Soviet Union. *Cancer Ward* and *The First Circle,* like their predecessor, are both set against the background of the 1930's Purges. But they are far more than documents of one of the most extraordinary phases of history. The prisoners in the camp, or the patients in the cancer hospital, form a microcosm of society, with the difference that they are *in extremis:* they daily confront the worst in cynicism, in treachery, in suffering and in death. But, in spite of this, qualities of honor, generosity, self-sacrifice and love survive Optimism is one of the most notable characteristics of Solzhenitsyn's work: a sense that for all the evil, for all the millions of wasted and broken existences, many tragic examples of which he describes in his massive historical documentary record of the labor camp, *The Gulag Archipelago,* human life is not in vain. Now in exile, Solzhenitsyn has settled for the moment in the USA (Vermont), where he continues to write, and there are signs that his optimism has come to be based on a strong Orthodox religious belief while, politically, he has grown increasingly pessimistic about the prospects for his country.

In the period since the trial of Sinyavsky and Daniel, the control of Soviet literary and intellectual life has tightened. This is not to say that excellent work is not done by those who are accorded the privilege of publication. In prose, perhaps the most noteworthy talent to come to the fore since the Second World War among establishment writers is that of V. F. Panova (b. 1905). Her short stories and short novels, brilliantly and effortlessly evocative of everyday Soviet life, have undoubted affinities with Chekhov. The tradition of personal, lyrical poetry is best represented by B. Akhmadulina (b. 1937). Unlike her former husband, Evtushenko, she has avoided the temptation to descend to political and propaganda works.

But the margins of the permissible are relatively narrow: many subjects are taboo, neither non-realism nor, in dealing with contemporary subjects, too frank a realism is acceptable; originality of any kind is at a discount; and the penalties for non-conformity are unattractive and efficiently enforced. Several of Russia's front writers have emigrated, either voluntarily or involuntarily. Many of them, together with those of their colleagues still in Russia and who have courage enough to assert their freedom to publish where they will (like satirical prose writer Vladimir Voinovich), are contributing works of major importance to the journal *Kontinent.* In a sense, *Kontinent* has become the focus for all that is best in the Russian literary tradition. Solzhenitsyn's words in 1967 have been well borne out since he wrote them:

"Our literature has lost the leading position which it occupied in the world at the end of the last century and at the beginning of this: it has lost the passion for experimentation which distinguished it during the twenties. The literature of our country appears today to all the world as infinitely poorer, more flat and worthless than it is in reality, than it would look if it were not being restricted, if it were not being prevented from developing. The loser is our country . . . and world literature is also the loser."

But Russian literature lives on in exile, as it has so often done in the past.

THE LIVELY ARTS

Music, Cinema, Theater and Dance

BY
**HILARY STERNBERG, RICHARD TAYLOR
AND JOHN FINCHLEY**

You may be forgiven if the words "Russian music" conjure up a vision of the massed choirs of the Red Army accompanied at breakneck speed by an orchestra of three hundred ebullient balalaikas. They certainly are a part of the picture—but only a part. And you are more likely to see them abroad than in the USSR, for they are the "image" the Soviet Union likes to export, along with its top ballet companies, conductors, singers and instrumentalists. These people are, however, more than mere musical ambassadors; they have a remarkable popularity and following in their own country, too. The Russians are a music-loving people, and the visitor will be struck at once by the quantity and variety of musical entertainment, the relative cheapness of tickets, and the size and enthusiasm of audiences.

Music in Russia goes back to very ancient origins. In many ways, its development parallels that of Russian literature. Both are facets of a culture that has always been intensely influenced by social and political circumstances. Because of the centuries of geographical and political isolation of the Russian state, punctuated by periods of officially encouraged "Westernization" (under Peter the Great, for example), Russian music has been either entirely reliant upon native folk tradition and Orthodox Church conventions, or suddenly subjected to bouts of imported influence from abroad, whether Italian vocal style or German counterpoint. It was not until the 19th century, at about the same time as the flowering of Russian literature, that a national Russian music came into being.

Slavonic folk music can be traced back long before the birth of Christ. Many of its themes are pagan and relate to old Slav mythology, rituals and ancient festivals. There are wedding songs, funeral songs, and harvest songs. In its purest form, Russian folk music tends to use the natural minor and major modes; present day arrangements have modified and "Westernized" some harmonies, but the distinctive features of the melodic line remain. When Kievan Russia was converted to Christianity in 988 AD, Greek and Bulgarian chant was introduced, but later, Russian forms of the Byzantine chant have acquired a Slavonic character and sometimes use Russian modes.

Kievan Russia was closely linked with Byzantium and absorbed much ecclesiastical and secular culture. Music played an important ceremonial and entertaining role in court life. Those were the days of the *skomorokhi,* wandering minstrels and court buffoons, who appear in many Russian operas (Rimsky- Korsakov's *Snow Maiden* is an example). The balalaika, the triangular stringed instrument now so popular, only dates back to the 19th century, while the guitar and accordion used widely today were introduced even later. Early Russian folk music employed a whole range of bowed, plucked and wind instruments; some of them were of oriental provenance, like the 16th-century *domra,* a forerunner of the balalaika, which is still played today in India and elsewhere. A very ancient stringed instrument often mentioned in folk epics and ballards is the *gusli,* which the minstrels used to accompany their songs. Sadko, the 12th-century merchant from Novgorod, celebrated in a medieval ballad (*bylina*), reputedly played his *gusli* for three days and three nights to placate the Sea King when a storm threatened to wreck his 30 red ships laden with rich wares.

With the growth of the Muscovite state in the period between the 14th and 17th centuries Moscow was hailed as the "Third Rome" and the Church became the dominant influence. In the mid-17th century, the Patriarch of Moscow even ordered the destruction of all folk instruments that could be found in the city. The *skomorokhi,* now regarded as an evil, pagan influence, were forced to flee into the countryside.

Western Influence

By this time a new, urban, Western European culture was developing, and Moscow was acquiring cultural ties as travelers visited Europe and Europeans came to settle in Moscow, foreign musicians among them. In 1586, incidentally, the English Queen Elizabeth I had made a gift of a gilded clavichord to the Czar's wife and, according to the description by the English envoy, crowds gathered in their thousands round the palace windows to hear the novel sound. In the mid-17th century, European musical notation was finally adopted—until then a variety of inconsistent and now only partly decipherable systems had been in use in Russia.

In the early 18th century Czar Peter the Great, who professed a great admiration for things European, introduced many "Western" features into Russia in his determination that his country should not lag behind. German musicians were employed at court and many wealthy nobles followed suit and hired private musicians to play in their homes. By the 1740's, Italian opera was well established in the new capital, St. Petersburg, and there were even resident foreign composers. It was at this time, too, that the first native soloists of repute emerged, and with them, Russian craftsmen—the violins of Ivan Batov (born 1767) were reckoned among the finest in the world.

In the 18th century a large scale revival of interest in folk music (by then contaminated by "urban" harmonies) led to the first methodical compilations of folk song collections. These were to prove very important to the first native composers, who made extensive use of folk material, either by way of direct quotation, or, later, by more subtle composition in the folk idiom. The first Russian operas date from the late 18th century and tend to be, musically, something of a hotchpotch, and dramatically primitive. They did, however, start a fashion for using Russian folklore that was to continue right through the 19th century and produce some of the greatest Russian operatic and orchestral music.

Glinka

It was not until the early 19th century that there came a composer of real stature who was able to transcend the melodramatic and fuse the folk idiom with an accomplished, professional technique and a classical feeling for melodic and harmonic flow, and to create an end product that was not simply a pastiche. He was Mikhail Glinka (1804–57), whose sense of balance and form, general sophistication and indeed innovation have been compared with those of the poet Alexander Pushkin. If the latter formulated the basis of a modern literary language, Glinka did the same for Russian music. Glinka is chiefly remembered for his two operas, based on folklore and historical legend, *Ivan Susanin or A Life for the Czar* (1836) and *Ruslan and Lyudmila* (1842), both of which are still performed today. He also wrote many orchestral and chamber works and a large quantity of piano music and songs. The Russian "romance", the lyrical, sentimental or passionate song, also developed with Glinka, and he was one of the first to introduce exotic and oriental material from Turkey, Persia, Arabia and the Caucasus, and to suggest oriental effects by the use of what were then unusual orchestral combinations, including nasal wind instruments (*cor anglais* and oboe).

A lesser-known, younger, contemporary of Glinka's was Alexander Dargomyzhsky (1813–69). He too composed an opera based on folk legend (*Rusalka,* 1848). Greatly influenced by Glinka, he exercised considerable influence in his turn upon the embryonic Russian "nationalist" school of music. Some of his later music, particularly his opera *The Stone Guest* (1868), a setting of Pushkin's poem, was, by the standards of the day, quite revolutionary, making use of vocal and instrumental motifs that anticipate Wagner, and attempting to reproduce the inflections of human speech. It was completely misunderstood by many critics.

"The Mighty Handful"

The 19th century was one of social, cultural and political ferment, and also of unprecedented fertility in the arts. Naturally, music was somewhat less affected than other cultural fields by philosophical and political argument. Nevertheless, there was a rough division in the musical world between the "Westernizing," pro-European Anton Rubinstein, a confirmed supporter of Teutonicism in music; middle-of-the-road Tchaikovsky; and the nationalist, "Slavophile," school represented by a group of young composers known collectively as "The Mighty Handful" or "The Five": Balakirev (1836–1910), Borodin (1833–87), Cui (1833–1918), Mussorgsky (1839–81) and Rimsky-Korsakov (1844–1908). United by their admiration for Glinka and his musical principles, "The Five" were an extraordinary musical phenomenon—a group of musicians who began largely as amateurs untrained in either instrumental technique or formal musical composition. Under the tutelage of Balakirev, the only one among them to have received some semblance of a professional training (the other four were a chemist, an army engineer, a guards officer and a naval cadet), these men composed some of the finest 19th-century Russian music. Often they composed jointly, suggesting themes and libretti, and criticizing each other's work. Had it not been for the efforts of Rimsky-Korsakov in particular, Mussorgsky's opera *Boris Godunov* and Borodin's *Prince Igor* might never have been completed in the form in which we know them today.

"The Five" met with a good deal of criticism and direct opposition from the musical establishment of the day, but eventually won recognition. Rimsky-Korsakov went on to become professor at the St. Petersburg Conservatory in 1871 and conductor of the Russian Symphony concerts in 1886–1900. As professor, he taught many young musicians who were later to become the first generation of 20th-century and Soviet composers, including Lyadov, Ippolitov-Ivanov, Grechaninov, Glazunov, Stravinsky and Prokofiev. Balakirev played a leading part in founding the Free School of Music in 1862, an institution which did much to promote the works of The Five and also the music of Berlioz, Schumann and, later, Liszt. A detailed list of the works of The Five is beyond the scope of this chapter. Their main feature, however, is the use of folk motifs from all over Russia and from more exotic lands (for instance, Balakirev's oriental fantasy *Islamey,* Borodin's *In the Steppes of Central Asia,* a musical picture; Rimsky-Korsakovs *Sheherazade;* and perhaps the most well-known piece by Borodin, the *Polovtsian Dances* from *Prince Igor*).

Mussorgsky developed away from the rather romantic orchestrations of his mentor Balakirev and embarked upon a new, "realistic" style best exemplified in his piano suite *Pictures from an Exhibition* (1874), in which he attempts to depict himself strolling through an exhibition of water colors by his friend Victor Hartmann, whose death the music commemorated. His historical opera *Boris Godunov* (1868–72) was an even further cry from the early days of The Five; its unusual, sometimes stark harmonies, powerful historical atmosphere and massive scale were an entirely new departure in the field. Indeed, much of Mussorgsky's music was more original and ahead of its time than his contemporaries knew. You can see *Boris Godunov* today at the Bolshoi Theater in Moscow; it is one of the most exciting spectacles, both musically and visually, that you are likely to experience during your visit.

Tchaikovsky

Before leaving the 19th century, a word should be said about Tchaikovsky (1840–93), perhaps the best known and most loved Russian composer. You will find his music played all over the Soviet Union today, whether at the Bolshoi or Kirov Ballets or in the countless concert halls.

His operas and ballets are lavishly produced and beautifully performed—they are not to be missed! A very personal composer, and a master of brilliant orchestration and rhythm, Tchaikovsky was able to express the whole gamut of emotions from the despair of his *Symphony No. 6* (*Pathétique*) to the exuberance of his *1812 Overture* and the passion of the *Romeo and Juliet Fantasy Overture*. His best known opera, *Eugene Onegin*, is a firm favorite in the Bolshoi repertoire.

A group of composers who form a bridge between the 19th and 20th centuries include Ippolitov-Ivanov (1859–1936), Glière (1875–1956), who was essentially a classical Russian composer although his life spans the first 40 years of Soviet power, and the solitary, mystically-inclined Alexander Scriabin (1872–1915), whose *Poem of Ecstasy* frequently figures in Western concerts. (Scriabin's nephew was also famous, in the political field however—he was V. Molotov, Stalin's long-time Foreign Minister.)

The Bolshevik Revolution in 1917 led to a complete break in the continuity of musical development, especially after the first few years of relatively free experimentation. Many composers and musicians, old and young, emigrated. They included Sabaneyev, Medtner, Grechaninov, Glazunov, Loure, Lyapunov, Rachmaninov, Cherepnin, Prokofiev and Stravinsky—and the singer Chaliapin. Of these, only Prokofiev returned, in 1936, after a series of visits. Some of these *émigré* composers were not played or even mentioned for many years in their homeland. Stravinsky in particular was designated the archvillain of them all, and it was not until the relatively liberal 1960's that he returned to the Soviet Union and made a tour (in 1962).

"Socialist Realism" and the Present

By 1932, the new criteria in all the arts, music included, were those of "socialist realism": patriotism, comprehensibility and accessibility to the masses. This entailed self-imposed isolation from contemporary Western musical experimentation in such fields as dodecaphonic, serial music and *musique concrète* (in much the same way as abstract art was shunned). Nevertheless, some composers with genuine talent have emerged within these limitations: Nikolai Myaskovsky, for instance, the most prolific Soviet symphonist (he had 27 to his credit when he died in 1950 at the age of 69). Among the few really individual and controversial Soviet composers are Sergei Prokofiev (1891–1953), many of whose works were not played until recently in Russia, and Dmitri Shostakovich (1906–75), who earned a worldwide reputation and now ranks as a great, if uneven, 20th-century symphonic composer. (Shostakovich has the unique distinction of being the only Soviet composer to be awarded an honorary doctorate by Oxford University.) An opera *The Nose*, composed in 1927–8 by the young Shostakovich, was successfully revived in 1979 by London's English National Opera. Based on Gogol's short story, it was first performed in 1930 but was withdrawn after controversial reviews and official disfavour.

There are well over 1500 listed Soviet "composers", that is, members of the official Union of Composers. Among them, Aram Khachaturian (1903–78) and Dmitri Kabalevsky (b. 1904) are known abroad, though their output has been on a lesser, more superficial scale and cannot be compared to the creative individuality of Prokofiev or Shostakovich. The visitor to Russia will find that concert programs usually include at least one work by a Soviet composer in amongst the Beethoven and Tchaikovsky—the name of Tikhon Khrennikov is one frequently met. As head of the Union of Soviet Composers, he is probably the most "official", or establishment composer today.

The visitor who wishes to enjoy the best of Soviet music-making should come for one of the annual music festivals. There is the "Moscow Stars" festival held each May in the capital; the "White Nights," a celebration of the long summer nights in the north (Leningrad, each June); and the "Russian Winter," a New Year festival in Moscow (December 25-January 5). At these festivities you can see and hear the finest folk music and dance ensembles from many of the Soviet republics; the Moscow Chamber Orchestra, the Leningrad Symphony Orchestra, the Kirov Opera and Ballet, the Bolshoi Opera and Ballet, and the finest conductors and soloists.

Don't miss the Tchaikovsky Piano Competition in Moscow, at which some of the best young international talent as well as Russia's up-and-coming pianists may be heard.

Another musical attraction is Moscow's Gypsy Theater, extremely popular with the Russians. One or two cafés in Moscow and Leningrad have jazz groups. Light music and variety concerts are plentiful. Tickets for most things can—and preferably *should*—be booked through your hotel or an Intourist bureau, especially where theater, opera and ballet are concerned. Incidentally, gramophone records are inexpensive, and the quality of recent recordings compares well with that of Western discs.

The Soviet Cinema

Lenin once observed, "Of all the arts for us the cinema is the most important", and, despite the rapid growth of radio and television as media for communication and entertainment, cinema attendances in the Soviet Union continue to grow year by year. Official figures show that the average Soviet citizen goes to the cinema 23 times a year. This is the highest attendance figure in the world; compared with this, for example, the average British citizen goes to the cinema only once every two years.

The Russian cinema was in a parlous state when the Bolsheviks seized power in 1917. Before the First World War, Russian films had been heavily dependent on foreign capital and raw materials and these supplies had now dried up. During the Civil War that followed the October Revolution, many people active in the cinema fled abroad, taking their much-needed skills, and often even their equipment, with them. In August 1919, the remains of the film industry were nationalized and the world's first state film school was established in Moscow to train new actors and technicians.

The cinema was regarded as a vital weapon in the struggle to unify the country; as the silent film was not hampered by the restrictions of language or the written word, it was ideally suited for the task of propagating Bolshevik ideology to the illiterate and multinational masses. Poets and painters lent their talents; from their midst emerged Eisenstein, formerly a stage designer. His films (*Strike, Battleship Potemkin, October*) characterize the heroic era of the Soviet silent cinema and blazed a trail across the world. He was not, however, alone; equally important, if less well-known, directors from this period include Pudovkin and Dovzhenko, and the documentary film-makers, Vertov and Shub. All their films were strongly visual, full of powerful revolutionary imagery aimed at the masses. But it was not until 1927 that the Soviet Union was able itself to produce the majority of films shown in its cinemas; Mary Pickford and Charlie Chaplin had been the real popular heroes.

With the advent of sound, which reached the USSR several years later than the West, the spontaneous exuberance of the Twenties gave way to a stale conformism. The dead hand of Stalinism had fallen; the crudest propaganda films date from the Stalin period and include *Peter the First, Lenin in October* and *The Rainbow*. These films are no longer shown; they now seem as dated to a Soviet audience as they would to its Western counterpart. But even at the height of the purges, some films still managed to display a subtle complexity; Eisenstein's two sound master-pieces, *Alexander Nevsky* and *Ivan the Terrible* may be overtly propagandist, but they are at the same time covertly subversive.

In the years since 1956 there has been a general relaxation. The state still controls all branches of the cinema: production, distribution and exhibition. It can thus determine what is produced and what is shown. In addition to an extensive chain of conventional cinemas, the Soviet Union has a larger number of projectors installed in youth clubs, work-ers' clubs and collective farms, as well as a network of traveling cinemas to serve the remoter areas such as Siberia. All this ensures blanket coverage of the entire country. But what kind of films do they show?

Nowadays the program in a Soviet cinema usually begins with the newsreel *Novosti dnya* (News of the day). Similar in style and structure to a Western newsreel, *Novosti dnya* concentrates on items like party functions, industrial output targets, the progress of the harvest and space or sporting triumphs. Negative news is never reported unless a moral can be drawn. The newsreel is often followed by one or more short films on similar topics, or the preservation of folklore or wild life; the aim is always to uplift the audience, never to depress it. Finally there comes the full-length feature film. The propaganda content in most current Soviet feature films is negligible; if it were otherwise, audiences would not go to see them—they sometimes only barely tolerate the newsreel and the shorts.

Long, but Not Always Boring

The Western viewer, however, should be warned that, in a country where time often seems to be on a different scale, length is no obstacle for the cinema audience. The pace of many Soviet films is therefore very slow by our standards; the classic examples are Sergei Bondarchuk's epic films *War and Peace* and *Waterloo,* with their extensive battle scenes. In its original four-part version, *War and Peace* lasted nearly 12 hours and was shown in sections on consecutive nights. More recently, the USSR has produced a similar epic about the Second World War entitled *Libera-tion.* Apart from such epics, the Soviet cinema also excels at biographical and historical films and adaptations from literary classics. Amongst more recent films in the first categories, *Tchaikovsky, The Sixth of July, Andrei Rublev* and *Lenin in Poland* should be noted. Many of the adapta-tions are already known in the West; Kozintsev's film versions of *Hamlet* and *King Lear* have been widely acclaimed, as has Heifits' *The Lady with the Little Dog,* but *The Seagull, A Nest of Gentlefolk,* and *The Brothers Karamazov* have also been successfully adapted to the screen. Soviet film-makers have recently begun to explore what are for them new fields: the detective film, the spy film and the science-fiction film. In the latter genre, Andrei Tarkovsky's superb *Solaris* must reign supreme. *Kalina Krasnaya* (The Red Snowball-Tree) caused a sensation in Russia and the West. It dealt with the problems of the Soviet village, the twilight world of provincial towns (a miniature Mafia), and even went on record as the first film to include scenes of life in a corrective labor camp.

Colorful folk customs are sometimes used as a basis for films. The Hatsuls, a Slav tribe of great antiquity, were lyrically portrayed by the Soviet director Paradzanov in *Shades of Our Ancestors.* This talented artist was consigned to a labor camp for his unorthodoxy; now released, he is struggling to regain a toehold in his profession.

There is by now a film studio in every one of the 15 union republics, producing films in the local language or languages and reflecting local cultural traditions. Nevertheless, Moscow and Leningrad remain the centers of production for films, as for almost anything else, and the Mosfilm studios in the Soviet capital are the largest in Europe after Cinecittà in Rome.

The Soviet film industry has just begun to co-produce films with western countries. *Tchaikovsky* resulted from a collaboration with the Americans, and *The Red Tent,* with Peter Finch, from a similar arrangement with the British. Nevertheless the USSR imports few Western films for general exhibition. Some are films which show Western society in a negative light, such as *If.* Then there are innocuous musicals like *West Side Story* or *My Fair Lady.* In tourist centres at the height of the season there is now quite a wide choice of foreign viewing. *Murder on the Orient Express* and *Blue Water, White Death* were reportedly among Western films on general release in Leningrad. Many other foreign films are given only a restricted release; on the one hand, Indian flesh-and-blood epics are imported for distribution in Central Asia, on the other, the products of the European avant-garde are shown only to restricted audiences of artists and intellectuals.

The Theater

The first recorded theatrical performance in Russia took place in 1662, but it was during the reign of Peter the Great (1682–1725) that the theater, like so many other Western fashions and institutions, first entered Russian life. Though the first theatrical companies in the country were foreign, it was not long before native performers emerged. Fydor Volkov (1729–63) established the first truly Russian ensemble. The Czarina Elizaveta Petrovna founded an Imperial Theater by royal decree in 1756. By the reign of Catherine the Great (1762–96), herself a writer of several plays in the French style, the tradition was fully established. Thereafter, there was no looking back.

So popular, indeed, did the theater become among the upper classes of Russia that, in parallel with the development of distinguished metropolitan theaters in St. Petersburg and Moscow, many landowners began to set up theaters on their own estates, using their serfs as actors. The serf theater, which reached its climax in the first half of the 19th century, became a major feature of Russian provincial life and produced a number of most distinguished actors and actresses who later gained their freedom and became the leading stars of the Petersburg stage. The most famous of these was Mikhail Shchepkin (1788–1863), an exponent of natural acting and the leading theatrical figure of his day.

Until the mid-eighteenth century all the plays produced in Russia were foreign, but the country was not slow to produce its own dramatists. A. P. Sumarokov (1718–77) is generally recognized as the first Russian playwright. He worked closely with Volkov. Denis Fonvizin (1745–92) was the first native dramatist to move on from mere imitation of foreign models. His satire *The Minor* is still sometimes performed in the Soviet Union. The first Russian play of real literary importance was *Woe from Wit* by A. S. Griboedov (1795–1829). A perceptive satire on the contemporary Russian scene, many of its pithy and epigrammatic lines have remained in the language as popular sayings.

The great Russian writers of the Romantic period, A. S. Pushkin and M. Yu. Lermontov, both wrote plays. The former's *Boris Godunov* (later set to music as Mussorgsky's opera of the same name), and the latter's *Masquerade* both display the hold exercised by Shakespeare over their authors. But the drama of great conflicts and isolated heroes, so typical of Romanticism, gave way by mid-century to more mundane themes, to the depiction of particularly Russian characters and situations and to the cult of realism which similarly characterized the contemporary novel.

Gogol's plays, of which *The Inspector General* is the best known, with their memorable (if caricatured) characters, their apparent humor and underlying pathos, are of a piece with his novels, as is Turgenev's *A Month in the Country*. The first Russian professional playwright, whose nearly 50 works have remained the backbone of the repertoire of the Russian theater, was A. N. Ostrovsky (1823–86). His work represents the high point of realism on the stage: both characters and dialogue are drawn, unaltered and unembroidered, straight from life. In his earlier works he was content to depict, and to satirize, the contemporary scene, and especially the world of the materialistic Moscow merchant class. But his later plays, *The Ward* and *The Thunderstorm* in particular, were written in a more gloomy and pessimistic vein, and show up the human misery under the surface of respectable society.

Chekhov

Turgenev and Ostrovsky both influenced the greatest of Russian dramatists, Anton Chekhov (1860–1904). His major plays, *Ivanov, The Seagull, Uncle Vanya, The Three Sisters* and *The Cherry Orchard,* have been variously interpreted as tragedy and as comedy, as reflecting a negative, individualistic and essentially despairing view of life, and as looking beyond the apparent frustration of their characters to a more glorious future. In truth, Chekhov's plays seem imbued with a stoical acceptance of the irony of life. His characters are both conscious of the brevity of existence, and bored with it; time is painfully limited and yet hangs heavy on their hands. Only occasionally does this sense of futility appear to be challenged: usually by the incursion of love with its new and sudden, if fleeting, conviction of purpose and hopes; or, as with Colonel Vershinin in *The Three Sisters,* by dreams of a new and better life for humanity in the future.

Though all such aspirations seem but pathetic self-delusions, doomed to final frustration, Chekhov is remarkable in that, having analyzed the human condition with such uncompromising directness and honesty, he does not draw his characters with cynicism or contempt, but rather with a warm sympathy that is greater for the excision of the pretensions and illusions with which men generally seek to give significance to their lives.

Chekhov's reputation was made in his own day largely by the performances of his works staged at the newly-founded Moscow Arts Theater by K. S. Stanislavsky (1863–1938). Stanislavsky, the foremost exponent of realism in the theater, who insisted on strict authenticity of scenery and costume and taught his actors to "live" their parts, has left a permanent mark on the Russian stage and, indeed on the Western theater through the Method School of acting, an offshoot of his theorics. Chekhov himself frequently quarreled with his "slice of life" and generally tragic interpretations of his plays, which he considered failed to catch some of their nuances of irony and comedy. Maxim Gorky's *The Lower Depths*, set in a doss house, provided the ideal material for Stanislavsky's technique, and its first production at the Moscow Arts Theater in 1902 was one of the latter's great triumphs.

Stanislavsky's most talented pupil, V. Meyerhold (1874–1940), took an entirely different direction, turning his back on realism and abolishing the conventional stage set altogether. He became the interpreter of Futurist drama, and his name is as closely linked with the first performances of Mayakovsky's *The Bedbug* and *The Bath* as that of Stanislavsky is linked with Chekhov.

Experimentalism of the type of Meyerhold came to an end with the cult of "Socialist realism" during the 1930's (Meyerhold himself was arrested in 1937 and shot in 1940). The Soviet theater, so alive and influential during the first quarter of the new century, became largely monopolized, so far as new works were concerned, by propagandist works by N. Pogodin (1900–62), E. Schwartz (1904–58), K. Simonov (1915–60) and others. M. Bulgakov, whose *The Days of the Turbins* had enjoyed a considerable success during the 1920's, under Stalin wrote plays on the lives of Molière and Pushkin, and dramatized Gogol's *Dead Souls*.

Since the death of Stalin, and more particularly since 1960, the Soviet theater has seen a revival, less in the quality of new plays being staged than in the variety, originality and talent with which classical, contemporary and foreign works are produced. Moscow presents a range of styles of production as wide as New York and wider than London or Paris. In the place of the ephemeral drawing-room comedies or romantic musicals of the West, the Soviet stage displays a high proportion of worthless propagandistic works. But the visitor to Moscow can still see virtuoso acting performances in the Stanislavsky manner in productions of Chekhov at the Moscow Arts Theater, while the non-theatrical, un-rhetorical, modern-dress tradition of Meyerhold lives on in full vigor at the Sovremennik and Taganka theaters, the latter famous for its striking productions of Shakespeare (using the Pasternak translation), of Brecht, and of daring contemporary plays including the unexpectedly popular *Rush Hour*.

The Ballet

Ballet in the 20th century has been inextricably linked with Russia, but the art form did not start there. It was introduced from France during the great period of Westernization which began in the last decades of the 17th century and continued throughout the 18th. The first ballet performance in Russia—perhaps it would be more accurate to refer to the first formal dance spectacle—was staged at the Russian court by Czar Alexei in 1672. The popularity of the new medium steadily grew throughout the reigns of Peter the Great and of his successors, and the Empress Anna founded the Imperial School of Ballet in St. Petersburg in 1738.

The ballet during all this period had drawn its inspiration from the West. It first became an innovative force of its own with the arrival in 1801 of Charles Didelot (1769–1837), a refugee from the French Revolution. With an interval during Napoleon's invasion of Russia, Didelot was to remain, and to dominate the ballet in his newly adopted country, for 30 years. He was responsible for three decisive innovations: the use of the *pointes* (the tips of the toes), the development of the *pas de deux* as a "conversation" between two dancers, and the introduction of expressive dancing, inspired by Caucasian and Russian folk dancing, with which he abandoned the courtly and classical dance of the 18th century in favor of a figurative and dramatic style more in tune with the spirit of the contemporary Romantic movement. Under Didelot's pupil, Aram Glouzhkovski, who became its director in 1811, these tendencies were still further developed in Moscow's Bolshoi Ballet (founded in 1776).

The long career of Marius Petipa (1819–1910), who came to Russia as a dancer from his native France in 1847 and who remained as chief master of the Imperial Ballet, spans the Romantic and the modern ages. It was he more than anyone who introduced the great sense of spectacle, and the cult of the virtuoso solo part, that have remained features of the Russian ballet to this day. Together with his deputy Lev Ivanov (1834–1901), he was responsible for the choreography of all the major ballets of Tchaikovsky, still the foundation of the repertoires of all Russian companies—and indeed many Western ones—*Sleeping Beauty* (1890), *The Nutcracker* (1892), and *Swan Lake* (1895). Their choreographies combined a unity of dance and music that marked a return to the precepts of classicism and a lyricism and taste for the spectacular that were the legacy of the Romantic Movement.

While Petipa and Ivanov dominated the St. Petersburg ballet in their day, a rather different direction was taken by Moscow's Bolshoi under the leadership of Alexander Gorsky (1871–1924).Gorsky was the pioneer of realism in the ballet, the counterpart of his contemporary Stanislavsky, whom he much admired, in the theater. His choreography was designed to achieve the dramatization of character and plot; his *corps de ballet* acquired individual dancing roles, so that his crowds appeared as collections of living people. In the 20th century, he abandoned some of his concern with the representation of real life and fell considerably under the influence of Isadora Duncan, with her ideas of free self-expression in dancing, which he did much to popularize in Russia. Gorsky's influence, both on Fokine and the Ballets Russes, and on the "socialist realist" style of the Soviet period, has been profound.

Diaghilev

The fantasy and the spectacle of the St. Petersburg tradition, and the dramatic legacy of Moscow, were both evident in the Ballet Russe (founded by Sergei Diaghilev, 1872–1929), which has had a decisive and permanent influence on the development of the art. Determined to evolve a new art form, in which dancing, painting and music would be inseparably combined, Diaghilev brought together a most remarkable group of choreographers, dancers and artists. He employed, in succession, the choreographers Mikhail Fokine (1880–1942), Leonid Massine (1894–1979, Bronislava Nijinskaya (b. 1891) and George Balanchine (b. 1904); the dancers Anna Pavlova (1882–1931) and Vatslav Nijinsky (1890–1950), to name only two immortals, and artists, who were responsible for the sets, of the caliber of Leon Bakst, Alexander Benois, Natalia Goncharova, Derain and Picasso.

Diaghilev's choreographers differed in many ways. But they were alike in their rejection both of the conventions and artificialities of classical ballet and of heavy-handed realism; their assertion of the role of the vigorous male dancer; and their insistence on natural movement. Consistent with his role as a founder member of the "World of Art Society", Diaghilev devoted himself to the creation of his new art for its own sake, permitting no extraneous, didactic or literary preoccupations to enter his work. His objective was simply to excite in his audiences a pure—and quite novel—esthetic emotion. For the same reason, he avoided figurative representation in his stage sets, granting full rein to the imaginations of the leading artists he employed, the sensual effects of whose works were to complement those of the dancing and the music.

As for musicians, Fokine achieved some notable successes with the music of earlier musicians including Tchaikovsky, Chopin (in *Les Sylphides*)and Schumann (in *Carnaval*). But Diaghilev's choreographers were most at home, and his productions most original and striking, when they employed contemporary music. The Ballet Russe made use of many modern composers, including Debussy (*L'Après-Midi d'un Faune*), Ravel (*Daphnis and Chloe*) and, above all, Stravinsky (*Petrushka, The Firebird, The Rite of Spring*). The combination of unfamiliar harmonies and daring rhythm, the exotic and fantastic colors and designs of the scenery, and the uninhibited, sometimes primitive, force of the dancing combined to produce a pantheistic festival of modernism that stunned the Europe of the pre-1914 years. Diaghilev transformed the ballet into a major art form, and brought it a cosmopolitan recognition that it has never lost.

The October Revolution condemned the Diaghilev Ballet to permanent exile, and though some of its greatest successes date from the 1920's, its history no longer belongs to that of the Russian ballet. Diaghilev's two youngest choreographers, Balanchine and Sergei Lifar, have had a dominating influence on the development of ballet in the West during the remainder of the 20th century, Lifar in France, and Balanchine in America. The latter, as director of the New York City Ballet, has been the pioneer of the abstract approach to the art which perhaps represents the major contribution to it of the mid-20th century.

Soviet Spectacle

Paradoxically enough the Diaghilev ballet had less influence in Russia itself since 1917 than it had in the West. The 19th-century ballet of Petipa with its emphasis on spectacle, and the ideas of Gorsky, and specially the latter's insistence that his performers should act as well as dance, have been the models chiefly followed. This approach achieved its greatest successes in the 1930's and 1940's, with the works of Leonid Lavrovsky (b. 1905) and in particular with his *Romeo and Juliet* (1940), set to Prokofiev's music and with the great ballerina Galina Ulanova (b. 1910) in the title role. Lavrovsky's production aimed to transmit through the dancing the full dramatic impact of the original play.

As in literature and in art, the 1920's had been a period of experimentation in the Soviet ballet, inspired by the contemporary Futurist and Constructivist movements. Kassian Goleizovsky (b. 1892) had tried to break away entirely from the lyricism and harmony of traditional ballet, as well as from its technical conventions, with his introduction of acrobatic effects. But this interval was not to last. With the 1930's ballet, in common with the other arts, was brought under strict Party surveillance and control. Leading figures whose productions were approved, including Lavrovsky, continued to be allowed relative freedom of expression. But the guidelines for young choreographers and composers were clearly set out: ballet must serve a useful social purpose, its aim should be to tell an uplifting story, to point a moral, above all to adopt a realistic idiom which would be immediately comprehensible to every audience. One of the pioneering works in the style, *Flames of Paris* (1932), on the theme of the French Revolution, with music by Asafyev and choreography by Vainonen, is still one of the stock works of Soviet repertoires.

But it should not be thought that "socialist realism" has produced only propagandistic and inferior works. Indeed, the style has been the major contribution of the Soviet Union to the development of ballet during recent decades. Among leading examples of the genre are *Spartacus* (1956; music by Khachaturian, original choreography by Jacobson) and *Icarus* (1971; music by S. Slonimsky, b. 1932).

The Soviet ballet of today shows undiminished vigor. There are 33 companies in 31 cities (Moscow and Leningrad have two companies each, including, respectively, the Bolshoi and the Kirov—among the foremost in the world). But the great tradition of technical mastery, spectacle and lyricism inaugurated by Petipa remains, and nowhere in the world are classical interpretations of the ballets of Tchaikovsky better performed than by the Bolshoi and the Kirov. The Russian ballet also retains its reputation for the power of its virtuoso male dancers, one of the characteristics for which the Diaghilev Ballet Russe was famed: Vasiliev, the male lead at the Bolshoi, Nureyev, his Kirov predecessor, and Baryshnikov, both currently stunning Western audiences with their vivid portrayals, are all fully in this tradition.

In contemporary choreography, modernism, abstraction and the concept of dance as pure movement continue to be rejected. Instead—and most happily for the variety of ballet, and for the world—the Soviet Union has continued to explore the theatrical possibilities of the medium. The requirement that every production should convey a crude ideological message has been relaxed, but Soviet ballets still tell a story. As a result, Russian performers retain their reputation for combining technical mastery with the power to convey human emotion and character, and a dramatic sense of pathos or excitement. Good examples of this approach have been provided by two of the great successes of the Bolshoi, both written by Rodion Shchedrin for his wife, Maya Plisetskaya (b. 1930), the ballerina-actress *par excellence:* the *Carmen Suite* (first performed 1967) and *Anna Karenina* (first performed 1972).

FOOD AND DRINK

Meals Slow, Meals Fast

BY
GABRIELLE TOWNSEND

"Russian cooking? Well, there's borshch, and chicken Kiev and
. . . beef Stroganov . . . and . . . " How many people could name more
Russian dishes than that, or even claim to have tasted an authentic
version of these? The cooking of the Soviet Union—the real cooking—is
pretty unfamiliar to us in the West, and those who haven't traveled there
or at least sampled Russian cooking in the home of émigré friends won't
have any idea of its richness and variety. Sadly, we know only the two
or three dishes that have passed into the depersonalized repertory of
international restaurant cuisine and in the process lost all their authentic
flavor.

You may doubt that in a monolithic, utilitarian society such as the
USSR there can be any time or inclination for such frivolous activities
as creative cookery or gourmet eating. It would be understandable if the
periods of privation and austerity to which the Russians have been
subjected at many times in their history had killed their culinary traditions completely. Gratifyingly, as the interested tourist will discover, this
isn't true at all. (After all, music and ballet flourish, and *they're* not
utilitarian!) And the general level of prosperity in the USSR, despite the
occasional shortage of certain commodities, is probably higher now than
at any time in the past.

Having said this, we must admit that it's not always easy to find the
best cooking. The kind of food you'll eat from day to day depends on
several factors: the category of accommodations you've reserved, the

area of the USSR you're staying in, the season, and whether you have Russian friends or acquaintances who will invite you into their homes or show you their favorite restaurants.

Since your hotels and most of your meals are probably prepaid, you may not have a lot of choice; unless you're in the deluxe class (and possible even then) you may find your daily fare rather monotonous. Hotel meal-times are similar to ours in the West (outside hotels they tend to be more chaotic, random and prolonged). In hotels dinner is usually served from around 7 to 8 or 8.30 and it may be difficult to get a hot meal later in the evening. Breakfast will be tea or coffee with bread, butter and jam or cheese and perhaps cold meat as well; lunch is soup, meat or fish and dessert, and dinner the same. Meat in hotels tends to be served in a thick sauce, garnished with sour cream and dill and accompanied by mashed potatoes or perhaps *kasha,* a kind of buckwheat gruel. What you're most likely to miss, if you're staying in Moscow and the north, is fresh fruit and vegetables. They are often in short supply and pickled vegetables, particularly red cabbage and cucumber, are much used instead. But if you go down to the south, to the Crimea or Georgia, you'll see lush, delicious vegetables and fruits aplenty—huge golden watermelons, green beans, big ripe tomatoes, purple grapes and plums ripening to sweetness in the southern sun.

Regional Specialties

The Soviet Union is, of course, not one country, but a federation of 15 republics, each with its own climate, natural features, language and culture. Though the Moscow administration and centralization have destroyed some of the republics' individuality certain things survive intact; especially language, costume and cooking. Indeed, people seem to cherish them all the more: the regional restaurants in Moscow are immensely popular and very good. (You'll find more about regional food in the chapters dealing with the different areas of the USSR, but if you don't have time to visit all the places, you can at least get a taste of what they're like from the representative restaurant. It's the best way to vary your meals if you're tired of hotel food.)

You can try chicken *tabaka* in a Georgian restaurant, *shashlik* from the Caucasus, *pilaff* in an Uzbek restaurant, lamb stew with pine kernels in an Armenian one, and honey-cake in a Ukrainian establishment. (In the chapters on Moscow and Leningrad, we've listed the best restaurants in each city.) The problem, though, is not so much what to choose as how to get in. These regional restaurants are popular both with local people who enjoy their novelty and exoticism and with homesick provincials who have been longing for some home cooking. It's very hard to reserve a table, though you can ask your Intourist guide or hotel service desk to try for you. Otherwise you can go along and either join the long line of Russians waiting patiently to get in, or, if you have the nerve, walk right in and hope that someone will give you special treatment as a foreigner. This sounds boorish, but in fact most Russians are so hospitable to tourists and so proud of their country in all its aspects that they prefer to see foreigners take precedence over themselves so that the guests, with less time, shouldn't get a bad impression.

Meals Slow, Meals Fast

Reports you may have heard about the slow service in restaurants are not exaggerated: nowhere does the fatalistic and resigned side of the Russian character reveal itself more than in the way that restaurant patrons uncomplainingly wait hours for waiters. Maybe the restaurants are understaffed or badly managed; more likely it's just because the waiters don't *have* to hurry: people really are *happy* to wait. Probably dining out is such a rare treat for the average citizen that he's determined to make the evening last as long as possible. In the long gaps between courses he's either laughing and drinking with his friends or, in an establishment with music, he and his partner are doing a sedate foxtrot to thirties jazz or, if younger, boogie-ing wildly! "So why don't you do the same?" the waitress will ask if you get impatient. You can take along *War and Peace* to read between courses (you may not *quite* finish it but you'll have made a good start). Or you can try tipping the waitress in advance (not officially approved of, but sometimes effective). Or you can leave. What doesn't help is to get angry—it'll only spoil your digestion and make the Russians think how rude foreigners are.

If you do want a quick meal, there are plenty of alternatives. You'll find self-service cafés and stand-up snack bars where you can have anything from caviar to a plate of *borshch, pirozhki* (little pastries filled with ground meat or anything else) to a glass of tea. There are also parlors serving ice-cream and sweet champagne—these, too, are very popular and there's something very touching about the comrades standing stoically in line to sample these peculiarly bourgeois delights. Russian ice-cream is excellent and you can also try it at kiosks on the streets and in the parks—the word to say is *morozhenoye.*

A Little History

Traditionally, Russian food was always hearty and substantial, with plenty of farinaceous matter to fill the stomachs of the hungry peasants. *Kasha* was the staple and cabbage was the other main element in the diet; in *shchi,* soup containing perhaps only cabbage and potato, enriched with bone stock if you were lucky; also in *goluptsy,* cabbage rolls stuffed with whatever was available. There's a famous Russian saying:
Shchi da kasha
Pishcha nasha
(Cabbage soup and gruel are our food.)
The other basic item was, and is, bread. Most commonly coarse and black, it was, with salt, the symbol of hospitality offered to the guest in even the humblest household. (Russians today still take great pride in their bread, and rightly so: they probably have a greater variety than any other nation in the world and its quality is greatly superior to the mass-produced, steam-baked blotting-paper we have grown used to in the West.) Fresh meat and fowl were something of a luxury to most people, but fish from Russia's vast lakes and many rivers was more plentiful. Vegetables were salted and pickled and fruit preserved to last through the long winters. Since ingredients were not widely varied, Russian cooks became skilled in the use of herbs and spices to make their dishes more interesting. In the north, onions, parsley and dill are much used, with sour cream as the almost inevitable accompaniment. In the

south, particularly in the Caucasus and Georgia, the cooking resembles that of the Middle East, with the use of paprika, cayenne, ginger, sesame seeds, garlic and coriander.

For centuries, the food of the rich differed from the food of the poor more in quantity and variety than in refinement. It was not until the beginning of the 18th century, in the reign of Peter the Great (1682–1725), that the Russian nobles became aware that the preparation and consumption of food could be an enjoyable art, not merely a means of satisfying hunger. Peter, that most Western-looking of rulers, was determined to modernize and civilize his backward and, as he considered, barbaric people. He built a beautiful city on Western models, employing Italian architects, and to it summoned Western musicians, dancing-masters and teachers to train his courtiers in the manners of polite society. He also got a French cook who started producing remarkable delicacies such as the Russians had never seen.

His heirs and their courtiers took their lessons to heart. Feasts became more and more elaborate and extravagant. Contemporary accounts tell of the staggering opulence of the table settings—one family had gold plates for a thousand guests—and the expensive and fantastic dishes served. The object was clearly to astound and impress the guests with the host's wealth rather than with his taste. Nevertheless, by the early 19th century every wealthy household had its own chef, and as a result Russian cooking did become more delicate and subtle. But the old customs still prevailed—French cuisine did not disrupt the daily rhythm of life in Russian families. Chekhov's plays show how, even at a later date, the rituals of eating and drinking were the welcome punctuation of the tedium of the long provincial days. The *samovar* was always on the boil, and meal followed meal: breakfast, lunch, dinner (often six courses) preceded by *zakuska* (which will have a few words later) and followed eventually by supper, known as evening tea, which, though simpler, was another meal in its own right.

Home Cooking Today

The food you'll have if you're invited to a Soviet home today is obviously not so extravagant nor so vast in quantity as in rich people's houses in pre-revolutionary days. But Russians still enjoy a feast as much as they ever did and the tradition of hospitality is just as lively.

In the evening, you'll probably be offered *zakuska* before dinner. In the old days this was an elaborately decorated table laid with savory tidbits—different kinds of caviar (the best is black Beluga but there are also red and golden varieties), cold sturgeon in aspic, cheeses, pickles, liver pâté, cold cuts—which guests washed down with a choice of different vodkas. It was enough to constitute an ample meal in itself, though it was only meant to be a light snack for those who got too hungry to wait for the real dinner. Today you'll probably still be offered vodka and perhaps caviar (*ikra* in Russian), though it's scarcer and more expensive than it used to be. It's most likely to be served with *blini,* thin buckwheat pancakes in which the caviar or other filling is rolled and then covered in sour cream. Other likely *zakuski* are *pirozhki,* mentioned above, which might alternatively be served as an accompaniment to soup as the first course of the dinner proper. Or your hostess might have made a *kulebia-ka*—a flaky pastry loaf with a savory filling, often salmon. Whatever you're offered, temper your enthusiasm and politeness (you are bound to be pressed to eat more than you can manage) with prudence, in the knowledge that you've still got a long way to go: what follows the *zakuska* may not be a Czarist feast, but it will be fairly substantial and your hostess will be hurt if you can't last the course. Since Russian housewives don't have as many labor-saving devices and convenience foods as we do, an elaborate dinner party is all the more an honor for the guest and a source of pride to the hostess.

The dinner will probably start with soup such as *borshch,* but probably a more interesting and substantial version than any you've tasted before, perhaps with ham and cabbage added to the basic beetroot liquid. Or in summer it might be *akroshka,* a chilled soup of vegetables or meat in *kvas* stock. (*Kvas* is that strange beverage that characters in Russian literature are always drinking and which never seems to find an adequate translation; in fact it's a kind of beer most commonly made by adding a yeast mixture to stale black bread and allowing it to ferment.)

The main course will be either fish or meat. The fish you are most likely to be served are sturgeon, halibut or herring, though of course if you are near the sea in one of the Baltic republics or by the Black Sea there will be a wider variety of local fish available. If the main dish is meat, perhaps you'll be lucky enough to have a well-cooked chicken Kiev—at its best a miraculous creation and very tricky to make. When you pierce the lightly-fried chicken breast, a fountain of golden butter shoots forth. Or you might get an authentic beef Stroganov, succulent with little mushrooms and sour cream. Or *pelmeni.* light boiled dumplings filled with meat and again served with sour cream. The possibilities are infinite and depend very much on where the family comes from: as we've said before, people in the Soviet Union are very attached to the cooking of their birthplace and take it with them wherever they move.

For dessert there might be *vareniky,* sweet dumplings filled with fruit, fruit purée, charlotte russe or some of that delicious ice-cream. The meal will probably last a long time, there will be a lot of toasting, and everybody will eat and drink far too much and enjoy themselves thoroughly!

What's On the Menu?

Here are a few names of the more common dishes that you may come across: *borshch*—beet soup; *akróshka*—cold soup with a base of *kvas* (a kind of beer); *beef Stroganov*—beef stewed in sour cream with fried potatoes, not rice; *bliny*—small pancakes, which you then fill with caviar, fish, melted butter or sour cream; *aládyi*—crumpets, with the same filling but also with jam; *ikrá*—black caviar. Ask also for butter (*maslo*) and toast (*tost*); *krásnaya ikrá*—red caviar, excellent with sour cream (*smetána*); *kotlyety po Pozhársky*—chicken cutlets; *kotléta po Kiyevsky*—fried breast of chicken, rich with butter; *pirozhky*—fried rolls with different fillings, usually meat; *ponchiki*—hot, sugared doughnuts; *prostakvasha*—yogurt; *pelmémi*—meat dumplings; *rassólnik*—hot soup, usually made of pickled vegetables; *shchi*—cabbage soup; *morozhenoye*—ice cream.

Drink

The two most typical drinks you'll be offered in the Soviet Union are tea (*chai*)—usually with a pile of sugar—and vodka.

Russians drink their tea black, often with lemon and with a spoonful of fruit jelly stirred in. It comes in tall glasses with metal holders. The boredom of long train journeys is relieved by frequent refreshment dispensed by the conductor from the steaming samovar kept on the boil night and day in every car. In the Central Asian republics try visiting a local *chaikhana* (tearoom) where you may sit outdoors or indoors and sip *green* tea.

Coffee is generally available with meals and in cafés, though the standard is variable. We recommend taking a jar of instant coffee along (like gold dust in the USSR) so that you can ask for hot water in the hotel and make your own. Soft drinks, fruit juices and mineral waters are obtainable everywhere.

Vodka is a drink the Russians treat with respect, and so should you. Legends that it never causes a hangover are just that—legends. But that doesn't mean you should sip it slowly and nervously: you should knock it back in one go and then savor the afterglow. With it, you nibble *zakuski* —Russians *never* drink vodka without eating something. Apart from the colorless, almost tasteless drink that we are used to, vodka in the USSR is often flavored and colored with herbs and spices for added interest. For instance, there's *zubrovka*, flavored with a particular kind of grass, *ryabinovka*, in which ashberries have been steeped, *starka*, the dark, smooth old vodka, *pertsovka*, with hot pepper, or cherry or lemon vodka. You can buy these readymade or take home a bottle of pure vodka and experiment with it yourself.

The Soviet Union also produces its own table wines, which are well worth trying. The best-known wine-producing areas are Georgia and the Crimea, where the grapes ripen through the long hot summers to be made into sweet full wines. You may well find some of them too sweet for your taste, but they go well with desserts. Russian champagne is reasonably good, too—an inexpensive luxury here. Beer in the USSR compares well with its Western counterpart and, if only from curiosity, you should try *kvas*—it's a refreshing and unusual drink on a hot day.

Finally, you should learn two words of Russian—*na zdorovie*—which means, literally, "to your health", but is the all-purpose toast. It's a phrase you may be saying and hearing quite a lot.

THE FACE
OF THE
SOVIET UNION

MOSCOW

Capital of Communism

Jerusalem, Mecca, Rome, Moscow—all are places of pilgrimage, whether the faithful come to pray at the Wailing Wall, circle the *kaaba*, be blessed by the Pope or file past Lenin's embalmed body in the great mausoleum of Red Square. Holy Moscow—that was the name for centuries and it has remained the symbolic heart of this vast country. Though Leningrad now bears the name of the founder of the modern state, by the spring of 1918 the Communist regime moved from what was then St. Petersburg to Moscow, which has been the center of government ever since.

Peter the Great, who built his city as a "window onto Europe", had deliberately turned his back on the old traditions; some three centuries later, equally deliberately, the young Soviet Republic transferred itself back to the heartland, for the former capital was too close to the besieged frontiers. And while Napoleon managed to occupy Moscow briefly, for 168 years since the great city has remained inviolate, defying the most violent onslaught, resisting the most determined foe. Moscow is more than a metropolis of some eight million people, more than the administrative, legislative, educational and cultural capital of the USSR—it is the embodiment of the Russian character and of Russian destiny.

It is the official capital not only of the Soviet Union, but of the Russian Soviet Federal Socialist Republic, the seat of the Central Committee of the Communist Party, the citadel of Soviet power, of the Supreme Soviet and all other federal government organs and offices.

The city lies in the central zone of the great Russian Plain, between the Rivers Volga and Oka, on the banks of the Moskva (a tributary of the Oka), some 360 feet above sea level. All the great rail lines radiate from it; it is the focal point of all air traffic. Centralization is an ancient Russian tradition which has been strengthened under Soviet rule, and whatever autonomy other republics and cities possess, they are all subordinate to Moscow. And while in the old times the oppressed and the dispossessed, sighing for justice, kept on saying, "The Czar, our Father, is far away," today, with modern communications, Moscow keeps the reins tight and the supervision constant.

Moscow's history covers about two thousand years, though the earliest annals set the date as 1147 A.D., which is the official "birthday" of the city (the eighth centenary was celebrated in 1947). The first, wooden Kremlin was erected by Prince Yuri Dolgoruky in 1156. By the 13th century it had become the center of the Moscow principality. Before very long it was destroyed by the Mongolian Tatar invasion, but the rule of Batu Khan did not last very long. In 1326 the foundations of the first stone building, the Uspensky Cathedral, were laid, and in 1380 it was from Moscow that the army of Prince Dimitri set out to defeat the Tatar forces at Kulikovo on the Don. The Kremlin rose to become both the ruling princes' residence and a fortress which withstood Mongolian, Lithuanian and other attacks.

By the 15th century, Moscow had established its paramount rule over the various Russian principalities and its urban area was over three square miles. A hundred years later it had grown into the capital of a strong and prosperous state, one of the largest in the world. A system of concentric fortifications with the Kremlin as its center enclosed Kitai-Gorod and Bely Gorod, new and large sections of the city with two other outer rings; the city had spread to over ten square miles. The Cathedral of the Archangel, St. Basil's Cathedral in the Red Square, the Great Bell Tower in the Kremlin were built and Russia's first printing plant was set up in 1563. And though civil war and Polish invasion ravaged the city in the first two decades of the 17th century, with Peter the Great a new era of stability and development began at the end of the 17th century—even though he favoured his own new capital on the Neva.

Moscow still remained the economic and cultural center of the country. The first university opened in 1775. By the end of the 18th century, the city had a population of 217,000 and a quarter of its buildings were of stone. Then came the Napoleonic invasion in 1812; the French occupation ended with a conflagration in which three out of every four buildings were gutted. But Moscow rose from its ruins; by 1840 it had a population of 350,000 and it was completely rebuilt. A major industrial and cultural center, its limits expanded to the so-called Kamer-Kollezhsky wall, with an area of 50 square miles.

In March 1918, Moscow became the capital of the new Soviet state. There followed years of much suffering and hardship, and the rebuilding and development of the capital were again interrupted by the Nazi invasion. Moscow, in the early stages of the war, was hard pressed; the enemy was stopped during the bitter winter of 1941 almost under the walls of the city and for many months Moscow was repeatedly attacked from the air. The post-war years saw the end of the Stalin era and the realization of the second urban plan, which emphasized housing. In 1960, the city limits were extended to the great outer ring of freeways and many villages and settlements were included in the urban area, while the district known as Yugo-Zapadny Rayon (Southwestern Region) was completed. Since then the city has continued its expansion and many new housing developments have been completed, while parts of central Moscow have been renewed and redesigned.

Exploring Moscow—The Kremlin

The nucleus of Moscow is the Kremlin and its Red Square. This is the oldest, most characteristic part of the Soviet capital, the site of its finest architectural monuments, and symbols of Russian and Soviet power. (Kreml means "citadel".)

We suggest you start your tour at the Metro station on Karl Marx Boulevard (Prospekt Marxa). From the corner of the Hotel Moskva, you'll have a general view of Red Square and two sides of the (roughly) pentagonal Kremlin. The first thing that you see is the red-brick battlemented walls, some 1½ miles in circumference and in some places 65 feet high, 10 to 20 feet thick. The walls are reinforced by 20 towers, five of which are also gates. In their present form they have stood practically unchanged since the end of the 15th century.

Cross under the square named after the 50th anniversary of the October Revolution to the northernmost point of the Kremlin, the so-called Sobakina Tower. More than 180 feet high, this was once an important part of the Kremlin's defenses. Its walls are more than 12 feet thick at the foundations; it was built so solidly because it concealed a secret well (important in time of siege) and also a way out to the Neglinnaya River, which now flows underground. Passing through a huge wrought-iron gate, we enter the Alexandrovsky Garden, which stretches along the northwestern wall. Not far from the entrance there is a grey obelisk, a memorial to the revolutionaries. Close to it stands the grave of the Unknown Soldier, dedicated on May 9, 1967, the 22nd anniversary of the victory over Nazism. The body resting under the red granite slabs is that of an unidentified Soviet soldier, one of those who, in the autumn of 1941, stopped the German attack at the village of Kryukuvo, outside Moscow. To the right of the grave there are six urns holding soil from the six "heroic cities", Odessa, Sevastopol, Volgograd, Kiev, Brest and Leningrad, which so stubbornly resisted the German onslaught.

Looking up from the garden to the Kremlin walls, we see a large yellow building, the Arsenal. Begun in 1701 by Peter the Great, it was finished only at the end of the 18th century; its present form dates from the early 19th century. The simple, yet impressive, two-floored building was originally intended to be an arsenal and museum; today it houses offices.

Walking along in the garden, we reach a double bastion linked by a stone bridge on nine pillars. The white outer bastion defended the approach to the bridge. The tower is called Kutafya, which in Old Slavonic means "clumsy or confused", and its shape is different from the other towers of the Kremlin. The massive inner tower, the Troitskaya (Trinity) is the tallest in the Kremlin wall, rising 240 feet above the garden. Its deep subterranean chambers were once used as prison cells. Napoleon's army entered the Kremlin in 1812 through this gate.

The Alexander Garden continues beyond the bridge and ends at the western corner of the Kremlin. You'll hear the noise of traffic beyond the iron railing. On the left a sloping path leads from the garden to the Kremlin wall. Here stands the pyramid-shaped Borovitsky Tower, rising to more than 150 feet; at its foot, a gate pierces the thick wall. The slits

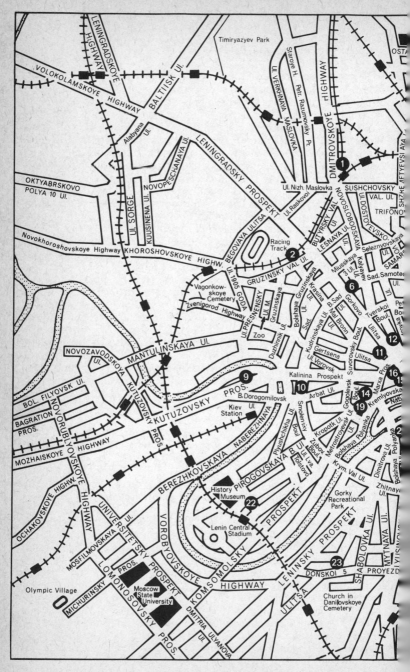

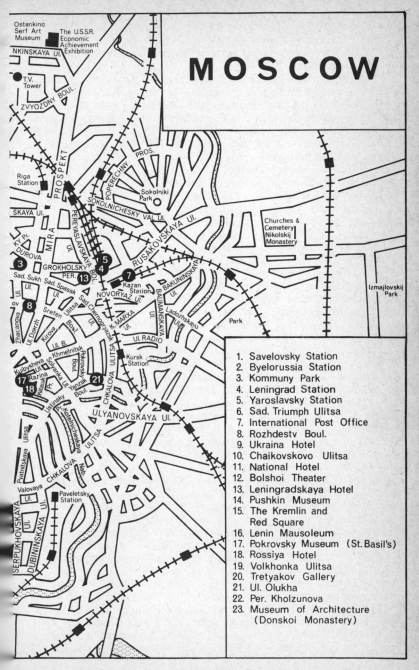

MOSCOW

1. Savelovsky Station
2. Byelorussia Station
3. Kommuny Park
4. Leningrad Station
5. Yaroslavsky Station
6. Sad. Triumph Ulitsa
7. International Post Office
8. Rozhdestv Boul.
9. Ukraina Hotel
10. Chaikovskovo Ulitsa
11. National Hotel
12. Bolshoi Theater
13. Leningradskaya Hotel
14. Pushkin Museum
15. The Kremlin and
    Red Square
16. Lenin Mausoleum
17. Pokrovsky Museum (St. Basil's)
18. Rossiya Hotel
19. Volkhonka Ulitsa
20. Tretyakov Gallery
21. Ul. Olukha
22. Per. Kholzunova
23. Museum of Architecture
    (Donskoi Monastery)

for the chains of the drawbridge are still visible beside the gate. Vehicular traffic passes through here now, with a separate entrance for pedestrians. This is one of the two pedestrian entrances (the other is through the Sobakina Tower), for touring the sights of the Kremlin. Both are open from 10 A.M. daily.

The road climbs steeply, as the Kremlin was built on a hill for defense reasons. A few yards away is the entrance of the famous Armory (oruzheinaya Palata), the oldest museum of the Kremlin and the place where the regalia and ambassadorial gifts were kept. Arms, armor and valuable objects from the country's chief armories and storehouses were gathered here. The present building was erected in 1849–1851, after the Great Kremlin Palace was completed.

Hall I has a large collection of Russian and foreign arms and armor, with a striking display of helmets (of which the earliest dates to the 13th century and is ascribed to Prince Yaroslav, father of Alexander Nevsky). Here, too, is the helmet of Prince Ivan, son of Ivan the Terrible, whom his father killed in a fit of rage when he was 28. Russian chainmail, battleaxes, maces, arquebuses, German and Dutch muskets, ceremonial armor and Russian and original sabers are also in this hall, together with the large Greek quiver belonging to Czar Alexei, his Oriental saber and a heavy golden mace presented to him by the Persian Shah Abbas. European suits of armor of the 15th-17th centuries, pistols and firearms complete the display. Admission to the Crown Jewel Room ("The Diamond Fund") is by special ticket.

In *Halls II and III* the work of goldsmiths and silversmiths of the 12th to 19th centuries is shown. In Hall II there is also a collection of Russian and foreign clocks and watches of the 16th to 19th centuries. The gilt copper watch in the shape of a book was Ivan the Terrible's and the wooden watch was made by Russian craftsmen in the 19th century. In Hall III there is a collection of 18th- to 20th-century jewelry, including a silver egg on the surface of which a map of the Trans-Siberian railroad is engraved; inside there is a golden clockwork model of a train with a platinum engine, windows of crystal and a headlight made of a tiny ruby.

Hall IV has vestments of priceless silk, velvet and brocade, embroidered with gold, encrusted with jewels and pearls, once worn by Czars, Patriarchs and Metropolitans.

Hall V is filled with foreign gold and silver objects, mostly ambassorial presents to the Czars.

Hall VI contains the regalia. Here are the thrones; the oldest, veneered with carved ivory, belonged to Ivan the Terrible. The throne of the first years of Peter I's reign, when he shared power with his older brother, Ivan, has two seats in front and one (hidden) in the back, where the Regent, their elder sister Sophia sat, and prompted the young boys to give the right answers to ambassadors' and others' queries. Another throne, covered with thin plates of gold and studded with 2,200 precious stones and pearls, was presented to Czar Boris Godunov by Shah Abbas of Persia; the throne of Czar Alexei (also of Persian make) is decorated with 876 diamonds and 1223 other stones. Among the crowns, the oldest is the "Cap of Monomakh", dating from the 13th century, refashioned in the 16th. Anna Ivanovna's Imperial Crown is encrusted with numerous diamonds and a large ruby. Russian and foreign orders and medals are also displayed here.

Hall IX holds court carriages, the oldest being an English one, reputed to have been presented by Queen Elizabeth I to Boris Godunov. The most attractive one is a French carriage painted by Boucher.

After visiting the Armory you'll see a courtyard on the left, closed off by a wrought-iron railing. The building on the left, adjoining the Armory, was once the home of the Czars. Today it is used for the visits of foreign heads of state. On the right is the complex of the Grand Kremlin Palace (Bolshoi Kremlyovsky Dvorets) that flanks the road.

Grand Kremlin Palace

This is a group of several buildings. The main section is the newest, built between 1838 and 1849 by the architects Chichagov, Gerasimov, Ton and others. Its 375-foot-long front faces south, overlooking the Moskva River. This was for centuries the site of the palaces of the Grand Dukes and Czars, but the immediate predecessor of the present building, dating from the 18th century, was badly damaged in the 1812 conflagration. This is the seat of the Supreme Soviets of the USSR and of the Russian Republic and is only open to visitors on special occasions.

The main entrance leads into a spacious marble hall with several marble chambers on the left. There used to be the imperial reception rooms; today they are the scene of the ceremonial signing of important state treaties.

A sweeping staircase leads to the first floor. Here is the great St. George's Hall, named after the highest military decoration of Czarist Russia, the Order of St. George, whose members are commemorated on marble tablets. They include Suvorov and Kutuzov, two famous generals. Eighteen spiral zinc columns topped by sculpted figures support the roof, the work of Ivan Vitali. Six immense gilt chandeliers and 3,000 lamps provide illumination. The parquet flooring is made up of 20 different kinds of wood. The hall is used for government and diplomatic receptions, youth balls and children's New Year celebrations.

Mirrored doors lead into the octagonal Vladimir Hall, the so-called "sacred ante-room". Its foundations were laid in 1487. A beautifully carved, gilt door opens from here into one of the most ancient chambers, the Palace of Facets (Granovitaya Palata), so called because of the shape of the stone facings on the side nearest Cathedral Square. Built in 1473–91 by the Italian architects Marco Ruffo and Pietro Antonio Solario, it is a large low-vaulted chamber, the roof supported in the middle by a rectangular pier. The iron ribs of the vaulting are gilded with inscriptions in Old Slavonic lettering.

From the Vladimir Hall there is access to the so-called Terem, or Golden Czarina Palace, also among the oldest parts of the Kremlin. It was in the gilt rooms of this palace that the Czarina received her official visitors. Another passage with wooden stairs and a gilt iron door leads to the Terem Palace. This was the residence of the early Czars; its furnishings have been preserved in the richly decorated vaulted chambers.

The Supreme Soviet's council chamber is the second largest in the Kremlin, with seating for 3,000. It was created by combining two existing halls. Here the party congresses were held until 1967, when the modern steel-and-glass Palace of Congresses, begun in 1961, was completed.

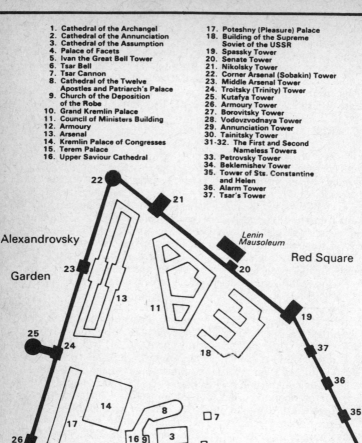

1. Cathedral of the Archangel
2. Cathedral of the Annunciation
3. Cathedral of the Assumption
4. Palace of Facets
5. Ivan the Great Bell Tower
6. Tsar Bell
7. Tsar Cannon
8. Cathedral of the Twelve
   Apostles and Patriarch's Palace
9. Church of the Deposition
   of the Robe
10. Grand Kremlin Palace
11. Council of Ministers Building
12. Armoury
13. Arsenal
14. Kremlin Palace of Congresses
15. Terem Palace
16. Upper Saviour Cathedral
17. Poteshny (Pleasure) Palace
18. Building of the Supreme
    Soviet of the USSR
19. Spassky Tower
20. Senate Tower
21. Nikolsky Tower
22. Corner Arsenal (Sobakin) Tower
23. Middle Arsenal Tower
24. Troitsky (Trinity) Tower
25. Kutafya Tower
26. Armoury Tower
27. Borovitsky Tower
28. Vodovzvodnaya Tower
29. Annunciation Tower
30. Tainitsky Tower
31-32. The First and Second
       Nameless Towers
33. Petrovsky Tower
34. Beklemishev Tower
35. Tower of Sts. Constantine
    and Helen
36. Alarm Tower
37. Tsar's Tower

Alexandrovsky

Garden

Lenin
Mausoleum

Red Square

The Kremlin

Kremlin   Embankment   Moskva River

MAP PRODUCTIONS LTD,

Near the council chamber are the former apartments of the imperial family. Their marble walls are covered with silk tapestries. There are statuary and china of great value and substantial inlaid furniture. The walls of the so-called Catherine Chamber are supported by green malachite columns valued at several million gold roubles.

Square of Cathedrals

After visiting the Grand Kremlin Palace, cross to the other side of the roadway and look down upon the Kremlin Garden, which is in the hollow below. The shady park has huge oaks and fir trees. If you return to the left side of the road, a few steps bring you to the ancient center of the Kremlin, the Square of Cathedrals. The paved square is framed by three large cathedrals in old Russian style, the massive bell tower and the Granovitaya Palace. The side-entrance of the Uspensky (Assumption) Cathedral is opposite. This is one of the oldest edifices of the Kremlin. The present building, which became Russia's principal church, follows the style of the Uspensky Cathedral at Vladimir. It was built in 1475–79 by the Italian architect Aristotle Fiorovanti, who had spent many years in Russia studying traditional architecture. Topped by five gilt domes, it is both austere and solemn, with a spacious interior, illuminated by two rows of narrow windows. It contains rare ancient paintings, including the ikon of the Virgin of Vladimir (the work of an 11th-century Byzantine artist) and the ikons of St. George (12th century) and the Trinity (14th century). The carved throne of Ivan the Terrible also stands here. The church is still open for religious services.

The smaller, single-steepled Rispolozheniye (Church of the Deposition of the Robe), built 1484–86 by master masons from Pskov, stands next to the Uspensky Cathedral, on the northwestern corner of the square. This was for a while the personal church of the Patriarchs of Moscow. It was rebuilt several times and restored to its original 15th-century condition by Soviet experts. In 1965 it was re-opened as a museum. The building boasts brilliant frescos dating from the mid-17th century covering all its walls, pillars and vaults. Its most precious treasure is the iconostasis by Nazary Istomin (1627).

The carved stone facade of the Granovitaya Palace stands on the west side, close to the Grand Kremlin Palace with the Blagoveshchensky (Annunciation) Cathedral next to it. This is a remarkable monument of Russian architecture, linking three centuries of art and religion. Its foundations were laid in the 14th century and a triangular brick church erected in the early Moscow style on them in the 15th century. Fire partly destroyed it; during the reign of Ivan the Terrible six new gilded cupolas were added when it was rebuilt. The 16th-century carved stone portals are particularly fine. Inside, look for a beautiful iconostasis and striking murals. These were painted in 1508 by the Russian artist Feodosy and his father and brother. The fine ikons of the second and third tiers of the iconostasis were painted by Andrei Rublyev, Theophanes the Greek and Prokhor of Gorodets. The floor is covered with polished tiles of agate jasper, given by the Shah of Persia. The cathedral served as the private chapel of the Czars. In the South Gallery, ikons and paintings are exhibited.

On its opposite side, the square of Cathedrals is bordered by the Cathedral of the Archangel. This is a five-domed edifice, built by the

Italian architect Aleviso Novi in 1505–09 to replace the original 14th-century church. Its ornate decorations have distinct elements of the Italian Renaissance. Between 1540 and 1700 this was the burial place of the Russian princes and Czars; their likenesses are painted on the walls above each of the 46 tombs, including those of Ivan Kalita (d. 1340) and Ivan the Terrible. The carved wooden iconostasis is 43 feet high. The ikon of the Archangel Michael is attributed to Andrei Rublyov. In 1953–55 some outstanding medieval murals, depicting battle scenes, were discovered beneath the layers of centuries. Other murals depict historical, religious and domestic scenes.

The tallest building of the square, and of the Kremlin, is the Ivan the Great Bell-Tower, which forms a splendid ensemble with the adjoining buildings. The octagonal main tower with its 329 steps is 263 feet high—three feet higher than the Hotel Rossia across the Square, in accordance with a tradition that the Tower must be the tallest building in Moscow. The Bell Tower is one of the most unusual structures built in the 16th century. The first tower was erected in 1505–8, the second in 1532–43. The first was rebuilt in 1600, when it was crowned with an onion-shaped dome covered with gilded copper. Originally it served as a watchtower; from it Moscow and its environs could be observed within a radius of 20 miles. The first tower has 21 bells, the largest weighing 64 tons. Both towers together have 52 bells, the largest weighing 70 tons. The Czar Bell, standing on a stone pedestal nearby, is the biggest bell in the world; cast in the Kremlin in 1733–35, it weighs more than 200 tons, is 20 feet high and 22 feet in diameter. The basreliefs on the outside show Czar Alexei Mikhailovich and the Czarina Anna Ivanovna. Not far from the Bell is the Czar Cannon, with the largest caliber of any gun in the world, cast in bronze in 1586 by Andrei Chokhov. It weighs 40 tons, its length is 17 ft. 6 in., and its caliber is 35 inches in a barrel six inches thick. It bears the image of Czar Fyodor Ivanovich. Its present carriage was cast in 1835, purely for display purposes.

Leaving the Czar Bell, let's walk around the large square into which we have emerged. It contains the Church of the Twelve Apostles and the Patriarch's Residence. The Church was built in 1655–56 and served as the Patriarch's private church. The buildings now house (since 1963) the Museum of 17th-Century Applied Art; the exhibits were taken from the surplus of the State Armory Museum and include books, items of tableware, clothing and household linen.

The Seat of Government

Passing the Cathedral of the Twelve Apostles and the former Patriarch's Palace we arrive at the most recent building of the Kremlin, the Palace of Congresses. A glass and aluminum building, it was added to the Kremlin complex in 1961 and completed six years later, much of it underground to avoid clashing with the old Kremlin architecture and ruining the skyline. Its vast stage is fully equipped for opera and ballet, concerts and recitals and wide-screen film projection. Simultaneous translation apparatus is built into the seats. Above the auditorium there is a banqueting hall for 2,500 people. The covered promenade circling this hall provides a splendid view. In addition there are more than 800 different premises—halls and lobbies, conference rooms, accommodations for the diplomatic corps and the press.

Beyond the palace you'll see the façade of the Arsenal, with the French cannon captured in 1812 by Kutuzov's forces.

On the other side of the square stands a two-storied, classical building with a central dome. This is the Council of Ministers, once the Senate, an 18th-century building by Matvei Kazakov. It was in this building that Lenin lived and worked; his fourth-floor study, with its original furniture and books, is sometimes open to the public. Next to it is the hall where Lenin chaired the meetings of the Council of People's Commissars and other committees. Lenin's apartment can be reached by a corridor from this hall. Four medium-sized and simply-equipped rooms have also been preserved in their original condition.

Next to the Council of Ministers Building is the Kremlin Theater, also in classical style. Walking past it, we reach the gate of the Spassky Tower, the finest and most ornate of the 20 bastions built to defend the main entrance of the Kremlin. Designed originally in 1491 by the Milanese architect Solario, it was given its present form in the middle of the 17th century. Rising to almost 210 feet, it has an ornamental clock, made in 1851–52, with a carillon marking every quarter hour.

Red Square

Near the Spassky Gate is a pedestrian exit into Red (Krasnaya) Square. Turning right along the descending broad road, we stop briefly on the Moskvoretsky Bridge over the Moskva River. The center of the bridge offers an excellent view of the southern part of the Kremlin; the garden behind the tall, crenelated wall with towers and bastions, the façade of the Grand Kremlin Palace, the forest of the gold-and-silver spires of the cathedrals make striking subjects for photographs.

Return now up the slope to Red Square. Its history reaches back to the 15th century when it was known as the *Torg* (Slavonic for "market place"). In the 16th century it became a ceremonial place. The Lobnoye Mesto (the elevated round platform in front of St. Basil's Cathedral) was built in 1534; from here the imperial *ukases* (decrees) were proclaimed and later it also served as a scaffold. The present-day appellation of the square dates from the 17th century, though in the usage of those days *krasnaya* meant "beautiful" and not "red". For centuries it remained the center of Moscow life, and since the establishment of the Soviet regime it has been the venue of the November 7 and May Day military parades.

Apart from the Kremlin, the oldest building in Red Square is the Cathedral of the Intercession (Cathedral of St. Basil the Blessed, or Pokrovsky Cathedral). Built in 1555–60 on the orders of Ivan the Terrible by the Russian architects Barma and Postnik, it is a unique achievement—a combination of nine churches. The central structure is 107 feet high, surrounded by eight tower-like chapels linked by an elevated gallery, and each with a differently patterned exterior. To commemorate the conquest of the Tatar city of Kazan, Czar Ivan dedicated each of the eight subsidiary churches to the saints on whose days he had won battles. Today the Cathedral is a museum. The antechamber provides a history of the building, the story of its construction and specimens of the materials used. In the 16th century, the crypt became the state treasury; in 1595 two nobles decided to rob it, first diverting the city guards by starting fires at different suburban spots. Their plan failed and they were executed. The Cathedral contains the iconostasis of the Trinity Church, the famous *Entry into Jerusalem* ikon in the church named after it, and some magnificent decorations in the Church of St. Alexander of Svir. In 1588 a church was built close to the cathedral and dedicated to a Muscovite holy man named Basil who had considerable influence over Ivan the Terrible. It was his name that was finally given to the Cathedral complex.

Near the cathedral on the lower corner of Red Square along the Moskva River stands the Rossiya Hotel, a huge block whose central tower houses luxury apartments.

In the small garden outside St. Basil's Cathedral stands the monument to Kuzma Minin, a Nizhni-Novgorod butcher, and Prince Dmitry Pozharsky, who liberated Moscow in October 1612 from Polish-Lithuanian occupation. The work of Ivan Martos, it was erected in 1818, paid for by public subscription.

Red Square is bordered on the east by two look-alike buildings. Before the Revolution they housed commercial offices and shops. Today one is the home of GUM, the state department store.

At the north end of the Square is the History Museum, built in typical Moscow style in 1874–83. Originally the first building of the Moscow University, the Museum, with 300,000 exhibits, now houses the largest collection of historical material and documents about the origin and history of the peoples of the Soviet Union from their beginnings to the end of the 19th century. It is the oldest museum in Moscow and its unique and fascinating collections include coins and medals, ancient implements, furnishings, manuscripts and early hand-printed books (including 11th-century Greek and 13th-century Byzantine works), Novgorod birch-bark scrolls dating from the 10th century, samples of the arms of Kiev Rus, robes of Ivan the Terrible, the iron cage in which the captured Pugachov, leader of the 1773–75 peasant uprising, was brought to Moscow, and Napoleon's bed which he abandoned when leaving Russia. The museum is engaged in ambitious research work, sponsoring historical and archeological expeditions to various parts of the country.

The center of Red Square is the Lenin Mausoleum, sited beside the Kremlin Wall between the Spassky and Nikolsky Towers. It contains the embalmed body of the founder of the Communist Party and the Soviet state. The opening hours are Tuesdays, Wednesdays, Thursdays and Saturdays from 10 to 2 and on Sundays from 10 to 6. There are always long queues, but escorted foreign tourists usually receive precedence. The line starts outside the History Museum. Behind the mausoleum is a cemetery with the remains of many leading Soviet politicians, including Sverdlov, Frunze, Dzerzhinsky, Kalinin and Stalin. The urns set in the Kremlin wall contain the ashes of Gorky, Orzhonikidze, Kirov, the astronauts Gagarin and Komarov, and others. From the balcony of the mausoleum Soviet leaders watch the great Moscow parades.

From Red Square you'll have an excellent view of the Kremlin Wall, including the Czar's Tower (1680), the Senate Tower, the Nikolsky Tower and the corner tower of the Arsenal.

The Heart of Moscow

Start your exploration from the metro station in the basement of the Hotel Moskva. The southeastern front of the hotel faces the Ploshchad Revolyutsii (Revolution Square). Opposite is the approach to Red Square, with the History Museum on the right, and another, similar building on the left. Before the Revolution this was the building of the Moscow Duma (council). In 1936 it became the Central Lenin Museum. Opened in 1936, its 22 halls contain many thousands of exhibits, covering the main periods in the life and work of the founder of the Soviet State. Among the exhibits are Lenin's personal belongings—his desk, with secret drawers, a coat with bullet-holes (after an attempted assassination) and his car. Newsreels from 1917–24, in which he appears and speaks, are shown.

The metro station next to the museum is linked by an underground passage with our starting point. Behind it there are some remnants of a red brick wall, similar to that of the Kremlin. This is part of the wall of the so-called Kitai-Gorod, built in the 16th century by the architect Petrok Maly. Kitai-Gorod, adjoining the Kremlin, was one of the oldest quarters of Moscow; from the 14th and 15th century it was a center of commerce and contained many noblemen's mansions.

Climbing the staircase that crosses this wall and through an arcaded house, we reach this former merchants' and artisans' district. Three parallel streets, the October 25th, leading into Red Square, the Kuibyshev, and Stepan Razin, with numerous cross-streets and lanes, occupy the site. The great merchant houses that developed in the 19th and the early 20th centuries built their headquarters and warehouses here and there are still numerous shops in this quarter.

One of the few surviving original houses was the home of the first Russian printing works at No. 15 October 25th Street, founded in 1563 by Ivan Fyodorov, at the request of Ivan the Terrible and rebuilt in the 17th century on the site of an earlier wooden building. Its carved stone ornaments and doorway are remarkable. Another surviving monument is the lovely Trinity Church in Nikitniki (1635–53), now a museum with murals by Simon Ushakov (Razin Street, Nikitnikov Pereulok). Most of these buildings now house public offices and institutions.

If we now go along Vetoshny Street, which runs parallel with Red Square, past the GUM department store, we'll reach Kuibyshev Street. Turning left on it, we soon arrive in busy Nogin Square. On the right stands the building of the Central Committee of the Communist Party of the Soviet Union. In the park opposite there is an octagonal tower-like monument, commemorating the Russian soldiers who fell in the Battle of Plevna in the Russo-Turkish war (1877). Across the street there is a huge block, housing the Polytechnical Museum. Built in the 1870s, its 55 halls and more than 20,000 exhibits illustrate the achievements of Soviet science and technology, and there are working models of the latest machines and machine tools. It has a large technical library.

The Innermost Ring

Moscow's basic plan consists of concentric rings bordered by the main boulevards. The innermost ring is a complex of squares and short thoroughfares which starts on the banks of the Moskva, near Nogin Square, and returns to the river not far from the walls of the Kremlin. Exploring this inner ring, we next reach Novaya (New) Square. Here stands the Museum of the History and Reconstruction of Moscow. Housed in the former Church of St. John the Baptist, dating from 1825, the museum was founded in 1896 and provides an outline of the history of Moscow's development, showing the city's role in different periods of Russian history. The reconstruction section deals with the modernization of public services, building programs and plans for the future.

A short distance away is another circular "square" named after Felix Dzerzhinsky, the Soviet revolutionary leader (1877–1926) whose statue stands in its center. From the far side of the square two streets start. On the right, next to the Polytechnical Museum, Kirov Street leads northeast almost to Komsomol Square. On the left, next to a large department store, Dzerzhinsky Street runs up to Mira Prospekt, the Permanent Exhibition of Economic Achievements and the Olympic indoor Stadium and swimming pool. The department store is Detsky Mir (Children's World). It serves the Pioneer movement and sells everything from baby clothes to camping gear.

From the western side of Dzerzhinsky Square the wide Marx Prospekt crosses a number of squares, among them Sverdlov Square and the one named for the 50th Anniversary of the October Revolution. The Hotel Berlin stands on the right-hand side of the avenue; on the left is the statue of the first Russian printer, Ivan Fyodorov. Across the road is the beginning of Neglinnaya Street, with the central building of the State Bank close by.

Marx Prospekt now reaches Sverdlov Square, which is linked to Revolution Square. Karl Marx's statue by Kerbel stands in the center of the square, carved from a 200-ton block of granite on the spot and unveiled in 1964. Opposite stands the Bolshoi (Big) Theater, the oldest in Moscow. Formerly known as the Great Imperial Theater, it was completely rebuilt after a fire in 1854 and now seats 2,155 people. Its ballet company is justly world famous; there are many Russian and foreign works in its opera repertory; its orchestra is also outstanding. The Bolshoi's building is remarkable architecturally, with its monumental colonnade topped by a quadriga of bronze horses. The color scheme of the interior is red and gold.

To the right is the fine building of the Maly (Small) Theater, with the statue of the satirist Ostrovsky in front of it. The Maly, formerly the Little Imperial Theater, is famous for its staging of Russian classics, especially those of Ostrovsky. Founded almost 150 years ago, it was once called by Gorky "the Russian people's university". It seats over 1,000. The associated studio theater in Bolshaya Ordunka Street is for more intimate productions.

Behind the Maly Theater the art nouveau outline of the GUM Department Store forms an interesting contrast. Between GUM and the Bolshoi, Petrovka Street begins, one of the main commercial thoroughfares. It has many specialist shops and a department store. Petrovka Street leads to the Hotel Budapest and its restaurant.

To the left of the Bolshoi Theater in Sverdlov Square is the Central Children's Theater. Pushkin Street starts just behind it, with the Operetta Theater at Number 6, and the Stanislavsky and Nemirovich-Danchenko Musical Theater is further along. This ballet and opera theater shows classical and modern works in both genres, as well as light operettas.

On the corner of Karl Marx Prospekt and Pushkin Street the *Dom Soyuzov* (House of the Trade Unions), painted green, with a classical façade, is the work of the distinguished architect Kazakov. The Dom Soyuzov was once a club for the nobility. Its famous hall of columns is one of Moscow's most beautiful halls and has seen many historic occasions—Lenin's lying-in-state, for instance. Today festival gatherings and concerts are held here. Next to the House of the Trade Unions is the building of the State Planning Committee, while across Marx Prospekt stands the 14-storied Hotel Moskva.

An underpass leads under Gorky Street, perhaps the best-known Moscow thoroughfare. Here, also, Marx Prospekt again broadens into a square. This is named after the 50th anniversary of the October Revolution. On the corner of Gorky Street and the square stand the twin buildings of the National and Intourist Hotels, the former erected in 1903 and the newer, 21-floor Intourist opened in 1970 with a dozen restaurants, cafés and bars. Walking along the right we reach the Lomonosov University building (Russia's oldest university), another design by Kazakov, dating from the end of the 18th century. The more recent university complex is on the Lenin Hills.

Passing Herzen Street (which contains the famous Moscow Conservatory, the Mayakovsky Theater and the Zoological Museum, with its huge collection of thousands of mammals, birds, amphibians and reptiles, and almost a million insects), we find on the other side of the square the former imperial riding school, the Manezh (Manège), since 1957 an exhibition hall. Built in the early 19th century, its huge roof has only the walls, not a single internal column, to support it.

Arriving at the busy corner of Kalinin Prospekt, we have a good view of the central building of the Lenin Library, one of the largest in the world. The most recent part, by Vladimir Shchuko and Vladimir Gelfreikh, was built in 1939–40. Bronze busts of outstanding writers and scientists stand in the niches along the façade. The portico, supported by square black pillars, is approached by a wide ceremonial staircase. Beyond this new building, on a small rise, stands the fine old building of the library, known as Pashkov House, designed by Vasily Bazhenov, one of Russia's greatest architects, and erected in 1784–86. Once the home of a rich family, its graceful, light and harmonious composition makes it one of Moscow's most attractive buildings.

Next is the mouth of Frunze Street, which leads steeply to the Borovitsky Gate of the Kremlin and the Great Stone Bridge of the Moskva River. Continuing straight ahead, however, we reach the Volkhonka Road that takes us to the Pushkin Museum, standing in the middle of a small park. Founded by Professor Tsvetayev, the museum was supported originally by private donations. The present building dates from 1895–1912 and was first known as Alexander III's Museum. It is the largest museum in the Soviet Union after the Leningrad Hermitage. There is a fine collection of ancient Egyptian art; Greece and Rome are well represented, though mostly by copies. The art gallery has works by most of Europe's greatest painters—Botticelli, Rembrandt, Rubens, Van Dyck, and Constable among them; a vast selection of French pictures from Poussin and Watteau to Cezanne, Gauguin and Matisse; there are also representative canvases by Picasso.

At the end of Volkhonka Road, on the left side, is one of the largest swimming pools in Europe, between the street and the quay of the Moskva River. It is divided into several pools for training, competitions, diving, etc. Its heated pool is open in winter; you reach it from the changing rooms through covered tunnels.

We have reached the end of the ring of squares and streets enclosing the center of the city. Here the tourist, if tired, can board the metro at Kropotkinskaya station. But it is also possible to return along the Moskva River, under the Kremlin walls, to our starting point near Nogin Square, taking a brief look at the island in the River Moskva. Beside the Great Stone Bridge, on the island, stand the Estradny (Variety) Theater and the Udarnik, one of the most popular cinemas. The island is laid out as a park; there are several interesting old houses, former noble mansions, including the British Embassy. At the far end of the island, near the Moskvoretsky Bridge which spans the river from the bottom of Red Square, we find the Hotel Bucharest. Crossing the bridge, we reach the Zamoskvorechye (Beyond-the-Moskva River) district which was inhabited mainly by merchants before the Revolution. There are few interesting architectural sights here, but not far from the river bank stands the massive Soviet Radio building behind the Novokuznetskaya metro station and the Tretyakov Gallery.

This is Moscow's finest art gallery and is devoted to the history of Russian art. The foundations of the collection were laid in 1856 by the brothers Pavel and Sergei Tretyakov, who made a gift of it to the nation in 1892. The exhibits illustrate the whole development of fine arts from unique 11th-century mosaics to the works of contemporary artists: more than 5,000 paintings, 3,000 works of ancient Russian art, about 900 sculptures and 30,000 drawings and engravings. They include the works of Andrei Rublyov, the brilliant 14th-15th-century ikon painter, Alexander Ivanov's *Apparition of Christ,* the canvases of Ilya Repin and Vasily Surikov, the landscapes of Isaac Levitan, Arkhip Kuinji, Alexei Savrasov and Vasily Polenov, the marine painter Ivan Aivazovsky, the portraits of Ivan Kramskoi and characteristic examples of "socialist realism". Examples of the work of the constructivists are, however, conspicuously absent.

Among the sculptures there are a few by Mark Antokolsky, the great 19th-century realist, and works of Sergei Konenkov and Anna Golubkina. The large section devoted to Soviet art features many examples of contemporary painters, sculptors and graphic artists, both traditionalists and, added to the display in more recent years, many examples of the art of the experimentalists.

The Tretyakov has been overcrowded for years and a new Art Gallery of the USSR is about to open on Krymskaya Embankment, opposite Gorky Park. It is huge, with 150 display halls, lecture rooms and workshops.

Down Gorky Street

For our next walk we can start again from the Hotel Moskva, in a more or less northerly direction. Gorky Street was given its present form in the middle thirties, during the first plan of reconstruction, though it has been an important route for centuries—the line of the road that led from the Kremlin to ancient Tver, today's Kalinin. Until the rebuilding, Tverskaya Street was narrow and twisting, lined in places with wooden houses. Today's Gorky Street is a broad, modern boulevard, with considerable traffic and many attractive shops.

Starting on the left-hand side, from the building of the Central Planning Committee, we see the tall block of the Hotel National and the Yermolova Theater (named after a famous actress). At the corner of the first major side street stands the very busy Central Telegraph Office, with a striking semi-circular entrance and a large, electrically-lit, constantly revolving globe. Glancing right into the side street we see a small green building—the Moscow Arts Theater, famous for its productions of the Russian classics, Chekhov in particular, and for major versions of foreign works. Founded in 1898 by the celebrated actor and director Konstantin Stanislavsky (1863–1938) and Nemirovich-Danchenko (1858–1943), here were given the first presentations of Chekhov's and Gorky's plays and here Stanislavsky developed his theories into "the Stanislavsky Method", based on the realistic traditions of the Russian theater. After the production of Chekhov's *The Seagull,* they chose this bird as their emblem. (A new, modern Moscow Art Theater with a seating capacity of 2,000 was opened in 1973 on nearby Tverskoi Boulevard, near Stanislavsky's former home.)

Another short stretch brings us to the small Soviet Square. On the right, at the back of the square, stands the Institute of Marxism-Leninism with Lenin's statue, by S. Merkurov, in front of it; closer to Gorky Street is the monument of Prince Dolgoruky, the founder of Moscow, an equestrian statue, the work of the sculptors Orlov, Antropov and Stamm, erected in 1954 to commemorate the 800th anniversary of the city.

Opposite this monument stands the building of the Moscow Town Council (Mossoviet), built at the end of the 18th century by M. F. Kazakov as a governor's palace. It was moved to widen the street. Next to the Town Council is the bookshop *Druzhba* (Friendship), specializing in publications of other Communist countries.

Passing the Hotel Central on the right, we reach the mouth of Stanislavsky Street (on the left), which contains the memorial museum of the great Russian stage director. Next we reach the so-called Yeliseyevsky Store (officially known as No. 1. Gastronom), which specializes in Russian and foreign food products.

Our next stop is Pushkin Square, where Moscow's first outer ring, the Bulvar (Boulevard), crosses Gorky Street. The boulevard is divided by a wide green strip in the middle. On the right hand, the Bulvar widens into an impressive park. A bronze statue of the great Russian poet after whom the square is named stands at its entrance. It is the work of the sculptor Opekushin, and was erected by public subscription in 1880. Summer or winter, fresh flowers on the pedestal prove that the poet's admirers are still ardent and numerous. There is a red granite fountain behind the monument, illuminated on summer evenings.

On the right, Pushkin Square is bordered by the huge Rossia cinema, inaugurated in 1961 for the Second International Moscow Film Festival.

Pushkin Square is also the home of *Izvestia* (News), the largest Soviet daily (circulation, 8½ million copies); the editorial offices were built in 1927. Behind the Rossia cinema are the offices of the Novosti (APN) press agency and nearby *Trud* (Labor), the newspaper of the trade unions, is edited.

Continuing along Gorky Street, we reach the railings of the former English Club, once the social center of Moscow aristocracy. Built by Giliardi in 1787, it now houses the exhibitions of the Central Revolutionary Museum. A little further away is another 18th-century building, the Central Ophthalmic Clinic. It is close to the Hotel Minsk, opened in the middle 1960's.

The grand boulevard of Moscow, the Sadoyava Ring, crosses Gorky Street at Mayakovsky Square. Traffic passes here by a tunnel under

Gorky Street and there is an underpass for pedestrians. Mayakovsky's statue by Kibalnikov, erected in 1958, stands in the center of the square.

Mayakovsky Square is one of the centers of Moscow's cultural life. The Tchaikovsky Concert Hall stands on the corner of Gorky Street; seating 1,500, it was opened in 1940. Nearby is the Mossoviet Theater, and on the far side of the square, the Sovremennik (Contemporary) Youth Theater. The tall tower of the Hotel Peking rises off to the left.

Gorky Street ends in the square of the Byelorussian Railway Terminus. Vera Mukhina's Gorky monument stands here. The railway station itself is built in Russian style, with the metro next to it. From here, you can return to the center either by the subway or by a trolley-bus. You can also take a trolley-bus down Leningradsky Prospekt, one of the fast, modern routes of the Soviet capital, divided into six lanes and 118 yards wide.

On the right, the second cross-street is Pravda Street, where you'll see the editorial offices and printing works of *Pravda* (Truth), the second largest-selling daily paper in the Soviet Union (7 million copies). The next corner is marked by the Hotel Sovietskaya. Here, too, is one of the most important sports centers of Moscow. On the right are the Dynamo Stadium (60,000 seats) and the covered swimming pool; the wide avenue branching to the left leads to the race course. The Cycling Stadium and the Pioneer Stadium are also in the vicinity.

A few hundred yards more brings us to the striking, crenelated Petrovsky Palace, one of the most characteristic creations of the celebrated Kazakov. Today it houses the Zhukovsky Academy of Aeronautical Engineers, whose students include the Soviet cosmonauts. Two monuments outside the academy commemorate Soviet achievements in the conquest of space—one of them, erected in 1962, is the work of G. Postnikov, the other, the statue of Konstantin Tsiolkovsky, "the father of space travel", is by S. Merkurov. Two high-rise buildings the other side of the street: one is the Ministry of Civil Aviation (Aeroflot), the other Aeroflot transit hotel for air passengers.

At the next metro station along Leningradsky Prospekt, we reach one of the newer quarters of Moscow, the Novopeschannaya district. This is a housing project surrounded with parks and gardens and built in the early 1950's.

After the Sokol metro station, Leningradsky Prospekt curves right. The left-hand street leads to Tushino, with its airfield for amateur fliers, and then on to Volokolamsk. Keeping right, still on Leningradsky Prospekt, we can take a trolley-bus to the Khimki Harbor, the starting-point for Volga cruises. The station building is in the shape of the hull of a ship. The modern motorway continues past new housing developments, crosses the River Moskva and, more than 20 miles from the center, reaches Sheremetyevo, the international airport.

The Kalinin and Kutuzov Prospekts

One of central Moscow's most modern avenues is Kalinin Prospekt, linking the Kremlin through Arbat Square to the Moskva River. It can be divided into two sections. The first leads from the Karl Marx Prospekt to Arbat Square. This was formerly known as Novodvizhenskaya Street and has retained some of its pre-revolutionary character. The second section, built in the 1960's, is a completely new thoroughfare, driven through the former maze of narrow streets and alleys. The pre-revolutionary stretch has now been widened and modernized and Kalinin Prospekt is now completed, the showcase of the Soviet capital.

Starting from the Kutafya Tower of the Kremlin (with the Riding School on the right) we cross Karl Marx Prospekt at the Lenin Library. The first important building, on the left, is the Shchusev Museum of Architecture. The building, by M. F. Kazakov, dates from the 18th century; between 1921 and 1924 it housed the Central Committee of the Communist Party. A little further on, the Central Military Department Store stands on the right. This was established before the First World War; it is open to civilians as well.

The next building of note on the right-hand side is the headquarters of the Association of Soviet Friendship Societies, which also occupies the adjoining house, called the House of Friendship. The latter was once the home of the wealthy industrialist Morozov and was designed by V. A. Marizin at the end of the 19th century. It is almost an anthology of interior decoration styles, ranging from imitation Tudor to classical Greek and Baroque. This is the regular meeting place of foreign visitors and Soviet artists and writers. Opposite these two buildings, several departments of the Soviet Foreign Ministry occupy a large house in classical style; here press conferences for foreign correspondents are usually held.

Beyond Arbat Square, nine tall buildings, rising to 23, 24 or 25 stories, mark the start of the second section of Kalinin Prospekt. Before reaching them, there are two other interesting landmarks on the corner of Arbat Square, however. On the left is the Praga restaurant complex, which contains several restaurants, banqueting and reception rooms. The right-hand corner building is the Dom Svyazi, the House of Communications, containing a very large post office and the largest telephone exchange in Moscow, together with video-phone studios for transmissions to other Soviet cities.

Next to the Post Office building is the small 17th-century church of St. Simon Stylites, with its cluster of domes.

On the right-hand side of Kalinin Prospekt there are five apartment blocks, each of 23 stories and containing 280 units. The ground floor and the first floor of these buildings are occupied by the *Malachite Box* jewelry shop, the *Ivushka Café,* a chemist shop, the record shop called *Melodiya* and the *Sireny* (Lilac) perfume shop. Here, too, you find in a separate building the *Dom Knigi* (House of the Book), the largest bookshop in the Soviet Union, and the *October Cinema* together with a large bakery and pastry shop.

On the left-hand side of the Kalinin Prospekt, there are four 25-storied office buildings, accommodating different industrial ministries. A glassed-in elevated gallery links them and contains specialized stores, service enterprises and places of entertainment. They include the *Café Valday,* the *Novo-arbatsky Gastronom* (one of the largest, partly self-service food shops in the USSR), a shop for philatelists, a large newspaper kiosk, an excellent flower shop, the *Transagenstvo* travel bureau, the *Pechora* restaurant and café (mostly frequented by young people), which has a popular jazz ensemble, the *Moskvichka* dress shop, the *Charodeika* (Witch), a fashionable hairdresser, and the *Institut Krasoti* beauty salon. There is also a photographer's studio, the self-service restaurant *Angara,* the photo and amateur film shop *Jupiter,* the *Sintetika* (selling synthetic fabrics and dresses), the *Metelitsa* pastry shop (with a summer terrace), the *Vesna* (Spring) gift shop, a take-away food shop, the *Café Biryusa* and finally, the *Restaurant Arbat,* which has a nightly cabaret.

After crossing Tchaikovsky Street, Kalinin Prospekt begins to descend towards the Moskva River. Not far from the river, on the right-hand side, we find the new headquarters of the Council of Mutual Economic Assistance, built in the 1960's. It houses the executive committee, secretariat and offices of COMECON, the East European equivalent of the EEC. Adjoining it is the twelve-storied Hotel Mir (Peace), which houses mainly foreign employees and guests of COMECON. Nearby is the recently completed palace of the Russian Soviet Federal Republic's Council of Ministers.

Passing across the bridge towards the Hotel Ukraine, we reach the Kutuzov Prospekt. Some 180 feet wide, it runs west, past new apartment houses and office buildings. Soon you reach the Borodino Panorama, with the triumphal arch commemorating Kutuzov's victory over Napoleon in 1812, and Kutuzov's wooden hut. It was in Kutuzov's hut that the Russian Council of War, headed by Field-Marshall Mikhail Kutuzov, decided that the army would retreat from Moscow. The painting by Kivshenko (1880) shows the Council in session. The Battle Panorama is housed in a cylindrical building, built in 1962 to commemorate the 150th anniversary of the Battle of Borodino between Napoleon's Grand Armée and the Russian forces. The huge canvases were painted by Roubaud (1856–1912) in Munich. The Panorama stands on a small rise, the Poklon hill. Kutuzov Prospekt continues towards the suburb of Fili-Mazilovo.

Our next excursion is to explore the Moscow of the early nineteenth century. We start from the Kropotinskaya metro station on the bank of the Moskva River, southwest of the Kremlin. From here, the semi-circle of the Soviet capital's lesser ring-road starts off, northwesterly, then curves eastwards and south finally to reach the river bank again after several miles, close to the mouth of the Yauza River and east of the Kremlin.

The Bulvar (Boulevard) was built on the site of the wall enclosing the former White City (Bely Gorod). Running along its center is a broad strip of trees and flowers, playgrounds and benches.

Leaving the metro station, we see the large open swimming pool to the east. Several roads converge in a little square. Volkhonka Street leads towards the Kremlin; two others start opposite, Metrostroyevskaya (Metro Builders) and Kropotkin Street. The former crosses, farther south, Zubovsky Boulevard by a high bridge and runs into the Komsomolsky Prospekt, which, in turn, leads to the Lenin Stadium.

These two streets and the river form the southern end of one of the most interesting quarters of Moscow, stretching roughly to Zubovskaya Square, while on the west it is bordered by the Sadovaya (Boulevard Ring). In the 18th and 19th centuries this was predominantly the quarter of court nobility, where they built their small private mansions, mostly single-storied. Alexander Herzen, the writer and philosopher, compared it with the St-Germain quarter of Paris.

The streets to the left of the Bulvar have many houses marked with plaques showing that eminent writers, artists and thinkers have resided in them. At No. 4 Gagarin Street (near the Kropotkin metro station), Pushkin lived for a while; the revolutionary poet Ryleev also stayed in the same street. At No. 25 Sivtsev Vrazhek Street, which is the next cross-street of the Bulvar. Herzen had his home; it was here that the Czarist police arrested him. When he returned from his exile, he moved into the neighboring house.

The first section of the Bulvar bears the name of Gogol. A pleasant walk takes you to Arbat Square, the center of the quarter, where the writer's statue stands. The large block of the Ministry of Defense catches the eye. There are two metro stations in the square, with the Khudoz-hestvenny Cinema beside them. The Kalinin Prospekt crosses Arbat Square, and here Arbat Street, one of the oldest thoroughfares of Moscow, begins. In the 16th century, this was the quarter of court artisans; the street names still recall their names—from Plotnikov (Carpenter) to Serebryany (Silversmith) and Kalachny (Pastrycook). Early in the 19th century it became the district of the aristocracy, while a century later it was a favorite shopping street, a role which has recently been revived. The whole area is now under a preservation order and redevelopment follows strict guidelines. In contrast to the Kalinin Prospekt, the Arbat has conserved its picturesque character. At number 26 is the Vakhtan-gove Theater, named after Stanislavsky's pupil, Evgeny Vakhtangov (1883–1922)—an excellent traditional theater. Arbat Street continues down to the Bouvlevard Ring; at the corner is the skyscraper of the Foreign Ministry.

Getting on a trolley-bus on the corner of Arbat and Suvorov Boule-vard, go to the next stop, which will be the so-called Nikitskiye Vorota (Gate), where Herzen Street crosses the Bulvar. Setting out to the right, we pass the famous Mayakovsky Theater, and a short walk brings us to the Moscow Conservatory. Alexei Tolstoy Street branches off on the left, with the memorial museum of the writer (nephew of Leo). The small square contains the statue of the botanist Timiryazev (1843–1920).

The next stop north along the Bulvar is opposite the Pushkin Theater, which brings us to Pushkin Square. Take a tram from the far end of the square if you wish to explore the Bulvar further. Two stops along is Trubnaya Square. On the left, the Tsvetnoy Boulevard branches off at a right angle. A few yards along stands the Mir Panoramic Cinema's circular building with the permanent home of the Moscow Circus next to it.

The Circus, a very popular form of entertainment with the Russians, is well worth a visit. It has a long, varied and spectacular program which changes every year and often includes an appearance by Popov, the famous clown. The building is so modest in size for a circus that it gives a great sense of immediacy to the performance—there is audience par-ticipation in jokes with the clowns. (A large, modern New Circus has been opened at 7 Vernadsky Prospekt, and has drawn off many of the top performers, though it lacks the intimacy and folksy feeling of the old circus.)

The Bulvar then crosses several avenues radiating from the center of the city—the Sretenka, famous for its shops, and Kirov Street. The Central Post Office is on the corner of Kirov Street. The next stop is the

Chistiye Prudi (Pure Water Reservoir), with a small artificial boating lake.

The semi-circle of the Bulvar reaches the Moskva River again at the mouth of the Yauza. Here, on the Kotyelnicheskaya Quay, we find another "Stalin Gothic" skyscraper with a 32-story central tower.

The Two-level Grand Boulevard and its Avenues

The Grand Boulevard of Moscow, the so-called Sadovaya, was also built on the site of the former city walls. It is more than ten miles long, which makes it somewhat too long to explore on foot. But trolley-cars travel its entire length.

Let us start not on the Sadovaya itself, but at Komsomol Square, northeast of the Kremlin en route to Sokolniki, a few hundred yards away from the Grand Boulevard. Emerging from the Komsomolskaya metro station, we find ourselves on a vast and busy square. It contains three large railway stations: the Leningrad, the Yaroslavl and the Kazan terminals. The narrow, 26-story tower of the Hotel Leningradskaya rises above the square. Starting from the hotel, pass southwest along busy Kalanchovskaya Street to reach Lermontov Square where it joins the Sadovaya. There is another high rise here: the 24-story headquarters of the Ministry of Railways.

If we board in front of this building a No. 10 trolley-bus, it will take us in a westerly direction along the Sadovaya Boulevard. We pass the Ministry of Agriculture; then stop in front of a palace with a classic central part and a semi-circular wing of columns. Once the home of the Sheremetyev princes, today it is the headquarters of the Moscow ambulance service, housing also an emergency hospital and a medical research institute.

After the Skifovsky Institute (named after a famous surgeon), we reach the corner of the Prospekt Mira (Peace). This is an important route, running north towards the Riga Railway Station, the Exhibition of Economic Achievements of the USSR and one of the main Olympic stadiums and swimming pool.

The next square, the Kolkhoznaya (kolkhoz means "collective farm"), is spanned by a fly-over. On the left, Tsvetnoy Boulevard joins the Sadovaya, which widens here into a square; on the right, another parkway leads out of the city. The pentagonal building of the Soviet Army Theater marks its end. Here, too, is the Central Army House and Memorial Museum. Its large park is the scene of concerts and variety performances in the summer.

The Sadovaya is lined by tall apartment houses; traffic moves on two levels, eliminating crossovers. The trolley-bus emerges on Mayakovsky Square from its tunnel in front of the Hotel Peking, then stops outside the Moscow Planetarium. Here there are illustrated lectures on the structure of the universe, on comets, meteorites, eclipses, the weather and on Soviet space exploration.

Almost exactly opposite there is a narrow, small building—the Chekhov Memorial Museum, once the home of the great playwright. The front door still bears his original physician's brass plate. Heading south now, a tour of the Ploshchad Vosstaniya (Square of the Uprising) brings us to the left-hand side of the Sadovaya (this section is called Tchaikovsky Street), by which point the Moscow "Saint-Germain" district has already begun. The other side is the Krasnaya Presnya, a working-class quarter.

Beside the high-rise building on the Square, a sloping road leads to the main entrance of the Zoo. (Another zoo entrance is on the Sadovaya, next to the Planetarium.)

On the far side of the square, Herzen Street and Vorovsky Street join the Square of the Uprising. Vorovsky Street is one of the main thoroughfares of the diplomatic quarter. There are a good many embassies and legations in the neighboring, quiet streets. Close to the Square of the Uprising, two important buildings face each other: the headquarters of the Soviet Writers' Union and the constructivist-style Dom Kino, the former home of the Association of Cinematic Arts.

Continuing along the Tchaikovsky Street section of the Sadovaya, we pass the American Embassy. The trolley-bus once again dips underground at the point where Kalinin Prospekt crosses the Grand Boulevard. (Down a gentle slope Kalinin Prospekt continues towards the Moskva River and, crossing the 500-yard long Kalinin Bridge, it reaches the Hotel Ukraine.)

If we pursue our exploration of the Sadovaya, however, we next pass the 27-story building of the Foreign Ministry and Ministry of Foreign Trade. Opposite, the Hotel Smolenskaya stands on a recently-developed square (Smolenskaya Square). Next to the ministry block, the Sadovaya reaches Arbat Street. On the right there is an attractive view of the River Moskva and the Borodino Bridge, decorated with reliefs commemorating the famous battle. Beyond the river on the right we can see the glass-domed building of the Kiev Railway Station.

The next broad avenue, the Bolshaya Pirogovskaya (Great Pirogov) Street, opens from the wide Zubovskaya Square. Named after a celebrated Russian surgeon, Great Pirogov Street contains several hospitals and clinics. Leo Tolstoy Street, running parallel with the Sadovaya, opens from Pirogovskaya Street. The great writer's former home is now the Tolstoy Museum. Sixteen rooms are preserved as they were when Tolstoy and his family lived there from 1872 to 1901. Pirogovskaya Street continues past Novodevichy Convent and cemetery, to the Lenin Stadium.

Beyond the Pirogovskaya the Grand Boulevard reaches the Moskva River, where the Crimea Bridge spans it. Another bridge crosses the Sadovaya itself, carrying rapid transit traffic from the Kremlin, towards Lenin Stadium and the southwestern part of the capital. This route is called the Komsomolsky Prospekt and was opened in 1957. On the right we can enter the Gorky Park station of the metro and beyond it stands one of the finest churches of Moscow with its onion-shaped gilt dome (Church of St. Nicholas in Khamovniki, 1679–82). The Crimea Bridge provides a fine vantage point for the river banks. Along the northwestern side there are tall blocks; this is Frunze Quay, a 1950's housing estate. On the far side, the green expanse of Gorky Park is dominated by two giant Ferris wheels. Gorky Park is the most popular of the city's parks. Situated along the River Moskva, its 300 acres include the Neskuchnyi Sad (Happy Garden) and the Zeleny Theatr (Green Theater), which is an openair one, seating 10,000. The park also has sports grounds, a boating station, cafés, a beer hall and various exhibition halls. Unfortunately, the place is getting a reputation for petty crime.

The trolley-bus stops at the ornamental gate of the park, then continues towards October Square. From this point, the Sadovaya continues to the industrial quarters of Moscow. The largest building on October square is the Hotel Warsaw. An underground line starts here towards the Southwestern District, New Cheryomushki. Nearby, one of the principal thoroughfares of Moscow, Lenin Prospekt, starts. Running parallel with this avenue, the Shabolovka, another wide street, branches off; Moscow Television used to have studions here. Opposite the mouth of Lenin Avenue, Dimitrov Street begins, leading to the center.

The Southwestern District

Board a trolley-bus at October Square if you want to travel along Lenin Prospekt to one of the Soviet capital's model housing developments, the Southwestern District.

The first part of Lenin Prospekt was once called the Kaluga Road. Here the city's first hospitals were built, some distance from the noisy and crowded center. The first of them, on the right-hand side, was designed by Bove, the architect who directed the rebuilding of the capital after the 1812 conflagration; the second, with a colonnade and dome, is even earlier, built at the beginning of the 19th century by M. F. Kazakov.

On the right, in the middle of an ornamental park, there is an old building with a gate decorated with statues. This is the seat of the Soviet Academy of Sciences, the former Neskuchny Castle. Scientists occupy the surrounding apartment houses, while on the left side of the road various research and planning departments of the Academy have been established. Between them, a street leads to Donskaya Square, where the Architectural Museum is housed in a 15th-century monastery.

Lenin Prospekt next crosses the circular Gagarin Square. Two tall ornamental buildings stand on either side. Up to the 1950's this square was at the city limits of Moscow and the buildings, somewhat over-decorated, were intended to greet the arriving tourist. Today they mark the beginning of the Southwestern District, consisting of several large, interconnected developments. These include the Lenin Hills and the site of the former village, Cheryomushki. The extensive building program began in 1952 and still continues.

At Gagarin Square the Vorobyovskoye Highway branches off from Lenin Prospekt and runs along the Moskva River on the ridge of the Lenin Hills. To the left Profsoyuznaya (Trade Union) Street leads towards Cheryomushki. On the right the Hotel Sputnik rises. Here too is the headquarters of the Central Council of the Soviet Trade Unions. On the left, several research institutes are housed in a block. Opposite, the Moskva Department Store specializes in men's and women's clothing; it is larger than the GUM store.

The first major crossroads is that of University Prospekt (right), and Cheryomushkinskaya Street. At the next crossing we leave the Lenin Prospekt, which continues for several miles, flanked by tall apartment blocks, passing the student hostels of Lumumba University, and then runs towards Vnukovo airport.

Let us instead follow the broad Lomonosov Prospekt to the right. This was the site of the first blocks of the Southwestern District and today is one of the busiest traffic arteries in the district. Ahead, off to the left, is the Olympic Village, a housing estate for 15,000 Muscovites with a range of shops, entertainment facilities etc.

Turning right from the Lomonosov Prospekt, we pass the railings of the Lomonosov University campus. This is the Vernadsky Prospekt where the humanities faculty of the university has been completed recently, and the new premises of the Moscow Circus opened. It borders, on one side, the apartment blocks of the new quarter. Near the Prospekt Vernadskogo metro station, is the recent Hotel Druzhba. On the other side, the dome of the Sternberg Observatory can be seen among the trees.

We have now almost come full circle, reaching University Prospekt once again. Turning left, we start for the distant, tall building of the Lomonosov University, which can also be reached by metro or one of the numerous buses. Standing on the Lenin Hills, this much-criticized complex was built between 1949 and 1953. Individual visitors need special permits to visit it, but there are regular group tours. From the top of the commanding tower there is a panoramic view of the Soviet capital.

Across the pleasant park in front of the university we can find the Lenin Hills Lookout Tower rising above the Moskva River. Offering a panorama of the greater part of Moscow, it has a wide terrace built of red polished granite. From here, we can see the wide loop of the river with the gentle slope of the Lenin Hills continuing on the left. There is a clear view, to the distant left, of the new quarter situated behind the Mosfilm Studios, the grey block of the Kiev Railway Station and the tower of the Hotel Ukraine on the corner of the Kutuzov Prospekt. Nearer to us, the golden domes of the Novodevichy Convent glitter; directly opposite the lookout tower, at the bottom of the river loop, we see the stadiums of the Lenin Sports Grounds, at Luzhniki. Far in the background, the golden domes of the Kremlin cathedrals can be seen in good weather. On the immediate right, a two-level metro bridge spans the river; inaugurated in 1958, its two main spans were manufactured on the spot.

On the lower level of the bridge, the metro runs towards the university; it has a stop on the bridge itself, from which we can reach both the stadium and the Lenin Hills. On the upper level, traffic moves from the Komsomol Prospekt towards one of the main traffic arteries of the Southwestern District, the Vernadsky Prospekt. On the flank of the Lenin Hills (though not visible from this vantage point) spreads the new diplomatic quarter.

To the left of the lookout tower there is a small church. To the right, a shady promenade takes us to the crossing of the Vernadsky Prospekt. We pass the ski jump and arrive at a glassed-in hall, marked by the red *M* of the metro (subway or underground). An escalator takes us down to the station on the bridge. Before we descend, let's look at the complex of the Central Palace of Pioneers, a group of all-glass buildings including a winter garden, a stadium and a domed observatory. The foundations of this young people's center were laid on the 40th anniversary of the founding of the Soviet Youth Organization, the Komsomol, and it was built mostly by young labor.

The Sports City, Novodevichy Convent and Frunze District

This exploration should start at the Lenin Hills metro station on the lower level of the double bridge referred to in the previous paragraph. We leave the station at the stadium exit. Inaugurated in August 1956, the main stadium seats more than 100,000 people; there are more than 130 halls, training courses, stadia, as well as several restaurants and cafés in the large park. The Lenin Stadium complex was converted and enlarged for the Olympics, but even before that it was probably the largest sports centre in the world.

Nearest to the metro station is the open-air swimming pool, which has more than 13,000 places for spectators. There is a separate diving pool. The Great Stadium is reserved for soccer, athletic meets and displays. It is equipped for night matches; the 100,000 spectators are able to leave the place within six minutes through skillfully planned exits. Inside the stadium building there is a covered course for sprinters, training and dressing rooms, a sports hotel, restaurant, cinema, a post office, press rooms for journalists and TV and numerous other service installations. The Lesser Stadium is reserved for basketball, volleyball, tennis and boxing matches; in the winter it's used for ice hockey and skating. It seats 16,000.

The Sport Palace is one of the largest indoor sport halls of Europe, with seats for 17,000 spectators. It can easily be converted into an indoor skating rink or a theater.

Leaving the sports center, walking north along the Moskva River, we pass under the railway embankment and come to the Novodevichy Convent and cemetery. Its entrance is on the southern side, through a small park, from Bolshaya Pirogovskaya Street. One of the finest examples of 16th- and 17th-century architecture, the Convent is enclosed by a crenelated wall with 12 battle towers, and consists of a group of several buildings. It was founded in 1524 by Grand Prince Vasili Iovanovich to commemorate the union of Moscow and Smolensk; it formed a stronghold on the road to Smolensk and Lithuania, besides being a convent for ladies of noble birth. Evdokiya, Peter the Great's first wife, and Princess Sophia, his troublesome sister, both spent part of their lives here and are buried here.

The huge, five-domed Smolensky Cathedral (1525) is dedicated to Our Lady of Smolensk; it was built by Aleviz Fryazin. The iconostasis has 84 wooden columns; the ikons of the 16th and 17th centuries were painted by outstanding Moscow masters. Since 1922, the Convent has been part of the Museum of History. It boasts rare and ancient Russian paintings, both ecclesiastical and secular, woodwork and metalwork, fabrics and embroidery of the 16th and 17th centuries. There is also a large collection of 16th- and 17th-century illuminated and illustrated books, decorated with gold, silver and jewels. In the cathedral, Boris Godunov was elected Czar in 1598.

The old cemetery within the convent wall is the burial place of eminent artists, generals, political and public leaders and scientists. Gogol, Chekhov, Mayakovsky, Scriabin (Molotov's uncle), Prokofiev, Stanislavsky, Eisenstein and Nikita Khrushchev rest here among the 270 monuments.

Outside the cemetery we can board a trolley-bus; but we can also walk southeast along the railway embankment, back towards the sports complex. Almost opposite the stadium stands the Hotel Yunost (Youth).

Farther away we reach the Sportivnaya metro station, and beyond that, the site of the Moscow Fair. From spring to autumn, many Moscow department stores have their own pavilions here.

Continuing, we arrive at Komsomol Prospekt, which links the center, by means of a two-level bridge, with the Southwestern District. It is lined by apartment houses.

Northwest of Komsomol Prospekt the modern Frunze District has some Russian classical buildings near the Sadovaya (Zubovsky Boulevard). These military barracks were built early in the 19th century. The nearby Church of St. Nicholas in Khamovniki dates from the 17th century; it used to be the parish church for the weavers who had settled in considerable numbers in this quarter.

At the end of the Komsomol Prospekt there is an overpass above the Sadovaya. From here we can continue by subway (or underground railway) from the Gorky Park metro station. If we take the trolley-bus back to the center, we pass the open Moskva swimming pool. The bus continues along Metrostroyevskaya (Street of the Metro Builders) towards the Bulvar—here, too, we can change to the metro at Kropotkinskaya Station—or continue along the Volkhonka as far as Karl Marx Prospekt and the Kremlin.

Economic Achievement Exhibition and Ostankino Palace

If time permits, a whole day can be devoted to these two; they are best approached by the metro from the Prospekt Mira station; or alight at VDNKH station (for the Exhibition).

Occupying 553 acres and including about 80 large pavilions and many smaller structures, the permanent Exhibition of Economic Achievements renewed annually, has a three-mile circular road served by various forms of public transport, including small buses, open miniature trains and motor-bike taxis. The pavilions are built in the architectural styles of the different Soviet republics; many large buildings are devoted to different branches of agriculture, industry and science. The exhibition grounds also include a circus, a Cinerama (*circorama*) cinema, two theaters, and an open-air theater. There are many restaurants and cafés of which the *Golden Ear* (*Zolotoi Kolos*) is the best.

Outside the North Gate is the gigantic steel statue by Vera Mukhina *Worker and Farm-Woman*, designed for the Paris Fair of 1937. Also just outside the Gate is a 295-foot monument to commemorate Sovet space exploration, and inside the exhibition grounds you will find gigantic multistage rockets, a replica of *Vostok* (Gagarin's first manned flight vehicle), the spaceship *Voskhod*, moon satellites, the automatic space station which made a soft landing on Venus, and the space station *Cosmos*, among others.

Most of the other pavilions are devoted to exhibitions covering almost every facet of national life from atomic energy to art. There are displays of work by contemporary artists and sculptors, graphic artists, stained glass panels by Lithuanian craftsmen and carpets by the famous Turkmen carpet weavers. A cinema shows selected Soviet films. Nearby are several hotels and hostels, some used for youth tourist groups.

A little further on, behind the Exhibition site, is the Ostankino Palace Museum. This timber palace was erected in the 18th century by the serf craftsmen of Count Sheremetyev under the direction of the serf and artist

Pavel Argunov. The estate itself was over 2 million acres, with 210,000 serfs and an annual income of 1½ million roubles. The decorations, in excellent taste, include delicate, lace-like gilt carvings on the portals and doors, cornices, columns and walls. All the furniture was also fashioned by the serfs. The floors are masterpieces of parquetry and from the painted ceilings hang ornate crystal chandeliers. Stoves and fireplaces are faced with varnished tiles, marble malachite and bronze. There is a fine collection of 17th- and 18th-century carvings, crystal, porcelain and fans.

The palace theater had its heyday in the 18th century when the company included some 200 actors, singers, dancers and musicians—all of them serfs. One of the stars was Parasha Kovalyova, daughter of a blacksmith, whose talent and beauty captured the heart of Count Sheremetyev; she became his wife and one of the Ostankino streets is named after her. The chairs in the theater were movable so that the auditorium could be transformed into a ballroom within minutes. The devices for scenic, light and sound effects, invented by the serfs, are still extant. The large park has many marble sculptures. Trinity Church, just to the left of the main entrance, was built in 1963 by the serf-architect Pavel Potekhin.

Near the Ostankino Palace Museum we find the new headquarters of Soviet Television, with the TV Tower just opposite. This was finished in 1967 and rises to over 1,750 feet. It serves five TV channels and six UHF radio programs. In the middle section of the tower, the *Sedmoye Nebo* (Seventh Heaven) *Restaurant* offers a splendid view (on three levels) of the whole Moscow area. It is a revolving restaurant, taking 45 minutes to describe a complete circle. Visits to the TV tower must be reserved well in advance; the tickets are 7 roubles, entitling you to a two hours' tour and a meal at the restaurant.

Excursions from Moscow

Within easy reach of the city for half-day excursions are some beautiful old palaces, estates and former noble residences, set in typical countryside. To see them to the best advantage you should try and time your visits to coincide with spring or summer.

Arkhangelskoye Estate Museum

This museum is in the village of Arkhangelskoye, 16 miles from Moscow. Motorists can reach it by leaving Moscow along the Leningradsky Prospekt, then the Volokolamskoye Chaussée, taking the left fork to the Petrovo-Dalnive Chaussée.

The estate, with the former palace of Prince Yusupov, is a striking 18th- and 19th-century group of buildings; the architecture artfully blends into the landscape. The main complex was built at the end of the 18th century for Prince Golitsyn by the French architect Chevalier de Huerne. Bought in 1810 by the rich landlord Yusupov, a descendant of the Tatar Khans, who at one time was the director of the Imperial Theaters and of the Hermitage Museum, it became the home of his extraordinary art collection.

The classical palace contains paintings by Boucher, Vigée-Lebrun, Hubert Robert, Roslin, Tiepolo, Van Dyck and many others, as well as antique statues, furniture, mirrors, chandeliers, glassware and china. In the study there are portraits of royalty and nobility. Samples of fabrics, china and glassware (all produced on the estate) are also on show.

In the French Park, the avenues are lined with many statues and monuments to commemorate royal visits; there is also a monument to Pushkin, whose favorite retreat was Arkhangelskoye.

In the western part, a small pavilion known as the Temple to the Memory of Catherine the Great depicts the Empress as Themis, goddess of justice. The Estate Theater, on the right side of the main road, was built in 1817 by the serf-architect Ivanov; it seated 400 and was the home of the biggest and best-known company of serf-actors. It now houses a special exhibition. The well-preserved stage decorations are by the Italian artist Gonzaga.

Arkhangelskoye is open between 11 and 5, closed Mondays and Tuesdays.

The Kuskovo Palace Museum

The Kuskovo Palace Museum is about 6 miles from Moscow along the Ryazanskoye Chaussée, but can be reached by train from the Kursk Railway Station. It was built in the early 18th century as a summer residence by Prince Pyotr Sheremetyev, who owned more than 150,000 serfs. Designed by Alexei Mironov, another serf-architect, it is a timber structure on a white stone foundation. The palace is the center of the estate, standing on the banks of a lake. It has been a museum since 1918; the main collection is devoted to Russian porcelain, ranging from the early works of Dmitry Vinogradov (1748), who introduced the manufacture of china into Russia, to new work by Soviet craftsmen. There are also Chinese, Danish, English, French and German porcelain, faïence, majolica and glassware, including many antique pieces.

In addition there are some 800 *objets d'art* including one of the best collections of 18th-century Russian art, with some 200 portraits. The White Hall, the dining room, the nursery, the oak-panelled study, the drawing room and the gallery of tapestries are of special interest. There are several smaller buildings in the French Gardens (including the Hermitage, where dinner tables were raised mechanically from the ground floor to the first-floor dining room), the Dutch House, the Italian House and the Grotto.

Kuskovo is open from 10 to 7, closed on Tuesdays and the last day of each month.

Kolomenskoye Estate

This estate was once the favorite summer residence of the Grand Dukes of Moscow and later of the Czars. It stands on the Kashirskoye Chaussée overlooking the Moskva River.

The most striking part of the large complex is the beautiful Church of the Ascension of Christ (1532), built in the old Russian "tent" style. There is a partly-rebuilt 16th-century iconostasis. The belfry also dates from the beginning of the same century. The royal estate was centered around a wooden palace which Catherine the Great had demolished in 1767; only the Main Gate, the Clock Tower and the Water Tower remain, but a full-restoration is in progress. The log cabin in which Peter the Great lived in Archangelsk has been transferred here. Other examples of Russian wooden architecture are the Prison Tower from Siberia (1631), the Defense Tower from the White Sea (1690) and a 17th-century mead brewery from the village of Preobrazhenskoye. The 17th-century Kazan Church, with five onion-shaped domes, is open for religious services.

The Museum is housed in the former servants' quarters of the estate. There are displays illustrating the peasant wars of 1606–07, the "Copper Mutiny" of 1662 against the introduction of copper coins in place of silver, exhibitions of Russian woodcarving, metalwork and ceramics.

Kolomenskoye is open 10 to 7 daily except Tuesdays.

PRACTICAL INFORMATION FOR MOSCOW

 WHEN TO GO. Moscow's climate is changeable; the winter is cold with plenty of snow; the summers are frequently very dry, though sometimes rainy. Winter, too, is changeable, with low temperatures—though there have been years when they rarely dropped below freezing point. June, July and August are the hottest months, August particularly; cloudbursts and thunderstorms are frequent. The average amount of sunshine is 250 hours in July and 211 in August. Winter rarely brings long periods of frost; December, January and February, however, can be rather grim for stretches of a week or ten days. Spring is late and short, so is fall; snow often arrives early in November. So for tourists, the summer months might be preferable, with May and September the best at either end. The festivals are held in May (5–15, Moscow Stars) and in mid-winter (December 25–January 5, Winter Festival). Choose the season that suits your tastes and interests best; if you have no preferences, stick to late spring and early autumn.

 HOW TO GET THERE. By air: You can fly to Moscow from practically every capital in Europe and many in Africa, Asia and the Americas. There are many regular flights from Leningrad, from all the Union Republics, the health resorts of the Crimea, the Caucasus, the Ukraine and the Baltic seaboard, from the Far East, Siberia, the Far North.

The City Air Terminal is at 37 Leningradsky Prospekt; the nearest subway stations are *Aeroport* and *Dynamo.* It is open 24 hours a day; after checking in you can go by cab, bus or helicopter to the airports. Planes of 20 foreign companies land at *Sheremetyevo International Airport,* from which Aeroflot and *major* foreign airlines take off for scores of countries. *Sheremetyevo-Two* services passengers on other international airlines. *Domodedovo,* the largest airport in the Soviet Union (and one of the largest in the world), is on the Kashira Highway, some 30 miles southeast of Moscow. Here the largest and fastest planes land, servicing the bulk of domestic flights. *Vnukovo Airport* is on the Kiev Highway, some 18 miles from the center of Moscow.

Telephone numbers—*City Terminal:* 155-50-04 (05) (Also Aeroflot Service Bureau).

Sheremetyevo: 158-79-26 (Cargo dispatch, *fret*); customs: 158-79-96 and 158-79-23. Intourist representative: 156-94-35 and 158-79-12.

Sheremetyevo-Two: 155-50-04(05).

Domodedovo: Intourist Representative: 234-09-32.

Vnukovo: Intourist Representative: 234-09-32.

General enquiries about all airports: 155-50-05.

Aeroflot: Reservations: 155-50-03; International enquiries: 245-38-77.

BY RAIL. Moscow has nine railway stations, which handle 400 million passengers annually. Railways are electrified. From Moscow to Leningrad, by the famed *Aurora Express,* traveling time is 4 hours 59 minutes, at an average speed of 85 m.p.h.

The Byelorussian Railway Station (Byelorussky Vokzal Square): Trains to and from Berlin, Warsaw, London, Paris, Smolensk, Minsk, Brest and Vilnius.

The Kazan Railway Station (2 Komsomolskaya Square): Trains to and from Rostov-on-Don, Kazan, Volgograd, the Central Asian Republics and Siberia.

The Kiev Railway Station (Kievsky Vokzal Square): Trains to and from Chop, Belgrade, Bucharest, Budapest, Karlovy Vary, Prague, Sofia, Cierna, Jassy, Kiev, Kishinev, Lvov, Odessa, Uzhgorod and Chernovtsy.

The Kursk Railway Station (29 Chkalov Street): Trains to and from the Crimea and the Caucasus, Armenia, Azerbaijan, Georgia, the Mineralniye Vody spas, Kursk, Tula, Orel and Kharkov.

The Leningrad Railway Station (1 Komsomolskaya Square): trains to and from Helsinki, Leningrad, Kalinin, Novgorod, Murmansk, Petrozavodsk, Pskov and Tallinn.

The Paveletsky Railway Station (Leninskaya Square): Trains to and from the Donets Basin and Volgograd.

The Riga Railway Station (Rizhskaya Square): Trains to and from Riga and Baltic health resorts.

The Savelovsky Railway Station (Butyrskaya Zastava Square): Trains to and from Leningrad and Uglich.

The Yaroslavl Railway Station (5 Komsomolskaya Square): Trains to and from Siberia and the Far East, Moscow-Peking Express.

The Central Railway Enquiry Office (tel. 266-90-00) will provide information about departures and arrivals.

BY SHIP. You might be adventurous and arrange with Intourist to arrive in Moscow by ship along the Moscow-Volga canal. With a length of some 80 miles, it links the Soviet capital directly with the Caspian, the Baltic, the Black Sea, the White Sea and the Azov Sea. The port for long-distance passengers is the North Port on the Khimki reservoir.

BY CAR. It is possible to reach Moscow along the autoroutes which we have described in *Facts at Your Fingertips. Intourist* will provide transportation from the airport either by bus or by taxi; also from railway stations and the landing stage of the Moscow-Volga boats, for those on Intourist package tours.

CITY TRANSPORTATION. Moscow spreads some 28 miles from north to south and 20 miles from east to west. There are eight subway (underground) lines with 181 kilometres of track and 107 stations.

The **Metro** (marked with a large illuminated *M* sign) runs from 6 A.M. to 1 A.M.; on Sundays, half an hour longer. It is the fastest and most convenient mode of transport; during the rush hours, trains leave the stations every 90 seconds. Six million passengers use it daily. Pocket maps are available from stations or Intourist offices. Plan your route beforehand and have your destination with you written down *in Russian* to help you spot the station. The fare is 5 kopeks regardless of distance; a coin must be inserted into the slot at the turnstile at the entrance to the platforms (as in the New York subway). Another 5 kopeks must be paid for each piece of luggage—whose length must not exceed 3 feet (except skis), and whose width must not exceed one foot or height 16 inches.

Trolley-buses, buses, trams and **minibuses** carry more than 8 million passengers daily. Most trolley-buses, buses and trams have no conductors; passengers drop the fare into a cash-box and tear off a ticket. The stops are sometimes announced by the driver. The 170 bus and 57 trolley-bus services start at 6 A.M. and the final runs begin at 1 A.M. The bus fare is 5 kopeks, the trolley-bus 4 and the tram 3 kopeks. The trams start at 5.30 A.M. on 52 routes, mostly in the suburbs, finishing at 1.30 A.M. "Microbuses" link points which are difficult to reach by other means of transport. They provide a shuttle service every 10 minutes, but there are intermediate request stops.

River-boats provide a pleasant, if leisurely way of getting about. Small boats ply the Moskva River within city limits, from May-June until September-October, depending on the weather. There are two routes. The first runs from the Kiev Terminal via the Lenin Hills-Gorky Park-Krymsky Bridge-Bolshoi Kamenny Bridge-Bolshoi Ustyinsky Bridge-Krasnokholmsky Bridge-Novospassky Bridge, passing the Novodevichy Convent, the Lenin Stadium, Moscow University, the Moskva swimming pool, the Kremlin, the Rossiya Hotel, the Novospassky Monastery and other Moscow landmarks. This cruise takes an hour and 20 minutes and the fare is 20 kopeks. The second route also begins at the Kiev Terminal via the Krasnopresensky Park to Kuntsevo-Krylatskoye. It takes you to the Fili-Kuntsevo Park and the river beach, lasting one hour. The fare is 20 kopeks.

There are more than 11,000 **taxis** in Moscow, available at 300 taxi stands marked by a special sign. They can be distinguished by a checkered line on their doors and a green light on the windshield. If this light is on, the taxi is free. You can also hail a taxi in the street by raising your hand. The charges are 20 kopeks per kilometer plus a 20 kopek service charge. The waiting charge is one rouble per hour. You pay according to the meter, irrespective of the number of passengers or the amount of luggage.

You can order taxis by phone. The number for all regions is 225-00-00 or 227-00-40; for Kutuzovsky, Gruzinsky, Sadovaya and the Center 257-00-40; for the Leninsky and Yugo-Zapad district 137-00-40. Expect up to 1-hour wait.

Car rentals. Intourist will provide a private car to tour Moscow with or without driver; either a four-seater Volga or a Lada. For an excursion outside the city, you can rent a car or bus, with or without a driver. Rentals must be paid in foreign currency. Please contact Intourist for the latest cars available and for current rates of hire.

For the **pedestrian,** the following traffic rules are prescribed:
Traffic moves on the right. Some central streets have one-way traffic. Cross the street only where crossings are indicated by zebra stripes or arrows and at a green light. Use the underpasses where available. If caught in the middle when traffic starts moving, stay put, do not run. Cross *behind* parked buses and trolley-buses; only *in front* of stationary trams. As drivers are not allowed to use their horns, look out—do not count on any audible warning.

 WHAT TO SEE. The principal sights (which we have described in more detail earlier in this chapter) are: The Kremlin—a city within a city. Much of it is open to the tourist, though, of course, the governmental offices, etc. are not. Visit the four great cathedrals: the Cathedral of the Archangel, the Cathedral of the Annunciation, the Cathedral of the Assumption and the Cathedral of the Twelve Apostles with the Patriarch's Residence; also the Church of the Deposition of the Robe and the Ivan the Great Bell Tower. See as much as

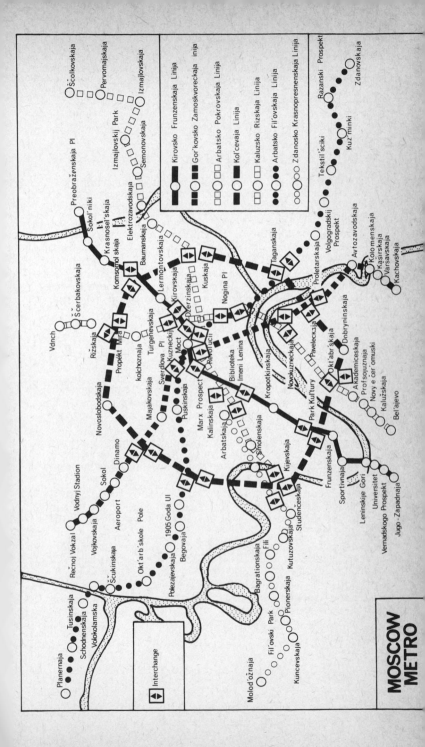

MOSCOW
METRO

WORDS TO THE WISE
A Few Useful Travel Hints

Whether you are on holiday or have important business to do, after a flight through several time zones give your body's clock a chance to catch up. It is easy to underestimate the effects of jet-lag.

Don't carry all your cash, travellers' checks, passport etc. in the same place, spread them around a bit – and never carry your wallet in your hip pocket.

Experienced travellers travel light. Don't forget that the hand luggage you carry with you onto the plane is a vital part of your travel equipment. Make sure you have your essentials in it, not in your other baggage.

With strikes and the cost of excess baggage always in the background, you would be sensible when flying not to take more than you could comfortably carry yourself – in a pinch.

Don't leave already exposed film in your pockets or in any hand luggage while passing through airport X-ray machines. The process can sometimes fog the film and you may find a whole trip's photographs ruined. Put the film on one side while passing through.

Never make long-distance phone calls from your hotel room without checking first on the likely price. Some hotels have been known to mark up the cost of a call as much as 200 %.

Several airlines will provide a cardboard carrying box for any loose items you might arrive clutching at the checking-in desk. It saves leaving a trail of last-minute purchases all the way to the plane.

You would be amazed the amount of free information that you can get from National Tourist Offices to help you plan your trip – all the way from brochures to movies.

Put a tag with your name and address on it *inside* your suitcase as well as outside. It will greatly help identification if the case goes astray.

Never leave valuables in your hotel room – put them in the hotel safe.

you can of the Palace of Facets, the Grand Kremlin Palace, the Armory, the Arsenal and the Palace of Congresses. You may want to take a glance at Lenin's Study and Apartment and the Council of Ministers Building.

In Red Square, outside the Kremlin walls, people queue up outside the Lenin Mausoleum to gaze at the remains of the Soviet Union's founder. The Cathedral of the Intercession (Cathedral of St. Basil the Blessed) is one of the most remarkable architectural monuments of Russia. Here, too, is the Monument to Minin and Pozharsky, the History Museum and the great GUM department store.

Other landmarks—apart from the main museums which we have already described—are the Academies of Medical Sciences and of Sciences, the first at 14 Solyanka Street, the second at 14 Leninsky Prospekt; the Alexandrovsky Garden on Marx Prospekt, the Andronikov Monastery, containing the Rublyov Museum (10 Pryamikov Square) the great panorama of the Battle of Borodino (38 Kutuzovsky Prospekt), the two Botanical Gardens—one of the Academy of Sciences in Botanicheskaya Street, Ostankino, and the other of Moscow University at 26 Prospekt Mira. The Tchaikovsky Conservatory (13 Herzen Street) and the housing developments of Cheryomushki in the south and Medvedkovo in the north might be of interest. Some smaller specialized museums are listed below.

There are some eight outstanding churches (described earlier) that should be included on a reasonably full itinerary; so should the Donskoi Monastery (now a Branch of the Museum of Architecture, 1 Donskaya Square), the Gorky Park near the Park Kultury Metro station, the Izmailovo Park (Metro station: Izmailovskaya), and several others for outdoor recreation and seeing the Muscovites at play.

 HOTELS. Normally, for American, British and most other Western tourists, Intourist uses the top seven hotels— *Rossia, Intourist, Metropole, National,* and *Ukraine* and the New *Belgrade* and *Kosmos.* If these are full, Intourist sometimes directs the overflow to the *Leningradskaya, Ostankino,* and *Sovietskaya.* Other hotels, though officially rated first class, are considered by Intourist not suitable for western tourists, though they may be used on special occasions for international meetings and congresses or special cut-rate tour groups. A number of new hotels were completed for the 1980 Olympic Games—the 28-story Kosmos, a Franco-Soviet venture, is the most luxurious of these.

Aeroflot, 37 Leningradsky Prospekt. This is generally used for transit air passengers and is next to the air terminal.

Altai, 12 Gostinichnaya Street, near the Exhibition of Economic Achievements. Inconvenient location.

Armenia, 4 Neglinnaya Street. Restaurant. Better-than-average service. Rarely used by Western tourists.

Belgrade, 5 Smolenskaya Square, new, near the Arbat and Kalinin Prospekt. Nominally Yugoslav, the restaurant serves good Russian food in an imaginative décor.

Berlin, 3 Zhdanov Street. 90 rooms; rating: *first-class,* atmospheric, with Victorian elegance. Restaurant quite good. This was formerly known as the Savoy. Also an Intourist Hotel. Favorite with businessmen.

Bucharest, 1 Balchug Street. Restaurant. No private baths. Opposite Kremlin across Moscow River.

Budapest, 2/18 Petrovskiye Linii. Restaurant. Central location.

Intourist, 3–5 Gorky Street. Opened in 1970. 466 rooms. Rated as *first-class superior.* Restaurants, cafés, shops. Finnish furnishings. Intourist Bureau. Basement night bar open till 2 A.M. (foreign currency only). Central location.

Izmailovo, in district of the same name. A luxury skyscraper complex; new in 1980.

Kosmos, Prospekt Mira, near Economic Achievements Exhibition. New 1980, French-built and equipped, down to the last doorknob. "Four-star prices". 28 stories, 1777 rooms, mostly twin-bedded. Bars, restaurants.

Leningradskaya, 21/40 Kalanchevskaya Street. A 28-floor hotel, near the Leningrad, Yaroslavl and Kazan railway stations. Baroque, medium grade. Less convenient to city center than hotels above. Less comfortable than it looks.

Metropole, 1/4 Marx Prospekt, 400 rooms. Rating: Well-located, recently renovated, *first-class.* A pre-revolutionary building, it bears three memorial plaques to mark important historical events associated with it. One of them commemorates the battles fought by revolutionary troops in November 1917 to occupy it, another the fact that Lenin spoke frequently in the assembly hall of the building, and the third the news that Yakov Sverdlov, the first Chairman of the Executive Committee of the Russian Soviet Federal Republic had offices here in 1918–19. The hotel was built in 1899–1903 by W. Walcott in the style then fashionable; the facade is still adorned with a large majolica relief, "Dream Princess" a replica of a famous drawing by Michael Vrubel. A kind of historical monument that is also quite a pleasant Intourist hotel. Good restaurant and café. Night bar (foreign currency) open till 2 A.M. on ground floor.

Minsk, 22 Gorky Street. Large central, often used to house foreign delegations. Restaurant and coffee-shop. Near Mayakovsky Square, theaters and concert halls.

Mir, 9 Bolshoi Devyatinsky Per.

Moskva, 1 Marx Prospekt. Faces the Council of Ministers Building; the two were the first to be built under the reconstruction program launched in 1932. (Not an Intourist Hotel.) Restaurant. In 1977 a new annexe was opened next door.

National, 1 Gorky Street. Rating: recently enlarged, traditional leader handsome, *first-class superior.* Erected in 1903, but expanded in the 1960's, it has retained some of its original plush atmosphere. The flat roof is designed as an observation platform, from which there is a splendid view of the Kremlin and much of the city center. Another Intourist hotel. Good restaurant.

Orlyonok, on the Lenin Hills, 17 floors, recent. Better-than-average, with friendlier-than-usual service. Food is acceptable. Mostly for foreigners.

Ostankino, 29 Botanicheskaya Street. Some distance from the center of the city, near the Ostankino Palace, the Botanical Gardens and the Exhibition of Economic Achievements. Positively *not* recommended.

Peking, 1/7 Sadovaya Street. Near Mayakovsky Square and the Planetarium. Restaurant.

Rossia (near Red Square) 6, Razin Street, is one of the world's largest hotels, with accommodation for 6,000 people. Its rating is *first class*. Lovely view from 21st-floor restaurant (over Kremlin). Designed by a group of architects led by Dmitry Chechulin. It has 3,150 rooms, two cinemas, a large concert hall seating 3,000, several restaurants, cafés and shops. Adjoining a park in which there are several old churches, including the Church of the Conception of St. Anne (16th century). Minimal room service, reasonably efficient staff. This Intourist hotel is the first to add a service charge (5%) to encourage promptness.

Sovietskaya, 32 Leningradsky Prospekt. Near the Dynamo Stadium and the Hippodrome Racecourse.

Tourist, 17/12 Selskokhozyaistvennaya Street. Poor location and appearance. Many student tourist groups end up here. Try not to!

Tsentralnaya, 10 Gorky Street. Restaurant.

Ukraine, 2/1 Kutuzovsky Prospekt. Near the Kutuzovskaya Metro Station, close to parks and the Kiev Station. 1,500 rooms, rated as spacious, modern first class. A skyscraper building (29 floors) on the banks of the Moskva River.

Ural, 40 Chernyshevsky Street.

Varshava (Warsaw), 1/2 Oktyabrskaya Square. Fairly recently-built, near the Leninsky Prospekt, the university and three metro stations. Restaurant.

Yunost, 36 Frunzensky Val. Operated by the International Youth Tourist Bureau. Pretty Spartan.

Yuzhnaya, 87 Leninsky Prospekt.

 RESTAURANTS. Russian cuisine (with some regional exceptions) is more nourishing than palate-tickling, but you can eat well in Moscow if you forget any *cordon bleu* pretensions. There are about 7,000 catering establishments, in which two and a half million people eat every day. It is advisable to reserve a table at the more popular restaurants—something which Intourist or your hotel's service bureau will do. As we have said before, reserve ample time for your meal; if you are alone, take a book; if you are in company, practice the art of conversation. Many restaurants have dance orchestras of the Palm Court or Saratoga Springs variety.

All the Moscow hotels have their own big restaurants. And there are various establishments for special cuisine. There are also restaurants in all Moscow parks, on the TV tower in Ostankino, at the Exhibition of National Achievement of the USSR, at the Khimki Riverport and the Lenin Stadium in Luzhniki. On a warm day, you might enjoy dinner aboard the floating restaurant near the Krymsky Bridge, the Lastochka or at the Burevestnik in Gorky Park. Light meals are provided at the cafés. Ice-cream, enormously popular in the Soviet Union, is sold at special ice-cream parlors, open year-round.

Here is a list of restaurants we can recommend:

Airline Terminal Restaurant, at the terminal on Leningradsky Prospekt. Modern elegance fine food.

Aragvi, 6 Gorky Street, Georgian specialities. Ask for *lobio,* butter beans in a spicy sauce; *kharcho,* a spiced meat soup; *osetrina na vertelye,* sturgeon roasted on a spit; there is also *tsiplyata tabaka,* roast spring chicken, flattened between hot stones. With good wine and vodka a splendid meal can be had for about 10 roubles a head. Reserve! Private rooms available at a price.

Ararat, 4 Neglinnaya Street. An Armenian 'haven' where you can enjoy *forel v tyestye,* trout cooked in a pastry; *solyanka,* a special soup; *tolma,* vine leaves stuffed with rice, meat and prunes. Small Armenian orchestra.

Arbat, 29 Kalinin Prospekt. A modern but uninteresting place. Seats 2,000. Reservations needed; pay 1 rouble to get in. Most expensive restaurant in town. Music, dancing, floorshow. Open till midnight. Typical food. Popular with the privileged class.

Baku, 13 Shvernika Street. Azerbaijani cuisine, kindred to Turkish. Specialities: *dovta,* a soup made with sour milk and meat; *plov* (pilaff), of which there are well over 20 varieties, all with a rice base. One of the better nationality restaurants. Music.

Belgrade, in the new Belgrade Hotel, 5 Smolenskaya Square. Russian and Yugoslav specialties. Good reputation.

Berlin, 3 Zhdanov Street. In the Berlin Hotel. Good, if rather heavy, German cooking with a dominant Bavarian influence. Old-fashioned atmosphere with fountain, gilt mirrors. Music, dancing. English spoken. Considered by foreign residents to be one of the best in town.

Bucharest, 1 Balchug Street. Romanian and Transylvanian cooking. Refurbished 1979 with new kitchens, improved dining-room and decor.

Budapest, 2/18 Petrovskiye Linii. Hungarian cooking, with plenty of paprika and sour cream. Good, if perhaps not quite up to the native standards.

Co-op at Tarasovo, about 30 minutes drive from center up Prospekt Mira. For those with a sense of adventure. Often the venue for wedding or retirement parties. Adequate shashlik, very good hot cheese and hot bread.

Intourist. 3–5 Gorky Street. In the hotel. Very good food. Sometimes there is a smorgasbord (all you can eat for 3.10 roubles, not including liquor).

Lastochka, good riverboat restaurant near the Krymsky Bridge on Moskva River. Not expensive.

Lefortovo, Krasnokursantsky Street, suburban, new. Repellant location near security police interrogation center of same name—if you go by taxi make it clear it's the *restaurant* you want, not the prison. Interesting experience—set lunch costs 1 rouble only. Clientele mostly military and seem to enjoy it.

Metropole, 1 Marx Prospekt. Attached to the hotel. Old-fashioned, but pleasant.

Minsk, 22 Gorky Street. In the hotel. Very good mushroom dishes, soporific orchestra and dancing in the evenings.

Mir, 9 Bolshoi Devyatinsky Per. A hotel restaurant. Average food and services. People living at this hotel get seated and served first. Small dining room.

Moskva, 7 Marx Prospekt. In the hotel. Open-air roof terrace in summer. Large main restaurant on 3rd floor. Music.

National, 1 Gorky Street. In the hotel. There is an upstairs bar in which hard liquor is served for foreign currency, and here you will also find music (an accordion) and *blinis* (pancakes with salmon, caviar and sour cream). Delicious! Restaurant is among the good ones in Moscow, a bit more expensive than average. Dancing. Female balalaika band, folk songs.

Praga, 2 Arbat Square Czech and Russian cuisine. Recommended, especially for the Kiev Cutlets and the chocolate cream cake! Pleasant open-air roof garden.

Rossia, 1 Moskvoretskaya Embankment. Located in the large hotel, which has nine restaurants, some of them massive and notable for slow service! One, on the 21st floor, has a lovely view overlooking the Kremlin and St. Basil's, one of the best sights in Moscow. Waiters in this restaurant also speak English. Food is good, and higher-priced than average. The basement restaurant is considered by young foreign residents in Moscow as the best in town for dancing. Good orchestra and music. Floor show. Other restaurants here are large and a bit impersonal.

Russian Hut (Russkaya Izba), a 40-minute drive from Moscow center on the road to Archangelskoye. Very pleasant for afternoon drive and meal. Set menu. Excellent *zakuski* (Russian hors d'oeuvres). More expensive than most. Reservations must be arranged well in advance (two days or so) through Intourist, which will have to supply car and driver for the trip to restaurant.

Slavyansky Bazaar, 13, 25th October St. Good food and service. A fun place to go, though music can be loud. Excellent private room for groups only. Ask Intourist guide to reserve it for your group.

Sofia, 32 Gorky Street. Bulgarian and Russian cooking. Food is fair; service, slow. Loud all-girl dance band playing polkas, gypsy music and bouncy 1920's style pop. Moderate prices.

Tsentralnyi, 10 Gorky St. Attached to the hotel. Traditional Russian dishes of great variety. Music, dancing.

Seventh Heaven (Sedmoye Nebo), TV Tower, Ostankino. So-so food, but the view is the main thing.

Ukraine, 10 Kutuzovsky Prospekt, in the Ukraine Hotel. Ukrainian cuisine. Try Ukrainian *borshch* (beetroot soup) or *vareniki,* very small dumplings filled with meat, rice vegetables or various fruits. Service and food vary considerably.

Uzbekistan, 29 Neglinnaya Street. Specialities include: *lagman,* meat and noodle soup; *maniar,* meat and egg soup; *pilaffs* ("plov") and *shashliks; tkhum-dulma,* Scotch eggs (breaded boiled eggs, if you can believe it!). Allow plenty of time, but the wait may be worth it. One of the better nationality restaurants. Must have a reservation. Colorful.

Varshava, Oktyabrskaya Sq. 2/1, in the Varshava (Warsaw) Hotel. Polish dishes. Food fair.

Yakor (Anchor) 49 Gorky Street. Neat little fish restaurant, fast service. Good dishes include King prawns when available and sturgeon Moscow-style with rich cream sauce.

Yunost, 36 Frunzensky Val. In the Yunost Hotel.

Of the **cafés,** the following deserve listing: *Aelita,* 45 Oruzheiny Pereulok; *Adriatika,* 19/3 Ryleev Street; *Ararat,* 4 Neglinnaya St.; *Arctica,* 4 Gorky St.; *Arfa,* 9 Stoleshnikov Pereulok; *Artisticheskoye,* 6 Proyezd Khudozhestvennogo Teatra; *Druzhba* (Friendship), Kuznetsky Most; *Krasny Mak* 20 Stoleshkinov Pereulok; *Ogni Moskvy* (Lights of Moscow), 2 Marx Prospekt, in the Moskva Hotel.

NIGHTLIFE See *Facts at your Fingertips* section earlier in this book.

OPERA AND BALLET. Evening performances at 7.30, sometimes earlier, matinees at 12 noon, but always check ahead. The **Bolshoi Opera and Ballet Theater,** Sverdlov Square. Tickets from 1 rouble to 5 roubles. Its ballet company is justly world famous; there are many Russian and foreign operas in its repertory, and its orchestra is also outstanding. The Bolshoi also presents regular performances on the stage of the Kremlin Palace of Congresses. (Entrance to this is through the white-washed Kutafia Gate, by the Manege, which leads to the Trinity Gate.) This seats 6,000.

Stanislavsky and Nemirovich-Danchenko Musical Theater, 17 Pushkinskaya Street. For classical and modern operas, ballets and operettas.

The Operetta, 6 Pushkinskaya Street. 2,000 seats. Classical and modern works. Obtain tickets for all performances through your hotel service bureau.

THEATER. Even if you do not speak Russian, you might want to explore the dramatic theaters and compare their productions of Shakespeare, Molière, Ibsen, Gogol and Chekhov or of modern playwrights like Arthur Miller or Arnold Wesker with the Western versions. Evenings at 7 P.M.; matinees at 12 noon; puppets at 7.30, but always check ahead. The puppet theater is excellent. There are 16 drama theaters; the most popular are: *Taganka, Sovremennik, Moscow Art Theater, Vakhtangov, Mayakovsky,* and *Moscow Drama Theater* (known as "Malaya Bronnaya").

The Maly Theater has *two* houses. The major is at 1/6 Sverdlov Square, its associated studio theater at 60 Bolshaya Ordynka Street.

Moscow Art Theater (MKhAT), 3 Proyezd Khudozhestvennogo Teatra. An affiliated smaller house, the MKhAT Filial, is at 3 Moskvila Street.

Vakhtangov Theater, 26 Arbat.

Central Soviet Army Theater, 2 Commune Square, has two auditoria.

Satire Theater, 18 Bolshaya Sadovaya Street, specializes in satirical comedies such as Mayakovsky's *The Bathhouse, The Bedbug* and *Mystery Bouffe.*

Poezia Hall, 12 Gorky Street. For poetry recitals and experimental drama.

Romany Theater, 26 Pushkinskaya Street, in the Hotel Sovetskaya. The only gipsy theater in the world.

Mayakovsky Theater, 19 Herzen Street.

Sovremennik Theater, Chistiye Prudy, in its new building. One of the youngest of Moscow's theaters; experimental, with a company of young actors and good designers.

Pushkin Drama Theater, 23 Tverskoi Boulevard.

Yermolova Theater, 5 Gorky Street.

Lenin Komsomol Theater, 6 Chekhov Street. The student and youth theater, presenting new plays by young authors.

Taganka Drama and Comedy Theater, 75 Chkalov Street. The best known of Moscow's avant-gardist and experimental companies. Very interesting staging by director Yury Lyubimov.

The Variety Theater, 20/2 Bersenevskaya Embankment, also known as the *Estrada,* the center of Moscow's music hall life.

The Moscow Music Hall has no premises of its own but performs at summer theaters in the parks, in the Variety Theatre, the Exhibition of Economic Achievements, etc.

Obraztsov Puppet Theater, 3 Sadovo-Samotechnaya. Puppetry is a particularly popular art form in the USSR and this is a world-famous troupe. Though primarily a children's theater it also puts on excellent satirical shows for adults which the visitor can enjoy even without Russian language ability. It also boasts an unusual "puppet cuckoo clock" which, at noon or midnight, is one of Moscow's tourist attractions.

Moscow Drama Theater,   (also known as the Malaya Brownnaya) on Malaya Brownnaya.

Moscow Theatre of Miniatures, 3 Karetny Ryad, offers popular programmes of "witty melodrama, merry tragedy, dramatized songs and dances"; its motto is brevity.

There are four *children's theaters* in Moscow: **The Central Children's Theater,** 2/7 Sverdlov Square; the **Moscow Children's Theater,** 10 Pereulok Sadovskikh; the **Moscow Puppet Theater,** 26 Spartakovskaya Street; and the **Children's Musical Theater,** now in its beautiful new premises on Vernadsky Prospekt. There is a **Mime Theater** (Teatr Mimiki i Zhesta) at 41 Izmailovsky Boulevard, which has been praised by no less a master than Marcel Marceau.

 CONCERTS. The musical life of Moscow is particularly rich; there are a number of symphony orchestras and song and dance ensembles, and the soloists are often world famous—from Igor Oistrakh to Sviatoslav Richter. The State Symphony Orchestra gives a long series of concerts through the season and then tours abroad and within the country. The Pyatnitsky Choir's performances of modern and old Russian songs are highly popular. There is Moiseyev's *Folk Dance Ensemble,* well-known in Western Europe and America, while the *Soviet Army Song and Dance Ensemble,* the *Beryozka Dance Ensemble,* the *Beethoven Quartet* and the *Osipov Russian Folk Orchestra* are equally (and justly) celebrated.

Variety and symphony concerts are given in the *Hall of Columns* (Kolonnyi Zal) of the House of Trade Unions, 1 Pushkinskaya Street. Chamber music is performed in the October Hall of the House of Trade Unions, and the Hall of the

Gnesin Music Institute, 30–36 Vorovsky Street, while symphony concerts and solo recitals, oratorios and concert performances of operas are given in the *Grand Hall of the Conservatory,* 13 Herzen Street, and the *Tchaikovsky Concert Hall,* 31 Gorky Street. Organ recitals are held in the *Small Hall* of the Conservatory and there are poetry readings in the *Lenin Library Hall,* 5 Kalinin Prospekt, and in the concert hall of the Rossia Hotel. There are scores of excellent halls where concerts are frequently given.

 THE CIRCUS. Often a hit with foreign tourists. The old *Moscow circus* is at 13 Tsvetnoi Boulevard. *New Circus* at 7 Vernadsky Prospekt. In summer there are tent circuses in the Gorky Park and at the Exhibition of Economic Achievements. There is a *circus on ice* which claims to rival the great ice shows of the West and has one extraordinary feature, *Bruins Play Hockey,* a troupe of bears playing on skates. The *Moscow Ice Ballet* usually performs in the Palace of Sport of the Lenin Stadium. For times and places of performance check with Intourist.

 MUSEUMS. Moscow has about 150 museums and permanent exhibitions. Some of the most important have already been described. Here we list their addresses, as well as some smaller and more specialized museums you may want to visit. Their hours of opening change frequently, so it is advisable to enquire at the service bureau of your hotel if you are not visiting them in the course of your Intourist group sightseeing. The opening times we give here are according to the latest information but it is still best to check them. *They may close early on days preceding holidays.*

REVOLUTIONARY MUSEUMS

Central Lenin Museum, 2 Revolution Square, near Red Square. Open daily 11–7, except Mondays.

Train of Mourning at Paveletsky Railway Station, 1 Kozhevnichesky Square. The engine and carriage which brought the coffin with Lenin's body to Moscow.

Lenin's House Museum In Gorky, 85 kilometers (about 50 miles) from Moscow. Open from 11 to 7, closed on Tuesdays. This is where Lenin spent the last years of his life and where he died on January 21, 1924. The furnishings have remained unaltered and documents and manuscripts are on display. Built in 1830, the house stands in a park of 175 acres, with 150-year-old oaks and a number of ponds; it was the home of the Mayor of Moscow before the revolution. Old motor cars stand in the garage, including Lenin's Rolls-Royce, adapted for use in heavy snow.

Karl Marx and Friedrich Engels Museum, 5 Marx-Engels Street. Open 1–7 Monday, Wednesday, Friday; 11 A.M.–5 P.M., Thursday, Saturday, Sunday; closed Tuesday. The exhibits include letters, early editions, documents and photographs of Marx and Engels and their close associates and friends, together with drawings and paintings. Marx's personal belongings, including his armchair and the easy chair in which he died on March 14, 1883, are also on view.

Museum of the Revolution, 21 Gorky Street. Open 10 –6, Tuesday, Saturday, Sunday; 12–8, Monday, Wednesday, Friday; closed Thursday. Originally built in 1780, rebuilt in classical style after the Moscow Fire of 1812. From 1831 until the 1917 revolution it was "the English Club", for noblemen. The six-inch gun in the yard was used by the revolutionary troops to fire on the Kremlin in

October, 1917. Opened in 1926, the 37-room museum guards the relics and mementos of the Revolution, starting with the history of the first worker's organisations in the 19th century. They include the battle-standards of the revolutionary groups, the horse-drawn machine-gun cart of the First Cavalry Army, the texts of the first decrees of the Soviet Government on peace and on land, dioramas and paintings portraying revolutionary battles, and thousands of other relics.

Mikhail Kalinin Museum, 21 Marx Prospekt, devoted to Kalinin's life and revolutionary activities.

Underground Press of the C.C., 55 Lesnaya Street. The premises of a revolutionary printing press deep below a house where the newspaper *Rabochii* (Worker) was printed.

Krasnaya Presnya Museum, 4 Bolshevitskaya Street. A small, one-storied timber house where the Presnya District Revolutionary Committee met in October 1917; one of the headquarters of the armed uprising.

HISTORICAL MUSEUMS

Historical Museum, 1–2 Red Square. Open 10:30–5:30 on Mondays, Thursdays and Sundays; from 12–7 on Wednesdays, Fridays and Saturdays; closed on Tuesdays and the last day of each month.

Cathedral of the Intercession Museum, St. Basil's Cathedral, Red Square. Also known as the Pokrovsky Cathedral Museum. Open 10–5 Wednesday to Sunday, closed Tuesdays.

 MOSCOW KREMLIN MUSEUMS. The churches and cathedrals within the Kremlin have all been converted into museums. Many have been specially repainted, restored and cleaned by master craftsmen have been using traditional methods and materials. They include: *Cathedral of the Archangel; Cathedral of the Annunciation; the Armory; Cathedral of the Assumption; Ivan the Great Bell Tower; Applied Art of the 17th Century Museum in the Cathedral of the Twelve Apostles and Patriarch's Residence* and *the Church of the Deposition of the Robe.* Detailed descriptions are given in the text of this chapter.

The Novodevichy Convent, 2 Bolshaya Pirogovskaya Street (near Sportivnaya Metro Station). Open 11–5.30; from November 1–April 30, 11–4.30; closed Tuesdays and the first Monday of each month.

Soviet Armed Forces Museum, 2 Commune Square. Open 10–7 on Tuesday, Friday, Saturday, Sunday; 12–8 on Wednesday, Thursday; closed Monday.

Battle of Borodino (1812) Panorama and Kutuzov's Hut, 38 Kutuzovsky Prospekt. Panorama open 9.30–8; closed Fridays; Hut open 10.30–7; closed Fridays.

Museum of the History and Reconstruction of Moscow, 12 Novaya Square. Open 10–6 on Saturday, Monday, Thursday; 2–9 on Wednesday, Friday; closed Tuesday and the last day of each month.

ART GALLERIES AND MUSEUMS

Tretyakov Art Gallery, 10 Lavrushinsky Pereulok, near Novokuznetskaya Metro Station. Open 10–8 (but Ticket Office closes at 7), except Mondays.

Pushkin Fine Arts Museum (New Gallery), 4 Marshal Shaposhnikov Street. Open 11–8 (Sundays 11–6).

Ostankino Palace (Museum of Serf Art) 5 Pervaya Ostankinskaya Street. Open 11–5 from May to September; 10–4 from October to April. Closed Tuesdays and Wednesdays, also Sundays at 2, except in summer.

Arkhangelskoye Estate Museum in the village of Arkhangelskoye, the **Kuskovo Palace Museum** and the **Kolomenskoye Estate Museum** are described in the section Excursions from Moscow earlier in this chapter.

Museum of Victor Vasnetsov, 12 Pereulok Vasnetsova. The former home, "a typical Russian fairyland house", of the famous 19th-century Russian artist, in which he lived and worked for 30 years. It contains his paintings, sketches, engravings and pencil drawings.

Museum of Russian Folk Art, 7 Stanislavsky Street, Open 12–7 daily; Mondays 12–6. Closed Tuesdays and the last day of the month. Antique and modern objects of art, such as pottery, ceramics, glassware, metalware, wood, bone, embroideries, lace and popular prints. In the Naryshkin House (17th century), 22 rooms have been restored.

Other museums worth visiting include the *Andrei Rublyev Museum* in the *Andronikov Monastery* (10 Pryamikov Square), the *Exhibition of Russian 17th- to 19th-Century Chattels,* 18/2 Razin Street (in the *Boyars Romanov Museum*), which shows fabrics, embroidery, lace and other garments; the *Central Exhibition Hall* (in the Pyatidesiatiletiye Oktyabrya Square), designed as a riding school, which has Russian and foreign exhibitions of art, textiles, furnishing and glass; the *Exhibition Hall of the USSR Academy of Arts* at 21 Kropotkin Street; and the *Exhibition Halls of the Union of Soviet Artists,* which are located at 20 Kuznetsky Most, at 25 Gorky Street, at 5 Chernyakhovsky Street, at 46b Gorky Street, at 7/9 Begovaya Street and 17 Zholtovsky Street. For the various exhibitions and opening times, check with Intourist or the galleries themselves.

ECONOMIC, SCIENTIFIC AND TECHNICAL MUSEUMS, EXHIBITIONS AND EXPOSITIONS

Exhibition of Economic Achievements of the USSR, Prospekt Mira, Metro: VDNKh. Open 9.30 A.M. to 10 P.M., Monday through Friday; 9.30 A.M. to 11 P.M. Saturday and Sunday. From September 1 to May 1, the pavilions are open 10 to 6.

Polytechnical Museum, 3–4 Novaya Square. Open 10–5 Wednesday, Friday, Sunday; 1–8 Tuesday, Thursday, Saturday; closed Mondays and the last day of the month.

The Zhukovsky Memorial Museum, 17 Radio Street, is dedicated to the work of the "father of Russian aviation", a founder of modern hydro- and aeromechanics, illustrating the development of Soviet aviation and space exploration.

The Frunze Central House of Aviation and Cosmonautics, 14 Krasnoarmeiskaya Street, is another museum devoted to the history of Russian aviation, especially the work of pioneers.

The Soviet Marine Exhibition is at 3 Stretenka Street.

The Timiryazev Biological Museum, 15 Malaya Gruzinskaya Street, is open daily from 10–6, but from 12–8 on Wednesdays and Fridays, and closed on Mondays. Its material covers plant and animal life and the origins and development of life on earth. It is named after Kliment Timiryazev (1843–1920), a botanist.

The Anthropological Museum, 18 Marx Prospekt, has an excellent collection of fossils of primitive man, including the Pithecanthropus, the Sinanthropus, a Neanderthaler and a Cro-Magnon.

The Palaeontological Museum, 16 Bolshaya Kaluzhskaya, one of the oldest in the country, a successor of Peter the Great's *Kunstkamera,* with fossils of past geological eras.

The Zoological Museum, 6 Herzen Street, Thousands of exhibits of mammals, birds, amphibians, reptiles and almost a million insects. Open 10 A.M.–6 P.M.; Wednesday and Friday 12–8 P.M.; closed Mondays.

The Mineralogical Museum, 14–16 Leninsky Prospekt, has a large collection of minerals of the Soviet Union and other countries, including rare crystals and precious stones.

The Darwin Museum, 1 Malaya Pirogovskaya Street, is open 10–5, closed on Saturdays and Sundays. It is devoted to the works and discoveries of Charles Darwin.

The Planetarium, 5 Sadovaya-Kudrinskaya Street, is open 12–7 in summer, 1–7 in winter, closed on Tuesdays.

LITERARY, MUSICAL AND THEATRICAL MUSEUMS

Museum of Literature, 38 Dimitrov Street. A fine collection of published and unpublished manuscripts, archives, portraits and first editions of Russian writers, whose recorded voices can be heard.

Gorky Museum, 25a Vorovsky Street, and the **Gorky Memorial Museum,** 6/2 Kachalov Street, are dedicated to the memory of the writer. The Memorial Museum is the house where he lived from 1931 to 1936; the Gorky Museum itself, which is open Tuesdays and Fridays, 1–8, Wednesdays, Thursdays and Sundays 10–5, and on Saturdays, 10.30–4 (closed on Monday), has a large collection illustrating the writer's life.

The Leo Tolstoy Museum and the **Tolstoy Home** are, respectively, at 11 Kropotkinskaya Street and at 21 Lev Tolstoy Street. The Museum is open 11–5 Thursdays, Saturdays and Sundays, 10–3 Mondays, 2–8 Wednesdays and Fridays, and is closed on Tuesdays. The Moscow Tolstoy Home can be visited every day 10–4.30, except Mondays.

Dostoyevsky Museum, 2 Dostoyevsky Street, open 11–6 Thursday, Saturday, Sunday, Monday 10–4, Wednesday and Friday 1–9, closed Tuesday. Devoted to the life and work of the great novelist.

Pushkin Museum, 12/2 Kropotkinskaya Street. Open on Saturdays, 1–7:30, Sundays 11–5:30.

Chekhov Museum, 6 Sadovo-Kudrinskaya Street. Open Mondays, Thursdays and Saturdays, 11–6, Wednesdays and Fridays 2–9, closed Tuesdays and Sundays.

Gogol Museum, Suvurov Street, in Gogol's former apartment.

Mayakovsky Library and Museum, 5/13 Mayakovsky Pereulok. This is installed in the poet's former home.

Alexander Ostrovsky Museum, 31/12 Bakhrushin Street. Open Thursdays, Saturdays, Sundays and Mondays 12–7, Wednesdays and Fridays 2–9, closed on Tuesdays. It presents the history of Russian drama, opera and ballet theaters from the 18th century to our own time. Founded in 1894 by the theater lover and collector in whose former home it is housed. Portraits of actors and scenic designs by well-known artists, theatrical costumes, famous manuscripts, rare editions, playbills, programs, and 200,000 photos.

Glinka Museum of Musical Culture, 12 Herzen Street. Open 9 A.M.–5.30 P.M., Saturdays 10 A.M.–3.30 P.M.; closed Sundays. A collection of musical instruments, some from the 16th and 17th centuries, drawings, photographs, pictures and recordings; also scores and letters by Tchaikovsky, Beethoven, Wagner, Liszt, Glinka, Prokofiev and other composers.

Puppet Museum. 3, Sadovaya-Samotechnaya. The Obraztsov-Puppet Theater has a collection of old and modern theatrical puppets from over 30 countries

There are **theatrical museums** attached to the *Bolshoi, Maly, Art* and *Vakhtangov* theaters. Others include *Konstantin Stanislavsky's,* 6 Stanislavsky Street; *Vladimir Nemirovich-Danchenko's* at 5/7 Nemirovich-Danchenko Street; *Yevgeny Vakhtangov's* at 12 Vesnin Street; *Boris Shchukin's* at 8a Shchukin Street, and *Alexander Scriabin's* at 11 Vakhtangov Street.

 SHOPPING. Most of the stores in Moscow are open Monday through Saturday 8 A.M. to 8 P.M., and closed Sundays. There is a one-hour lunch period (which varies) during which they are closed—except the big department stores GUM and Central. A few food shops open on Sundays.

What to buy and where to buy will depend on your taste, how much you want and how much you can spend. According to most recent information, the best buys seem to be fur hats, blouses and shirts, chess sets, books, records, silver tea-glass holders, lacquered and burnished boxes, ceramics (small vases and cups), balalaikas, pencil boxes, cigarette cases, nests of dolls, scarves and *babushkas;* also ivory carvings, miniature counting toys and dolls in peasant dresses. Electrical and medical instruments, guitars and educational toys are reasonably priced.

Though there is a restriction on their export, the famous Russian furs—sable, mink, polar fox, karakul, red, silver and blue fox—are usually available. So is North Russian lace, Lithuanian amber, jewelry, trinkets made of Ural gems, Ukrainian embroidery and inlaid woodwork, Georgian, Ukrainian and Baltic ceramics, Byelorussian linen, etc. Cameras, vodka, Armenian cognac, Georgian and Moldavian wine are low-priced. Soviet watches, champagne, caviar, Uzbek gowns and gold-embroidered skull caps, Georgian inlaid silver wine horns, accordions and harmonicas might also tempt you. The main shopping streets are Gorky Street, Arbat, Kuznetsky Most, Petrovka, and Stoleshnikov, but there are several other newly established districts. Try the new, elegant Kalinin Prospekt for records, photographic equipment or gourmet goods.

The **Beryozka** shops only accept payment in *Vneshtorgbank coupons* or in foreign currency; and here the goods are duty-free. You may get change in some exotic foreign currency, not your own! Come prepared with an assortment of notes and coins to avoid this.

Note: Many of the above items are for sale in these Beryozka (Birch Tree) shops, which are located in all the large Intourist hotels. Here the prices are lower and the selection better than in regular Russian stores. The Rossiya and Ukraine have the best shops.

Here is a select list for the shopper:

Gastronom, 62 Gruzinskaya, open Monday-Saturday, 10–1 2–7, closed Sundays. For food supplies, cigarettes and drink.

Gastronom, 60 Dorogomilovskaya, open 10–1, 2–7.

Department Store, 25a Luzhnitsky Proyezd, near the Lenin Stadium. Open Monday-Saturday, 9 to 7, closed Sundays. The best **Beryozka,** large selection. Good for souvenirs, transistor radios, watches.

Book Shop, 1812 Goda Street, near Kutuzovsky Prospekt, turning right before the Borodino Panorama, open Monday-Saturday, 10–2, 3–7. Closed Sundays.

Clothing Store, 5/9 Krasnokholmskaya Embankment. Open Monday-Saturday, 11–8.

For clothing, 31 Kropotkinskaya Street. Open Monday-Saturday 11–8, closed Sundays.

Knitwear and Shoe Shop, 60/2 Leninsky Prospekt. Open Monday-Saturday, 10–8.

Clothing Store, 5 Fersmana Street (up Leninsky Prospekt, then left, opposite Moskva Department Store). Open Monday-Saturday, 9–8.

Clothing and Fur Shop, 16 Profsoyuznaya Street. Open Monday-Saturday 9–8.

Gift Shop and Furs, 9 Kutuzovsky Prospekt.

Vneshtorgbank Gold Shop, 9 Pushkin Street. Gold, silver, precious stones. Open Mondays-Fridays 10–4, Saturdays 10–2.

The GUM Department Store, 3 Red Square, is open Monday-Friday 11–9, on Saturdays 8–9, closed Sundays. This is one of the Moscow sights but it also offers a reasonable selection of clothes, fabrics, shoes, watches, jewelry, handicrafts, souvenirs, perfumery, toys, etc.

It has a number of branches: **Podarki,** at 4 Gorky Street, has a broad range of gifts and gift sets, ladies' bags, gloves, confectionery and wines; **Izdelia Khudozhestvennykh Promyslov,** 17 Kutuzovsky Prospekt, specializes in arts and crafts lace, ceramics, bone and wood articles, prints and other works of folk art; **Khrustal** (Cut-Glass) at 15 Gorky Street sells vases, wine glasses, salad dishes and other cut glass articles.

The TSUM (Central) Department Store is a shopping center of 12 shops on Petrovka Street, Stoleshnikov Pereulok and Kuznetsky Most. Open Monday-Friday 11–9, Saturdays 8 A.M.–9 P.M. and closed on Sundays.

The Detsky Mir Children's Department Store, 2 Marx Prospekt, is open Monday-Friday 8–8, Saturday 8 A.M.–9 P.M., closed Sundays. A wide range of children's wares; it has 24 branches throughout the city.

There are two **markets** you might like to visit: **Tsentrainy Rynok** (Central Market), 15 Tsvetnoy Boulevard, and the **Cheryomushkinsky Rynok,** 3 Lomonosvsky Pr. A real Soviet institution, very colorful. Often farmers from Georgia or Central Asia bring their fruits, vegetables and flowers to sell. Fancy prices in winter.

An East European specialty modelled on the Russian original is the **Commission Shop,** in which private individuals offer their possessions for sale. One of the best is at 54–58 Dimitrov Street, near the French Embassy. It has samovars and paintings. Two others are particularly popular: the first is at 46 Gorky Street and specializes in china; the other is at 32 Arbat, it also has glass and bronze ware. At either of them, you might conceivably pick up something unusual, but prices are high and you may have difficulty exporting your purchase.

Art galleries which sell paintings, small scuplture, etc. include two on Gorky Street (the first at No. 25 and the second at 46b, the latter selling mainly graphic art), and one each at 24 Kutuzovsky Prospekt, 8/1 25-Oktyabrya Street, and 12 Petrovka Street.

The Beryozka shop at 32 Gorky Street specializes in *jewelry* and the **Yantar** at 13 Stoleshnikov Per. in *amber.* Other **Beryozka** shops: 5 Rostovskaya Naberezhnaya, 12 Eighteen Twelve Street, 21 Bolshaya Dorogomilovskaya (food).

Perfumes and cosmetics can be found at 6 Gorky Street, 7 Marx Prospekt and 20 Kuznetsky Most.

Crystal and glass (in addition to the commission shops and the big stores) at 15 Gorky Street and 8/2 Kirov Street.

For **carpets,** 9 Gorky Street.

For **flowers,** 1 Sretenka Street, 16 Arbat and 4 Arbat (commission flower shop) can be recommended.

Toys are of good quality at the **Dom Igrushki** shop, 8 Kutuzovsky Prospekt, which is open 11–8 and closed on Sundays, **souvenirs** at 4 Gorky Street and at 9 Kutuzovsky Prospekt, open Monday-Saturday 10–9, closed Sundays.

Other high quality goods are available at:

19 Arbat and 46b Gorky Street for antiques, china, cut glass, bronze, marble, ivory, paintings, and miniatures.

Druzhba, "Friendship", 15 Gorky Street, for books in the languages of the Communist countries; 18 Kuznetsky Most for books in other foreign languages.

Second-hand foreign books at 16 Kachalov Street.

Moskva, 8 Gorky Street, books in Russian and foreign languages, stamps and postcards.

Moscow House of Books, 26 Kalinin Prospekt, the largest bookstore of the city.

Stamp Collector's Shop, 16 Dzerzhinsky Street, stamps and postcards.

Records at 6/2 Arbat and 17 Kirov Street.

Amethyst, 9 Kutuzovsky Prospekt, for jewelry, souvenirs. Soviet and foreign currency accepted.

Wanda, a Polish gift shop, is on Leninsky Prospekt. Other Polish shops are **Morozko** (for food products including fresh-frozen berries), **Polish Carnation** (for flowers) and **Polish Fashions.** Addresses unknown.

TOURS. *Intourist* runs regular city tours which will be part of your individual or group arrangements. If you have special interests, consult the service bureau at your hotel or your Intourist guide.

MEDICAL SERVICE. Medical service in the Soviet Union is free and available in any city or town. When feeling ill, immediately call a doctor through your interpreter or through the hotel desk. First aid administration and doctors' visits are free, but you will have to pay for medicines, and for hospitalization at 16 roubles a day. Normally this is offset against the value of unused tourist services per day, and the difference is refunded where the unused amount is greater, or paid by the tourist if hospitalization costs exceed hotel or other pre-paid costs.

There is a *special clinic* in Moscow which cares for foreign visitors. Its address is 12 Herzen Street, the telephone numbers 229-73-23 and 229-03-82. Its staff includes qualified doctors and nurses, and there are X-ray, physiotherapy, dental and other departments.

There is a *diplomatic polyclinic* at 3 Sverchkov Per. (tel. 221-59-92 and 221-49-11, day and night). It has a *children's section* (228-07-25) and the director can be reached at 223-55-15. The *Botkin Hospital,* 5, 2nd Botkinsky Proyezd. tel. 255-00-15, ext. 268, has a Diplomatic Block (Korpus 5).

For *First Aid and Ambulance,* dial 03; people in hospital, dial 294-31-52.

CHURCH SERVICES. Protestant church service is held on alternate Sundays at Spaso House (US Embassy) and the British Embassy, 14 Nab. Morisa Toreza, at 10.30 A.M. The chaplain (according to most recent information) is the Rev. Raymond Oppenheim (telephone 143-35-62, 38 Lomonosovsky Prospekt, Apt. 59–60.) The visiting Anglican chaplain (who normally resides in Helsinki) can be contacted at the British Embassy.

Baptist services are held on Sundays at 1 P.M. and 6 P.M. and on Tuesdays, Thursdays and Saturdays at 6 P.M. at 3 Maly Vuzovsky Per.

Catholic services: St. Louis des Français, 12 Malaya Lubyanka (masses in Latin, sermons in Polish and Russian); Sundays 8 A.M. and 11 A.M., 6 P.M. (after Easter, 7 P.M.); Mondays, Tuesdays, Wednesdays and Thursdays, 8 A.M., Fridays and Saturdays, 6 P.M.

Chapel of Our Lady of Hope, 12/24 Savodo-Samotechnaya, Apt. 23. Masses in Latin; sermons in English and French.) The Chaplain is Father Joseph Richard. A. A., tel 294-41-78. Services: 7 P.M. (after 1st October, 6 P.M.) in the Chapel of Our Lady of Hope, which fulfils Sunday obligations. Sundays: 9 A.M. and 10.30 A.M., 12 noon, in the Community Room, American Embassy, 19/23 Tchaikovskaya Street. Mondays, Tuesdays, Thursdays, Fridays 8.30 A.M., Wednesday 7 P.M., all at the Chapel of Our Lady of Hope.

Synagogues: 8 Arkhipova Street. Services daily at 10 A.M. and one hour before sundown; also at 8 Bolshoi Spasoglinischchevsky.

Russian Orthodox churches open for worship include: Yelokhovsky Cathedral, 15 Spartakovskaya; Uspensky Church, in the Novodevichy Convent, 2 Bolshaya Pirogovskaya Street; Ivan Voin Church, 46 Dimitrov Street; Voskresenskaya Church, on the Brusovsky Per.; The Old Believers' Cathedral, 29 Rogozhsky Per.; and the Moscow Patriarchate at Kropotkin Street, 5 Chisty Per.

Mosque: 7 Vypolzov Per. The *Hamaz* is recited five times daily.

 MAIL, TELEPHONE AND CABLES. For general information, see *Facts at Your Fingertips.* In Moscow: The *International Telephone Call Office* is at 7 Gorky Street, tel. 295-92-68 (enquiries). Incoming telegrams can be collected here; tel. 294-47-50.

Long distance calls within the USSR: (a) the Caucasus, Central Asia, the Far East, Kazakhstan, Siberia, Belgorod, Kherson, Kursk, Odessa, Orel, Tula and Voronezh, dial 08. (b) Crimea, Archangelsk, Kaluga, Kazan, Kharkov, Ryazan & Yaroslavl, dial 06. (c) Kalinin, Leningrad, Murmansk, Novgorod, Petrozavodsk and Pskov, dial 225-10-03. (d) Kiev, Kharkov and Volgograd, dial 225-11-00. (e) The Baltic countries, Byelorussia, Donbas, Moldavia and the Western Ukraine, Chernigov, Poltava, Vinnitsa and Zhitomir, dial 245-00-00. (f) Ulyanovsk, Vladimir and Ivanovo, dial 271-90-21. (g) towns in the Moscow area, dial 00 (h) long distance enquiries, dial 07. For dialling codes for most places in the USSR dial 09.

International Telephone Exchange: 271-91-03; 295-10-20 (if you have an account); 272-06-14 (enquiries); 271-25-85 (supervisor).

Cables by phone within the USSR: 225-20-02.

International Post Office, la Komsomolskaya Square. Tel. 294-75-55 (enquiries); enquiries about incoming parcels: 295-47-94.

Telex Center: 229-63-06.

 READING MATTER, LIBRARIES. We have mentioned foreign-language bookshops under our shopping information. Foreign (American and British) newspapers are rarely available, though there has been some relaxation in the kiosks of the principal Intourist hotels. There is a foreign literature *lending library* at 3/5 Ulyanovskaya Street, which is open 10 A.M. to 10 P.M., closed first day of the month; another is located at No. 1 Petrovskiye Linii. *Reading Rooms* are situated at 12 Razin Street.

Other libraries with foreign-language material include:

Lenin Library, 3 Kalinin Prospekt, open 9 A.M.–10 P.M. This is the largest in the Soviet Union, with over 21 million titles, receiving a copy of every book printed in the country. The rare books and manuscripts section has a collection of early documents, old manuscripts and incunabula, and, dating back to 1587, the first Russian printing press.

Central Polytechnical Library, 2 Politekhnichesky Proyezd, Entrance 10. Open 9 A.M. to 10 P.M.

Public Library (History) 9 Starosadsky Per. Open 9 A.M. to 10 P.M.

Theatrical Library, 8/1 Pushkin Street. Open 11–9.45, Mondays to Fridays. Closed Sundays.

 **SPORTS.** Many facilities were re-equipped or extended for the 1980 Olympic Games. *The Lenin Stadium and the Palace of Sports,* Luzhniki, provide the largest complex of facilities.

The Dynamo Stadium, 36 Leningradsky Prospekt, is the second biggest stadium, accommodating 60,000. It has a large indoor swimming pool and is set in a park. There is a cycling track nearby (31 Leningradsky Prospekt), where there is a Young Pioneers Stadium for Children.

The Army Palace of Sports is at 39 Leningradsky Prospekt.

Moskva Open Air Pool, 37 Kropotkinskaya Embankment is open all year 7 A.M. –11 P.M. Heated pool. *The Dynamo Bathing Beach* is at 69 Leningrad Chaussée, Khimki Reservoir. *Seryebryany Bor Bathing Beach* is at Seryebryany Bor. At these places swimming, bathing and boating are available.

For skiing and skating there is ample opportunity in the large parks. Moscow has snow on 164 days a year (on average). Artificial ice-rinks are open throughout the year. There is a ski-jump on the Lenin Hills.

Football matches, track-and-field competitions and mass sports pageants are held in the Lenin and Dynamo Stadiums; hockey games at Lenin Stadium and in Sokolniki.

The race course (Hippodrome) is at 22 Begovaya Street. Racing begins at 5 on Wednesdays and Saturdays; there is racing at 1 and 5 on Sundays. An Equestrian Sports Center has been laid out in *Bitsa Forest Park* outside the city. A new cycle track has been constructed at *Krylatskoye* to the north-west, and in Moscow itself a large multi-purpose *stadium and indoor swimming and diving pool* has been built on Prospekt Mira.

The Central Chess Club is at 14 Gogolevsky Boulevard.

PARKS AND GARDENS. *Gorky Park,* 9 Krymsky Val. Open 10 A.M.–11 P.M. The most popular in Moscow.

Sokolniki Park, 62 Rusakovskaya Street. Open 10 A.M. –11 P.M. Named after the falconers *(sokolniki)* who used to live here. Openair theater, an amusement park, a shooting gallery, restaurants and cafes. There are bicycles to hire, which you may need to explore all 1,530 acres of the park, including part of an ancient forest.

Izmailovo Park, 17 Narodny Pr. Covering almost 3,000 acres, it includes large stretches of pine forest. Once the manor of the Romanovs, a favorite retreat of the Czars. Amusement park, open air theater and several cafés.

Hermitage Garden, 3 Karetny Ryad. Open May 1–September 1, 10 A.M.–11 P.M. This is a small park in the center of the city, in which there are concerts and variety and puppet performances during the summer. Several cafés and a restaurant.

Main Botanic Garden of the USSR Academy of Sciences, at Ostankino, (trolley buses 36 or 9) covers an area of some 900 acres and has been planted in and among the original beech-oak-spruce forests of the Moscow area. One large landscape section has nearly 3,000 species of native plants of the USSR, from the Carpathians to Vladivostok, arranged in naturally landscaped areas; over 1,700 kinds of trees and shrubs are planted in the dendrarium. Another smaller botanical garden, belonging to the University is at 26 Prospekt Mira.

Pet Market, Saturdays and Sundays, Kalitnokovskaya Street, south-east of Taganka Square. Hard to find but a taxi-driver will know where it is. Birds, dogs, fish—a fascinating glimpse of Russians and their pets.

The Zoo is at 1 Bolshaya Gruzinskaya Str Open 10–5.

With the parks, the puppet theaters and the sports grounds, there will be always plenty of things of *special interest to children,* including the various museums which have guided tours for young people.

 GENERAL INFORMATION AND EMERGENCIES. Emergency and information phone numbers in Moscow: *Fire* (dial) 01. *Police* 02. *Ambulance* 03. *Emergency Gas Service* 04 *Enquiries* about Moscow telephone numbers 09 (if you speak Russian). *Correct time* (speaking clock) 100. *Lost Property:* if in subway (metro), 220-20-85; if in tram, trolleybus; 233-00-18, extension 139 *Lost children,* 02 and 232-07-22. *Tracing people* in hospital, 294-31-52.

Intourist telephone numbers and addresses are listed in *Facts at Your Fingertips,* earlier.

Embassies: *United States of America:* 19/23 Tchaikovsky Street, tel. 252-00-11/19. Telex 429. Monday to Friday 9–1; 2–6.

Great Britain: 14 Nab. Morisa Toreza, tel. 231-95-55/57. Office hours: Monday-Friday 9–12; 2:30–5. Consular Section: same hours. Commercial and Cultural Offices: 7/4 Kutuzovsky Pr., tel. 241-10-33.

Canada: 23 Starokonyushenny Per., tel. 241-90-34; 241-91-55; 241-96-98; 241-50-70. Night 241-90-34 Open Monday-Friday, 9:30–1; 2–6.

Australia: 13 Kropotkinsky Per., tel. 241-20-35; 241-20-36; 246-31-24; 246-02-09 and 246-83-35. Telex 474. Office hours: Monday-Friday, 9:30–1; 2:30–6.

Anglo-American School: 26 Kropotkinsky Per.

Foreign Airlines and Travel Agencies: *Air Canada.* Hotel Metropole, Room 383. tel. 225-63-83; 225-60-83; 225-69-26. Open Mondays-Fridays 9:30–6, Saturday 9:30–2. At Sheremetyevo (on flight days only) 156-94-96; 155-60-06, ext. 846.

British Airways, Hotel National, Rooms 375-376. Tel. 203-94-63; 203-55-87. Office hours: Mondays-Saturdays, 9:30–1; 2–5:30. Sheremetyevo: 158-79-65 (Mondays, Wednesdays and Fridays 12–6).

Pan-American Airways, Hotel Metropole, Room 239. Tel. 223-51-83; 225-64-06. Mondays-Saturdays, 9–6. Sheremetyevo: 156-94-43.

American Express, Hotel Metropole, Room 384. Tel. 225-63-84.

LENINGRAD

Elegant and Heroic

"Leningrad," a young, devoted guide said, "is the Number One rival of every city in the Soviet Union—because the Czars built so many palaces and churches here. For a tourist there is far more to see in our city than in Moscow."

This is not just local patriotism: many people would agree that the second largest metropolis of the USSR deserves the proudly-claimed name of *Venice of the North*. Voltaire declared: "The united magnificence of all the cities of Europe could but equal St. Petersburg." There are magic cities whose names alone inspire you to dream—and to travel. Leningrad belongs io this privileged company, celebrated equally because it is a unique treasure-house of 18th-century architecture, has one of the richest collections of French and other paintings—and at the same time provides an object lesson in urban planning. Leningrad proves the Russian genius for museums.

It is, by European standards, a young city—less than 300 years have passed since Peter the Great built his first log cabin here to supervise the creation of his own city. Called St. Petersburg until 1914, when the Germanic-sounding name was changed to Petrograd, in 1924 it was renamed the City of Lenin. Today the city and its immediate area are the home of some 4,372,000 people. The central area is divided into 14 districts and five other towns (Kolpino, Kronstadt, Petrodvorets, Pushkin and Sestroretsk) also belong to the community.

Lying in the delta of the Neva River, Leningrad is only a few feet above sea level. The huge delta has formed 110 islands, which are linked by some 700 bridges; the city is built partly on these islands and partly on the mainland. The city is susceptible to floods—one such flood inspired

Pushkin's dramatic poem *The Bronze Horseman*. Severe flooding in 1977 led to plans for a 26-kilometer flood barrage to be laid across the Gulf of Finland.

The climate is moderate, with cold winters and warm but not excessively hot summers. The average temperature is 4°C. (39.2°F.), with a July average of 18°C. (64.4°F.) and a January one of − 8°C. (17.6°F.). But though winter begins in December and ends around March 21 (the vernal equinox), Leningrad is warmer than Moscow, as the climate is influenced by the Baltic. The atmosphere is humid, fogs are frequent and the rainfall is heavy; it is changeable enough to be compared to London.

Early in the summer the "White Nights" are an unusual phenomenon; there is only a brief interval of semi-darkness between the late sunset and the early sunrise and even then it is light enough in the streets to read large print. These White Nights last from June 11 to July 2. They inspired Dostoyevsky to write his *White Nights*, and are nowadays the occasion for Leningrad's annual summer festival of music and the arts.

After Peter the Great decided to "open a window to Europe," he commissioned the most outstanding Russian and foreign architects of his age to build his capital. He made it the imperial residence in 1712. During the second half of the 18th century and during the 19th century the rapid growth continued unabated. By 1862 there were some 300 factories in St. Petersburg; in 1837 the first railroad line linked it with the town of Pushkin (formerly Tsarkoye Selo). The Academy of Sciences was founded here in 1725, followed by the university, with medical and technical faculties. Military Academies, high schools, the opera, theaters and museums were also quickly established. St. Petersburg (and later Petrograd) was the cultural and scientific center of the country, and also the scene of the major political movements. Here the Decembrists rose in 1825 and the theoreticians and ideologists of the peasant revolution, Chernyshevsky, Dobrolyubov and Pisarev, directed in the 1870's the Narodnik (populist) movement.

Pushkin, Gogol, Lermontov, Goncharov, Belinsky, Turgenev, Dostoyevsky and Gorky all lived and worked for longer or shorter periods on the Neva; it was the home of Glinka, Rimsky-Korsakov, Mussorgsky, Borodin and Tchaikovsky among the musicians; of Repin and Vereshchagin among the painters. By the end of the 19th century it was also the headquarters of the revolutionary workers' movements.

The first, abortive Russian revolution of 1905 began when Czar Nicholas II's soldiers massacred scores of workers who were demonstrating outside the Winter Palace. Lenin, of course, was closely linked with the subsequent political events; it was to Leningrad's Finland Station that a sealed train brought him from Germany. The city was the scene of the October Revolution (on November 6–7, according to the Western calendar) which established Soviet power. Though in the twenties Moscow became the capital of the Soviet Union, Leningrad remained, if not the equal, at least the close rival of the larger city.

During World War Two Leningrad withstood the assault of 43 German and 22 Finnish divisions—about a million men. The grim statistics show that some 107,000 bombs and 250,000 shells fell upon it and the engines of war that battered the city included 12,000 guns, 1,500 tanks and 1,200 aircraft.

It was an almost unparalleled ordeal—much longer than the siege of Stalingrad. There was no electricity, no transportation and no water (except that drawn from the rivers and canals). The winter of 1941–2 was particularly severe. Seventeen thousand people were killed by bombs and shells: a million died of starvation. The bread ration was 400 grams for manual workers (reduced later to 125). Milk was made from soya beans: tobacco from the leaves of trees. Drink was brewed from the soil in which sugar had soaked after the warehouses burned down. When, on January 26, 1945, Leningrad was awarded the Order of Lenin, it was a fitting reward for heroism and endurance. In the past 35 years the city has been practically rebuilt, rising triumphantly from its ruins.

Exploring Leningrad

The Neva is one of the shortest rivers in the world, less than 50 miles long. It flows from Lake Ladoga, divides at Leningrad into many smaller and larger branches and then disappears in the Gulf of Finland. Its flow, however, is so strong that the water of the Gulf near Leningrad is barely salty and the silt it carries bars the city from the sea except along a constantly dredged channel. From the beginning of November to the beginning of April it freezes over—and the ice is thick enough most of the time to bear the weight of pedestrians. There are two thaws in Leningrad—the first when the ice of the river melts, and, a few weeks later, usually early in May, when the ice-floes of Lake Ladoga float down into the Gulf of Finland.

Most of Leningrad's bridges are comparatively low. Only small ships can pass under them during the day. At night the bridges are opened for an hour or so, according to a strict time-table, as this interrupts road traffic. Some are raised, others have their center section floated out.

Several times during the year, usually on May 1, the last Sunday of July (the Day of the Soviet Fleet) and on November 7, the units of the Baltic Fleet steam up the Neva and anchor in the heart of the city. In the spring and summer, hydrofoils and small water-buses ply the river. One of the best ways to explore the city is by one of these; it only costs a few kopeks, depending on how far you go.

The finest view of the Neva can be had from the Kirov Bridge. The river is at its broadest here and opposite the bridge, at the tip of Vasilevsky Island, it divides in two. On the right you'll see the gilt towers of the Peter-and-Paul Fortress while to the left is a whole row of the splendid palaces of long-vanished courtiers.

The Peter-and-Paul Fortress

Peter the Great built the fortress that formed the nucleus of St. Petersburg on a small hexagonal island on the Neva. Started in 1706, the fortress was not completed until 1741; later the walls were faced with granite slabs. Peter's successors added barracks and bastions within the fortress walls, most of which are still standing. After losing its military importance the fortress became a prison, here Peter I's son, Alexei, was tortured to death on his father's orders. From the end of the 18th century it was a prison for political offenders; Gorky was a prisoner in 1905, Dostoyevsky in 1849. In 1917 its arsenal was used to arm the revolutionaries.

The dominant edifice is the Cathedral of Peter-and-Paul, founded in 1712 but rebuilt in 1753 by Rastrelli and his pupil Savva Chevakinsky.

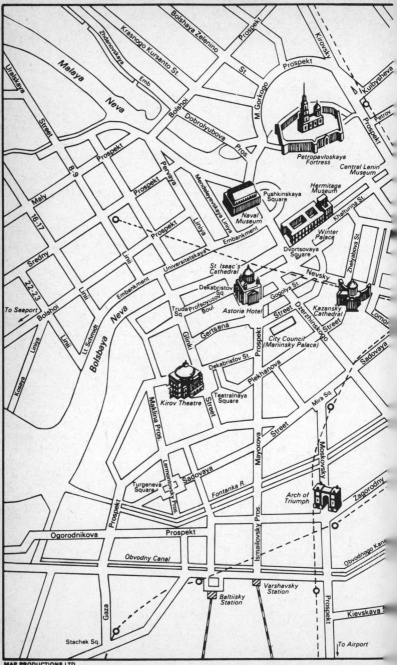

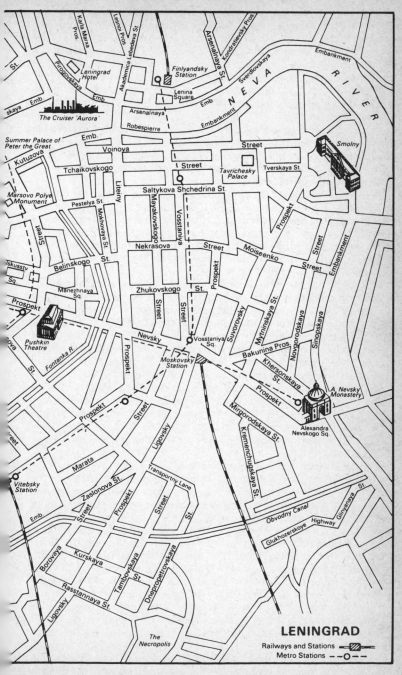

LENINGRAD

Railways and Stations
Metro Stations

All the rulers of Russia (except Peter II) were buried here from Peter I to Alexander III, after Petersburg became the capital of Russia. The imperial tombs are of white marble with gilded eagles at the corners. The iconostasis was designed by Zarudnyi in 1726. The upper part of the cathedral's tower is a needle-like spire covered with gold leaf. (When this had to be renewed in recent years the only people who would undertake the task were experienced mountain climbers.) Under the cross at the top an angel hanging on a chain swings in the wind. The clock strikes every quarter of an hour.

Since 1922 the Fortress has been a museum; guided tours explore the bastions, the battlements and the casemates. The Artillery Museum and the Museum of Military Engineering are also housed here. The Old Mint still functions within the walls. The cannon on the battlements is still used to fire salvoes on festive occasions.

Near the Fortress, on the bank of the Neva, stands Peter the Great's wooden hut. Built in 3 days in 1703, it was the summer residence of the great Czar. The pine logs of which it was constructed were painted to resemble bricks; it has two rooms and a cabinet. It is enclosed within a stone building set up in 1784 by Catherine II to protect it. Inside the cottage is the boat in which the Czar saved the lives of some fishermen on Lake Ladoga in 1690.

Vasilevsky Island, one of Leningrad's largest, contains 2,000 acres. It is bordered on both sides by the two arms of the Neva and at its lower end by the Gulf of Finland. The upper tip was mostly occupied by public offices; on the rest, throughout most of the 18th and 19th centuries, stood two- to four-storied tenement houses. Peter wanted to turn this part of the island into a miniature copy of Venice but only some of the small canals were dug and these were later filled in. However, their memory still survives in the names of the streets—called "lines." They cross the three avenues which run parallel to the axis of the island, the Great, Middle and Small Prospekts; instead of names they bear numbers, one to each side of each street. The island forms the north-west corner of the map on page 000, just across the Neva from the Winter Palace. Since 1967 it has been accessible by subway; take the train to Vasileostrovskya station.

The upper, semi-circular tip of the island is a park, a favorite spot for Leningrad lovers. Two lighthouses which stand in the square before the park, called the Rostralniye Columns, are decorated with ships' prows. They were erected in 1806 to serve as signal towers for the ships; in those days this was the commercial harbor.

The main building of the square, the former Stock Exchange, dates from the same period. Built in 1804–10 and designed by the Swiss Thomas de Thomon, it is an imitation Greek temple with Doric columns. Today it houses the Central Navy Museum. The museum was founded by Peter the Great, who ordered a model to be kept of every vessel under construction. It now has over 1,500 exhibits. Of its four sections the first is devoted to the history of the old Imperial Russian Fleet from the date of its inception up to the 1917 Revolution; the second covers the navy's role in the October Revolution, the Civil War and its development up to 1941; the third deals with the activities of naval vessels and aircraft in World War Two; the final section is devoted to the post-1945 period. The vast collection includes paintings and sculpture on marine subjects by Russian and foreign artists, battle flags, medals, decorations and photographs.

On the side of the island facing the main branch of the Neva, along the Universitetskaya Quay is the Zoological Museum of the USSR Academy of Sciences, opened in 1782. Its Hall of Mammoths is unique; discovered in perma-frost, their bodies have remained almost intact, with part of their fur. There are about 100,000 exhibits. Adjoining the Zoological Museum to the west stands George Mattarnóvi's fine building in the so-called Peter-the-Great baroque style. Finished in 1727, it was the home of the first Russian museum of the natural sciences, then called the Kunstkamera. Today it houses various scientific institutes, including the Anthropological and Ethnographical Museum of the USSR Academy of Sciences and the Lomonosov Museum.

Collected during expeditions and archeological excavations by Russian scientists and travelers, the exhibits in the Ethnographical Museum show the culture and life of the peoples of Asia, Africa, Australia and Oceania, native peoples of South and North America and those of the Arctic. The first section deals with the development of primitive societies. The Far Eastern section is devoted to the history, handicrafts and national costumes of China, Korea and Vietnam. A unique collection of noblemen's clothes from 17th-century China is a special feature. The "Peoples of India" section shows a rich selection of objects and utensils, silk, cotton and brocade garments, theatrical costumes and masks. Many items were gathered by 19th-century Russian explorers, among them Nikolai Miklukho-Maklai who explored the Polynesian islands. Models, life-sized figures and dioramas complete the displays. Peter the Great's original Exhibition of "Rarities, Curiosities and Oddities" is in the gallery of the upper floor.

The next building also serves science; erected in 1783–1789, designed by the Italian Giacomo Quarenghi, it was the original home of the Soviet Academy of Sciences until 1924, when it was transferred to Moscow. Today it houses various learned societies and research laboratories.

The next group of buildings is that of the Zhdanov State University (or Leningrad State Univ.) whose predecessor, the famous University of Petersburg, was founded in 1819. The main building was designed by Trezzini, again in Peter I's baroque style. In the great Czar's days it housed the "Twelve Colleges" (or, as we would call them today, Ministries.) In the vicinity of the university there are a number of other research institutes and one of the largest libraries in the Soviet Union, that of the Academy of Sciences.

Another notable building on the University Quay is the Repin Academy of Painting, Sculpture and Architecture. The building itself was designed by Alexander Kokorinov and a Frenchman, Jean Vallin de la Mothe. Its style is a transition between baroque and classicism; it was built in 1764–88. Two Egyptian sphinxes of the 15th century BC stand on either side of the ramp leading to the river harbor. These were brought to Petersburg in 1862.

The Kirov Cultural Palace stands on the Bolshoi (Grand) Prospekt. Finished in 1937, it was designed in the prevailing constructivist style.

The center of Vasilevsky Island is industrial. At its lower tip, on the seashore, there is a beach near the passenger harbor from where ships link Leningrad with Finnish, Swedish, Danish, British and North American ports.

Palace Square and the Hermitage

Dvortsovaya (Palace) Square is the historical, architectural and topographical heart of Leningrad. From the middle of the 18th century, Russia was governed from this spot; it is the site of the former imperial residence, the Winter Palace. In the winter of 1905, "Bloody Sunday" occurred here; peaceful demonstrations were gunned down by soldiers. During the days of the October Revolution the Winter Palace was the temporary refuge of the Kerensky Government, which was finally overthrown by the Bolsheviks.

Leningrad's architecture is characterized by "group building": the planning of whole vistas and ensembles of palaces and public offices. This style is most evident in Palace Square. The dominant Winter Palace was built between 1754 and 1762 by Rastrelli. After the great fire of 1837 it was reconstructed by Stasov and Bryullov. It is an immense building, three stories high; one side faces the Neva, while the main façade gives on to the square.

The baroque palace has 1,047 rooms and halls and 117 staircases. The white marble main staircase is still as it was in the 18th century. Many of the halls are decorated with delicately worked Ural stone. The Heraldic Hall (1,200 square yards) has some splendid chandeliers, carrying the coats of arms of Moscow, St. Petersburg and all the regions of the Russian Empire.

Later in the 18th century, other buildings were added and the complex now houses the Hermitage Museum, one of the world's great museums. Its origins go back to the early 18th century, but the official foundation date is 1764 when a large collection was acquired in Europe. In the next three years a special Hermitage Pavilion was built, called the Small Hermitage, to house this collection. Outside is the Hanging Garden, laid out on a platform supported by vaults. In 1775–84 the Old Hermitage was constructed by Felten and was notable for its brilliant interior decoration. In 1788 Quarenghi designed a replica of the Raphael Gallery in Rome in the Old Hermitage. By 1850 still another building, the New Hermitage, was added, linked to the main building by a system of corridors. It contains the Hall of Twenty Columns made of Karelian granite and a white marble Roman courtyard.

Until the middle of the 19th century the Hermitage held the private collection of the czars and few outsiders had access to it. Since the 1917 Revolution the collection has been more than tripled, and now consists of well over two million items and occupies more than a thousand rooms and halls.

The collections of the Hermitage are divided into seven main sections and subdivided into 40 smaller ones.

The first section is devoted to the history of Russian culture from the 7th to the 20th century. Its subdivisions include Russian silverware and malachite objects. In the Malachite Hall more than two tons of this semi-precious stone were used for the columns alone. Two other galleries have exhibits of Russia's military history including the 1812 "Patriotic War". The majority of the portraits of Russian senior officers are by the British painter George Dawe, nearly all painted from life. The St. George Hall, known as the Large Throne Room, has 48 Italian marble columns and a huge map of the USSR (covering 300 square feet) made of Ural stones and jewels; Moscow is marked by a diamond hammer and sickle.

The second section deals with prehistoric cultures, showing the discoveries made within the Soviet Union, including examples of Scythian culture and art and evidence of the prehistoric nomads of the Altai region.

The third section covers the history of oriental culture and art of peoples now living on Soviet territory, mainly in Central Asia and the Causasus. The fourth section is concerned with the same subject outside the Soviet Union: Ancient Egypt, Babylon, Assyria and Palmyra, Byzantium, the Near and Middle East, China, India and Japan.

The fifth section contains much striking material from the antique culture and art of Greece, the Greek colonies on the Black Sea, Rome and ancient Italy.

The sixth section is devoted to Western European art—from medieval European applied art to the art of Italy, Spain, the Low Countries (Dutch and Flemish) Germany, Austria, France, Sweden and Denmark, Finland, England—with separate sub-divisions devoted to European silverware and decorative china. In the art collections there are outstanding works by da Vinci, Titian, El Greco, Velazquez, Rubens (42 canvases), Van Dyck, and Rembrandt (21 paintings). One of the rooms in the German section was originally the Small Throne Room, also known as Peter's Hall. The French collection includes works by Renoir, Matisse, Gauguin and others.

The final section is devoted to Russian and foreign medals, badges and decorations.

Opposite the Winter Palace stands the semi-circular building of the former General Staff (Glavny Shtab), erected in 1819–29 and designed by the Italian architect Carlo Giovanni Rossi in classical style. The center of this building (opposite the main entrance of the Winter Palace) is pierced by a street spanned by a Triumphal Arch which commemorates the Russian victory in the 1812 campaign. A triumphal chariot by Demut-Malinovsky and Pimenov crowns the monument.

In the center of Palace Square stands a huge memorial column, raised in 1832–4 and designed by the Frenchman Auguste Ricard Montferrand, also to celebrate the 1812 victory over Napoleon. This is one of the tallest memorial columns in the world, rising to some 150 feet. On the east, the architectural complex of Palace Square is completed by the building of the former Guards Corps Headquarters, built in 1840–8 and designed by Alexander Bryullov. The Admiralty (originally a shipyard and the GHO of the Fleet, built in 1806–23 by Andrei Zakharov) is also part of the Palace Square design.

Along the Left Bank of the Neva

The western façade of the Admiralty (which stretches along the Neva) overlooks Decembrists' Square. It was in this square that on December 14, 1825, during the interregnum following the death of Alexander I, the Decembrists, the insurrectionist noblemen, attempted to launch their rising. The former building of the Senate and the Holy Synod (two important institutions of the Czarist regime) faces the Admiralty; it was built by Rossi in classical style, between 1829–34. The building now houses the Historical Archives and is decorated with statues and reliefs by Pimenov, Demut-Malinovsky and Nikolai Ustinov.

One of the finest statues in Leningrad, Peter the Great's Monument, by the French sculptor Etienne-Maurice Falconet, stands in the center of the square. This is the subject of Pushkin's famous poem, *The Bronze Horseman*.

The south side of Decembrists' Square is occupied by the majestic building of St. Isaac's Cathedral, now a museum. The largest church in Leningrad, designed in Russian Empire style and built by Auguste Montferrand between 1819 and 1858, it covers some 2½ acres. It is of granite and marble, in the shape of a cross, with an enormous gilt dome from which an excellent view of the city and the river spreads out in front of you. (Photographing is forbidden from this height unless special permission has been obtained.) The four colossal oak and bronze doors and the iconostasis deserve special attention.

The main entrance of St. Isaac's Cathedral faces Isaac Square (Isaakiyevskaya Ploshchad). The equestrian statue of Czar Nicholas I by Klodt and Montferrand stands in the center of this square. Another building on the square is the headquarters of the City Soviet (Town Hall) on the banks of the Moyka River. This was the Mariinsky Palace, a wedding gift from Nicholas I to his daughter Maris in the early 1840s. In 1917 the Kerensky Government had its seat here. Most other buildings on Isaac Square house scientific research institutes. The Intourist Hotel Astoria (dating from 1912) is also here.

If we return across Decembrists' Square to the Neva, walking downriver, we soon reach Ploshchad Truda (Labour Square). It is the landward end of the Bridge of Lieutenant Schmidt, linking the "mainland" with Vasilevsky Island; completed in its present form in 1938, it was named after the leader of the 1905 Black Sea sailors' revolt.

Near the bridge is the Dvorets Truda (Palace of Labour), the Leningrad center of the Trade Unions. This was originally built by Nicholas I for his eldest son. It was designed by A. Stakensejder.

Continuing along the Neva, we come to a marble tablet marking the anchoring place on November 7, 1917 of the cruiser *Aurora*. (Nowadays the *Aurora* is permanently moored where the Bolshaya Neva branches off from the Neva, near the Nakhimov Naval College and the Leningrad Hotel.) This was the battle cruiser which, on November 7, 1917, sailed up the Neva river and trained her guns on the windows of the Winter Palace, then used by the Provisional Government. Her first, blank shot was the signal for the revolutionaries to attack. For a long time she was used as a training ship, but during World War Two her guns helped to defend the city. In 1948 she became a floating museum.

Nearby, on Red Navy Embankment (Naberezhnaya Krasnogo Flota) there is an attractive neo-classical building, dating from the 18th century, restored by C. V. Glinka in 1826–7. This has been a museum since the middle of the 19th century; now it houses the Museum of the History of Leningrad. Founded in 1918, the museum houses collections donated by members of the Society of Lovers of Old St. Petersburg, including a rare collection of manuscripts, printed maps and plans of the city beginning with the projects of Peter I; original designs by Rastrelli, Quarenghi, Starov, Voronikhin, Zakharov, Rossi and other outstanding architects. There are also paintings, engravings, photographs and other historical relics. In 1953–4 the exhibits were supplemented by collections from the former Museum of Leningrad's Defense during the Great Patriotic War. There are exhibits showing modern Leningrad and plans for the future.

Before leaving the Neva, start out in the opposite direction from the Hermitage (to its east) for a visit to the Summer Garden and the Summer Palace. The Summer Garden, in Pestel Street, was founded more than 250 years ago by Peter the Great. With its ancient oaks, limes and elms, it is a popular place of recreation. Its lanes are decorated with marble sculptures dating from the 18th century—though these are hidden under wooden covers from the early fall. Here is the monument to Ivan Krylov, the Russian La Fontaine (by Peter Klodt, 1855) and the Summer Palace of Peter the Great. Designed and built in 1710–14 by Domenico Trezzini, the palace was only used occasionally. There are six halls on each of the two floors, with kitchens, servants' rooms, etc. The tiled kitchen, the entrance hall with a carved Minerva, the Green Study and a number of blue-and-white tiled stoves are particularly attractive; so is the statuary by Schluter and the ceiling frescos.

The Field of Mars (Marsovo Polye) lies between the Hermitage and the Summer Palace (Sadovaya and Khalturin Streets), the former parade ground became a park in 1920 and was earlier the site of mass meetings and firework displays. Known formerly as the Tsarina's Meadow, it was renamed at the end of the 18th century when the statue of Field Marshall Suvorov was erected here. It now stands near the Kirov Bridge. The paths meet in the center at the monument of the Victims of the Revolution, designed by Rudnev in 1919, with its eternal flame. The buildings surrounding the Field of Mars (the former Marble Palace which is now the Leningrad branch of the Lenin Museum, the barracks of the former Paul Guards Regiment, and others) were erected at the end of the 18th and at the beginning of the 19th centuries in classical style and they form a pleasantly harmonious whole.

The Lenin Museum has exhibits illustrating the Communist leader's activities before and during the 1917 Revolution. It is housed in the Marble Palace which Rinaldi built in 1768–85 as Catherine II's present to her lover Count Orlov. The marble hall and grand staircase have been preserved in their original state. The armored car (inscribed *Enemy of Capital*) stands in the small garden in front of the main entrance. Lenin made his famous speech at the Finland Station from its turret on April 3, 1917. (Various homes of Lenin in the city have also been turned into memorial museums; 7 Ilyich Street, Apartment 13; 52 Lenin Street, Apartment 24; 5 Khersonskaya Street, Apartment 9; the Shalash (Straw Hut) at the Razliv Railroad Station, and the Smolny Institute.)

Walks in the Inner City

There is no coherent "downtown district" in Leningrad; it is dissected and broken by the delta of the Neva and the various branches of the river. By and large the inner city is the district stretching south from the Bolshaya Neva. This includes Palace Square, Isaac Square, Decembrists' Square, the Field of Mars and the Summer Garden (already mentioned), but there are some other interesting sights, above all, the Nevsky Prospekt.

The roughly oval-shaped district is bordered by a semi-circle that starts at the Neva and swings back to it. The innermost ring is the Moyka River and the streets that developed along its banks (especially Herzen Street); the second is Sadovaya Street and the third the Fontanka River which flows in an arc from the Neva and back to the Neva. This quarter is cut into segments by great avenues starting from Palace Square which are like spokes of a wheel: the Nevsky Prospekt, Dzerzhinsky Street and Mayorov Prospekt.

The Nevsky Prospekt and Neighborhood

This is the main artery of central Leningrad, where the majority of the theaters, hotels, cinemas, libraries and other cultural institutions can be found.

The Nevsky (as the Leningraders call it) runs for about three miles, interrupted only at Revolution Square, near the Moscow Railway Station. The section that begins here, the Old Nevsky, is no longer considered to belong to the main Nevsky Street. It carries only vehicular traffic, the tramlines having been removed after the Second World War. Our tour goes from west to east.

On the right-hand, odd-numbered side, at the corner of Gogol Street, is the Aeroflot ticket office, housed in a most peculiar building; erected originally in 1912 by the Wawelberg banking house, it is a mixture of the Doges' Palace in Venice and the Medici Palace in Florence. Almost every second or third house is marked with a tablet proclaiming it a monument. Some date back to World War II, for example the sign proclaiming: "Comrades! In case of shelling, this side of the street is the more dangerous!"

On the corner of Gertsena (Herzen) Street, the *Mir* bookshop carries a wide assortment of foreign (mostly East European) books and interesting postcards and greeting cards. It also has a good selection of art books. Herzen Street runs, a few steps from Nevsky Prospekt, into Palace Square, reaching it under the arch of the former General Staff building. Here, just before the arch, we find the Central Telephone Exchange, where international calls can be booked.

Further along we cross the small Moyka River. On the odd-numbered side of the Nevsky is the green-colored former Stroganov Palace, built by Rastrelli in 1752–4. With its white columns, it is one of the finest examples of Russian baroque. Opposite this palace, running diagonally into Nevsky, is the tree-lined Zhelyabov Street. The Leningrad Estradny (Variety) Theater directed by Arkady Raikin, is to be found here. Next to it stands the four-storied *DLT* (House of Leningrad Commerce), one of the largest department stores.

Walking along the even-numbered side (left-hand) of the Nevsky, we find a Romanesque-style church, the Peter-Paul Evangelical Church, built by Alexander Bryullov in 1833–8, and originally attended mainly by German artisans living in Petersburg.

The next noteworthy building on the even side stands on the banks of the Griboyedov Canal (which is really a river). Opposite the *Dom Knigi*, The huge bookshop, is one of the finest examples of Leningrad architecture, the Kazan Cathedral, built 1801–11 by Andrei Voronikhin. Here Kutuzov, Napoleon's great opponent, is buried; his statue stands by the cathedral. The cathedral is now the Museum of the History of Religion and Atheism, and its main purpose is anti-religious propaganda. The exhibits illustrate the history of religion, the origins of Christianity, the history of the Inquisition and the evolution of agnosticism and atheism. You may find some of it tasteless, even offensive, but it does offer an insight into the official attitude to such matters in the Soviet Union.

From the Kazan Bridge, crossing the Griboyedov Canal at the axis of the Nevsky Prospekt, you'll notice a typical old Russian-style onion dome. It belongs to the Church of the Bleeding Savior, built in 1883–1907 by Alfred Parland on the spot where revolutionary terrorists assassinated Czar Alexander I.

Farther down the Nevsky Prospekt we find on the even side the Small Hall of the Philharmonia; the house used to belong to V. V. Engelhardt, Pushkin's close friend. In the middle of the 19th century many public concerts were held here—Berlioz, Liszt and Wagner appeared in the hall. Next to this is a theater-booking office ("teatralnaya kassa") where tickets can be booked for all major concerts, opera and ballets right up to the day of the performance. Next to the Philharmonia, set back, stands the St. Elizabeth Church, built to the designs of Vallin de la Mothe in 1763–83, in a style between baroque and classicism.

Across the street, on the corner of Duma Street, on the odd-numbered side of the Nevsky stands the building of the former City Duma (Municipal Council); today it is a railroad ticket office. Quarenghi designed it in 1784 but it has been rebuilt several times.

Opposite the former Duma, the short Brodsky Street reaches the Nevsky, linking the latter with the Square of Arts. Here is the Intourist Hotel Europe (Yevropeiskaya), reconstructed in 1910 in a style reflecting the European art nouveau movement.

Square of Arts

The Ploshchad Iskusstv (Square of Arts) is one of the largest and finest architectural complexes in Leningrad. Its central building is the State Museum of Russian Art, formerly the Michael Palace, built by Rossi in 1819–25. The museum was opened in 1898. The Michael Palace is so called because it was built for Grand Duke Michael, youngest son of Czar Paul I. A second building (designed by Benois and Ovsyanikov) was finished in 1916 and rebuilt from 1948 to 1953. The first of the buildings contains pre-revolutionary Russian art; the second, Soviet art. Temporary exhibitions are also shown here. There are extensive collections of drawings, paintings and engravings, examples of handicrafts, folk art and a large collection of ancient icons. All the outstanding Russian masters and the main periods and movements in the development of Russian art are well represented.

The eastern block of the Michael Palace houses the Museum of the Ethnography of the Peoples of the USSR. Five halls are devoted to Russian material including works by the master craftsmen of Palekh and Khokhloma, and others. There are toys from Vyatka and Vologda, embroidery and lace, Turkmenian carpets, jewelry, coins from Armenia and Georgian leatherwork, carvings and ceramics from the Baltic Republics, and fine bone-carvings from the Far North. Documentary films are projected regularly.

Opposite, on the corner of Brodsky Street, we find the Philharmonia, designed by P. Jacquet with a façade by Rossi, built in 1834–9 to house the Nobles' Club. The main hall with its marble columns has served as a concert hall since 1921. The Leningrad Symphony Orchestra is one of the world's leading musical ensembles. Here the Seventh Symphony of Shostakovich, written in the besieged city, was first performed. A smaller hall of the Leningrad Philharmonia is at 30 Nevsky Prospekt.

The Operetta Theater is next to the Philharmonia. The Maly (Small) Opera House, designed by Alexander Bryullov and Rossi, on the northwestern side of the Square of Arts, was built in 1831–33. Originally called the Mikhailovsky, up to 1918 it was occupied by a more or less permanent French company. In 1918 it became an opera house; a ballet company was founded in 1933. It is known as "the laboratory of Soviet Opera" and continues to stage new operas and experiments in modern choreography while also presenting classical ballets.

Near the Maly Opera Theater is the former home of Isaak Brodsky, one of the pioneers of modern Russian painting. The house itself was built in the 1820's (its façade designed by Rossi) and Brodsky lived here from 1924 to 1939. The memorial museum contains some 80 of his own paintings and over 500 works of his friends and contemporaries.

The other buildings on the square are all organically combined in the general architectural scheme. The center of the Square of Arts was turned into a park after the war. Pushkin's statue (by M. K. Anikushin and V. A. Petrov) was placed here on the 250th anniversary of Leningrad's foundation.

Between Brodsky and Sadovaya (Garden) Streets the Nevsky Prospekt is at its widest (some 180 feet) and busiest, especially around the Nevsky Prospekt Metro station. Leningrad's Metro was only opened in 1955, but now the fourth line is in the process of being built. The lines, linked together, connect the busiest industrial districts and all the important railway stations. The total length is over 38 miles. After its completion, it will have 142 stations. In some of the existing ones, the system of the Paris Metro is adopted—but in a reverse manner. Access to the platforms is barred and the doors only open when the trains arrive. Mayakovskaya station, on the Nevsky Prospekt, is one of these. Otherwise the escalators, platforms and trains, though less elaborate, are similar to those in Moscow. Avtovo, one of the largest new districts, has a particularly ornate station you may want to visit just for the experience.

Several large department stores can be found along this busy section of the Nevsky; on the odd-numbered side, the Gostinyi Dvor, built in 1761–85, is an arcade of shops almost a mile long. You can enter it from the Nevsky Prospekt Metro station, on one of the lines that intersect there. On the sidewalk and in the roadway facing the City Duma are kiosks and stalls selling secondhand books, cigarettes, newspapers and snacks. Opposite is the Passage Department store and the Komissarzhevskaya Theater, named after a great tragic actress. Here many Gorky, Chekhov and Ibsen plays were premièred early in this century.

The Sever (North) Pastryshop is in the neighboring house; that is a the favorite meeting place of young Leningrad writers and artists. Set back from the street, near the Passage, is the former Armenian Church, designed by Felten and built in the 1770's.

On the corner of the Nevsky Prospekt and Sadovaya Street is the Saltykov-Shchedrin Library, the second largest in the Soviet Union. Its first building was designed by Yegor Sokolov and built in 1796–1806. The semi-circular corner building was added by Rossi in 1828–32. The statues in the loggias, of Homer, Plato, Demosthenes, Virgil, Tacitus, etc., are also by Rossi, while the reliefs were contributed by Demut-Malinovsky, Pimenov and Mikhail Kirov. The library was opened in 1814; its regular visitors included Tolstoy, Gorky, Pavlov, Mendeleyev and Nekrasov. It contains the most complete collection of books published in pre-revolutionary Russia and there is a full array of the literatures of other nationalities of the Soviet Union, in 90 languages. The incunabula and manuscript collection is unique and there is a special section devoted to the works of Russian writers published abroad. Voltaire's library, early Russian linguistic relics, and the correspondence of Peter the Great, Suvorov, Kutuzov, etc., can also be found here.

The library stands on Ostrovsky Square, which opens off Nevsky Prospekt. The most important building in the Square is the Pushkin Theater, designed by Rossi in Empire style and built between 1828 and 1832. The statues in the niches are by Russian sculptors after Rossi's original drawings. This is one of the city's leading theater companies, with a repertoire of classical and modern drama.

Ballet on Architect Rossi's Street

In the square outside, the small park is centered around the statue of Catherine the Great, erected in 1873, the joint creation of Mikeshin, Chizhov and Onekushin. The street behind the theater, named after Rossi, is his extraordinary creation. It is bordered by two identical, yellow buildings with white columns; its breadth equals the height of the buildings, and the street's length is exactly ten times its width. On one side is the Theatrical Museum and the Theatrical Library, with a rich collection illustrating Russian and European stage history. The collection was started by a group of leading Petersburg actors at the end of the 19th century. The museum was founded in 1908, after the first Russian Theatrical Exhibition; it has been housed in the present building since 1918. Portraits, stage designs, photographs, personal memorabilia of leading performers, manuscripts of plays, magazines, programs and records are exhibited. (Most Leningrad theaters have similar, though smaller, exhibitions in their foyers.) The building along the other side of Rossi Street other is the Ballet School (founded in 1738), whose graduates include Anna Pavlova, Nijinsky, Ulanova and many others.

Beyond Rossi Street on the river banks leading southwest, we find the editorial and printing offices of the two Leningrad dailies, the *Leningradskaya Pravda* and the youth paper *Smena;* next door, also on the banks of the Fontanka River, is the Gorky Theater, founded by the writer himself in 1919. Since the 1960s it has acquired a reputation for highly experimental productions, and is worth a visit if your Russian is good enough.

If you now return to Nevsky Prospekt, you'll find in the corner house opposite Ostrovsky Square the largest and most luxurious delicatessen of Leningrad, built by the wealthy merchant Yeliseyev in 1903–7. This shop with its elaborate decorations is worth a visit just for itself. Two further, modern sections are round the corner. The top stories are occupied by the Comedy Theater, one of the best in the country.

Not far away, at No. 60 Nevsky Prospekt, in the Aurora Cinema Building, is the Visas and Registration Office. Foreigners who are not staying in a hotel must call here to register and arrange their permits to stay.

Crossing the Nevsky again, we find between Ostrovsky Square and the Fontanka River the Palace of Pioneers, formerly the Anichkov Palace, whose garden is called the Garden of Rest. In the open-air theater, jazz groups, and Soviet and foreign musical ensembles appear during the summer. The Anichkov Palace was built by the Czarina Elizabeth in 1741–50 for her lover Count Razumovsky. It is a mixture of styles. Only the side-entrance opens from the Nevsky Prospekt; its main entrance faces the Fontanka. In 1937 the building was turned over to the Pioneers Communist Party youth organization. It caters for all sorts of activities and special interest groups, and it has its own planetarium, puppet theater and dancehall. Tourists can only visit it in groups, but usually after a short wait, enough people gather there for a group tour.

The Fontanka River, which flows into the Neva and which is lined by some fine buildings, crosses the Nevsky Prospekt here. This is the site of the Anichkov Bridge, one of the finest in Leningrad. Designed by Gotman, its balustrade was the work of Alexander Bryullov. Its bridge-head is decorated by four fine statues, the work of Klodt. These were buried for safe-keeping in the garden of the Palace of Pioneers during the siege of the city.

The rest of the Nevsky Prospekt was built at the turn of the century. Along this section there are several more cinemas and a good many small cafés, restaurants, cheap food shops and snack-bar kiosks. The Baltiiskaya Hotel is also here.

The Nevsky Prospekt leads into Insurrection Square (Ploshchad Vosstaniya) named after the demonstrations and mass meetings that took place here in 1917; the mutineers of the Paul Regiment opened fire on the mounted police and then went over to the side of the revolutionaries.

The Moscow Railway Station, dating from 1891, stands opposite the Nevsky on the Square. Two other large buildings on the same square are the Moskovskaya and October Hotels. Here, too, is the Ploshchad Vosstaniya Metro Station of the Nevsky Prospekt line. The stretch of the Nevsky from Insurrection Square to Alexander Nevsky Square has little architectural or other interest for the foreign tourist.

Beyond Nevsky Square, however, is one of the most interesting artistic monuments in Leningrad, the Alexander Nevsky Monastery, which can also be reached by the Metro. The Monastery of the Holy Trinity and Alexander Nevsky was founded by Peter the Great in 1710, together with the Cathedral of the Annunciation and the Holy Trinity Cathedral. The latter is still functioning as an Orthodox church, to which a theological seminary is attached. The necropolis of the Alexander Nevsky Monastery has been preserved by the State, and a part of the complex now houses the Museum of Urban Sculpture, containing models and photographs of Leningrad's many monuments.

The Rings of the Inner Town

We have just described the semi-circular rings stretching from the Neva to the Neva and enclosing the Inner Town. Some of these are rivers, carrying pedestrian and vehicular traffic along their quays. The innermost ring, the Naberezhnaya Reki Moyki (Moyka Embankment), is one of these. The Moyka starts from the Fontanka at the Field of Mars and flows into the Neva, near Labour Square, winding through the central part of the city. Many historical and other important cultural buildings stand on its banks.

One of these, at No. 12 Moyka Quay, is the Pushkin Memorial Museum, the poet's home from October 1836 until his death. Here he spent his last night before the fatal duel that was to end his life, and here he died of his wounds on January 29, 1837. His furniture and personal effects—study, books, lamps, writing materials, etc.—are all here, almost exactly as they were on the day he died. There is a brief synopsis in English you can take with you as you walk around, and there is also an English-speaking guide.

Near the Nevsky Prospekt, on the bank of the Moyka, stands a block housing the Herzen Pedagogical College. The main building was designed by Vasili Bazhenov and Vallin de la Mothe and built in 1761–5. One of the specialties of the college is the Faculty of Northern Peoples, where students are trained as teachers for the Lapps, Chukchi, Evenki and other Arctic tribes.

Beyond Isaac Square, close to the Moyka, we find the Central Post Office (built in 1803, designed by Sokolov, rebuilt several times) and, beside it, the Museum of Communications.

The second musical center of Leningrad is also close to the river and just south of it. (The first is the Square of Arts.) This is Theater (Teatralnaya) Square, with the Conservatory, the oldest musical academy of Russia, whose pupils have included Tchaikovsky, Glazunov, Shostakovich and many others. Statues of Glinka and Rimsky-Korsakov flank the entrance. Concerts are often held in the main hall and the Opera Studio of the Academy also presents its productions here.

On the far (west) side of the square stands the famous Kirov Opera and Ballet Theater, designed by Albert Kavos and built in 1860. (It was formerly called the Mariinsky.) Early in the 19th century this was the cradle of Russian ballet; later, Anna Pavlova danced and Chaliapin sang here. More recently, Ulanova and many other famous ballerinas began their careers here, as did Rudolf Nureyev and Mikhail Baryshnikov.

Sadovaya Street, some three miles long, links the Field of Mars with Repin Square and is one of the busiest streets of Leningrad. At its beginning, near the Moyka River, is the Michael Garden, laid out by Rossi. Opposite we find the College of Military Engineering, the "Engineers' Castle". In front of it stands the statue of Peter the Great by Carlo Rastrelli (father of the architect). The Michael Palace, on the right, we have described earlier.

Continuing along Sadovaya Street, if we glance down Malaya Sadovaya Street on the left, we see Manezhnaya (Riding School) Square, with the Winter Stadium where many national and international athletics meetings are held. In the same square stands the headquarters of Leningrad Radio; the square's name originated from the former Michael Riding School, built in 1798–1801 by Brenna; in 1824 Rossi remodeled it. In 1917–8 it was the headquarters of the armored car division of the Red Army.

Crossing the Nevsky Prospekt, on the left side of Sadovaya we see the Suvorov Military College, designed by Rastrelli in the 1740's; this was the home throughout the 19th century of the most exclusive military academy. On the same side, the block-long building of the Apraksin Bazaar begins at the next corner.

Walking on along the Sadovaya we soon cross Mir (Peace) Square, which was previously called Hay Square, and was the former haymarket. The slum district of Petersburg with its drinking-shops and dives, the scene of several Dostoyevsky novels (among them *Crime and Punishment*) used to be behind this square. In the 1930's the square was rebuilt and part of it was turned into a park. Here one of the city's more modern thoroughfares, the Moscow Boulevard, begins.

At No. 50 Sadovaya Street we find the Museum of Railroad Traffic, one of the oldest in the USSR; it presents the history of Russian rail-building, engine and wagon manufacture.

The Smolny and its Neighborhood

Suvorovsky Prospekt, leading northeast from Moscow Railway Station, starting at the Old Nevsky Prospekt, suffered grievously during the Second World War. Many of the apartment houses here were built in the late forties and early fifties in a pseudo-classical style aiming at monumental stature rather than attractiveness. Along the section of the Suvorovsky Prospekt approaching the Neva and in the same neighborhood there are three important architectural and historical monuments.

The Smolny Institute is the local headquarters of the Communist Party and has a fascinating history. The present building stands on the site of several predecessors—first the Swedish fort of Sabina, then a storing place for tar (*smolny dvor,* tar yards), and later a summer palace for Elizabeth, daughter of Peter I. This burned down and Elizabeth decided to build a convent for orphans in its place. In 1748 Rastrelli designed the new baroque building, the Cathedral of the Resurrection (1744–57), a school for the daughters of the nobility and a widow's house (this last designed by Giacomo Quarenghi in classical style). The huge building of the Institute (its façade is 200 yards long) is a characteristic example of the Russian classical style. In front of the ceremonial court enclosed by the two wings, there are Grecian columns forming an outside gate. These were added in 1925 but are in harmony with the style of the main building.

From August 1917, the Smolny was the central headquarters of the Bolshevik Party. In its ceremonial hall the Second All-Russia Congress of the Soviets opened on November 7, 1917, electing the Council of Commissars with Lenin as its president. The Smolny remained the seat of the Soviet government until it moved to Moscow. It was here that Kirov, the Party Secretary of Leningrad, was assassinated. Today it and its adjoining territory belong to the Leningrad Party Committee; special passes are needed for entry, but there are frequent guided group tours.

North of the Smolny Institute is the Smolny Nunnery and Cathedral, fine examples of Russian baroque. The cathedral with its five steeples stands in the center of the complex of buildings. It was completed in 1823. Further north yet is the first building of the Smolny Institute, of little interest.

The third large building of the Suvorov Prospekt district is the Tauride Palace (Tavrichesky Dvorets), on Voinov Street, leading westwards from the Smolny Cathedral. This was built by Prince Potemkin, Catherine the Great's favorite, in 1783–9. In its day it was one of the largest buildings in Europe, with an area of 66,000 square yards. A large park and several fishponds surrounded it and it had its own port on the Neva. The State Duma (Parliament) met here early in the 20th century, and after February 1917, the Petrograd Soviet. In March 1918, it housed the Seventh Congress of the Bolshevik Party and in July 1920 the Second Congress of the Communist International.

The Narva Gate and the Kirov Factory

On the site of the Narva City Gate, in southwest Leningrad, a triumphal arch was erected in 1814 (designed by Quarenghi) to welcome Russian troops returning from Paris after their defeat of Napoleon. In 1834 the wooden arch was replaced by a granite-and-brick one. The neighborhood of the Narva Gate was the scene of several skirmishes during the 1917 Revolution; the workers' brigades gathered here for the assault on the Winter Palace.

This is one of the largest industrial districts of the city today. Its main thoroughfare, Stachek Prospekt (Avenue of Strikes) leads to the Kirov Factory (the former Putilov Works), which had been one of the largest pre-revolutionary enterprises in Russia. Founded early in the 19th century, it saw the first strike in Russia and during the Civil War some 10,000 of its workers joined the Red Army.

The New Districts of Leningrad

By and large Leningrad's atmosphere, and its historical monuments and past, are being carefully preserved. The New Leningrad has been built beyond the original area of the city, on empty land or by absorbing villages. Since the early 1960's whole settlements have been established in Avtovo, Kupchino, Polyustrovo, in the Neva District and the Vyborg Quarter.

Arriving by air or by car from the direction of Moscow, the traveler passes along Moskva Prospekt, on which there are examples of every period and style of Soviet architecture.

Driving from the Inner Town, the first section of the boulevard, stretching from Peace Square as far as the Obvodny (By-Pass) Canal, dates largely from the 19th century. There are a good many colleges and research institutes. The section leading from the Canal to the city limits has factories, apartment houses and public buildings.

The broad avenue has trees and flowerbeds along its entire length. The buildings here include the Kapranov Cultural Palace, the town-hall of the Moscow District, the large but plain apartment houses of the pre-1939 years, the gigantic, pseudo-classical-style tenements of the Stalinist years and the more well-appointed and better-planned dwellings of recent times.

Passing under the Moscow Triumphal Gate (built between 1834 and 1838 according to Stasov's design) which commemorates the victories over Persia and Turkey, we turn left on Ligovsky Prospekt, thence right on Rasstannaya Street, and soon reach the famous Volkov Cemetery. Many statues and plaques mark the graves of outstanding Russian scientists and writers, including Belinsky and Blok, Mendeleyev and Pavlov.

Returning to the Moskva Prospekt we pass one of the largest hotels in Leningrad, the Rossiya. The second line of the subway passes under the boulevard. At the end of the Moskva Prospekt, near the town limits, the Park Pobedy (Victory Park) occupies some 175 acres. Crossing the park is an "Avenue of Heroes", with an enormous fountain and several monuments dedicated to Soviet heroes.

After the park the avenue divides. One fork continues to become Moscow Highway, the other leads to the Pulkovo Observatory and the airport.

The Observatory was built in 1839, based on the designs of Alexander Bryullov. It was rebuilt in its original form after the Second World War. The Observatory plays an important part in the Soviet space program.

The Kirov Islands

Before visiting the Kirov Islands, we might explore Lenin Park, a favorite spot for walkers and courting couples, which stretches from the beginning of Kirov Prospekt, along the limit of the Peter-and-Paul Fortress. The Zoological Gardens (founded in 1895 with animals of the Arctic, such as polar bears and seals, as its main attraction as well as about 250 other species including aurochs, black rhinos and the Tien Shan panther) are in this park; so is the Komosomol Theater, popular with youth, the three-dimensional Stereokino the Velikan (Giant) Movie House and the Planetarium.

The Kirov Prospekt leads north towards the islands. This is the main thoroughfare of the district. Some of its houses were built in the art nouveau style at the beginning of the 20th century but the majority were erected in the last two decades. Not far from the Peter-Paul Fortress there is a Moslem mosque. It was built in 1912, modeled on the famous Gur Emir mosque at Samarkand.

One of the largest film studios of the Soviet Union, the Lenfilm, is on Kirov Prospekt; and near it stands the 945-foot-high tower of Leningrad Television.

Three of the several islands in the lower part of the Neva delta, close to the sea, are of importance. They are: Krestovsky Ostrov, Trudyash-chikhsya Ostrov and Yelagin Ostrov (collectively known as the Kirov Islands). Before the Revolution the summer residences of the czars and aristocrats and the villas of rich merchants occupied the large parks. Today they are public places of recreation.

Five bridges lead to Krestovsky Island. There are half-a-dozen smaller and medium-sized stadia here and one of the finest sports centers of the USSR: the seaside Kirov Stadium which seats 100,000 people. It was built after the Second World War and more than a million cubic yards of earth had to be moved for its construction. Kirov's statue stands in front of it. It is surrounded by the Primorsky ("Seaside") Park of Victory, the city's second Victory Park, established in the 1950's. It has several artificial lakes with salt- and fresh-water swimming pools. The island has many other recreational facilities, including boat-houses.

Trudyashchikhsya Island (Island of Workers), formerly known as Stony Island, has several dozen palaces and villas which are now mostly sanatoria and rest-homes. Here is Czar Paul I's former palace built in 1776–1781, in early Russian classical style.

The third Kirov Island (Yelagin) has a beautiful park, designed by Rossi and now known as the Kirov Park. Near its fine avenue of trees we find the Great Open Air Theater and the Musical Theater. There are open-air concerts in the spring and summer, and a huge open-air dancing floor attracts the young, while in winter it is transformed into a skating rink. The old Yelagin Palace (1818–22, designed by Rossi) rises behind a wide stone terrace. It was the home of Yelagin, the nobleman who owned the island after 1780. From the island's tip (known as the Strelka, Little Arrow), there is a lookout point over the sea, with a pink marble terrace. There are bathing and boating facilities. Yelagin Island is the annual scene of celebrations to mark the start and end of the summer White Nights.

Excursions from Leningrad

The old castles, parks and other attractions near Leningrad are well worth visiting, especially in summer. At other times of the year, check whether they are open before making the journey. The finest of the summer resorts is Petrodvorets (formerly Peterhof), some 18 miles from the center of Leningrad, on the shores of the Gulf of Finland. It can be reached by local train from the Baltic Railway Station, by bus from Riding School Square or by hovercraft from Makarov Quay.

Petrodvorets was started in 1704 and building continued through many decades. It was occupied by the Germans during World War Two and many of its buildings were destroyed by artillery fire. The buildings have been partially restored but many of their contents were irretrievably lost.

Petrodvorets is divided into an Upper and Lower Park, of which the second is particularly interesting. It has spectacular fountains and elaborately designed lakes. The most important architectural features are Peter the Great's Monplaisir Palace (1714–23 to the designs of Braunstein, Leblond and Michetti); the Catherine Wing on its left (built by Rastrelli in 1784) and the Hermitage, Braunstein's fine palace (not to be confused with the Leningrad Palace), built 1721–7.

The façade of the Grand Palace has been restored but there is nothing behind it—the interior was totally destroyed and its furnishings lost. There is a fine view from the northern front of the huge park of the Gulf of Finland, which is linked to the palace by the so-called Sea Canal, with its many fountains.

The town of Pushkin (formerly Tsarskoye Selo) is about 15 miles from Leningrad to the south. It can be reached by local trains from the Vitebsk Railway Station (cost: 90 kopeks return) or by bus from Riding School Square.

The building of the town began in 1710, together with the two large parks named after Catherine and Alexander, with many large and small buildings. You may like to visit first the three-storied Lyceum building in which Pushkin studied from 1811 to 1817. Built in 1794, today it is a museum (NB: closed on Tuesdays according to latest information).

The Catherine Palace was built in the middle of the 18th century, designed by Kvasov and Rastrelli. Its interior was remodeled at the end of the 18th century by the Scottish architect Charles Cameron who also designed the attractive arcade. The central building of the Alexander Park is the Alexander Palace (1795), a work by Quarenghi of great simplicity, perfect balance, lightness and extraordinary harmony.

Pavlovsk is about 25 miles from Leningrad and can be reached by train from the Vitebsk station. The main sights of Pavlovsk are the obelisk on the right bank of the Slavyanka River (Cameron's work, 1782), the building of the former hospital (designed by Quarenghi, built 1796) and the 1,500-acre park where the Grand Palace stands. It is closed on Fridays, and Thursdays only the main buildings are open (according to information at presstime).

The Grand Palace is situated on a high bluff overlooking the Slavyanka. It is golden-colored and its dome, supported by 64 columns, is its outstanding feature. Cameron designed it and it was built in 1782–6. Several adjoining buildings were added in the following decades by Brenna, Voronikhin and Rossi. The throne room, the Knights' Hall and the Greek Hall are decorated with paintings, reliefs, marble, gilt and Gobelin tapestries. There are many other fine architectural monuments in the Pavlovsk Park, large and small pavilions, among which the Khram Druzhby (The Temple of Friendship) is the most interesting. It was built on the model of classical rotundas by Cameron in 1782. The greatest feature of Pavlovsk is the magnificent park with flowerbeds and alleys laid out in geometrical patterns.

The town of Lomonosov (formerly Oranienbaum) is on the shore of the Gulf of Finland, opposite the island of Kronstadt, some 25 miles from Leningrad. It can be reached by local trains from the Baltic Railway Station. It was founded by Menshikov, a statesman during the reign of Peter the Great, and it developed swiftly during the reign of Catherine the Great.

Its large park is divided into Lower and Upper sections. The most interesting building in the former is the Grand Palace, built in 1710–25, after the designs of Giovanni Fontana of Switzerland and Gottfried Schädel, a German architect. The Summer Palace of Peter III (part of the former fortifications), built in 1757–62 by the Italian Arnoldo Rinaldi, today houses a collection of Chinese arts and crafts.

The pride of the Upper Park is the Chinese Palace (by Rinaldi, 1762–74). Its 17 main halls include a Hall of Muses, a blue drawing-room and a small Chinese room.

A rather lengthy excursion from Leningrad of about 250 miles to the northeast will take you to the Island of Kizhi in the middle of Lake Onega, one of the natural lakes forming part of the White Sea-Baltic Canal ("Belomorkanal"), built in the 1930's by convict labor with terrible loss of life. The nearest town is Petrozavodsk, with an Intourist hotel. It is a trip best done over a weekend, and the pleasantest way is by boat from the Ozernaya River Station. The journey threads through the rivers and lakes the whole way. You can also get there by plane, bus or train. You may have some difficulty arranging the trip but it is worth trying.

The Island of Kizhi is one of the most ancient sites in all Russia. It was an early pagan center and is now an openair architectural museum, preserving some of the few remaining wooden churches in the Soviet Union. Among the really splendid ones, the Church of the Transfiguration (1744) stands out with its 22 timbered onion domes. During the long summer days, the evening light and vivid skies make Kizhi a place set apart.

The city of Vyborg, close to the Finnish border, was recently reported open to tourists; but it does not appear on official lists—check first. Day excursions to Novgorod by coach cost about $15 per person.

PRACTICAL INFORMATION FOR LENINGRAD

WHEN TO GO. The people of Leningrad claim that their city is a year-round attraction. In winter you can go skating or ice-fishing, take a ride on a Finnish sled (a chair mounted on long steel runners), and ski (there are two ski-jumps at Kavgolovo, some 20 miles from the center). The end of the winter is marked by special festivities. There is tobogganing, riding in horse-drawn sleds *(troikas)* and snow-ball fights, and the traditional *blini* (pancakes) are served.

The spring draws the first sun-worshippers to the Peter-and-Paul Fortress—though they have to sunbathe well wrapped up and leaning against the warm stone blocks of the fortress. The openair stadia start their soccer season. Rowing, yachting and cycling are the favorite spring sports.

In summer the White Nights Art Festival runs from June 21–29. You can spend a white night on a ship sailing out into the Gulf of Finland. Arts festivals fill the theaters and concert halls. There are fireworks at Petrodvorets, "the town of fountains," some 18 miles from Leningrad.

Autumn brings the 30-kilometer race between the center of the city and the town of Pushkin and the celebration commemorating the October (or, rather, November) Revolution. But the autumn is mostly rainy and cold; if there is a snowfall, it does not last. Life is largely restricted to indoor activities and of course the theaters and concert halls are in full swing.

HOW TO GET THERE. There is a plane from Moscow to Leningrad almost every hour, covering the distance in an hour, for 18 roubles. The fare is less than the first-class sleeper; but as the airports in both cities are some distance from the town center, not much time is saved.

There are 15 express trains linking Leningrad with Moscow each day, of which six are by day (additional services in peak holiday periods), and the fastest now doing 410 miles in about 4½ hours. The *Red Arrow* is the prime overnight express. There is a daily express between Helsinki and Leningrad taking 8 hours.

Cruise ships and ships of the regular Soviet Baltic passenger line and foreign liners call at the Leningrad seaport.

You can also approach the city by car along the transit highway that runs from Finland, via Vyborg. The road into the city from the north runs along Primorsky Prospekt past the gasoline and service station and over a bridge to Kirovsky Prospekt which leads straight to the Palace Embankment. If you are traveling to Moscow, you follow the main Leningrad-Moscow highway which leads out of the city near the Varshavsky (Warsaw) Railroad Station, close to Izmailovsky Cathedral.

Intourist will arrange for you to be met at the docks, the railway stations or the airport. The city air terminal is on Nevsky Prospekt in a remarkable building called Dvorets Dozhei (Palace of Doges) described earlier.

Taxis are available at the stations and terminals; they can also be ordered in advance through Intourist.

HOW TO GET ABOUT IN THE CITY. There are 39 streetcar (tram) lines, 17 trolley-bus lines, 68 bus lines and three subway lines. The streetcars are not only marked with numbers but each line has its own color. For instance, the No. 1 streetcar is distinguished by a red and orange lamp at the front, and the No. 2 with blue and red, so that they can be recognized even after dark and from some distance away.

Within the city limits water-buses ply on the Neva between the Academy of Arts and the Victory Park and between the Summer Garden and Kirov Stadium. The fare is 10–30 kopeks.

The suburbs and outlying parks are best approached by local trains. There are also buses which mostly start from Riding-School Square *(Manezhnaya Ploshchad)* which is also the starting point for the airport buses. There are boats from the harbor for Petrodvorets, Zelenogorsk and Lomonosov.

Of the three subway lines the first, completed in 1955, links all the railroad stations: Moscow, Finland, Vitebsk, Baltic and Warsaw. It is marked *red* on subway maps. The second (blue) connects the district at the end of the Leningrad-Moscow highway with the Petrograd District. The third (green) runs across town. In December 1978 a new section of the line out to Vyborg was opened, to cater for people in the new residential districts. The overall length of all lines is now 38 miles; a total of 2,730 trains operate daily, carrying several million passengers. Taxis are available at stands and can be ordered by telephone. If you order through your hotel you have to pay an extra 50 kopeks service charge. Many taxi-drivers seem to dislike relatively short distances—under 2½ miles. Sometimes drivers of private cars will offer their services and generally at very reasonable rates.

 WHAT TO SEE. Nevsky Prospekt, the oldest and main street of the city, running from the Admiralty building to the Alexander Nevsky Monastry.

Palace Square (Dvortsovaya Ploshchad) with the Winter Palace and other early 19th-century buildings.

The Peter-and-Paul Fortress (Petropavlovskaya Krepost) in Revolution Square. Peter and Paul Cathedral (Petropavlovsky Sobor) with the imperial tombs. Peter Gate (Petrovskiye Vorota) and Neva Gate (Nevskiye Vorota). The Mint (Monetnyi Dvor) and Arsenal (Gaupt Vakht), both within the fortress. Peter I's Cottage (Domik Petra) in the Petrogradskaya Storona, 1 Petrovskaya Naberezhnaya.

The Admiralty and the Summer Palace. Smolny Institute (with the Cathedral of the Resurrection). The Little Arrow (Strelka) lookout on Vasilyevsky Ostrov, near the Peter-and-Paul Fortress.

The Cathedral of Saint Nicholas, Kommunarov Ploshchad. The Church of the Transfiguration, Radishchev Square; the Church of Saint Vladimir (or Church of the Assumption), Petrogradskaya Storona, 16 Blokhin Street; the Church of the Resurrection, north side of Nevsky Prospekt, near by the Griboyedov Canal.

The Alexander Nevsky Monastery, Alexander Nevsky Square, once the second largest in Russia, containing the Museum of Urban Sculpture, the Trinity Cathedral (Troyitsky Sobor), the Gate Chapel, and the Mitropolichy Korpus.

St. Isaac's Cathedral Isaakyevskaya Square, now a museum. Kazan Cathedral, Kazanskaya Square, housing the Museum of the History of Religion and Atheism.

The Hermitage Museum (former Winter Palace), the greatest museum in the Soviet Union. The Winter Palace, the Small Hermitage, the Old Hermitage and the New Hermitage are all part of the same complex.

Porcelain Museum, Oborony Prospekt. The Russian Art Museum, 4/2 Inzhenernaya Street, in two buildings.

The Leningrad Artists' Permanent Exhibition, 8 Nevsky Prospekt. History of Leningrad Museum, Krasnogo Flota Embankment 44.

Planetarium, 60 Krasnaya Street. Arctic Museum, 24 Marat Street. Central Naval Museum, Vasilyevsky Ostrov, 4 Pushkinskaya Square. Artillery History Museum, 7 Lenin Park. Museum of Ethnography of the Peoples of the USSR, 1/4 Inzhenernaya Street.

Lenin Museum, 5/1 Khalturin Street, Pushkin Museum, 2 Moika Naberezhnaya. Suvorov Museum, 41b Saltykov-Shchedrin Street. The Cruiser Aurora, near the Nakhimov Naval College. Kirov Museum, 26/28 Kirov Prospekt. Museum of the Revolution, 4 Kuibyshev Street.

The monuments of Peter the Great, Decembrists' (Debakristov) Square; of Catherine II, Ostrovsky Square; of Nicholas I, Isaakyevskaya Square, and of Rimsky-Korsakov, in front of the Conservatory.

Summer Garden (Letny Sad), containing Peter's Summer Palace, 2 Pestel Street.

Field of Mars, a 25-acre park, surrounded by the Summer Garden, the Mikhailovsky Garden and the Marble Palace.

Botanical Gardens, 2 Prof. Popov Street, Petrogradskaya Storona. Zoo, 1 Lenin Park, Petrogradskaya Storona.

Repin Museum, Repino Railroad Station.

 HOTELS. As in Moscow, Intourist uses only a handful of the better hotels for Western tourists and normally does the assigning of hotel space. The choice hotels are the *Astoria, Evropeiskaya* and *Leningradskaya* and *Leningrad,* and they are normally used for tour groups. The new *Pribaltiskaya* has joined their ranks. Overflows go into *Oktyabraskaya,* which is right across the square from the Moscow-Leningrad railroad station. The rates are generally the same as in Moscow for top, deluxe-class hotels. All listed here have restaurant or café attached.

Astoria, 39 Herzen (Gertsena) Street. Leningrad's best all round, ageing but well-preserved, retains its air of faded glory. Very good restaurant, most convenient location. 380 rooms, rated "deluxe" Full of atmosphere and certainly the most famous hotel in town. Bar open to 2 A.M. Restaurant opens at 8.30 A.M. Tel. 219-11-00.

Evropeiskaya, 1/7 Brodsky Street. Old like the Astoria. Centrally located. 268 rooms, rated first class by us, "deluxe" by Intourist. Service reportedly good. *Vostochnyi Restaurant* in hotel quite good. Bar open to 2 A.M. Tel. 211-91-49.

Leningradskaya, 10/24 Mayorov Prospekt. Centrally heated; another good traditional hotel.

Leningrad, 5/2 Pirogovskaya Embankment, is the place to stay if you want a new hotel at any price or perhaps if you plan a very long sojourn in this city. Opened in 1970, this Finnish-decorated hotel is very elegant by Soviet standards. Rated as deluxe. Breakfasts recommended, excellent dining room. Entertainment nightly including variety show, jazz and dancing in restaurant. You are expected to eat a 4-course supper with it. Three late bars; best one on 10th floor has lively balalaika and disco music—foreign currency only, expensive. Other bars are 2 roubles entrance charge. Located across the Neva but only a short ride from the center. 650 well-furnished, smallish rooms all with own bathroom. Ask for waterfront rooms overlooking river. (One suite has a sunken bath, Japanese style.) Tel. 242-91-23.

Oktyabrskaya, 118 Nevsky Prospekt, opposite Moscow Railway Station. A massive place used as overflow for Top Three. 740 very ordinary rooms. Rated as moderate by us, "first class" by Intourist. Poor service (you may have to carry your own bags), and very ordinary facilities throughout.

Pribaltiskaya, Primorsky Boulevard on Vasilevsky Island; opened December 1978, this is one of the USSR's largest, 2,400 beds, 4 restaurants, 7 banquet halls, 6 bars and snack-bars seating 3,200 people. Swedish built; attractive interior decor. Saunas, swimming-pool, gym, bowling-alley, car park run by computer!

Rossia, 163 Moskovsky Prospekt, has 414 rooms. Moderate category. Tel. 296-73-49.

Severnaya, 21, Lenin Prospekt, Petrozavodsk. 218 rooms.

Others: All in the official secondary category, and ranking with us as mixed moderate to rock-bottom, are: *Moskovskaya,* 43/45 Ligovsky Prospekt; *Neva,* 17

Tchaikovsky Street; *Baltiskaya,* 57 Nevsky Prospekt; *International Seaman's Club,* 166 Griboyedov Naberezhnaya (this latter not generally used for accommodating foreign tourists). All have restaurant or café attached.

 RESTAURANTS. Hotel restaurants open at 8.30 (Astoria, Leningrad) or 9 A.M. Hot dishes served until 11.30 P.M. Others include: *Neva,* 44–66 Nevsky Prospekt, the largest restaurant in Leningrad, seating more than a thousand. It has the *Sever Café,* a cocktail lounge and banquet hall. The *Sever* is famous for its cakes. The *Neva* prides itself on its *Leningrad* salad, Neva-style *shchi* (soup) and fish fillet, its ice-creams and pastries.

Baku, Sadovaya Street between Rakov Street and Nevsky Pr. A new Azerbaijani restaurant with spicy Caucasian food and good bread. "Remarkable" is one visitor's description of the *zakuski,* which included smoked sturgeon, herb cheeses, mild pickled peppers. One of the most popular restaurants in town, with more prompt service than normal. There is a 2-rouble cover charge in the evenings for the upstairs dining room, which offers a quite good dance band. Reservations needed. Up to 20 roubles a head for a slap-up meal.

Del'Fin: One of the floating restaurants, in front of the Admiralty. Atmosphere rather than food.

Kavkazsky, 25 Nevsky Prospekt. One of the most popular restaurants, specializing in spicy Caucasian dishes. Not as well decorated, clean or expensive as the Baku.

Metropol. 22 Sadovaya Street. Near Nevsky Prospekt and the Main Library, the oldest restaurant of Leningrad, originally a co-operative. It's famous for its meat and fish dishes, and for its cakes, pies and tarts. Attached to the restaurant is a shop for take-away food. Indifferent service, but Leningraders claim it has the best Russian food in town. Rarely frequented by tourists, so waiters do not speak English (or any other foreign language).

Moskva, 49 Nevsky Prospekt. Specializes in good Russian cuisine.

Okolites, 15 Primorsky Pr. (en route to Helsinki). A small restaurant with good food and interesting decor. Worth a try for travelers going by car either to or from Helsinki.

Sadko, corner of Nevsky Pro. and Brodsky Street, practically next door to Evropeiskaya Hotel. Traditional Russian cooking with folk music and occasional, quite lively floor shows. Food has generally good reputation. Hard currency bar in cellar. In summer, it is jammed with tourists, so book reservations well in advance. Few Russians can get in during tourist season, so you will mingle mostly with foreigners. Good *blini.* Fixed price dinners.

Volkhov, Liteiny Pr., near Chernyshevsky Street, a pleasant-looking, small restaurant which American students have liked.

Other Restaurants. (All officially open until midnight, but often turn customers away earlier); *Primorsky,* 32 Bolshoi Prospekt, Petrogradskaya Storona, *Severny,* 12 Sadovaya Street, *Chaika,* 14 Griboyedov Naberezhnaya; *Universal,* 106 Nevsky Prospekt. *Airport,* in Air Terminal, second floor, Manezhnaya Square, has a good reputation. *Kronverk,* a floating restaurant at 3 Mytninskaya Naberezhnaya, has a nice atmosphere. *Austeriakh,* in the Peter-and-Paul Fortress, has "decent food" with good modern music. *Zakuski* are 5 roubles. The *Evropeiskaya* and *Leningrad* hotels each have a "Swedish Table" where for 2 roubles you can eat all you want. "Fantastic" is how one of our correspondents described it—"and cheap!"

CAFES. *Druzhba,* 15 Nevsky Prospekt. Open from 8 A.M., it serves a wide assortment of breakfast, dinner and supper dishes. *Minutka,* 20 Nevsky Prospekt. Quick-service snacks, coffee, cocoa, tea, clear soup, small pies with a tremendous variety of fillings. *Avtomat Café* (Self-Service) at 45 Nevsky Prospekt.

Ogonyok, 24 Nevsky Prospekt. Specializing in ice-cream and liquid refreshments. Especially popular on hot summer days. *Lakomka,* 22 Sadovaya Street. Near Nevsky Prospekt, attached to the Metropol Restaurant. Great variety of pies, cakes, pastries. *Children's Café,* 42 Nevsky Prospekt. Catering specially for the young with a staff of experienced dieticians.

Aurora, 60 Nevsky Prospekt. Specialists in dairy dishes; also special food, both hot and cold, for people on diets. *Blinnaya* 74 Nevsky Prospekt. A cellar café, specializing in pancakes, black and red caviar, salmon, etc.

Kafe Fregat, Vasilevsky Island, Bolshoi Pro. 39/4, is a café near Leningrad University frequented by students; clever decor and good traditional Russian cooking. Inexpensive. No smoking allowed. Champagne and "cocktails", but no vodka.

Leningrad, 96 Nevsky Prospekt. Sugar-free and other low-calorie diet dishes are specialties here.

NIGHT LIFE. The situation in Leningrad is the same as in Moscow; desperate. No real nightclubs and fairly early closing times in most cafés, bars and restaurants. Of the latter, Sadko has the best music and atmosphere if you don't speak or understand Russian, and its foreign currency bar stays open till 2 A.M. See under hotel listing for details of other bars. Things are improving all the time. A surprisingly good selection of Western pop music is played in the handful of hotel discos.

CULTURAL ACTIVITIES. Opera and ballet: The *Kirov Academic Opera and Ballet Theater,* to give it its full title (sometimes called the Big Opera or Bolshaya Opera) is at 2 Teatralnaya Square.

The Academic Maly Theatre of Opera and Ballet, 1 Ploshchad Iskusstv (Arts Square).

Musical Comedy Theatre, 13 Rakov Street. The only theatre that continued to perform throughout the siege of Leningrad. Mainly operettas.

Theatre of the Music and Drama Institute, 35 Mokhovaya Street, also presents musical productions.

Great Puppet Theatre is at 10 Nekrasov Street.

Gorky (Bolshoi) Drama Theatre, 65 Fontanka Naberezhnaya, founded in 1919 by the writer himself.

Pushkin Theatre, 2 Ostrovsky Square, classical and modern drama.

Comedy Theatre, 56 Nevsky Prospekt.

Komsomol Theatre, 4 Lenin Park.

Youth Theatre, 46 Zagorodny Prospekt.

Concerts: Leningrad has a very intensive musical life; the concert halls include: *October Concert Palace,* Ligovsky Prospekt (three minutes from the Ploshchad Vosstaniya Metro station).

The Leningrad Philharmonia Concert Hall. 1 Brodsky Street. A smaller hall of the Leningrad Philharmonia is at 30 Nevsky Prospekt.

The *Glinka Kapella* (Choral Hall) at 20 Moyka Naberezhnaya was built in 1880 by L. N. Benois; the choir was founded by Peter the Great in 1713. Glinka, Rimsky-Korsakov and other famous musicians appeared here.

Circus: The *Leningrad Circus* is at 3 Fontanka Naberezhnaya. Designed in 1876 it is one of the oldest circuses in the country. Its programs feature many Soviet and foreign artists.

Cinema: The most important movie-theaters are: *Aurora,* 60 Nevsky Prospekt; *Barrikada,* 15 Nevsky Prospekt; *Velikan,* 4 Lenin Park; *Gigant,* 44 Kondratyevsky Prospekt; *Kolizey,* 100 Nevsky Prospekt; *Molodezhny,* 12 Sadovaya Street; *Neva,* 108 Nevsky Prospekt; *October,* 80 Nevsky Prospekt; *Primorsky* 42 Kirovsky Prospekt; *Rodina,* 12 Tolmachov Street; *Saturn,* 27 Sadovaya Street; *Smena,* 42 Sadovaya Street; *Stereokino,* 4 Lenin Park (stereophonic films); *Titan,* 47 Nevsky Prospekt; *Khronika* 88 Nevsky Prospekt, (newsreel); *Khudozhestvenny,* 67 Nevsky Prospekt.

Movie theaters have fixed program times and tickets must be bought for a specific performance. As on public transport, in museums, theaters, etc., smoking is not allowed. Foreign movies are usually dubbed into Russian.

Note: All times of opening may vary according to season—earlier closing in winter. Check before setting out.

 MUSEUMS. Historical, Revolutionary and Military: *Lenin Museum,* 5/1 Khalturin Street. Open 10.30–18.30 weekdays, 11–5 Sun.; closed Wed. Other memorial museums are at Lenin's various homes scattered throughout the city. (see page 13). The *Shalash* (Straw Hut) is at the Razliv Railroad Station. All these are open every day except Wednesday.

Smolny (see page 220). Group tours only; special pass needed for individual entry.

Museum of the Great October Revolution, 4 Kuibyshev Street. Open daily 11–6, except Thur.; 10–5 Sat., Sun. Housed in the former mansion of Mathilde Kshessinskaya, the famous ballerina and mistress of Czar Nicholas II.

Kirov Museum, 26/28 Kirov Prospekt. Open 11–7 weekdays, Sun. 10–6; closed Sat. Commemorates the Bolshevik politician who was assassinated in Leningrad.

Cruiser *Aurora* is moored in the Neva near the Nakhimov Naval College. Group and individual visits daily 10.30–16.30, except Fri.

Central Naval Museum, Vasilyevsky Ostrov, 4 Pushkinskaya Square. Open 10.30–5 weekdays, Sun. 11–6, closed Tues.

History of Leningrad Museum, 44 Krasnogo Flota Embankment. Open Mon., Thur. Sat. and Sun., 11–6 and Tues. and Fri., 1–9; Closed Wed.

Museum of the History of Religion and Atheism (in the Kazan Cathedral), 2 Kazanskaya Ploshchad. Open Mon., Thur., 1–8, Fri., Sat. and Sun. 11–6, Tues. 11–4.

Peter-and-Paul Fortress (Petropavlovskaya Krepost), Revolution Square. Open 11–7, closed Wed. Entrance 30 kopeks. Part of the History of Leningrad Museum.

Ethnographic, Literary and Theatrical: *Anthropological and Ethnographical Museum of the USSR Academy of Sciences,* 3 Universitetskaya Naberezhnaya. Open Thur. and Sun., 11–5.

Museum of the Ethnography of the Peoples of the USSR, 1/4 Inzhenernaya Street, Open 11–6 daily, except Mon.

Pushkinsky Dom (Pushkin House—Literary Museum of the Academy of Sciences), 4 Naberezhnaya Makarova. Open daily 11–6, last tour 5.15 P.M., Sat. 11–4. Closed Tues. (Not to be confused with the next item, Pushkin's House.)

The *Pushkinsky Dom* is so-called because it was founded in 1899, the centenary of Pushkin's birth. It has a vast collection of manuscripts and books illustrating the life and works of Pushkin, Lermontov, Gogol, Turgenev, Dostoevsky, Tolstoy, Gorky, Mayakovsky and other writers. The archives contain over half a million items. There are regular special exhibitions and the institution is a meeting place for Soviet writers and their official foreign guests.

Pushkin's House, 12 Moyka. The poet's last residence. English-speaking guide available.

Theatre Museum, 6 Ostrovsky Square, open daily (except Tues.), 12–7, entrance 20 kopeks.

Circus Art Museum, 3 Fontanka Naberezhnaya, open daily 12–5 except Sun. A collection illustrating Soviet and world circus history: posters, programmes, photographs, costumes, models, large library, 6,000 postcards.

Museums of Fine Arts and Art History. *State Museum of Russian Art* known as the "Russian Museum", 4/2 Inzhenernaya Street. Open daily 11–6, except Tues.

Hermitage Museum, Winter Palace, 36 Dvortsovaya Naberezhnaya, open 10.30–6.30; closed Mon. Entrance 30 kopeks. One of the world's great museums. Ideally make several visits, if time permits.

Repin Museum. 'Penates), Repino Railroad station, on the Karelian Isthmus, in the resort region of Leningrad. Open from May to September daily, from October to April daily except Tues. This was the estate of the Russian painter Ilya Repin (1844–1930). A characteristic memorial museum, its exhibits span almost a century. Entrance 20 kopeks.

St. Isaac's Cathedral, Isaakyevskaya Square. Open as a museum 11–5. Closed Tues.

The *Summer Palace,* in the Summer Gardens (see under *Parks and Gardens*) is open May to November, 12–8, closed Tues.

Peter I's Cottage (Domik Petra), Petrogradskaya Storona, 1 Petrovskaya Naberezhnaya. Open May to November, 12–7, except Tues.

Monastery of the Holy Trinity and Alexander Nevsky, 1 Alexander Nevsky Square. Containing the *Museum of Urban Sculpture.* Open daily 11–7, except Thurs.

Permanent Exhibition of Leningrad Artists, 8 Nevsky Prospekt. Open everyday 10–9. Various exhibitions of contemporary work.

I.I. Brodsky Museum, 3 Ploshchad Iskusstv. Open daily 11–8 except Thurs. A memorial museum to the artist, well-known for his revolutionary scenes, portraits of Lenin, etc. Rather a matter of taste.

The palaces and museums in the environs of Leningrad are generally open every day from the end of May until September 15 (depending on the weather) from 11–8. The museums of *Lomonosov* are closed on Tuesdays. *Petrodvorets* is open 11–8 daily, except some Mondays, from 1 January to 25 September. The *Monplaisir Palace* there is open 11–5 except Wednesdays, as is the *Hermitage Palace.* The *Lyceum* at *Pushkin* is reported closed on Tuesdays. *Pavlovsk* is closed on Fridays, and on Thursdays only the main buildings are open.

Technical and Scientific Museums: *A. S. Popov Communications Museum,* 4 Podbelsky Street, near the Central Post Office. Open daily 12–6; Mon. 12–3. Closed Tue.

Railway Museum, 50 Sadovaya Street. Open daily, 12–6; Mon. 12–3. Closed Tue.

Zoological Museum, 1 Universitetskaya Embankment. Open daily 11–5, except Mon.

The *Zoo* is at 1 Lenin Park, Petrogradskaya Storona. Open from May to August 10–10, from September to November, 10–6, from December to February, 10–4, in March and April, 10–7.

The Komarov Botanical Gardens, 2 Professor Popov Street, is open from May to October daily; the hot-houses are open every day, except Fri., 11–4 in summer and 10.30–3 in winter. Entrance 20 kopeks.

Arctic Museum, 24 Marat Street, open 12–7 daily, 11–5 Sun. Closed Mon.

The Field of Mars, between Sadoyava and Khalturin Streets.

Mikhailovsky Garden, 1 Sadovaya Street, near the Field of Mars; *Garden of Rest,* 39 Nevsky Prospekt.

 **PARKS AND GARDENS.** The *Kirov Park* on Yelagin Ostrov (Island). The park was laid out in 1932; more than 18,000 trees have been planted in recent years. There is a summer theater, seating 1600, a variety theater, movie-theater, exhibition halls, boating facilities and a bathing beach.

Park Pobedy (Park of Victory), Moskovsky Prospekt. Leningrad has two victory parks, both established in 1945. The second is the Seaside Victory Park *(Primorsky Park Pobedy)* at 7 Rubin Street on Krestovsky Island.

Lenin Park, Maxim Gorky Prospekt, a crescent-shaped strip of land on Kronwerk Strait, is not very large but a favorite spot for walkers and lovers.

Botanical Gardens, 2 Professor Popov Street, and the *Zoological Gardens* in Lenin Park have already been mentioned under the *Museums* section.

Summer Garden, 2 Pestel Street, was founded more than 250 years ago by Peter the Great.

SHOPPING. The great Leningrad department stores and most of the specialist shops are either on or near the Nevsky Prospekt. The main department stores are: *Gostinyi Dvor,* 35 Nevsky Prospekt, on the corner of Sadovaya and Dumskaya Streets; *Dom Leningradskoi Torgovly,* 21/23 Zhelyabov Street; *Passage,* 48 Nevsky Prospekt, built in 1848, specializing in women's wear, perfume, household goods; *Apraksin Dvor,* Sadovaya Street, (from Lomonosov Street to Apraksin Pereulok).

Souvenirs can be bought in the kiosks and foreign currency shops of the Intourist hotels and in the Beryozka shops on Herzen Street and in the Nevsky Prospekt. The *Sovetskaya* hotel reportedly has a particularly large *Beryozka.*

Nevsky Prospekt offers the best array of shops; in particular, the following:

No. 55 machine- and hand-made carpets with ethnic designs of the various republics, mainly from Central Asia.

No. 53: cheeses—Altai, Dorogobuzh, Lithuanian, Swiss.

No. 51: national handicrafts, bone and wood carvings, tooled leather, embroidery, ceramics, Palekh caskets, toys.

No. 78: stamps, both foreign and Soviet, match-box labels.

No. 76: Soviet perfumes and cosmetics.

No. 72: prints and engravings, reproductions of works in the museums, postcards and albums. In the same building the *Mechta* (Dream) shop sells sweets and confectionery (one of the largest selection in the country).

No. 64: machine- and hand-made laces and embroidery. In the same building are tobacco shops selling cigarettes, cigars and the Russian *papirosi* (cigarettes with long cardboard mouthpieces). Still another shop at the same number sells glassware, crystal and china from the Lomonosov Porcelain Factory.

No. 60: for the hunter and fisherman; also other sports goods.

No. 56: is the largest foodstore in the city with meat, fish, dairy produce, cakes, fruit, wine, brandy, vodka. Still called the "Yeliseyev shop" after its pre-revolutionary owner.

No. 54: a gift-shop with a wide assortment of haberdashery, souvenirs, candy.

No. 52: a government-owned "commission store" where antiques, paintings, sculptures, china and bronze are on sale. It also has a recording studio for making your own disc.

No. 50: the largest sheet-music shop in Leningrad.

No. 44: The *Sever* shop, in the basement, is known for its cakes and tarts. The neighboring shop specializes in sausages.

No. 34: one of the largest record shops.

No. 28: The Book House *(Dom Knigi)*. The building also houses several publishers; the shop occupies two floors. Foreign-language publications can also be found here.

No. 26: souvenirs.

No. 18: everything for the artist: brushes, paints. The same building houses a wine and spirits store.

No. 16: *Mir* (Peace), a bookshop specializing in the arts, and work published in the Socialist countries.

No. 12: a dressmaker—garments in knitted fabrics made to measure.

No. 9: Birch Tree *(Beryozka)* shop, with a wide assortment of souvenirs. The Urals supply the shop with caskets, brooches, ear rings, bracelets of malachite, lazurite, rhodonite and jasper; amber from the Baltic Republics (check on export rules); brightly painted clay figures (called *Dymkovo* toys) from Kirov; wooden articles from Khokhloma, near the Volga. There are also Palekh miniatures made in the Palekh village of Central Russia, once well known for its ikon painters. There are records of Russian folk songs and guitars, mandolines and balalaikas. Russian perfumes are also on sale; so are souvenir sets of liqueurs and vodkas, champagne, boxed chocolates, canned caviar, headscarves and fur hats.

 TOURS are available through the Intourist offices in the city and in hotels, including visits to museums, opera, ballet and theaters. These are either pre-packaged in your trip or can be arranged individually (more difficult) once you have arrived. Be warned that tours arranged via Intourist work out considerably more expensive than doing it yourself. For example, you can get to Pushkin (15 miles outside the city) on your own for about 90 kopeks return. The advertised excursion rate is 4 roubles per person by coach, 30 roubles in a 3-seater car! For longer trips, more distant excursions, e.g. a 10-hour trip to Novgorod, it may be worth paying the advertized rate ($12 per person) for the convenience of door-to-door travel and guide services. This one is good value. There are also excursions available to Petrodvorets (formerly called Peterhof) in summer only, some 18 miles from the city on the Gulf of Finland; to Pushkin (formerly Tsarskoye Selo, some 15 miles from Leningrad), to Pavlovsk (17 miles), Lomonosov (formerly Oranienbaum, 25 miles), to Gatchina (a former imperial castle and park) and to the Sanatorno-Kurortnaya district, consisting of fifteen spas and resorts along the Gulf of Finland of which Sestroretsk and Zelenogorsk are the best known. We have already mentioned Repino under *Museums*. The Finnish border city of Vyborg can now also be visited. Petrozavodsk (for Kizhi Island) is a lengthy trip, and can be undertaken individually or in group tours.

 SPORTS, SPORTING FACILITIES. Lenin Stadium Krestovsky Ostrov, and Kirov Stadium. The latter is on Krestovsky Island, the sports center of Leningrad. Seaside Victory Park (Primorskoi Pobedy) Park was laid out in 1945 and the Dynamo Stadium was built in 1925.

Jubilee Sports Palace, 2 Zhdanovskaya Street; Winter Stadium, 6 Manezhnaya Ploshchad.

Winter swimming pools are available at: 11 Pravda Street, (only for training); 20 Bolshaya Raznochinnaya Street; Krestovsky Ostrov, 44 Prospekt Dinamo; 38 Dekabristov Street; 5a Novocherkassky Prospekt; 22–25 Nevsky Prospekt; Litovskaya Street (at the corner of Lesnoi Prospekt).;

Outdoor swimming pools and aquatic sports centers: 6 Olginskaya Street; 2 Prospekt Dinamo; 4 Vyazovaya Street; 24 Naberezhnaya Bolshoi Nevi; 11a Deputatskaya Street; 2 Vyazovaya Street; 15 Deputatskaya Street.

Cycling Track: 14 Vyborgskoye Chaussee; Cycling Stadium: 81 Engels Prospekt.

The summer skating rink is at 2,15th Liniya. Open-air skating rink: Central Recreation Park, Tavrichesky Sad (for children).

Skiing Station, within the city limits: Central Recreation Park.

Beaches, open in summer, are in the Central Recreation Park and the *Park Pobedy* (Victory Park).

For events see foreign language press and Intourist offices.

MEDICAL SERVICES. These are available on the same basis as in Moscow and other Soviet cities. Emergency ambulance service: dial 03 (24-hour service) but be prepared to wait up to 2 hours. Eye clinic (accidents or other treatment): 38 Mokhovaya Street, tel. 73-16-31 (24-hour emergency service). Ear, nose and throat clinic: 9 Bronnitskaya Street, tel. 92-28-41 (24-hour service). The Central Chemist Shop (Drugstore) is at 63 Nevsky Prospekt, tel. 12-89-78. Here, too, there is a round-the-clock service.

CHURCH SERVICES. Orthodox Russian churches open for worship: *Saint Nicholas,* 13 Ploshchad Kommunarov, open daily 8 A.M.–7 P.M., Sundays and holidays, 9, 11.30 A.M. and 7 P.M.; *Trinity Cathedral,* Ploshchad Alexandra Nevskogo, open daily 9 A.M.–6 P.M., Sundays 9 A.M.–7 P.M.; Others: *Baptist Church,* 29a Bolshaya Ozornaya (in suburbs), open Tues. and Thurs. at 7 P.M., Sundays 10 A.M., 2 P.M. and 6 P.M.; *Roman Catholic Church,* 7 Kovensky Pereulok, open daily at 7 A.M., 10 A.M. and 6 P.M., on Sundays at 1 P.M. too; *Synagogue,* 2 Lermontovsky Prospekt, open daily 10–12, Saturday 10–2; *Mosque,* 7 Maxim Gorky Prospekt, open Fridays 1 P.M.

Check times of services at your hotel or at the Intourist office; or, if the information is not forthcoming, visit the church itself.

MAIL, TELEPHONE AND CABLES. The same rules and regulations prevail here as in Moscow (which see). The Central Post Office is at 9 Soyuza Svyazi Street, open 9–9, tel. 06; Central Telegraph Office, Soyuza Svyazi Street 15, tel. 06 (24-hour service); Central Telephone Exchange, 3/5 Herzen Street (24-hour service). At this building you can also send telegrams. Leningrad-Moscow telephone exchange: tel 10-00-20; Telephone exchange: 07; Telegrams on credit: 06 (24-hour service). Enquiries for private telephone numbers: 00; Enquiries for office telephone numbers: 09.

ENGLISH READING MATTER. A limited number of English and American papers are available at the Intourist offices and in hotels. Books at the foreign-language bookshops (see *Shopping*). The choice is limited.

GENERAL INFORMATION. The following useful telephone numbers and addresses, together with emergency numbers (except medical) cover everything you'll need to know in Leningrad: Weather Service: dial 13-62-18; time clock: 08 (24 hours).

Taxi hire: tel. 10-00-22 (24-hour service); arrival and departure of trains: tel. 15-00-48 (24 hours); air terminal; tel. 15-00-18; Intourist Service, airport: 93-09-27; air, rail and ship tickets, Intourist: 29 Herzen Street (in the Hotel Astoria), tel. 12-65-53; merchant ship harbor, tel. 16-40-63; Vasilevsky Island harbor; 17-03-20, 17-10-38; information about movies: 05.

Fire alarms: 01; militia (police); 02; lost property: general: tel. 97-00-92. If lost on trolley-buses: 15-18-62; in trams: 10-98-97; visa and registration office: 60 Nevsky Prospekt, tel. 11-67-49.

City Soviet of Workers' Deputies, Reception Room, 6 Isaakyevskaya Ploshchad, tel. 19-13-66; House of Friendship and Peace, 21 Fontanka; Union of Societies for Friendship and Cultural Ties with Foreign Countries: tel. 15-96-66; Peace Committee: tel. 14-66-88.

Service Station No. 3, 3 Novaya Derevnya, Liniya 5, tel. 33-69-30 or 33-87-04. (Open 8–11 for overhauls, checking cars; 9–4.30 for repairs. Closed on Sundays.) Filling Station No. 30, at the Service Station; 24-hour service. Filling Station No. 2, 10 Klinicheskaya Street; 24-hour service. Filling Station, No. 3. Moskovsky Prospekt 100; 24-hour service. Filling Station No. 12, 18 Dnepropetrovskaya Street; diesel oil also available.

International airline offices in Leningrad: *SAS,* Gogol Street, 19, tel. 12-09-59. *Finnair,* Gogol Street, 19, tel. 12–42–28. *BA.* Hotel Astoria, Room 22, tel. 19-11-82 (open in summer only). *Interflug* (GDR), Airport, tel. 13–55–66. *LOT* (Poland), Hotel Astoria, Room 23, tel. 19–11–83. *Aeroflot:* 7/9 Nevsky Prospekt, tel. (information): 215-00-18 or 210-00-77, (tickets): 225-25-29. *Aeroflot* for flights to Baltic republics and northern USSR: 36 Herzen Street.

U.S. Consulate-General, 15 Petr Lavrov Street, tel. 72-52-17, 72-45-48. Residence of the U.S. Consul-General, 4 Grodnensky Pereulok, tel. 72-84-07.

WEST, CENTRAL AND NORTHERN RUSSIA

European Russia and Byelorussia

We have previously described the Russian Soviet Federal Socialist Republic, the largest republic in the Soviet Union. The Russian SFSR occupies 6,593,391 square miles in both Europe and Asia, with a population of almost 133 million, made up of more than 40 nationalities.

This huge territory is divided by the Urals into two main areas: European Russia and Siberia. The former occupies the lesser half of the Republic's territory but the majority of its population lives here.

To the east, the European half is bordered by the Ural mountains; to the southwest is the "second Baku," the oil fields between the Volga and the Ural rivers, lying north of the border with Kazakhstan; southwest again are the Caspian plain, the wheat-growing expanse of Krasnodar and Stavropol (the "waving sea of Kuban," as Russian poetry calls it) and the Black Sea Riviera as far as Sochi. To the west it is bordered by the iron ore deposits on the edge of the Ukraine, the district of Kursk, the forests of Bryansk, and further north, Byelorussia, Latvia, Estonia and the Baltic (in the Gulf of Finland).

The 10,000-square-mile Kaliningrad Territory also belongs to the Russian Federal Republic, though it has no direct territorial link with it: it lies between the Baltic Sea, Lithuania and Poland. This is a district which was added to the Soviet Union by the Potsdam Agreement of 1945, dividing East Prussia; one-third was handed to the Soviet Union, two-thirds to Poland. Thus the former Königsberg and its surrounding area became Kaliningrad and the Territory of Kaliningrad. Here is the westernmost point of the USSR.

To the northwest, European Russia is bordered by Finland; at the Kola Peninsula the Soviet Union and Norway meet. This is a district rich in nickel, copper and other rare metals. On this peninsula we find the western gateway to the Soviet Union for northern shipping lines: the ice-free harbor of Murmansk. This is the northernmost metropolis in the world, where "night" lasts three weeks in winter and "day" lasts three weeks in summer. The northern limit of European Russia is the North Polar Sea (the Barents Sea and White Sea). Until the foundation of Petersburg, Arkhangelsk was Russia's only sea port. From its neighborhood the vast Siberian forests reach almost as far as Vorkuta, where there is a vast complex of labor camps.

We will deal with European Russia in various sections, beginning with the territory west of Moscow (from its borders with Byelorussia), moving next northeast of the capital, then northwest and south and, finally, to Byelorussia. The Volga deserves a chapter to itself.

WEST OF MOSCOW

Smolensk, some 210 miles from Moscow, standing on both banks of the Upper Dnieper, is an important district center. It is also a rail and road junction which, in the former frontier region, was "the Key to Moscow" three times between the 16th and 20th centuries against the Polish and Swedish conquerors, in the Napoleonic invasion, and, finally, during the Nazi assault.

Since 1949 there have been systematic archeological researches in Smolensk and its neighborhood and these have established the presence of Slavs in the sixth century—but human habitations have been traced back to the Later Stone Age. The excavations within the city limits among others on the Sobornaya Gora, Temple Hill—have uncovered the relics of Slav settlements of the sixth to eighth centuries, while about nine miles west, in Gnyozdovo, there were rich finds of a pagan burial site.

Smolensk was thus one of the oldest Slav settlements; in the ninth century it was already known as a "big" city, compared to Kiev. Russian historical sources mention it as the center of the Krivich tribe in 865 AD. We know that it was an important industrial and trading town; its name probably derives from the caulking of ships (*smoleniye*—which means tarring). Its prosperity was due to the fact that it lay on the famous waterway linking the Baltic and the Black Sea, of which the Dnieper was an important section. As such, it was mentioned in the famous work of Constantine Porphyrogenitus (912–59 AD), *De administrando imperio*.

Excavations at the so-called Dnieper Gate uncovered many layers of wood dating back to the 11th century when the swampy soil of the Dnieper shore was covered with fallen trees. The excavators also found traces of ancient wooden houses, agricultural implements and documents written on birch bark.

In the 12th century Smolensk became the capital of an independent principality. Prince Rostislav enclosed it with walls and battlements. In the 13th century it was annexed by the Lithuanian Grand Duchy. After 110 years of Lithuanian rule, the Russians reconquered it in 1514. In the 16th, 17th and 18th centuries it developed further; its defensive walls date from this period. Early in the 17th century, when Poles and Swedes attacked it together, it was besieged for 20 months and fell only because of its betrayal by three local nobles. Those who did not fall in the battle died under the ruins of the cathedral built by Prince Vladimir Monomakh in 1101, which was blown up at the last moment. One of the ruined bastions of the city walls still bears the name of the Voivode Seyin who commanded the defense. After the fall of Smolensk, the 1618 truce handed it again to Poland. It returned to Russia at the end of the same century and soon became a regional capital. In 1812 it was the scene of a great battle with the French which lasted for two days and ended in a retreat by the Russians after they had set fire to the city and blown up the arsenal.

In the 19th century Smolensk became an important commercial and cultural center. The building of railways, starting in 1856, increased its importance, but its industries mainly developed under the Soviet regime. In the Second World War, the battle of Smolensk lasted from July to September 1941. During the Nazi occupation all but 300 of its dwelling houses were destroyed. It was liberated on September 25, 1943, and since then has built up significant textile, metallurgical and machine plant industries.

Exploring Smolensk

In the center of the city, next to the Rossiya (Intourist) Hotel in Marx Street if we turn right to Marx Square, we find the House of Soviets (Dom Sovietov) built in the constructivist style of the early thirties. The theater at 4 Marx Street is an eclectic building dating from a little later. Radovka, a characteristic residential district, can be reached by No. 1 bus traveling in the direction of Krasninskaya Street. (Take the bus to Chernushenskaya Street.) The No. 1 can be boarded on the Bolshaya Sovietskaya, the main street of Smolensk, at Smirnov Square southeast of Marx Square. You can reach this point by turning left when leaving the Rossiya Hotel on Marx Street, then south to a point near the Smolensk Hotel.

If you take the No. 1 bus traveling in the opposite direction (north towards Kolkhoznaya Square) and get off beyond the Dnieper bridge, at the terminus, you have reached the so-called Gorodnanka District. Here, between Kachin Street, opening from Kolkhoznaya Square, and the railway station, we find the oldest architectural monument of Smolensk, the Church of St. Peter and St. Paul (12th century). To the west stands the Episcopal Palace (17th century) and the Church of St. Barbara (Varvarovskaya), also 17th century. The Peter-and-Paul Church was built in 1146, largely in Byzantine style. Its gleaming majolica floor is particularly attractive. In the 17th century it was turned into a Unitarian Church and the Unitarian Episcopal Palace next to it was built in 1632. The Church of St. Barbara is typically Russian Baroque.

The Church of St. John the Divine (Tserkov Ivana Bogoslova) is roughly contemporary with the Peter-and-Paul Church. It was built by Prince Roman Rostislavich in 1173; it stands in Krasnoflotskaya Street, on the left bank of the Dnieper, downstream at the next bridge.

The nearby Svirskaya Church on Malaya Krasnoflotskaya Street, near the Smyadinka river, was erected by Roman's brother, David Rostislavich, in 1191–4. It was intended as a court church and its size and shape symbolize the princely intentions. It is particularly interesting to see how the form of the earlier wooden architecture was imitated in a brick building.

Returning to the Bolshaya Sovietskaya, let us climb away from the river to Temple Hill, where we find Kutuzov's life-size equestrian statue (erected in 1954, sculptured by Motvilov). On Temple Hill the first, wooden, church was erected by Vladimir Monomakh in 1101. This was destroyed five centuries later in the siege of Smolensk; in the 17th century the local people began to build the Cathedral of the Assumption (Uspensky Sobor) on its site on the model of similar Moscow churches. The first architect (in 1677) was the Moscow master Korolkov; his work was continued early in the 18th century by Sedel, and it was according to his designs that the cathedral was finished in 1740. Its bell tower was rebuilt in 1767 in the Petersburg Baroque style; at the same time its stone wall and the triumphal arch of the pedestrian approach road were added. The stairway leading from the Bolshaya Sovietskaya was completed in 1767 by Obukhov with Baroque brick columns and granite steps; but in 1784 it was reshaped by Slepnev with classical elements.

The cathedral is used for services today. It stands 229 feet high and 140 feet wide; the central dome is built of wood and decorated. The iconostasis of gilded limewood is 33 feet high; ten people worked for 12 years to complete it. The principal treasure is a reputedly wonder-working icon of the Virgin, said to have been painted by St. Luke for the ruler of Syria. There are other valuable icons.

Continuing uphill on the Bolshaya Sovietskaya we reach, at Smirnov Square, the city wall, built under the reign of Boris Godunov. The wall continues left to Krasnoznamyonnaya Street and right, crossing the Kutuzov Park, to the City Park. The section between Smirnov Square and Krasnoznamyonnaya Street includes the Seyin Bastion, where the restoration work is most advanced. Built in 1595–1602, the wall stretches for four miles; it is a striking combination of architectural beauty and military utility. Boris Godunov called it "the pearl of Russia" and it received its first baptism of fire soon after completion, when the Poles besieged Smolensk.

After visiting the wall and the bastions, we can go back down Krasnoznamyonnaya Street, following the lines of the No. 1 tram westwards towards the Hotel Smolensk. This will take us down Glinka Street. The building of Number Three Hospital is the former mansion of the Engelhardt family, built in the 18th century. It was originally baroque but was later rebuilt in a constructivist style.

Glinka Street ends at the Town Park of Smolensk, which bears the composer's name. His statue by the sculptor Bok and erected by public subscription stands near the entrance. The iron railing around it skilfully incorporates several of Glinka's melodies, reproducing the actual musical notes from *Ruslan and Lyudmila* and other operas.

Crossing the Glinka Park, (also known as the Blonye, the Flat Meadow), we reach October Revolution Street. Starting uphill, to the left, we find, after the first crossing, Smolensk's other important park, the Kutuzov Garden. Near the city wall (of which a section stands within the park) we find the burial place of several illustrious figures in Russian military history, including that of Maria Oktyabrskaya, a Heroine of the Soviet Union who fell in the battles for the liberation of Smolensk in the autumn of 1943.

On the central promenade of the Kutuzov Garden we find Kutuzov's bust, by Strakhovskaya, unveiled in 1912, the centenary of the Battle of Borodino. The Eagle Monument at the end of the promenade was also erected on the same occasion; a heavily symbolic work by Sukman and Nadolsky, it includes a number of allegorical figures, a stylized bronze map of European Russia and the names of the Russian generals who led the armies against Napoleon. An even more elaborate memorial to the 1812 campaign is at the entrance of the Park Kultury (Cultural Park).

The sights and the history of Smolensk are summed up in the Museum of Local Lore on Temple Hill. Other museums include the Local History Museum on Lenin Street, which contains exhibits from local archeological excavations, including the Gnyozdovsky tumuli and some birch-bark writings. Several halls are devoted to the region's past from the 17th century until the Second World War, with the emphasis on revolutionary leaders and activities. A section deals with the first cosmonaut, Yuri Gagarin, including his personal effects and the gifts he received after his first flight in space.

The Art Gallery, 7 Krupskaya Street, contains Russian classical paintings and works by Soviet and foreign artists. The native artists include Ilya Repin and Isaac Levitan; there is also an interesting collection representing the Italian, Dutch, Flemish, Spanish and German schools. Murillo, van Ostade, Claude-Joseph Vernet and Kaulbach are the most important artists represented.

The Smolensk Museum of Local Lore has a branch in the village of Talashkino, 8 miles from Smolensk on the Roslav highway. (Intourist can arrange an excursion.) Here, on the former estate of Princess Maria Tenisheva, stands Teremok, a wooden chalet built in 1901–3, in Russian "fairy-tale" style, designed by Malyutin. The museum has some 2,000 items of folk art; the woodcarvings are of particular interest. Close to Teremok is a small family chapel with a striking mosaic over the entrance. Many prominent Russian artists worked here to revive their native folk art.

Gnyozdovo, the site of the archeological excavations, is some eight miles from Smolensk, along the Vitebsk highway. It can be reached easily by the Koltso line on the local train system or by No. 2 bus to the Vtoraya dachnaya. Gluschenki and Belaya Stantsiya stops. Gnyozdovo is a protected area and the taking of any souvenirs—even a stone—is frowned upon. More than 3,000 graves, mostly from pre-Christian times, have been found on the site, which extends over two square km. A number of kurgans (burial mounds) date from the tenth century. Many Byzantine and Arab coins, Scandinavian jewelry and Russian tools were found here. The excavations began in 1874 and, with some interruptions, have continued ever since.

The Road to Moscow

Passing Yartsevo, northeast of Smolensk, on the tourist highway to Moscow, you come to another industrial center, Safonovo, the second-largest town of the Smolensk region. The ancient town of Dorogobuzh-on-the-Dnieper and its regional electric power station are close to Safonovo.

Vyazma was first mentioned in an 11th century manuscript. It stands on the Vyazma River, a tributary of the Dnieper. Until the 18th century it was a place of great military and economic importance and was seized several times by Poles and Lithuanians. During Napoleon's retreat in 1812 it was burnt down. Once among the largest dairy centers of Russia,

Vyazma is now a light industrial town. Among its products are jam-filled cookies, famous throughout the Soviet Union, called *vyazemskiye pryaniki.*

Trinity Cathedral, dating from the 17th century, is on Nagornaya Street. It has a copy of a miraculous icon, the Virgin of Iberia, and is open for services. The buildings of the St. John the Baptist (Predtecha) Monastery date roughly from the same time. The Ascension Church (1650) is lavishly decorated with pilasters and small columns, and an arcade extending around practically the whole circumference. The Arkadievskaya Church (1661), with its traditional five cupolas, is also a remarkable monument.

Gagarin (Gzhatsk) stands on the banks of the Bolshaya Gzhat River, which is a tributary of the Vazuza. The river, 60 miles long, used to be an important waterway, and is now used mainly for floating timber. The most interesting monument in Gzhatsk is the Kazanskaya Church (1794), a singular example of Russian Baroque. The town was renamed in honor of Yuri Gagarin, the astronaut, who studied here and who spent his childhood in the nearby village of Klushino.

Mozhaisk, some three miles off the main road, is one of the oldest cities in Russia, first mentioned in a document of 1231. From the 13th century to the 15th century, it was the capital of a princely state. The remains of the Luzhetsky Monastery (16th-17th centuries) and the Cathedral of St. Nicholas (19th century) are both worth visiting. The battle of Borodino took place about eight miles from Mozhaisk and it is a good base for exploring the famous battleground with its various monuments. This can be reached along a side road which branches off from the main Minsk-Moscow road at the 96 or 108 km. stone. Founded in 1903, the museum is now located in a building erected in 1912 to commemorate the centenary of the 15-hour battle between French and Russian armies on August 26, 1812. The collection includes guns, pictures and personal relics. Over 30 other monuments are scattered over Borodino Field, most of them erected in 1912, dedicated to Field Marshal Kutuzov and other generals and to whole regiments. There is also a monument to French soldiers and officers.

There was another battle of Borodino in 1941, and the city was retaken by the Russians in January 1942. A large reservoir, "the Mozhaisk Sea", has been built here and a hydroelectric power station spans the Moskva River.

Zvenigorod, nine miles off the main road, is an ancient town of the Moscow Region. The earliest recorded references to it date from 1328. For more than 150 years it remained the center of a principality subordinate to Moscow. Situated on the Moskva River on high hills cut by ravines and surrounded by forests, it was an important stronghold protecting Moscow on the west. It lay on the old Smolensk-Moscow road leading from Lithuania and Poland.

The most ancient part of Zvenigorod, Gorodok, is an earth fortification rising 150 feet above the Moscow River. The stone Cathedral of the Assumption, also known as the Sobor na Gorodke, is a striking monument of early Moscow architecture, built in 1400. It has a single dome and is rectangular in shape, similar to the Vladimir Cathedral. The narrow windows show that in wartime it served as a fortress. The decorations are unique, with remnants of ancient frescos.

The Savvino-Storozhevsky Monastery, on Storozha Hill, a mile up the Moskva River, was founded in 1398 under Prince Yuri Zvenigorodsky, whose confessor, Sava, was the first abbot. Ivan the Terrible visited the place frequently; young Peter I, his brother Ivan and his sister Sophia took refuge within its walls in 1682 during the Rebellion of the Streltsy (imperial guard). Today some of the monastery buildings have been turned into a sanatorium and the Zvenigorod Museum of Local Lore. The most ancient and interesting building is the Cathedral of the Nativity of the Virgin, erected in 1404. Though the exterior has changed considerably, the interior walls still have some of their 15th to 17th century frescos. The five-tier iconostasis also dates from the 17th century. The four-story former refectory, built between 1652 and 1654, is also quite distinctive. The Transfiguration Church, built in 1639 by the order of the Princess Sophia, has striking light stucco decorations contrasting with the dark-red walls. Other monastery buildings include the Holy Trinity Church (1652) and the former palace of Czar Alexei Mikhailovich (1652–4), son of the founder of the Romanov dynasty.

The Zvenigorod countryside is very lovely, resembling the foothills of the Alps. Many famous Russian artists spent their summers here. Zvenigorod was also associated with well-known Russian writers and composers, including Herzen, Chekhov (who worked as a doctor at the hospital in Lermontov Street) and Tchaikovsky.

Bakovka and Kuntsevo are the last two towns on the road to Moscow. The former is a popular place for *dachas* (country villas); in the nearby village of Peredelkino, Boris Pasternak lived until his death in 1960. His simple grave in the village churchyard may be visited. It is not officially signposted, but if you mention Pasternak's name to any passing local, he will direct you there with great pride.

Bakovka has a motel, a restaurant and a camping site. Kuntsevo is famous for its "Farewell Hill," where Muscovites would say goodbye to relatives and friends going on a long journey. From here, the Kutuzov Prospekt leads straight into the heart of Moscow.

PRACTICAL INFORMATION FOR WESTERN EUROPEAN RUSSIA

WHEN TO GO. Summer is the best season to visit European Russia, unless you are a winter sports addict. June, July and August are warm and sunny but less humid than in Central Europe. The early autumn is often a true Indian Summer, dry and sunny. October is usually windy and cool; by early November it begins to snow. The winter in the European part of the Russian Federal Republic is cold but seldom wet or windy.

HOW TO GET THERE. By train from Warsaw and other cities west of the Soviet Union; there are good connections from Hungary via Chop. Direct trains both from Moscow and Leningrad. **By car:** the Intourist motor route runs from Minsk to Smolensk and then on to Moscow. Detours are only possible if advance notice is given.

WHAT TO SEE. In **Smolensk:** The Cathedral of the Assumption, the Church of St. Peter and St. Paul; Church of St. John the Divine; Svirskaya Church; Kutuzov Monument; Glinka Monument. In **Talashkino** (8 miles off the main road, along the Roslav Chaussée): the museum of Teremok (folk art). **Vyazma:** Trinity Cathedral. **Mozhaisk:** St. Nicholas Cathedral; Luzhetsky Monastery ruins; Borodino Museum. **Peredelkino:** Pasternak's grave.

HOTELS. Smolensk. *Smolensk,* Glinka Street, with guarded car park; or *Rossiya,* 1/2 Lenin Square, with Intourist office therein. *Motel Fenix* (Intourist services), 2/1 Lenin Square.

There is a camping site 1 mile to the left of the Brest-Smolensk road, at 384 km. stone, sited in the woods. Café, bathing and shopping facilities, post office, telephone, etc.

RESTAURANTS. Gagarin (formerly Gzhatsk). A pleasant restaurant on the banks of the river in town.

Kuntsevo. Adequate restaurant on the Moscow Road.

Smolensk. In *Rossiya Hotel,* the *Dnepr Restaurant* in the Smolensk Hotel, or one of the following: *Sputnik,* Nikolayev Street; *Zarya,* Kommuna Street; or *Otdykh,* in the Glinka Gardens.

CULTURAL ACTIVITIES. In **Smolensk** there is a Drama Theater, 4 Karl Marx Street; a Puppet Theater, 5a Lenin Street, and a Philharmonic Concert Hall, 18, Bolshaya Sovietskaya Street.

MUSEUMS. Smolensk: *Local History Museum,* 9 Lenin Street.

The *Local Natural History Museum,* 7 Soborny Dvor, presents a survey of the natural resources of the Smolensk region and their economic utilization.

The *Art Gallery,* 7 Krupskaya Street.

The *Smolensk Museum of Local Lore* in Talashkino, 8 miles from Smolensk on the Roslav highway. (Intourist can arrange an excursion.) Open 10–4, Wed. and Sun.

Borodino Museum, near Mozhaisk, open 10–6.

SHOPPING. The *Smolensk* Department Store is at 1 Gagarin Prospekt; a *Beryozka* Souvenir Shop is located at 22 Kommunisticheskaya Street; special souvenirs of Smolensk can be found at 11/1 Lenin Street. There is a *Central Bookshop* (18 Bolshaya Sovietskaya Street), a good jeweler's shop (33 Bolshaya Sovietskaya Street) and a well-stocked tobacconist at 10 Lenin Street.

TOURS by bus or car will be arranged by Intourist starting from Moscow or, if you travel in the Smolensk region on your way from the west, included in your itinerary on the way to Moscow.

USEFUL SMOLENSK ADDRESSES. *Intourist:* 2/1 Marx Street, (tel. 3-35-08). *Railway Station.* on the right bank of the Dnieper, at the terminus of No. 1 tram. *General Post Office:* October Revolution Street including International Telephone Office. *Address Bureau,* 12 Dzerzhinsky Street.

NORTHEAST OF MOSCOW

If we set out northeast from the Soviet capital, after passing the first few towns (Pushkin, Abramtsevo and Zagorsk), there are three old Russian cities which have many ancient monuments: Pereslavl-Zalessky, Rostov-Veliky and Yaroslavl. Beyond them lie Vladimir, Suzdal, Ivanovo and Palekh, all of which deserve to be visited.

Exploring the Northeast

Situated 44 miles from Moscow, the town of Zagorsk can be seen from a distance, easily identifiable by the huge fortified monastery of Trinity-St. Sergius, founded in 1340 by Sergius during his evangelizing crusade. It rapidly became the nucleus of Sergievo, (now Zagorsk), and in 1550 the complex of buildings was surrounded by imposing white walls. The Church of the Trinity used to contain famous paintings by Andrei Rublyev, but they have been replaced by copies and the originals taken to the Tretyakov Museum in Moscow. In 1585 the Cathedral of the Assumption was built, its five enormous bulb-shaped towers, in blue and gold picked out with stars, adding to the already vivid richness of the town's architecture. Near the Cathedral is a tiny colorful chapel with a miraculous fountain. Beside the chapel stands the tomb of Boris Godunov and his family. The elegant baroque belfry in the main square was built in the middle of the 18th century, following the plans of Rastrelli.

For five hundred years this monastery has been one of the most important centers of pilgrimage in Russia. After the Revolution it was converted into a museum, but now almost all the churches are open again for worship. There is even a flourishing theological college. Zagorsk should unquestionably be included in every modern traveler's pilgrimage. The town is, incidentally, often used as a location for costume films.

Pereslavl-Zalessky, "the city of waters," the birthplace of Peter the Great's fleet, was founded by Yury Dolgoruky in 1152, five years after the foundation of Moscow. It lies on the shore of Lake Pleshcheyevo, framed by numerous tributaries of the Trubezh River—a Russian Venice in miniature.

If you set out from town on the right-hand shore of the lake, you'll have a fine view of Pereslavl and the water from Mount Alexander (Alexandrova Gora), named after Alexander Nevsky who, in the 13th century, was co-ruler of the city. About two miles on the other shore, near Thunder Mountain (Gremyachaya Gora), stands the Nautical Museum housing Peter the Great's ship, *Fortuna.* It was here that the future Czar built a toy fleet in anticipation of the first real one which he launched in the last years of the 17th century.

The heart of the town is Red Square (Krasnaya Ploshchad) with the Cathedral of the Savior, erected by Yury Dolgoruky in 1152. The cathedral was linked to the palace of the prince (near the northern city walls) and to the fortifications; it was part of the defenses. Its single dome, apse and the clean lines of its façade make it an impressive and powerful building. The Church of the Metropolitan Peter, on the western side, was built in 1585. It is also known as the Shatrovaya Church. Its cellar was once a treasury; today it houses the Alexander Nevsky Museum.

There are large monasteries both north and south of Pereslavl. The northern one is the Nikitsky Monastery, founded in the 12th century, with most of its monuments dating from the 16th. Its compound includes the Cathedral of St. Nicholas and the Church of the Annunciation, joined by the *trapeza,* the rather grim and solemn refectory. The monastery walls are divided by six bastions of different shape.

To the south at the approach to the town stands the Goritsky Monastery with its churches (the Cathedral of the Assumption and the Vsesvyatskaya), and its 17th century murals. Its chief feature is the richly-carved Holy Gates (17th century). Today it is a museum, especially rich in icons and wood carvings. There is an art gallery featuring mainly the works of Dmitri Kardovsky (1866–1943), who was born in this region. The Czar Gates from the Vedenskaya Church and Peter the Great's live plaster mask (1719), and Falconnet's original model for the Bronze Horseman are also here.

Rostov-Veliky is 40 miles from Pereslavl and about 120 miles from Moscow. Founded in 862 AD, it was the capital of a principality in the 11th and 12th centuries. Its earliest architecture has been destroyed but in the 17th century the Metropolitan Iona Sisoyevich, a man of both ambition and taste, inspired many outstanding buildings.

Of these, the Metropolitan Palace (actually a fortress) close to Lake Nero, is perhaps the most impressive. Today it houses the local museum, established in 1883 when the kremlin was first restored. The museum has collections of porcelain, icons and woodcarvings of the 16th-20th centuries. There is a small prison cell called the "stone sack". Though it was built in 1670–83 as the Metropolitan's residence, the Palace has something of a medieval castle about it; the high church dignitary wanted it to symbolize the triumph of "the sword of religion" over the "saber of laity". Also known as the White Palace (because of its white-painted walls), it stands in Rostov's Kremlin, close to the town center.

The center of the Kremlin (also known as the Metropolia, as it was fortified only for the purpose of protecting the metropolitan, or archbishop), is a spacious courtyard with a small lake in the middle. This is the actual residence, the so-called Samuilov Corpus, with the remnants of the Krasnaya Palata (Fine Palace) on the right. Beside it stands the five-domed Church of St. John the Divine (Ivan Bogoslov) built over one of the gates. Skirting the Metropolitan's Palace we reach the single-domed Church of the Redeemer, the chapel of the Metropolitan, which had a direct passage linking it to the palace. The murals are truly impressive both in this chapel and in the Church of the Resurrection, built over the other gate.

The Church of the Savior is linked by a gallery to the Belaya Palata (White Palace) and the Otdatochnaya (Ceremonial) Hall. The hall has an area of some 300 square yards, with a huge column in the center and resembles the Granovitaya Palace of the Moscow Kremlin. From the hall you can go on to the castle walls; its open gallery provides access to the whole Metropolitan Courtyard, its bastions and its gate-churches.

The Uspensky Cathedral (built in the 15th century) and the four-domed belfry (1680–2) stand outside the Kremlin. The latter has 13 bells which play four different carillons. On the north the Church of the Resurrection is bordered by the so-called Holy Gates, where the Metropolitan made his ceremonial entry. The best view of all this is from the lake. Take a boat and see.

Yaroslavl

Yaroslavl, on the bank of the Volga, is where the highway from Moscow, around 150 miles away, ends. It is not only an important industrial centre but an ancient city, rich in monuments. According to tradition, it was founded by the Kiev Grand Prince Yaroslav the Wise.

The harbor is a good place to start our exploration. Turning left, we reach the bank of the Volga. Crossing the Krasny Syezd (Red Congress) bridge, we reach the monument (1958) to the 19th-century Russian poet Nekrasov, who spent most of his life in this region. His home at Kara-bykha, ten miles south of Yaroslavl, is now a museum.

Pervomaysky Boulevard starts at the Nekrasov Monument; there is a park here in which three of the former bastions of the Yaroslavl city wall have been preserved.

Pervomaysky Street leads from the boulevard of the same name to Volkhov Square, where stands the city theater, in which Stanislavsky and many outstanding Russian actors appeared. On a No. 5 tram we can travel to the Lenin Industrial district and further on to a typical modern residential quarter, finally returning along Svoboda Street to the railway station. From here we can travel by trolley to Trud (Labour) Square, the former Haymarket. Our route is again along Svoboda Street; at its end we find the Znamenskaya Bastion (1660). From the Tefolev Street stop we can walk along Sovietskaya Street to Sovietskaya Square, where an 18th-century classical building, formerly the Governor's Palace, now houses the regional government.

Yaroslavl became the regional seat in 1777 when it was rebuilt. The groundplan of the center has remained largely unchanged mostly because this was the residential Inner Town with massive stone houses, and industry therefore, could only be established in the outskirts. The center is Sovietskaya (formerly Ilyinskaya) Square, from which the main streets (Sovietskaya, Kirovskaya and Bolshaya Oktyabrskaya) radiate.

The finest feature of Sovietskaya Square is the Church of Elijah the Prophet with its ancient pews, 18th-century iconostasis and 17th-century icons and murals, several of them masterpieces by Yury Nikitin and Sila Savin.

Another walk from Sovietskaya Square takes us down Narodny Street to the Volga quay, which was built in 1825–35. To the left along the quay, called Volzhskaya by the locals, in the courtyard of No. 2–4, we find the Nikoly Nadena Church; its murals date from 1640. At No. 5, the Ilinsko-Tikhonovskaya Church, built in 1825–31 and a masterpiece of 19th-century classicism, is now in rather bad repair. Further along, we can turn left into M. Fevralskyaya Street (running parallel with Narodny) where No. 1 (on the quay corner) is the Church of the Nativity (1644), which has a mid-17th-century bell tower and a gate-church attached.

Coming from the railway station northward to the main part of the city, we find, at the bridge and Medveditsky Ravine, and the Volga Bastion (1658–68), the area of the former kremlin.

From here, going eastwards along the Kotorosl River, we reach the Strelka Point which offers a fine view of the stream's confluence with the Volga. Along the Kotorosl, there is a whole series of monuments: the Nikolai Rublenov Church (1695), once adjoining the wall of the kremlin; the Church of the Redeemer, with its beautiful murals of 1896; and the Church of St. Michael the Archangel, built in 1657–80. Its frescos, painted by local artists, are particularly noteworthy.

The important complex of the Spaso-Preobrazhensky (Transfiguration of Our Savior) Monastery is behind us on the bank of the Kotorosl (at 25 Podbelshov Square). It was there that the only copy of the *Song of Igor's Campaign* was discovered—and, sadly, lost again when Napoleon invaded Moscow, where it had found its way into the personal library of the nobleman Musin-Pushkin. The opera *Prince Igor* was based on this national epic. The monastery, founded at the end of the 12th century, was converted into a bishop's palace in 1787. The entrance gates date from 1616. The murals inside the archway illustrating St. John's apocalyptic visions were painted in 1664. Within the walls is the Transfiguration Cathedral, built in 1516 but altered several times during the centuries. The frescos were painted in 1563–4 by several local artists; others were added in 1782. Besides the cathedral the monastery also contains a 16th century refectory, the Church of Yaroslavl Miracle-Workers (1831), now used as a cinema and meeting hall, a 16th century bell tower (reconstructed) and monks' cells dating from the same period. Parts of the local Art Museum are now housed in the monastery.

South of the monastery is the Kotorosl Bridge. Beyond the river, there are two important architectural monuments. One, to the left, is the Church of St. John Chrysostom, built in 1649–54 in the Korovniki District, with its 17th century iconostasis and frescos dating from 1732–3; the other, to the right of the bridge, upriver, is the Church of St. John the Baptist (1671–87) with 15 domes, bricks imitating woodcarvings, colored tiles and some outstanding murals. There are an 18th century bell tower and iconostasis.

Vladimir

Vladimir, founded by Prince Vladimir Monomakh, Grand Prince of Kiev, in 1116, is attractively situated on the River Klyazma, a small tributary of the Volga. Enlarged in the 12th century by Andrei Bogoliubsky, it was destroyed by the Tatars in 1238 and came under the rule of Moscow in the 15th century.

The first striking monument on the way from Moscow is the Golden Gate, built in 1164. This was not only the ceremonial gate of the city, but one of its important fortifications, rising to two stories and still accessible by a stairway. The actual gates were defended by platforms supported by oak columns.

Behind the Golden Gate, Vladimir rises on a semicircular hill on the riverside. The Cathedral of the Assumption (Uspensky Sobor) stands on the eastern summit. Originally it was built as a single-domed church in 1158–61 but after a fire it was enlarged in 1185–9; it was given another four domes, among other improvements. There is much gilt, fine majolica tiles and some remnants of the old murals. The other frescos (1189) were restored in 1408 by Andrei Rublyev and Daniel Chorny.

It is thought that the palace of Vsevolod III stood close to the cathedral. Its church, the Dimitri Cathedral (1194–7), is the finest in Vladimir, and one of the most outstanding in the whole country. Its high reliefs are quite sensational; carved on the cathedral front, they represent a strange mixture of subjects from the Scriptures and classical history—Alexander the Great and King Solomon, for example, are both represented.

The rest of Vladimir's monuments belong to the 17th-19th centuries; many of these are concentrated in the Street of the Third International, where the Intourist Hotel is located. Here is the Monastery of the Nativity, the Church of the Assumption, the classical Dvoryanskoye Sobranye (Diet of the Nobles) and Torgovy Ryad (Merchant Row).

The Cathedral of the Princess (Knyagini) at the Vorovsky Settlement was built in the 16th century on the site of an earlier church and named after the wife of Vsevolod III. Its 17th century murals were restored in 1947.

Note: you cannot travel individually to Vladimir unless you are a motoring tourist, so trips must be arranged through Intourist, either in groups or individually, with a guide.

Suzdal

Along the road from Vladimir to Suzdal, the villages evoke ancient times. Batiyevo (from the name of Batu Khan) recalls the Tatar invasion. Pavlovskoye and Borisovskoye, the estates of the medieval Princes of Moscow. Suzdal, a holy city, is in itself an entire museum—the multitude of its monuments, towers and domes enables the visitor to follow the history of Russian architecture from the 12th to the 19th centuries. It is similar, in fact, to Colonial Williamsburg, the Rockefeller-restored capital of old Virginia.

Suzdal's name figures in the annals for the first time in 1204, but excavations have proved that there was already a settlement here in the tenth century, in the bend of the Kamenka (a tributary of the Nerl). The smiths and bricklayers who lived here bartered with the villagers farming the black soil of the district. The coins found in the pagan burial grounds show that traders from distant lands visited Suzdal regularly. At the end of the 11th century, Suzdal came under the rule of the Grand Prince Vladimir Monomakh and under the influence of Kiev architecture. It was in the 12th century that Monomakh built the first stone church. In the same century, Yury Dolgoruky transferred here the capital of the Rostov-Suzdal principality though his son and heir moved it to Vladimir. Suzdal was almost destroyed by the Tatars; invasions of Poles and Crimean Tatars followed each other; there were fires and plagues—the last one in 1719—but it rose again after each disaster. Today it is more an overgrown medieval village than a town.

The kremlin, perched on the left bank of the Kamenka, represents a strange amalgam of church and lay architecture. It was a princely residence and (in the 16th century) an archiepiscopal seat; but some remnants of Monomakh's church were also uncovered. Within the walls, protected by 15 bastions, the people of Suzdal found temporary safety. Nowadays, the Cathedral of the Nativity of the Mother of God dominates the panorama of the Suzdal kremlin, a monumental building with five domes. It forms a harmonious whole with the belfry (1636) and the snow-white archiepiscopal palace, whose carved window-frames are particularly attractive (16th and 17th centuries).

While in other cities the castle, or kremlin, is usually in the center of the community, here it was built in the southwestern district; the center is occupied by the Torg (Market), the settlement of artisans and traders. In the middle of the Torg, the steeple of the Church of the Resurrection (17th century) rises with exquisite entablatures. The main square is bordered by the Merchants' Row (Torgovy Ryad), with its characteristic double columns. Around the main square are a number of churches, built in the 17th and 18th centuries, simply designed but with elaborate internal decorations: the churches bear names such as Entry into Jerusalem, Nikolskaya, Kare-Konstantinovskaya (the latter has most impressive domes). The Church of Mary Magdalene shares its belfry with the former edifice. The churches stand more or less in pairs, close to each other, with a less-richly decorated building next to a more ambitious one. The richly-decorated ones with several domes were the "summer" churches, opened at Easter, while the "winter" churches, identifiable by their belfries, were for regular services. The domes of the Suzdal churches, generally built on a drum base, have varied forms and decoration. The helmet-shaped belfries are handsome and imaginative.

The Monastery of the Lament of Christ (Spaso-Efimievsky Monastery) has a 180 feet high belfry. It stands on the main street and is in an entirely different style than its neighbors. The Holy Gate is one of the finest treasures of 17th-century Suzdal architecture. The gate barely rises above the enclosing wall, yet it draws the eye with its asymmetric composition underlined by the symmetrical double "helmet" of the steeple. The yellow and green tiles are decorated with botanical motifs; the carvings of the façade and its splendidly human proportions give an impression of airiness and joy.

Walking down along the monastery wall to the river, we find the Monastery of the Intercession of Mary (Pokrovsky Convent) in the northwestern part of the city, on the level bank of the Kamenka. Founded in 1364, it was built practically as a redoubt of the castle; its walls date from the 17th century. It has a three-domed cathedral and two churches: that of the Annunciation (Blagoveschenskaya) and that of the Immaculate Conception (Zachatievskaya); these are still being restored. Vasily III, the father of Ivan the Terrible, exiled his first wife to Suzdal having condemned her for barrenness; the churches were built in her time, the 16th century. Ivan the Terrible followed his father's example: his wife was a prisoner here and so was the first wife of Peter I. In the crypt of Pokrovsky Cathedral we can still see the graves of the exiled Czarinas.

Opposite the monastery, on the hills of the far banks of the Kamenka, stands the Spaso-Efimievsky Monastery, founded in the 14th century and resembling a fortress. Up to the 20th century it was the Russian Bastille, the prison for disgraced courtiers, free-thinkers and political hotheads. Its walls are several miles long and divided by 12 towers, of which only one served as an entrance—and then only once a year, on the day of the Easter Procession. Within the red-and-white walls, the most outstanding building is the Cathedral of Spaso-Preobrazhensky (Transfiguration) with its five domes and fine murals, dating from 1389. Beside it are the gate-church (Nadvratnaya, 17th century) and the square belfry (16th century), which are also remarkable buildings.

Two and a half miles from Suzdal, in the village of Kideksha, we find the Church of Boris-and-Gleb (on the banks of the Nerl, near the mouth of the Kamenka), erected by Prince Yury Dolgoruky in 1152, on the pattern of churches in Kiev.

Ivanovo and Palekh

On the way to Vladimir, some 60 miles from Moscow, we pass the textile center of Orekhovo-Zuyevo. A sister city is Ivanovo, beyond Vladimir, some 80 miles by train, on the banks of the Uvod River. Here, in 1905, the first workers' council *(soviet)* was founded when 80,000 men went on strike. In the 19th century, Ivanovo became known as the "Russian Manchester." Its museum traces its evolution. It has a collection of fabrics illustrating the progress of the textile industry, as well as local folk art, including miniatures of papier-mâché. The folk artists of the nearby village of Palekh (30 miles away) are famous for their fairy-tale paintings on the familiar black lacquered boxes. The murals of the Ivanovo Palace of Pioneers are also their work and the artists of Palekh were responsible for the restoration of the murals of the Moscow Kremlin in 1946.

In 1935 an art school was opened in the village to preserve and nurture its traditions. Today 120 local artists work here, painting lacquer boxes. The museum of Palekh has a large selection of their work but they are also represented in the Russian Museum in Leningrad and in the Tretyakov Gallery in Moscow.

PRACTICAL INFORMATION FOR NORTHEASTERN RUSSIA

WHEN TO GO. The climate of this area is similar to that of Moscow and the territory west of the capital though a little colder in the winter. Summer is the recommended time for a visit unless you are interested in winter sports.

HOW TO GET THERE. Rostov-Veliky and Yaroslavl can be reached from Moscow **by train** from the Yaroslavl Railroad Station. Pereslavl-Zalessky is not on the railroad line and it's best to go **by car**—the nearest railroad station is 12 miles away. All three are on the Moscow-Yaroslavl highway, which passes through Babushkin, Mytishchi, Pushkino, Novaya Derevnya, Bratovshchina, Rakhmanov, Zagorsk, Novoye-Glebovskoye to Pereslavl and then through Slobodka, Petrovsk, Rostov-Veliky and Karabykha to Yaroslavl. The total distance to Yaroslavl is 150 miles. You can also get there **by boat** down the Volga.

Vladimir can be reached from the Kursk Station in Moscow by taking a train in the direction of Gorky and Kirov and traveling some 120 miles east. From Vladimir, Suzdal is only 18 miles by train; the road leads between the hills and meadows.

Ivanovo is 80 miles from Vladimir; Palekh is a further 30 miles away. Both can be reached by train and road.

WHAT TO SEE. Zagorsk: Trinity-St. Sergius Monastery, Uspensky Cathedral, Tomb of Boris Godunov, belfry, paintings by Rublyev, 13 other churches.

Pereslavl-Zalessky: Botik Museum. Goritsky Monastery, the Cathedral of the Savior and the Transfiguration, the Convent of St. Nicholas and the Convent of St. Theodore, The Danilov Monastery, Smolenskaya Church, Novovladimirsky Cathedral, Simeonovskaya Church, Sorokosvyatskaya Church, Pokrovskaya Church, Alexander Nevsky Church, Church of the Metropolitan Peter, The Kremlin, Nikitsky Monastery (on the road to Yaroslavl).

Rostov-Veliky: The Church of the Smolensk Mother of God, The Church of the Redeemer, The Metropolitan's Palace and the Belaya Palata, (White Palace), The Uspensky Cathedral, The churches of St. Gregory, the Savior-in-the-Market-Place and of the Ascension, The Epiphany Cathedral, The Spaso-Yakovlevsky Monastery, the local museum.

Yaroslavl: The Spaso-Preobrazhensky Monastery, The churches of Nikoly Nadina, of the Nativity, of Elijah the Prophet. The group of churches in Korovniki. The Cathedral of the Kazan Monastery. The Historical and Local Museum, the Art Museum, the Planetarium and the Nekrasov Monument. Ferry-boat excursion along the Volga, one hour (costs 20 kopeks).

Vladimir: The Golden Gate, the Uspensky Cathedral, the Cathedral of St. Dmitri, the Cathedral of the Dormition, the Monastery of the Nativity, the Church of the Intercession of the Virgin on the Nerl.

Suzdal: The Kremlin, the Cathedral of the Annunciation, the Spaso-Efimievsky Monastery (north of the town), the Monastery of the Intercession. In the village of Kideksha: Church of Boris and Gleb.

Ivanovo: Museum, Headquarters of the General Staff of the Marxist Organizations (1890–5), The Zubkov House, The Pioneers' Palace.

Palekh: Cooperative of Folk Artists.

HOTELS. Suzdal. *Suzdal Intourist,* modern, first-class. *Motel Suzdal,* Ivanovskaya Zastava.

Vladimir. The *Vladimir Hotel,* Third International Street (Intourist), and *Klyazma Hotel,* Lenin Street.

Yaroslavl. *Volga Hotel,* Kirov Street (with Intourist office); *Tsentralnaya Hotel,* Volkov Square; and *Hotel Yaroslavl,* 40/2 Ushinsky Street, 150 rooms, moderate.

Zagorsk. Proximity to Moscow makes day-trip feasible.

RESTAURANTS. Pereslavl-Zalessky. Hotel of same name.

Pokrov. The *Druzhba Restaurant* on the highway.
Rostov-Veliky. Hotel of same name on Karl Marx Street, or *Beryozka Restaurant,* especially for foreign tourists.

Suzdal. Try the *Suzdal Hotel* on Lenin Street, the *Trapeznaya Restaurant* in the kremlin, *Sokol Restaurant* on Lenin Street, or *Pogrebok Restaurant* on Kremlyovska Street.

Vladimir. Eat in the hotels or at *Dieticheskaya Restaurant* on Frunze Street.

Yaroslavl. The restaurant in the *Volga Hotel,* the *Medved Restaurant* in the Yaroslavl Hotel, or the following restaurants: *Moskva,* 1 Komsomolskaya Street; *Konditerskaya,* Volzhskaya Naberezhnaya; *Yevropa,* Svoboda Street; *Chaika,* Lenin Street; or *Rossiya,* Chkalov Street.

 CULTURAL ACTIVITIES. Yaroslavl: Volkov Drama Theater, Volkov Square—built in 1911, Puppet Theater, 8 Komitetskaya Street; Concert Hall: Komitetskaya Street. **Ivanovo:** three theaters: dramatic, musical comedy and puppet; House of Culture.

 MUSEUMS. Pereslavl-Zalessky: Botik Museum near the village of Veskovo, 2 miles from the town. Open 10–4; closed Tue. Formerly part of the Botik Estate, with a wooden palace, a triumphal arch (1852) and a monument to Peter the Great, designed by Campioni, with some of the great Czar's naval guns and relics of the flotilla.

Local Museum and Picture Gallery, both housed in the Goritsky Monastery, Kardovsky Street, reached before entering the town on the way from Moscow; follow an arrow pointing left. Open 10–4; closed Tue.

Rostov-Veliky: *Local Museum,* in the kremlin. Open 9–5, closed Wed.

Yaroslavl: *Local Museum and Art Museum* housed in the Spaso-Preobrazhensky Monastery, 25 Podbelshov Square.

Museum in the Church of Elijah the Prophet, Sovietskaya Street. If closed, apply to the museum authorities in the Spaso-Preobrazhensky Monastery.

Historical and Local Museum, 19/1 Sovietskaya Square. Open 10–5; closed Sat.

Art Museum, 2 Chelyuskintsev Square. Open 10–5; closed Tue.

Planetarium, 20 Trefolev Street. Open 11–7; closed Tue.

Ivanovo: *Local Museum.*

Palekh: *Museum of Folk Art.*

 SHOPPING. Pereslavl-Zalessky: *Bookshop,* 8 Rostovskaya Street. Yaroslavl: *Bookshop,* 5 Komsomolskaya Street; *Gift shop,* 16 Svoboda Street; *Department Store,* Svoboda Street.

 TOURS. Intourist arranges two-day tours by train from Moscow to Vladimir with one night spent at the Intourist Hotel. On the second day a bus or car excursion is made to Suzdal, 18 miles away.

 USEFUL YAROSLAVL ADDRESSES. *Intourist:* 40/2 Usinsky Street. *Railroad Station:* Privokzalnaya Square. *Bus terminal:* Moskovskoye Road. *Harbor:* Flotsky Spusk.

Setting out from Moscow in a northwesterly direction, we have to cover 300 miles to reach Novgorod, one of the most ancient cities of the Soviet Union. It is possible to do the trip in five hours: first to Klin (60 miles) where the memorial museum to Tchaikovsky is located; then on to Kalinin (called Tver in pre-revolutionary times), 100 miles away, which is an important stop on the Moscow-Leningrad railroad line. After Kalinin the route leads on through Vyshny-Volochek (186 miles from Moscow) along the Valday Ridge to our destination.

Exploring the Northwest

Starting from Moscow towards Klin, we find, some 35 miles away, near the settlement of Solnechnogorsk (Sunny Hills), the large Lake Senezhskoye, a favorite place for Moscow anglers and hikers. It is a reservoir, originally part of a large-scale canalization scheme which Peter the Great had planned. Ten miles farther along, we reach the village of Frolovskoye, where Tchaikovsky composed his *Fifth Symphony* and finished his opera, *The Queen of Spades.* Another few miles and we are in Klin, at the great composer's memorial museum, where on May 7 and November 6 (his birthday and the anniversary of his death), outstanding Soviet pianists give special concerts.

Klin was Tchaikovsky's home in 1892–3, though he had lived in the district from 1885 onwards. Here he composed his *Pathétique Symphony,* his *Third Piano Concerto* and the music for the *Nutcracker* and *Sleeping Beauty* ballets. The two-story building is decorated and furnished as it was in Tchaikovsky's lifetime, and contains his books, paintings, piano and other personal possessions. The Tchaikovsky archives contain 50,-000 items and are an important source for researchers.

Beyond Klin, at the 125-kilometer stone, we reach Bezhorodovo, the huge expanse of the "Moscow Sea," a reservoir which was built at the time of the Moscow-Volga canal's construction (1932–7). This section, at the confluence of the Sosa and the Volga, is another favorite excursion spot for Muscovites.

Kalinin, 100 miles from Moscow, is an important regional seat. It lies on the Upper Volga and is also an ancient trading port. Formerly known as Tver, it was named after Kalinin, the President of the Soviet Union from 1919 to 1946.

The early architectural monuments of Tver-Kalinin were almost all destroyed during the years of feudal strife; the rest were devastated by the great conflagration of 1763. But the White Trinity Church (founded in 1563–4 and built by Tushinsky during the reign of Ivan the Terrible) is still standing. The Transfiguration Cathedral, built at the end of the 17th century and following the pattern of the Uspensky Cathedral in Moscow, has also survived; the belfry, dating from the middle of the 18th century, recalls that of the Troitsa-Sergeiyevsky Monastery.

Following the great fire of 1763, the Moscow architects Nikitin and Kazakov redesigned the town, and the main lines of their plan can still be followed. The heart of the city was the Moscow-Petersburg highway (today called Sovietskaya Street), from which two avenues fanned out left and right. The Sovietskaya crosses three squares: the Pushkinskaya, the Pochtovaya and Lenin Square. The last is octagonal. Among the town's outstanding architectural features are the Putyevoi Dvorets, the seat of the Municipal Council (built 1770–80), the building of the city Party Committee (formerly the Noblemen's Diet, 1766–70) and the Youth Theater (1786, originally a school).

The Putyevoi Dvorets on Sovietskaya Street, was erected as a palace for Catherine II, so that she could break her journeys between Moscow and St. Petersburg. It was built by Kazakov in 1763–75; Rossi redesigned it in 1809. The Church of the Ascension (1813, designed by Lvov) today houses the local museum.

Ostrovsky, the Russian dramatist, lived here in 1856; in 1859, Dostoyevsky spent a few months at No. 1 Pushkin Street, while Saltykov-Shchedrin worked here as deputy governor of Tver in 1860–2, gathering material for several of his satirical works.

On May 1st Quay (Pervomayskaya Naberezhnaya) stands the Nikitin Monument, commemorating the Russian merchant and explorer who traveled to India in the mid-15th century and wrote about his trip. It is close to the spot whence, according to tradition, he set sail. Kalinin's war memorial, at 48 meters, is one of the world's tallest monuments.

From Kalinin, you can make an excursion to Volgino-Verkhovye, near the source of the Volga. (The excursion will be arranged by the Kalinin Intourist Office, located in the Hotel Seliger, named after nearby Lake Seliger.)

Vyshny-Volochek (186 miles from Moscow) is an industrial town and the starting point of the canal system of the Upper Volga. It was here that Peter the Great built the first canal in Russia (1703–9). The first barges passed through in 1790, putting an end to the laborious overland transport of goods; it was in use until the second half of the 18th century. Later, this was the place where those exiled to Siberia gathered to start their long journey.

Novgorod

Situated four miles from Lake Ilmen, on both banks of the Volkhov River, this city is a regional center and, with a history of 11 centuries, is perhaps the Russian city richest in art treasures and monuments. Its story, in some ways, has mirrored the history of Russia.

We start our exploration at the castle (kremlin) and then continue along the western or left bank, Sofiskaya Storona (Sophia side), following with the right bank, Torgovaya Storona (Market Side), and ending with the monuments in the areas surrounding Novgorod.

The kremlin is certainly the most striking landmark in Novgorod. Its historic character has been carefully preserved, even though its buildings have been adapted to house the city's most important cultural institutions: the museum, theater, library and lecture hall. There is now even a restaurant in this evocative building.

If we enter the castle's grounds through the entrance on the Volkhov River side, under the 19th century arcades (formerly the site of the Prechistenskaya Bastion), we find to the right the most important monument in the city, the Saint Sophia Cathedral, built with six domes by Greek architects between 1045 and 1052. Opposite is the central square of the kremlin with the Millenary Monument, which can serve as a central signpost for our walk. It is shaped like a bell and was erected in 1862 to commemorate 1,000 years of Russian history.

Crossing the square in front of the monument we stand in front of the oldest stone building in Northern Russia, the Cathedral of Saint Sophia. It has three apses—the apse became the most important external feature in all subsequent typical Russian architecture. The central dome is a huge copy of the helmet of a warrior, capped by a bronze dove and a cross. (Legend says that Novgorod will remain in existence until the dove flies away.) At the west entrance is the Korsun bronze door, supposedly brought from Magdeburg as booty in the 12th century. It depicts scenes from the Old and New Testaments, with Latin and Slavonic inscriptions. The murals are much later, having been painted over earlier ones in the 1830's. The best frescos are in the southern part of the cathedral.

The Vladichny Dvor (Archbishop's Palace, 1436) is northwest from St. Sophia. This was the "fortress within the fortress" of the Archbishop of Novgorod; its entrance was at the passage where today there are some stone cannon balls. But first, adjoining the cathedral, is the 15th century porch where the miraculous icon and the sacrificial bread were kept. Leaving the passage we find a large, one-storied building, the Nikitny Corpus, today a department of the Museum of History and an art gallery showing 18th to 19th century Russian art.

The Historical Museum has 11th-century mosaics and many other items of interest; over 80,000 exhibits in 35 halls, including letters dating from the 11th to 15th centuries written on birchbark. The Nikitny Corpus dates from the 12th century; until the middle of the 14th, this was the archiepiscopal residence. It was remodeled in the 17th century. In the palace itself is the Granovitaya Palata (Faceted Palace), actually a massive Gothic hall on the second floor. The beautiful interior decoration of the hall is particularly fine. It was in this palace that Ivan the Terrible gave the banquet in 1570 at which the stubborn Novgorod prelates and magnates were killed at the Czar's prearranged signal. Today it houses a collection of icons and other church treasures from local monasteries and churches.

The former apartments of the archbishop now house the Regional Library, with 250,000 volumes: next to it, further west, we find the Sergei Church (1463). Linked to it is the Giant Bell of Yevfimy inspired by the Archbishop Yevfimy, the militant apostle of Novgorod's independence (1443). The 155 ft. high tower was originally a watch-tower.

The next building on the kremlin-wall side is the 17th century Prikaz (Law Court); between the Prikaz and the section of the castle wall lying to the north was the archiepiscopal farmyard. (Today it houses the central architectural offices of the region.) South of the Prikaz, sharing its entrance, is the Likhudovsky Corpus (a former school-building of the 15th century, rebuilt in the 17th and 18th centuries) which is the center of the restoration work of Novgorod.

Passing through the archway in front of St. Sophia to the "main street" of the castle (actually a square), where the Millenary Monument stands, we find on the right a one-storied building (1670) which served in the 17th-19th centuries as the residence of the Metropolitans. Today it is the administrative headquarters of the Novgorod region. It occupies the site of the Church of St. John Chrysostom, built by Archbishop Yevfimy. Excavations in its courtyard carried out in 1923 uncovered some church plate and vessels buried in the 15th century. To the right, the next building is the Regional Theater.

Setting out in the opposite direction from St. Sophia, we pass the Lecture Hall; opposite, at the castle wall, we find the Sofiskaya Zvonnitsa (15th–17th centuries), the belfry of St. Sophia's Cathedral. The additions to the tower (among them the porch) belong to the 17th century. The three bells, exhibited outside, used to hang in the belfry. (The heaviest weighs 26.5 tons; it was placed in the tower in 1650 but fell and shattered nine years later, after which it was recast.) The bell on the right was the gift of Boris Godunov to the Dukhov Monastery in 1589.

Returning to the block of the Prisutstvennoye Mesto (1783–1822), which stretches the width of the castle and was originally the Treasury, we find the City Library and the Historical Museum of the Revolution. Turning left here, we can walk to the Andrei Stratilates Church, where excavations are still in process. It has been established that, from the 15th century, this was the artisan quarter of the castle.

Between the excavations and the Prisutstvennoye Mesto there are three single-storied houses. They were built in 1781, paid for by Catherine II, to house the local clergy. Past them, near the castle-wall we find the 14th-century Pokrov (Intercession) Church. It was remodeled in the 17th century. The next tower is named after St. John Chrysostom; nearby the dead of the 1917 Revolution were buried, and in front of the arcade opposite are the graves of the Soviet soldiers who died liberating Novgorod in the last war.

Outside the Kremlin

Passing through the western gate of the kremlin (away from the river) we enter Victory (Pobeda) Square and the Sofiskaya Storona (Sophia Quarter), the heart of Novgorod. Opposite we see the House of the Soviets, on the right Merkurov's Lenin Statue.

Turning left in Pobeda Square, we find in the next square, at the meeting of three streets, a typical monument of 15th century Novgorod architecture: the Vlasiya (St. Blasius) Church, built in 1407 on the site of a much earlier wooden church and recently restored. Its square groundplan and its single dome are repeated in several other churches. Walking upstream (south) and leaving the kremlin behind, we reach the Uvereniye Fomi (St. Thomas) Church, built in 1463 on the shore of Lake Myachino. It is a masterly imitation of 12th century style—so much so that experts until recently believed it to be the 1195 church which once stood on this site. The adjoining Ioanna Milostivovana-Myachinye (St. John) Church has preserved few of its original 15th century features.

West of Lake Myachino, in the middle of the Sinichya Gora cemetery, the Church of Petra-i-Pavla-na-Sinichei-Gorye (Peter-and-Paul on Blue-tit Hill) has remained (with the exception of its flat roof) exactly as the inhabitants of nearby Lukina Street built it in 1185–92. Half a mile away, further west, stands the Blagoveshcheniya-u-Arkazhi (Annunciation) Church. This was built in 1179 and its lower parts are still in the original form while its vaulted roof and dome were rebuilt in the 16th century. Some fragments of murals in the sanctuary are interesting examples of the late 12th century Novgorod school.

Returning to the city and following the line of the original ramparts (Great Earthwork Fortifications), we find several important monuments. The first, directly west of the kremlin, is the Church of Twelve Apostles, in Leo Tolstoy Street, dating from 1454. The next, the Feodor Stratilates

Church on Komsomolskaya Street northeast of the kremlin, belongs to the 13th–17th centuries and has good murals. The Petra-i-Pavla-v-Kozhevnikakh Church in Zverinskaya Street north of the kremlin and nearer the river dates from 1406 and is outside the fortifications; it is one of the most characteristic Novgorod churches of this period. Its fabric is halfbrick, half-limestone; the decorations of the front, the vaults, the supporting pillars and the dome itself are all of brick. Continuing north, near the little Gzena River are the three churches of the Zverin Monastery: the Pokrov (Intercession), the Nikolai Byelov (St. Nicholas the White) and the St. Simeon. The latter was built in 1467 and apart from its disproportionately large dome, invokes the shape of the Twelve Apostles Church. The original murals have been preserved but they have been only partially uncovered.

The Trinity Church in the Dukhov (Holy Spirit) Monastery, built in 1557, is in Molotovskaya Street, along the highway to Leningrad. It reflects the influence of Muscovite architecture.

The Market Side of Novgorod

On the right (eastern) bank of the Volkhov, the Torgovaya Storona (Merchant Quarter) with its gridiron streets is a reminder of Catherine the Great's city planning endeavors. The original center of the quarter was the Yaroslav Court, opposite the kremlin on the left bank. It is first described as a "court" in the chronicles of the 13th century and we know that public meetings were held here. The partly-enclosed complex is dominated by the St. Nicholas Cathedral (Nikolo-Dvorishchensky), built in 1113 in Kiev style, with three naves; under its roof the remnants of the original four domes still exist. The graphic quality of its partially surviving murals is quite remarkable.

South and southwest of St. Nicholas are the churches of Zheni-Mironositsi (Myrrh-Bearing Women) and Prokopy, both dating from the 16th century and built entirely of brick, though the roof of the former is wood. Northwest from St. Nicholas Cathedral we see the two-level gate-house of the Gostiny Dvor (Market Hall), with its double archways; its octagonal helmet-crowned tower dates from the 1690's. One of the other churches of the Torg, the Paraskeva-Pyatnitsa (1207), is one of Novgorod's most original monuments though it was somewhat modified in the 16th century. The other church, the Uspensky (Assumption), has retained only the groundplan of the 12th century original. North of it in Pervomayskaya Street the Church of St. George belongs to the 17th century with the exception of its lower walls. West from here the Ioannna-Opokakh (St. John) Church (1127–30) was the headquarters of the Ivanovskoye Sto merchant guild, housing its civil courts, and the depository of the weights-and-measures officials. The church was demolished in 1453 but its successor was an almost exact imitation of the original.

Southeast from the Yaroslav Court, across the street, a brick passage connects the churches of St. Michael (Mikhail-na-Mikhailovye) and of the Annunciation (Blagoveshchenie). The former was extensively rebuilt in the 19th century; the latter (though built in the 15th century) survives in its rebuilt form dating from the 16th century, when the octagonal belfry was added.

If we walk eastward from the Church of the Annunciation to Ilyinskaya Street, the Filippa (St. Philip) Church is the next point of interest.

Built in 1383–4, it was rebuilt in the 16th century but its square ground-plan with single apse has been preserved and so has much of its original wall. Interestingly, the upper façade (16th-century) follows a 12th-century style.

North of St. Philip's on Ilyinskaya Street is the Znamensky (Apparition of the Cross) Cathedral (17th century), a classic example of Moscow architecture with its five onion domes, the brick balustrade of the façade and the murals of its tympana.

The Spas-na-Ilyine (Redeemer) Church stands to the north, at the corner of Ilyinskaya and Pervomayskaya streets. Built in 1378, it is one of the masterpieces of Novgorod architecture; compared to its simple groundplan, its wall-decorations, apse and tympanum appear a little over-rich. But its murals, which have been restored in our century, are quite extraordinary. Their creator was the Byzantine master Theophanes (1378). Using only brown, red and white, the artist has worked with superb virtuosity.

The Dmitriya Solunskogo (Dmitri of Salonika) Church (1383) on Moskovskaya Street, the town's main road, was recently restored. The nearby Klimenta (St. Clement) Church, though built by a Moscow master in 1386, reflects the local Novgorod style.

Novgorod's second Feodor Stratilates Church stands on Moskovskaya Street, the Moscow-Leningrad highway on the market side of Feodorovsky Ruchei Street. (The first is on the other side of the river.) Built in 1360–1, it created a new school of Novgorod architecture. Its murals —uncovered in 1910—show considerable Byzantine influence and may also be by Theophanes. On Molotovskaya Street, near Feodorovsky, the Rozhdestva-Bogoroditsy (Nativity of the Virgin) Church (1379) has also recently been restored. It is the Feodor Stratilates's contemporary but has a simpler groundplan and is less ornate. However, its murals (some of which date back to 1125) are of great splendor. Some parts of the building date back to the 12th-century Antonius Monastery, founded by a Roman.

Returning along Krasnaya Street to the city center, let us turn right into the Moskovskaya, off which to the right is the Nikita Church built in 1557, most probably by Ivan the Terrible. Turning westward on Moskovskaya to the bridge, then turning right, we can walk downstream (north) to the point where the fortifications and the river meet. Here the Borisa-i-Gleba (St. Boris and Gleb) Church is an example of the 16th-century style, based on ancient traditions. Beyond the earth wall the Church of St. John the Divine (Ioanna Bogoslova) is one of the best-preserved examples of 14th-century Novgorod architecture.

Excursions around Novgorod

The important sights of Novgorod's environs are mostly on the Volkhov River and on Lake Ilmen. The best way to approach them is by water. The first stop, on the right (east) bank of the river, is the village of Gorodishche, which may have been Novgorod's ancient Old Town. When the feudal republic was declared in the 12th century, this became the ducal residence; Mstislav, son of Prince Vladimir Monomakh of Kiev, had the Church of the Annunciation built about the same time. It was rebuilt in the 14th century but destroyed in 1941. Opposite, on the left bank, the monastery and church of St. George (1119) resembles in its proportions and size the St. Sophia Cathedral. Its murals were largely ruined during the 19th-century restoration, the remainder were salvaged in 1935; the fragments show a Byzantine-Kiev influence.

East of Gorodishche, beyond the small Spasovka River, stands the Church of the Redeemer on Mount Nereditsa, built in 1198 by Prince Yaroslav Vladimirovich and restored after the 1941–5 War. Though it was a prince's church, it had a single dome and resembled the small churches erected by merchants. The priceless murals were totally destroyed during the war and only remain in reproductions.

The other great architectural monuments, churches and chapels on the right bank of the Volkhov were also heavily damaged but have now been mostly restored.

West of Gorodishche, near the St. George Monastery, postwar excavations on Perun Hill have uncovered the ruins of the temple of the pre-Christian god, Perun. His idol was destroyed with the triumph of Christianity and a monastery was built on the spot—the Our Lady of Perun Monastery, whose 13th century church has been restored. South of here, on the northeastern shore of Lake Ilmen, the Church of St. Nicholas the Miracle-Worker has also been restored in Lipna. North of Novgorod, along the Volkhov we can visit two partly-ruined churches at the Derevyanitsky Monastery some two and a half miles from the city: the Cathedral of the Resurrection (1700) and the Uspensky (Assumption) Church, dating from 1725.

Pskov

Leaving Novgorod, traveling along the highway towards Riga, we reach Pskov (130 miles by road, 150 miles by train), another ancient Russian city. During the ten centuries of its existence, this regional capital has been the scene of many important historical events.

It was at the Pskov railway station that Nicholas II abdicated in March 1917; and in and around the city several decisive battles of the ensuing civil war were fought. Lenin lived here from March to May of 1900, preparing his underground newspaper, *Iskra* (Spark).

But many centuries before these events, Pskov was the advance post of the Eastern Slav drive towards Estonia and Livonia and the base of the Teutonic Knights. It was first mentioned in tenth century chronicles, having been in all probability founded in the reign of Ryurik. For many years it was ruled by the Novgorod Republic, but it also intermittently had its own princes. In 1348 an independent republic which survived for a long time was established, though it was constantly at war with the Teutonic Knights and the Grand Prince of Lithuania and withstood no less than 26 sieges. But in the 15th century it yielded to the might of Moscow. Later, Pskov was an important commercial center, still repulsing attacks from Livonia and Sweden. Only at the end of the 18th century, when Byelorussia became a dependency of Russia, did Pskov lose its strategic importance. It was badly damaged during the Second World War but has been almost completely rebuilt in the last decades. It now has considerable heavy industry as well as its traditional plants for processing flax.

Though its urban structure was partly rearranged in the 18th and 19th centuries, Pskov still has many monuments dating from the 12th to 17th centuries: two castles, the remnants of its 14th- and 15th-century Old

Town, and the newer quarter developed on the left bank of the Velikaya and the right bank of the Pskov rivers.

The kremlin deserves to be seen first; here, on the romantic limestone cliffs at the confluence of the two rivers, was the cradle of today's city. The kremlin was an important fortress by the 11th century though its stone walls were only raised in the 13th. Its most important monument is the Trinity Cathedral, built in 1699 on the site of the 13th century church. Here was the center of the feudal republic of Pskov: the princes set out to do battle from the cathedral; here the treasures were kept, foreign ambassadors received, dignitaries buried. Through the arcade that stretches under the cathedral we reach the assembly square which extends to the southern castle walls. (Here Alexander Nevsky was acclaimed in 1242.) The restoration work on the bastions and walls has been in progress for some years. The Greblya moat under the castle originally linked the Velikaya and Pskov rivers but has now been filled in.

From the south the Dovmontov Gorod wall, named after Prince Dovmont, was linked to the kremlin in the last third of the 13th century. In the 12th to 14th centuries there were no fewer than 19 churches in this area; the foundations of some of them have been uncovered during recent excavations. Part of the kremlin's southern wall can be seen at the Prikaznaya Palace; this was the administrative center of 17th-century Pskov, an interesting example of civil architecture. The western wall of the Dovmontov Gorod has been restored and a replica of its original Vasilyevskaya Tower erected.

The fortifications of Pskov were built in the 13th and 14th centuries from local limestone and extend about six miles. They defended the two castles and the Central (Sredny) and Suburban (Okolny) quarters, south of the Dovmontov Gorod and the Zapskovye district (the quarter on the right bank of the river) to the north.

From the Dovmontov Gorod there is a fine view of the medieval center of Sredny Gorod, the Torg (Market Place), today called Lenin Square. Setting out along Sovietskaya Street towards October Square, we see, next to the Central Post Office, the first stone church of Pskov's Old City, the Church of the Archangel Michael, built in 1339 and later remodeled. Its courtyard is bordered by a belfry (17th century) on the street side. Along the Sovietskaya, it is worth climbing the hill to the Vasily-na-Gorke Church (1413), whose tympanum and apse retain their original decorative carvings. Some of the special features of the Pskov architectural school can be seen here: in the tympanum, the belfry above the gate, the loophole-like windows, the inner vaults and the semi-circular arches upon which the roof-structure rests. Across the street the Nikola-na-Usokhe Church (1371) was rebuilt in 1573 and partially restored after the last war. West of it, the ruins of the Odigitria Church (1537–1685) indicate a Moscow influence.

In the Stary Torg (Old Market), the house at 10 Marx Street, with its vaulted ceremonial halls and its attic store-rooms (it had no cellar) recalls the merchant houses of the Baltic (17th century). Also in Marx Street we find the Peter-and-Paul Church, built on the site of a 1299 wooden church in the 15th century and rebuilt in 1540. Its restoration in 1962 emphasised its original style.

Walking along the banks of the Pskov in the direction of Krasny Partizan Street, we can drop into No. 6 Yedinstvo Street, the 17th century home of the merchant Yamsky, an interesting survival of the old, picturesque Pskov quarter of Okolny. (In 1710 Peter the Great stayed here.) No. 10 Krasny Partizan Street, the Guryev Mansion, was built somewhat earlier. We can now continue along Ostrovok Quay to No. 42 Gogolevskaya Street, the so-called Malt House (Solodezhnya). Perhaps this is the most typical of the 17th century Pskov houses. Its verandah has cross-vaulting, with a rare stone icon-stand and lampholder. It has two large vaulted rooms, a smaller one, an attic and a courtyard. Of the gates, only the iron one is original. Opposite, the Pechenko House (17th century) has been restored. As we continue southwest towards the Polonishche Quarter, along Mikhailovskaya and Nekrasovskaya streets, we reach the St. Nicholas (Nikolai-ot-Torga) Church (1676) and the Pokrov-ot-Torga (The Intercession of the Virgin) Church (17th century). The proportions of the Anastasia Church at October Avenue show that in the 16th century it was one of the finest ecclesiastical buildings of Pskov. Continuing along Nekrasov Street, we see the Church of the Ascension (1467), which has been rebuilt several times; only the belfry has preserved its original charm.

Between Nekrasov, Gogol, Museum and Komsomol streets, the 17th century Pogankin House today contains the historical section of the Art and Historical Museum of Pskov. Pogankin House, consisting of three buildings, was once a fortress. The staircases between the warehouses, the shop and the apartments are lined with six-foot-thick walls; there are double iron gates and the 105 loophole-shaped windows are of the barred-and-shuttered variety. The Menshikov mansion, home of another merchant family (50 Sovietskaya Street), differs somewhat from the traditional 17th-century Pskov style; the barrack-like exterior is relieved by the carved limestone decorations of the windows.

From Sovietskaya Street we can approach the Joachim-and-Anna Church through Sverdlov Street. This has been restored to its original 16th century condition. On the riverbank, in the 15th-century St. George Church on the corner of Uritsky and Liebknecht streets, only the mosaic decoration of the tympanum under the dome is preserved, though the loophole-windows of the apse also date from that century. Finally, after visiting the 16th-century Double Church of the Nativity and the Intercession of the Virgin (also restored), we can stop at the Pokrovskaya bastion and gate, on the riverbank. Here the restoration work of recent years shows us how the city walls must have looked centuries ago. (In 1701 Peter the Great ordered the removal of the tower's wooden parts and had the bastion itself stuffed with earth so that it could bear the weight of heavy cannon.)

The bridge at Sovietskaya Square leads into the Zapskovye quarter. The Kozma-and-Damian Church stands close to the bridge. Built in the 15th century, it was badly damaged in 1507 by an explosion of gunpowder stored inside. But its enclosing wall is of rare interest, especially its gate, which resembles a triumphal arch. On Herzen Street we find one of the largest churches of 15th-century Pskov, the partly-restored Bogoyavleniye (Apparition of the Lord). On Leon Pozemsky Street, the main thoroughfare of the quarter, the Trubinsky House is one of the masterpieces of lay architecture of the 17th century. The men's and women's apartments had separate dining halls; the former had an adjoining guest room and access to the wine cellar. But the staircase to the garden led from the men's apartments through the women's, so the isolation was not complete.

Opposite the Trubinsky House, the Elijah Church (1677) has an open verandah and a gallery built on high columns. The Postnikov House, on the corner of Leon Pozemsky Street and Moskovskaya, dates from the turn of the 17th and 18th centuries. The Church of the Resurrection also stands on Leon Pozemsky Street (1522). On nearby Varlaamovsky Proyezd, we find the Varlaam Church (1495); during the 1615 siege this was transformed into a supporting bastion of the nearby Varlaamovskiye Gates. Finally, visit the Obrazskaya Church (1487), on the Ilyinsky Proyezd.

In the Zavelichye quarter, on the left bank of the Velikaya, the Cathedral of the Savior, within the Mirozhsky Monastery, stands about a mile from the kremlin. The monastery was founded in the 11th century; the cathedral is one of the oldest monuments in Pskov (12th century) and has remained fundamentally unchanged. It is built of limestone and brick; its Byzantine elements are probably due to the taste of Nifont, Archbishop of Novgorod, who initiated the building. Its interesting murals also show a Byzantine influence. The 19th-century restoration did much harm to the murals but more recently some of the original beauty has been regained by skilful work.

The Clement Church, down on the riverbank at the ferry, has more or less preserved its 16th-century form. Close to the bridge we find the Church of the Blessed Virgin (1444–1521), and opposite the castle, the Cathedral of St. John the Baptist (or the Cathedral of the Ivanovsky Monastery). The latter, according to tradition, was founded by the wife of Yaroslav, Prince of Pskov. Murdered by her stepson, she was buried in the cathedral.

PRACTICAL INFORMATION FOR NORTHWESTERN RUSSIA

WHEN TO GO. This district has the same climate as the region northeast of Moscow and therefore the summer is likely to be the best season—especially as there are good facilities for swimming and boating.

HOW TO GET THERE. By train. Trains from Moscow and Leningrad to Novgorod. From Moscow, change at Chudovo. From Novgorod by train to Pskov (150 miles). **By boat.** To Kalinin by boat on the Volga. **By car and bus.** Klin, Kalinin, Vyshny-Volochek, Novgorod are on the Number 1 tourist highway. There is no highway open to tourists from Novgorod to Pskov—but Intourist runs buses on the Novgorod-Riga road (130 miles).

WHAT TO SEE. Klin: Tchaikovsky Museum. 16th-century church in the compound of the Uspensky Monastery. **Kalinin:** White Trinity Church, Engels Street; Transfiguration Cathedral; Convent of the Nativity; Church of Elijah the Prophet; the Palace of Catherine the Great.

Vyshny-Volochek. 18th-century church.

Novgorod: The Kremlin; Church of Ioann-na-Opokakh, Herzen Street; Uspenie-na-Torgu Church, Moskovskaya Street; Georgiy-na-Torgu Church, Pervomayskaya Street. In addition there are six 12th-century churches, 19 churches built in the 13th–15th centuries and eight in the 16th and 17th centuries.

Pskov: Cathedral of the Ivanovsky Monastery, Trinity Cathedral, merchants' homes.

HOTELS. Ivanovo. The only hotels are *Tsentralnaya* on Engel Street (450 rooms, moderate) and the *Sovietskaya*, 64 Lenin Prospekt.

Kalinin. *Motel Tver,* best, recent and comfortable; then *Seligger Hotel,* Sovietskaya Street; the *Volga Hotel,* Uritsky Street; or the *Tsentralnaya,* Pravda Street, the last a modest-sized but 5-story hotel.

Murmansk. Two equal-ranking hotels, the *Artika* and the *Severnaya,* can be recommended.

Novgorod. A choice of four: *Intourist,* 16, Dmitrievskaya Street, 238 rooms; *Sadko,* Yuri Gagarin Street; *Volkhov,* Nekrasov Street; or *Ilmen,* Gorky Street. Camping: *Savino,* Novgorod–6.

Pskov. Either *Oktyabrskaya,* October Prospekt; or *Tourist,* on Krasnoznamenskaya.

Vyshny Volochek. The *Vyshny Volochek Hotel* on Pervomayskaya Street. (Note: can be used in transit only.) Restaurant too.

RESTAURANTS. In addition to the hotels above, all of which have restaurants, you can try the following:

Kalinin. The *Orel Restaurant,* Naberezhnaya Stepana Razina, or the restaurant at the *boat landing.*

Murmansk. We suggest eating at your hotel, but if you're not satisfied, you can always try the *Sport Restaurant* on Karl Marx Street.

Novgorod. *Detinets Restaurant.* Set in the medieval Kremlin. New but old! Beautiful atmosphere.

Pskov. Outside the city at the *Pechora Monastery,* there are adequate little restaurants on both Svoboda and Oktyabrskaya streets.

CULTURAL ACTIVITIES. Kalinin: Drama Theater, 43/18 Svobodny Pereulok (Puppet Theater in the same building); Youth Theater: 44 Sovietskaya Street. **Vyshny Volochek:** Drama Theater in Pervomayskaya Street. **Novgorod:** Drama Theater and Concert Hall, inside the kremlin.

MUSEUMS. Klin: *Tchaikovsky Museum,* 48 Tchaikovsky Street, open 11–5; closed Wed. **Kalinin:** *Local Museum,* 3 Sovietskaya Street, in the left wing of the Palace. Founded in 1866; closed Tues. *Picture Gallery* in the Church of the Ascension.

Novgorod: *Historical Museum,* inside the kremlin. *Art Museum,* also in the kremlin (Granovitaya Palata) with a collection of icons and other church treasures gathered from the monasteries and churches. *History Museum of the Revolution,* in the former treasury, Prisutstvannoye Mesto, which shares the building with the City Library.

Pskov: *Historical Museum,* in the former Pogankin Court.

SHOPPING. Kalinin: *Central Market,* **Ploshchad Kommuny;** *Department Stores:* 84 Sovietskaya Street and 35 Uritsky Street.

TOURS. Intourist arranges a nine-hour bus tour to Klin from Moscow. There are two- and three-day tours to Novgorod and its neighborhood and similar tours to Pskov.

USEFUL PSKOV ADDRESSES. *Tourist Bureau:* 4 Krasnoznamenskaya Street; *Railway and bus station:* Privokzalnaya Square, at the end of October Boulevard.

SOUTH OF MOSCOW

Starting from Moscow to the south—either along the Moscow-Yalta highway or from the Kursk railway station in the Soviet capital—the most important stops are Podolsk, Tula, and Kursk. Lesser places deserving exploration include Chekhov, Serpukhov, Yasnaya Polyana, Plavsk, Mtsensk, Verkhnii Lyubazh. Oboyan and Belgorod, south of which the Ukrainian Soviet Republic, the subject of a separate chapter, begins.

Exploring South of Moscow

Driving along the Moscow-Yalta highway you will come across the Butovo camping site some 16 miles from Moscow and about 500 yards on the right. It is situated on hilly ground among pine trees which keep it pleasantly cool. There is a self-service kitchen, a buffet and shops. The railway station is only 400 yards away, making it possible to visit the capital without having to drive there.

Podolsk, less than 25 miles from Moscow, stands on the Pakhra River and has large marble and limestone quarries which have been worked since the 18th century; its coat-of-arms, granted in 1781, carries two crossed pick-axes. It has several gardens and parks and many historical and literary associations. Around the turn of the century, Lenin lived here (on Moskovskaya Street) after returning from his exile. The house where he lived is now a museum. The little estate of Melikhovo, 8 miles from Chekhov (near Podolsk), was the home of Anton Chekhov, the great playwright, who lived here between 1892 and 1898. He was responsible for building the local school and worked as a doctor during a cholera epidemic. The museum contains his personal belongings and manuscripts; there is a monument on the estate. The nearby town was formerly known as Lopasnaya, but it has been renamed Chekhov in the writer's honor.

Sixty miles from Moscow we reach Serpukhov, with important textile, paint and machine factories. Eight miles to the east, on the banks of the

Oka River there is a Nature Reserve, spreading over 5,000 hectares between the villages of Dubki and Luzhki. It has a special preserve for bison, spread over 60 hectares where these rare animals are carefully guarded and registered. Another interesting feature of Serpukhov is the riverside house of the Russian painter Polenov, with a fine collection of paintings by Repin and Levitan. The museum assistants practice the art of flower arrangement and display samples of their art in which they use more than 500 flowers and herbs. The History and Art Museum on Chekhov Street, located in a century-old building, houses a collection of icons and Western European works of art, once the property of the local nobility.

Some 112 miles from Moscow is Tula, a city lying on either side of the Upa River, a tributary of the Oka. It is one of the oldest industrial settlements of Russia because of the early discovery of its rich iron ore deposits. The arms forged here were famous as early as the 16th century; the first small arms factory was founded by Peter the Great in 1712. It employed 1,160 workers and produced 16,000 muskets and 4,000 pistols annually. By the end of the 19th century, there were 177 workshops and factories in Tula, turning out both weapons and samovars. Among its museums is the Museum of the History of Arms, opposite the kremlin on Lenin Prospekt. Established in 1724, it has a fine collection of Russian arms of all ages as well as many miniatures—well worth a visit.

Less than 10 miles from Tula is Yasnaya Polyana, the home of Leo Tolstoy. Tolstoy's grave, surrounded by oak trees, is in the estate park, on Stary Zakaz Hill. The house contains his portraits by Repin and Kramskoy, a library of 22,000 books in 20 languages, a phonograph presented by Edison, and many other souvenirs. The literary museum is in the building where Tolstoy ran a school for the peasants. Allow plenty of time for this beautiful place—you'll want to linger there and soak up the atmosphere, which really is something special.

As we return from the Tolstoy estate to the highway, we find Shchekino, a mining town, next on the road, then Plovsk and—within the Orel region—Mtsensk. Six miles before reaching the town, there is a signpost indicating the road to Spasskoye-Lutovinovo, the Turgenev estate. The turning is marked by a bust of the writer and the estate is 3½ miles from the main road. The estate is now a branch of the Orel Museum with 8 halls of exhibits in the Exile's House (to which Turgenev was exiled in 1852–3 by Czar Nicholas I). The main part of the house was burned down in 1906 but the remaining wings have been restored as they were in 1881 when Turgenev last visited the place. Some of his works were written or completed here, among them *Fathers and Sons*. The park was laid out in 1808; it contains a church and mausoleum.

Mtsensk itself is a swiftly developing industrial city. It is also the scene of Leskov's famous novella, *Lady Macbeth of Mtsensk,* upon which Shostakovich based his opera.

Orel

The next stop is Orel (pronounced *Ahr-yol*), a district capital standing on the upper Orel River, 220 miles from Moscow. Founded in the reign of Ivan the Terrible, it became an important settlement in the 18th century when the grain destined for Moscow was shipped from here. The first steam engine in Russia was set up in Orel. Today it is an important railway junction and industrial center. During World War II, it was occupied from 1941 to 1943 and liberated after the battle of Kursk.

The Turgenev Museum, of which the estate of Spasskoye-Lutovinovo is a branch, is at 11 Turgenev Street in the Trubitsyn House; it contains not only the great novelist's possessions, but also manuscripts and books left by his friend Belinsky, the critic and reformer. The Granovsky (Local Writers) Museum nearby is also worth a visit. In a hilly part of the town, it is housed in the former home of the historian and writer Timofei Granovsky. It is devoted to the work and life of Turgenev, Leonid Andreyev, the Nobel Prize winner Ivan Bunin and many other outstanding men of letters who were born or lived in the district.

Close to the city park you can visit the Tolstoy House, where the author, working on his novel *Resurrection,* collected material on prison conditions.

Orel has one of the Soviet Union's oldest permanent theaters, the Turgenev Drama Theater in Theater Square. It was established in 1815 as a theater of serf-actors by Count Kamensky on his estate 7½ miles from Orel; the count, a real tyrant, kept careful records of any mistakes his actors made and punished them severely after each performance. Yet the company thrived and in a single period of six months produced 18 operas, 15 dramas, 41 comedies, 6 ballets and 2 tragedies; the plays included not only those of Shakespeare and Schiller and the Russian classics, but also works by serf-playwrights. The present building dates from 1779 and originally housed the Town Council.

Continuing towards Kursk we first pass Kromy, where the third act of Mussorgsky's *Boris Godunov* takes place; then come some villages with unusual names: Kuri (Hens), Butilka (Bottle), Sayka (Breadroll). The district seat Ponyri is famous for its apples, known as *antonovskiye yabloki.*

Kursk and Belgorod

Kursk, 325 miles from Moscow and one of the junctions of the Moscow-Yalta highway and railway line, stands in the Dnieper basin, at the confluence of the Tuskor and Seym rivers. Lying around the city is one of the largest iron ore fields in the world. It was here that one of the greatest battles of World War II on Soviet soil took place.

The chronicles mention Kursk as early as the 11th century. But the Tatar invasion of 1240 destroyed it completely. It was rebuilt in the 16th century as a frontier fortress against the Crimean Tatars. From the end of the 18th century it was a district capital but until 1917 it remained mostly a market town. Today it is an industrial center with machine, chemical and agricultural machinery plants.

Kursk has a simple groundplan. From north to south its main streets are Marx and Lenin avenues, leading to Red Square; from the Square, Engels and Dzerzhinsky streets lead in a southwesterly direction from the town. The building of Red Square began in the 18th century. Postwar reconstruction has preserved the old gridiron system so it's easy to find your way about.

The center of the city is Krasnaya Ploshchad (Red Square), with the Lenin Monument and the more important public buildings. The main streets all converge here, and along them we find the outstanding sights. Among them, the St. Serge Cathedral in Gorky Street (which runs parallel with Lenin Street) is the most interesting. It was built in the years 1752–78 according to a design by Rastrelli. Inside you will find a fine carved iconostasis, about 55 feet high.

The local picture gallery at 3 Sovietskaya Street (a side street of Dzerzhinsky Street) is worth visiting; it has several canvases by Repin, Shishkin, Levitan and Vereshchagin. In the Local Museum (6 Lunacharsky Street running parallel with Dzerzhinsky Street from Red Square), there are some 50,000 items reaching back to the Stone Age.

The Ufimtsev Museum on Semenovskaya Street is devoted to the inventor and aero-engine constructor who was born in Kursk. He built the windmill standing beside his house, which is now a club for young engineers.

Traveling from Kursk towards Belgorod, at the 624 km. stone, you can visit the Park of the Battle of Kursk, where relics of the long and bitter conflict are preserved. Some deadly souvenirs still lurk underground: in 1957 an immense arsenal was discovered during excavations near the railway station. The shells and bombs have, of course, been rendered harmless.

At the 662 km. stone of the Moscow-Yalta road, lies Belgorod at the foot of the chalk and limestone hills of the Northern Donets. Its public buildings and apartment houses are all painted in light colors to suit its name—"White City". Old Belgorod, which was already known in the 13th century, was almost completely destroyed in World War II, but has now been reconstructed and is a district center.

PRACTICAL INFORMATION FOR SOUTH OF MOSCOW

WHEN TO GO. Late spring and the summer are the best times; the fall is also fairly mild.

HOW TO GET THERE. By train: from Moscow from the Kursk Station. From the south via Kharkov. **By road:** from Moscow by the Yalta (Number 8) tourist road. Yasnaya Polyana and several other smaller places are off the railroad and only accessible by car or bus.

WHAT TO SEE. In **Podolsk:** Trinity Cathedral. In **Melikhovo** (8 miles from **Chekhov**) the home and memorial museum of the great playwright. In **Serpukhov** The Trinity Cathedral and the Church of St. Nicholas the White, the Church of the Prophet Elijah, the Uspensky Church the Vladichny Convent and the Vysotsky Bogoroditsy Monastery. In **Tula** the kremlin, the Church of the Uspensky Monastery and the local museums. In **Yasnaya Polyana** the Tolstoy memorial museum. In **Orel** St. Nikita's Cathedral, the churches of the Archangel Michael, of St. Nicholas-on-the-Sand, the Smolenskaya Church, and the Turgenev Museum. In **Kursk** St. Serge's Cathedral, the Church of the Sign of Our Lady, the Trinity Convent, St. Nikita's and St. Catherine's Church. In **Belgorod** The Church of the Annunciation.

HOTELS. Kursk. *Kursk Hotel,* 2 Lenin Street, with Intourist bureau and car park; or *Oktyabrska Hotel,* 72 Lenin Street. Also in Kursk. *Motel Solovinaya Roshcha* (Intourist), 142–a, Lenin Street.

Mtsensk. *Tourist Hotel,* with restaurant and car park, both open all day. *Note:* can be visited only in transit on automobile tours.

Orel. *Orel Hotel,* Pushkin Street; *Rossiya Hotel,* 37, Gorky Street. Also in Orel, *Motel Shipka,* off Moskovskoye Highway, 3 miles out. Intourist facilities.

Serpukhov. *Moskva Hotel,* Lenin Square. *Note:* can be visited only in transit.

Tula. *Tula Hotel,* Lenin Prospekt; or *Central Hotel,* Sovietskaya Street. *Note:* can be visited only in transit.

Voronezh. Try *Rossia Hotel* on Teatralnaya Street; then either *Voronezh Hotel* or *Don Hotel,* both on Plekhanovskaya Street.

 RESTAURANTS. Belgorod. *Urozhai Restaurant,* Parkovaya Street; *Belgorod Café,* on the main road at the corner of Khmelnitsky and Narodnaya streets.

Chekhov (Lopasnya). Fairly good restaurant here. Also a restaurant at Melikhovo, 8 miles from Chekhov.

Kursk. *Seym Restaurant,* Solyanka Street; *Kursk Café,* Lenin Street.

Orel. *Orlik Restaurant,* 228 Komsomolskaya Street; *Oka Restaurant,* 16 Lenin Street; *Tson Restaurant,* between town and Orel camping site; *Druzhba,* Moskovskaya Street.

Podolsk. Better-than-average restaurant in center of town.

Tula. *Moskva Restaurant* in Central Hotel

Voronezh. If you don't want to eat at the hotel, ask for the *Chaika Restaurant.*

Yasnaya Polyana. Restaurant just outside the gates of the Tolstoy estate.

 MUSEUMS. In Podolsk: *Lenin Museum,* Moskovskaya Street. This is a house where Lenin's family lived for some time during the 1890's. **Melikhovo,** eight miles from Chekhov, is the estate of Anton Chekhov.

Serpukhov: *History and Art Museum,* 87 Chekhov Street.

Tula: *Local Museum,* 68 Sovietskaya Street; *Art Museum,* 44 Lenin Prospekt; *Museum of the History of Arms,* Lenin Prospekt, on the main Moscow-Yalta road, opposite the kremlin. Open 11–3, closed Mon.

Yasnaya Polyana is the birthplace and *home of Leo Tolstoy* lying a mile 69 the main road, 125 miles south of Moscow. The museum ticket office is at the main gates. Opening hours are 9–5; closed Wed.

Spasskoye-Lutovinovo, the *home of Turgenev,* can be reached by a sideroad which branches off from the main road north of Mtsensk, at the 303 km. stone from Moscow. The turning is marked by a bust of Turgenev and a signpost indicating the way to his former estate.

Orel: *Turgenev Museum,* 11 Turgenevskaya Street. Closed Fri. *Museum of Local Writers,* 7th November Street, No. 24 (in Granovsky's home). Closed Fri. *Local Museum,* 1/3 Moskovskaya Street. *Picture Gallery,* 3 Sovietskaya Street.

Kursk: *Ufimtsev Museum,* 13 Semenovskaya Street. *Picture Gallery,* 3 Sovietskaya Street.

Belgorod: *Local Museum,* 42 Frunze Street.

CULTURAL ACTIVITIES. Serpukhov: Drama Theater, 58/27 Chekhov Street. **Tula:** Gorky Drama Theater, 51 Lenin Prospekt; Youth Theater, 10 Komintern Street; Puppet Theater, 78 Sovietskaya Street; Zenith Stadium, in the eastern half of the Kremlin area. **Orel:** Turgenev Drama Theater, Teatralnaya Square. Puppet Theater, 1/3 Moskovskaya Street in the 18th-century building of the Epiphany Church; Hippodrome, near Troitskoye Kladbishche (Cemetery).

Kursk: Pushkin Drama Theater, 1 Perekalsky Street; Summer Theater, Lenin Street, in the May 1st Garden, opposite the Kursk Hotel; Puppet Theater, 99 Lenin Street; Dynamo Stadium, 36 Lenin Street; Trudovye Rezervy Stadium, 58 Lenin Street, seating 17,000—the Local Agricultural Exhibition is held here between September and November. (Near the Kursk Camping site.)

SHOPPING. Orel: *Department Store and Souvenirs,* 5 Moskovskaya Street. **Kursk:** *Department Store,* 12 Lenin Street; *Jeweler's,* 2 Lenin Street.

TOURS. Intourist will arrange visits to the Tolstoy and Turgenev estates and to Chekhov's home.

USEFUL ADDRESSES. Orel: The *Intourist* office is at 37 Gorky Street; 2 miles from the city there is a *camping* site, off the main Moscow-Simferopol road, 330 yards to the left. Telephone and hot showers, car-wash and repair ramp are available; another 330 yards away on the Tson River there are facilities for fishing and bathing.

Kursk: *Camping.* At the southern end of the city, 220 yards left from Engels Street, on the Solyanka Park on the River Seym. *Railroad station.* Privokzalnaya Square. *Bus terminal* Marx Street (north) and 1 Engels Street (south).

Belgorod: There is a *camping* site half a mile to the left of the main road, just south of the town. The site covers 7½ acres and has a buffet, self-service kitchen, hot showers, a laundry, post office, telephone, a sports ground equipped for volleyball and a car-wash and repair shop.

BYELORUSSIA ("WHITE RUSSIA")

The "White Russian" Byelorussian Soviet Republic is bordered by Poland on the west. Lithuania and Latvia on the north and northwest, with the Russian Federation in the east and the Ukrainian Soviet Republic in the south. Its total area is some 80,154 square miles and it has mild winters and moderately warm summers. Forests cover more than one-third of its total area and it has over 4,000 lakes. The great Dnieper (Dnepr), Niemen (Neman), Pripyat and Berezina rivers flow through it; its wild life includes moose, deer, wild boar, beaver and many species of game birds. It is well-supplied with oil and coal, peat and rock salts.

Byelorussia was once the site of many ancient Russian principalities whose centers were, at various times, Kobrin, Nesvizh, Minsk, Pinsk, Polotsk and Slutsk. It was the Byelorussians who finally defeated the Tatar and Mongol invaders in the battle of Koydanovo (now Dzerzhinsk), barring their way into Western Europe. Napoleon suffered a decisive defeat on the banks of the Berezina. It was the scene of long and bitter fighting during the Second World War and guerrillas were active here throughout the years of German occupation.

The republic has developed considerably both in agriculture and industry. It now has its own engineering, chemical, power and automobile industries. New cities have been built but there are still beautiful old towns, rich in history, to explore. The population (predominantly Slav) has its own distinctive culture, unusual cuisine (rich in mushroom dishes) and its own national drinks.

The major cities are along the Brest-Smolensk highway (which continues to Moscow) and include Brest, Kobrin, Beryoza, Ivatsevichi, Baranovichi, Stolbtsy, Dzerzhinsk, Zhodino, Borisov, Tolochin, Orsha, and Yurtsevo. The capital is Minsk.

Exploring Byelorussia

Brest, a mile and a half from the Polish-Soviet border, a busy railway junction and port on the Dnieper-Bug Canal, is also a fairly large center for food production and light industry. The Moscow-Warsaw-Berlin express passes through daily and regular passenger and freight trains leave here for Moscow, Kiev and elsewhere. The Warsaw-Moscow international highway intersects Brest; highways from Lithuania and Transcarpathia, etc., all converge on it.

Although it's quite a sizeable town, its sights can be explored in about two hours. Begin at the railway station, where a memorial tablet marks the defense of the city by a handful of partisans between June 22 and July 2, 1941. They held out for ten long days west of the station, then withdrew into a basement and finally fought their way through the encircling Germans, to reach the forests beyond where they joined the Byelorussian partisans.

From the station, an overpass leads to Lenin Street and a public park. At the main entrance, there is a monument to the war dead above a communal grave. From the park, Lenin Street leads to the Central Square, where various municipal and regional institutions, a drama theater and the Museum of Local Lore are situated. Moskovskaya Street will take you to the newly-built districts of town.

The Brest Fortress is on the southwestern outskirts. It can be reached from downtown Brest by Lenin Street and the Street of the Brest Fortress Heroes. Here Soviet soldiers held out for almost six weeks in the underground casemates. By then, the German forces had rolled past Brest, advancing as far east as Minsk (nearly 200 miles). The Soviet Army liberated Brest on July 28, 1944 and the fortress was almost reduced to rubble. It has been rebuilt—though it still bears battle scars—and turned into a museum.

An alley leads from the Street of the Brest Fortress Heroes to the northern gate of the Kobrinsky Bridgehead, the largest in the fortress. To the left of the Northern Gate is the Eastern Fort; outside the gate, the alley leads to the bridge spanning the right fork of the Mukhavets. Beyond the bridge is the citadel, erected on a natural island. Left of the alley is the Brest Fortress Defense Museum, opened on November 8, 1956. It has four sections divided over ten halls, illustrating the history of Brest and the Brest Fortress, the Nazi attack, the part played by the defenders of the Fortress in the 1941–45 battles, and, finally, one devoted to war veterans. Portraits, sculptures and photographs complement the historical exhibits and documentary films are shown.

Kobrin and Eastward

Kobrin, an ancient town, stands on either side of the Mukhavets River. It was first mentioned in the Ipatiev Chronicle in 1287 as a fishing settlement. At different times through the years it has belonged to Lithuania and to Poland. Here, on July 15, 1812, the Russians achieved their first victory (albeit temporary) over Napoleon. It is associated with General Alexander Suvorov, whose former estate is now the municipal park: the lime trees date from his time. A monument commemorating the 1812 war stands on the right bank of the river, near the highway.

The Suvorov Military History Museum on Suvorov Street is in the general's former house. It contains numerous exhibits associated with his life and activities. Suvorov lived in Kobrin from 1797 to 1800.

Kobrin has been rebuilt since the last war and is now mainly notable for its food processing industry. The 60-mile-long Dnieper-Bug canal, linking the Mukhavets and Pina rivers, starts in its vicinity. The canal was built between 1775 and 1848 by serf labor; it was reconstructed after 1917 and then again after its partial destruction in the Second World War.

Beryoza is about 60 miles east of Brest. Its name means "Birch Tree". Under Polish rule, the remains of a Catholic monastery here were utilized as a prison; years later, the Nazis established a large concentration camp on the site. Ivatsevichi, 95 miles from Brest, has a large saw mill, but nothing else to recommend it. Kossovo, ten miles from Ivatsevichi, is an ancient settlement where the Byelorussian Academy of Sciences operates an experimental station for the study of the conditions and methods of farming on former marsh-land.

Baranovichi is 120 miles from Brest, two miles off the main road. Founded in 1870, it is still an important rail junction. Before the Second World War it had a large Jewish population. The two main streets are Sovietskaya and Komsomolskaya. Near the railway station there are extremely dense pine woods and another pine forest has been turned into a park. Near its entrance stands the memorial to Sergei Gritsevets, "twice hero of the Soviet Union", who was killed in the Russo-Japanese War of 1939. Baranovichi (Baranowicze in Polish) has many associations with the Polish poet Mickiewicz.

Stolbtsy, about 140 miles from Brest, is a rapidly growing town, a mile off the main road on the upper reaches of the Niemen River. The countryside is particularly attractive around here: the wide Niemen Valley has meadows and woods stretching to the far horizon. The grave of Avenir Kostenchik, who captained the first heavy military aircraft of the Soviet Union, lies in Stolbtsy. Seven miles away is the village of Nikolaevshchina, birthplace of Yakub Kolas, the Byelorussian folk poet.

Dzerzhinsk (formerly Koydanovo) is about 180 miles from Brest and is a district center for the Minsk Region. Originally it was named after the Tatar leader Koydan who was defeated here in 1241. The first mention of the place is in the 12th century. It was renamed in honor of Felix Dzerzhinsky (1877–1926), born in the nearby village of Petrivolichi. Dzerzhinsky was a close associate of Lenin and a founder of the Cheka, the Soviet Secret Police. His monument stands in the center of town.

The Minsk Sea (a large reservoir) 10 miles before Minsk offers good bathing facilities.

Minsk

Minsk, the capital of Byelorussia is the republic's biggest industrial, scientific and cultural center. People first settled on the banks of the Svisloch 900 years ago and the city was marked on an old map of the world drawn by the famous Arab traveler Abu Abdallah Muhammed in 1154, when it was already a large and well-known city.

Much of the city was razed to the ground during the war. Today the reconstructed Minsk is a center of heavy and light industry. It is laid out with broad avenues and wide embankments flanking the Svisloch River, which winds through the city. The symmetrical design of its straight streets, wide squares, numerous parks and gardens is particularly striking from the air.

Most foreign tourists usually stay in the Hotel Minsk, where the Intourist offices are also housed. The hotel stands on one of the most attractive avenues in the city, the Lenin Prospekt. If you are staying at the Hotel Byelorus, you can easily reach Lenin Prospekt from Kirov Street by taking Krasnoarmeiskaya Street. The first cross-street is Karl Marx Street (running parallel with Kirov Street) and the second is the Lenin Prospekt.

The Lenin Prospekt is the direct continuation of the Brest-Moscow highway and leads from Pobeda Square straight south to the square in front of the railway station.

In the center of Pobeda Square there is a tall gray granite obelisk commemorating the heroes of World War II. It is part of a whole complex of monuments, the work of Zaborsky and Korol, and is a landmark of the city.

Starting along Lenin Prospekt towards the center of Minsk, we see on the right hand corner of the square, on the river bank, the one-storied house in which the Russian Social Democratic Workers Party held its first congress in 1898. Today it is a memorial museum surrounded by a small park. It consists of two sections. The first documents the social and economic position of Russia in the second half of the 19th century, the second is the former home of P. Rumyantsev, in whose apartment the secret Congress sessions were held.

The Lenin Prospekt, which is lined with modern apartment houses and public buildings, now crosses the Svisloch River. The next crossing is named after Yanko Kupala, the great Byelorussian poet; a short distance beyond the corner to the right is the literary museum dedicated to his work and life. After passing it, you once again cross the twisting river to reach Kuibyshev Street to the west. After this crossing, we find ourselves on the square named after the Paris Commune. The building dominating this square is the Opera House. Turning left on Kuibyshev Street, we cross still another bridge over the Svisloch, where Kuibyshev Street becomes Herzen Street. At its far end, off Svoboda Square, we find the Museum of the Great Patriotic War.

At the crossing of Lenin Prospekt with Krasnoarmeiskaya Street we come to the other large square into which Lenin Avenue broadens. It is called Central Square and is the heart of the city. If we walk down Engels Road, which crosses Lenin Prospekt on the far (north) side of Central Square, we reach the Byelorussian Dramatic Theater (named after Yanko Kupala) at the Karl Marx Street crossing.

South of Central Square, Lenin Prospekt widens into Lenin Square, which has many public buildings. The huge Government Building, is the largest and tallest building in Minsk. Lenin's statue (by Manizer) stands in front of it. Facing the Government Building is the complex of Lenin University.

The tourist might like to visit Zhdanovichi, a pleasant recreation area, about 11 miles from the city, with beaches, swimming pools, islands and lakes.

East of Minsk

Minsk is about 140 miles west of the border between Byelorussia and the Russian Republic. As you drive along the Intourist-approved motor route, you cross the Minsk and Vitebsk regions. The important places here are Zhodino, Borisov, Tolochin, Orsha and Orekhovsk.

Zhodino is in the heart of Byelorussia, 30 miles from Minsk, and manufactures heavy vehicles.

Borisov, on the Berezina River, is 40 miles from Minsk, situated where the Brest-Moscow highway and railway cross the Berezina, the largest tributary of the Dnieper. An important industrial center, it was allegedly founded by Boris, Prince of Polotsk. Between the 14th and 18th centuries it belonged to Lithuania and Poland. North of the town, near the village of Studenka, where remnants of Napoleon's *Grand Armée* were hastily retreating across the Berezina, the French suffered a serious defeat. The center of the town lies between the river and the railway. Prospekt Revolyutsii, the main thoroughfare, runs through the town from the railway station to the Berezina. There is a fine park and a stadium.

About 350 miles from Brest the road crosses the Kiev-Leningrad Highway. Twelve kilometers (about seven miles) away is Orsha, an ancient Byelorussian town. It was first mentioned in chronicles in 1067 and became part of Russia in the late 18th century. Today it is a large industrial center.

Orekhovsk lies several miles north of the above mentioned highway crossing, in the direction of Leningrad. Once a small town surrounded by swamps it is now a well-planned town, servicing a peat-burning power station which uses fuel from the neighboring Osinovsk peat mines.

The last town in Byelorussia on the way to Moscow is Yurtsevo, 73 miles from Smolensk.

PRACTICAL INFORMATION FOR BYELORUSSIA

 WHEN TO GO. The best seasons for Byelorussia are spring and fall, though the summer months are pleasant and rarely too hot.

 HOW TO GET THERE. The main railroad from Poland runs via Brest, Minsk and Borisov to Smolensk and Moscow. The main highway crosses the Polish frontier at Brest, then goes to Kobrin, Ivatsevichi, Stolbtsy, Minsk, Borisov, Malyavka and on to the east and Moscow.

Minsk has an airport with direct flights from and to Moscow and Leningrad.

 WHAT TO SEE. In **Brest,** the Semyonovsky Church. In **Kobrin,** the Alexander Nevsky Cathedral, the Church of St. Peter and St. Paul (15th century), the Suvorov Museum of Military History and the Suvorov Park.

In **Baranovichi,** the Intercession Cathedral in Kuibyshev Street and, in nearby Novogrudok, the memorial museum of Poland's greatest poet, Adam Mickiewicz, who was born in the adjoining village of Zaosie.

In **Minsk,** the Cathedral of the Holy Spirit, 3 Bakunin Street; the Church of St. Catherine, Ostrovsky Street; the World War II and the Byelorussian Art Museum (the first is at 23 Svoboda Square, the second at 20 Lenin Street), the Gorky and Cheluskintsev Parks.

In **Borisov,** the Cathedral of the Resurrection in Svoboda Square.

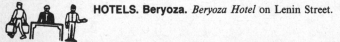 **HOTELS. Beryoza.** *Beryoza Hotel* on Lenin Street.

Brest. *Intourist Hotel,* 15, Moskovskaya Street, or *Bug Hotel,* 2 Lenin Street. *Note:* only one-night stay allowed at presstime. For transit only.

Kobrin. *Byelorus Hotel,* Svoboda Square. *Note:* can be visited only in transit.

Minsk. *Yubileinaya,* 19, Parkovaya Avenue, a modern high-rise overlooking an attractive square, is best, with 249 rooms. First class. Then comes *Minsk,* 11 Leninsky Prospekt, also first class, with 250 rooms.

Also-rans: *Byelorus,* 3 Kirov Street; *Pervaya,* 13 Komsomlskaya Street; *Tretya,* 3 Tolbukhin Street; *Vtoraya,* 6 Volodarsky Street; and *Sputnik,* 30 Brilevskaya Street.

Minsky Motel and Camping Site, 11 miles outside of Minsk on the road to Brest. Set within a forest, this new motel has a restaurant and souvenir shop selling local Byelorussian crafts. Nearby is a car service and filling station, post office, open-air cinema and sports ground.

RESTAURANTS Borisov. *Borisov Restaurant,* small but adequate.

Brest. *Byelorus Restaurant,* corner of Pushkin and Sovietskaya streets.

Minsk. Apart from the restaurants attached to the hotels, try any of these: *Neman Restaurant,* 22 Lenin Prospekt (best); *Raduga,* Privokzalnaya Square; *Zarya,* 2 Lenin Street; *Chaika,* 2 Tolbukhin Street; *Teatralnoye,* 34 Gorky Street; *Leto* 8 Pervomayskaya Street.

 CULTURAL ACTIVITIES. In **Brest** there is a Drama Theater in Lenin Street. The city also has a pedagogical institute, a medical and music school, cinemas, clubs and several museums.

In **Minsk** there is a Trade Unions' Palace of Culture in Central Square, containing a theater. The Byelorussian Academy of Science and the Lenin University are the cultural centers; the 12 different faculties have around 35,000 students. The Polytechnical Institute is the second major educational establishment and the Byelorus Film Studio is also located in Minsk. In nearby Grushevski, a small village, important archeological excavations have continued for many years. Minsk has the large Lenin Library (with 2½ million books) and several theaters: the Bolshoi Theater, 7 Ploshchad Parizhskoi Kommuni, where opera and ballet are performed and which is the home of the Capella Byelorussian Choir and the Byelorussian Folk Choir; a puppet theater; the Yanko Kupala Byelorussian Theater, 23 Engels Street; the Gorky Russian Drama Theater. 5 Volodarsky Street; a Youth Theater, Engels Street, and a circus on Lenin Prospekt.

 MUSEUMS. In **Brest** are the *Regional Museum of Local Lore,* 34 Lenin Street, the *Museum of the Brest Fortress Defense,* Street of the Brest Fortress Heroes (take buses nos. 1, 5 or 12); *the Regional House of Folk Art,* 1 Komsomolskaya Street.

Kobrin. The *Suvorov Military History Museum,* 16 Suvorov Street.

Baranovichi. A *local museum* displays Byelorussian folk art and costumes. (We have elsewhere mentioned the memorial museum at Novogrudok devoted to the life and work of Adam Mickiewicz.)

Minsk. *World War Two Museum,* 23 Svoboda Square, also known as the Museum of the History of the Great Patriotic War, with 25 halls. *Local History and Folklore Museum,* Revolyutsionnaya Street. *Yanko Kupala Memorial Museum,* Yanko Kupala Street. Open 10–3, closed Fri. Housed in the former home of the Byelorussian poet (1882–1942). Ten rooms. *Yakub Kolas Museum,* 66 Lenin Prospekt. Open 9:30–3:30, except Sat. This was the home of another outstanding Byelorussian poet (1882–1956).

Museum of the First Congress of the Russian Social-Democratic Party, Lenin Prospekt. Open 11–6, closed Fri.

State Art Museum, 20 Lenin Street.

 **SHOPPING.** The best place for shopping in Minsk. The local department store is at 21 Lenin Prospekt. There is a *Children's World Store* at 12 Lenin Prospekt, a gift shop *(Podarki)* at 22 Volodarsky Street, a sports shop at 16 Lenin Prospekt, a jeweler's at 22 Lenin Prospekt, an antique and art shop at 19 Lenin Prospekt and a florist in the same building.

TOURS are arranged through Intourist, mostly covering the cities and towns along the Brest-Smolensk highway. It is recommended that those traveling by car or bus should take three or four days for the trip from Brest to Moscow. Individual tours of the area south and west of Minsk can also be arranged. The tours include a visit to the Katyn Memorial Complex, the site of a massacre in which thousands of Polish soldiers were killed. You will be very unpopular with your Soviet guide if you challenge the official version of exactly who was responsible for the slaughter. Best be diplomatic or politely walk away.

There are excursions to the Minsk Sea—as the Zaslavskoye Reservoir is known—and to the Minsky camping site on the thickly forested bank of the Ptich River.

A striking war memorial in the Siberian city of Novosibirsk

A street in the old city of
Tallinn, capital of Estonia

Part of the Arabian Nights' architecture of Shahi Zinda in Samarkand

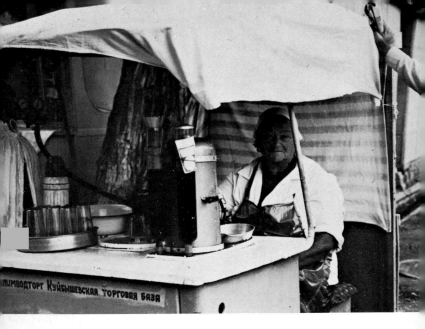

A lemonade seller in the Worker's
Market in Tashkent. Relaxing on
the Shaikhana in Bukhara

THE BALTIC REPUBLICS

Estonia, Latvia and Lithuania

The three present-day republics of Estonia, Latvia and Lithuania have a long and checkered history. Lithuania's is perhaps the most distinguished and is characterized by her ancient association with Poland. The other two, Estonia and Latvia, have for centuries been intermittently at the mercy of a variety of powerful neighbors—the Teutonic knights, then the Danes, Poles, Swedes and the Russian Czars. They enjoyed a brief period of precarious independence between the two World Wars and are now, all three, Soviet republics.

Lying along the Baltic coast in the northwestern corner of the USSR, in many ways they are different from the rest of this vast empire. They use the latin alphabet (though street signs are also in Russian), their traditions are completely Western, their religion Catholic and Protestant. Of the three, Estonia is the smallest but its capital, Tallinn, offers the most interesting medieval architecture. Latvia, the traditional "work-shop of the Baltic", was an important industrial area in Czarist times, and Riga, too, has some extremely fine architecture. Lithuania, the "land of amber", on the great Amber Road that ran from the Baltic to the Mediterranean, has supplied this mysterious and rare product of the seashore from time immemorial. It has picturesque landscapes, fine monuments in its historic capital, Vilnius, and a magnificent carillon in Kaunas.

Exploring Estonia

Estonia lies on the shores of the Baltic and the Gulf of Finland, between the Russian Republic to the east and Latvia to the south. It has an area of 17,413 square miles, including 800 islands and 1,500 small and large lakes. Its population is one and a half million of whom 75 percent are Estonians, a people belonging to the Finno-Ugrian group which also includes the Finns and the Hungarians. The 20 percent Russian population lives mostly in the cities and in the oil shale basin. On the western shore of Lake Chud there are some predominantly Russian settlements; these are the descendants of the Orthodox "Old Believers" who fled here in the 17th centruy.

Tallinn

Tallinn, the Estonian capital, is the republic's largest industrial and cultural center. It is also an important Baltic harbor. Its climate is tempered by the sea; the coldest month is February, the warmest July. While the days are very short in winter, in summer they stretch well into the nights, especially in June, when you can see the "White Nights".

In many ways Tallinn is one of the most attractive cities in the Soviet Union. A wonderfully preserved city of the old Hanseatic League, it has as many atmospheric streets as a really good stage setting. Just across the Gulf of Finland from Helsinki, it is the goal of swarms of Finnish tourists, not always well behaved, and seems to Russian visitors, who also arrive in their thousands, a "little version of the West". Indeed, it may well be the city in which tourists from the West may feel most at home.

It's hard to lose your way in Tallinn. All you have to do is to use the tallest tower, the steeple of the Oleviste Church, as a landmark. If you get tired visit a café, open from 8 or 9 A.M. till late evening.

You can start from the Palace (Intourist) Hotel on Victory Square (Voidu Väljak), which is one of the centers of the New Town. True, the word "new" simply means in this case that these quarters are outside the ancient city walls. They grew up in the mid-19th century. Here you will find the Russian Drama Theater, and the headquarters of the Estonian Association of Fine Arts.

Climbing the promenade up Harju Mägi (hill), you will come to a bastion with a red roof called Kiek-in-de-Kök (Look-Into-The-Kitchen), built in 1470, when it was the tallest edifice in Estonia. From it, watchmen were able to peer into the kitchens of the houses below. It still has some iron cannonballs in the massive walls, souvenirs of the siege of 1577.

To the right of the bastion you will see the onion domes of the Alexander Nevsky Cathedral (1894–1900).

The nearby tower is the Long Hermann (Pikk Hermann), which now houses government offices. Before entering the castle area, continue south along Noukogude Street. On the castle side you will see the former Governor's Garden, on the other Linda Hill. Linda was a legendary lady, the widow of Kalev, hero of an Estonian national epic: an episode of the folk poem supplied the inspiration for Welzenberg's statue on Linda Hill. The semicircular Deer Park (Hirvepark) on one side of the hill is a favorite walk for the people of Tallinn.

From Noukogude Street a stairway leads down on the right to Snellevsky Lake. The park around the lake, which stretches as far as the railway station, is known as Bastion Square (Tornide Valjak); it has a number of horseshoe-shaped towers in which marksmen used to be

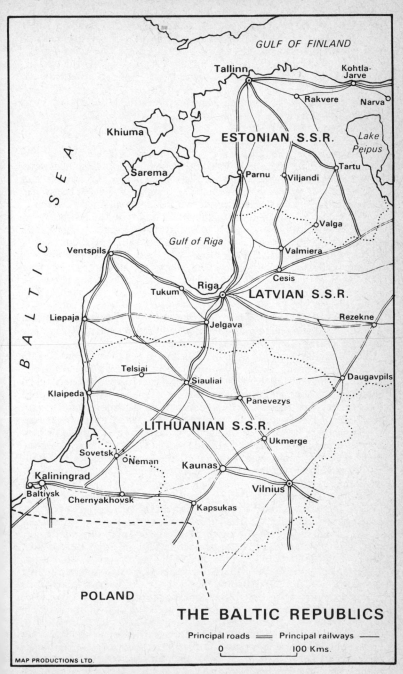

GULF OF FINLAND

Tallinn

Kohtla-
Jarve

Rakvere

Narva

Khiuma

ESTONIAN S.S.R.

Lake
Peipus

B A L T I C   S E A

Sarema

Parnu

Viljandi

Tartu

Valga

Gulf of Riga

Ventspils

Valmiera

Cesis

Tukum

Riga

LATVIAN S.S.R.

Liepaja

Jelgava

Rezekne

Telsiai

Siauliai

Daugavpils

Klaipeda

Panevezys

LITHUANIAN S.S.R.

Ukmerge

Sovetsk

Neman

Kaunas

Kaliningrad

Vilnius

Baltiysk

Chernyakhovsk

Kapsukas

POLAND

THE BALTIC REPUBLICS

Principal roads ═══ Principal railways ───

0   100 Kms.

MAP PRODUCTIONS LTD.

stationed. The Patkulskaya Stairs lead up to Castle Hill; their upper end emerges into the courtyard of 3 Ravhakohtu Street, a classical-style building dating from 1792. From here you have a fine view over Bastion Square and of the sea.

Castle Hill and the Lower Town

You are now on the Toompea, Castle Hill. In the Middle Ages it was divided into the Great and the Small Castle. The palace, which today houses the Council of Ministers, was the Small Castle, and the rest of the Toompea's area the Great Castle.

"Long Hermann" and the other two surviving bastions of the fortress (Pilstiker and Landskrone), together with the 60-foot-high western, northern and eastern walls, belonged to the Small Castle. This was built in the early 13th century, soon after the Danish conquest, but the system of fortifications you see today dates from the 14th century and was built by the Teutonic Knights to strengthen their hold over the territory they had purchased from the Danes. The Small Castle changed hands several times and underwent several alterations—the most important at the end of the 18th century, during the reign of Catherine the Great, when its eastern wall was demolished to make way for a new baroque building, and the moat was filled in. Much of the Great Castle was destroyed in the great fire of 1684, and the houses that replaced it were built for the most part in the classical style. The most important surviving monument is the Cathedral, which was first mentioned in the 13th century. But it, too, has undergone numerous alterations and refurnishings. It has a fine baroque altar and many interesting tombs.

The most characteristic quarter of Tallinn is the Lower Town. From the courtyard of No. 12 Kohtu Street and the little platform at the end of the same street the whole panorama of the Lower Town unfolds in front of you. Towers and steeples rise above the cluster of red tiled roofs. Below is the bastion of Pikk-Jalg, opposite the Town Hall: to the left, some distance away, rises the steeple of the Oleviste Church, a familiar landmark. This was the center of ancient Tallinn: the Pikk-Jalg, whose fortified gate was the only entrance in the Middle Ages to the Toompea; the Town Hall Square, meeting-point of seven streets, and beyond it, the Vanaturg, the Old Market, reached by a short street from the Town Hall Square.

The streets radiating from the Vanaturg all have a history. Vene Street leads to the harbor; Viru Street started where the two gate-bastions now stand; along Harju Street cattle were driven to graze for many centuries. Vene runs left, Viru straight ahead, Harju to the right. Niguliste Street runs from the corner of Harju towards the Pikk-Jalg and Lühike Jalg, across Harju Hill.

The steeple of Oleviste Church is flanked by two streets, running parallel, almost a continuation of Pikk-Jalg. One of them is Lai (Broad) Street, the other Pikk (Long) Street, which once linked the old city center with the harbor.

Descending into the Lower Town, you can start your exploration at the 15th-century bastion of Lühike Jalg Street which runs into Pikk-Jalg Street. Next to it you'll notice an iron-studded wooden gate (17th century). Going along Pikk-Jalg you pass the grey limestone of the remains of the former city wall: this was built in 1454 by the municipal council of the Lower Town as a defense against the masters of the castle. The square gate-house of the Pikk-Jalg dates from 1380.

Turning along the flank of Castle Hill towards Bastion Square, follow Nooruse Street, where you can see clear traces of the former fortifications of the city, three-quarters of which are still standing. They were begun in the 13th century, and in their present form date from the 15th–16th centuries. Some of the bastions were named after the town councillors who were the keepers of the keys. But the Saunatorn Tower in Nooruse Street commemorates the baths of the nearby convent. The 13th-century convent's site is now a school, while its medieval cellars are topped by a soft-drinks factory. The convent has in fact housed a school since the 17th century. The assembly-hall of the high school, divided into two Romanesque sections, was once the convent's refectory. The convent church later became an Orthodox cathedral. Its main feature is the baroque iconostasis, a gift from Peter the Great. Turn left from Nooruse Street into Lai Street. No. 29, a characteristic 15th-century burgher's mansion, is well worth a visit. The entrance to the Museum of Natural History is from its courtyard. The Museum displays 92,000 items illustrating Estonia's fauna, flora and mineral wealth. There is a rich *Herbarium Balticum.*

Passing along Lai Street, turn right into any cross-street and walk down to Pikk Street. Turning left at the end of the street you'll see "Fat Margaret", a large bastion, built between 1510 and 1529. This was the right-hand defense of the Suur Rannavarar, the Great Sea Gate. "Fat Margaret" and the adjoining building house the Municipal Museum which explores the history of Tallinn since the 17th century. (Earlier history is displayed in the permanent "Old Tallinn" exhibition in the Town Hall.)

Turning back along Pikk Street, notice to your right the 375-foot-high steeple of the Oleviste Church, named after St. Olaf, King of Norway. Destroyed and rebuilt several times, and restored between 1820 and 1840, it is a fine example of the Gothic style. Continuing along Pikk Street, notice No. 26 (on your left). Now a House of Culture, it used to be the seat of the Society of Blackheads, founded in 1399 by the sons of Tallinn merchants and other bachelors. The members of this society supplied the city's cavalry in times of war. The next house, No. 24 Pikk Street, was once the home of the Olaf Guild, which was founded in the 13th century as a religious body and later became a society of non-German-speaking craftsmen. It survived until 1698.

No. 17, on the other side of the street, was the center of the Great Guild, formed early in the 14th century by the richest merchants; only its members could be elected to the city council. The house was built around 1410 and is a splendid example of Northern Gothic. The white cross against a red background on its facade was the coat-of-arms of both the city of Tallinn and the Great Guild. Inside there are fine vaulted ceilings and richly decorated columns: the ceremonial hall was the scene of great festivities, including the election of the "Countess of May", a medieval beauty contest. The "Count of May", her consort, had the privilege of freeing one prisoner from the municipal jail. The building was also used for theatrical performances until the beginning of the 20th century. Today it houses the Historical Museum of the Estonian Academy of Sciences. This museum presents the history of the Estonian people from prehistoric times to the present day. It has vast resources of coins, parchments and other documents, archeological finds in abundance, articles of folk art and craft, and over a thousand pieces in the weapon collection covering seven centuries.

At the next corner you'll see on your left the Church of the Holy Ghost, built at the end of the 14th century—the oldest Tallinn church that still stands in its original form. It was also once called Town Hall Church. Just past the Church of the Holy Ghost, turn left into any of the four streets leading off Pikk Street, and you will find yourself in the Raekoja Plats—Town Hall Square. (Two of these streets are the winding Voorimehe and Saja Käik, so narrow that only pedestrians can use them.) Entering the square by Saja Käik Street watch out for a remarkable wrought-iron sign bearing the traditional snake symbol of the apothecary. This is the municipal chemist's shop, which has been functioning since 1422.

Town Hall Square was originally called Market Square; excavations have shown that it was a market as long as a thousand years ago. The remains of a 12th century sewage system have also been found, together with pieces of a triumphal arch erected in 1711 for the visit of Peter the Great. The Town Hall, begun in 1317–74 and completed in 1401–4, has been preserved almost intact in its original Gothic form and still serves as the City Hall. Perched on top of its tower you can see a weather vane carved in the shape of a Tallinn municipal guard; this is the Vana (Old) Toomas—or rather, its replica, for the original is kept in the municipal museum inside the Town Hall.

Another fascinating walk starts at the Niguliste (St. Nicholas) Church. This church, built in the 13th century, was dedicated to the patron saint of seamen. Much of its interior has been preserved, including the Gothic high altar, the work of the Lübeck master Hermann Tode (1481). The altar has several dozen carved figures. The church is now being restored and will eventually house a museum of medieval art and architecture.

Leaving the church you can walk down Niguliste Street (away from Castle Hill), across Harju Hill as far as Vana Turu and then straight down Viru Street to Viru Gate. Medieval Tallinn had six gates, all of them bastion-forts with moats and drawbridges. The city walls were protected by an extra moat and other defensive fortifications. In Viru Street you will see the two surviving bastions of the outer gate (15th century).

Continuing your walk, you will soon find yourself back in the New Town, in the Park of October 16, with the Estonian Opera and Ballet Theater close by. From the parking lot outside the theater a broad promenade leads to Lenini Puiestee (Boulevard) where you can take a No. 1 or No. 3 tram at the stop marked "Forumi" to Kadriorg Park.

Excursion to Kadriorg

Kadriorg (Kateriyna Org, Catherine's Valley) was built in 1718 at the request of Peter the Great in honor of his wife Catherine. It was designed by the Italian architect Niccolo Michetti. One of the original features of the park is the Swan Lake with the statue of F. Kreutzwald, the poet who gave Estonian national epic, the *Kalevipoeg,* its final form. The Kadriorg Palace was built in 1718–24 in the baroque style typical of the age. Erected on a hillside, it has two stories in the front and one at the back. The pillared balcony was added later. Today it houses the Estonian State

Fine Arts Museum which boasts a fine collection of the Estonian realist school as well as some canvases of Repin and Breughel the Elder. There is also a permanent exhibition of 20th-century Estonian art and sculpture.

A few hundred yards away is the House of Peter the Great (open May to October, 11 A.M. to 5 P.M., except Tues). It is a very modest, simply-furnished building with only three rooms—a drawing room and a bedroom on the ground floor and a dining room on the mezzanine, all of them light and spacious.

One of the modern buildings in Kadriorg Park, on the Pirita Tee, is an openair bowl created in 1960 for the Tallinn Song Festival. At 12 and 24 Pirita Tee, beyond the bowl, you will see the pavilions of the National Economic Exhibition. The Pirita Gardening Commune also has a permanent display (closed Sun).

Tallinn's beach and water sports center is at Pirita which you can reach by buses Nos. 1, 8 and 34. There is swimming in fine weather in the sea, but if the waves are too high, you can walk over to the mouth of the Pirita River, where there is a pleasant beach on both banks, with good facilities and cafés. The popular Pirita-Kloostrimetsa motor-racing circuit passes through the pine-woods at the river mouth. There are boathouses here too. Nearby is the huge yachting marina, constructed for the 1980 Olympics.

Tartu is Estonia's second largest city, and lies on the Emajõgi River (which flows into Lake Peipus), some 20 miles from its mouth and about 110 miles from Tallinn. Its German name was Dorpat.

It is Tartu's cultural reputation that is the chief attraction for visitors, tourists and scholars alike. The city is famous for its excellent University which is housed in an early 19th-century classical-style building and has expanded into several specialized institutes. The University has had many outstanding philologists, scientists, physicians and philosophers among its alumni. It has an excellent library, founded in 1802 and housed in the sacristy of the Cathedral of Tartu Castle. It is said to contain almost two million volumes. The University's Botanical Garden, established in 1803, also attracts many visitors.

Tartu's medieval monuments were destroyed partly by the great fire in 1775 and partly during the Nazi occupation. One of them, destroyed in 1944, was the 14th century Ivan Church, with three naves.

Pärnu, Narva, Kohtla-Järve

Pärnu, founded in 1251, is a harbor town with a population of about 49,000 and also an important health-resort at the mouth of the River Parnu on the Bay of Riga. From Tallinn it is 30 minutes by air (summer flights only) and 2 hrs. 15 mins. by bus. Excavations have proved that this site was inhabited in the early Stone Age; many flints, axes and fishing hooks have been found. You will see some of the finds on display in the local museum.

Pärnu has a northern climate, with a mild winter and a short and cool summer with a fair amount of rainfall; its two-mile-long sandy beach is nevertheless very popular with Estonians. Pärnu has an important medicinal feature—the mud dredged from the gulf of Riga—and several sanatoria have been built.

Narva, with a population of 71,000, lies on the banks of the River Narva, eight miles from its mouth on the Gulf of Finland. It has been the scene of great battles—the Russian defeat by the Swedes in 1700–1 and the Red army victory on February 23, 1918. Narva is about 120 miles from Tallinn, 4 hrs. 30 mins. by bus. Its oldest monuments are the castle (14th century) and the Fortress of Ivangorod (built in the 15th century by Czar Ivan III). The City Hall and the former Stock Exchange date from the 17th century, and there are various towers and bastions of the same vintage.

Kohtla-Järve lies between the main Leningrad-Tallinn railway line and the Gulf of Finland. It is 3 hrs. by bus from Tallinn. With a population of 71,000, it is a center of gas-manufacture from oil-shale and supplies both Leningrad and Tallinn.

Exploring Latvia

The Latvian Republic lies on the Bay of Riga between Estonia and Lithuania. Its inland frontiers also border on Byelorussia and the Russian Republic. It has an area of 24,695 square miles. Of its population of 2.5 million plus, more than 60 percent are Latvians, a quarter Russians, and the rest Byelorussians and Poles. In Czarist times Latvia was one of the most highly industrialized areas of the empire. In 1899 almost half the population of Riga were German.

Riga

The most important Soviet Baltic port after Leningrad, Riga, has a long, historic past. The capital of the Latvian Republic, it lies at the mouth of the Daugava River (also known as the Western Dvina). The center of the city is about ten miles from the Bay of Riga. Although Riga is a sizeable city covering almost 90 square miles, its clear layout makes it easy to explore.

A good starting-point for exploration is the River Daugava which is 1,150 feet wide in the city center. Three bridges span the rivers; most traffic uses the middle one, which is also served by public transport.

The left bank, Pardaugava, has always been the industrial side. On the way from the airport to the city center you will pass the Dzeguzkalna Park; the 60-foot-high hill in the middle is the highest point in the city. The park also has a large openair theater. The next "green spot" is a cemetery, and behind it the 40-acre University botanical garden. The first river bridge has a landing stage and you will also see several water sports centers here.

Riga's main sights are on the right bank of the river. If you cross the second bridge you will come to the main seven-mile-long thoroughfare, the Lenin. Lenin Street, called Alexander Street in the last century, divides the right bank into almost-equal areas, cutting across the Vecriga, the Old City. This district stretches from Komjaunatnes Krastmala, the Daugava Quay, to Padomju Boulevard, which runs parallel with it; the other two edges are marked by Gorky Street (parallel with Lenin) and 13 Janvara Street. Perhaps you will get a clearer idea of the Old City if you remember that it stretches along the canal between the river and the boulevards, in a semicircle that starts and ends at the river Daugava. The canal (1½ miles long) was formerly the castle moat.

Vecriga is a typical old city; some of its streets are so narrow that you can touch the walls of the houses on both sides by stretching your arms out.

But beyond Padomju Boulevard, farther away from the river and the Old City, the boulevards and main streets running parallel with the Padomju are wide and shady: the three biggest are Raina, Komunaru and Kirov. Kirov Street crosses Lenin Street and emerges, beyond Gorky Street, into Kronvalda and Eksporta boulevards, the continuations of Padomju. The other end of Kirov Street runs into Kr. Barona Street (parallel with Lenin Street). Beyond Kr. Barona Street and parallel with it runs Suvorov Street, the continuation of 13 Janvara Street.

If you arrive in Riga by train, you'll find yourself outside the station on the corner of Raina and Suvorov Streets and you will easily find your way. Walking down Suvorov Street toward the river, the first main crossroads you come to is Padomju; turn right and you will find the Hotel Riga (Intourist). The somewhat unattractive skyscraper behind the station, incidentally, is the seat of the Latvian Academy of Sciences.

One Castle, Three Museums

Riga offers a wide variety of architectural styles: Romanesque and Gothic, Renaissance and Baroque, Classical and ultramodern. Let's start our walking tour from the old castle:

The castle of Riga (Pils) stands on Pionieru Square, where Gorky Street and Komjaunatnes Krastmala Quay meet. It houses the Riga Pioneer Palace and three museums: the Historical Museum, presenting Latvia's history; the Fine Arts Museum, containing works of Dutch and German masters as well as French graphics and sculpture; and the Rainis Literary Museum. Jan Rainis was Latvia's greatest poet, but the museum is not devoted exclusively to him, other writers are represented and there is a section on the history of Latvian theater.

From Pionieru Square turn into Torna Street. No. 1, on the corner of Arsenal Street, is the Arsenal, a long, low building (erected 1828–32), which includes part of the former city wall and the "Maiden Bastion". Passing it, turn right into Komjaunatnes Iela (not to be confused with Komjaunatnes Krastmala, the riverside walk). On your right is the Church of St. James (or Jacob), originally built outside the city walls in the 13th century. Its parishioners were the Latvian and Livonian inhabitants of the nearby settlements. It has been remodeled several times; but its tall sanctuary and three-naved basilica are still in their original form. The 240-foot-high steeple bears the traces of 16th and 18th century restorations. The church opposite, which also dates from the 13th century, is that of Mary Magdalene.

Turning left into Vestures Street at St. James's Church, walk to the corner of Maza Pils Street. Nos. 17, 19 and 21/23 Vestures Street, jointly called the "Tris Brali" (Three Brothers) are typical examples of the architecture of medieval Riga. No. 17 is a 15th century house—the oldest surviving residential building in Latvia. The benches on either side of the gate end in a vertical stone slab bearing the "sign of the house". The ground floor of the house consisted originally of a single room with an open fireplace at its far end. Holes were cut through to the cellar and the upper stories, with a wooden hoist above the openings for the transport of goods into the warehouse. In 1687 a bakery was established here; it has been carefully restored.

The neighboring house (No. 19) was built in 1646, with a similar ground floor plan. The front of No. 21/23 has preserved its original form intact but the inside has been modernized.

Continue back along Maza Pils Street to Komjaunatnes Iela, turn left, then right at the first corner into Smilsu Street. At the end of this street you will find the Pulvera, the Gunpowder Tower. Instead of walking all the way to the Pulvera, you can turn left into Aldaru (Brewer) Street. At the end (No. 11 Torna Street) you come to the Zviedru Varti, Swedish Gate, the only surviving city gate of Riga. It was built in 1698 as an addition to the 13th century city walls, the adjoining bastion and the neighboring houses. The name "Swedish Gate" refers to this whole complex.

Returning to Smilsu Street, turn left and continue towards the Gunpowder Tower. This was first mentioned by the chroniclers in 1330. Erected on oak foundations, it was rebuilt in 1650, and now houses the Latvian Revolutionary Museum.

Opposite the Gunpowder Tower, turn right into Kaleju Street and walk down towards the river as far as the corner of Zirgu and Meistaru Streets. Turn down Meistaru Street to Amatu Street, pausing en route in front of Nos. 5 and 6. No. 5 now belongs to the Latvian Trades Union Council, and was formerly the headquarters of the Maza Gilde (Small Guild); No. 6 is now the home of the Philharmonia; it once housed the Liela Gilde (Great Guild). Both houses have been rebuilt several times through the 14th century "Munster Chamber" in No. 6, scene of many festivities, has been preserved. In 1521 a smaller chamber was added, the "Bridal Suite". It has many features typical of the late Gothic style.

Continuing down Amatu Street (away from Meistaru), turn right. A few more steps, and you come to 17 Junija Square and the magnificent Lutheran Cathedral (now a museum). Its building was begun under Bishop Albert in 1211 and 500 years were to pass before it was completed, which accounts for the mixture of architectural styles, including Romanesque and Gothic elements. The Russian Orthodox convent next to the Cathedral is still open and has 50 nuns at the moment. It also reportedly houses a Historical Museum (entrance from 4 Palasta Street) with good archeological and numismatic collections. The Cathedral itself has a world-renowned organ which still draws large crowds for weekly recitals. It is a marvellous 6,768-pipe structure, built by German craftsmen in 1884 and still one of the largest in the world.

From Palasta walk down Muzeya to Komjaunatnes Krastmala, the river quay. Turning left onto the promenade, look out for a plain residential building just before the corner of Lenin Street. This was once the mansion of Czar Peter the Great, who came to Riga in 1711 and lived here for a while. Originally the Czar had a hanging garden on the roof, where he exercised his "green fingers".

Continue along the quay as far as Marstalu Street (the third turning after Lenin Street); then, turning left into Marstalu Street, notice No. 21, a fine baroque mansion built in 1696 by Donnerstern, a rich burgher. Further up Marstalu Street, No. 2/4 is the former Reitern mansion (1685), also built by a well-to-do merchant. It still has its original 17th century facade, with a delicately ornamental portico.

Returning along Marstalu Street past the 18th century Protestant church, keep turning left, first into Great Kaleju Street then into Sarkanas Gvardes Street. Notice Nos. 7 and 11, and also No. 10 Vecpilsetas Street. These are 17th century warehouses. Their frontages are quite narrow but they go a long way back. On the ridge of the double roof you will see the drum of a hoist, and over each main entrance the relief of animals—camels, elephants and other quadrupeds. These served as identifying signs.

From Vecpilsetas Street you can walk down to Audeju Street, turn left, then right at the next corner into Skarnu Street and you will find yourself back in the Middle Ages. The first building on your right (24 Skarnu Street) is the Romanesque-Gothic Church of St. John, first mentioned by the chroniclers in 1297. As it was in a built-up area by the time it was enlarged in 1330 the buttresses had to be placed inside the church. Four alcoves were thus formed and they accommodated the side-altars. At the end of the 15th century the interior was decorated with star-vaults and the church's northern wall was heightened by a 100-foot-high, graduated tympanum. At the end of the 16th century the church was lengthened: to the Gothic nave a new part was added with three naves whose Tuscan pillars display Renaissance features. The baroque altar dates from the 18th century.

Next door to St. John's church, at 22 Skarnu Street is the Eka Convent, Ek's Home for Widows (Ek was a Mayor of Riga). Built in 1435 as a temporary shelter it was transformed into a dower house at the end of the 16th century. Its original structure, wooden staircase and former open fireplace have all survived. There is a memorial plaque to the charitable mayor on the facade.

The next building, 10/16 Skarnu Street, was erected in the 13th century. This is St. George's Church, one of the oldest religious edifices in Riga. In the 15th century it became a poorhouse, in the 16th a warehouse. At the end of the 17th century a vaulted passage was added running from the courtyard to the street.

Turning back along Skarnu Street you will see on your right a monumental church. Its main entrance is on Vecrigas Square. This is the 13th-century, late-Gothic Church of St. Peter, patron saint of Riga. Its elegant, 380-foot steeple was the tallest structure in the Old City until Intourist built the new 27-story Latvia Hotel right in the middle of this historic precinct, topping the steeple by three feet to the fury of many of Riga's citizens.

Between the palaces bordering Vecrigas Square there are glimpses of the Daugava embankment. Passing between the palaces, turn right, and the first corner is Lenin Street. Turn up this street and, after passing the Russian Drama Theater and reaching the corner of Padomju Boulevard, you have come to the edge of the Old City.

One final word on the Old City: if you have the chance, to stroll through it on a Sunday morning and you will be pleasantly surprised at how many churches are open for worship, and amazed how crowded they are. There are 18 functioning Lutheran churches and a Lutheran seminary, 14 Russian Orthodox churches and 16 Roman Catholic Churches still in use. As well as the Orthodox convent we have mentioned, there is a Catholic seminary with 30 students. A single synagogue serves Riga's 28,000-strong Jewish community, many of whom still speak Yiddish, which has practically died out in other parts of the Soviet Union.

Roaming the Boulevards

Pausing at the corner of Lenina and Padomju, notice at the beginning of Raina (Rainis) Boulevard the Statue of Liberty (also called the "Allegory of Latvia"). Turning left out of Lenin Street, walk into Bastejkalns Park (Bastion Hill) which was built on the site of the former fortifications. It has a fine waterfall, which is illuminated at night. On the far side from Padomju Boulevard, the park is bordered by the municipal canal.

Follow the canal north across Gorky Street into Kronvalds Garden, which has an attractive playground. The garden is flanked by Kronvalda Boulevard, a continuation of Padomju. The building on the corner of Gorky Street is the Latvian State Drama Theater, where Gorky supervised in person the production of *The Lower Depths,* in 1904.

On Eksporta, the continuation of Kronvalda Boulevard, notice the Vestura Garden on your right. Peter the Great himself helped to plant it in 1721. In 1873 the first Lativan national song festival was held here. The triumphal arch at the entrance was transferred from Lenin Street in 1935; it commemorates the Russian victory over Napoleon in 1812.

Leaving the Vestura Garden, walk back either along Eksporta or along the parallel Sverdlov Street to Kirov Street; then, turning left, continue south along Kirov which is the outer line of the park and boulevard ring around the Old City. The residential streets beyond it were mostly built in the second half of the 19th century.

No. 10 Gorky Street is the Latvian and Russian Museum of Fine Arts. Further down Kirov Street you'll pass Komunaru Park on your right. No. 34 Lenin Street the Latvian Supreme Court, is one of the 70 palaces which the Latvian architect Baumanis designed in the 19th century.

Continue along Kirov Street past Lenin Street to the Kirov Park which was laid out in 1816. The park has a rose garden, fountains, an openair concert-platform, cafés and playgrounds. Turn right out of Kirov Street into Kr. Barona Street. On the corner of Raina Boulevard is the Museum of Natural History. Raina Boulevard and the parallel Komunaru have several important institutions; the Conservatory on the corner of Raina and Kr. Barona, opposite the museum, the University at No. 13 Raina, the Aeroflot office on the corner of Lenin Street (Raina 11) and opposite, on Lenin Street itself, the Central Post Office. Raina 7 is the Riga City Soviet—the City Hall.

The two important features of Padomju Boulevard are the State Opera and Ballet Theater (No. 3) and, opposite, the Hotel Metropol.

The Pantheon of Riga

One of the moving, though rather grim, sights of the Latvian capital is the double Pantheon—the Bralu, Cemetery of "Brothers" (or Heroes) and the Rainis Cemetery.

At the bus terminal take No. 4 or 9 to Bralu Kapi, the Bralu Cemetery. The cemetery entrance is by the Berzu Aleja, which branches off on the left. When the road divides into three, continue along the middle one which takes you straight to the entrance of the Bralu Kapi. At its far end is a statue of a female figure symbolizing Latvia; many of the unknown soldiers who fell in battle are buried here.

As you leave the Bralu, you will see on your right the entrance to the Rainis cemetery. Here is the red marble tomb of the great Latvian poet; behind the Rainis monument several outstanding Latvian artists and writers are buried.

Riga's Parks and Resorts

The 500-acre Mezaparks—laid out in 1949—is Riga's main park. It contains a Zoo, an amusement park, the National Economic Exhibition and a Pioneer Railway run by children. There are several openair theaters and, on Kiso Ezers (Lake), a number of boathouses. The park is accessible from the city by water bus along the Daugava and the Kiso Lake: from the stop outside the two cemeteries by bus No. 30: and from the Old City by tram No. 11, which starts from Gorky Street and runs via Padomju and Kr. Barona.

The "Skansen", the openair Museum of Peasant Life on the shores of Lake Jugla, occupies almost 200 acres. Lake Jugla is linked by a canal with Lake Kiso; the two lakes are divided by Lenin Street. You can reach Jugla Park by taking buses No. 1, 18 or 19 at the bus terminal, getting off at the Balozi stop and walking down the road that branches off to the right. This brings you to the entrance to Jugla Park.

Riga's seaside beach, Jurmala, is a separate district of the capital, several miles from the city. Over 100 trains daily run there from the main station. Jurmala extends for ten miles along the shore of the Gulf of Riga as far as the Lielupe River; it's a two-mile-wide belt of pines and dunes, with sanatoria, hydrotherapy clinics, boarding houses, rest homes, children's camps and small weekend houses. Jurmala is recommended especially for those suffering from high blood pressure; it is also an ideal holiday spot. There is a branch of the Historical Museum here, an openair theater, and facilities for water sports.

Beyond Jurmala, three miles from the Gulf of Riga and about 27 miles from the capital, is the forest resort of Kemeri, which can also be reached by local trains from Riga.

Liepaja is an industrial center and an excellent winter harbor about 140 miles west of Riga. It is an ancient city, mentioned as long ago as 1263 as Portas Liva, because it was surrounded by groves of lime trees.

Kaliningrad

The region of Kaliningrad has, at time of writing, no Intourist facilities and is therefore not visitable as part of the normal tour programs. The area, between Lithuania and Poland, is a mild, lowland countryside, verging on the humid, with fertile soil and extensive forests. Although geographically isolated from the Russian Republic, it forms a part of it.

The city of Kaliningrad (population 345,000) once called Königsberg, was the seat of the dukes of Prussia, who were crowned there. During the 18th century it became the capital of East Prussia and a long-time a bone of contention between Russia and Germany. The city was captured from the Germans, in April 1945, after a two-month-long siege, during which almost all the old town was flattened, including the cathedral with its tomb of Kant. The new city, built in the residential northwestern suburbs, is an important industrial center, as well as being an icefree port, linked with the Baltic by means of a 26-mile canal.

Exploring Lithuania

Amber Land—or, to give its official Soviet name, the Lithuanian Soviet Socialist Republic, lies immediately south of Latvia on the Baltic, and also borders on the Kaliningrad Region of the Russian Republic, Poland, and Byelorussia. Its area is 25,173 square miles. Of its population of 3½ million, the majority are Lithuanians with Russians, Poles, Byelorussians, Latvians and Germans making up the remainder. The Lithuanian coastal area is for the most part a flat plain, but inland, especially to the east, there is some hilly ground.

The capital of ancient and modern Lithuania, Vilnius, lies among these eastern hills, on the river Neris, the second largest river in Lithuania. The Neris joins the country's main waterway, the Niemen, at Kaunas, the second largest Lithuanian city. Of the two rivers only the Niemen is navigable, from Kaunas to the sea.

Lithuania has a moderate, continental climate with a mean annual temperature of 43°F. The coastal climate is milder than that of the inland plain; July is the warmest month. Arctic currents, though, can bring frost even in June and autumn frosts can begin as early as September. August is the rainiest month in central Lithuania and October is the wettest along the coast.

At the moment, Vilnius is the only city in Lithuania where tourists are allowed to stay overnight. Intourist provides several 1-day trips to other locations: Kaunas, Trakai, Druskininkai, Rumsiskes.

Vilnius

Vilnius, the capital, occupies an area of 100 sq. miles. The city's name first appears in historical documents in 1323, although archeological findings indicate that the area was inhabited as early as the 9th century. By the 16th century Vilnius was one of the biggest and most important Eastern European cities.

The city is built on the terraces of the Neris Valley surrounded on the south, southeast and east by wooded hills (Paneriai, Rasos, Antakaliis). The river divides it into two. The southern, left-bank, side is the ancient and modern center of Vilnius, and contains the most interesting sights.

When you plan your route of exploration you can make Castle Hill your main landmark. This bastion, the Tower of Gediminas, flying the red-white-and-green flag of Lithuania, dates from the 14th century. It has recently been restored and now houses the Museum of Municipal History.

Castle Hill (Piles Kalnas) is situated at the confluence of the rivers Neris and Vilnele. The Old City stretches south from here, away from the river, with Gorkio (Gorky) Street as its axis. The main thoroughfare of modern Vilnius is Lenin Prospekt, running parallel with the Neris for over a mile from the foot of Castle Hill. (The Neris incidentally, although 300 miles long, is navigable only along a five-mile stretch above Vilnius).

Both Gorky Street and Lenin Prospekt start from Gedimino Square, the heart of Vilnius.

Exploring the Old Town

Vilnius has a large, interesting old quarter, constructed over 5 centuries. If properly restored, it could be one of the most interesting old towns in Europe. Unlike the old towns of Tallinn and Riga, it is not of Germanic origin. The old architecture is a synthesis of various Western European influences with that of Italian architects probably dominant. The old quarter is best explored on foot and it is highly recommended to spend a few hours just walking around. You should be able to see the most interesting places by following our suggested route. While you will inevitably get lost here and there, you should be able to follow the most important landmarks.

Your tour could start in Gedimino Square, dominated by a classical building reconstructed in 1784. Once the Roman Catholic cathedral, it now houses an art gallery, mainly old pictures gathered from various private and public collections. More interesting here than the actual pictures are the interiors and statues of the various chapels, especially St. Casimir's. The body of St. Casimir himself, one of the most revered of Lithuania's princes, has been removed and now lies in the St. Peter and St. Paul Church. On Sundays the cathedral is used for organ recitals or symphony concerts. The lonely tower in the square is a former bell tower of the cathedral. Its foundation dates from the 13th century.

From Gedimino Square take Tallat-Kelpsos Street to Kutuzov Square, where the late classical palace was the residence of Vilnius bishops. Later reconstructed in the Russian empirc style (1824–32), it became the residence of Russian governors and now houses the Artists' Union. From Kutuzov Square follow Universiteto Alley to the University area.

The historic University of Vilnius was founded as a Jesuit college in 1570 and in 1579 had its university charter granted by the Polish-Lithuanian King Istvan Bathory and by Pope Gregory XIII. Walk around the university precincts and visit its 3 main inner courtyards (Sarbievijaus, P. Skargos and M. Pocobuto). The latter courtyard contains a 17th-century former observatory. The arcades of the great courtyard give a Renaissance feel to the place. Among the university's distinguished students was the poet Mickiewicz.

The nearby St. John's church is now a museum of the university's history. From the church, make a left turn on Gorky Street and continue to Pilies Alley. Walk down this quaint street to St. Anna's church, a beautiful example of 16th-century Gothic architecture, still in use as a Catholic house of worship. Beside it stands the church of St. Bernard, another 16th-century Gothic building which also served as a fortress. No. 11 Pilies Street is a memorial museum to Adam Mickiewicz. Most of the architecture here is 17th and 18th century.

Return to Gorky Street via Biliuno Street. Notice the perfectly preserved Renaissance church of St. Michael (Svietimo 13), finished in 1625, which now houses a Museum of Architecture. Make a left turn in Gorky Street and continue as far as Antokolskio Street which passes through the old artisan district. You will see several small souvenir shops (Suvenyrai) and two restaurants housed in the buildings "Lokys" (No. 8) and "Amatininku Uzeiga" (No. 2). Look into courtyards in this quarter.

Return again to Gorky Street which is the main thoroughfare in the old town, to "Dailes Muziejus" (Museum of Fine Arts), 55 Gorky Street. Housed in the former City Hall, it contains a permanent exhibition of official modern Lithuanian art. The hall itself was rebuilt in 1783 in classical style. Notice the Doric columns.

Here, on and around Gorky Street, you will find many interesting monuments to Vilnius' past. On the right side of Gorky Street the massive, stylistically eclectic home of the Philharmonia (No. 69). No. 84 is an old restored building with cellars housing the restaurant *Medininkai.* No. 73 Gorky Street has an attractive rococo portico; the street ends at the Medininkai Gate, the only surviving city gate in Vilnius. The gate and wall (once 1½ miles long) were built early in the 16th century. The Medininkai is a typical example of Gothic and Renaissance architecture. Its traditional historic name is Ausros Vartai (The Gate of Dawn), and it houses a painting of Our Lady of Vilnius, famous since the 17th century. The shrine is located above the street in a small chapel, reached through a side door.

Return to Gedimino Square by walking back to Gorky Street and follow Gorky Street to Muziejaus Street. The modern building at No. 2 is "Dailes Parodu Rümai" (Art Exhibition Hall) which has several permanent exhibitions of contemporary art and a store where you can buy art and craft objects. Muziejaus Street starts from the Museum of Fine Arts and leads north towards the river. During World War II the Nazis established the Vilnius ghetto in this neighborhood, between Garelio, Traku and Muziejaus streets. Watch for interesting small streets on your left (Kretingos, Medininku, etc.) Turn right on Traku Street, right on University Alley. Reach Gediminas Square via Tallat-Kelpsos Street.

The only important historical site you have still to see is the Castle, which can be reached from the Square by taking a path leading up the hill. The present-day "castle" is a restored corner tower of the original castle, built by Lithuania's Grand Duke Gediminas in the 14th century. The roof of the tower offers a good view of the city and the tower contains an exhibition of Vilnius' history. At the bottom of the hill (Vrublevskio Street 1) stands the Museum of History and Ethnography, the main historical museum in the city.

The New Town

The more interesting places away from the center of the city can be visited either by bus or by taxi. Taxi transportation is inexpensive and for an extra fee they will wait. Taxis are most easily found in their offical parking places (32 in the city); they don't cruise looking for passengers.

If you want to do a tour on foot of parts of the new town, Gedimino Square is again a good starting point. Walk down Lenin Prospekt. On your right (No. 1) is a good souvenir store "Daile". On the opposite side of the street you will come to Chernyakhovsky Square, named after the general who commanded the troops that "liberated" Vilnius in 1944.

Continuing on Lenin Prospekt, pass the Vilnius Hotel and restaurant. Make a detour to the right on Vienuolio Alley, past the popular restaurant-night-club *Dainava* (No. 4), to the new Opera and Ballet Theater. Return to Lenin Prospekt and continue past a small square with a statue of the writer Zcrmaite to Lenin Square. This is Vilnius' Tyburn: after the

Belorussian and Lithuanian peasant revolts of 1863 against Russian rule, the leaders of the uprising were executed here.

Make a left turn on Kudirkos Street and climb up Tauras hill, from where there is a good view of the city. One of the buildings on the hilltop is the Wedding Palace, where marriages are performed. Go left on Kalinausko Street, turn left on Roziu Street and down the stairs to Cvirkos Square. Kapsuko Street will lead you back to Lenin Prospekt. The tour is about two miles.

One of the most imposing monuments in Vilnius is the gleaming white Baroque building of the St. Peter and St. Paul Church. You can reach it be walking from Gedimino Square toward the river. As you cross the Vilnele, with Olandu Street behind you, you will see the church. The original building dates from the 14th century; it was renovated in 1668–84 and is still used for worship today. It is the most characteristic example of Baroque in Lithuania with a splendid interior on which 200 artists worked under the direction of the Italian masters Galli and Peretti. It contains more than 2,000 life-size statues and reliefs as well as the tomb of St. Casimir.

Vingis Park is Vilnius' favorite recreation area. You get there by turning from Lenin on to Sierakausko Street and then turning right into Ciurlionio Street.

Trakai, Kaunas, Klaipeda, and Druskininkai

Trakai, some 18 miles from Vilnius, lies on the route to Kaunas, the temporary capital of Lithuania between the two World Wars. The castle (dating from 13th century) now houses the Ethnographic Museum. Trakai lies on the shore of a picturesque lake where international swimming and sailing events are regularly held. There is also a tourist center, about which Intourist in Vilnius will provide you with detailed information. Boat rides are available.

Kaunas has a population of 353,000 and is an important industrial and cultural center with particularly good theaters. Architecturally, it is not nearly as interesting as Vilnius. The old city has 11th-century castle ruins at the confluence of the rivers Niemen and Neris and an old city hall now used as a wedding palace. The city hall square has several old restored houses. The Gothic basilica (on the bank of the Niemen) is worth seeing.

Ciurlionis Museum houses the work of the most famous Lithuanian artist, M. K. Ciurlionis, who painted and also composed music at the turn of the century. It is claimed by some that his art influenced Kandinsky and thus contributed to the development of abstract art. The permanent exhibit is very interesting and any art lover should visit the museum. The nearby historical museum is also worth visiting. An added attraction is the carillon recital at 11 A.M. on Sundays and Holidays. The residential quarter of Zaliakalnis (Green Mountain) has a funicular linking it with the city.

Klaipeda with a population of 169,000 is an important sea and river port on the Baltic, at the mouth of the Akmene (Dange) River. A canal links it with the mouth of the Niemen. It is the main harbor in Lithuania and an important fishing center. It also produces ornaments and other articles in amber.

From Klaipeda you can make an excursion by bus to Palanga (18 miles to the north), a popular seaside resort.

Druskininkai is a small resort on the River Niemen about 100 miles from Vilnius. Intourist sometimes brings visitors here for a few days' relaxation.

PRACTICAL INFORMATION FOR THE BALTIC REPUBLICS

 WHEN TO COME. To **Estonia:** Definitely in the summer, during the "White Nights" in June. Riga (**Latvia**) should be visited early in August for the Festival of Song. The climate is varied but at the end of July and the beginning of August there is little wind and the sea is at its warmest though it never rises above 60°–62°F (17°–18°C). In **Lithuania** July is the warmest month and the only time when you may find the weather too hot. August is the rainiest in Central Lithuania and October has most rain on the coast.

 HOW TO GET THERE. You can reach **Tallinn** in about 6 hours by train from Leningrad (1 hr. 15 mins. by air) and 19 hours from Moscow (3 hrs. 30 mins. by air). There are connections to all major Soviet cities. Finnish and Soviet steamers sail regularly on the Tallinn-Helsinki Line. You can also travel by car or coach from Leningrad. Tartu is 3–4 hrs. by train from Tallinn, 3 hrs. 15 mins. by bus, 1 hr. by plane (summer only).

Riga is 16 hrs. 45 mins. from Moscow by train (1 hr. 35 mins. by plane), and there are air connections with most other Soviet cities. You can travel from Tallinn by plane, train or Intourist coach.

Vilnius is 14 hrs. 10 mins. by train from Moscow, 1 hr. 15 mins. by plane. From Poland, it can be reached via Grodno and Minsk.

 WHAT TO SEE. Tallinn: The citadel and cathedral, the Church of St. Olaf, the medieval houses in Lai Street and Pikk Street, the Town Hall, the Church of St. Nicholas, Kadriorg Palace.

Tartu: The Castle and the Cathedral, the University.

Riga: The museums, the old town, Riga Castle, the Church of St. James (or Jacob), St. Peter's Church, the old rooms in the Great Guildhall, the 24 storehouses, the Cathedral organ.

Vilnius: Old town, Cathedral, Gediminas's Castle (ruins), St. Anne's Church, Baroque residences, the Church of St. Peter and St. Paul.

Kaunas: The carillon, the Gothic Basilica, the Town Hall.

 HOTELS. Tallinn: *Hotel Viru,* Viru Square, New, Scandinavian-style, high-rise hotel (23 floors) on edge of old city in down-town Tallinn. Rated deluxe. Finnish-built and furnished. One of the best hotels in the Soviet Union. Good food. Nice views from top rooms and restaurant.

Hotel Tallinn, 27 Gagarin St. 114 rooms. Rating: first class. Service and food are good. A modern, 5-story hotel.

Also: *Palace,* 3 Voidu Väljak; *Europa,* 24 Viru Street.

Riga: *Riga* (Intourist), 22 Padomju. 300 large rooms, centrally located; outer rooms, near main square, get noisy traffic din. Hotel has aged. Food only fair. *Latvia,* (also Intourist establishment), new 1980. 700 rooms, 27-floor skyscraper, 1st class, in Old City.

Also: *Metropol,* 36 Padomju Bulvar (with restaurant); Daugava, 38 Kugyu Street.

Vilnius: Best is *Vilnius,* 20 Lenin Prospekt, then *Gintaras,* 14 Sodu Street, first class, modern, good restaurant. *Draugyste,* 84 Ciurlionis Street, rarely available for Intourist guests although probably Vilnius' best hotel.

Also-rans: *Neringa,* 23 Lenin Prospekt (small), old, good, and *Turistas,* 14 Ukmerges Street.

 RESTAURANTS. It is generally agreed that the restaurants and the service are better in the Baltic Republics than anywhere else in the USSR. Each of the three republics has its own specific cuisine; ask the waiter for advice.

Hors d'oeuvres are very good, usually the best part of the meal. Soup and local specialties also will be good, plain meat dishes might be disappointing. Order several different hors d'oeuvres plates to share.

Local specialties in Estonia *"sult"* (jellied veal), *"taidetud basikarind"* (roast stuffed shoulder of veal and *"rossolye"* (vinaigrette with herring and beets). In Latvia: meat patties, *Alexander Torte* (raspberry-filled pastry strips). In Lithuania *"skilandis"* (like Canadian bacon) is a local snack meat, in summer cold soup "salti barsciai". Various patato-based dishes are very popular: *"oepelinai"* (dumplings), *"bulvinai blynai"* (potato pancakes), *"vedarai"* (potato sausage). Also various ravioli-like dishes—*"virtinukai"*—are popular.

Hotel restaurants vary throughout the area, but those in new hotels are generally better than hotels in other parts of the Soviet Union. In Tallinn several US/European-style bars (*baar* in Estonian) have opened, serving Western drinks for roubles, but they are pricy. See below.

Riga. *Pearl of the Sea* (*Juras Perle* in Latvian), on the beachfront at Jurmala resort. Beautiful location jutting out over the sand, overlooking Riga Bay. Good food. Western-style floor show and dancing. Be sure to reserve through Intourist in advance. A modest charge is made for reservation. There is a cover charge for the floor show. Try seafood fish soups. More expensive than most Soviet restaurants, but not high-priced by world standards.

Blow Wind! (*Put, Vejinii* in Latvian), around the corner from the Dom Cathedral, off 17th of June Square. One of the best restaurants in the Soviet Union, with excellent cooking, intimate atmosphere, good service. Try *okroshka,* a milk soup with onions, herbs, cucumbers sour cream; *mestinsh,* a Latvian Lemonade-honey drink; and any entrée the waitress recommends. No entry without reservation made through Intourist. Do it when you arrive in Riga. There is a charge for the reservation. Prices are higher-than-average for USSR. Well worth it.

Univermag Restaurant, 1½ blocks from Riga Hotel. Latvian specialties. Good food. Dancing.

Apollo Café, young people's gathering place, with Latvia's best combo, the Rigonda.

Staburags, 55 Suvorov Street, is good for fish specialties.

Others: *Astoria,* 16 Audeyu St; *Kavkaz,* 13 Merkelya Street; *Tallinn,* 27 Gorky Street; *Moskva,* 53 Kirov Street; *Daugava,* 7 Stuvkas Street. *Health restaurants:* 65 Kirov Street and 9 Suvorov Street.

Tallinn. *Viru Hotel* restaurant, top floor, lovely view, very nice food. Bar with western selection of drinks.

Vanatoomis across from City Hall on Town Square, in the cellar. Very good Estonian food, attractive decor, good service. In all, a treat. (There are other cellar restaurants near and in the old town, also recommended, but put Vanatoomis high on your list.)

Others: *Flower Pavilion,* a café-restaurant on outskirts, with excellent sandwiches and pastries; *Gloria,* 2 Murivahe Street; *Kevad* 2 Lomonosov Street; and in Pirita, a suburb by the sea, *Pirita,* 1 Merivälya Voidu Väliak.

Cafés: Tallinn, 48 Hariu Street (with a garden, on Hariu Hill); *Moskva,* 10 Voidu Väljak; *Energia,* Lenin Street.

Bars: Munde, cover charge of around 2 roubles include one tiny *Kokteil.* More *Kokteily* cost at least 1 rouble 50 kopeks a shot, and there's a queue to get in. You can buy tickets in advance—before 4 P.M. you stand a chance!

Vilnius. *Gintaras,* Sodu 14; *Draugyste,* M.K. Ciurlionis 86; *Erfurtas,* Architektu 19; *Vilnius,* Lenin 20. All except *Erfurtas* are in the hotels of the same name. These restaurants have a dance band at night.

For old town atmosphere: *Medininkai* M. Gorky 84 and *Lokys,* M. Antokolskio 8. Both are located in old restored buildings with rooms on several floors including cellars. *Lokys* serves moose and wild boar meat, highly recommended.

Food is also served in night clubs: *Dainava* Vienuolio 4; *Erfurtas* (night-club is separate from the main dining room), and *Saltinelis,* Zirmunu 106.

CULTURAL ACTIVITIES. Tallinn: Russian Drama Theater (5 Voidu Väljak). State Opera and Ballet Theater (4 Estonia Puiestee). Openair musical theater (Lauluväljak), in the Kadriorg Park. In *Tartu:* Vanemuyne Theater.

Riga Cathedral for concerts and organ recitals. Russian Drama Theater, Lenin Street. Latvian State Drama Theater, corner of Kronvalda Boulevard and Gorky Street. Conservatory, corner of Raina and Kr. Barona Streets. Academy of Art, Komunaru Street. State Opera and Ballet Theater, 3 Padomju Boulevard. Openair theater. Mezaparks (scene of the Song Festivals). *Liepaja* has two theaters.

Vilnius: Opera and Ballet Theater Vienuolio; good opera in season. Philharmonia, M. Gorky 69 symphony and chamber concerts etc. Lithuanian Drama Theater (J. Basanaviciaus 13); Picture Gallery (Cathedral) for organ recitals and orchestral concerts on Sundays; Puppet theater "Lele" (Arkliu 5); Openair Theater (Vingis Park). Kaunas has several theaters.

MUSEUMS. Tallinn: *Gallery of the Estonian Artists' Union,* 6 Voidu Väljak. *State Museum of Natural History,* 29 Lai Street (open 12–7, except Tues; closed on the last day of every month).

City Museum, 70 Pikk Street (open 11–6, except Tues; Sat 11–5).

Historical Museum of the Estonian Academy of Sciences, 17 Pikk Street, (open 12–6, except Wed: Tues. 12–4).

State Fine Arts Museum, Kadriorg Palace, (open 12–7 daily, except Tues.

Tartu has *six museums*—ethnographic, literary, geological, zoological, fine arts and archeological. Parnu has a *local museum* with a rich collection of Stone Age artifacts. Here, too, is the *Lydia Koidula Museum,* in the home of Estonia's great poetess (1843–86).

Riga: *Historical Museum of the Latvian Republic.* In the castle.
State Museum of Fine Arts, also in the castle.
Rainis Literary Museum, in the castle.

State Latvian and Russian Fine Arts Museum, 10/a Gorky Street. Paintings, graphics, sculpture.

Latvian State Museum of Natural History, 34 Kr. Barona Street, the oldest in the Baltic Area.

"*Skansen*" (officially: Open Air State Museum of 17th–19th Century Peasant Life), on the shore of Lake Jugla.

Ljepaja has a *local museum.*

Vilnius: *Museum of History and Ethnography,* Vrublevskio 1; *Fine Arts Museum,* M. Gorky Street 55; *Picture Gallery* Gediminas Square; *Art Exhibition Hall* Muziejaus 2.

Kaunas: *M.K. Ciurlionis Gallery; Historical Museum* Donelaitis Street; *Velniu Muziejus* (collection by a private artist of mainly folk art of devil images). Stained glass gallery located in former Russian Orthodox church, (Laisves Blvd.).

Rumsiskes: "Skansen", open-air museum of Lithuanian peasant life.

 SHOPPING. Amber is the best buy in the Baltic Republics, especially in Lithuania, but check on export restrictions. You may enjoy browsing around the following stores: **Tallinn:** the *Central Department Store,* 2 Lomonosov Street (gifts and folk art), also at Voidu Väljak 8 (closed on Sundays), 27 Pikk Street (closed on Sundays), and 19 Viru Street (closed on Mondays). For *souvenirs:* 8 Raekoya Plats (Town Hall Square). The hard-currency shops in Estonia are called "Turist". A must in Tallinn is a bottle of "Stary Tallinn" (Old Tallinn) Liqueur.

Riga: *Souvenirs:* 12 Lenin Street. *Arts and crafts:* 52 Lenin Street. *Maksla Art Gallery,* 20 Padomju Boulevard.

Vilnius: *"Daile",* 1 Lenin Prospekt; *Souvenirs:* 5 Lenin Prospekt, 6 Antokolskio Street. Amber, linen goods and local crafts are good buys.

Kaunas: *"Daile",* in the old Town Hall Square.

 USEFUL ADDRESSES. Tallinn: *Intourist:* 27 Gagarin Street, 3 Voidu Väljak *Rail ticket reservations:* 10 Oleviyagi Street. *Air reservations:* 10 Voidu Väljak. (There is a half-hourly Aeroflot bus service from here to the airport.) *Central Post Office:* 20 Suur Karya Street. *Central Telegraph Office:* 9 Vene Street (open 24 hours). Long-distance calls. 9 Vene Street.

Riga: *Intourist:* 22 Padomju Boulevard. *Railway tickets:* 2 Suvorov Street, 6 Smilsu Street. *Aeroflot City Office:* 11 Raina Boulevard. *Bus terminus:* 13 Janvara Street, near the central station. *Boat landing stage:* Balasta Damvis *Central Post Office* (long-distance calls): 21 Lenin Street. Central Telegraph Office: 33 Lenin Street.

Vilnius: *Intourist:* 20 Lenin Prospekt. *Aeroflot City Office:* 21 Lenin Prospekt. *Railway station:* Gelezinkelio Street (corner of Komjaunimo).

THE UKRAINE AND MOLDAVIA

Breadbasket of the USSR

The Ukrainian Soviet Socialist Republic borders on Hungary, Czechoslovakia, Poland, Romania, and the Soviet Republics of Byelorussia, Moldavia and the Russian Federal Republic. The Black Sea forms its southern frontier. The capital of the Ukraine is Kiev; a part of the so-called Soviet Riviera on the Black Sea belongs to it, but you will find a description of this resort area in the chapter devoted to the Crimea and Southern Russia.

With an area of 232,046 square miles and a population of almost 50 million in 1980, the Ukraine is the second largest in population and the third in size in the Soviet Union. Forty-six precent of the population is urban; three-quarters are Ukrainian, the remainder Russians, Jews and others. Ethnographically the Ukrainians are Eastern Slavs. They have a strong national consciousness and an independent history.

Ever since the Kievan period of Russian history, the Ukrainian regional dialect has had distinctive features, and Ukrainian is now a separate language—although Russian is spoken in all the big cities except Lvov.

It was in Kiev that Christianity first found a foothold in Russia when Prince Vladimir had his people collectively baptized in the river Dnieper in 988 AD. After the Tatar invasion and the decline of the Kiev Principality (13th and 14th centuries), the Ukraine was held by Poland and Russia, with sovereignty repeatedly changing hands; it was devastated, sometimes completely and sometimes in parts, by the Crimean Tatars. In the mid-17th century the Cossacks, the most militant of the Ukrainian population, led by their Hetman, Bogdan Khmelnitsky, won independence from Poland and established their own state, occupying the central part of the modern Ukraine. In 1654 the new state was annexed to

Muscovy. Ukrainian nationalism, with its demands for autonomy, had a strong revival early in the 20th century. During the Civil War of 1918–22, Germans, white Russians, Communists and various separatist groups struggled for control of the rich Ukrainian agricultural lands. Proclaimed the Ukrainian Soviet Socialist Republic in December 1917 it was one of the four original republics to form the Soviet Union in 1922. In 1939 the western part of the Ukraine, together with Lvov, until then a part of Poland, was returned to the republic, followed in 1945 by Transcarpathia, which had belonged to Hungary and Czechoslovakia. In 1954 the Crimea was transferred from the Russian Federal Republic and annexed to the Ukraine.

The huge Ukrainian Soviet Republic can be roughly divided into three zones: the forests bordering on Byelorussia in the north; the wooded steppe with oak and beech forests; and the treeless steppe zone with its fertile black soil. The climate is much warmer than that of central Russia. Both industry and agriculture are well-developed; there are also rich deposits of coal, iron ore, natural gas and oil.

The major cities are Kiev, Kharkov, Lvov, Dnepropetrovsk, Lugansk, Uzhgorod, and Mukachevo.

Exploring the Ukraine

Kiev, the capital of the Ukrainian Soviet Socialist Republic, has a population of over two million and is one of the most important industrial and cultural centers in the Soviet Union. It lies on both sides of the Dnieper River; the right bank (western) is hilly, the left an extensive flat plain. Kiev has developed rapidly in recent decades, absorbing several suburbs, and on the eastern bank of the river a whole new industrial area, the Darnitsa, has sprung up. Machinery plants are the chief industry, with light industries and chemicals coming second in importance. Kiev is also a major road and rail junction, a great river port and a busy airport; and a traditional cultural center with excellent colleges and universities. It is the seat of the Ukrainian Academy of Sciences and numerous research institutes. Its museums are richly endowed, and the city abounds in theaters, opera, ballet and other cultural institutions and entertainments. It is one of the most ancient of Russian cities; in the chronicles it is described as the "Mother of Russian cities."

Kiev suffered severely during World War II; many irreplaceable architectural and art treasures were destroyed and the city center was systematically demolished. Since 1945 the wounds have been treated and the monuments that could be saved have been restored. Today Kiev is the most popular tourist city after Moscow and Leningrad, and attracts large numbers of foreign visitors.

Tours of Kiev—First Tour

Exploring Kiev is best done in four instalments. The starting point of the first tour is the Hotel Dnieper, where many Intourist groups are lodged. It stands at the eastern end of Kreshchatik, Kiev's main boulevard; its entrance is on Lenkomsomol Square, a central location from which the main streets branch off like the points of a star. Opposite is the continuation of the Kreshchatik, the Vladimirsky Spusk, leading down to the river bank; the street to the north, named after the Heroes of the Revolution, leads to the famous St. Andrew's Church, and Kirov Street, leading south, also starts from this square. Lenkomsomol Square is an important traffic center and the terminus of several tram, trolley-bus and bus lines. The Kreshchatik subway station is nearby. An under-pass with several branches crosses beneath the square. Opposite the Hotel Dnieper, left of the Vladimirsky Spusk, you can see the building of the Philharmonia (1882).

If you are staying at the Hotel Moskva, you can walk down to the Kreshchatik and turn right, and you will soon reach the Hotel Dnieper. From the old Intourist Hotel on Lenin Street you can get to the Dnieper Hotel via Lenin Street; and from the Hotel Ukraine, via Shevchenko Boulevard, walking downhill and then along the Kreshchatik.

The main Street of the Ukrainian capital and its busiest thoroughfare are in a valley (there was once a deep ditch along here) and hills rise steeply on the left-hand side.

Clinging to the hill on this side is the 16-story Hotel Moskva; alongside the hotel October Revolution Street (Zhovtnevoi Revolutsii in Ukraini-an) leads up to the top of the hill where the government buildings are situated. At the beginning of October Revolution Street, already a steep slope, you will find the October Palace of Culture. Constructed in 1838–42 as a finishing school for young ladies of the nobility, it was restored and enlarged in 1953–57; its main hall seats over 2,000 and is chiefly used for concerts.

On the other side, the Kreshchatik broadens into Kalinin Square, once the site of the southeastern gate of the city wall, built by Yaroslav the Wise. House No. 2 was once the Noblemen's Diet; today it is a Teachers' Club. The large and elaborate building on the corner of the square and Kreshchatik is the main Post Office.

On the left of the Kreshchatik, Karl Marx Street leads uphill, with the Tchaikovsky Conservatory on the corner. If you turn into Karl Marx Street and follow it up the hill, you come to Ivan Franko Square. Here stands the Ukrainian Drama Theater (built in 1898 and named after the great Ukrainian poet), which has followed the ideas and spirit of the Moscow Arts Theater in its presentation of modern Ukrainian plays.

Back down on the Kreshchatik, you will notice that the odd-numbered side has been made into a sort of parkway with trees, flower beds and benches. The buildings on this side are mostly apartment houses, cine-mas, restaurants and hotels—while the other side consists mainly of public buildings and offices. The Kreshchatik underground station (cen-ter of the public transport network) is on the odd-numbered side; the largest restaurant in Kiev is in the same building. There is an escalator leading to the booking hall of the Metro (it costs five kopeks to use and this also gives you access to the trains). The escalator on the far side travels a much longer distance and takes you to the hill that rises above the river bank and forms Kiev's administrative district.

Continuing along the Kreshchatik, with its uniformly designed facades, you come to the passage which links the Kreshchatik and Zam-kovetskaya Street. The entrance is under an arcade between two wings of a huge building. The building on the far side of the Kreshchatik (with the tall antenna) is the Kiev Radio and Television. On the passage side are Kiev's best shops, among them the Children's Department Store (Nos. 15–17). Sverdlov Street starts on the opposite side; carrying on farther along the Kreshchatik you come to the Ukrainian Ministry of

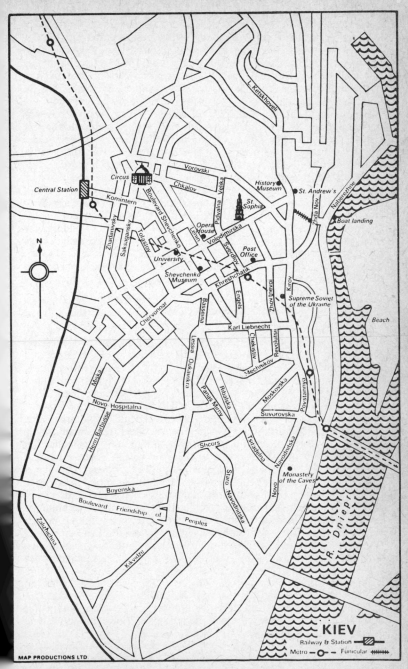

Central Station

Komintern

Circus

Vorovski

Chkalov

Boulevard Shevchenko

Pidvalna Velika

History Museum

St. Andrew's

St Sophia

Izda Nov.

Naberezhne

Boat landing

Zhdanivsky

Suksagansky

Tolstoy

Lenin

Opera House

Volodimirska

Sverdlov

Post Office

University

Shevchenko Museum

Khreshchatik

Zhov Jnevoi

Kirov

Supreme Soviet of the Ukraine

Beach

Chervonar

Bassenna

Engels

Karl Liebknecht

Miska

Oukrainka

Lessia

Panus Mirny

Ribalska

Chekistiv

Revolutsu

Mechnikov

Moskovska

Povstannya

Novo Hospitalna

Henri Barbusse

Suvorovska

Navodnitska

Shcors

Tsiradelna

Staro Nawodnitska

Novo

Monastery of the Caves

Boyenska

Boulevard Friendship of Peoples

Zaliznichna

Kikvidze

R. Dnieper.

KIEV

Railway & Station   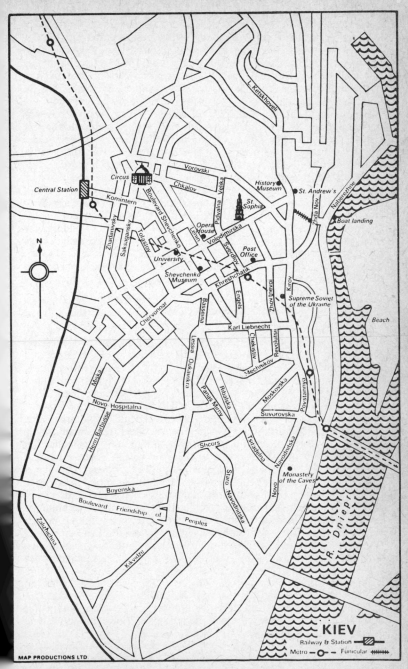

Metro —O— — Funicular

MAP PRODUCTIONS LTD

Culture and then the tall City Council building. A little farther on is the Central Department Store, at the corner of Lenin Street.

Lenin Street climbs the hill rather steeply. Opposite the Central Department Store is the Pervomaiskaya Hotel. No. 5 Lenin Street houses the Russian Drama Theater, which is named after the Ukrainian poetess Lesya Ukrainka. Next comes the Teatralnaya Hotel, and across the street, on the corner of Pushkin Street, the technical bookshop; No. 26 is the Intourist Hotel.

Returning to the Kreshchatik you will see an impressive stairway leading up the hillside to the Druzhba cinema. Then you come to the vast Central Market (Krity Rinok). You are now in Bessarabskaya Square, one of the most important in Kiev. The avenue on the right is the wide Shevchenko Boulevard, with Lenin's statue at the entrance.

The Kreshchatik continues as Krasnoarmeiskaya (Red Army) Street, another busy main thoroughfare. No. 12 is a permanent exhibition hall for Ukrainian artists. Passing Saksagansky Street you come to the Operetta Theater and then the massive block of the Central Stadium and Sports Palace. It has a covered swimming pool as well as facilities for ice hockey, handball, tennis, football and athletics. The Druzhba Narodov (Friendship of the Peoples) Boulevard, which starts here, leads to the mile-long Paton Bridge. This bridge links the historical quarters of Kiev with the Darnitsa district on the far side.

Second Tour

Leaving the Hotel Dnieper, turn right into Kirov Street. Next to the hotel is the sociology department of the Ukrainian Academy of Sciences. The building also houses the Institute for the History of Literature and the ground floor is the Academic Bookshop. Still on Kirov Street, climb the slopes of the hill that rises above the Dnieper. The right side of Kirov Street is built-up, while the left is a series of large, well-kept parks. No. 1 Kirov Street, set in one of these parks, is the Republican Library. On the right-hand side, No. 6 Kirov Street, is the Museum of Ukrainian Art. Built in 1898–1900 on the lines of an ancient Greek temple with huge granite steps and a six-columned portico, the museum has a collection of Ukrainian art of the 15th to 19th centuries and of Soviet artists.

Next you pass the headquarters of the Ukrainian Council of Ministers and, a few hundred yards further up, on the left, the Supreme Soviet of the Ukraine with its entrance in the adjoining square. No. 5 across the street is the former Marinsky Palace designed by Rastrelli and built in 1747 as a local residence for the Czar. The upper wooden story, which burned down in 1819, was reconstructed in 1870 and has survived in its 18th-century baroque form. Outside the palace stands the memorial to the Civil War, with black marble and red granite decorating the mass grave.

On your left, in a park, is the entrance (No. 3 Kirov Street) to the Dynamo Stadium. The other side of the stadium faces on to the Petrovsky Promenade. A bridge divides the former Petrovsky Park into two parks; the northern part is called Pioneer Park and the lower, southern part, Pervomaisky.

In Karl Liebknecht Street (the sidestreet opposite the Supreme Soviet), you will see the headquarters of the Znaniye Educational Society, and in Rosa Luxemburg Street (Nos. 15–17), the Youth Theater. Chekist

Street crosses both these streets further west; here is the Ukrainian Foreign Ministry, and the headquarters of the Composers' Union. The writers, too, have their home nearby at No. 2 Ordzhonikidze Street, which runs parallel with Liebknecht Street towards the Kreshchatik. The editorial offices of several literary reviews are also here. Ordzhonikidze Street passes behind the Ukrainian Drama Theater (the Ivan Franko Theater), and you can see a statue of Ivan Franko himself by Suprun (1956) in the square beyond the theater.

Reaching the end of Kirov Street you come to Moskovskaya Street on your right. This leads eventually into Lesya Ukrainka. On your left, at the corner of Kirov Street and Sichneve Povstannya Street, stands the monument to the Arsenal Workers, commemorating their dead in the Civil War. Sichneve Povstannya Street is named after the January 1917 rising in Kiev. Suvorov Street begins on the right; its left side is a large park in memory of the dead of the Second World War. A street called Dneprovsky Spusk leads downhill on the left from the park. Here stands the monument to the Unknown Soldier.

Monastery of the Caves

On the right of the street named after the January Rising, Citadel Street leads to the Pecherskaya Lavra, the Monastery of the Caves. Nearby is the Museum of the History of the Theater.

The Monastery of the Caves, founded in 1051 by the monks Anthony and Theodosius, comprises a whole series of churches, cathedrals and monuments. Outside the complex of buildings stands the ancient church of the Redeemer of Berestovo, built early in the 12th century by Prince Vladimir Monomakh as a burial place for the princes of Kiev. The founder of Moscow, Yury Dolgoruky, was buried here in 1157. The church is built in characteristic late 11th- and early 12th-century style: a crossdome with six pillars. Its eastern wing, which faces the Dnieper, was added in 1640–4. In 1947 a marble sarcophagus was installed here in memory of Yury Dolgoruky.

The Pecherskaya Lavra is the most important and most famous historical site in Kiev. Most of its buildings have been turned into museums, though some still function as churches. They include the Trinity Church, built over the entrance gate (today 21 Sichneve Povstannya Street), which dates from 1108, and has 18th-century wooden iconostases; the walls of the Upper Monastery, built between 1698 and 1701, stretch from this gateway around the compound. Another gateway is topped by the five-domed All Saints' Church (17th century). The main court of the Upper Monastery centers around the ruins of the Assumption Cathedral, built 1073–89 and destroyed by the Nazis in 1941. The majority of the surrounding houses are 18th century. The bell tower, the highest in Russia (316 ft.), was built in 1731–45; it has been completely restored and the dome regilded. Local ledgend speaks of the belfry being built by 12 brothers so saintly that heaven aided them—as they worked, the bell tower sunk deeper and deeper into the earth, needing no scaffolding, and when it was finished, it rose again to its full height in a single night!

Of the various museums in the Monastery, the Historical Museum is particularly interesting. Among its exhibits are 17th to 20th-century fabrics, 16th to 19th-century handicrafts, wood carvings, metal work, ceramics—all examples of Ukrainian folk art. Highlights are the delicately painted *krashenki,* Easter eggs.

The St. Anthony Caves contain 73 tombs and three underground churches. In the St. Theodosius Caves there are 47 tombs and another three churches. The two series of caves are quite separate from each other, and are reached by way of a covered gallery. The belfry of the St. Theodosius or Further Caves was designed and built in the 18th century by the architect Stefan Kovnir. The most famous tomb is that of the chronicler Nestor, who died in 1115.

Near the walls of the refectory are the graves of the Cossack leaders Kochubei and Iskra, executed by Ivan Mazepa in 1708.

If you leave the Lavra and walk along Citadel Street you come to Novo-Navodnitskaya Street, which leads to Staro- Navodnitskaya Street and then on to the broad highway of the People's Friendship.

Cross the highway and you will find yourself in the Botanical Garden, which covers some 500 acres and affords beautiful views of the Dnieper and Kiev itself. Here, too, on the bank of the Dnieper, you will see the ruins of the Vydubetsky Monastery. According to archeologists, there was a river ferry here in earliest times. In 1070–77 Vsevolod Yaroslavich, Prince of Kiev, had a monastery built on this spot; only the western side of a part of it, St. Michael's Cathedral (1070–88), has survived, but there are fine murals. In 1701, following a landslide, St. George's Church, a five-domed masterpiece of Ukrainian architecture, was built in its place. The refectory (early 18th century) and the three-storied belfry (1730's–40's) are also interesting. Between the two churches lies the grave of Konstantin Usinsky, the eminent Ukrainian educationalist.

From the Paton Bridge you can return to the hotel by tram or trolleybus. Or you can walk along the quay until you reach the Dneprovsky Spusk, mentioned earlier. This is one of the sloping roads leading along the riverside parks. Askold's Grave, erected in 1809–10, is a rotunda where, according to legend, a Prince of Kiev was buried in 1882. This is perhaps the most picturesque spot in Kiev and a favorite promenade.

One of the park roads leading north will take you to the openair theater; its sloping amphitheater seats 4,000 people. It is used for musical and dance shows and rallies. In the summer there are film shows. Nearby is the Kukushka openair restaurant.

Descending to the quay again, you can cross by the footbridge (Peshekhodny Most or Parkovy Most) to the parks on Trukhanov Island and the city's bathing beach. Near the bridge is the monument built by Molensky in 1802–8 to commenorate the charter of the city of Kiev.

You can go back to the Hotel Dnieper by ascending the Vladimirsky Spusk. Nearby, overlooking the river, is the St. Vladimir Monument. Vladimir holds aloft a cross commemorating the conversion of Russia to Christianity. The monument was erected in 1853.

Third Tour—St. Sophia's Cathedral

To explore the northern and western sections of Kiev, start out along the Street of Revolutionary Heroes walking west. Turn left into Chelyuskintsev Street, and you will find the Planetarium at No. 17 housed in a former Roman Catholic church. This street leads to Kalinin Square. Mikhailovsky and Kalinin Street will take you to Bogdan Khmelnitsky Square, with the statue of the Cossack Hetman who freed the Ukraine from the Poles and later subjugated it to the Russian state. St. Sophia's Cathedral stands behind the statue; like the major part of the Monastery of the Caves, St. Sophia's has also now become a museum.

The cathedral was dedicted in 1037 by Prince Yaroslav the Wise as a mark of gratitude for the battle he won against the Pechenegs, an invading tribe from the east. Here the first Russian library was founded and the earliest chronicles were written. St. Sophia is a stylistic combination of the traditional wooden church and the principles of stone building, with interesting mosaics and frescos in the central part and on the main dome. In the northeast part is the marble tomb where Yaroslav the Wise was buried in 1054. The iconostasis dates from the 18th century.

The bell tower (256 feet) was erected between 1744 and 1852. The Zavorovsky Gate is the main entrance to the Metropolitan's residence and is decorated with elaborate stucco ornamentation. The cathedral's surrounding wall was built in the 1740s. The whole complex is now a museum which also displays architectural models of other ancient Russian towns and local archeological discoveries. The entire precincts, as a "ancient monument," are maintained under a preservation order.

Leaving the Sofisky Sobor (cathedral) walk along Streletsky and Polupanov Streets until you reach a park-like square containing the ruins of the Golden Gate, once a part of Kiev's fortifications. The gate consists of two parallel walls built of brick and stone in 1037 by Yaroslav the Wise to guard the main entrance into the city. The arch was topped by the tiny Church of the Annunciation. It was through this gate that Bogdan Khmelnitsky entered Kiev in 1648. In 1751 the Golden Gate was covered with earth; in 1832 it was excavated and reinforced with bricks.

The far side of the square is the continuation of Vladimirskaya Street. Walking southwest along it you come to the Opera House, then, at No. 57, on your left, to the Kiev branch of the Central Lenin Museum.

At the junction with Shevchenko Boulevard, on your left, is the Shevchenko Park, where you can see a statue of the great Ukrainian classical writer erected in 1939 on the 125th anniversary of his birth. The large and impressive building opposite the park, on Vladimirskaya Street, is Kiev University, named after Shevchenko, and founded in 1834. It is flanked by the University Library and the Faculty of Humanities.

The far side of Shevchenko Park borders on Repin Street, which runs parallel with Vladimirskaya. Here there are two museums: No. 9 is the Museum of Russian Art and No. 15 the Museum of Oriental and Western Art. The former covers the 12th to the 17th centuries and includes icons of the Novgorod, Moscow and Stroganov schools; the 18th- and 19th-century rooms also have works by outstanding Russian artists. There is a fine collection of 18th–20th-century china, glass and crystal. The Museum of Oriental and Western Art has a collection that includes works by Bellini, Franz Hals, Rubens and Velasquez.

Passing Repin Street, continue along Shevchenko Boulevard. Between Repin and Pushkin Streets, at No. 12, you will find the Shevchenko Museum, which is devoted to the life and work of the poet. Turn back to cross Vladimirskaya Street again and walk on further northwest and you come to one of the newer but important monuments in Kiev, the Vladimir Cathedral. Built in the 19th century, designed by Beretti and Bernhardt, it has seven gilded domes, three naves and several striking murals.

Further along Shevchenko Boulevard on the left you will see the University Botanical Gardens. Then after a short distance, the boulevard arrives at Pobeda (Victory—Peremogi in Ukrainian) Square. Here you can visit the circus, and shop in the Ukraine State Department Store. Here also is the newest Intourist Hotel (Lybed), one of the country's best.

From here on, the Shevchenko Boulevard continues as the Brest-Litovsk Highway. Along it you will find the Kiev Zoo, which can be reached from Victory Square by trolley-buses No. 5, 6 or 7 and trams No. 2, 9 or 47. Close to it is the Medical Faculty of the University and the Dovzhenko Film Studio.

Fourth Tour

For your final walk, start again from the Hotel Dnieper but follow the Street of the Revolutionary Heroes until you reach Vladimirskaya Street. No. 2 is the Historical Museum. From there turn northeast, down Andreyevsky Spusk. Here is St. Andrew's Church, designed by Rastrelli and built by the Russian architect Michurin between 1744 and 1753, an important example of Russian baroque architecture. This is the highest point of Old Kiev, overlooking the Podol district, the river and the plain to the east where, according to tradition, the Apostle Andrew, who first preached the Gospel in Russia, erected a cross.

Built at the command of Elizaveta, the pios daughter of Peter the Great, St. Andrew's Church stands on a terrace at the top of a broad flight of steps. Its proportions are perfect. Today the domes are restored in silver-gilt and the walls painted in turquoise and white. The iconostasis was painted by Andropov and local masters. The church is still used for religious worship.

Behind the church you can descend the Andreyevsky Spusk into the Lower Town, the Podol. At the foot of the hill turn left into Zelinsky Street and a few steps will take you to Krasnaya (Red) Square. The House of Contracts (Kontraktovy Dom) built here in 1817 expressly as a headquarters for the negotiating and signing of agreements, is an interesting example of the early 19th century Russian classicist style.

The building on the corner of Red Square and Naberezhno-Nikolskaya Street (designed by Sedel and built in 1735) is a branch of the Academic Library. The courtyard wall has baroque decorations. The building used to be the home of the Kiev Academy, which was founded in 1701 at the command of Peter the Great, to replace the former Kiev College. It had many distinguished graduates in its time.

Also on Red Square are the ruins of the Bratsky Monastery; the old house in the northwestern corner was Peter the Great's headquarters in 1706 when he prepared the attack on the Swedes, who had advanced to within 25 miles of Kiev.

East of the square, at No. 15 Kreshchatik Quay, which curves in from the river, is the former dormitory of the students of the Kiev Academy, the "Bursa." The ground floor was built in 1778; in 1809–11, two stories were added, with a four-columned gate, and the facade was remodeled in the style of the early 19th-century classicism.

Turning along Kreshchatik Quay towards the harbor, you can see Trukhanov Island on the far side. The island has been developed into an aquatic sports center. A wide promenade lines the riverbank where railway lines and warehouses once stood. Behind the harbor is Pochtovaya Square, a traffic center and terminus for the funicular which links the Lower and Upper Cities. Take the funicular to the Upper City terminal and you are back at the starting point of your tour.

Excursions around Kiev

The permanent Ukrainian Economic Exhibition covers 750 acres on Sorokichya Zhotvnya Prospekt, to the south of the city. It can be reached by No. 11 trolley-bus directly from Lenkomsomol Square.

Darnitsa is on the far bank of the Dnieper; once an independent village, it became a part of Kiev in 1927. It has a camping site; follow the arrows carefully from the roundabout on the Kharkov road and you will find it on the left side of the Dnieper, on Chernigov Chaussée.

The site has a café, a self-service kitchen, showers and laundry facilities. It has been recently enlarged.

Pushcha-Voditsa is one of the finest parks in Kiev's green-belt. It extends over 1,875 acres, about 13 miles from the city center. It used to be a hunting preserve and also a refuge from enemies who attacked Kiev. It can be reached by tram No. 25 from the railway station or No. 12 from the Red Square in Podol.

Lvov

Lvov is a regional capital, the traditional economic, transport, cultural and administrative center of the western Ukraine. For six centuries it was the scene of much strife and war between hostile powers, irreconcilable nations and opposing religions. Yet the monuments of the past, the different styles, ranging from Ukrainian traditional to Italianate Renaissance, German baroque and Polish, today form a unique whole and demonstrate that different cultures need not necessarily clash at their meeting-point but can also merge and mingle harmoniously.

The statue of the great Polish poet Adam Mickiewicz (by Popiel and Farashcuk, 1905) stands in Mickiewicz Square and has come to be a symbol of Lvov. Also in the square is the Intourist hotel, built in 1901, and close by, the shady promenade of the Shevchenko Prospekt to Rosa Luxemburg Square. The most important monument here is the Roman Catholic Cathedral, dating from 1270–1480, but never completed. It is still used today for services. The old Gothic houses in the square burned down in 1527 but their foundations, ground floors and, here and there, parts of their first floors have survived and become incorporated into more recent dwellings. The cathedral has 18th-century frescos and many decorative carvings and statues dating from the 17th and 18th centuries. The chapels and the 214-feet-high Gothic tower were added between the 16th and 18th centuries. The Boim Chapel, built 1609–17 in baroque style, belonged to a family of Hungarian origin, whose ancestor was private secretary to King Stephen Batory of Poland and Transylvania.

No. 2 Rosa Luxemburg Square (with its classicist facade) was built in the 18th century. No. 3 dates from 1630.

You entered Rosa Luxemburg Square from the southwest; now you leave it at its northeastern corner, where it is crossed by Russky (Russian) Street, the only street where Russian Orthodox believers were allowed to live at the end of the Middle Ages.

No. 2 Russian Street dates from the 16th century and has Gothic details. No. 8 is 18th century; notice the four relief carvings symbolizing the occupant's trade. But the most important landmark is the Church of the Assumption, one of the most beautiful in Lvov. After two previous churches had burned down, the present one was built in 1590–1629. In the courtyard there is a bell tower 226 feet high, dated 1572–8, with a bell called Cyril, cast locally in 1783 and weighing almost five tons. The outside walls of the church are decorated with a sculptured frieze depicting Biblical scenes; the interior contains 18th-century sculptures and 17th- and 18th-century icons. Russian Orthodox services are held here regularly.

Rinok Square

Rinok (Market) Square is like an architectural sampler of the centuries, so we will describe it in some detail. The old City Hall (now the City Soviet) stands in the center, and almost all the buildings around the edges of the square are worth close inspection. Of the 44 houses none is less than 200 years old.

No. 2 is a Gothic one-storied house dating from the 16th century, with a sculpture by Bellon and dolphin-reliefs on its façade. In 1627 this was the home of the first Lvov post office. No. 3, with its 18th-century façade, is typical of the transitional style between rococo and classicism. No. 4, built in 1577 and known as the Black House (Chornaya Kamonica), houses a section of the Historical Museum. (The museum occupies several buildings, including also Nos. 6 and 24 in Market Square.)

No. 6 has also had a varied past. It is called the Korniakt or Sobieski house; it was built at the end of the 16th century by one of Lvov's richest burghers, a Greek merchant, who had special permission to erect a broad façade with six windows instead of the usual narrow frontage. In the 17th century the Polish King Jan Sobieski bought the house. No. 7 has many basic Renaissance features. No. 8 was built at the end of the 18th century in classicist style but its front, stylistically a survival from the 16th century, was later decorated with balconies, wrought-iron railings and reliefs symbolizing shipping and trade. No. 9 dates from 1680; No. 10 with its rich baroque and rococo decorations belongs to the 18th century.

No. 12 has also acquired Renaissance features during its long life; the ornamentation shows the plump-cheeked faces and bold moustaches of contemporary Polish figures. The portals of No. 14 display a winged lion, the symbol of Venice, denoting that this was once a diplomatic dwelling; Antonio di Massari, the Venetian consul, lived here in 1600. Nos. 15 and 16 are 17th century, but their façades are in early classicist style. No. 16 has preserved some Gothic vaulting.

No. 17, built in Louis Quinze style, is noteworthy for its elegance and air of serene luxury. No. 18 dates from 1523 and was one of the most richly-decorated mansions of its age. Nos. 19 and 20 have preserved the baroque lines of the 18th century; under the balcony of No. 19 there are fantastic, half-human, half-animal masks. No. 20 has intricate rococo vase decorations.

No. 23 is massive, almost oppressive in its effect. The details, and decorative elements, the splendid masks, the stylized lions' and angels' heads belong to the traditions of the Italian Renaissance but their excessive use and the heaviness of the whole ornamentation betrays German and Flemish influences.

No. 24 is the third section of the Historical Museum; it dates from the 16th century but its front was rebuilt in the 20th. In 1707 Peter the Great received a deputation of the Stavronigy Brotherhood here and granted them a charter to sell their books freely in the Ukraine.

No. 28 is a real architectural anthology: its left side still displays the Gothic arches and flying buttresses of 1510, its Renaissance portico and window frames are 17th century, while its second story dates from the baroque period. Built by an anonymous architect, it has a particular gracefulness and charm.

No. 29, in classicist style, was built by peasant rebels captured at the end of the 18th century; as soon as it was finished, they were executed.

Almost the entire northern side of Rinok Square dates from the second half of the 18th century, but some buildings have earlier elements. The decorations are especially interesting, ranging from a laurel-wreathed, bearded head with a lion's body, the hermit figures supporting the balcony of No. 40, and the grinning stone face with a huge moustache on the façade of No. 41.

Elsewhere in Lvov

Leaving the square at one of the northern corners, you come next to Armyanskaya (Armenian) Street, which is also filled with historical associations. Its most interesting building is the Armenian Cathedral, founded in 1363, with a bell tower dating from 1571. It includes the house where the Armenian Archbishop resided in the 16th century. A 16th-century column topped by a statue of St. Christopher stands in the courtyard.

Other interesting buildings in Armenian Street are: No. 13, an 18th-century house with early classicist façade and balcony; Nos. 16 and 17, of the same period; No. 21 with three allegorical reliefs and decorative friezes; No. 20 built in 1560 by Pietro di Lugano; No. 22, from the 17th century; and No. 23 dating from the 18th century, with a classicist façade bearing the signs of the zodiac and the symbols of the four seasons.

From Armyanskaya Street, turn into Krakovskaya, which crosses it behind the Armenian Cathedral. On your right is Daniel Galitsky Street, named after the founder of Kiev. On the square named after the 300th anniversary of the Russian-Ukrainian union stands the Church of the Virgin of the Snows, once the oldest Catholic church in Lvov. It dates from the end of the 13th century.

Reaching Bogdan Khmelnitsky Street, you will notice the Church of St. Nicholas, constructed between the 13th and 18th centuries. Russian Orthodox services are now held here. At No. 63 in the same street, there is another Orthodox church, the Pyanitskaya, built in 1645, with a very old iconostasis. No. 34 is the St. Onufri Monastery, with a 17th-century church in which Orthodox services are still held; the bell tower and walls are 17th to 19th century. Ivan Fyodorov, the first Russian printer is buried here. He died in 1583, having produced his first book in 1563 in Moscow, shortly after which he fled from persecution to continue his work in Lithuania and Poland.

This quarter is called Podzamese (Precincts of the Castle); on Bogdan Khmelnitsky Street there is a railway station of the same name. To get to the castle turn to the right, uphill. There is a Number 12 tram along this route which you can use to return to the October Hotel, if you are staying there.

Zamkovaya Gora (Castle Hill) is the name of the former Prince's Hill where a fortress was built in the second half of the 13th century. Only parts of the southwestern walls remain today. The fortress survived many sieges and occupations; in 1957 Lvov's television mast was erected here in the middle of a park and a playground.

If you have any more time and energy for exploration, you may like to walk down Lenin Prospekt, the most important thoroughfare in Lvov. At No. 15 you can visit the Ethnographical and Handicraft Museum, established in 1951, which has an extremely rich folklore collection of over 70,000 items. No. 16 is the Pioneer Palace, opened in 1959; No. 20 the Lenin Museum. You pass large apartment houses and public buildings, until, at the end of the boulevard, you come to the Lenin statue by Merkurov (1952). Behind it stands the large and impressive Opera House, built between 1897 and 1900 in a Viennese eclectic style.

Another place well worth visiting is the Heroes' Cemetery in Lenin Park (No. 2 tram). Not far from Rinok Square, going eastwards, there is a fine baroque building, the Church of the Dominican Monastery (1748). Nearby stands the former royal arsenal (1630), now used to house the Historical Archives (13 Podvalny Street), and the City Arsenal (5 Podvalny Street) which was built in 1554–6. Another medieval monument is the Gunpowder Tower, opposite the Archives, built in 1554, with walls nine feet thick. Restored in 1954, it is now the headquarters of the Architects' Union. All these sights can be reached by trams Nos. 1, 2, 4, 7, 9 or 12.

To the south, on Vechevaya Square, stands the former Benedictine Convent, looking rather like a fortress, and its church, which was built between 1600 and 1630 in Renaissance style by Paolo Romano and Ambrogio. It contains many valuable paintings and statues dating from the 17th and 18th centuries.

As well as the Roman Catholic, Armenian and Russian Orthodox churches, the Greek Catholics also had their cathedral in Lvov, built on a hill in the southwestern part of the city: the St. George Church, built in 1743–60 by Bernardo Meretini; it is a rich storehouse of Ukrainian baroque, with a splendid equestrian statue of St. George on its roof. Its bell tower contains one of the oldest bells in the Ukraine, cast in 1341.

The square fronting the cathedral is called after Bogdan Khmelnitsky; in 1648 the Cossack forces besieging Lvov camped here.

The Museum of Ukrainian Art, with its fine collection of 14th–18th-century icons, is housed at 42 Dragomanov Street, while the Ivan Franko Museum in Franko Street was opened in 1940 in the house where the poet spent the last 14 years of his life.

Kharkov

A regional capital with a population of almost one and a half million, Kharkov is an economic and cultural center accessible by rail, road and air. It is characterized by a preponderance of monumental buildings erected in the last few decades, but it has also several important historical and artistic monuments.

The Lopan River cuts through the city from north to south; near the upper city the little Kharkov River runs into it from the east. The Intourist Hotel is at the beginning of Sverdlov Street. Turning left out of the hotel you soon reach the traffic and architectural heart of the city, the hugh Dzerzhinsky Square, some 750 yards long. Part of it is a regular square, opening on to Sumskaya Street, which leads towards Moscow in a northeasterly direction, while the remainder is a circle from which Lenin Prospekt opens.

Among the huge buildings in the square the Palace of State Industry catches the eye. Built between 1925 and 1928, it was the first skyscraper in the Soviet Union. The building of the Gorky University, dating from the 30s, was almost totally wrecked during the war but was rebuilt with new ceramic decorations. The Party Headquarters stands at the corner of the square and Sumskaya Street. The seven-storied Hotel Kharkov is on the corner of Dzerzhinsky Square and Trinkler Street.

To the northeast of the main square lies another of Kharkov's main squares, the Tevelev, which was designed in the 1890s by the architect Beketov. The City Hall, (now the City Soviet), was erected in 1885 on the corner of what is now Moskovsky Prospekt. Here too is the Tsentralny Restaurant, and several shops. The Yuzhny Vokzal railway station is one of the largest in the Soviet Union.

Kharkov's historical buildings are best approached from Tevelev Square. The fortress that formed the nucleus of the city once stood in the triangle formed by this square, Rosa Luxemburg Square and Proletarian Square. Of its 12 cannon, two can still be seen in the courtyard of the Historical Museum. The Pokrovsky Cathedral on the bank of the Lopan River was built in 1689. The Uspensky Cathedral (1777) on Universitetskaya Gorka has also survived. Situated on top of a hill, it can be seen from every part of the city, by virtue of its prominent bell tower (1841), which commemorates the 1812 victory over Napoleon and has a fine carillon.

Kharkov University was established in the 19th century on the former castle hill. It is now surrounded by a park. The Historical Museum illustrating Kharkov's story is at 10 University Street and is served by trolley-buses Nos. 1, 2 and 4. Kharkov's other great museum is the Fine Arts Museum at 11 Sovnarkomovskaya Street; tram Nos. 5, 7, 10, 11, 20 and A will take you there, as will the trolley-buses 1, 2 and 4. It has 19 halls devoted to Russian and Ukrainian pre-revolutionary art, icons of the Novgorod, Pskov and other schools of the 16th century. There is a good collection of paintings by Repin, who was born at nearby Chuguyev, and Soviet artists are well represented.

Poltava

Lying 80 miles to the southwest of Kharkov, this is the administrative center of the Poltava Region of the Ukraine. The city is of ancient origins; its first mention dates back to the late 12th century.

In 1709 Russian troops, led by Peter I and aided by Ukrainian Cossack detachments, routed the invading army of Charles XII of Sweden near the city. The 17th-century Holy Cross Monastery and the Savior Church still stand, and there are some fine examples of 19th-century public building, notably the administrative offices encircling Round Square.

Poltava has an interesting Museum of Local Lore. The largely rebuilt city has several fine parks, theaters and a philharmonic society.

Vinnitsa

Vinnitsa 150 miles south of Kiev is the administrative and cultural center of the region of the same name. It lies in an area famous for folk handicrafts: pottery, embroidery, weaving and carpet-making. Beneath Mayakovsky Street are the ruins of a fortress 600 years old. The origins of Vinnitsa, however, go back much earlier—archeological excavations have proved that Slav tribes inhabited the area in very ancient times. During the war of 1648–54, Cossack troops routed Polish royal forces near Vinnitsa. A commemorative obelisk has been erected on the site of the battle.

Although Vinnitsa, like many cities in the Ukraine, suffered terribly during World War Two, some remnants of early 17th-century architecture remain. The city is the birthplace of Ukrainian writer M. Kotsiubinsky, (1864–1913), and the house where he was born and lived is now a museum. Modern Vinnitsa, too, has a Museum of Local Lore, a musical drama theater, a philharmonic society, and is a city of parks.

Down the Dnieper from Kiev to the Black Sea

The great Dnieper River flows through three Soviet republics—the Russian, the Ukrainian and the Byelorussian—and is the third largest river in Europe (after the Volga and the Danube). Rising to the north of Smolensk, in the Valday Hills, it runs past Smolensk, then continues southwest till it reaches White Russia. Here it flows through the town of Mogilyov; its first great tributary is the Berezina. Later it is swollen by the waters of the Sozh and the Pripyat (Pripet), the latter gathering the waters of the huge Pripet marshes. After that for some 550 miles, more than half its length, it flows through Ukrainian territory. This is its widest section and it flows through such important cities as Kiev, Dnepropetrovsk and Zaporozhye; its waters are exploited to the full for hydroelectricity with immense dams and power plants.

Many tragic and triumphant episodes in Ukrainian history have been connected with this river; Ukrainian poets, painters and composers have devoted innumerable works to its moods and landscapes; not surprisingly, it has become a national symbol.

There are ample facilities for excursions along the huge river and its tributaries. There are regular cruises, from Kiev northwards to Gomel (on the Dnieper and Sozh), from Kiev to Mozir (along the Dnieper and Pripet), to Chernigov (on the Dnieper and the Desna, with the Kiev hydroelectric plant just above their confluence). But the most popular and most interesting cruise is of 600 miles from the Ukrainian capital to the mouth of the river, to the city of Kherson on the Black Sea. Comfortable fast or slow passenger steamers ply regularly to Kherson; at major points en route there is time for short excursions. Even the express steamers stop for two hours in Dnepropetrovsk and an hour in Zaporozhye, about two-thirds of the way to Kherson.

Leaving Kiev, the boat first starts upstream, then swings south. On the right bank, huge public buildings rise above the parkland, and then you glimpse the domes of the ancient Monastery of the Caves. You pass under the Navodnitsky and Paton bridges—to the left lies the district of Darnitsa—and finally under the railroad bridge, the last landmark of Kiev.

The villages of Osokorki on the left and Korchevatoye on the right are still part of Greater Kiev, but Visenka, on the left, and the vacation settlement of Plyuyi on the right are outside its boundaries. The hills on the right bank begin to rise more steeply. The village of Tripolye takes its name from archeological finds discovered there dating from the Bronze Age to the so-called Tripolye culture of the fourth-to-second millennium BC.

After Stayki and Kalnoye, you come to the first stop—Rzhishchev. This is the town where in 1654 the envoys of the Czar negotiated the union of Russia and the Ukraine with the Cossack *hetman* (commander), Bogdan Khmelnitsky.

Khodorov, on the right bank, is a small town, founded in 1506; Trakhtimorovo is dominated by the cone-shaped Mount Baturin which rises opposite the harbor of Peryaslav-Khmelnitsky, some eight miles from the river; it was here that on January 8, 1654, the union was voted by a council assembly ot Ukrainian nobles.

Grigorovka (another stop) is on the right bank. It was here that, in the autumn of 1943, the Russian troops crossed the Dnieper, in a bitterly contested battle. On the right you will see Kanev, about one mile from the river. This is the home town of the great Ukrainian poet, Taras Shevchenko; hc is buricd here and there is a large museum devoted to his life and work.

Prohorovka follows on the left bank; a former mansion where both Shevchenko and Gogol were visitors is now the holiday rest home of the Ukrainian Academy of Sciences.

Some six miles beyond Prohorovka, the river widens into what looks almost like a sea—it is the reservoir of Kremenchug. At the far end is a huge hydroelectric plant. The ship stops on the right, at the mouth of the Olshanka River.

Cherkassy, one of the greenest cities in the Ukraine, is a major administrative and cultural center. Highways and railway lines converge here and there is an airport. The Museum of Local History displays the development of the city since the 16th century, through the Cossack-Tatar wars and later vicissitudes. Since the great reservoir was completed, Cherkassy has become an important river port as well.

Kremenchug is a district capital and a railway junction. Its fortress was built in 1590 against the Tatar marauders and peasant rebels.

The next stop is Misurino, one of the Ukraine's agricultural centers. On the left bank is the port of Perevolochno, where the remnants of the defeated Swedish army tried to cross the Dnieper after the Battle of Poltava (which Peter the Great won). Only King Charles XII and his ally, the Cossack hetman Mazeppa succeeded.

Now the Dnieper reaches the environs of Dneprodzerzhinsk, and traffic on the river becomes much heavier. Dneprodzerzhinsk is a center of the iron and steel industry. It has an interesting Museum of Local History.

Dnepropetrovsk

Dnepropetrovsk is the next main stop. A regional capital and major railroad junction, it boasts a large mechanized harbor and an airport. Founded in 1784 by Catherine II and originally called Yekaterinoslav, it has been an industrial town almost since that time.

Its main thoroughfare is the Karl Marx Prospekt, lined with a double row of shady trees. The Shevchenko Park, the favorite recreation area of the city, is on a hill where you can see the poet's statue and the co-called Student Palace, built on the ruins of the former Potemkin Palace (1787–89). The Preobrazhensky Cathedral (1830–35), designed by Zakharov, is also here.

After Dnepropetrovsk, the ship enters Lenin Lake, which covers what used to be dangerous rapids and whirlpools. On the left bank is the Lenin Harbor, close to the great dam of Dneproges, one of the largest hydroelectric installations in the world.

Zaporozhye, a city with a large mechanized port, is the next stop. This, too, is a largely industrial community, built on the site of the former Fort Alexandrovsk. Since 1927 its population has increased tenfold. The Dnieper Power Plant was built next to Khortitsa Island, where the famous Zaporozhskaya Sech, a self-governing Cossack Community, was established in the 16th, 17th and 18th centuries.

In Zaporpzhye itself, the main street is the Lenin Prospekt, linking the old and new quarters of the city. There are few historical buildings, but many modern apartment blocks and offices, large parks and gardens.

After Zaporozhye the left bank of the river opens out into a plain crossed by many small streams and dotted with copses and woods. Belenka has a large camping ground for Pioneers (rather like Boy Scouts). After this, the river enters one more huge reservoir, the 150-mile-long Kakhovka Sea. The next stop is Kamenka, on the left bank, the center of a large irrigation area. Crossing the reservoir you come to Nikopol on the right bank. Nikopol, a district center, has a Museum of Local History: a settlement on the site was first mentioned in 1530. Between 1638 and 1652 it was the capital of the Zaporozhskaya Sech.

Kherson is your final stop on the Dnieper. Founded as a fortress in 1778, it is both a river and sea port. From here you can visit the new town on Novaya Kakhovka and see the hydraulic power plant, or make an excursion to the steppe preserve at Askania Nova, with its ostriches, bisons, antelopes and wild horses. This is where you leave the Dnieper, but you can take a 300-seat hydrofoil to Odessa, which is only two hours' ride.

Transcarpathia

The Transcarpathian Region (Zakarpatskava Oblast) is part of the Ukraine and was established on January 22, 1945 as an administrative unit. It extends from the basin of the Tisza River to the ridge of the Carpathians; it is surrounded by Romania, Hungary, Czechoslovakia, Poland and the Lvov and Ivano-Frankovsk regions of the Ukrainian Republic. Until 1914 it was a part of Hungary, between 1918 and 1939 of Czechoslovakia. When Hitler carved up the Czechoslovak state, Transcarpathia passed partly to Ruthenian and partly to Hungarian rule. It was occupied by the Soviet Army in the autumn of 1944. Its population is just over a million, and includes Ukrainians, Russians, Hungarians, Romanians and Slovaks. Its capital is Uzhgorod.

The region can be explored by following the valleys of the various rivers from the Tisza basin to the Watershed Range mountains and springs with their many cataracts and falls. The highest peaks do not rise abruptly but unfold slowly as you gradually climb out of the plain. Your tour will take you through a wonderful region of hills, ravines, steep cliffs, wide valleys, and, in the upper parts, mountain lakes.

After the Caucasus, the Black Sea and the Crimea, Transcarpathia is one of the most popular holiday areas in the Soviet Union. Much of it can be reached by car, but in the mountains the best way is to hike or use whatever local transport is available.

Uzhgorod is the largest town in Transcarpathia. It is an important rail and road junction and the best base for exploring the region. Situated on either side of the River Uzh, in the midst of a wine-growing region, Uzhgorod is mentioned in chronicles as early as in the ninth century.

Teatralnaya Square with the Intourist (Verkhovina) Hotel and the opera and drama theater is about halfway between Lenin Square and the castle. Nearby is the Philharmonia Concert Hall, a former synagogue. The square also has an Art Gallery where you can buy souvenirs and gifts made by local artists.

Behind the theater is the river Uzh embankment and a foot-bridge. Turn right here towards Lenin Quay. At the next bridge, turn right into Lenin Square. On either side of the huge City Hall there are other public buildings; on the eastern side the Trade Union house, on the corner of Lenin Quay the medical faculty of the University.

Turning back along Kalinin Street, you pass the Central Post Office overlooking Pochtovaya Square, then reach Koryatovich Square, with its colorful local market. Suvorov Street will take you back to Teatralnaya Square and the Verkhovina Hotel.

You can make another excursion in the opposite direction to climb Castle Hill. The castle dates from the ninth century; Slav Prince Laborets lived here until his murder in 903 by invading Hungarians. In 1312 Uzhgorod was presented by the Hungarian Anjou King Charles Robert to an Italian court, whose family held it until 1692, when it passed to a Hungarian count. After that, it changed hands several times in the course of religious and national wars.

The castle as it stands today has a 16th-century façade; it was reconstructed in 1598 and in 1775 was given to the local bishop, after which it housed a seminary until 1945. A statue of the mythological Hungarian *Turul* bird stands in the garden. The Museum of Local History is at 27 Kremlyovskaya Street, inside the castle.

The slope between the castle and the river is the Gorky Park; there is a swimming pool here. Turning towards the river bank and walking towards the city center you pass the Botanical Garden and the Pioneer (Children's) Railway, then reach the theater and your hotel.

For your third walk, you might like to climb up the Hill of Glory. Turning into Kladbishchenskaya Street at the corner of Koryatovich Square, near the Hotel Kiev, follow a road that climbs the hill. After passing under a monumental arch, you enter the Cemetery of Heroes, where victims of the last war lie.

There are many long and short excursions and hikes you can take starting from Uzhgorod. The local Intourist office will provide guides, maps and information.

Mukachevo and Other Towns

A district center. Mukachevo is a lively town and is another good base for excursions. Standing on the river Latoritsa, it was first mentioned in 903 AD, when the Hungarians arrived as invaders. After 1919 it became part of Czechoslovakia; it returned to Hungary in 1938, but became part of the Soviet Union in 1946.

The most interesting sight is Palanok Castle, on the top of a hill just south of the city. Dating from the 14th and 15th centuries, this 200-food-high building has served as a prison since 1782. A wooden Russian Orthodox Church stands in Bogomoltsa Street. This was brought from a nearby village in 1927 as an example of early architecture (1777).

Chust (Huszt) is a district center and a busy road junction. The mountain rising above the town is topped by the ruins of a 16th-century castle built to protect the nearby salt mines. The castle was destroyed in 1766 when a bolt of lightning caused gunpowder stored in a tower to explode. The town's Gothic church dates from 1459.

Tyachev is another district center lying on the Tisza River (Theiss) near the frontier with Romania. The road here follows the river through Solotniva, the site of a large salt mine and some interesting caves.

Rahov is the center of the Hutsul region. The Hutsuls are a Slav tribe of great antiquity and colorful folk customs. It is an industrial and tourist center. The highway and railway lines lead from here along upper reaches of the Tisza towards its source. On the right is Kvasi, a spa known for its mineral waters. Yasina is 1,800 feet up (in a broad valley) on the bank of the Black Tisza. It has a 200-bed hotel, open in the tourist season, and Hutsul folk art (woodcarvings, embroidery) is on sale here. After this rather large village comes the Yablonitsky Pass (2,700 feet), after which the road continues towards Delatin and Komomiya.

Transcarpathia has several other popular health resorts and holiday centers.

PRACTICAL INFORMATION FOR THE UKRAINE

WHEN TO GO. As we have indicated, the climate of the Ukraine (except for the mountainous Carpathian region) is much milder than that of Russia. The spring starts earlier and the autumn lasts longer, so April and October are pleasant months for a visit. However, most of the Dnieper river cruises run in the summer months only. There are winter sports facilities in the Carpathians.

HOW TO GET THERE. By train, From the West via Czechoslovakia or Hungary to Uzhgorod and then to Kiev and points east and south. From Moscow and Leningrad to Kiev. From the southwest via Romania. Trains from Eastern Europe to the Ukraine are always full so reservations are adviseable, indeed vital if you want sleeping-car accommodation.

By plane. Regular connections from Moscow and Leningrad to Kiev.

By road. No. 3 tourist route begins at the Czechoslovak-Soviet frontier and continues via Uzhgorod, Mukachevo to Strij, Rovno, Zhitomir and Kiev. Route No. 7 takes you from Kiev to Kharkov and No. 8 from Moscow directly south to the Black Sea. No. 6 route runs from Kiev to Odessa. (These are the authorized routes for tourists; Intourist will provide up-to-date information about any possible changes.)

By ship. Regular sailing to Kiev via Kanev, Cherkassy, Zaporpzhye from Kherson and Odessa. Intourist cruises include air travel from London to Kiev and back via Moscow (15 days).

 **HOTELS. Chernovtsy** (formerly Cernauti when part of Romania). *Bukovina Hotel* 41 Lenin Street is best, followed by any of following: *Kiev Hotel,* Lennin Street, *Radyanska Hotel,* Universitetskaya Street. *Motel:* one mile east of city.

Donetsk. *Druzhba Hotel,* 48 Universitetskaya Street, is best, followed by either the *Ukraina Hotel,* 88 Artyoma Street, with 305 rooms or the *Donbas Hotel,* 80 Artyoma Street. The *Oktyabr Hotel,* 20 Pushkin Prospekt, is an old wreck. *Hotel Shakhtior,* recent, 15 German Titov Prospekt, 12 floors, 402 rooms, airconditioned. Sounds promising but we have no details.

Kharkov. *Intourist,* 21 Prospekt Lenina, moderate, *Motel Druzhba,* 185 Gagarin Prospekt.

Kiev. *Lybed Hotel,* Victory Square, a new Intourist hotel (1970), 280 rooms, reportedly among the Soviet Union's best hotels. *Intourist Hotel,* 26 Lenin Street, is officially classed as deluxe but we call if first-class. Only 44 rooms at last look. Of equal rank are: *Dnieper Hotel,* Lenkomsomol Square, 200 rooms, good restaurant, moderate facilities; *Moskva Hotel,* in October Revolution Street skyscraper, with 370 rooms, adequate; and *Ukraine Hotel,* 5 Shevchenko Boulevard, 319 rooms, relatively modern, so-so.

Also-rans: *Desna Hotel,* 3 Shevchenko Boulevard; *Mir Hotel,* Goloseyevsky Forest; *Leningradskaya Hotel,* 4 Shevchenko Boulevard; *Kiev Hotel,* 36 Volodimirska Street; *Pervomaiskaya Hotel,* 1/3 Lenin Street; *Teatralnaya Hotel,* 17 Lenin Street.

Lvov. *Lvov Hotel,* 3,700-Letiya Street, 226 rooms, Lvova is best of the older hotels, and first-class (faded). *Intourist Hotel,* 1 Mickiewicz Square is best of newer (relatively). First class moderate. 85 rooms. Third choice is the *Dnieper Hotel,* 45 Pervomaiskaya Square, adequate.

Also-rans in Lvov Include: *Ukraina Hotel,* 4 Mickiewicz Square; *Narodnaya Hotel,* 1 Kostushko Street; and *Kolkhoznaya Hotel,* 14 Vossoyedineniye Square.

Poltava. Try the *Kiev Hotel,* 2 Leningradskaya Street, or the *Poltava Hotel,* 19 Oktyabrskaya Street. *Motel Poltava,* 2 Sovnarkomovskaya Street, (Intourist services).

Uzhgorod. Best is *Kiev Hotel,* Koryatovich Square, which boasts an open air terrace in summer; then *Verkhovina Hotel,* Teatralnaya Square.

Vinnitsa. *Ukraina Hotel,* with an Intourist office. on Lenin Street, is first choice; second choice, *Vinnitsa Hotel,* on same street. *Yuzhniy Bug Hotel.* Then *Oktyabrskaya,* Gagarin Street.

Zaporozhye. Best is *Dnepro Hotel,* 202 Lenin Prospekt, with Intourist office; then *Teatralnaya Hotel,* 23 Chekista Street. *Zaporozhye Hotel,* 135 Lenin Prospekt, is also an Intourist establishment.

 RESTAURANTS. Ukrainian specialities include soups like *borshch* (beet base) and cutlets of meat fried in egg and breadcrumbs. Chicken Kiev was born here—the white meat of fat hens or capons stuffed with butter. *Kolbasa,* a long, thick, circular sausage, is always a reliable choice, and ask for *vareniki,* small dumplings filled with sugared sour cream. Ukrainian dishes make lavish but skillful use of garlic, pepper, and vinegar.

The wines of Livadia and Massandra are perfectly drinkable, and you may come across a sparkling wine somewhat misleadingly called champagne. Experts also recommend *medivnyk* (spiced honey cake) and *kartoflia solimkoi* (deep-fried matchstick potatoes).

In addition to the restaurants of the hotels listed above, we recommend the following:

Chop. Try the restaurant of the *Ukraina Hotel,* Privokzalnaya Street.

Donetsk. The following are all average: *Moskva Restaurant, Troyanda Restaurant* and *Metallurg Restaurant,* all on Artyoma Street; then *Sport,* on Universitetskaya Street.

Kharkov. *Tsentralny Restaurant,* Tevelev Square, and *Teatralnaya Restaurant,* 2 Sumskaya Street, share top billing. Then any of these: *Lux Restaurant,* Rosa Luxembourg Street; and *Vareniki Café,* 14 Sumskaya Street, specializing in the Ukrainian national dish, a small dumpling with various fillings.

Kiev. *Kiev,* 35 St. Vladimir Street; *Abkhaziya,* 42 Kreshchatik; *Metro,* 19 Kreshchatik; *Record,* 5 Suvorovskaya Street; *Dynamo,* 3 Kirov Street (at the Stadium); *Sport,* 22 Chervonoarmiiska Street; and *Stolichny,* 5 Kreshchatik.

Also: *Leipzig,* German specialties (what else?), 30 Volodimirska Street; and *Ostrokvo,* at the Economic Achievements Exhibition.

There are several restaurants which open only in summer and are mostly in the open air: *Poplavok,* Naberezhnoye Chaussée; *Priboy,* on the Rechnoi Vokzal wharf; *Chervoni Mak,* 8 Kreshchatik; *Riviera,* Parkovyi Pereulok; *Automat,* 30 Sverdlov Street; *Kukushka,* near the open air theater; and *Snezhinka,* on Kreshchatik, near Tolstoy Square.

Not far from *Kulushka* is the *Kureni,* where you can get private cabins. Food is excellent, and there's open-air dancing to a good band. There are few tourists; the waiters speak only Russian or Ukrainian. Cover charge 8 roubles includes *zakuski* (starters), and a hot dish, ½ litre of vodka and 200 grams wine. Not bad!

Lvov. *Moskva Restaurant,* Mickiewicz Square; *Leto Restaurant,* 17 Gorky Street; and *Pervomaisky Restaurant,* 17 Lenin Prospekt, are best three.

Mukachevo. *Zvezda Hotel* restaurant is best.

Poltava. Either of these two: *Poltava Restaurant* on Lenin Street or *Vorskla Restaurant* on main road out of town.

Uzhgorod. *Konditerskaya Café* on Sholokhov Street is a good bet.

 WHAT TO SEE. Kiev: The Monastery of the Caves, Vydubetsky Monastery, Mikhailovsky-Zlatoverkhy Monastery, St. Sophia's Cathedral, St. Andrew's Church, St. Vladimir's Cathedral, St. Nicholas's Cathedral, St. Cyril's Church (largest collection in the USSR of 11th–12th-century frescos and later masterpieces by Vrubel—one of the few churches virtually untouched by the war), Goloseyevo Forest. Babi Yar (site of massacre of Jews).

Kharkov Pokrovsky Cathedral, Uspensky Cathedral, Cathedral of the Annunciation. Three Saints' Church, Yekaterinsky Palace, Museums, Botanical Garden.

Lvov: Count Potocki's Palace, Gunpowder Tower, Saint Yuri's Roman Catholic Cathedral, Armenian Cathedral, Church of St. Nicholas, St. Onufri's Monastery. Pyanitskaya Church, Benedictine Church and Convent, Cistercian Church and Monastery, St. Martin's and St. Voitsekh's R.C. Churches the Roman Catholic Cathedral, Church of the Assumption, Church and Monastery of the Barefoot Carmelites, Church of the Dominican Monastery, Jesuit Monastery, Prince's Hill, 16th-century cemetery.

Uzhgorod: Russian Orthodox Cathedral, St. Paul's Church, University, Botanical Garden, Gorky Park.

Mukachevo: Palanok Castle, Convent, Wooden Orthodox Church.

 MUSEUMS. Kiev. *Historical Museum in the Monastery of the Caves.* Open 10:30–6, closed Mon. *Ukrainian Theater Museum,* also in the Monastery. Open 10:30–5, closed Mon.

Museum of Eastern and Western Art, 15 Repin Street, open 10–5. Closed Fri.
Historical Museum, 2 Volodimirska Street, open 10–6, closed Wed.
Museum of Russian Art, 9 Repin Street. Open 10–6, closed Fri.
Museum of Ukrainian Art, 29 Kirov Street, open 10–5, closed Fri.
Shevchenko Museum, 12 Shevchenko Boulevard, open 10–5, closed Tues. Also: *Shevchenko's House,* 8a Shevchenko Pereulok, open 1–5:30 closed Fri. The great Ukrainian poet lived here for some months in 1846.
Lenin Museum, 57 Volodimirska Street. Open 10–7, closed Mondays.
Planetarium, 17 Chelyuskintsev Street.
Ukrainian Economic Exhibition, Sorokichya Zhovtnya Prospekt.

Kharkov. *Historical Museum.* 10 Universitetskaya Street (with another nearby building). Open 10–6, closed Tues.
Fine Arts Museum, 11 Sovnarkomovskaya Street, Open 11–7, closed Fri.

Lvov. *Historical Museum,* 4/6 Rynok. Open 11–7, closed Wed. and Sun.
Museum of Ukrainian Art, 42 Dragomanov Street, Open 12–7, closed Mon.
Art Gallery, 3 Stefanik Street. Open 12–7, closed Mon. Over 10,000 works, including some by Goya, Rubens, Tintoretto, Titian and many Russian masters.
Lenin Museum, 20 Lenin Prospekt. Open 10–7, Closed Mon.
Ethographical and Handicrafts Museum. Lenin Prospekt. Open 11–6, closed Mon.
Museum of Natural History, 18 Teatralnaya Street. Open 11–5, closed Mon.
Ivan Franko Museum, 152 Franko Street. Open 10–7, closed Tues. Devoted to the life and works of the famous Ukrainian writer.

Yaroslav Galan Museum, 18 Gvardeiskaya Street. Open 12–5, closed Wed, Fri. and Sat. Galan, a publicist and political writer, was murdered in 1949.

Botanical Garden. Shcherbakov Street.

Uzhgorod, *Local Museum,* 27 Kremlyovskaya Street, inside the castle. Open 11–7, closed Wed. Sections on natural history and local handicrafts.

There is also an *Art Gallery* inside the castle, open 11–7, closed Mon. Russian and Ukrainian artists.

 CULTURAL ACTIVITIES. Kiev. Shevchenko Opera and Ballet Theater, 50 Volodomirska Street. Ivan Franko Ukrainian Drama Theater, 2 Franko Square. Lesya Ukrainka Russian Drama Theater, 5 Lenin Street. Musical Comedy Theater, 51a Chervonoarmiiska Street. Puppet Theater, 13 Rustaveli Street. Philharmonia Concert Hall, 16 Kirov Street (the former Merchants Hall). Zhovtnevy (October) Palace of Culture. Circus, Victory Square. Cinerama, 19 Rustaveli Street.

Kharkov. Lysenko Opera House, 19 Rymarskaya Street. Musical Comedy Theater, 28 Karl Marx Street. Krupskaya Puppet Theater, 3 Krasin Street. Pushkin Russian Drama Theater, 11 Chernyshevsky Street. Shevchenko Ukrainian Drama Theater, 9 Sumskaya Street. Regional Drama Theater, 18 Sverdlov Street. Circus, 17 Krasnogo Militsionera Street, Philharmonia Concert Hall, 10 Sumskaya Street. Ukraina Concert Hall, opened in 1965, in the Shevchenko Garden. Seats 2,000.

Lvov. Franko Opera and Ballet Theater, Torgovaya Square. Zamkovetskaya Ukrainian Drama Theater, 1 Ukrainskaya Street. Russian Drama Theater, 6 Gorodetskaya Street. Gorky Youth Theater, 11 Gorky Street. Puppet Theater, Galitsky Street. Summer Theater, Khmelnitsky Park, 43 Dzerzhinsky Street. Concert Hall, 25 Franko Street. The famous Lvov *Trembita* choir performs here. Spartak Swimming Pool. 49 Instrumentalnaya Street.

Uzhgorod. Ukrainian Drama Theater, Teatralnaya Square. Philharmonia Concert Hall, Teatralnaya Square. It is the home of the Transcarpathian Folk Choir. Avangard Stadium (seats 10,000).

Mukachevo Russian Drama Theater, Mir Street.

 SHOPPING. The best buy in the Ukraine is ceramic ware. **Kiev:** *Main Department Store,* 2 Lenin Street, at the corner of Kreshchatik. *Podarki* (Gift Shop), 9 Karl Marx Street and at the corner of Kreshchatik and Shevchenko Boulevard. *Jewelers:* 19 and 53 Kreshchatik. *Porcelain:* 34 Kreshchatik. *Ukrainian Handicrafts:* 23 Chervonoarmiiska Street and 93 Kirov Street. *Dom Knigi* (Bookshop): 30 Kreshchatik. *Bessarabka* (Covered Market), Shevchenko Boulevard. *Kashtan* shops are the Ukrainian equivalent of *Beryozkas*—gift shops for tourists. In Kiev they are located at: 24/26 Boulevard Lesya Ukrainka, Monastery of the Caves, Borispol Airport, Prolisok campsite/motel, Hotel Lybed and Hotel Dnieper.

Kharkov. *Department Store,* Rosa Luxemburg Street. *Antique and Second-Hand Shops:* 29 Engels Street and 4 Sverdlov Street. *Jewelers:* 16 Trelov Street and 3 Sumskaya Street.

Lvov. *Antique and Second-Hand Shops:* 3 Shevchenko Prospekt (near Intourist Hotel) and 11 Volovaya Street. *Jewelers:* Mickiewicz Square and 29 Lenin Prospekt. *Gift Shop:* 1 Kopernik Street. *Arts and Crafts* Mickiewicz Square (near Intourist Hotel).

Uzhgorod: *Souvenirs, art gallery,* Teatralnaya Square. *Gift Shop,* 10 Suvorov Street. *Jeweler's:* 8 Suvorov Street.

TOURS. Intourist organizes tours to Kiev, Kharkov and Uzhgorod with various stopovers, either as separate excursions or as part of general tours. It also offers a special river cruise down the Dnieper. Up-to-date details are available from Intourist offices.

USEFUL ADDRESSES. Kiev: *Railway Station:* at the end of Komintern Street on Vokzalnaya Square. (City Ticket Office. Pushkin Street.) Trams 2, 6, 7, 10, 13, 25 and 30 serve the station. *Bus Terminus:* Avtovokzalnaya Square, served by trams 9, 10, 24 and trolley-buses 1, 11, 12. *Boat Terminal:* Pochtovaya Square, in front of No. 2 Naberezhno-Kreshchatitskaya Street. Local boats serving the environs and excursion boats can be taken from the *Prigorodnaya pristan* landing-stage in front of No. 3 Naberezhnoye Road. Trams: 3, 16, 21, 28, 31 and 32. *Airport:* Borispol, 18 miles from the city. City terminal: 6 Karl Marx Street.

Kharkov: *Railway Stations:* Yuzhny Vokzal (South), Privokzalnaya Square. (City Ticket office, 7–9 Ufinsky Street.) Trams 1, 9, 11, 14, 17 and 19: trolley-buses 2 and 3. The other two stations are the Vokzal Levada (Sigelnikovsky Street), accessible by trams 13, 14 and 16, and the Vokzal Balashovsky (Pichanovskaya Street) by trams 5, 13, 14, 16. *Bus terminus* 22 Gagarin Prospekt. *Airport:* 8 miles from town. City terminal: 2 Rosa Luxemburg Square. Buses start from Kosturensky Street. *Information bureau:* 11 Ufinsky Street. *Central Post Office:* 7 Privokzalnaya Square.

Lvov: *Railway Station:* Privokzalnaya Square. (Ticket office: 20 Gorky Street.) Served by trams 1, 6. 9 and No. 1 trolley bus. *Autobus terminus:* 5 Yaroslav Mudry Square. *Airport:* about 4 miles from the city. *City terminal,* tickets: 2–5 Pobeda Square. *Information Bureau:* 1 Mir Street. *Kolkhoz Market:* 11 Bazar Street. *Main Post Office:* 1 Slovatsky Street.

Uzhgorod: *Railway Station:* 9 Stantsionnaya Street. *City Ticket Office,* 46 Vossoyedineniye Square. *Bus terminus:* 11 Kirov Street. *Airport:* 2 miles from the town, 145 Sovietskaya Street. *City terminal and airport buses* Koryatovich Square.

Ulyanovsk: *Intourist:* 13 Goncharov Street. *Aeroflot office:* Sovietskaya Street. *Railway Station:* Privokzalnaya Square.

MOLDAVIA

The Moldavian Soviet Socialist Republic is in the southwestern corner of the Soviet Union, between the Prut and the Dniester rivers and on the left bank of the Dniester. The Prut forms the western boundary of Moldavia and Romania while in the north, east and southeast, Moldavia borders on the Ukraine.

Moldavia is a small republic, extending for some 200 miles from north to south and 100 miles from west to east. It has a population of getting on for 4 million.

It can be reached from the Romanian border by rail via Ungheni and by motorway via Leusheni. Kishinev, the capital, is linked by road, rail and air with all the major cities of the Soviet Union.

In pre-Christian times, the rich pastures and wooded slopes of the Carpathian mountains were inhabited by Thracian, and later, by Slav tribes. The Volokh ancestors of the Moldavians later left the mountains for the East Carpathian lowlands, where in 1359 they formed an independent principality. For more than 400 years there were many foreign invaders. In the 19th century, the territory between the Dniester and the Prut was annexed to Russia; in 1917 Soviet power was established here. During World War Two, Moldavia suffered considerably during the Nazi invasion and occupation. Today it is an industrial and agricultural republic which has undergone considerable development. Moldavian folk art, especially carpets, has become widely known; so has Moldavian music, especially the dances and songs of the Doina Choir, the Zhok Folk Dance Company, and the Fluierash Orchestra of rare folk instruments, which include the *cimpoi* (bagpipe), *fluier, nai* and *tarogato* (ancient clarinet). The orchards, vineyards and wineries produce excellent fruit and wine.

Kishinev, the capital, stands on the banks of the Bik River. With an average summer temperature of 68–74F°, it has a warm autumn and a mild winter.

The streets and squares are a striking mixture of Western and Eastern elements. Near the banks of the Bik you can still find the Old City, with its picturesque winding alleys and streets. There is much rebuilding going on, though, and gradually the old houses are disappearing. Surrounded by picturesque hillocks planted with flowers, Kishinev's Russian Orthodox Cathedral of the Nativity (opposite the Lenin Monument on Lenin Prospekt) is perhaps the outstanding architectural feature of the Moldavian capital. It was built in 1836; the bell tower dates from 1840. The town's main street is Lenin Prospekt, and the two best hotels are on or close to it. The streets of the new district run parallel with Lenin Prospekt the Bik River's right bank.

The Fine Arts Museum on Lenin Prospekt has 14 large halls devoted to Russian, Moldavian and Western European painting, sculpture and applied art. The Pushkin House on Antonovskaya Street, where the poet lived while in exile in Kishinev between 1820 and 1823, is now open as a museum. It was here that Pushkin began working on his long poem *Eugene Onegin.*

Pobeda Square is in the city center. The Mazaraki Church of the Nativity, in the old city, was built in 1852; there is an old synagogue near Armyanskaya Street.

In addition to Kishinev you might like to visit: Tiraspol, one of the centers of Moldavia's canning and wine-making industries. Here on the bank of the Dniester less than 50 miles from Kishinev, you can sample the Moldavian brandies *Yubileiny, Tiraspolsky, Nistru, Doina* and *Solnechy,* and a variety of wines.

Benderi, near Tiraspol, is one of the oldest towns in Moldavia. It has a 17th-century fortress and a fine view of the Dniester, and it is famous for it silk mills. Destroyed during the last war, it has been completely rebuilt and now has attractive parks and wide boulevards.

Beltsi, a major industrial center north of Kishinev, produces sugar, vegetables oil, wines, brandies—and fur coats.

PRACTICAL INFORMATION FOR KISHINEV

 HOTELS. *Kishinev,* 7 Negruzzi Boulevard. *Moldova Hotel and Restaurant,* 81a Lenin Prospekt. *Motel Strugurash,* 230 Kotovsky Highway, Intourist facilities, about 4 miles from center.

 THEATERS. Moldavia Opera House, 79 Lenin Prospekt. Pushkin Music and Drama Theater—in the same building. All performances in Moldavian. Chekhov Russian Drama Theater (formerly a synagogue), 28th June Street. Philharmonia Concert Hall, at the corner of Komsomolskaya Street. Symphony orchestras, the famous Doina Choir and other national ensembles perform here. Puppet Theater in the Likurich (Glow-worm) Theater, 7 Fontannaya Street, at the corner of Kotovsky Street. Youth Theater, at the same address.

CINEMAS, Patria, Biruinca, Kishinev, all in city center.

 MUSEUMS. Local Museum, 82 Pirogov Street, open 12–7, closed Wed. Good collection of carpets and national costumes. Fine Arts Museum, 115 Lenin Prospekt. Closed Tuesdays. Pushkin Museum and Pushkin House, Antonovskaya Street. Open 11–6, closed Mondays.

 **SHOPPING.** Kolhozny Rynok (market), at the corner of Benderskaya Street and Lenin Prospekt. Sells peasant ware and Moldavian national handicrafts as well as food. Department Store: 136 Lenin Prospekt. Podarki (Gift) Shop, Komsomolskaya Street, at the corner of Lenin Prospekt. Jeweler's: 85 Lenin Prospekt. Secondhand and Antiques: 36 Pushkin Street.

USEFUL KISHINEV ADDRESSES. *Airport:* 9 miles from city. *City terminal:* 132 Lenin Prospekt.

DOWN THE VOLGA

The "Little Mother" from Kazan to Rostov

Matushka—"Dear Little Mother" Volga, as the Russians affectionately call it—is a somewhat contradictory name, for this is the greatest river in Europe, twisting, meandering and flowing from the Valday Hills to the Caspian Sea for almost 2,500 miles, draining an area of a million square miles, and linking five oceans and seas with Moscow through its canals. It is navigable for most of its length until it divides into 80 branches at its vast delta. Yet the Russians call it by a diminutive to express their affection—for, as one of the river captains once put it, "the Volga flows in the heart of every Russian".

To travel its whole length would take a month or more, so Intourist recommends a somewhat shorter cruise, from Kazan along the Middle and Lower Volga and then through the Volga-Don Canal to Rostov-on-Don. From Moscow, a plane will take you to Kazan in a little over an hour. From Rostov, you can return by air to Moscow in less than two hours or you can continue with a visit to the Ukraine or go further south to the Caucasus.

Exploring Along the Volga

Kazan, the capital of the Tatar Autonomous Republic, lies some 800 miles east of Moscow. It has a population of almost one million. The city is built on the left (eastern) bank of the Volga and is one of the most important industrial and cultural centers in the Soviet Union and a major road and rail junction for traffic from Moscow to the Ural Mountains. Until 1956, when the Kuibyshev Reservoir was built, its harbor was some four miles from the city, but now Kazan is a Volga port in its own right.

Founded in the 14th century, Kazan was once the capital of the Kazan Khanate, annexed to Russia by Ivan IV in the 16th century.

A good place to start your exploration of Kazan is the kremlin (No. 2 trolley-bus to Kuibyshev Square, then No. 1 trolley-bus to the Krem-levskaya stop). Opposite the kremlin entrance is the Tatar State Museum, whose collections present a remarkable survey of the history of the Volga region.

The Spasskaya Bastion, through which you enter the castle, has four levels and with its adjoining walls forms the oldest part of the kremlin (16th century). Originally the fortress only occupied three-quarters of its present area and consisted of the Khan's palace and the mosque (both built of stone) and several other, wooden, buildings. (Kazan also has two 18th-century mosques: the Apanayevskaya and the Mardzhani.) The Church of the Annunciation (1561–2) was designed by the Pskov architect, Postnik Yakovlev. The seven-story Syumbek Tower (17th century) was built by Moscow masters, as was the 19th-century White Palace. Today the White Palace houses the Supreme Soviet and the Council of Ministers of the Tatar Republic.

From the hill next to this palace, or, if you feel like climbing higher, from the Syumbek Tower, there is a fine view of the city. You will see that Kazan lies partly below the level of the Kuibyshev Reservoir and therefore has some 18 miles of protecting dams along its riverfront. In the distance, on a small island, you will see a truncated conc-shaped monument. This is the memorial to the heroic dead of the 1552 siege of Kazan.

Leaving the kremlin by the Spasskaya Bastion, continue along Lenin Street. Here you will find the Kazan Branch of the Soviet Academy of Sciences. In front of the building there is a statue of Lobachevsky, the famous mathematician who studied at the local university and became its rector. Lobachevsky is celebrated in the Soviet Union as the founder of non-Euclidean geometry. Kazan University, by the way, has more than 60 faculties and a library of two million volumes; its former students include Leo Tolstoy—and Lenin.

No. 68 Ulyanov Street is where Lenin lived with his family from October 1888, when he returned from exile. Today the wooden building is the Lenin Memorial Museum, and Lenin's room has been reconstructed with its original furnishings. Maxim Gorky worked in Kazan from 1885 to 1886 as a baker's assistant. The Gorky Museum (10 Gorky Street, take No. 2 trolley-bus to the Dynamo Stadium) has many souvenirs of his stay in Kazan. Nearby, at 13 Gorky Street, is the Kamal Tatar Drama Theater, one of the five theaters in the city (Sharif Kamal was a classic Tatar writer). The Tatar Opera and Ballet Theater stands on Svoboda Square, opposite the Lenin Statue. It is named after Musa Dzhalil, a resistance fighter excuted in 1944 by the Nazis in Berlin. He was posthumously awarded a Lenin Prize in 1957 for the poems he wrote while in prison.

Ulyanovsk

Boarding the boat in Kazan, a journey of 11 hours takes you to Ulyanovsk, a regional capital. This is Lenin's birthplace, and here he spent his childhood and youth. As such, it is naturally a Soviet place of pilgrimage. The squat wooden house on the former Moskovskaya Street (now Lenin Street), now refurbished as the Lenin Memorial Museum, has been visited by several million people.

Previously called Simbirsk, the town adopted the surname of its famous son (Lenin's real name was Vladimir Ulyanov) in May 1924. Simbirsk was founded in 1648 by Czar Alexei Mikhailovich as a frontier fortress; in the 1780s Emelyan Pugachev, the leader of the Pugachev Rebellion, was brought here after his capture and later taken to his execution in Moscow; by then, the city was an important trading centre for the Volga district and in 1796 became an administrative capital. Today it manufactures automobiles, machine tools and electrical equipment.

The best place to start exploring Ulyanovsk is in the center on the right bank. The Lenin Memorial Museum (58 Lenin Street) was the home of the Ulyanov family until 1887, when the founder-to-be of the Soviet Union left to enter the University of Kazan. There are a number of other museums, all devoted to the life and career of Lenin; the central one is at 39 Tolstoy Street. Walking towards the river, you come to the crossroads with Goncharov Street—the main thoroughfare in Ulyanovsk. No. 16 on the left is the birthplace of Goncharov, the author if *Oblomov*.

Crossing into Kommunisticheskaya Street, you reach Lenin Square, which is on the embankment. Before you come to the square you can, if you wish, turn left into Sovietskaya Street, where No. 12 is the former Simbirsk High School, where Lenin studied from 1879 to 1887. A former classroom (next to the assembly hall on the first floor) has been turned into yet another shrine in Lenin's honor.

Opposite the school in the Karamzin Garden you can see the memorial to the first Russian historian, Karamzin, who was born here. Following the park railing along Gimov Street, you come to Ulyanov Street. Lenin's birthplace is No. 12. Today it houses a children's library.

Returning along Ulyanov Street to the corner of Kommunisti- cheskaya Street, and turning down Kommunisticheskaya Street, you pass the Palace of the Book (a library used by the young Lenin) and then come to Novy Venets (New Wreath) Quay. Nos. 3–4 are known as the Goncharov House, and house the Museum of Fine Arts and Local History. One of the rooms contains souvenirs of the writer's life and work.

Your walk takes you back to Lenin Square, and, at the northern end on the corner of Sovietskaya Street, to the Drama Theater.

The "Sea of Kulbyshev" and Volgograd

From Ulyanovsk you will reach Togliatti in eight hours. There used to be a small town on this site called Stavropol, but the building of the huge Kuibyshev Reservoir swallowed it up and its population was transferred to the present-day Togliatti. The city is one of the industrial settlements that have developed around the Kuibyshev Hydroelectric Plant; this is where the Italo-Soviet Fiat works were recently established, hence the Italian name of the city commemorating the long-time leader of Italy's Communist Party.

Tourists on Volga cruises can take an Intourist excursion to the Lenin Power Works, which were built in 1950–6. The main dam is more than half a mile long.

The landscape on either side of this section of the Volga is particularly attractive. On the right the Zhiguli Mountains block the river's course and it makes a 100-mile-long detour through hills with oak and pine forests. Here the Volga turns east; then, at the Hill of the Royal Grave (Karev Kurgan) where archeologists have found Scythian burial places, it suddenly curves south. Originally the Karev Kurgan rose well above the river, but now it barely protrudes out of the Kuibyshev "Sea." On the left you catch your first sight of the Sokoli Gori (Hawk Mountains) which extend as far as the city of Kuibyshev. The part you see is called Tip-Tav, and is even more picturesque than the Zhiguli. Here the Volga narrows at the Zhiguli Gate, beyond which the holiday settlements of Kuibyshev begin. Kuibyshev, formerly Samara, is a large industrial city, the wartime capital of the Soviet Government; but the ship does not stop here. From Togliatti, there is an unbroken journey of 15 hours to Khvalinsk, which is pleasantly situated and has an agreeable climate, a sandy beach and other attractions. From Khvalinsk, you sail straight on to Volgograd, passing Saratov which is the city of natural gas (a pipeline carries it straight to Moscow). (Here again there is no stop.) The total journey time to Volgograd is 36 hours.

Volgograd, formerly Stalingrad, was the site of the great, fierce and decisive battle which the Russians consider, with some justification, a turning point in World War Two. The city was totally destroyed in the battle. Today, Volgograd is a regional capital with a hugh power plant and a number of important industrial plants; the Volga-Don Canal begins close by. There are direct rail and air connections with Moscow. Spreading for almost 50 miles along the river, the city has vast tracts of industrial areas. The residential quarters are set apart from these, separated by a green belt covering well over 20,000 acres.

From Volgograd there are excursions to the Hydroelectric Plant on the left bank of the river, where a whole town called Volzhsky has been erected. The plant is the largest on the Volga; only those in Siberia can compete with it in size and output. The reservoir has an area of over 2,000 square miles.

Exploring Volgograd

From the harbor of Volgograd, climb the solemn gray granite steps of the quay and make your way to the center of the city via Alleya Geroyev (Heroes' Promenade). The Square of the Fallen Heroes is the center. At the entrance to the Promenade stands the Fountain of Friendship, while the road itself is lined with busts of the most famous of the city's defenders. The Square of the Fallen Heroes has a number of monuments commemorating the dead of the Civil War and World War Two. Here too, are several public buildings: the Intourist Hotel, the House of the Soviets, the Central Post Office, the Central Department Store and the Gorky Dramatic Theater. It was in the cellar of the department store that Field Marshal Paulus and his staff surrendered.

The Square of the Fallen Heroes is crossed on the west by Prospekt Mira (Peace Boulevard). On the corner of Prospekt Mira and Gagarin Street further north about three blocks is the Planetarium.

By walking along Gogol Street from the Square of Fallen Heroes, you soon reach the railway station. Close to it (to the south) is Komsomol Park. Lenin Street leads eastward from the park towards Lenin Prospekt, the longest thoroughfare in Volgograd. At No. 8 Gogol Street, the corner of the station square and Gogol Street, a single-story building houses the Museum of the Defense of the City.

After visiting the museum you might like to inspect the most important memorial places connected with the Battle of Stalingrad. Walk down the Promenade of Heroes to the tram station on Lenin Prospekt and take a tram to Lenin Square. Between the square and the river stands Pavlov House, named after Sergeant Jacob Pavlov, who defended it with a handful of men for 58 days until his group was able to join the Soviet counterattack. Outside the three-storied house is the statue of the Soldier of Volgograd. Beyond Pavlov House toward the river is Flour Mill (Melnitsa) No. 4, which has been left standing in ruins to commemorate the devastation caused by the fighting.

The highest point in Volgograd is the Mamayev-Kurgan, where the front line troops faced each other for five months. You can get to it be taking a bus along Lenin Prospekt. After the battle, 1,200 shell fragments were found for every square yard of this area. At the top of the Mamayev-Kurgan there is a 305-foot-high concrete memorial and a separate colonnaded hall inside which a model panorama of the Battle of Stalingrad has been reconstructed.

Down the Volga-Don Canal

Between Volgograd and the Caspian Sea there is only one important settlement—Astrakhan. This port city (with 458,000 inhabitants) is famous for its fish canneries—especially for processing caviar.

The Volga-Don Canal (Lenin Canal) begins some 18 miles south of Volgograd. You'll see a triumphal arch 120 feet high erected to commemorate the mingling of the waters of the two great rivers on the night of May 30, 1952. The first nine locks are still on the Volga: the tenth lowers ships onto the Don. The 13th lock is the entrance to the Tsimlyansk Reservoir which not only feeds the canal and the hydroelectric plant, but also irrigates the Lower Don area, which is often threatened by drought.

On the right as you enter the reservoir (some six miles) upstream on the Don—the other way, and not on your cruise—ships sail from the harbor of Kalach for the Cossack village of Veshenskaya where Mikhail Sholokhov, the author of the famous "Don" novels, lives. You will turn south down the reservoir and into the bluish-green waters of the Don as you journey towards Rostov, the final stop.

Rostov (officially Rostov-na-Donu) is a regional capital. It lies on the high, right bank of the river, 30 miles from the Sea of Azov. Founded in the eighteenth century, it is both a river and a sea port and the "Gateway to the Caucasus," the rail and road junction for people traveling from Moscow to the holiday resorts in the Caucasus and on the Black Sea Riviera. By train it is 28½ hours from the Soviet capital, by air 1 hr. 50 mins. The Moscow-Yalta highway branches off at Kharkov towards Rostov; the distance from Kharkov and Rostov is 320 miles.

Rostov is a large industrial city, but it has something to offer the tourist, too: the great wheatfields of the surrounding countryside, the fish specialties in its restaurants, and the produce of its champagne factory are all enjoyable. It is well worth visiting the racecourse (at the end of Universitetsky Prospekt), while the traditions of the Cossack past are faithfully preserved in the Museum of Local Lore (87 Engels Street). Its collection includes the sword of Frederick the Great seized during the Seven Years' War. The Museum of Fine Arts (115 Pushkinskaya) has some splendid canvases by Vereshchagin, Levitan and Repin.

The streets of Rostov are laid out on a rectangular plan around Engels Street. The Gorky Theater (170 Engels Street) has an excellent company, while in summer Rostov beach (on the left or south bank) offers good swimming.

PRACTICAL INFORMATION FOR THE VOLGA

WHEN TO GO. Summer, late spring or early autumn are the best seasons. The Intourist cruises are mainly in July and August but regular steamers run year round. The average temperature in summer varies from a maximum of 84°F (29°C) to a minimum of 65°F (18°C). The humidity is low.

HOW TO GET THERE. By train. From Moscow to Kazan, then by ship. **By air.** Regular flights from Leningrad and Moscow to Kazan. The Intourist cruise combines rail and air travel; it takes you by air from London or other Western capitals to Moscow and after two days' sightseeing there, flies you to Kazan. After the river cruise you fly back from Krasnodar to Moscow and then leave the Soviet Union by air after a day's stopover. There are other flights from various points in the Soviet Union to Kazan.

By road. From Moscow by Route 8 to Kharkov; from Kharkov by Route 10 to Rostov.

By ship. Extended cruises can be arranged directly from Moscow. The Kazan-Rostov-on-Don cruise takes 9 days. The cruise boat offers various classes of accommodations including, if you wich, all meals and excursions; for current prices check with Intourist.

WHAT TO SEE. Kazan. The Kremlin. The Church of the Annunciation. The Syumbek Bastion. The White Palace. **Ulyanoysk.** Lenin's birthplace and museum. The Freedom House. **Volgograd,** Square of the Fallen. Mamai Burial Mound. Sergeant Pavlov's House. Volgograd Hydroelectric Station. Locks on the Volga-Don Canal. **Rostov.** Cathedral of the Nativity of the Virgin. Ulyanov Park. Museums.

HOTELS. Kazan. *Kazan Hotel,* 9/15 Bauman Street, is the best in town, but by no means outstanding. Centrally located. Restaurant is very popular with the locals. Then come either the *Soviet,* 80/7 Bauman Street, or *Tatarstan,* 86 Bauman Street.
Note: Kazan can be visited in daytime only, at presstime.

Rostov. Best is *Moskovskaya Hotel,* with an Intourist office, at 62 Engels Street. Or *Intourist* at 115 Engels Street, 273 rooms, with Intourist services. Then come the *Rostov,* with 524 rooms, first-class contemporary, but without character. Then either the *Don Hotel,* 34 Gazetny Pereulok, or the *Yuzhnaya Hotel,* 20 Karl Marx Prospekt. Camping in Rostov: on Novocherkassk Highway, 9 miles out.

Ulyanovsk. Best is the *Venets Hotel,* in town centre, with Intourist office; then, in order, *Volga Hotel; Rossiya Hotel,* Marx Street; and *Number One Hotel,* Sovietskaya Street.

Volgograd. Equal choice between *Intourist* and the *Volgograd,* both on the Square of the Fallen (Ploshchad Pavshikh Bortsov).

 RESTAURANTS. If you travel by boat down the Volga, you will be taking at least your main meals on board. Fish from the Volga is excellent, and the meals are usually ample, though they can be somewhat monotonous. Apart from the hotels listed above, most of which have at least better-than-average restaurants, we can recommend the following:

Kazan. *Parus,* the floating restaurant at Lenin Bridge; then *Vostok,* Kuibyshev Street, and *Mayak,* Dekabristov Street.

Novocherkassk. Best is the *Novocherkassk Hotel's* dining room, 90 Podteklov Street; then *Yuzhnaya Restaurant* on Moskovskaya Street; finally, *Durzhba Restaurant* on the outskirts of town.

Rostov. *Teatralny Restaurant,* in October Revolution Park, is fine in summer. Other restaurants include the *Tsentralny,* 76 Engels Street; *Volgadon Restaurant,* 31 Beregovaya Street; *Zoloty Kolos,* 45 Engels Street; *Druzhba,* 90 Engels Street; *Cosmos,* 128 Engels Street; and *Molodyozhnoye Café,* Teatralnaya Square.

Volgograd. *Leto Restaurant* in the City Gardens (best in summer); then *Mayak Restaurant* on the Embankment and *Molodyozhnoye Café,* 19 Lenin Prospekt.

 CULTURAL ACTIVITIES. Kazan: Soviet Academy of Sciences and University. Kamal Tatar Dramatic Theater. Tatar Opera and Ballet Theater. **Ulyanovsk:** Drama Theater, corner of Lenin Square and Sovietskaya Street.

Volgograd: Drama Theater, The Square of the Fallen. Theater of Musical Comedy, 2 Vorovsky Street. Puppet Theater, 15 Lenin Prospekt. Philharmonic, Embankment. Circus: Volodarsky Street. Cinemas: Pobeda, 1 Kommunisticheskaya Street. Rodina, 29 Nevskaya Street. Novosti Dnya, (Newsreels), 4 Heroes' Avenue, Gvardyeets, 5 Akademicheskaya Street.

Rostov: Gorky Drama Theater, 1 Teatralnaya Square. Youth Theater, 170 Engels Street. Musical Comedy Theater, 88 Serafimovich Street. Open Air Theater (Zeleny Teatr), Oktyabrsky Park Revolutsii. Circus, 45 Budyonnovsky Prospekt.

 MUSEUMS. Kazan: *State Museum of Tataria,* 2 Lenin Street. *Gorky Museum,* 10 Gorky Street. **Ulyanovsk:** *V.I. Lenin Memorial Museum,* Lenin Street. *Museum of Art and Local Museum,* 3/4 Novy Venets Quay.

Volgograd: *Defense Museum,* 8 Gogol Street. Open daily, except Tues, 11–6. *Local History Museum,* 38 Lenin Prospekt. Open daily, 11 to 6, except Tues. *Fine Arts Museum,* 21 Lenin Prospekt. *Planetarium,* 14 Yury Gagarin Street.

Rostov: *Local History Museum,* 79 Engels Street. Open 10–6, closed Mon. Interesting stone idols worshipped by nomads in 11th–12th centuries. The Planetarium is in the same building. *Fine Art Museum,* 115 Pushkinskaya Street. Open 10–6, closed Mon. *Museum of the Revolutionary Past and the Glory of Labor,* 2 Guzev Street.

SHOPPING. The large *Volga boats* all carry souvenir shops; you may be able to pick up items by local craftsmen when you stop en route. There is a large *department store* on the Square of the Fallen in Volgograd.

In Rostov-on-Don you will find *department stores* at 46 and 65 Engels Street; good *jewelers'* at 43 and 58 Engels Street, and a *gift shop* at 60 Engels Street. The main *market* is in Oborony Street.

USEFUL ADDRESSES. Kazan: *Intourist Office:* Intourist Hotel, tel. 2-05-00. *Aeroflot City Office:* 7 Universitetskaya Street. *Harbor,* at the end of Tatarstan Street (from Kuibyshev Square along Kuibyshev Street). **Volograd:** *Intourist:* 14 Mir (Peace) Boulevard. *Aeroflot Office:* 5 Promenade of Heroes. *Railway station:* Privokzalnaya Square. **Rostov:** *Intourist,* 62 Engels Street. *Aeroflot,* 68 Engels Street. *Port:* 14 Beregovaya Street. *Railway Station:* Engels Street.

THE CRIMEA AND THE BLACK SEA

From Odessa to Batumi

Tourist brochures often speak of the Soviet Riviera. This is a somewhat misleading description of the northern and northeastern coast of the Black Sea. It is only in the east, at the foot of the Caucasus, that its latitude reaches that of the Mediterranean; and it is only in the Crimea and the coastal areas of the Caucasus that the mountains protect the sea from the cold northern currents. In these regions the vegetation is truly Mediterranean. And the attractions are genuine enough—long and seldom crowded beaches, pleasant if not luxurious hotels, plenty of sunshine, cultural activities and other attractions.

The area is a large one, and in this chapter you will find a general description of the Crimean and Black Sea resorts covering the facts you need to know as a tourist. The main places are: Odessa, the western gate of the Soviet Riviera; the cities of the "Liman" (Ochakov, Nikolaev, Kherson); the Crimean Peninsula with Simferopol, Alushta, Artek, Gurzuf, Yalta, Livadia, Oreanda, Miskhor, Alupka, Simeiz, Bakhchisarai and Sevastopol; the Western Crimea with Yevpatoriya and Saki; the cities east of Yalta, Feodosia, Planerskoye and Sydak; Kerch and its peninsula; the Caucasian coast with Anapa and Novorossisk, Gelendzhik and Dykhankhot, Tuapse, Sochi and its environs, Matsesta, Hosta and Adler; the region of Abkhazia with Gagra, Gudauta, Akhali Afon, and the Abkhazian capital, Sukhumi; and Batumi, only 12 miles from the Turkish frontier.

Exploring the Black Sea Coast and Crimea

Odessa, the "Western Gate" of the Soviet Riviera, with its picturesque situation, has been described as the "pearl of the Black Sea". It is connected by regular steamship lines with ports in Romania, Bulgaria, France, Italy, Greece, Turkey, the United Arab Republic and Lebanon. Many foreign tourists prefer to come by rail or air (the 950 miles between Moscow and Odessa are covered in 23 hours by express train and 105 minutes by air) and then continue from here by ship on a Black Sea cruise. This takes about 18 hours to Yalta, 45 hours to Sochi and 66 hours to Batumi, the last port on the Soviet coast before the Turkish border.

The best starting-point from which to explore Odessa is the seaside promenade, high above the water. This is the Primorsky Boulevard, with one of the Intourist Hotels, the Odessa, at No. 11 (the other Intourist hotel, the Krasnaya, is at 15 Pushkin Street; these two and the newer Chernoye Morye hotel are recommended for tourists).

The walk along Primorsky Boulevard not only reveals the picturesque panorama of Odessa Bay but also introduces you to the city's historical and cultural monuments, many of which you will find on this boulevard and on neighboring streets.

The southern part of Primorsky Boulevard ends at the Pushkin Statue, erected in 1888 by public subscription. The poet spent the years 1823–4 here during his exile, living in a house which is now the headquarters of the Ukrainian Writers' Association.

The palace situated at the far end of the boulevard was once the residence of Count Vorontsov, Pushkin's strict and intolerant boss when the poet was employed as a civil servant. Built in 1826–7 by Boffo, it became the headquarters of the Odessa Soviet after the revolution. To-day, restored to its original form, it houses the Odessa Pioneers.

Walking north along Primorsky Boulevard you pass a cannon mounted on a wooden carriage which recalls the days of the Crimean War. It was salvaged from the British frigate *Tiger* sunk by shore batteries.

Close to the boulevard, at 8 Lastochkin Street, stands the Odessa Opera House, one of the finest in Europe, where Caruso and Chaliapin once sang; its ceiling is decorated with frescos depicting scenes from Shakespeare. Designed in 1884–87 by two Viennese architects (and resembling the Vienna Opera and the Dresden Court Theater), its interior is in Louis XVI style. Tchaikovsky, Rubenstein, Glazunov and Rimsky-Korsakov all conducted here.

Passing the corner of Pushkin Street and Primorsky Boulevard, beyond Kommuna Square, you will see the Archeological Museum with its graceful columns. Dating from 1825, it illustrates the history of the peoples who lived on the northern shore of the Black Sea from ancient times until the 13th century. It also has one of the largest collection of Egyptian relics and exhibits from ancient Greek settlements on the Black Sea.

Farther along stands the impressive, classicist palace of the city Soviet, another Boffo-designed building with some attractive allegorical statuary. No. 9 Primorsky Boulevard used to be the residence of the military commander of the city; today it is the Sailors' Palace. In front of Nos. 7 and 8 the street opens out into the square and two buildings border it in a semicircle. Built in 1827–8 by Melnikov, No. 8 was a private mansion, which in the 1840's became a hotel. No. 7 used to house various offices and, for a while, the municipal library.

The Potemkin Steps

From these buildings a long stone stairway leads down to the harbor. Originally Boffo intended this to be the main entrance to the city, with an unusual triumphal arch at the top. These are the famous Potemkin Steps, the scene of the traumatic sequence in Eisenstein's great film in which czarist soldiers massacre the crowd as they descend towards the mutineers from the *Potemkin* anchored in the bay.

Descending the historic stairway you reach the harbor. At the entrance to the Customs House stands a memorial to Vakulenchuk, one of the Potemkin mutineers, on a red granite base. Now you can see the full panorama of the largest port on the Black Sea. There is another large harbor, built some 15 miles from the city at Sukhoi Liman. This harbor is the base of the Russian whaling fleet, whose headquarters, built in the rather ornate style of the early 1950's, are on the corner of Marx and Deribasovskaya Street.

After visiting the harbor, continue along Primorsky Boulevard (to which you can return by the funicular to the left of the Potemkin steps). Opposite the top of the steps stands a statue of the Duc de Richelieu erected in 1826 in honor of the French aristocrat who for a time was Mayor of Odessa.

Nearby there is an openair café, where you can take a rest and enjoy the view. Then, between the semicircular houses, you can walk on to the Deribasovskaya, the busiest thoroughfare in Odessa.

No. 16 was formerly a college; later Mickiewicz lived here and in 1855–6 the famous scientist Mendeleyev taught at the same institution. The courtyard has kept its original atmosphere.

Deribasovskaya Street, with its hotels and shops, leads into the Square of the Soviet Army, in the corner of which stands a bust of Count Vorontsov. Not far from the city center is Shevchenko Park, which can be reached by trolley buses Nos. 2 and 3 and trams Nos. 1, 4, 23, 28. It has many pleasant walks, a stadium, an openair theater and a beach. On the seashore are some remains of the old Odessa quarantine station. From the park you can walk across the Square of the October Revolution, which used to be the market place.

Your exploration of Odessa would not be complete without a visit to the catacombs which run for several hundred miles under Odessa and its environs. They must be visited with a proper guide as any individual exploration can be highly dangerous. The catacombs have been used as hiding places by revolutionaries and criminals; during World War Two they served as a command post for the Resistance and were never occupied by the Germans. A mock-up of the Resistance headquarters can be seen in the Local Museum (accessible by trolley buses No. 1 and 2 and trams 2, 3, 12 and 23). The Art Museum and the Museum of Western and Eastern Art are also well worth a visit.

Among the numerous scientific institutions in Odessa the distinguished Filatov Clinic of Ophthalmology deserves special mention; also important are the astronomical and geophysical observatory and the laboratory researching increased plant yields. Odessa's university, founded in 1865, is named after Mechnikov, the famous bacteriologist.

Health Resorts

It is also a pleasant spa and vacation resort with sandy beaches stretching for some 25 miles, a mild climate and plenty of sunshine. The bathing season starts in mid-May and ends around September 25th; September is the sunniest month. Apart from the Shevchenko Park Beach there are a number of other spas and beaches. Lermontov is within the city limits, on a high plateau above the seashore. It has a large park, mud baths, hospitals and sanatoria and can be reached by trolley buses 2 and 3 and trams 4 and 28.

Arcadia, three miles from the city, is a pleasant health resort which can be reached by tram No. 17, by bus and by waterbus.

Kuyalnitsky is eight miles from the city, reached by bus. Ukrainsky Artek, six miles away, is a spa for children. It has a shallow, sandy beach. No. 9 tram, or bus or boat takes you there. Malodolinsky, 12 miles from Odessa, is also a children's health resort, with mud baths and a beach. It is accessible by rail (Odessa-Ovidiopol line) or by car. Chernomorka, 11 miles from Odessa, is another children's resort, with shallow water and sandy beaches. No. 29 tram serves it. October Revolution, 13 miles from Odessa, is yet another children's health resort, with mud baths. There is a beach near the hospital. Go by rail to Dachnaya station, then take the bus.

Zatoka, 40 miles from Odessa, is a seaside spa. The beach is sandy and the water shallow. Get there by rail to the town of Bugaz.

The Towns of the "Liman"

Sailing from Odessa towards the Crimea, we see before long the bay formed by the estuaries of the Southern Bug and the Dnieper rivers. In Ukrainian, the bay is called Liman—narrow on the sea side, the peninsula makes a natural barrier some 25 miles long. The three towns Ochakov (at the "gate" formed by the peninsula), Nikolayev (in the mouth of the Southern Bug) and Kherson (on the right bank of the Dnieper) form an almost perfect triangle.

Ochakov is an agricultural and fisheries center. For tourists the nearby excavations some 22 miles from Ochakov are the interest. The excavations are on the site of the ancient city of Olvia, founded by the Greeks some 2,500 years ago, and now a protected area. A local museum houses archeological finds made over the years.

The second town on the Liman is Nikolayev, an important port and industrial center. Founded in 1788 soon after the Turks were driven out from nearby Ochakov, it was one of the cradles of Russian shipbuilding. The first Russian merchant ship and the first armored cruiser were launched here. Lazarev, the Antarctic explorer, also lived and worked in Nikolayev. The shipyards are still busy. The port is a center of manganese and iron ore export.

The third Liman city is Kherson, with a population of 315,000. It lies 15 miles inland from the bay but seagoing ships can enter its river harbor and sail as far upstream as Kiev on the river Dnieper.

Founded in 1778 on the instructions of Catherine the Great, Kherson was intended to be an outpost of the southern steppes and a shipbuilding center. The area was already part of the defense line developed during the 1735–9 Russo-Turkish War. The Alexander Fortification dates from this period and is a characteristic example of 18th-century military architecture. The walls and the main gate are still standing and inside you can visit the former arsenal.

Close by is the Basilica of St. Catherine, also 18th century. In 1783 the first ship of the Black Sea Fleet, the *Glorious Catherine*, a 66-gun frigate, was launched here, to be followed by many battleships and merchant vessels. The local history museum has many souvenirs of Field Marshal Suvorov, who supervised the building of the fortifications. An oak tree that he is supposed to have planted to commemorate his victory over the Turks still stands in the center of the city park.

Today Kherson is a major trading port and cultural center.

Near Kherson is a fish reserve in the Dnieper delta and a reservation for steppe animals and waterfowl. Some distance away is the Askania-Nova nature reservation, where large numbers of antelopes, zebras, bisons, llamas, ostriches and other animals roam freely. From Kherson, a short excursion will take you to the mudbaths of Golaya Pristan, 11 miles away, which has a fine park. Or you can make a longer trip to the hydroelectric plant at Kakhovka; here is the new town of Novaya Kakhovka, built in the '50s. The Intourist office in Kherson (Intourist Hotel, Svoboda Square) will provide information and make all arrangements for your visit.

The Crimea

Yalta, the best-known Crimean resort, is best approached by sea, skirting the wide arc of the Crimean Peninsula. Coming from Odessa you sail along the western coast, past the softly sloping sandy beach of Yevpatoriya, the majestic rock fortress of Sevastopol, the sheltered bay of Balaklava (where Ulysses once took refuge), and then the 60-mile-long string of picturesque vacation resorts along the southern Crimean shore. Traveling by air or rail you approach the Crimean coast across steppes from north to east. Simiferopol is the end of the railroad and the highway from Moscow. From here, buses and cars will take you along winding roads through the romantic countryside of the Crimea, descending over some 55 miles to the coast. Most of the three million or more tourists who visit the Crimea annually tend to stay in the smaller or larger coastal centers, but there is much to see inland as well.

Simferopol

Simferopol, a regional capital with a population of almost 300,000 lies on the banks of the river Salgir, which is rapid and swollen in spring and barely a rivulet in summer. This is the traditional starting or terminal point of Crimean tours. Roads connect the city with the main Crimean resorts. It is 60 miles from Yalta, 40 from Yevpatoriya, 45 from Sevastopol and 65 from Feodosia.

Simferopol has direct rail connections with the mainland, via Dzhankoy in the north and Kerch in the east, and by virtue of its airport and the excellent Crimean road network it is also an important junction for through traffic. From Moscow by rail (express) the journey takes 23 hours, by air less than two hours. From Moscow a 900-mile highway leads to the city via Kursk and Kharkov and continues to Yalta.

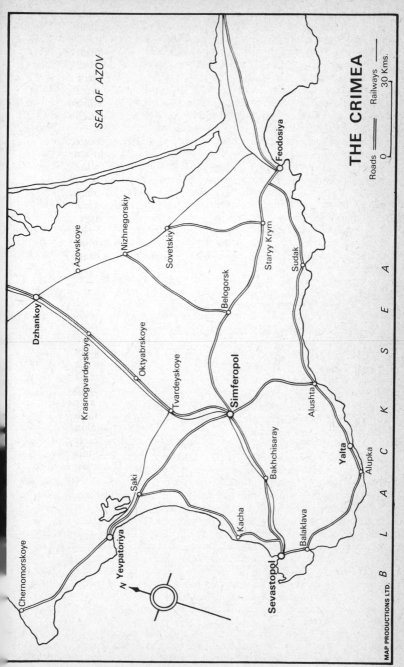

SEA OF AZOV

Chernomorskoye

Yevpatoriya

Saki

Dzhankoy

Krasnogvardeyskoye

Oktyabrskoye

Tvardeyskoye

Azovskoye

Nizhnegorskiy

Sovetskiy

Belogorsk

Simferopol

Bakhchisaray

Kacha

Balaklava

Sevastopol

Alushta

Staryy Krym

Sudak

Yalta

Alupka

Feodosiya

B L A C K S E A

THE CRIMEA

Roads

Railways

0   30 Kms.

MAP PRODUCTIONS LTD.

N

Simferopol was granted a charter in 1784. Built on the site of a former Tatar settlement, its coat of arms includes a bee hive and bees to symbolize its industriousness. Today the city has a university, numerous research institutes and theaters, and is an important cultural center. The vegetation is tropical and exotic; the terraced city park on the banks of the Salgir is particularly attractive.

A visit to the Local Museum with its specialized Tavrida (Tauria) Library, a collection of some 50,000 books about the Crimea, is very rewarding. The Regional Art Museum, too, is well worth seeing. But the main tourist attraction, in the environs of Simferopol, is Neapolis-Neapol Skifsky, an archeological site in the Valley of Petrovskiy (Peter's Rock), less than a mile from the city, on the Alushta highway. This "Scythian New Town" was the capital of the Scythian state in the 2nd century BC. It was destroyed by the Huns some 600 years later. Excavations started here in 1827; they revealed many marble and bronze statues, and a large burial ground with stone mausoleums and the graves of 72 Scythian noblemen with gold ornaments and weapons.

The Salgir Reservoir, on the Alushta highway, two miles from Simferopol, is also a pleasant excursion spot to visit. It is four and a half miles long and a mile wide, with a beach, a boathouse and a lakeside restaurant.

By prior arrangement, you can visit the astrophysical observatory of the Soviet Academy of Sciences. Although 20 miles away it is easily accessible by a regular bus from Simferopol.

From Simferopol to Yalta

Intourist has group excursions from Simferopol along the southern coast of the Crimea and you may find that certain localities can *only* be visited in a group.

You can take a helicopter from Simferopol to Yalta—it seats 10 passengers and the trip takes 20 minutes. There is also a bus and trolley line, or you can drive there yourself. The distance is about 60 miles. The winding road first follows the valley of the Salgir River then, passing Lozovoye and Zarechnoye, it climbs a 2,400-foot-high pass in the Crimean Mountains. This is one of the finest sections of the Simferopol—Yalta road, with the Chatir Dag (Tent Mountain) rising over 4,500 feet to your right, and a splendid panorama from the terrace of the Pereval Motel restaurant which you will find on the old highway here.

From here, the road descends quickly to the first large seaside resort, Alushta, almost exactly halfway between Simferopol and Yalta. Less than 10 miles from Alushta stands the Kutuzov Fountain, a monument to the Russian general who lost the sight of one eye in a battle fought nearby in 1774 against the Turks.

Alushta is less sheltered than Yalta because the mountain range is some five miles from the shore; and in the summer the heat is tempered by the mountain breezes. But sunshine hours are very high here and the sea is warmer than at Yalta. The sea bed shelves steeply so swimmers must take great care.

On the hill that forms the city center, the remains of the ancient fortress built by the Byzantine Emperor Justinian some 1,300 years ago are still visible. In the 14th century the Genoese captured the city and turned it into a fortified trading center. The main thoroughfare of the modern resort is Lenin Street, which runs along the shore and is edged with stone balustrades and decorated with flower beds and fountains. The hotels, restaurants, the best shops and the harbor are all on or near this street.

The sanatoria and vacation area is about one mile west of the center. Here, too, there is a camping site with a service station for motorists.

From Alushta you can visit the Chatir Dag. A walk of some two or three hours from the summit will take you to the famous stalactite caves on the northern plateau. The Suuk Koba (Cold Cave) has a cold spring; the Bin-bas Koba (Thousand-Headed Cave) has some splendid rock formations. Another favorite excursion is to Mount Demerdzhi (over 4,000 ft.), north of Alushta. A longer tour will take you to the Dzhur-Dzhur, 15 miles northeast from Alushta near the village of Generalskoye —this is the finest waterfall in the Crimean, in a picturesque ravine.

Alushta's most interesting sight is the game reservation, officially known as the Crimean State Nature Preserve; its central offices are in the city at 24 Putsatov Street. It can be visited only with an official permit. The reserve covers well over 70,000 acres—it is a huge openair museum, with ancient trees and a huge variety of native game, Crimean stags, moufflons, gazelles and foxes.

Alushta can be reached from Simferopol and Yalta. There is a water-bus service from Yalta. (Like other spots in the Crimea, it may be barred to individual travellers. Check with Intourist.)

On the way from Alushta to Yalta the road skirts on the left a strangely shaped mountain called Ayu-Dag (Bear Mountain), which looks like a bear bending over the sea. There is a local legend about the mountain: a greedy trio of bruins once tried to drink the Black Sea dry, and a fairy turned the greediest of them to stone. On the summit of Bear Mountain you can still see the ruins of one of the Genoan forts. Adam Mickiewicz, the Polish poet, devoted one of his Crimean sonnets to the Ayu-Dag in 1825.

Here begins the international children's vacation area called Artek, scattered over some five miles. In the summer, Pioneers camp here; while from autumn through spring it is a forest school for children of 10–14 who are tuberculosis-sufferers. Artek consists of several camps, some of them on the seashore (Primorsky). It has various activity centers and its own fleet of small motorboats. A cable-car lift now runs from the sea to the inland camps and pavilions.

Gurzuf is two miles from the highway, on a picturesque bay 10 miles from Yalta. It is surrounded on three sides by high mountains, which protect it from cold wind; on the northeast, Bear Mountain, on the north, Babugan-Yayla and Roman-Kos (4,600 feet). To the west, Gurzuf is enclosed by the bare cliffs of the Orliny Zalyot ("Where the Eagle Flies"), the nesting place of huge white-headed eagles.

Pushkin spent three happy weeks in Gurzuf in the spring of 1820 and the house of his friend, General Rayevsky, has been restored after being greatly damaged in the last war. A huge cypress stands in the garden. Sitting beneath this Pushkin began his long poem *Prisoner of the Caucasus.* Overlooking the sea at Gurzuf is the Souk-Su Cape with the Chaliapin Cliff, where the great singer liked to perform in the open air, singing to the fishermen.

The former Korovin mansion is now the holiday home of the Soviet Artists' Union. The international youth camp "Sputnik" is also here; the settlement can be approached by bus or waterbus.

Yalta

Yalta, the most popular Crimean resort, lies near the southern tip of the Crimean peninsula, in the valley of the Vodopadnaya and Bystraya rivers, in a horseshoe formed by spurs of the Crimean Mountains. Yalta is a port city and is the administrative center for the 80 sanatoria and health resorts stretching from Alushta in the east to the Baidar Gate in the west. It is linked by regular steamer services with Odessa, Sochi and the more important Black Sea coastal cities. It is ideally located and has an excellent climate. There are practically no north winds and the average annual temperature is 56°F (13°C). The winters are extremely mild (roses often bloom in the open at Christmas) and the town is rich with acacia, laurel, magnolia, and palm trees, and is surrounded by orchards and vineyards. The mountains are covered with oak and beech forests.

The heat of the summer months is tempered by the sea breezes. The annual sunshine hours equal those of Nice in the south of France. Even in September and October the average temperature is 60°–68°F (15°– 20°C.) The bathing season begins in June but the best time is in the early autumn, as the sea water is actually warmer then.

It is, among other things, the most important therapeutic research center on whole south coast. The Sechenov Climatic and Physio- therapeutic Institute is in Yalta; among many other projects, research is being done here into the therapeutic properties of sun, air and sea- bathing and of the (undeniably pleasant!) grape-cure. Experiments have proved, according to Soviet sources, that sleeping at night on the sea- shore is extremely beneficial to TB sufferers. The patients are taken from the sanatoria to the beach at 11 P.M. where they rest under canvas. They are woken at 7 A.M. for gymnastics followed by sunbathing and, in the summer and autumn, seabathing. This climatic therapy has the advan- tage that the patients can spend an extra eight or nine hours per day in the beneficial sea air.

Another scientific institution in Yalta is the Magarach Central Re- search Institute of Viticulture and Viniculture, which has worked to improve some 800 varieties of grape and several thousand hybrids from Algerian, French, Italian, Hungarian and Syrian vines. The well known Vinicultural Combine of Massandra, near Massandra Park, is closely connected with the institute. Its cellars hold some wine bottled in 1775— not for general consumption. You might like to visit the state wine- tasting establishment at 1 Litkens Street to sample Massandra, Livadia and other local wines.

Yalta consists of three more-or-less clearly defined districts: the Old City, whose main thoroughfare is called Roosevelt Avenue; the new city, where the hotels and tourist facilities are, and the former residential district, the Zarechye ("Beyond-the-River"), which is now the sanatoria district.

Yalta's main street is Lenin Street. You reach it by turning left out of Roosevelt Street. It is a seaside promenade and has the most important shops, hotels, restaurants, the post office and a branch of the State Bank.

Here, too, is the Polyclinic with its hydrotherapy and balneological departments and 58 other surgeries.

From the promenade, shady walks lead up the mountainside. One of them is Litkens Street (close to the motorboat-harbor) where the Chekhov Theater and Philharmonia Concert Hall stand. Voikov Street also climbs the hillside. Maxim Gorky lived at No. 9 in 1900, while the school on this street used to be supervised personally by Anton Chekhov.

The central section of Lenin Street runs into the city park. A little farther, beyond the bridge over the river Vodopadnaya, it reaches the huge Primorsky Park, renamed Gagarin Park. From the park you can walk down to the city beach and health station.

The Gagarin Park is large and pleasant, with statues of Gorky and Chekhov at the entrance and in its center. On Kirov Street (No. 94) you will find the Chekhov Museum, housed in the villa that the writer himself built in 1898 and where he lived for five years until his final illness. He planted the eucalyptus and Indian lilac trees with his own hands. The museum was privately maintained by Maria Chekhov, Anton's sister, until 1920, when she became its curator, a post she held until she died in 1957. Today it is run by the Moscow Lenin Library. Recently closed for repairs, it was expected to be open again by 1981.

Another attraction of Yalta is the Nikitsky Botanical Garden, four miles east of the city, with regular bus and waterbus connections. The garden was founded in 1812 by the Russian natural scientist, H. H. Steven; it rises in terraces from the seashore to the highway and covers some 500 acres. It has been a center for various acclimatization experiments. There are 7,000 trees and plants here, both native to the Crimea and imported from the five continents, and 80,000 leaves are preserved in its herbarium. Among its special treasures are a 1,000-year-old pistachio tree, a giant chestnut tree and Baby Ionian willows. Frost-resistant oranges and lemons are grown at what is known as the "Citrus Cape". The gardens are open throughout the year.

Another fine excursion can be made to the Uchan-Su waterfall (five miles from Yalta, via Livadia towards the Ay-Petri mountain). There is a regular bus connection for those who don't hike. At the waterfalls is a good restaurant with a fine view—the *Lesnoi*.

Leaving Yalta westwards, at Livadia turn off on to the Bakhchisarai road, which will take you through scented Crimean pine trees to the high plateau. From the bus terminus, a few minutes walk will take you to the waterfall, which descends into a huge wooded ravine. (Note: The waterfall is visible only in the spring and when it is swollen by the autumn rains.)

From the waterfall you can continue along the highway to the Ay-Petri Pass, where there is a fine panorama of the 3,600-foot-high plateau. A steep path leads from here to the summit, another 100 feet up. From here you can see the Ayu-Dag, the Bear Mountain of Artek and Gurzuf. The meteorological station of Ay-Petri is two miles away.

West of Yalta

Yalta is an excellent center for exploring the other Crimean resorts and cities, as well as the forests and historical monuments of the peninsula. West of Yalta, the spas and holiday resorts along the southern shore of the Crimea follow one after another: Livadia two miles, Oreanda (four miles), Miskhor (eight miles), Alupka (10 miles) and Simeiz (13 miles). All are accessible by bus or motor yacht (from Yalta's yacht harbor on Lenin Street, opposite the Polyclinic).

Livadia is only a 45-minute walk from Yalta. It is a picturesque place that was originally an imperial estate, an ideal summer residence near the Meganero springs. There was an early Greek settlement on the site; the artificial "Nymph Mountain" in Livadia Park was shaped in the form of an old sarcophagus. Many courtiers built villas here, but these have now been turned into rest homes and sanatoria and the grounds are a tourist attraction.

The most interesting sight is the Grand or Marble Palace, built by Nicholas II, the last Czar, in Renaissance style in 1911. Here, from February 4 to 11, 1945, Stalin, Roosevelt and Churchill met for the famous Yalta Conference, and here the American delegation stayed. The first floor has been restored as conference rooms, Roosevelt's office, etc., and one of the upper floors houses an exhibition of modern Soviet art.

On the western outskirts of Livadia lies a huge park which is already part of Oreanda, the next resort. Tolstoy spent many hours here beneath the huge and ancient trees. From here you can see the white building of the Nizhnaya Oreanda Sanatorium. After Oreanda, similar buildings follow each other closely. The most attractive spot is the Golden Beach, which is also the terminus of the shorter yacht trips starting from Yalta and calling at Livadia. Beyond Golden Beach is one of the most striking sights on the entire Crimean Coast, the Swallow's Nest (Lastochkino Gnezdo). It looks like a medieval castle with bastions and battlements, rising from the sea on the cliffs of Cape Ay-Todor. From Ay-Todor, which also has a lighthouse, the whole Bay of Yalta opens out in front of you. There are the ruins of a 2,000-year-old Roman fortress and a copse of juniper bushes on the northern slope.

Your next stop is Miskhor, which has the mildest climate of all the Crimean Riviera resorts (average July-August temperature 77°F (25°C), in June and September 70°F (21°C), in May and October 61°F (16°C)). Most of its sanatoria are built in Moorish style and favor the same climatic therapy as in other places in the region, with patients spending the night on the seashore, in the open air.

From the park at the Marat sanatorium you can see Gaspra, built on the mountainside opposite, with the gray twin-towered Yasnaya Polyana nursing home where Tolstoy spent several months in 1901–2 and where Gorky visited him several times.

Alupka and Simeiz are twin resorts west of Miskhor, on the steep slopes of the Crimean range. The summit of Ay-Petri (3,700 feet) rises over Alupka, the At-Bas ("Horse's Head") over Simeiz (3,600 feet). After Yalta these are the most important resorts on the southern shore. Their 22 sanatoria specialize in tubercular patients. One of them is exclusively for children.

Alupka's outstanding feature is the Vorontsov Palace, former home of the Governor General of Novorossisk. It has 150 rooms and took 18 years to build. Its northern elevation is in Tudor style and recalls a medieval castle, while the southern front has distinct Moorish elements. The gates open on to the splendid Lion Terrace, whose six marble lions are the work of Italian sculptors. During the 1945 Yalta Conference, the British delegations stayed here. Today it is a museum, including an art gallery of Russian, Soviet and Western European masters. The 120-acre estate is one of the finest on the southern Crimean coast, with 200 exotic plants and trees. In the Upper Park is the Alupka Chaos, the quarry from which the material for the palace was taken; it is now a picturesque and romantic labyrinth.

The area surrounding Alupka is particularly varied and attractive. The Koshka ("Cat") Mountain to the west of Simeiz is topped by the Simeiz branch of the Crimean Astrophysical Observatory. A little farther to the west is the 270-foot-high Krylo ("Swan's Wing") cliff. The nearby Divo ("Miracle") Cliff stretches far out into the sea and provides an excellent vantage point.

Katsiveli lies two miles west of Simeiz. Rising above the resort of Kastropol, the Devil's Staircase (Chortova Lestnitsa) used to be the only way to reach the pass over the northern ridge of the mountain range, the village of Bayderi and the more distant Bakhchisarai. Pushkin once did the climb—clinging to the tail of his little Tatar horse!

Bakhchisarai

Some 50 miles inland from Yalta, Bakhchisarai can be reached by bus; there are also rail connections from Simferopol or Sevastopol. The former capital of the Girays or Gireys, the old Tatar Khans, Bakhchisarai lies in the valley of the rivers Alma and Kacha. Today it is a district center. Near the railroad station you'll notice a large perfume factory, and some four miles from the city, on the road to Sevastopol you can see the tree nursery of the Soviet Agricultural Academy's Botanical Institute. Both can be visited by prior arrangement.

Bakhchisarai, a settlement long before the 13th-century invasion of the Crimean Tatars, has many historical monuments worth visiting. The Historical and Archeological Museum is housed in the former palace of the Khans. It is a setting that inspired both Pushkin and Mickiewicz. The palace was built by Khan Abdul Sahal Girey in 1519; more than two centuries later fire destroyed the original structure but it was rebuilt in 1787 for Catherine the Great when the Crimea was annexed to Russia. The harem is still in its original form, and so is the mosque, which dates from the 1700s; the cemetery of the Gireys has also been preserved—and so has the Fountain of Tears, the famous landmark of Bakhchisarai. There is a richly ornamented Ambassador's Gate, the work of an Italian master imported by Ivan III.

The Russian General Suvorov, who had his headquarters here during the Crimean campaign, is commemorated in a special section of the museum established in 1950, on the 150th anniversary of his death. The Historical and Archeological Museum is also responsible for the 14 cave cities in the neighborhood, or rather, their ruins. Fulla, about two miles from the museum, beyond the village of Staroselye, and 1,650 feet above sea level, is the most interesting. It was inhabited as long ago as the sixth century AD. The museum will supply you with a guide for group visits. A longer and equally interesting excursion can be made to the medieval fortress of Tepe-Kermen, on a picturesque plateau five miles east of Bakhchisarai. Here there are more than 200 caves, among them a cave church dating from the ninth and tenth centuries.

Sevastopol

Situated just above the southwestern tip of the Crimean peninsula, on the shores of a natural harbor, is Sevastopol, the terminus of the Moscow-Crimea railroad. It is 50 miles from Simferopol by rail or bus, and about 60 miles from Yalta by bus or boat. You may have difficulty getting information from Intourist about visiting Sevastopol—but perservere!

Sevastopol is a treasure-house of historic monuments; some 400 are listed in and around the city, not counting the archeological sites. The more important ones are concentrated in the center.

A good place to start exploring Sevastopol is Istorichesky Boulevard, in the southern part of the city on the site of the former Jason battlements. (All trolley buses will take you to Ushakov Square, while the bus to Kulikovo Pole will put you down at the upper end of Istorichesky Boulevard.) Here, in a tall, round building you will find a circular panorama painted by Roubaud of Munich and depicting the Defense of Sevastopol in the Crimean War (1855). From the tower of the exhibit hall you can enjoy a fine view of the city.

Some 100 yards south of the circular hall you will see a section of Bastion IV as it is called, with seven old cannon; it was here that Tolstoy was promoted lieutenant and began to write the first of his Sevastopol stories in the intervals between the fighting.

About halfway along the boulevard stands the statue of General Totleben who was in charge of the military engineering works during the siege of Sevastopol and commanded the sappers.

From Istorichesky Boulevard you can walk to Ushakov Square which closes the ring formed by Lenin Street, Nakhimov Boulevard and Bolshaya Morskaya—a ring surrounding the hill on which the center of Sevastopol stands.

Turning into Lunacharsky Street you come to Ploshchad Stroitelei (Builders Square). Opposite Gorky's statue is the Cathedral of Peter and Paul (1843), whose classical façade resembles the Theseion of Athens. Today it is a Palace of Culture.

Higher up on the top of the hill stands the former St. Vladimir Cathedral, designed in Byzantine style but badly damaged during World War Two. It is no longer used for worship.

The highest point of the hill, Nagornaya Square, is dominated by Bondarenko's 65-foot-high statue of Lenin. From here you can walk down to Matrossky (Sailor) Boulevard, where there is a monument to Captain Kazarsky, another naval hero of the Russo-Turkish War of 1829. From here a stairway leads down to Nakhimov Boulevard. No. 9 on the Boulevard is an art gallery, housing a collection that includes works by Repin, Levitan and others; also Western European works of the 14th to 17th centuries, among them a Raphael *Madonna,* canvases by Giordano, Rubens, Sneyders and Ruysdael.

From the adjoining Nakhimov Square, continue along Primorsky Boulevard, the seafront.

On the far shore of the bay you will see two stone battery emplacements and various war memorials.

Along Primorsky Boulevard you will find a biological station (founded in 1871) of the Soviet Academy of Sciences, with a museum and an aquarium. Passing the water sports center of the Black Sea Fleet, you come to Nakhimov Square and the striking ceremonial gate of the Grafskaya Pristan (Court's Harbor), which was the private landing stage of Admiral Voinovich, a count and Commander-in-Chief of the Black Sea Fleet. It was here, too, that the Soviet flag was hoisted on May 9, 1944 when Sevastopol was liberated.

Returning to Lenin Street, you can end your first tour by visiting the Museum of the Black Sea Fleet, established in 1869 by public subscription; its present home was opened in 1895. One of the oldest museums in the Soviet Union, it commemorates the long seige of 1854–55 and houses relics of the period. The museum also arranges guided tours, including excursions to Malakhov Hill and Mount Sapun.

Malakov Hill can be reached by bus or trolley plus a five-minute walk from the terminus. It was the command post of the first defense of Sevastopol. You will see the restored fortifications and the Eternal Flame in honor of Russian and Soviet naval heroes. Memorial tablets mark the spots where Admiral Nakhimov and Admiral Kornilov were mortally wounded. There are a number of other naval and military monuments both here and on Mount Sapun (four miles south of Sevastopol, on the Yalta road; regular buses from Ushakov Square). Mount Sapun was the scene of the bloody battles of May 1944. A large diorama depicts this struggle and a small local museum of documents and relics can also be visited.

Two miles from Sevastopol, the State Historical and Archeological Museum of Khersones (direct bus from Nakhimov Square) houses the heritage of a civilization 2,500 years old. Relics of the ancient Greek city state of Chersonesus are displayed in two sections and several halls.

Balaklava, scene of long and bitter clashes in the 1854–5 Crimean War, is 10 miles south of Sevastopol. Buses start from the city bus terminus, 7 Vosstavshikh Street. Balaklava may not be on Intourist's list of visitable places, but it may be possible to join a group, if there are any.

Halfway to Balaklava, you turn into a sideroad leading to a former monastery and to the rather forbidding seashore cliffs. Here, on the Feolent Cliff, mythology has placed the Temple of Artemis. It was to this spot that the goddess brought Iphigenia to save her from being sacrificed by her loyal father, Agamemnon; this is the setting of Euripides' tragedy, *Iphigenia in Tauris*. The ruins, admired by Pushkin in 1820, have now disappeared.

Returning to the highway, you soon reach the valley of Balaklava and then the city itself. The entrance to the narrow Balaklava bay is protected by red and yellow rocks; the waters are clear and calm even when a storm rages outside the bay.

Balaklava's history can be traced back to the Scythians and one theory ascribes its name to the Scythian King Palak. In the Middle Ages, when it was called Cembalo, the Genoese built a fortress here; its ruins can still be seen on the cliffs. During the Crimean War the British troops had their base here. In World War Two there was bitter fighting for the Bezimyannaya Heights above the city; a monument to the Soviet dead stands at the top of a 600-foot-high stairway.

Western Crimea

Yevpatoriya, an excellent children's resort, lies on the western shore of the Crimean Peninsula near Artek. (Direct rail link with Moscow; with Simferopol, 49 miles, rail and bus; with Sevastopol, 85 miles; and with Yalta 100 miles, regular bus connections.) Yevpatoriya can also be reached by boat but, as the port is extremely shallow, landings are made by motorboat. The clear, transparent water warms up very quickly, which makes Yevpatoriya an ideal place for children; the sea bottom shelves gently and gradually, the sand is fine, the beach wide and the sea very clean, so small children can bathe here in complete safety.

The season begins in May and lasts through October 1; the annual hours of sunshine are over 2,400. Sunbathing and swimming are both medically supervised.

Two miles west of Yevpatoriya, one of the largest spas in the Soviet Union exploits the salt water and mud of the Bolshoye Moynakskoye Lake. (Regular Trolley link with Yevpatoriya.)

Yevpatoriya's old city (a few minutes' walk from the harbor) has narrow, twisting alleys, relics of the old, oriental merchants' quarter. Some of the 16th-century battlements have been preserved. The gate through which the marauding Tatars drove their Russian and Ukrainian captives into the fortress still stands. The mosque of the Old City 1552–57) has also survived. To the right of the mosque, on the seafront promenade, stands the cathedral, which was erected in 1898 to commemorate the explusion of the Turks and the liberation of the city. The building is modelled on Hagia Sophia in Istanbul.

Continuing westwards, you come to the late 19th-century New City, once a center for wheat and salt exports. A number of monuments recall the Crimean War and the various struggles during the establishment of the Soviet regime, and during World War Two.

At Teatralnaya Square, the New City merges into the health-resort district, which stretches as far as Lake Moynakskoye. The whole area is a single huge park with white sanatoria dotted amid rich foliage. The greenery of Yevpatoriya was planted with considerable effort—there was only a thin layer of sand over the rocky foundation so this had to be replaced by specially imported black soil. The Gorky Promenade on the seafront, and the Frunze Park in the city, are proofs of the success of this painstaking work. The local museum organizes regular tours of the city on foot.

Some six miles from the city is the Mamaiskiye quarry, which has provided much of the limestone used in Yevpatoriya's buildings; the largest quarry in the Crimea, it can be visited in groups by prior arrangement.

Saki is 13 miles east of here and a little over two miles inland. Another well-known spa, it lies on the shore of Lake Saki. Beyond the lake some 800 yards of turf lead to the sea. Its mud is excellent for arthritic, nervous and vascular complaints—its curative effects were even praised by Pliny. In recent years a medicinal spring has been discovered a few miles from the settlement, and this is used to treat metabolic and digestive complaints. Saki's 80-ycar-old park has two artificial lakes: the Swan Lake and the Crimea Lake; the former is shaped like the Black Sea, the latter like the Sea of Azov.

East of Yalta

Feodosia, which lies on the hills surrounding its bay, is on the fringe of the Crimean range; beyond it the steppe zone begins. (Feodosia can be reached by rail from Moscow, by bus from Simferopol, 68 miles away, and by ship from the Black Sea Coast, including Yalta. On the way you pass the coast which has already been described between Simferopol and Yalta, the seaside resorts of Gurzuf, Artek and Alushta.) As the mountains are not very high here, Feodosia is exposed to the cold winter and warm spring winds. Its climate is therefore cooler and drier than that of the southern Riviera of the peninsula. Yet it is still an important health resort; its climate is tempered by the sea and there is no frost, even in the coldest months. The summer heat never becomes unbearable. Standing on the top of the Feodosia hills you can see the endless grassy plain to the north, the hills of the Kerch Peninsula to the east and the sea to the south. No wonder Chekhov declared that he could never tire of this panorama—"not in a thousand years!".

The sandy beach is over 10 miles long; the bathing season lasts from June through October. Swimming is particularly pleasant outside the city limits, near the station of Aivazovskaya, where the water is very clear and you can see the bottom at great depths. Close to Feodosia, at the foot of the Lisaya Gora (Bald Mountain), is a medicinal spring. The mud of the nearby Adzhigol Lake (with a strong Epsom salts content) is also used by the local sanatoria.

Feodosa itself is divided into two clearly-marked parts: the old quarter at the foot of Mithridates Hill, and the new city, the coastal health resort. Feodosia was founded by traders from Miletus in the sixth century BC. Formerly Theodosia, it became Kaffa in the 13th century, when it was a center of the Genoese Black Sea colonies with a famous slave market. These slaves built the harbor and the fortifications, whose ruins—towers, walls, battlements, bridges—have partly survived. The Local Museum, founded in 1811, contains many objects found in the ruins.

Feodosia's name is connected with that of Aivazovsky, a distinguished Armenian painter of seascapes (in the manner of Turner) and battle scenes. His home is now a museum, much enlarged from the original private collection, and there is a statue of the artist in the grounds. The building also houses an art school for children.

From Feodosia you can make an excursion to Sudak, one of the oldest health resorts in the Crimea. (Thirty miles, regular bus connection; from Simferopol 60 miles; from Alushta 55 miles. It can be reached by sea from Alushta.)

Halfway between Feodosia and Sudak lies the resort of Planerskoye, picturesquely situated on a spur of the Kara-Dag (Black Mountain) along the shores of the Bay of Koktebel. The Kara-Dag stretches for five miles between the highway and the sea. Many of the coastal cliffs and rocks have fantastic and romantic shapes—and names. Look out for Ivan Razboinik ("Ivan the Bandit"), Chortov Kogot ("Devil's Claw") and Peshchera Piratov ("Pirates' Cave"). Opposite the Kara-Dag, planted way out in the open sea, stands the rock called the Gate of Kara-Dag, whose arch is big enough for a large sailboat to pass under. You can sometimes pick up samples of jasper, agate, cornelian and other semi-precious stones on the shore. The bathing season is from May to October.

Sudak has a bay of its own. A mile south-west of the town you can see a medieval ruined castle perched on a cliff above the sea. The only approach is from the highway to the north. Beside the wall with its 12 bastions stands the citadel of the former "Consul Castle". From here you can have a fine view of the Sudak Valley and the sea. The little town lies in a valley dotted with vineyards, orchards and white houses. The semicircle of the bay is lined by a 300-foot-wide beach. The bathing season lasts from the middle of May through the middle of October. Although July and August are the hottest months, the sea temperature is 68°F (20.2°C) even in September. Sudak is a very congenial place for sufferers from bronchial and alimentary troubles, anaemia and loss of appetite. It is the center of a large agricultural area. The state farm in the Valley of Roses grows many acres of roses and sage.

Kerch

The eastern corner of the Crimean Peninsula is a separate peninsula in itself, about 1,150 square miles in area, protruding far into the sea. This narrow tongue of land, with its eastern neighbors, the Kerch Straits and the Taman Peninsula, separates the Black Sea from the Sea of Azov. The district has important iron ore deposits.

The Kerch Straits linking the Black Sea and the Sea of Azov lie between the Kerch Peninsula and the Taman Peninsula opposite. The straits are between three and 10 miles wide and about 25 miles long. North-east of Kerch is the Crimea-Caucasus rail ferry to the Caucasian side. The straits were orginally rather shallow so a canal was dug for ships of greater draught. This made it possible for the Volga-Don canal, built in 1948–52, to link the Black Sea, via the sea of Azov, with the Baltic, Caspian and White Seas.

The city of Kerch sprawls in a horseshoe-shaped bay over some 25 miles. It can be reached by rail from Simferopol and Krasnodar, by sea from Odessa, Sochi and Rostov-on-Don, by bus from Feodosia, Simferopol, Sevastopol and Yalta.

Kerch is one of the oldest settlements in the Soviet Union. Founded in the sixth century B.C. by the Greeks, who called it Pantikapaion, it later became the capital of the Bosporan Kingdom. In the fourth and fifth centuries A.D. it came under Byzantine rule; then in 1318 it became a Genoese colony, while from 1475 it was part of the Ottoman Empire until, in 1774, it was annexed by Russia. A visit to the Historical and Architectural Museum will give you a good idea of the city's history.

Kerch is not only a large port and industrial and cultural center but also one of the main fishing bases in the Crimea. The waters round about are particularly rich in plankton; in winter, when the Sea of Azov cools off, the fish migrate through the straits into the Black Sea and then return again in the spring to the Sea of Azov.

The Caucasus Coast

Crossing the straits to Cape Tuzla, on the Taman Peninsula, you are back in the territory of the Russian Republic. But by the time you have traveled along the several hundred miles of Black Sea coastline from north to south, from Anapa to Batumi, you will also have visited two Autonomous Republics which are in the territory of the Georgian Republic: Abkhazia (capital Sukhumi) and Adzharia (capital Batumi).

As you approach the port of Novorossisk you will see the first foothills of the Caucasus Mountains. These begin south of Anapa, a large resort. These mountains accompany you all the way to Batumi. Novorossisk is a port and an unloading point for goods transported by rail from Rostov and Volgograd, which are transhipped from here along the coast.

At Novorossisk, you join the famous Chernomorskoye Chaussée, the Black Sea coast road built in the 1890's and leading to Sukhumi. One of the road builders was Gorky, who worked here for a while.

The first important resort is Gelendzhik, 25 miles from Novorossisk, with an extremely mild autumn and winter. It has about 30 rest-homes and sanatoria—among them one for members of the Lomonosov University in Moscow. Close by Dzhanhot (10 miles), with its pine-wooded seashore and beach, is equally popular.

At Tuapse (an important oil-port), 120 miles from Novorossisk, the coast road meets the main Armavir-Tuapse-Sochi-Sukhumi railroad. From here the railroad and highway run parallel as far as Sochi, sometimes only a few yards from the blue expanse of the Black Sea, to the right, and the dense Caucasian forests to the left. The various resorts—Gizel-Dere, Dederkoy, Sepsi, Magri, Makopse, Aseba, Lazarevskoye and Dagomis—are all popular favorites with Russian vacationers. To the right of the highway at Lazarevskoye (50 miles from Sochi) and Dagomis (13 miles from Sochi) are campsites for motorists. All these little resorts lie at the foot of the mountains, in valleys with fast-flowing streams and rivers. As you approach Sochi the climate becomes more and more subtropical and the oak forests give way to cypresses and yews, palm trees and magnolias. Here the winters are warmer and the summers cooler than in the Crimea.

The bathing season lasts from June through the end of October.

Sochi

Sochi is the largest and best known of all the Soviet seaside resorts. It extends for over 20 miles at the foot of the Caucasus Mountains, between the Mamaika and Kudepsta rivers. You can come here from Moscow in two and a half hours by air; the rail journey takes 30 hours. During the high season, trains arrive almost every half-hour from major Soviet cities. By sea the journey from Odessa takes about 45 hours, from Yalta 24 hours. There are bus connections with all the Black Sea resorts.

Sochi owes its popularity to the proximity of the medicinal springs at nearby Matsesta (seven miles) and to its pleasant subtropical climate. The average temperature in January and February is 43°F (16°C), while in summer the heat is tempered by sea breezes. The season begins in mid-June and lasts through mid-October. In the summer and early autumn the water becomes very warm (up to 85°F, 29°C). Some of the beaches are pebbly rather than sandy, but they are all well equipped for swimming and sunbathing. Some covered pools have been constructed and are filled with preheated seawater for winter swimming.

The pleasantest season is the autumn when the humidity falls, there are long hours of sunshine and the mountain winds are warm. Spring comes early to Sochi and the flowers are in full bloom by the end of March.

Founded in 1898, Sochi's real popularity dates from the 1950's. Since then the number of visitors each year has exceeded the total population of the city. Sochi's history can be followed in the Local Museum (29 Ordzhonikidze Street). The sanatoria here are mostly for bronchial, lung and nervous complaints. They are quite palatial, most having their own clinics and beaches, with funiculars linking hillside buildings with the beach. Among the more recent the Avantgard (1960) and the somewhat earlier Chaika (Gull) and Lazurny Bereg (Azure Coast) attract the most foreign visitors. Of the older establishments, the Balneological Clinic and the Gorny Vozdukh (Mountain Air) sanatorium are outstanding.

Sochi's harbor building is one of the most attractive in the Soviet Union, with an excellent view from its restaurant. Ships arrive here from other points along the coast and also, via the Volga-Don canal, from Moscow, Leningrad and Murmansk. The Crimea-Caucasus line (Odessa-Batumi) operates throughout the year. There are special cruise lines linking Sochi with Venice and Beirut. Short trips can be made in motorboats and hovercraft. The port for these is near the main harbor.

From the harbor you come out into Voikov Street; here you will find the post and telegraph office. The street continues to Kurortny Prospekt, which traverses Sochi from the old Kavkazskaya Riviera Sanatorium in the north to the Sputnik International Youth Holiday Camp in the Matsesta valley to the south, a distance of six miles. If you stop at the beginning of Kurortny Prospekt and look to the left of the Kavkazskaya Riviera you will see the New City (Noviye Sochi) which grew up in the 1950's between the Mamaika and Sochi Rivers. To the right of the Kavkazskaya Sanatorium, Kurortny Prospekt, with its cypresses, laurel and camphor trees, continues to the city center, lined with hotels and sanatoria.

Between the promenade and the sea front, on Teatralnaya Square, you will find the Sochi State Theater with its 16 columns and allegorical figures of Art, Architecture and Sculpture on its façade. (Sochi also has an openair theater in the Primorsky Park.) From Teatralnaya Square, steps lead down to the sea. The city beach is near the Primorskaya Hotel. There is a footpath along the sea front from the State Balneological Institute to the Lenin Sanatorium, which takes you through several parks over a distance of some two miles.

On Kurortny Prospekt (take the bus to the Polyclinic stop) lies the Dendrarium (open 10 A.M.-6 P.M.). This botanical garden was founded at the end of the last century and extends over 30 acres; more than 1,500 trees and bushes have been planted here from all over the world. There are fountains, basins and statues; the Dendrarium is also an experimental research station, working to improve and increase the flora of the Caucasian Riviera's parks and forests. Another of Sochi's main sights is the Ostrovsky Museum, a memorial museum housed in the writer's home. Some fine excursions can be made in the immediate environs of Sochi and a little father away.

The Bolshoi Akhun Mountain (1,900 feet) can be reached by car along a nine-mile winding road. From its 90-foot-high lookout tower you get a panorama of almost the whole Caucasian Riviera, from Tuapse down to Cape Pitsunda. Behind you the snow-covered peaks of the Caucasus seem quite close, though in fact they are some 25 miles away. The Akhun Restaurant, near the lookout, is a very pleasant spot to take a rest.

From Staraya Matsesta (accessible by bus from the center of Sochi), a five-mile path lined with plantains and lime trees leads to the Orliniye (Eagle) Cliffs and the Agura Waterfalls. The Cliffs (1,200 feet above sea level) and the ravine of the River Agura below them are a most impressive sight. You pass by the three main waterfalls of the Agura, the largest of which drops 90 feet between two immense rocks.

In the valley of the River Hosta, about 15 miles from Sochi (one mile from the resort of Hosta (Khosta), accessible from Sochi by bus and motorboat), there is a forest of yew and box trees, covering some 500 acres on the southeastern slope of the Bolshoi Akhun Mountain. The area is a nature reservation; some trees are 400 years old, and some of the box trees date from around the birth of Christ.

13 miles from Sochi is the Dagomis Tea Farm, to which an excursion costing about 10 roubles can be made. Tea is served in delightful surroundings and souvenir packets presented.

Perhaps the most attractive excursion you can make on the Caucasian Riviera is to Lake Ritsa, 3,000 feet up in the mountains of Abkhazia. The excursion coach from Sochi goes along the shore of the Black Sea, the Chernomorskoye Chaussée, as far as Gagra (40 miles), then turns left into the valley of the River Bzipi, along a winding road that runs through forests and ravines. On your left, close to the village of Bzipi, are the ruins of a fortress (10th to 12th centuries) and a Christian church (eighth century). Eight miles from Gagra, just before the Yupsara Gorge, you can stop for a while on the shores of the small Goluboye Lake. This is almost a halfway point.

The Goluboye (Blue) Lake is a striking deep blue and in places as much as 200 feet deep.

Beyond the lake, at the confluence of the Gega and Yupsara Rivers, the bus enters the Yupsara Gorge. Its high walls rise to 1,500 feet and soon grow so narrow that only a thin strip of sky remains visible. Caves, pine forests and huge waterfalls follow, then another narrow tunnel-like defile. This brings you out on to a rocky plateau. A few hundred yards farther along, the bus stops outside the boarding house on the lakeshore.

Lake Ritsa lies in a most romantic setting, framed by forest and meadows. Mount Atsetuko rises to 7,500 feet and has a snow-capped summit even in July. Another forbidding mountain range to the southeast is the Riukhava, and there are also the twin peaks of Mt. Psegisva, almost split in two. Lake Ritsa itself is one and a half miles long and about half a mile wide. A motorboat will take you on a short cruise, after which you might feel like trying the local specialty—trout.

Matsesta, Khosta and Adler

Sochi's spa, Matsesta (eight miles from the city center towards Sukhumi), is a recent seaside development. Staraya Matsesta, the old city, lies in the valley of the river Matsesta, but not on the shore—it is situated some two miles inland along the river. A good road links the two.

Matsesta's name is of Cherkess origin. It means "Fiery Water", a reference to the hot sulphur springs that have been known here from ancient times. The first baths were built in the early 1900's but there was no real medical supervision until the 1950s when installations were built for treatment of various complaints. The water contains 27 different elements and the wells yield several million gallons a day. The reserves in the area are considerable, with springs spread over 90 miles from Lazarevskoye to Gagra.

Hosta is another pleasant health resort. The summers are particularly fine and dry here. The bathing season lasts from July through October. Hosta also has some medicinal sulphur springs, two dozen sanatoria and holiday homes. It boasts a huge plantation of cork trees imported from southern France.

The airport of Greater Sochi and the last sizeable resort on the coast, still within the territory of the Russian Republic, is Adler, 20 miles from Sochi, at the mouth of the river Mzimta. This is an important agricultural area with numerous tea plantations. One of the collective farms, "Yuzhniye Kulturi", produces flower seeds, trees and ornamental bushes, and supplies large quantities of flowers to other parts of the USSR by air. There is a 40-acre arboretum on the alluvial soil of the Mzimta, where more than 500 kinds of trees and bushes are grown.

From Adler you can make a pleasant excursion into the Caucasus, whose snow-covered summits are clearly visible from here (Fist, 9,000 feet; Chugus, 9,750 feet; Pseasho, 9,800 feet; Agepsta, 9,780 feet). Your destination is Krasnaya Polyana (30 miles), at the foot of the Caucasian range, on the river Mzimta, a mountain resort with medicinal springs. The road winds through a wild and picturesque landscape with views as fine as those along the famous Georgian Military Highway. Krasnaya Polyana itself has a lovely park (the former residence of a Grand Duke), with many rare plants. This is the headquarters of the State Nature Reservation of the Caucasus (Southern Section). The reservation covers over 300,000 acres around Krasnaya Polyana on the northern and southern mountain slopes. The fauna is extremely varied, ranging from the Caucasian heath-cock to the bison, which survives in only two other places in the Soviet Union.

Abkhazia

Abkhazia begins south of Adler, at the river Psou. It is a small autonomous republic with a population of half a million. Its capital is Sukhumi and more than two-thirds of its territory is mountainous. (The highest peak is Domay-Ulgen, 12,120 feet.) This is the area with the largest number of centenarians—some people are reputed to be 140 to 150 years old. A unique local speciality is the Abkhaz song-and-dance ensemble, consisting of these sprightly senior citizens. Their music and dances are very like those of the Basques and other interesting linguistic and folkloric similarities have been noted.

Abkhazia's mountains, with their dense forests, beautiful valleys and wild rivers, begin right on the coast. Paths from the coast lead up through woods of magnolia and cypress, oak and hornbeam to the sanatoria and rest-homes, in which more than 50,000 people stay annually. The climate is subtropical. Gagra, an Abkhazian resort, has the warmest climate in the European part of the Soviet Union. The winters are extremely mild; there is the occasional snowfall, but the snow rarely lies on the ground for more than a day or two.

Apart from tourism Abkhazia is also noteworthy for its coal deposits, its timber and its subtropical agriculture. Silkworms are cultivated and bees are kept; but the main agricultural areas are along the coastal strip. Tea, tobacco, tropical fruit and grapes are all grown.

Gagra is a health resort lying 40 miles from Sochi and 50 from Sukhumi, by rail, bus and sea. It has a two-mile-long seaside park with a great variety of tropical and subtropical trees. The openair theater and the sports center are also located here. The Gagra mountain range (dominated by the peak of Ah-Had, 8,300 feet) surrounds the town like the wall of some ancient amphitheater—the descending terraces contain sanatoria and rest homes concealed in the greenery. The Soviet Government also has several villas and guesthouses here.

Though the atmosphere is humid there is not too much cloud, and on the average, 200 sunny days per year. The bathing season lasts from May through mid-November. There is a well-equipped beach stretching for three miles and, as the sea shelves rapidly, the swimming is excellent.

Gagra was built on the site of the fortress of Tracheia, at the gate of the ancient Colchis. Many bastions, ramparts and churches still stand in ruins in and around the city, dating from the sixth, seventh and eighth centuries. Among them are the Marlinsky ruins in the valley of the river Zhoekvara, whose waterfalls are quite spectacular. There are several ravines, caves and underground streams in the limestone of the Gagra mountains. The source of the river Gagripei is near a stalactite cave with a beautiful spring. It will take you a day to climb from Gagra's subtropical gardens to Mount Mamzdiska (6,000 feet), where snow lingers even in summer. The Gagra Motel is on the Sochi-Gagra highway, some five miles before Gagra, to the left, near Kholodnaya Rechka (Cold Stream).

Cape Pitsunda, Gudauta and Akhali Afon

Cape Pitsunda, 15 miles south of Gagra, is one of the newest resorts on the Caucasian Riviera, planned as a second Sochi. Several 14-story hotels have been built since 1966. Details of the newest Pitsunda hotels are given in the Practical Information section.

Pitsunda's coastal pine woods (300 acres) are a nature reservation. Lake Inkit is a paradise for waterfowl; its shores also boast several mink farms. The fertile soil sustains several plantations of tropical fruit, and fresh figs and passion fruit are on sale in the market. A pleasant sandy beach is another attraction.

The garden city of Gudauta is 25 miles from Gagra and 20 from Sukhumi, in a miniature bay on the Black Sea. It can be reached by rail, bus and sea. Surrounded to the north and east by mountains forming a semicircle of about 10 miles, its climate is similar to that of Sukhumi, though a little less warm, with frost in winter and gentle heat in summer. There is an openair movie-house here, and a theater. The beach and the fruit market are the largest on the Abkhazian coast.

In the nearby village of Likhny (2½ miles) you can see the ruins of an 11th-century Byzantine church and palaces of the old Abkhazian princes.

Akhali Afon, a resort at the foot of the mountains (40 miles from Gagra, 11 from Sukhumi, accessible by rail, bus and ship), was named after a monastery, Novy Afon or New Athos, and was founded by monks from Mount Athos in Greece.

The surrounding mountains protect Akhali Afon from the northern winds, and give it a climate similar to that on the French Riviera, though with rather more sunshine. The little coastal settlement is enclosed by cypresses. Olive groves are scattered on the mountain slopes, and beyond them stands the former monastery, now a sanatorium. From the top of Mount Iverskaya (1,575 feet), which you can climb by a gently rising limestone path you can see as far as the lighthouse of Sukhumi. Two miles from Akhali Afon are the ruins of Prince Hassan Maan's palace. In 1954 the railroad station was moved inland, a little way uphill, and trains also stop at the lake side station of Agaraki.

Sukhumi

Sukhumi is the capital of Abkhazia. It lies on Sukhumi Bay and can be reached from Moscow by rail in 36½ hours and by air in 2 hours 40 minutes; by sea from Odessa it is 615 miles while from Sochi it is 100 miles by rail, bus and ship.

Sukhumi's subtropical climate has been compared with that of southern Spain and Sicily. It is an ideal resort for sufferers from cardiac and lung diseases. Six miles south, at Gulripsi, there is a TB sanatorium.

Except in December and January the day temperature seldom falls below 54°–61°F (12°–16°C). Spring comes early, in February. The bathing season lasts from April or May through early November. The beach is three-quarters of a mile outside the city, on the Tbilisi road; there are boat and bus connections. The water in Sukhumi Bay is warmer than that of the other Caucasian beaches; there is no current and there are 2,000 hours of sunshine a year. Early autumn is the most pleasant season.

As well as a resort Sukhumi is also an administrative, industrial and cultural center with tobacco and leather factories, shipyards and canneries. It is the site of the Abkhazian Section of the Georgian Academy of Sciences.

The Abkhazian capital has a past going back 2,500 years. Founded by the Greeks in the sixth and fifth centuries BC (when it was called Miletos Dioscurios), it became one of the most important trading ports on the Black Sea. Later a Roman fort was built here. In the city itself you will find interesting historical remains from the tenth, eleventh and twelfth centuries. The fort in the harbor, dating from the time of Colchis, defended the entrance to Sukhumi from the tenth to the twelfth centuries. In the southeastern part of the city, on Chelyuskintsev Street, close to the House of Tourism, stands Bagratid Castle, also dating from the 10th or 11th centuries. This fortress was built by one of the Bagratid rulers of Georgia above the steep banks of the river Besleti, and it offers a fine view of Sukhumi.

On the road to Tbilisi, 2½ miles outside Sukhumi, stands the Great Abkhazian Wall, built in the seventh century. It ran as a series of forts for 100 miles between the rivers Kelasura and Mokvi and much of it has been preserved.

A little farther from Sukhumi, in the ravine of the river Besleti, is a multi-arched stone bridge, an interesting 10th–12th century example of Georgian architecture. On the left bank of the river are the ruins of an ancient temple dating from the same period. Eleven miles east of Sukhumi, in the village of Dandra, stands another (restored) church dating from the sixth, seventh and eighth centuries.

The streets of modern Sukhumi are laid out on a regular grid-pattern, the longer streets running parallel with the coast while the smaller side streets climb the mountainside very steeply.

Primorsky Boulevard runs along the entire seafront. Where bazaars once stood there are now parks and gardens with palm trees, camphors and cedars, roses and camellias. The promanade is decorated with fountains and obelisks. Reaching Rustaveli Prospekt (a pedestrian precinct) you can follow Sukhumi's main promenade further, to the park with Rustaveli's statue and a large openair movie-house.

Around the middle of Rustaveli Prospekt, steps lead down to the sea; a floating restaurant offers specialties of Abkhazian cuisine. The Prospekt has a whole row of hotels and a Drama Theater, built in Georgian national style.

When you come to the ornamental pillars on Rustaveli Prospekt turn into Lenin Street. At the end of this street you will find the Baratashvili railroad station; the main rail station is outside the city, at the end of Chochua Street, and this is the city halt. At No. 20 Lenin Street you'll find the Abkhazian State Museum, with a varied collection of folklore items including a display illustrating daily life in an Abkhazian village.

The Botanical Gardens of Sukhumi are also on Lenin Street. Founded in 1840, they are a nursery for more than 800 varieties of trees and bushes including a Victoria Regia which flowers for just one day in August!

Trapetsia Mountain is perhaps the most striking peak in the range surrounding Sukhumi. In a park on this mountain there is an Institute of Medical Biology, with a large colony of monkeys and baboons imported from Central Africa, Indonesia and India, who live in the open; by the seventh generation they appeared to be completely acclimatized.

Mount Sukhumi can be reached along Kutaisi Street by climbing some basalt steps or driving up along a highway. The terrace of the restaurant on the summit offers a beautiful panorama. Here, at a Subtropical Plant Research Institute, experiments are conducted into the acclimatization of some 150 varieties of eucalyptus trees.

Some 40 miles from Sukhumi you can see the longest stalactite cave in the Caucasus. (Regular bus service from Ochamchire.) This is the Avlaskira Cave, the third largest in the Soviet Union. Its "Drapery Chamber" is particularly impressive and it also has an underground stream.

Foreign tourists can arrange visits to the tea and tobacco plantations, orchards and vineyards belonging to nearby collective farms; don't miss the opportunity to taste the "Buket Abkhazii", the famous "bouquet" of Abkhazia wine.

Batumi

Your final destination on this Black Sea tour is the southern-most city on the Soviet coast, 12 miles from the Turkish frontier—Batumi, capital of the Adzhar Autonomous Republic.

Batumi has the warmest winter, the heaviest rainfall and the most luxuriant vegetation of any place in the entire Soviet Union. From Moscow it is 40 hours 25 minutes by rail, and about three hours by air. From Odessa, Yalta, Sochi and Sukhumi it can also be reached by boat. The humid air and tropical showers have turned Batumi into something like a natural hothouse. The bathing season is from mid-May to mid-November but October is perhaps the pleasantest time for a visit. The winter is also extremely mild; some swimming-pools on the medicinal beaches are filled with preheated seawater.

Exotic trees and bushes growing with amazing speed, dazzling white houses, well-kept gardens and scrupulously clean streets are all typical of Batumi. There is practically no dust.

Of the more recent buildings, the Revolutionary Museum (9 Gorky Street), the pink marble Drama Theater (1 Rustaveli Street) and the Summer Theater (Primorsky Park) are the most important. The Adzhar State Museum (4 Dzhincharadze Street) has many exhibits showing prerevolutionary Batumi, especially the former slum district of Chaoba (Swamp); today this is a modern residential district.

The Primorsky Park is on the seashore and the Pioneer Park (4 Engels Street) provides another pleasant recreation area with a boating lake.

From Batumi you can make a rail or bus excursion to Zelyony Mys (six miles to the north), the Green Cape health resort. The heavily wooded mountain slopes come down almost to the sea, leaving a narrow strip of excellent beach. This is the site of Batumi's famous Botanical Garden, a large subtropical acclimatization and cross-breeding center.

Also to the north of Batumi are several resorts and sanatoria, many of them open in winter. They include Makhindzhauri (4 miles), Zelyony Mys and Tsihis-Diri (12 miles), Kobuleti (13 miles) has a drier climate than Batumi and the bathing season lasts eight or nine months.

North of Kobuleti the railroad and the highway both turn away from the coast but they swing back again at the district center of Ochamchire, continuing through nearby Sukhumi towards Gagra and Sochi.

PRACTICAL INFORMATION FOR THE CRIMEA AND BLACK SEA RESORTS

 WHEN TO GO. The high season in the Crimean and South Russian spas and resorts runs from early May through mid-October and the winter is fairly mild with snow practically unknown and temperatures rarely falling below 32°F in **Odessa**. September is the sunniest month; the July mean is 70°F (22.7°C) and though during the winter the sea is sometimes covered with a thin sheet of ice, this is easily cleared and the port is open year round.

Yalta has the mildest winters of any Soviet resort and frost is rare; the summer heat is tempered by sea breezes. Late May is particularly pleasant with an average temperature of 61°F (16°C). Autumn is the most popular season; sea bathing lasts until the end of October.

Sochi and its neighborhood enjoy permanent protection from cold winds, while snow and frost are very rare and the summer heat is never oppressive. Spring comes early—but the ideal season here, too, is autumn.

In Sukhumi spring starts in February and there is bathing from April through end November.

Batumi, however, has the highest rainfall of all the Transcaucasian cities (154 days annually) though mostly in short and heavy showers; August and September are rather unhealthy. October is the most enjoyable time here.

Summing up: mid-June, through August is worst time to go—over-crowded, too hot and humid, and inadequate airconditioning. So go in the "velvet season", when privileged Russians like to go—September and October.

 HOW TO GET THERE. By rail. Most of the places mentioned in this chapter are accessible by rail from Moscow, Leningrad, Kiev, Kishinev, Tbilisi and Yerevan, and are themselves interconnected.

By air. Odessa, Yalta, Simferopol, Sochi, Sukhumi and Batumi all have airports. These are linked to the places mentioned above with rail-connections and also with Baku, Ashkhabad, Dushanbe, Tashkent, Frunze, Alma-Ata, Riga, Vilnius and Minsk.

By road. Odessa can be reached from Central Europe via Chop, Lvov, Zhitomir and Kiev (from Kiev by highway No. 6). Yalta is the terminal of highway No. 8 from Kharkov. Sochi and Sukhumi are on highway No. 10 from Rostov-on-Don via Krasnodar and Novorossisk.

By sea. Cruise routes link Constanza, Varna, Istanbul, Piraeus, Alexandria, Latakia, Famagusta and Beirut with the Black Sea Coast. Motorships service the routes Marseilles-Odessa—Yalta—Batumi and vice versa; and Vienna—Izmail—Yalta. Odessa can be reached also from ports as varied as Naples, Bari, Dubrovnik, Venice and Genoa.

 WHAT TO SEE. Odessa: The Uspensky Cathedral, the Church of Elijah the Prophet, St. Peter's Church and the Greek Orthodox Church, the Odessa Fortress and Prince Vorontsov's Palace, the Potemkin Steps, City Hall and Catacombs, the four main museums, Shevchenko and Pobeda parks, the Charles Darwin Garden, the Lermontov Resort, the Uspensky Monastery, Chernomorka, Kuyalnitsky and Khazibeyevsky Liman—all the latter outside the city.

Ochakov: the excavations (the former Greek city of Olvia).

Kherson: the Fortress, the Greek Church of St. Sophia, the Cathedral of the Holy Spirit.

Simferopol: Archeological sites, Chokurcha Cave, local museums.

Alushta: the Zapovednik (Nature Reserve 75,000 acres). Special permit needed. Nearby is Artek, the largest children's health resort.

Yalta: Alexander Nevsky Cathedral, Chekhov Museum, wine-tasting hall, Nagorny Park.

Livadia (part of Yalta): the White Palace and park, state farm vineyards.

Miskhor and **Alupka:** famous sanatoria and the Golden Beach; the Vorontsov Palace.

Simeiz: the Observatory.

Bakhchisarai: The Khan's Palace.

Sevastopol: The Cathedral of St. Peter and Paul and the Vladimir Cathedral, the Tower of Winds, the Count's Quay, two main museums, Balaklava.

Yevpatoriva: Old City, museums, the lake and park of Saki.

Feodosia: The Mithridates Hill, museums, excursions to Planerskoye and Sudak.

Kerch: The museum and the Institute of Oceanography.

Sochi: Cathedral of the Archangel Michael, fortress, museums, excursions to the Ravine of the River Agur, Mount Akhun, Matsesta, Eagle Rock.

Adler: The state collective farm of Yuzhniye Kulturi, (Tropical Flowers), Krasnaya Polyana and the Caucasian State Park (Reserve).

Gagra: the sanatoria, New Gagra, Gagra Mountain Resort, Lake Ritsa.

Novy Afon: The monastery, excursions to Pitsunda, Gudauta and Likhni.

Sukhumi: The Fortress, Bagratid Castle, Besleti Most, Cathedral of the Annunciation, Monkey Colony, Botanical Garden, various parks.

Batumi: Museums, trip to Zelyony Mys, Makhindzhauri, Kobuleti.

 HOTELS. Adler. *Adler Motel,* 41 Pervomaiskaya Street, 10 minutes from the sea. Shop, café, parking lot. Central location. *Note:* Adler can be visited only in transit to or from the airport.

Alushta. *Magnolia Hotel,* 1 Naberezhnaya. *Note:* Alushta can be visited only in transit.

Askania-Nova. *Askania Hotel,* Krasnoarmeiskaya Street.

Batumi. *Intourist Hotel,* 11/1 Ninoshvili Street, is best. Set in a garden of palms and flowers, it has 123 rooms on 4 floors. First class and highly recommended.

Gagra. *Gagriosh Hotel* is best sited, but if you don't mind being 5 miles outside town, try the *Kholodnaya Rechka Motel,* near the sea with cinema, baths and showers, shop, post office, etc. *Note:* Gagra can be visited only in transit.

Kherson. *Intourist Hotel,* recently opened, on Svoboda Square, is best. Then the **Pervomaisky Hotel,** 26 Lenin Street. Also *Kiev Hotel* on Ushakov Prospekt.

Kobuleti. *Gorizont Hotel,* new 1978, 450 beds.

Novaya Kakhovka. *Druzhba Hotel,* Dneprovsky Prospekt, your only hope.

Odessa. *Odessa Hotel* (formerly the London Hotel), an Intourist hotel. One of the nicest hotels in the USSR, it overlooks the harbor and has a charming courtyard where you can have breakfast under the trees. First-class superior. Address: 11 Primorsky Boulevard.

Next is *Krasnaya Hotel,* 15 Pushkin Street, at Kondratenko Street. Also an Intourist hotel. First-class moderate. *Chernoye More Hotel,* 59 Lenin Street, a new Intourist hotel, 194 rooms.

Also-rans in Odessa: *Arkadya,* with 150 rooms, best in this category, then *Bolshaya Moskovskaya Hotel,* 29 Deribasovskaya Street; *Passage Hotel,* 34 Sovietskaya Armiya Street; and *Tsentralnaya Hotel,* 40 Sovietskaya Armiya Street.

Pitsunda. There are five Intourist hotels here, each 14 stories high, each open from June through October, the *Apsny, Bzyb, Zolotoye Runo, Mayak* and *Iveria.*

Each has dining rooms with European cuisine, bars accepting foreign or Soviet currency, shops, etc. The *Bzyb* has a heated sea-water pool, and guests may rent any kind of sports equipment they want. Facilities for water-skiing, motor-boating, basketball, tennis, volleyball and, for the indoor types, chess and billiards, concerts and movies (with an open-air cinema as well). This is essentially a health resort.

Sevastopol. Only recommendable one is *Sevastopol Hotel*, on Nakhimov Prospekt.

Simferopol. Best is *Simferopol Hotel*, 22 Kirov Street, then the *Airport Hotel* (but good for little except transiting); *Ukraina Hotel*, 9 Rosa Luxemburg Street; *Moskva Hotel*, 1 Yaltinskaya Street; finally *Yuzhnaya Hotel*, 7 Karl Marx Street, and *Vokzalnaya Hotel*, at the railway station.

Sochi. *Camellia Hotel*, 89 Kurortny Prospekt, leads the list. 184 cozy rooms finished in fumed oak. 17 first-class single rooms; 149 first-class double rooms; 18 deluxe two-room suites for two persons. From the Night Stars bar and the Russian Troika tea room on the 11th floor there is a panorama of the sea, the town and the majestic peaks of the Caucasian Range. The restaurant serves a wide variety of European, Russian and Caucasian dishes. A dance orchestra and variety ensemble provide entertainment. In the light and spacious lobby, you can book tickets to the theater, cinema, circus or sports stadium as well as make plane, train and boat reservations. The hotel stands in a large park amongst many evergreen trees and shrubs. Paths lead through the park to the beach nearby.

Sochi Hotel, two buildings, 50 Kurortny Prospekt. A modern, 5-story hotel. Rooms have balconies from which there is a good view of the sea. Also known as the "Magnolia Hotel". This large hotel is Number Two and almost deluxe.

Intourist Hotel, 91 Kurortny Prospekt, is third choice, and first-class superior. Small, 4 floors with 110 rooms, own bathing beach, souvenir shop, etc.

Zhemchuzhina, 3 Chernomorskaya Street, highrise, with 658 rooms, recently opened Intourist hotel, reportedly "adequate" rooms with fine view over beach, good restaurant, two swimming pools, concert hall, etc.

If you get sent to the *Primorskaya*, complain. We usually leave out hotels we don't like, but as you are assigned rooms by the bureaucracy, we must report that this hotel is old, badly maintained, and is known for its poor service and nothing else. 434 rooms.

Also-rans in Sochi include: *Yuzhnaya Hotel*, Teatralnaya Street; *Kavkaz Hotel*, 72 Kurortny Prospekt; and *Kuban Hotel*, 5 Gagarin Street.

If you want a good health sanatorium, we can recommend the *Chaika*, at 3 Moskovskaya Street, but Intourist has others on its list as well.

Sukhumi. Best is the *Sinop*, with Sinop camping site, just outside town on the Tbilisi Highway, among the lush trees and on the beach. Restaurant, shop. The Intourist hotel, called *Abkhazia*, is next, at 2 Frunze Street. Third is the *Tbilisi Hotel*, on Dzhguburi Street.

Yalta. *Oreanda Hotel*. 35/2 Lenin Street. An Intourist hotel, best in town, only 30 yards from the sea. In the center of Yalta, with restaurants, cafés, shops, small craft landing stage, a wine-tasting center all nearby. Deluxe suites, first-class and tourist-class rooms; restaurant open 11 to 11, café from 8 A.M. Intourist service bureau arranges excursions, reservations, etc. Highly recommended.

Yalta Hotel. First class, modern, over 1,000 rooms, on hill overlooking the sea. 100 steps down to pebble beach; 10–15 minutes' walk or bus to harbor. Superb view of city, harbor and mountains. Large, excellent dining-room, shops, post office, etc.

Tavrida Hotel. 13 Lenin Street, gets a moderate rating for its 53 rooms, and is second best.

Fourth on our list is the *Motel* at 25 Lomonosov Street, overlooking Vodopadnaya River, with restaurant, filling station, etc.

Moderate to inexpensive are: *Ukraina Hotel,* 18 Botkin Street, with restaurant open till 11 P.M.; *Yuzhnaya Hotel,* 12 Franklin D. Roosevelt Street, restaurant also open till 11 P.M.; *Crimea,* 36 Lenin Street; and *Gnyozdishko Hotel,* Kirov Street (near Chekhov Museum).

 RESTAURANTS. Alushta. Either *Poplavok* on Lenin Street or *Volna* on Naberezhnaya.

Feodosia. For people-watching, *Feodosia,* on the municipal beach, or for just food, *Yuzhny* on Semashko Street.

Gurzuf. The *Gurzuf Restaurant* on Leningradskaya Street is best.

Kherson. Best is *Kherson Restaurant* in Pervomaisky Hotel; then any of: *Ogonyok* on Ushakov Prospekt; *Dnieper,* at the harbor; or *Minutka,* on Suvorov Street.

Novaya Kakhovka. Try the *Tavriya Restaurant* on Dneprovsky Prospekt.

Novy-Afon. Try *Psyrtskha,* in the heart of town.

Odessa. *Ukraina,* 12 Karl Marx Street, is probably best. Then *Yuzhny,* 12 Khalturin Street. After that, any of these: *Teatralnaya,* 36 Armiya Street; *Chernomorsky,* 23 Karl Marx Street; *Primoriye,* 1 Tirapolskaya Street; *Volna Restaurant,* city harbor building.

Sevastopol. *Volna,* on the sea front, Primorsky Boulevard, is best, followed by *Primorsky,* on Lenin Street.

Simferopol. Dining room of the *Simferopol Hotel,* Karl Marx Street, is best, followed by *Chaika,* by the reservoir. Then any of these: *Dorozhny,* at the railway station; *Astoria,* 16 Karl Marx Street; or *Otdykh,* in the Kirov Gardens.

Sochi. *Cascade Restaurant* in downtown Sochi is best. Good food, colorful atmosphere, dancing. Nice terrace with view of the sea.

Izba Restaurant, outside Sochi on road to Gagra, is second, and as it is in a re-created Georgian village, in a fascinating setting. Ask your Intourist representative to reserve for you and take you there.

Pazhka Restaurant, is beautifully located in a hillside forest about 5 mins. drive from the center of Sochi. Pleasant atmosphere and excellent Armenian dishes.

The following are all about the same in service and atmosphere, so choose according to location: *Gorka,* 22 Voikov Street; *Svetlana,* 10 Pushkinskaya Street; *Goluboye,* 8 Voikov Street; *Dietichesky* (health foods), 10 Voikov Street; *Primorye,* 10 Chernomorskaya Street.

For atmosphere, try *Akhun Restaurant,* on the slopes of Mount Bolshoi Akhun, or *Morskoi* at the passenger wharf.

Sukhumi. Best is *Aragvi,* on Mir Prospekt. Next are *Kavkaz,* Frunze Street, and *Ritsa,* Lenin Street. The following are about the same and rank next: *Eshera,* Verkhnyaya and Eshera; *Psou Restaurant,* Tbilisskoye Chaussée.

For atmosphere, try the *Amra,* Rustaveli Prospekt, on the seafront; *Amza,* on top of Sukhumi Hill; or *Dioskuri,* in the Sukhumi Fortress overlooking the sea.

Yalta. Perhaps best is *Yalta Restaurant* in the Ukraina Hotel, 18 Botkinskaya Street. A close second is the *Ukraina Restaurant,* 34 The Promenade. Open till midnight, choice of self-service or otherwise.

For panoramic views over the city and sea, try one of the following (in order of their proximity to the city): *Gorka,* at the cable-car's mountain terminus; *Lesnoi,* at the *Uchan-Su* waterfalls up the Ay-Petri mountain; and *Shalash,* at the Baidarsky Gates on the road to Alupka and the west.

Also-rans include: *Aquarium,* Moskovskaya Street, over a small stream; two restaurants in Primorsky Park, both open till 1 A.M., the *Priboi* and *Leto;* and *Otdykh Restaurant,* a terrace restaurant atop the main port building at the harbor. At all the latter, the atmosphere or view is better than the food, which is at least adequate.

Yevpatoriya. Either *Zoloto Plyazh* on Gorky Quay, or *Krim,* on Revolution Street.

CULTURAL ACTIVITIES. In Odessa there is an excellent Opera and Ballet Theater at 8 Lastochkina Street. The October Revolution Ukrainian Drama Theater is at 15 Paster Street, the Ivanov Drama Theater at 48 Karl Liebknecht Street. There is a musical comedy theater (50 Karl Leibknecht Street), and the Ostrovsky Youth Theater, named after the Russian playwright, is at 12 Tchaikovsky Pereulok. The Philharmonia Concert Hall, 15 Rosa Luxemburg Street, dates from 1899. Originally it housed the stock exchange. The Nezhdanov Conservatoire is in Ostrovidov Street; the late David Oistrakh and many other leading Soviet musicians have been among its graduates. One of the best Soviet *circuses* is at 25 Podbelsky Street.

Kherson's Musical and Drama Theater is at 7 Gorky Street.

Simferopol: Gorky Drama Theater, 15 Pushkinskaya Street. Ukrainian Music and Drama Theater, 3 Mendeleyev Street. There is also a puppet theater.

Yalta: Chekhov Theater, 13 Litkens Street. Philharmonia Concert Hall: in the same building.

Sevastopol: Lunacharsky Theater, 6 Nakhimov Prospekt. Circus: Korabelnaya Storona, near the Sevastopol wide-screen cinema.

Sochi: Theater, Teatralnaya Square. Open-air theater, Primorsky Park, Chernomorskaya Square. Circus, 8 Deputatskaya Street, seats 1180. During the summer season many touring companies and individual performers visit Sochi.

Sukhumi: Drama Theater, 1, Pushkin Street. Built in 1952 in Georgian style, it incorporates a waterfall. Summer Theater, Kirov Street, in the park.

Batumi: Drama Theater (1 Rustaveli Street).

MUSEUMS. Odessa: *Archeological Museum,* Kommunarov Square. Open 10–8, closed Wed.

Kherson: *Historical Museum* with many exhibits connected with Field Marshal Suvorov.

Simferopol: *Local Museum,* 18 Pushkinskaya Street, Open 10–3, closed Wed. The Neapolis excavations are also part of the museum. These are on the main Alushta Road, not far outside the city; a signpost marked "1 km" points the way.
Art Gallery, 35 Karl Liebknecht Street, open 10–4, closed Tues.

Yalta: *Local Museum,* 21 Pushkin Street, open 10–4, closed Wed. Housed in a former Roman Catholic church.
Chekhov Museum, 112 Kirov Street, open 10–4, closed Tues.
History and Archeology Museum, 3 Zagorodnaya Street, open 10–5, closed Wed.
Literary Museum, 10 Pavlenko Proyezd, open 10–5, Thurs., Sat. and Sun. only.

Bakhchisarai: *Historical and Archeological Museum* in the Khan's palace. 9–5 daily, except Wed; guides provided. The museum also superintends the 14 cave-dwelling settlements in the neighborhood, including the one at Fulla.

Sevastopol: *Black Sea Museum.* 11 Lenin Street, open 10–5.
Sevastopol Panorama, Istorichesky Boulevard, open 9–8, closed Mon.
Art Gallery, 9 Nakhimov Prospekt. Open 12–6, closed Tues.
Kovalevsky Biological Station of the Academy of Sciences, Primorsky Boulevard. Aquarium and museum open 10–4, closed Mon.

Khersones (near Sevastopol) has a *Local Archeological Museum,* established in 1892, open daily 10–5 except Mon, direct bus from Nakhimov Square, Sevastopol

Yevpatoriya: *Local Museum* (11 Lenin Street, open 12–7, except Wed). Interesting natural history section, also an aquarium, with a huge swordfish as its prize exhibit.

Feodosia: *Aivazovsky Gallery,* 2 Galeremaya Street, open 12–5, except Wed.

Kerch: *Historical and Archeological Museum,* 16 Sverdlov Street, open 10–4, except Wed. Many important local finds; information about excavations now in progress.

Sochi: *Local Museum,* 29 Ordzhonikidze Street, open 10–4, closed Tues. Sections devoted to the natural history of the Caucasus and Black Sea.
Ostrovsky Museum, 4 Ostrovsky Lane. Open 10–10, closed Wed. A memorial museum.

Sukhumi: *Local Museum,* 20 Lenin Street. Open 9–5. Monkey Colony, Baratashvili Street. A large open colony of baboons and macaque monkeys.

Batumi: *Museum of the Revolution,* 8 Gorky Street. *Adzhar State Museum,* 1 Dzhincharadze Street. History of the city and its environs.

 **SHOPPING.** Local handcrafts, carpets, embroidery, Black Sea Coast and Crimean silverware can be obtained in the following shops: **Odessa:** *Department Store,* 75/73 Pushkin Street. *Podarki (Gift) Shop:* 33 Deribasovskaya Street. *Beryozka Souvenir Shop:* 19 Deribasovskaya Street. *Book and music shop:* 25 Deribasovskaya Street.

Sochi: *Souvenirs,* 40 Gorky Street. *Art Shop,* Boulevarnaya Street, opposite Morskoi Vokzal (Boat Station). *Jewelry:* 26 Kurortny Prospekt. *Market:* 30 Kirpichnaya Street.

Sukhumi: *Department Store,* 52 Mir Prospekt. *Bookshop,* same building. *Jewelry,* 1 Lenin Street. *Market,* 7 Tarkhinishvili Street.

 USEFUL ADDRESSES. Odessa: *Railroad station:* Privokzalnaya Square (with taxi stand). *Rail tickets:* 21 Marx Street (9–6). *Bus terminus:* 5 Martinovsky Square. *Boat tickets:* 1 Marx Square. *Airport:* outside city. *Aeroflot City Office:* 17 Karl Marx Street.

Simferopol: *Intourist:* 9 Luxemburg Street. *Railroad station:* at the end of Lenin Boulevard. *Aeroflot Office:* 18 Sevastopolskaya Street. *Camping:* (Intourist), "Delfin", Luzanovka, 7 miles out.

Alushta: Service bureau for paying guests: 9 Krasnoflotskaya. *Railroad reservations:* (station in Simferopol) 19 Lenin Street. *Air reservations:* (airport in Simferopol) 13 Lenin Street (telegraph office).

Yalta: *Intourist:* 1–3 Kommunarov Street. *Harbor:* 7 Roosevelt Street. *Railroad reservations office:* 12 Sverdlov Street. *Air reservations:* in the post office in the harbor building. *Car camping* (with service): 79/a Kirov Street.

Alupka: *Tourist Office:* 10 Kirov Street. *Paying Guest Service:* 10 Rosa Luxemburg Street. *Railway reservations:* 30 Rosa Luxemburg Street.

Simeiz: *Railway reservations:* Lenin Boulevard.

Sevastopol: *Intourist:* 8 Nakhimov Boulevard. *Railroad reservations and sales:* 28 Bolshaya Morskaya. *Boat reservations:* 1 Tamozhennaya. *Air reservations:* (airport in Simferopol) at rail station.

Yevpatoriya: *Spa administration:* 15 Gorky Quay. *Paying Guest Service:* 44 Revolution Street. *Railroad station:* by tram from Teatralnaya Square (reservations: 15 Revolution Street). *Harbor:* 1 Moryakov Square. *Air reservations:* 14 Gorky Quay (nearest airport: Simferopol).

Feodosia: *Paying Guest Service:* 23 Kuibyshev Street. *Rail station:* Lenin Boulevard. *Harbor:* Gorky Street. *Rail/air reservations:* 5 Voikov Street.

Sochi: *Intourist:* 91 Kurortny Prospekt. *Railroad station:* Privokzalnaya Square. *Rail reservations:* Gorky Street. *Harbor:* 1 Voikov Street. *Air reservations:* in harbor (nearest airport is Adler).

Adler: *Motel:* 41 Pervomaiskaya (near the beach). *Car camping:* in the eucalyptus woods at Veseloye village, towards the seashore, off to the right of the Adler-Gagra road, 6 miles from Adler.

Sukhumi: *Intourist:* 2 Frunze Street. *Railroad station:* Chochua Street (1½ miles north of city). *Aeroflot Office:* 1 Lenin Street. *Harbor:* 16 Rustaveli Prospekt. *Camping for motorists:* near the beach, on the highway to Tbilisi, ¾ mile from Sukhumi.

Batumi: *Intourist:* 11 Ninoshvili Street. *Harbor:* 2 Primorskaya Street. *Aeroflot:* 42 Marx Street.

Bakhchisarai: *Railroad station,* some distance from city center, but connection from Sevastopolskoye Road.

Gurzuf: *Paying Guest Service:* 26 Leningradskaya. *Rail reservations office:* 19 Leningradskaya.

Kerch: *Rail and air reservations:* 13 Tolstoy Square (nearest airport: Simferopol).

THE CAUCASUS

Georgia, Armenia and Azerbaijan

The Caucasus, a land of towering mountains and winding valleys, is a varied, colorful part of the Soviet Union—but is largely unknown to the traveler, though the tourist season lasts throughout the year. On the narrow strip of land between the Black Sea and the Caspian, snow-covered summits rise above the coast; in a single day one can travel from palm groves to the domain of eternal snow, from fresh, green tea plantations to rocky deserts. The three republics of the Caucasus have much to offer: Armenia has monasteries and chapels dating from the first century, Azerbaijan mosques and minarets almost a thousand years old, Georgia the ruins of 600-year-old castles.

In an area of some 170,000 square miles there is an immense variety of nationalities with different customs, traditions and ways of life—but of these customs, the tradition of hospitality seems to be all-enduring. And the inexorable laws of tribal revenge and masculine domination still linger.

Exploring Georgia

To the Russians it is Gruzia, to the Georgians, Sakartvelo—but whatever you call it, it is a country of rare variety and attraction. It is a republic of 26,911 square miles, with more than half of its area lying above 3,000 feet, crossed by the 9,000- to 12,000-foot-high ranges of the Great and Lesser Caucasus (highest peak, Mount Elbrus, is nearly 17,000 feet). It has some enclosed high valleys like Svanetia, wide basins like Kakhetia; only 13 per cent is lowland. A third of its length is bordered by the Black Sea.

Among the almost five million Georgians, 15 major nationalities are registered. The Georgians represent about 70 per cent of the population. Within the Republic's territory are two autonomous republics and an autonomous region: the Abkhazian Autonomous Republic (5,375 square miles, population 497,000, capital Sukhumi); the Adzhar Autonomous Republic (1,875 square miles, population 334,000, capital Batumi); and the South Ossetian Autonomous Territory (2,437 square miles, population 582,000). Most of the population live below the 3,000-feet level; the mountain districts are sparsely populated.

This is the area with the greatest concentration of centenarians, whose lives are being studied by a special gerontological institute.

Tbilisi

Tbilisi, the capital of Georgia, stretches along the River Kura for more than 13 miles; its population is over a million.

Surrounded by mountains, the city has an average elevation of over 1,200 feet. The Suran range, the watershed between the Black Sea and the Caspian, is west of Tbilisi, linking the Kavkasioni range (its highest summit is the 15,120-foot-high Kazbek) with the Mesheti Ridge. To the southwest, the spurs of the Trialeti Ridge close the circle; within the city, Mount Mtatsminda rises to 1,965 feet. The climate is temperate and continental, with somewhat more precipitation but a less variable temperature than average. Sycamore trees line the streets. July is the warmest and January the coldest month, often with snow, and frost frequently occurs in December, January and February.

Mount Mtatsminda (Mamadaviti) and Environs

Mount Mtatsminda is the highest point of Tbilisi and from the top you get a panoramic view of the surrounding countryside. You can reach it by cable car. The terminal is near the Rustaveli monument, at Elbakidze Street which can be reached by both bus and trolley-bus. There is a stop halfway up where the Mamadaviti (Father David) Chapel stands on a specially-built terrace. Today it is a pantheon honoring the celebrities of Georgian culture. From here you can continue by the funicular or on foot. At the top terminal there are a restaurant, reading and game rooms and children's nurseries. Around the building a large park contains an openair cinema.

From the summit you can descend on foot, first along the path leading to the Pantheon, then along Besiki Street, emerging on Rustaveli Boulevard, opposite the Hotel Tbilisi. Another, winding, serpentine path passes the resort of Okrokanya; then, along the Kodzhor highway, you reach the Komsomol Promenade, which runs along the Salalaki Ridge. The promenade stretches for almost a mile, lined with cypresses and linden trees. On the town side, a huge aluminum statue, the Deda-Kalaki (Mother of the Town), holds a sword in one hand, a cup in another—the symbolic welcome to foe and friend. On the same side you see the ruins of the former citadel. At the end of the promenade, a one-story brick building houses the Museum of Local History and Ethnography, containing archeological finds, costumes, arms and tools. From Komsomol Promenade, narrow, steep streets lead into the Old Town; but you can also visit on the far side of the mountain the Botanical Gardens, which

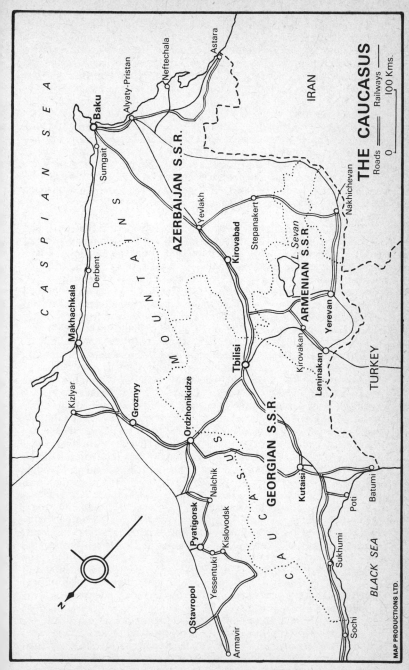

THE CAUCASUS

Roads ——— Railways ———

0   100 Kms.

CASPIAN SEA

IRAN

Astara
Neftechala
Alyaty-Pristan
Baku
Sumgait
Derbent
Makhachkala
Kizlyar
Groznyy
Ordzhonikidze

AZERBAIJAN S.S.R.

Yevlakh
Kirovabad
Stepanakert
L. Sevan

ARMENIAN S.S.R.

Nakhichevan
Yerevan
Kirovakan
Leninakan

TURKEY

MOUNTAINS

Tbilisi

GEORGIAN S.S.R.

Kutaisi
Poti
Batumi
Sukhumi
Sochi

BLACK SEA

CAUCASUS

Nalchik
Pyatigorsk
Kislovodsk
Yessentuki
Stavropol
Armavir

MAP PRODUCTIONS LTD.

are a cool, pleasant refuge with a waterfall. Next to the gardens is the former Moslem cemetery, with a number of characteristic funeral monuments.

Descending from Komsomol Promenade you reach the Salalaki District. Its main thoroughfares, Davitashvili Street and Kirov Street, lead to the Inner Town. In Salalaki the most interesting architecture is to be found on Alaverdi Square and on the streets intersecting it.

Tbilisi's Center

The town center is Lenin Square, where, on the north side, stands the Georgian Art Museum. The treasury section (which can only be visited by special request) contains some exquisite gold and silverware. The Museum also has a fine collection of icons, frescos and works by Georgian painters. It was once the Tbilisi Ecclesiastical Seminary; a plaque still records the fact that Stalin studied here from September 1894 to May 1899.

Tbilisi's finest thoroughfare, Rustaveli Boulevard, branches off from Lenin Square. It is a wide, sycamore-lined street with many public, scientific and cultural buildings and hotels; in the evening it is the favorite promenade of the local population. Not far from Lenin Square the boulevard widens. Here is the Pioneers' Palace, formerly the local governor's residence. Opposite, we find the Georgian National Museum, opened in 1929. Formerly the Caucasian Museum (founded 1852), it has a particularly rich ethnographical section. Next to the museum are the Shota Rustaveli cinema and the Intourst Hotel, built in the 1870's.

Close by is the Number One High School, with the statues of Ilya Chavchavadze and Akaky Tsereteli in front of it. The school also houses the Museum of Education; the adjoining huge building is the headquarters of the postal administration. (The main post office is on the far bank of the Kura.) Kashvety Cathedral, consecrated in 1910, stands in the center of a large garden on the other side of the boulevard. Behind the cathedral, the Garden of the Communards contains the statues of Gogol, Ketskhoveli and other notables. Before the park, on Rustaveli Boulevard, we also find the Georgian Art Gallery, which has seasonal exhibitions. It is housed in the former Khram Slavi (Temple of Glory), built in the 1880s to commemorate the conquests of the Russian Army in the Caucasus.

On the corner next to the park is the Hotel Tbilisi, built in 1915. Here the boulevard's straight line deviates at the Rustaveli Drama Theater, which also contains a concert hall. The Rustaveli Drama Company are world famous for their productions of Shakespeare in a bold, original style. They were acclaimed in London and at the Edinburgh Festival in 1979–80.

Nearby is the Paliashvili State Opera, a building in Moorish style, finished in 1896. The Opera House is named after a Georgian composer whose grave is in the garden outside. Their opera and ballet productions are well worth seeing.

On the same side of the boulevard is the Marxism Leninism Institute and the Lenin Museum. Opposite the institute stand the editorial offices of the *Zarya Vostoka* (Dawn of the East) newspaper. Here the boulevard curves towards the road leading to the top of the Elbakidze Hill. At the end of the boulevard we find a rather ornate building housing a café and post office. The cable-car station is in its courtyard. Rustaveli Boulevard ends in Rustaveli Square, which has a statue of Georgia's greatest poet, Shota Rustaveli.

Lenin Street is the continuation of Rustaveli Boulevard which divides, not far from the square, into Lenin Street on the right and Melikishvili Street on the left. In Lenin Street there is, on the right, the openair cinema, located inside Kirov Park. One entrance to the park is from Lenin Street which stretches to the bank of the Kura. There is another entrance from the river bank side. The Park has a large openair theater, sports stadia and a Chess Palace. In its southern part, at the end of Niko Nikoladze Street, stands the Lurdzhi (Blue) Monastery which was built in the reign of Queen Tamar, with some of the original 12th-century building surviving. Its once blue roof gave it its name.

Returning to the crossroad, we now continue along Melikishvili Street. The Hotel Sakartvelo is on the left with a restaurant on the ground floor. The Tbilisi wine cellars are at the bottom of the street, on a little rise to the left. Here one can not only taste the excellent Georgian wines but visit the "vinotheque" in which 126,000 bottles of 700 different vintages are kept—including 1806 Tokay and 1714 Kiev vodka.

The white-domed university building can be seen from the beginning of Melikishvili Street. It stands on Ilya Chavchavadze Boulevard, one of the main arteries of the Vake District. It follows the steep bank of the River Vere, only a block away.

From Chavchavadze Boulevard, a stairway leads into the 300-acre Victory Park, with its fountains, shady walks, open-air cinema and cafés. The Locomotiv Stadium is in the southwestern part of the park. Behind the stadium on the mountain slope is the favorite Tbilisi resort quarter, Tskhneti.

On the other side of the university, the sloping Varazis-Hevi Street leads to the Square of Heroes, an important traffic junction. From here Chelyuskintsev Street leads to the left bank of the Kura and the railway station. Lenin Street crosses the square from north to south, connecting the city center with the Saburtalo district and the Georgian Military Highway. On the north and east side, Heroes' Square is bordered by the slope of the Saburtalo Plateau, on the southwest by a tall mountain. On the southeastern side, the lower stretch of the Vere River and the quay of the Kura can be seen. Turning south, we see Lenin Street, and, in the distance, the outlines of the Mamadaviti. On the corner of Chelyuskintsev Street and the square a stairway leads to a hill where the municipal circus is located.

On the right of Chelyuskintsev Street we find some of the buildings of the Georgian Academy of Science. On Chelyuskintsev Bridge we cross to the left bank of the Kura. The street ends at the railway station; from here, another bridge takes us to the Lenin district.

The main street on the left bank is Plekhanova Road. At the corner of Chelyuskintsev Street stands a film studio: The nearby Dynamo Stadium, rebuilt in the 1970s, has a total capacity of 70,000. Ordzhonikidze Park, opposite the stadium, has one of the first Pioneers' Railways, built by schoolchildren and students of the railway engineering college. An openair theater and cinema, a parachute tower, a library, café and planetarium are among the park's other attractions. The Main Post Office is on Plekhanova Road on which also are two typical Tbilisi houses, Nos. 107 and 116. Walking south from Chelyuskintsev Street we reach the busy Mardzhanishvili Square.

Old Town

The old town is dominated by the castle, built in the fourth century. Of the citadel or western fort, known as Sahis Tahti (The Throne of the Shah) a few ruins on Komsomol Promenade have survived. The castle was a large complex and, beside the courtiers, many artisans and tradesmen lived within its precincts. Southeast of the castle walls a whole town developed. Its former site is most easily reached from Lenin Square by turning into Pushkin Street, then turning right again at the first cross-street. On the main street of the Old Town, in Shavteli Street, we find the Anchiskhati Church, founded in the sixth century and rebuilt several times—most extensively in 1675, when new gateways and a bell tower were added. On the right side of Shavteli Street is the Karis Ecclesia church, built in 1710 on the site of an earlier one. On its western side is a bell tower.

Shavteli Street runs into Irakly Square, center of old Tbilisi. It was the Royal Square where officials listened to complaints, where openair courts sat, sentences were carried out and royal commands proclaimed. The eastern part is occupied by the police headquarters, formerly the governor's palace. On the north side, at the corner of Shavteli Street, we find the Simon Palace. Most of the old houses have been extensively rebuilt in the 19th century; but part of the palace of King Rustum, next to police headquarters, has survived. This is known as the Mint and has eight vaulted rooms.

Near Irakly Square, on the left side of Sionskaya Street, is one of Tbilisi's oldest and largest churches, the Cathedral of the Assumption. Its 19th-century bell tower with Russian dome is opposite. The original church was built between AD 575 and 639, but little of that remains. On the left also, just before reaching the Cathedral, there is an early 19th-century caravanserai.

To the south, Sionskaya Street runs into Vakhtang Gorgasali Square, an important traffic junction, linked by a new bridge to the far bank of the river. Vakhtang Gorgasali Street, starting from the square, swings into Bath Street, named after the famous sulphurous baths, with a whole row of bath-houses in Turkish style. The newer medicinal baths, which have clinics attached, are back in Vakhtang Gorgasali Street.

On the left bank of the Kura, where the river curves east, there is a steep rocky hill with a slim church on top. This is the Metekhi Chapel, the most characteristic sight of Tbilisi. Founded in 1278–83 and reconstructed several times, it was for some time the chapel of the Georgian Catholics. In the 1820's it was turned into a prison. On the same heights we find the round, bastion-like palace of Daredzha (Darya), the wife of King Erekle (Irakly) II. It is called Sachino (Noble). Its circular balcony offers a panorama of the city.

Walking along Kura Quay, you can rest in the riverside gardens. At the Verei Bridge is the central bus terminal from which buses leave for every part of Georgia, Armenia and the Northern Caucasus.

The Georgian Military Highway

This road offers the finest tour of the high Caucasus mountains, which have inspired a great many poets. The Military Highway received this name only in the last century, though it is many hundreds of years old. It is the shortest route (130 miles), crossing the Caucasus ranges, linking Georgia with the Northern Caucasus and Transcaucasia. Its two terminals are Tbilisi and Ordzhonikidze, capital of the North Ossetian Autonomous Republic. The road from Tbilisi first skirts the River Kura, then swings sharply towards Mtskheta. From Mtskheta it runs up to Guduari and the Cross Pass in the valley of the Aragvi River, then continues in the Terek valley and reaches the plain after the Daryal Ravine. This is a spectacular and varied journey, with the landscape and the weather changing almost every mile, through a land of legends and striking beauty.

From Tbilisi we reach the Georgian Military Highway along Lenin Street. The road leads between the fields of the Digom State Farm, passes the Zemo-Avchala Power Plant and makes a sharp turn towards Mtskheta. Not far from the 1927 hydro-electric plant a cliff-top church stands on the horizon—this is already part of Mtskheta.

Mtskheta, some 14 miles from Tbilisi, is one of the most ancient cities in Georgia and was its capital until the 16th century. Though it is rather insignificant today, once it was a twin city at the confluence of the Aragvi and Kura rivers and excavations, which have been going on since 1925, have uncovered many valuable and interesting monuments. Here we find examples of both the styles of ancient church architecture: the basilica and the cruciform domed church. The oldest is the 11th-century Sveti Tskhoveli Cathedral, dedicated to the Twelve Apostles, with a carved façade and 16th- and 17th-century decorations. It contains the tombs of the last two kings of Georgia.

About 500 yards northwest from the Sveti Tskhoveli stands the Samtavro Convent also built in the 11th century. The main church is dedicated to Saint Nina, "the Enlightener of Georgia." Not far from the Sveti Tskhoveli, too, are the remains of the so-called Basilica of Antioch, with some parts dating from the fifth and sixth centuries, others much later. Opposite, on the left bank, in the mouth of the Aragvi and Kura, at the summit of the Sagurami ridge's rocky spur, stands the Dzhvari Church, built in AD 585–604. It is remarkably well preserved, with lavish decorations on the eastern and southern façades. It has served as the prototype of many other Georgian churches.

Leaving Mtskheta, we see on a cliff the ruins of the castle of Bebristsihe (Fort of the Old Man), of which only the main tower and the western wall are standing. This was an outpost of Mtskheta built as a defense against attacks from the north.

After Mtskheta the highway runs along the right bank of the Aragvi, descending to the village of Garzis-Hevi, then continues along the undulating Mukranai Valley. In the next village, Tsitsamuri, a white obelisk marks the spot where Ilya Chavchavadze, the Georgian poet, was murdered on August 21, 1907 by Czarist agents. North of the obelisk, in the village of Saguramo, there is a memorial museum in the poet's former home.

After Saguramo the highway turns southwest, to Mukhrana. This valley used to be the estate of a great and rich aristocratic family, the

Bagrations. Today there are vineyards in this area. In the courtyard of the central administrative building is an 800-year-old oak tree. After crossing the valley, the road reaches the community of Bulachauri. Close to it, on the right bank of the Aragvi, we find the Bodorna Monastery, rebuilt in 1772. There are many caves in the neighborhood which served as temporary refuges for the local people hiding from the hordes of Genghis Khan and Tamerlane. Close to Bodorna, the ruins of a medieval town can still be seen.

Zhinvali stands north of Bodorna, at the meeting of the Psava and White Aragvi rivers. Here, too, there are several ruined castles and watchtowers.

Here we can make a detour to Bari-Sabo. A road branching off to the right leads across woods to the village of Bodavi, then over two passes and another couple of villages to Tianeti, in a wide valley. From Zhinvali we can also make a side-trip to the town of Duseti and to the scenic Bazaleti Lake, south of it. Duseti became the capital of the Aragvi princes in the 17th century and in the late 18th century was given a municipal charter. The Bazaleti lake, some six miles to the south, has excellent fishing and there is plenty of game in the woods around. In summer, though the water is cold, it offers good swimming (but beware of leeches!). Legend has it that Queen Tamar deposited the cradle of her dead child here and that the lake was created by the tears of the Georgians.

Returning to the Military Highway, five miles from Zhinvali we reach the village of Ananuri with a 16th–18th-century fortress and, inside, the Church of the Assumption, built in 1689. Nearby is the 16th-century Bteba church and at the foot of the hill a domed Armenian church. A little further on is the village of Pasanauri, which has a new Intourist hotel, and an excellent restaurant.

North of Ananuri begins the Mtiuleti region with the highest mountains of the Caucasus. There are forests and Alpine-like meadows; bear, wolf, wildcat and fox roam the woods and the cold streams are well stocked with trout.

Mleti is 4,635 feet above sea level. Passing across a stone bridge, the road snakes uphill, flanked by a deep ravine. Gudauri, the next village, is on the summit—at 7,080 feet the highest habitation along the Military Highway, offering a spectacular view into the valley. To the northeast we see Mount Gud, with the Krestovy Pereval (Cross Pass, 7,837 feet) on the right and somewhat farther away the summits of the Red Mountains, with huge rock pillars far behind them. These are Svidi Dzma, Seven Brothers.

After Gudauri the road dips, then, having reached the Devil's Valley, it begins to climb again to the Cross Pass, which is marked by a cross erected in 1824. Beyond the pass is the region of Hevi, the finest section of the road. The narrow valley of the Terek is framed by majestic mountains; the highest is the Kazbek (16,508 feet), with glaciers covering its flanks.

The road now descends to the valley of Baydara, which is usually blocked throughout the winter. Here there are ten important mineral springs.

After passing a few smaller settlements we arrive in Kazbegi (known in the 19th century as Stepan-Tsminda), center of Mokhavia, a mountain region of Georgia. Excavations have unearthed many bronze and silver vessels, jewels and other objects dating from the sixth century BC.

The Kazbek, one of Europe's highest mountains, consists of two adjoining peaks, linked by a ridge. Amirani, the Georgian Prometheus, was chained to this soaring summit, according to local legend. The highest geophysical observatory in the Soviet Union stands on the Gergeti Glacier, at the foot of the Kazbek.

West of Kazbek, on a mountain on the left bank of the Terek, is the Trinity (Tsminda Sameba) Church, one of the finest examples of Georgian church architecture. From Kazbegi, a journey of 12 miles will take us to Betlemi which has a large network of caves on several levels. These were lost for a long time and only rediscovered in 1948. Today they are well signposted and lit, and open to tourists.

From Kazbegi the road runs alongside the Terek River, first climbing then descending to the village of Gveleti, near the Gveleti Falls. It descends further to the river, crossing the Devil's Bridge and arriving at the Daryal Gorge, into which the foaming, rushing river is compressed by steep rock walls, stretching for nine miles. Here we see the ruins of the Daryal Fortress, the inspiration of Lermontov's fine poem, *Tamara*.

After the fort, the road on the right leads to the Daryal Sanatorium, that on the left to the village of Chmi. A few miles farther on, we leave Georgia and enter the North Ossetian Autonomous Republic.

Excursions Around Tbilisi

Turning off from the Georgian Military Highway at the eight-kilometer stone, we reach Digomi, a village that has been inhabited for 2,000 years. Two of its originally seven churches have survived; one is St. George Church, on the outskirts, standing on the right-hand side of the road. It was built in the late 10th or early 11th century. There are some interesting votive tablets and reliefs. The other, the Mother of God Church, is at the northwestern end of Digomi, and is even older.

Kodzhori can be reached on foot from Tbilisi; the footpath is only five miles long, though the distance is more than ten miles by road. It lies some 4,200 feet above sea level. Once it was the favorite summer resort of the Tbilisi nobility. Southwest of it is a ruined castle, dating from the 1600's. A mile to the northeast, on the wooded flank of Mount Udzo, there is a church which was a place of pilgrimage for barren women. The top of the mountain provides an extensive and beautiful view.

Betania is 20 miles west from Tbilisi, with a monastery that is one of the masterpieces of Georgian architecture; its church has ancient portraits of several Georgian kings.

Tskhneti, another summer resort on a high plateau, lies five miles northwest of the capital. Rustavi, on the banks of the Kura and 16 miles from Tbilisi, is a new industrial center. Its local museum displays interesting finds discovered during its construction.

A good road leads from Tbilisi to Batumi, passing through Gori. This, too, lies on the Kura, and its ancient fortress, the Goris-Tsihe, stands in the center of the town, on a hill rising above the bank of the fast-flowing Liakvi River. It was founded in the first half of the first millennium BC, but has been rebuilt and altered many times. Gori is Stalin's birthplace and the house where he was born still stands, enclosed within a large, decorative building. On the way to Batumi we also pass Borzhomi, one of the most important health resorts in Georgia, famous for its mineral water. It has a monastery dating from the fifth or sixth century.

On the left bank of the Kura River, 11 miles from the town of Ahalkalaki is Vardzia, the famous cave city. Its caves are on five or six levels and more than 300 chambers. The church carved directly into the rock dates from the 12th or 13th century and has fine murals.

Kutaisi, Georgia's second largest city, stands on the road linking Tbilisi and Sukhumi. The remains of the Bagrat church and the fortress there date from the 1st century AD.

The Northern Caucasus

The northern part of the stretch of land between the Black Sea and the Caspian is occupied by autonomous republics which form part of the Russian Federation: Dagestan, Chechen-Ingush, North Ossetia and Kabardin-Balkar. It also includes the Stavropol territory.

The land of mountains, as Dagestan is translated, is a country of narrow valleys and towering cliffs. Most of the villages are in the mountains and are inaccessible for more than half the year. The houses are built very close together, on top of each other, forming strange fortress-like conglomerations. This is the location of Tolstoy's great *Hadji Murat*. Thirty-three nationalities live on the republic's 30,000 square miles; among the most numerous groups are the Lezgins, Avars, Dargins, Kumiks, Tabasaranians and Lakks.

The capital, Makhachkala, is an important port on the Caspian. In 1970 it suffered a devastating earthquake and has been mostly rebuilt. Its hotel is on the shore; it has a theater and a museum with exhibits of the local customs and rich folk art of all the 33 nationalities, especially carpets and jewelry. Kubachi, a mountain village, is famous for its jewelers and there is a good selection of their wares available in Makhachkala.

The other important Dagestan city, Derbent, is also a port—the oldest surviving settlement on the Caspian. It has some fine architectural monuments dating from the 6th to 14th centuries.

North Ossetia

The capital of this region is Ordzhonikidze, also called "The Gateway to the Caucasus", the northern entrance to the Georgian Military Highway. It is a small town which was the scene of embittered battles during the Civil War. The Revolutionary History Museum is at 50 Kirov Street.

The Kabardin-Balkar Republic

With more than 634,000 inhabitants and an area of some 4,825 square miles, this republic boasts within its borders the highest peak in Europe, the 18,481-foot Mount Elbrus. Nalchik, the capital is a health resort and university town, rich in greenery. There is a museum of local history, and close to the city are unearthed ancient burial places. Nalchik's main street is Lenin Road, linking Soviet Square and the Square of the 400th Anniversary, commemorating the fourth centenary of the Russian rule.

The pride of Nalchik is the city park, which provided the great silver pines decorating Moscow's Red Square. Two peaks rise above the park—

the Dih-Tau (Mount Heaven) and the Kostan-Tau (Tent Mountain). The statue of Sora Nogmov, the Kabardin poet who created the Kabardin alphabet and grammar and wrote the *Cherkess Legends,* stands in the center of the park. Dolinsk, near Nalchik, has many valuable mineral springs and is being developed into a large health resort. Nalchik itself is an important tourist center, from which four main routes branch out. One leads through the Balkar Valley to the Blue Lakes, of which the finest and most mysterious is the Cherek-Koel Tarn. Another route passes through the Bezengi Valley to the Bezengi Ice Wall, which stretches for nine miles and rises almost vertically. The route through the Chegem Valley winds past huge waterfalls. Finally, the road to Mount Elbrus goes through the Baksani Valley. Much of the latter trip can be taken by bus; from Nalchik the Terskol route passes through Staraya Krepost and Zayukovo (not far from the Baksan Power Plant) to Tirni-Auz. This recently-built town 3,900 feet up, is the center of molybdenum and wolfram mining. From here we continue our way in the Baksani Valley. For the walker there are splendid trails in these mountains. One leads to the forest-lined Adir-Su Valley; from here you can proceed to the 12,000-foot-high Adir-Su-Bashi and Cheget-Tau-Chan peaks. The even more picturesque Adil-Su Valley gives access to the Shkhelda Peak (a fantastic ice-palace); thence, through the Dzhan-Tugan Pass, we can reach Svanetia. On the way to Mount Elbrus the first town where the bus stops is Upper Baksan, with the castle of Prince Ismail Urusiev and his sons. It is a traditional base for Elbrus expeditions.

The next stop is Baksan-Basi-Ullu-Gara, where there is a large mineral spring whose water is bottled and sold all over the Soviet Union. A 300-room hotel has been built recently. Another six miles bring us to Terskol, one of the leading winter sport centers in the Soviet Union. A five-mile cable-car lift takes you from the Hotel Azau to the summit. There is an intermediate stop at Sary Krugozor.

Mineralniye Vodi

Mineralniye Vodi (Mineral Waters) is the collective name of the four well-known Caucasian resorts, all with a pleasant climate and delightful location. Their waters are rich in mineral salts and they attract many holidaymakers and visitors taking the cure. They are: Pyatigorsk, Kislovodsk, Yessentuki and Zheleznovodsk. In all four resorts there are a number of sanatoria and hotels. The treatments offered include drinking cures and mud baths.

In Pyatigorsk it is worthwhile visiting the Local Museum and the Lermontov Museum (devoted to the poet). There are pleasant walks on the Goryachaya Gora (Hot Mountain), where you can explore the Tsvetnik Park, the Lermontov Gallery or descend on the south side to the caves, among them the Proval, which has a sulphurous lake. You can actually walk underneath the lake bottom. The other interesting features of the town are the Perkal Spring and the tree nursery near Perkal Cliff. From here, less than a mile's walk takes us to the clearing in which Lermontov was killed in a duel on July 27, 1841. The ascent of Mount Masuk is also a traditional Pyatigorsk excursion; the path starts at the museum and it is a comfortable hike of 50 minutes.

Kislovodsk is in a valley, on the banks of the Olkhovka and Beryozovka rivers. There is a beautiful park on the banks of the Olkhovka which has several small waterfalls. From here we can take a trip to the valleys of the Olkhovka or Alikonovka, explore the five huge cataracts of the Honeyed River or Mount Ring (named after its ring-shaped cave), the 4,600-foot-high Great Dzhina Peak and Bermamit.

Apart from its baths, the chief feature of Yessentuki is its spectacular park near the Hotel Mayak. From here we can take an excursion to the Podkumka Gorge and its cave.

Zheleznovodsk lies 1,890 feet above sea level, in the midst of a thick forest. From here we can climb Iron Mountain (Zheleznaya Gora), which offers a fine view of the district. On Razvalka Mountain the air is always cool, about 10,000 square yards having a layer of permafrost; this is caused by carbon dioxide that has accumulated in the underground caves. The stations of Mineralniye Vodi are linked by electric trains.

Armenia

The Armenian Soviet Socialist Republic lies on the southern slope of the Armenian Mountains, along the northeastern part of the range, framed by the peaks of the Lesser Caucasus. Its area is 11,502 square miles and its population almost 3 million. On the north it is bordered by Georgia, on the east by Azerbaijan, on the west and south by Turkey and Iran.

This is one of the most picturesque and majestic parts of the Caucasus. Its average elevation is 4,500 feet; even the deepest valleys are 1,500 to 2,400 feet above sea level. Spring comes later here; the atmospheric and barometric pressures are different from ordinary.

Yerevan

Yerevan is one of the oldest and most attractive cities in the USSR. Its situation, its natural features and its colorful buildings all contribute to its beauty. Lying on the Armenian plateau, its elevation is 3,000 feet, with a remarkably pure atmosphere. It has hot summer days but cool evenings. In winter it can be very cold and sometimes there is snow, though mild winters are not infrequent. The city is surrounded by mountains; to the south the snow-covered peak of Ararat, on its left the somewhat lower Lesser Ararat (Masis) and to the northwest the four peaks of Mount Aragats. On the north it is bordered by the bleak rocks of the Kanaker Plateau, on the east by the greenery of the villas of the Nork Plateau, on the west by the deep ravine of the Razdan (Zanga) River with its riverside promenades and the vineyards of Mount Dalmin.

Modern Yerevan is a colorful city, its buildings constructed of basalt, marble, onyx and volcanic rock in many different styles, yet forming a fairly harmonious whole. Though some of them may look over-decorated, they avoid the monotony of the box-like concrete-and-glass structures of many other cities.

Lenin Square is the center of the city. The dominating building is the Government Palace, housing the Council of Ministers and the Supreme Soviet of Armenia.

Opposite, on the northern side of the square, we find the offices of several ministries. Between the two pink palaces, on the northeastern side of the square, is the House of Armenian Culture, with a huge, arcaded loggia and a large basin with fountains in front of it. This is the home of the Historical Museum and the Armenian National Gallery. The Historical Museum covers the evolution of art on Armenian soil from prehistoriic times. On the first floor are works by modern craftsmen and traditional costumes. Also in Lenin Square is the Armenia, Yerevan's biggest hotel—famous for the "best coffee in the Soviet Union" served in its lobby. The Yerevan office of Intourist is here too.

Lenin Boulevard and Neighborhood

Leaving the Hotel Armenia, turn left along little Amiryan Street and you will reach the boulevard in a few minutes. Turning left on Lenin Boulevard, we pass the minaret and mosque built in 1776. This houses the municipal museum illustrating the 2,000-year-long history of the city. Opposite is the Market Hall with its massive wrought-iron railings; it has a striking interior and a very colorful atmosphere.

Turning right from Amiryan Street and walking uptown along Lenin Boulevard, we reach the Armenian Opera House, standing in a park which is a favorite with Armenians. They are often to be seen here engaged in what look like violent arguments but is usually just friendly discussion. The finest street in the city, Bartskamuntsyun, begins at the park. It runs into a broad square, to the left of which Kiev Street starts. This leads to the Great Razdan Bridge, which crosses the river to Ordzhonikidze Boulevard. Turning from the boulevard into the Street of the 26 Commissars, we can reach Shaumyan Square. The Hotel Sevan stands here; the square is linked by a promenade with Lenin Square.

At the end of Lenin Boulevard a stairway leads to the Matenadaran, the famous Armenian archive which has a large collection of manuscripts, complete and fragmentary, in many languages as well as miniatures and some fine rare bindings. Most of the material in the archive originated in the church library of Echmiadzin. A memorial to Mesrop Mashtots, the creator of the Armenian and Georgian alphabets stands outside the Matenadaran.

The Banks of the Razdan

The fast-flowing Razdan (Zanga) River forms a deep ravine near Yerevan. The river's flow has been regulated and pleasant walks have been built along its banks. The shortest way to approach it is through Spandaryan Street to the Bridge of Victory. The other, somewhat more interesting route, is through Kiev Street to the Great Razdan Bridge.

The impressive bridge was built some years ago and connects the two banks at a height of 225 feet. After crossing it, we can take a footpath down to the quay. Walking upstream we reach Abovyan Park, a pleasant recreation area with an openair theater. The Pioneer's Railway, *Ayrenik,* will take us to a beach, which has a swimming pool. The river itself has a strong current and the bottom is stony here, so swimming in it is not recommended.

Walking downstream, we reach the aqueduct. Nearby, on the rocky left bank, there are some remains of a fortress, stormed by Russian troops in October 1827. On the right bank are the Stadium and Shaumyan Park. Near the aqueduct there is a three-span bridge and on the left bank a large building without doors or windows: the wine cellar of the Ararat

Trust. It is decorated with sculptures of Armenian wine jugs and has an arcaded loggia. The entrance is at the back. Opposite the wine cellar, on the far end of the Bridge of Victory, a steep stairway leads to a pink, elaborately decorated building—the brandy stills of Yerevan. Visitors are welcome (by previous arrangement only).

New Residential Quarters and Ancient Fortresses

One of the most pleasant recreation areas of the Armenian capital is the Nork Plateau, with its shady trees and villas. We can reach the TV tower either by bus or on foot along Abovyan Street and Norki Road. In Abovyan Street, running parallel with Lenin Boulevard, stand the Academy of Sciences and the University. The old observatory is opposite the university in a large park. The new one is not far from Yerevan, at Byurakan, on the side of Mount Aragats.

Abovyan Street, named after a prisoner of modern Armenian literature born nearby, runs into Abovyan Square. Two roads start from here—Kanakeri and Norki. Kanakeri Road leads us to the Kanaker Plateau, from which there is a fine view of the city. (At Kanaker itself, a village now absorbed in Yerevan, is a memorial museum to Abovyan.) Here we can rest in Akhtanak Park and return either by bus or on foot along the Tbilisi highway.

The newest quarter, named after the 26 Commissars, is being developed along the edge of Akhtanak Park. This industrial district has absorbed the village of Kanaker, where Abovyan was born—his birthplace has been turned into a museum.

If we set out from Abovyan Square along Norki Road, we pass a whole row of hospitals and rest homes and come to a residential complex. Turning right here, we soon reach a shady copse where we can sit down and rest and then continue towards the TV tower. From here a forest path leads south to Komsomol Park. South of the park, on the plain, we see the buildings of Nor-Ares and a bare hill. This is Arin-Berd, the former Urartu fortress, which has recently been excavated. Stone tablets were found here describing how the son of King Menua built a fortress and founded a city he named Argisti Ervuni. This was the predecessor of present-day Yerevan.

Southwest of Yerevan, on the left bank of the Razdan, is the Karmir-Blur, an Urartu fortress built in the eighth and seventh centuries BC. Excavations at the foot of the hill, on the southern and western sides, have uncovered the remains of the Urartu city of Teysehaini. This is best visited on Sunday mornings: the bus bound for the race course takes us here from town (get off one stop before the terminal). From here a short walk will take us to the ruins. The hilltop offers a beautiful panorama of Yerevan's buildings and the vineyards and orchards of the Ararat Valley. The Armenian Exhibition of Economy has been laid out near Karmir-Blur; it covers more than 45 acres and has a striking central industrial pavilion.

Armenian Landscapes and Cities

Yerevan is an excellent base for exploring some of Armenia's most typical towns and villages. Echmiadzin is the center of the independent Armenian-Gregorian Church, the seat of the Patriarch or Catholicos, elected by the national bishops. It can be reached from Yerevan by bus, car and cycle; the distance is about 12 miles. The Echmiadzin road, lined with poplars, begins at the Bridge of Victory and runs on the right bank of the Razdan past vineyards and orchards. At the 18th kilometer stone, an obelisk-like signpost marks a left fork. This leads to one of the most interesting architectural monuments in Armenia, Zvartnots Cathedral. Built in the years 640–660 AD, the Church of St. Gregory is in ruins but it still retains many striking features, among them a most unusual sundial and a relief of the architect, Master Ovennes. There is a museum nearby containing some of the finds discovered by local excavations.

About 2 kilometers before the Zvartnots turning stands the Ripsime Church, a beautiful 18th-century building on the foundations of a very much earlier church.

Echmiadzin is only a mile-and-a-half from Zvartnots. This was the ancient capital of Armenia, called Vagarsapat when it was founded in 117 AD. It is also a center of Armenian learning and culture, where many of the leading intellectuals were educated. It is a district capital and the hub of an agricultural area famous for its vineyards and orchards and also its cotton-growing. Its cathedral, in the center of town, dates from 302 AD and has been rebuilt several times. Its museum has many relics—including a lance said to have pierced the side of Christ.

The cathedral is separated by a park from the residence of the Patriarch. Nearby is the Armenian Theological School, and other institutions, including the 7th-century Gayane Convent.In this ancient city, even the swimming pool is a historic relic—its main basin dates from the 18th century and was originally part of a large irrigation system.

From Echmiadzin, it is worthwhile making a trip to Lake Aygerlich, ten miles away, accessible by both bus and car. It is a small lake, surrounded by mountains, in a very beautiful setting. There is excellent fishing, and otters are bred in the reeds framing its shores.

To the southeast of Yerevan, some 11 miles away, we find the ruins of Dvin, another former Armenian capital. It is best reached by car along the Artasat highway.

Garni and its Environs

Two important Armenian monuments, the Garni fortress and the Gegard cave monastery, are only 22 miles from Yerevan by car. The route goes through Avan, Dzhrvezh and Vokhchaberd. The twisting road passes through romantic landscapes, along the ridge of the Gegami Range, and descends through a pass into the Garni Valley. In the sheer rock walls of the pass there are caves, today almost inaccessible, though once a regular refuge from invaders.

Garni Fortress was built on a cliff, near the village, in the steep valley of the Azat River. Its walls are of huge basalt blocks. Once it was the summer palace of King Trdat I, who built it in the first century AD. Parts of the pagan sanctuary within the walls have still survived, a beautiful mosaic floor, for instance.

The Gegard (Holy Lance) Monastery is only five miles from Garni. After a few loops the road reaches a ravine where the Karmirget River flows far below. A gate-like opening in the rocks is followed by a sudden descent; then the valley narrows and emerges into the Gegard Basin. Its perpendicular walls are honey-combed with caves. The church, built beside the river at the foot of the rock, dates from 1215. It provides access to another building with a roof formed by stalactites. The convent is a cave adjoining this building; the only way in is through a narrow opening in the roof. It was carved out of the rock by a single craftsman who spent his entire life decorating and enlarging the cave chamber and its smaller alcove, which was used for burials.

Ashtarak, Byurakan and Amberd

Ashtarak is a district center, 12 miles northwest of Yerevan, on the southern slope of Mount Aragats. The whole district has been inhabited from time immemorial and there is hardly a village without some interesting feature. From Semiram (named after the Babylonian Queen) to Kos, the whole area is full of menhirs, cromlechs and dolmens.

Talis is famous for the cuneiform tablets found here. There are ancient burial places and fortifications in Parbi, Orgov, Mungi, Osakan and Egvard. Parbi has one of the oldest Christian basilicas in the world (fourth-century). In the village of Ahtse a fourth-century underground crypt with bas-reliefs has been preserved; it is supposed to be the burial place of the Arshakid rulers. On the road from Yerevan to Ashtarak the Kasan River is spanned by a fifth-century bridge, and on the rock rising above it are the ruins of the fifth-century Tsiranavor Church.

From Ashtarak the highway continues west; after six miles, it begins to twist and turn, leading finally to Byurakan, where there is an important astrophysical observatory. From here we can set out on a pleasant hike. The ascending road reaches the village of Antarur and its fine old oak forest (two miles). The path descending to the west takes us to the valley in which the Arkhansen and Amberd rivers meet. On the heights we can see the restored Amberd Church and Fortress, built in the age of the Bagratid dynasty, with a complex system of underground corridors. On the left bank of the Arkhansen, huge, fish-shaped carved stones, the so-called *visapos,* can be seen. These are several thousand years old, probably souvenirs of a prehistoric water-cult.

Arzni and Environs

Arzni, known for its mineral spring and medicinal baths, lies in the valley of the Razdan River, some 13 miles north of Yerevan, linked by a regular bus service to the capital. Its sanatorium was built in 1925 but its sulphur springs were known long before then. The baths are set in a huge park of pine and chestnut trees. The promenade leads to a 300-foot waterfall. Towards the north another road takes us to the Egvard highway; a side-road leads to the Arzni reservoir, which is also a boating lake.

Tsakhkadzor is one of the most picturesque valleys in Armenia, some 5,130 feet above sea level. From Yerevan you take a train to Razdan and then continue by bus. The Valley of Flowers is the home of several Pioneers' camps, a "city of children". It is possible to put up a tent near the forest springs but the nights are cold and you need blankets or a sleeping bag.

From the valley we can make a half-day excursion to Mount Tegenis, starting from the northwestern edge of the youth camp where the Kecharis, an 11th-century memorial, stands. The path descends to the Tandzhabyur spring, from where a forest trail leads to a valley opening on the left. Here the ascent begins through woods and mountain meadows. From the summit (8,463 feet) there is a splendid panorama of much of Armenia. In winter this is a favorite skiing area, with thick, powdery snow, little or no wind and only moderate cold.

Lake Sevan and Leninakan

Some 37 miles from Yerevan, at an elevation of 6,000 feet, we find one of the largest mountain lakes in the world—the Sevan. Fed by some 30 rivers and streams, it has only one outlet, the Razdan River. The lake has a shoreline of more than 120 miles. The Artanas Peninsula narrows it at one point to less than five miles, dividing it into the Grand and the Little Sevan (the latter is much deeper). It can be reached from Yerevan by train or car. Sevan is a quickly developing town on the western lakeshore and has a recently opened motel with extensive facilities.

The Sevan Peninsula is four miles from the town; its ninth-century monastery provides some beautiful views. Boating and sailing are best restricted to the morning and late afternoon hours because around noon there is usually a strong wind, often rising to a storm. The water is very cold, so bathing is only for the keen swimmer. In Sevan there is an interesting natural history exhibition in the Institute of Marine Biology.

Not far from Sevan, outside the village of Lohasen, prehistoric cave dwellings have been found and some once-submerged hills have turned out to be Urartu settlements dating from the ninth century. The cunei-form tablets identify King Argisti and the city of Istikuni. The archeolo-gists found an almost complete four-wheeled carriage, bronze vessels, axes, jewels and inlaid daggers, evidence of a highly developed Bronze Age culture.

Twenty miles from Sevan an ancient cave dwelling at Cape Noratus has been found. Four miles from the cave is the town of Kamo (Nor-Ayazet), founded in the eighth century BC and now a center of the fish industry.

Lake Sevan can also be reached from Tbilisi and Baku. On this route, the first Armenian town is Idzhevan, famous for its potters and carpet-makers. From Idzhevan the road leads through the wooded valley of Akstafachay to Dilizhan, one of the most pleasant and popular health resorts in the country. It is surrounded by dense pine forests and there are fast mountain streams, waterfalls and bracing air. From here Lake Sevan is only a few kilometers.

Among other Armenian cities we must mention Leninakan, in the northwestern part of the republic, at an elevation of 4,600 feet. Founded in 1837 by Armenian refugee artisans from Turkey, it has developed into a large city noted for its textile industry and theater life.

Azerbaijan

Azerbaijan, occupies the southeastern part of Transcaucasia, on the Caspian Sea. It is bordered by the Russian, Armenian and Georgian republics and by Iran; its northern area lies along the southern slopes of the Caucasus. Near Derbent there is a narrow land bridge, most impor-tant in the Middle Ages, for the caravans of Eastern traders passed along this route; the Arabs called it Bab-ul-Abvad (The Gate of the East). Almost half of Azerbaijan's area is a plain. The southwestern part is surrounded by mountains of the Little (Lesser) Caucasus. The flat eastern area is bounded by the Mugan, Mili and Shirvan steppes. The highest peaks are Bazar-Dyuki (13,500 feet) and Sag-Dag (12,750 feet) At the corner of the Sag-Dag and the Murov-Dag range lies one of the most beautiful features of the country, the Gök-Göl Tarn.

Baku

The Azerbaijan capital is finely situated, built on a hillside around the horseshoe-shaped bay of the Apsheron Peninsula, which stretches out into the Caspian. While its climate is generally mild, it is often plagued by the "Nord of Baku", a wind of devastating strength. Most of the new buildings lie from east to west to lessen their exposure to the wind.

There is little left of old Baku. Its famous oil wells are now on the outskirts and a determined effort has been made to end (or at least limit) pollution. In the fifties a pleasant promenade was built. It is the busiest spot in the city, with the main thoroughfare, the Boulevard of Oilworkers, running beside it.

The Intourist Hotel stands at one end of the Oilworkers' Boulevard. Next to it is the funicular station. The funicular will take us in a few minutes to the highest point of the city, the Kirov Monument, from where we can see the whole city and its bay.

Baku is a mixture of architectural styles. The rooms of the palace preserve the ancient traditions of Azerbaijan architecture; the flat-roofed ramshackle houses are medieval. Several buildings in the Inner Town date from the turn of the century. One of them is the present-day Marriage Palace, pseudo French Gothic. It used to be the headquarters of a big industrial concern and later a club for emancipated Turkish ladies. The State Philharmonia (2 Communist Street) was built at the same time in neo-classical style and the Ismailia Palace (10 Communist Street), imitating Venetian Gothic, today houses the Academy of Sciences. The headquarters of the City Council and the Opera (27 Nizami Street) are early 20th-century.

The early constructivist style is represented by the Intourist Hotel on the seashore and the Press Palace on Nizami Square. In contrast, a rather exaggerated, over-decorated oriental style is apparent in the Government Palace on the seashore and the House of Scientists, very close to the Intourst Hotel. Examples of more tasteful, recent architecture, can be seen in the Youth Theater, the new observatory and the new wide-screen movie theater on Kirov Road.

From the Kirov monument we can descend by an imposing flight of stairs to the shore. The hillside park has an openair theater, the design of which has cleverly made the most of existing topography.

The Shore and Lenin Square

Starting from the Intourist hotel along the shore, we find a square with an ornamental fountain and, on the shorter side of the square, the House of Scientists. The Oilworkers' Boulevard begins on the sea side of the square and so does the shore promenade. Here there are an openair movie theater, several modern restaurants, *chaikhanas* (oriental teahouses) and facilities for various sports. A miniature Venice has been built here for children, with a maze of boating canals. We can visit the big Exhibition Hall and rest a while in the openair Pearl (Zhemchuzhina) Café, listen to a concert on an openair stage or watch children's movies (also openair).

Continuing either by the seashore promenade or by the Oilworkers' Boulevard, you reach Lenin Square.

The Castle

From the Intourst Hotel we can walk in ten to fifteen minutes to the castle district of Baku. It is best to enter by the Shemakha Gate. The streets are so narrow and twisting that in some places you can barely squeeze through between the houses. It is easy to lose your way, but the many slender minarets and the Bastion of the Maiden (Kyz-Kalasy) serve as landmarks.

The Bastion of the Maiden is on the left side of the road leading into the maze from the Shemakha Gate. There are many legends linked with it, most of them centering on unrequited love and a cruel *khan,* and all of which have a tragic ending. Once it must have stood surrounded by the sea, which has now retreated some 500 yards; it probably dates from the 11th century. The oldest monument in Baku is the minaret of the Mohammed Mosque, the Sinik-Kala, a delicate edifice; its inscription states that it was built in 1093. The Mohammed Mosque itself is much later. The most important part of the castle is the 15th-century Palace of the Shirvan Shahs. It houses the Historical and Architectural Museum of Azerbaijan and consists of several buildings and courtyards. Near the main palace is the Divan Khan, an octagonal domed hall surrounded by arcades. A huge gate on the southern side is the entrance; the square courtyard is edged by a pillared gallery. There are several other interesting buildings in the castle, including caravanserais, mosques, minarets and baths. Many of the old houses are likely to disappear, but the most important and historical will be restored and preserved.

Nizami Square and Kirov Road

Nizami Square, one of the finest in Baku, is outside the Shemakha Gate, with the statue of Nizami, the outstanding poet of Azerbaijan's Persian literature. Opposite we find the building of the Nizami Literary Museum; its loggia is decorated with the statues of leading Azerbaijan writers. The entrance is from Communist Street. The museum's three halls illustrate the history of Azerbaijan, and there are ceramics, miniatures, carpets and paintings dealing with the work of the 12th-century poet.

Behind the Nizami statue is an interesting apartment house called the Monolith. On a smaller square close to the castle wall the statue of Sabir, the great satirist, stands in front of the Academy of Sciences.

On Communist Street, opening from Nizami Square, are the Kirov University of Baku, the local party and government offices and the State Philharmonia.

Kirov Street is one of the main thoroughfares, connecting the hill quarter with the sea. To the left is the Square of the 26 Baku Commissars with a monument and an eternal flame in their memory. Further along Kirov Street is Shaumyan Street, where the city's second modern hotel, the Yuzhnaya (Southern), is located. Along April 28 Street opening from

Kirov Street, or along Lenin Street which crosses it, we can reach the railroad station.

Not far from Baku there are the black rocks rising from the Caspian upon which the oil center of Neftaniye Kamni (Oil Rocks) is based. It was in 1949 that the first undersea wells were sunk and since then a whole city has been built upon the iron piles. Neftaniye Kamni can be reached by boat, either directly or from Artyom Island, which is accessible by local train or bus.

Azerbaijan's Countryside and Cities

Baku is not only the capital, but also the communications center of Azerbaijan. The trains and buses starting from here are an excellent means of visiting the more interesting places in the republic.

We can reach Kirovabad by train and then continue by bus to Gök-Göl, or travel all the way by bus. After leaving the capital, the road passes across the Kobystan Steppe. First we journey north, towards Dagestan, along the Hachmas-Derbent highway; from here, the road branches off after Hurdalan westward towards Shemakha-Kirovabad. Soon the first mountains appear. The bus stops first at Maraza with its 15th-century mausoleum (Derk-Baba).

After Maraza the road continues among the spurs of the Great Caucasus, which, though they do not approach the height of the main peaks, resemble them with their grim cliffs. Shemakha appears in the distance. It was the former capital and one of the oldest settlements of Azerbaijan, the seat of the Shahs of Shirvan, whose court was often visited by the ambassadors of European and Asian powers. The formerly splendid city was several times devastated by earthquakes—by 1902, only 20 buildings survived. The new city was built close to the old one. Outside Shemakha, on the slope of Mount Pirkuli, at a height of 4,200 feet, we find one of the largest solar observatories in the Soviet Union.

The road continues toward the Asuini Pass, up through the wine-growing villages of Sagayan and Matrasa. On the right we see the rocky ravine of the Harami Ridge with the houses of the town of Ahsu. High up on the mountainside the road passes the mountain village of Baskal, then Mugnali. The pass itself is the finest point of the route.

Descending, we see the mountains of the Little Caucasus on the far side of the Kura Valley, though they are 100 miles away. West of the pass there is a plain called Kara-Maryam (Black Maria), criss-crossed by mountain streams. On the right side of the highway the Ahsu (White Water) River emerges from a deep valley into the marshland of what was once the Kura's delta. The village of Ahsu is on the riverbank; from here we can get to the district center of Kurdamir, to the village of Kara-Maryam and then to Geokchay and Agdash. These two villages are famous for their huge orchards growing quinces and pomegranates. The grapes of the district are also excellent.

From Geokchay and Agdash we continue across the plain and we soon cross the Kura, arriving in Yevlah, a developing industrial center with a good restaurant and huge fruit market. After Yevlah the highway and the railroad run parallel for a while. Beyond Kasum-Izmailovo the outlines of the Mingechauri power plant appear. The dam here raises the level of the River Kura by 270 feet and beyond it the reservoir stretches for some 40 miles.

Villages and railroad stations follow each other, then a monumental tower appears on the right-hand side—the mausoleum of the poet Nizami. From here the road leads along the valley of the Gandzhachay River to the poet's birthplace, the former Gandzha, now called Kirovabad and the second largest city in Azerbaijan. Of its numerous architectural monuments the Dzhuma Mosque is the most interesting, built by the command of Shah Abbas in 1603; you can also see the 13th-century fortress wall, the 17th-century caravanserai and the Dzhavad Khan mosque. Architecturally the Hey-Mam Mosque (built in the 17th, rebuilt in the 19th century) is also significant. The town has a huge park, many gardens and shady squares—and an oil refinery.

The hotel is not far from the bus stop and the best restaurant is on the wide terrace of the riverbank.

After Kirovabad the route continues across the mountains. The mist-wreathed peak of the 9,090-foot-high Mount Kyapaz appears in the distance. The beautiful Gök-Göl Tarn lies amid dense forests at a height of 4,500 feet, its shores lined with sanatoria and holiday homes.

Kazah, Dilizhan and Sevan

From Kirovabad we continue along the right bank of the Kura, among orchards and vineyards. Samhor is famous for its dry wines. The small town of Tauz stands on the banks of the Tauzchay River. It has a market where good bargains can be found, and a pleasant restaurant. After Tauz we pass through Akstafa, famous for its wine, then through the ancient village of Kazah. From here the twisting road leads through romantic landscapes and soon reaches the frontier of Azerbaijan and Armenia. First we pass the resort of Idzhevan, then in the valley of the Akstafachay, we arrive in one of the prettiest resorts in Armenia, Dilizhan, known for its mineral waters and ozone-rich forests. From here it is a short distance to Lake Sevan, from where we can continue to Yerevan.

Nuha, Kah, Ilisu and Belokan-Lagodchi

At Yevlah, the road branches off toward Nuha. We leave Haldan behind us, then cross the bridge of the Aldzhiganchay, with the Mingechauri reservoir on the left of the road. Climbing for some distance, we reach the saucer-shaped basin of the Adzhinaur lake. A barren plain stretches out to the left of the road; the spurs of the Great Caucasus rise on the right, among them the Das-Yug. Our road crosses this mountain, then emerges into the valley of the Agrichay River. From here, passing through the fertile Alazan-Agrichay plain, we arrive in Nuha, an important industrial and cultural center which has some interesting monuments, including the castle of the Nuha Khans, dating from the 18th century. Richly decorated both outside and in, it has some remarkable frescos. The caravanserai and the minaret also are well worth visiting.

From Nuha to Kah the road leads among copses and fields. From Kah a wide, steep serpentine road branches off to the resort town of Ilisu, famous for its rich, sparkling mineral springs. There are a castle and mosque built in the 17th century and, Kah's outstanding feature, the Russian fort built in 1856. From here we can quickly reach the nature reserve Belokan-Lagodchi, where there is a wealth of flora and fauna.

Sumgait, Kuba and Hachmas

These are best visited by car. From Baku to Sumgait, the distance is 25 miles. On the way we pass the Altava quarry. Sumgait is an industrial center, with modern residential quarters and a fine coastal promenade.

From Sumgait, we continue along the Hachmas-Derbent road, crossing the irrigation canal of Samur-Divchini and reaching the dam and the huge Dzherainbatan Reservoir, which is helping to desalinate the soil and turning barren areas into fertile land.

Later along the road there is a large limestone cliff on the left side surrounded by four smaller cliffs. These are called Five Fingers (Bes-Barmak) and are surrounded by numerous legends; the local folk believe that the spring at their foot produces water only once a week—on Friday, the holy day of Moslems.

The road now turns, then starts to climb. On the right we see the drilling towers of the Siazan oil field. Soon we reach the village of Gizib Gurum which is a pleasant halting place. From here we can reach the little town of Divichi in an hour; here the lifeless, dry steppe suddenly ends. A few miles from Divichi the road branches off. On the left, a 25-mile-long row of poplars leads to Kuba, the town of apple orchards. It is the fifth largest town of Azerbaijan and famous for its carpets. Its buildings are all in oriental style and it has a fine park.

The road that branches off leads towards Hachmas and Derbent. Hachmas is a small place with only one street two-and-a-half miles long and lined with poplars. Near it the woods begin and north of here we enter Dagestan. We can continue to the 1,500-year-old town of Derbent, to Makhachkala, the Dagestan capital and to Astrakhan, the great port at the mouth of the Volga.

Kizilagach Reserve and Lenkoran

This excursion is best done by bus, which takes us past several oil fields. We can stop at the favorite bathing resort for Baku residents, Sihov Beach. Our next stop is the town of Primorsk, then Sangalachi, notable for its medieval tower. Next is Salyany, a small town, with several oil wells and a fishery center. From Neftechali, the road leads to the nature reserve of Kizilagachi, rich in flora and fauna. From the village of Massali onward, we are already in a subtropical area, with cypresses, vineyards, lemon and orange groves, rice fields and tea plantations. Its center is the town of Lenkoran, with the experimental subtropical gardens of the Academy of Sciences nearby.

PRACTICAL INFORMATION FOR THE CAUCASUS REGION

WHEN TO GO. With mountains offering winter sports, lakes and rivers for angling and fishing, medicinal springs and the beaches for swimming, the Caucasus is a year-round tourist attraction. The late spring and early fall are perhaps the most favored seasons.

HOW TO GET THERE. By train: There are rail links into Armenia from the main part of the USSR, running from Rostov-on-Don via Sochi to Tbilisi and on to Baku. There is also a direct line to Baku via Armavir. From Turkey there is a line from Erzurum via Leninakan and from Iran via Tabriz to Djulfa. A ferry service runs on the Caspian Sea from Anzali (Iran) to Baku. Check before setting out on all these routes, as there are restrictions for tourists.

By air it takes 3 hrs. 35 mins. from Moscow, about 5 hours from Leningrad, about 4 hours from Tashkent, 2 hrs. 30 mins. from Odessa, 1 hr. 40 mins. from Sochi, 1 hr. 10 mins. from Tbilisi. There is a **motor road** from Tbilisi which, in turn, is connected by Intourist routes with many other cities of the Soviet Union.

Azerbaijan and its capital, Baku, can be reached **by plane** from Moscow, Kiev, Tashkent, Ashkhabad, Yerevan and other Soviet cities; **by train** from Moscow, Kiev, Odessa, Tbilisi, Yerevan and other cities in the USSR. From Tbilisi, it is also possible to make a return trip by Intourist chauffeur-driven car.

The *Northern Caucasus* is accessible by plane, train or boat. So is *Georgia*. The capital, Tbilisi, is linked by rail, air and road to the main Soviet cities.

WHAT TO SEE. Apart from the many natural, scenic sights which we have described in our "exploration" section, the main points of interest in the towns and cities are: In **Tbilisi:** The Dzhvari Churches, Metekhi Chapel, Lurdzhi Monastery, Didubi-Pantheon, Narikala Fortress, Sachino Palace. The Ethnographic Village Museum is a new place of interest situated on the hill above the Victory Park, Chavchavadze Prospekt. **Ordzhonikidze:** St. George's Church, main museums. **Nalchik:** local museums, town park. **Pyatigorsk:** Lermontov House and Grotto, Diana Grotto, Kirov Park. **Kislovodsk:** St. Pantilemon's Church, Kurortny Park, Verkhniy Park. **Baku:** the Kirov Gardens, the old town of the Shahs of Shirvan.

HOTELS. Baku. *Intourist Hotel* is best. First-class comfortable hotel, 63 Prospekt Neftyanikov, with 124 rooms. Has an excellent restaurant by Russian standards; ask waiters for recommendations.

After the Intourist, we suggest *Azerbaijan Hotel,* 1 Lenin Prospekt, another Intourist hotel, 1,201 rooms, or *Yuzhnaya,* 31 Shaumyan Street, which is at least relatively modern.

Also-ran: *Baku Hotel,* 9 Darwin Street, with 744 rooms.

Gori. *Hotel Intourist,* 22, Stalin Prospekt, 54 rooms, swimming pool.

Kislovodsk. Best is the *Kislovodsk Motel,* outside town on the lake, with filling station, etc. An annex 2 miles further on, named the *Zamok Motel;* both have restaurants.

Also-rans: *Kavkaz Hotel,* Dzerzhinsky Prospekt, 246 rooms, and *Narzan Hotel,* Mir Prospekt.

Kutaisi. *Hotel Kutaisi,* 5, Rustaveli Prospekt.

Nalchik. Either of two equals: *Rossiya Hotel,* Lenin Street, or *Nalchik Hotel,* Lermontov Street. *Note:* Nalchik may not be visited except during the day, as of press time. Check with Intourist representatives locally.

Ordzhonikidze. The fine new *Vladikavkaz* hotel is sited near the River Terek close to the Sunnit Mosque. *Motel Daryal,* on the southern outskirts of town, is best. A modern 4-story motel for 260 guests. Spacious lounges (with television) on every floor, a bar on ground floor. Adjoining restaurant, post office and souvenir shop. Set amidst a pine grove, with views of the mountains.

Second best is *Kavkaz Hotel,* 50 Vatutin Street. best in the town itself. Third choice is *Intourist Hotel,* Mir Prospekt.

Also-rans: *Iriston Hotel* and *Terek Hotel,* both on Mir Prospekt.

Pasanauri. On Georgian Military Highway, 55 miles north of Tbilisi, *Intourist Hotel,* new, 70 rooms. Excellent restaurant.

Pyatigorsk. Best is *Mashuk Hotel,* 26, Kirov Prospekt, with an Intourist office therein. (Formerly known as the Bristol Hotel.) Otherwise, the *Pyatigorsk Hotel,* Krainy Street, but only if you are desperate.

Much better are the two *motels,* one on Kalinin Street, the other on Lumumba Street (with camping), both of them fairly recent.

Stavropol. You have a choice of two moderate hotels: *Stavropol,* on Karl Marx Prospekt, or *Elbrus,* on Gorky Street.

Tbilisi Iveria Hotel, 5 Inashvili Street, is best, with good food but the usual slow service. A first-class superior hotel, recently built. In the center of the Georgian capital, on the bank of the Kura River. 25 deluxe suites, 30 single and 223 double rooms in the first-class category. Public rooms airconditioned. Two restaurants (one on 16th floor), a café, Intourist Service Bureau, and many other facilities. Swimming pool on roof. All rooms have telephones. Complaints about terrible plumbing.

Adjaria Hotel at junction of Lenin Street and Pekin Street, is an Intourist establishment built in the early 70's. It compares with the Iveria but is in a poor location for tourists.

Intourist Hotel, 7 Rustaveli Prospekt (formerly the Orient Hotel and about 100 years old). First-class moderate, very small.

Tbilisi Hotel, 13 Rustaveli Prospekt, is only 63 years old, and its 113 rooms can be rated as moderate, or second-class.

Ushba. Motel at the 4th km mark on the Georgian Military Highway, better than average.

Yerevan. Best is the *Armenia Hotel,* Amiryan Street. Has 209 large, but plain rooms. First-class moderate rating. A modern building, with restaurant featuring dance bands (very popular with the locals). Also café, bar, wine cellar and Intourist Service Bureau.

Another Intourist hotel is the *Ani,* on Sayat-Nova Avenue, a high-rise building with café, bar, wine-tasting room and cinema (on the 14th floor). Large restaurant on second floor.

Also-rans: *Sevan,* on Shaumyan Square, and *Erevan,* Aboryan Street.

Yessentuki. Not much choice between the three moderate establishments: *Yessentuki Hotel,* Karl Marx Street, *Mayak Hotel* and *Yalta Hotel,* both on Internationalnaya Street.

Zheleznovodsk. Two very modest hotels of equal appeal: *Kavkaz Hotel,* on Gorky Street, and *Druzhba Hotel,* in center of town.

 RESTAURANTS. Georgian cuisine is probably the most original in the Soviet Union. The standard entrées are usually *shashlik, chicken satsivi, basturma* (a variety of shashlik), *sulguni* (cheese), and *bazha sauce* (of walnuts) *chicken tabaka,* and sausages, are the best known specialties. Other delicacies: *khachapuri* (cheese pie), *karabakh loby* (green beans in soured cream and tomato sauce), *tkemali* (sour prune sauce), and *tabaka* (pressed fried chicken). Good Georgian white wine: *Tsinandali;* a good red: *Mukuzani.* Excellent mineral waters (*Borzhomi* the most famous).

In Armenia there are *solyanka* (hot, herbed beef stew), *shashlik,* many kinds of pilaffs and mutton. Excellent wine and heart-warming brandies.

Azerbaijan has at least a dozen kinds of pilaff to offer—the food is always spicy. Try *dovta* (a meat casserole with sour milk), *piti* (soup served in earthenware crockery), *yariakh dalmasy* (meat and rice wrapped in vine leaves, Greek-style); *nar kurma* (roasted meat garnished with pomegranates). Splendid full-bodied red wines, less good white ones.

Apart from the restaurants attached to hotels, we list the following:

Baku. Try one of these three, all about the same: *Metro Restaurant,* Gogol Street; *Shirvan Restaurant,* Kirov Prospekt, or *Nargiz Restaurant,* Karl Marx Gardens.

Kislovodsk. *Chaika,* 4 Pervomaisky Prospekt, and *Zarya,* Herzen Street, are two favorites. But for scenery or atmosphere try the *Tourist Restaurant* on Lake Kislovodsk (outside town, near the motel); *Khram Vozdukha* in Nizhni Park; the *Park Restaurant,* near open-air theater in the Lower Park; or *Krasnoye Solnishko Restaurant,* also in the Lower Park, on Krasnoye Solnishko Hill.

Kutaisi. Two average places on Rustaveli Street: *Gelati Restaurant* and *Imeretia Restaurant.*

Nalchik. The following three restaurants are all of the so-so category: *Kavkaz Restaurant,* Kabardinskaya Street; *Nalchik Restaurant,* Respublikanskaya Street; and *Dorozhny,* Osetinskaya Street.

Ordzhonikidze. *Otdykh Restaurant,* Hetagurov Park; *Terek Restaurant,* Mir Prospekt; and *Ogonyok Restaurant,* Mir Prospekt; are about equal. For a view and atmosphere, however, try *Gorny Orel Restaurant,* atop Mount Lysaya, 7 miles out of town.

Pasanauri. Reportedly has a very good restaurant, probably in the *Intourist* hotel: we have no further details.

Pyatigorsk. *Druzhba Restaurant* in the Mashuk Hotel is best. Then comes *Kolos,* Shoseinaya Street; *Yug,* Universitetskaya Street; and *Tsentralnaya,* Kirov Street. For atmosphere, try *Lesnaya Polyana,* at the place where Lermontov fought his famous duel.

Sevan, Lake. If you have a choice at all, try the *Ishkhan Restaurant* near the Sevan Monastery.

Tbilisi: *Mount Mtatsminda Restaurant,* dinner for about 10 roubles and a nice view, if you want atmosphere. Best in town itself is probably *Daryal,* 22 Rustaveli Prospekt. Daryal boasts good service, surprising anywhere in the USSR, plus even better food. The walls are decorated with copies of interesting Georgian "primitive" paintings by Pirosmanishvili. Try their *kuptai* (looks like Georgian bagels), *cheezhi-peezhi* (egg and meat pan omelet).

The other top restaurant is *Aragvi,* Naberezhnaya Street, on the river below the Circus. It is related to the restaurant of the same name in Moscow.

For atmosphere and scenic views try the *Mtatsminda Restaurant* on the mountain, or the café in Victory Park, at the end of Chavchavadze Prospekt.

Stavropol. Two equally modest restaurants: the *Elbrus,* on Marx Street, and the *Gorka,* on Suvorov Street.

Yerevan. Four more-or-less equal in standing, thanks to the bureaucracy which determines such things: *Arabkir Restaurant,* Komissara Street; *Aragil Restaurant,* Victory Park; *Egnik Restaurant,* Spandarian Square; and *Massis Restaurant,* Krasnoarmeiskaya Street.

Yessentuki. Best place is *Kavkaz Restaurant,* Internatsionalnaya Street. In a pinch, try the *restaurant* just alongside the railway station.

Zheleznovodsk. Only place worth mentioning is the *Beshtau Restaurant,* Tchaikovsky Street.

 CULTURAL ACTIVITIES. Tbilisi: *Marx Library,* 5 Ketskhoveli Street founded in 1846 with a large collection of Georgian books: *Paliashvili Opera House,* 25 Rustaveli Prospekt. *Mardzanishvili Theater,* 8 Mardzanishvili Street, named after a well known Georgian theatrical producer. *Rustaveli Theater,* established in 1920, on Rustaveli Prospekt. *Gribovedov Russian Drama Theater,* 127 Plekhanova. Originally built as a caravanserai, the theater building dates from the 1850's. *Shaumyan Armenian Drama Theater,* 8 Shaumyan Street; opened in 1936. *Russian Youth Theater* in the same building as the Puppet Theater, 101 Plekhanova Prospekt. *Georgian Youth Theater,* 37 Rustaveli Prospekt. The *Georgian Puppet Theater,* is also here. At 123 Plekhanova is the summer home of the State Symphony Orchestra, the national dance ensemble, etc. Concerts are now mainly given in the new *Philharmonia Concert Hall,* Melikishvili Street. *Vano Saradzhishvili Tbilisi Conservatory,* 8 Griboyedov Street, named after the Georgian singer buried in the Opera House garden. *Concert Hall,* Melikishvili Street. *Abashidze Musical Comedy Theater,* 182 Plekhanova Prospekt. *Circus:* Ploshchad Geroyev Sovietskovo Soyuza (Heroes of the Soviet Union Square).

Ordzhonikidze: *Ossetian Music and Drama Theater,* 18 Naberezhnaya. *Russian Drama Theater,* 1 Lenin Square; founded in 1869. *Puppet Theater,* 3 Lenin Square. *Open-Air Theater,* Kirov Park. *Green Theater* (open-air), Tbiliskoye Chaussée. *Planetarium,* 14 Kirov Street, in an old mosque.

Nalchik: *Drama Theater,* in the park. *Pyatigorsk: Musical Comedy Theater,* 17 Kirov Street. *Philharmonia Concert Hall,* in the Lermontov Gallery, Tsvetnik Park. In the Kirov Park, 3 Dunayevsky Street, there is a *planetarium* and an *Open-Air Theater.*

Kislovodsk: *Gorky Theater,* 5 Krasnoarmeiskaya Street. *Concert Hall,* in Verkhny (Upper) Park. *Yessentuki: theater* in the park.

Baku: *State Philharmonia,* 2 Communist Street. *Opera House,* 27 Nizami Street. *Children's Theater,* Kirov Avenue. *Open-Air Theater,* on the seaside promenade.

Yerevan: *House of Armenian Culture,* Lenin Square. *Armenian Opera House,* Lenin Boulevard. *Open-Air Theater,* Abovyan Park.

 MUSEUMS. Tbilisi: *Lenin Museum,* 29 Rustaveli Prospekt. *Historical and Ethnographical Museum,* 11 Komsomolskaya Alleya. *Georgian Literary Museum,* 8 Georgiashvili Street. *Georgian Art Gallery,* 13 Rustaveli Prospekt; open 11–9. *Georgian Art Museum,* 1 Ketskhoveli Street; open 11–9, closed Tues. *Georgian Museum,* 3 Rustaveli Prospekt; open 10–4, closed Mon. *Chavchavadze's House,* 22 Ordzhonikidze Street, open 10–6, closed Mon. The home of the outstanding romantic poet of Georgia. *Museum of Children's Toys,* 6 Rustaveli Prospekt.

Nalchik: *Local Museum,* Lenin Prospekt; open 11–6, closed Sat. *Fine Arts Museum,* 35 Lenin Prospekt; open 11–6, closed Sat.

Ordzhonikidze: *Revolutionary History Museum,* 50 Kirov Street.

Pyatigorsk: *Lermontov Museum,* 9 Buachidze Street, devoted to the life and work of the great Russian poet. *Lermontov's House,* 18 Lermontovskaya Street. The poet lived here for two months and after he was killed in a duel his body was brought here. *Local Museum,* Sacco-and-Vanzetti Street 2; open 10–4.40, closed Tues.

Yerevan: *History Museum,* Lenin Square. *Mantenadaran,* Lenin Prospekt. *Museum of Fine Arts,* Lenin Square.

Baku: *Exhibition Hall,* on the seashore promenade. *Nizami Literary Museum,* Nizami Square (entrance from Communist Street). *Historical and Archeological Museum,* in the Castle.

Kislovodsk: *Yaroshenko Museum,* 3 Yaroshenko Street; open 11–6, closed Tues. Devoted to the work of the prominent Russian painter (1846–98). *Sergo Ordzhonikidze Museum,* in the Sergo Ordzhonikidze Sanatorium.

 SHOPPING. The carpets of Armenia and Turkmenia are certainly the best buys in the Caucasus; but wines, brandies, embroideries, miniatures can also be purchased at reasonable prices. The recommended shops are: **Tbilisi:** *Art Salon,* 19 Rustaveli Street, next to the Tbilisi Hotel; *Souvenir Shop,* Lenin Square; *Department Store,* 7 Mardzhanishvili Street. There is a new *Department Store* on Rustaveli at Lenin Square which is worth a visit, while the *Souvenir Shop* at 18 Rustaveli is a good one. There is a hard-currency store called *Tsitsinatela,* at 23 Rustaveli, which has some handicrafts from the Caucasus.

Ordzhonikidze: *Department Store,* 31 Mir Prospekt; *Souvenirs,* 33 Mir Prospekt, *Jeweler's,* 26 Mir Prospekt.

Nalchik: *Department Store and Souvenirs,* 15 Kabardinskaya Street, *Jeweler's,* 10 Kabardinskaya Street.

Kislovodsk: *Jeweler's,* Karl Marx Prospekt. In **Yessentuki:** *Department Store,* 11 Internatsionalnaya Street. In **Pyatigorsk:** *Department Store,* 1 Oktyabrskaya Street; *Jeweler's,* 42 Dzerzhinsky Street.

TOURS. Intourist offers several tours of the Caucasus. One (IML 9) takes you to Kiev, Tbilisi, Batumi and Moscow; departues from Gatwick Airport, near London, from late May through mid-September. Another (IML 3) takes in Tbilisi, Baku and Yerevan, as well as Moscow and Leningrad, with similar departure dates. Tour IML 7 takes you to Kiev, Tbilisi, Ordzhonikidze, Pyatigorsk, Leningrad, Moscow; departures May/June through early September.

Winter tours are offered for climbing and skiing in Dombai and Tebarda in the Northern Caucasus; in addition there are dozens of local tours which can be arranged either in advance or in the main stopovers of the two tours described.

TRANSPORTATION Baku is the only city with a subway (underground rail) system.

USEFUL ADDRESSES. Pyatigorsk. *Baths:* Lermontov (sulphurous), Tsvetnik Park; Pushkin Bath (upper and lower), Nos. 1 and 2 Kirov Road; radioactive baths, 17 Teplosernaya Street; mud bath, 67 Kirov Street. *Tourist office,* 38 Kirov Road. **Kislovodsk.** *Baths:* Central, 6 Glavny Prospekt; October Bath, 8 Main Road; mud bath, 5 Krepostnoy Pereulok; *Baths Administration,* 9 Glavny Prospekt. *Tourist office:* 5 Glavny Prospekt.

Yessentuki. Mud bath: 4 Semashko Street; *Administration,* 15 Andzhiyevsky Street.

Zheleznovodsk. Mineral water bath, 6 Gorky Street; Slav baths, Park; mud bath, 2 Pervomaiskaya Street; *Dietetic Restaurant,* 2 Park Street; *Administration,* 4 Horizontalnaya Street.

CENTRAL ASIAN REPUBLICS

Exotic Gateway to the USSR

Central Asia is a plain geographical term which, nonetheless, inspires exotic visions of fearful adventure. Definitely, it has something new to offer the tourist. There are, to be sure, hotels, airports, paved roads, water and electricity, department stores and theaters, even subways (underground railways), yet the climate, the rhythm of life, the dress and the architecture, the traditions and customs are all strikingly unfamiliar to the traveler from the West.

Soviet Central Asia consists of four republics: Turkmenistan, Uzbekistan, Tadzhikistan and Kirghizia. Geographically and ethnographically, moreover, Kazakhstan is also a part, though not officially so. The whole area stretches, north to south, from the Aral-Irtysh watershed to the Soviet-Iranian and Soviet-Afghan borders and, west to east, from the Caspian to the Sino-Soviet frontier.

Four of the five republics are inhabited by people whose languages belong to the Turkish family: the Turkmen, the Uzbeks, the Kazakhs, the Kirghizes and the Kara-Kalpaks. (The last of these form an autonomous republic within the Uzbek Soviet Socialist Republic.) Their languages are so similar that they understand one another and are able to communicate, more or less easily, with the Turks, Azerbaijanis, Tatars and Bashkirs. The language of the Tadzhiks, on the other hand, belongs to the Iranian family, related to Persian. The religion of the Central Asian population is largely Moslem. A good many Russians and Ukrainians also live in the area, especially in Kazakhstan, where, during the last two decades or so, hundreds of thousands of people were sent to open up the so-called "virgin" lands.

Much has been done to develop the culture of the various ethnic communities and the establishment of native arts and literatures as well as to provide a modern education, technological know-how and so on. For the visitor, there is a good deal to see—from the immense deserts of Kara-Kum to the cotton-fields of Turkmenistan, the longest irrigation systems in the world, nuclear research centers and hydroelectric plants, local arts and crafts, music and drama.

Exploring Turkmenia

The Turkmenia Republic lies in the southwestern part of Central Asia, bordering on Iran and Afghanistan in the south. It has an area of 188,417 square miles and a population of 2,430,000 of which the majority lives outside the towns. Over 60 percent are Turkmen, the others are mainly Russians, Uzbeks and Kazakhs. More than four-fifths of the republic's area is desert and only a small percentage is irrigated. The Kopet-Dag mountain range stretches along the south and southwest. The principal rivers are the Amu-Darya, the Murgab and the Tedzhen. The mean average temperature in the northern part is −4°C (25°F) in January, 28°C (80°F) in July; in the southern regions, +4°C (39°F), 30°C (86°F) respectively.

Ashkhabad

The capital of the Turkmenian Republic is Ashkhabad. It is the southernmost city of the Soviet Union. Sited in an oasis of the Kara-Kum desert near the Kopet-Dag mountains, it lies 660 feet above sea level and is only 25 miles from the Iranian border. The winter can be quite cold and the summers extremely hot; the rainy season is in the spring.

The finest view of Ashkhabad can be had from the lower slopes of the Kopet-Dag. It is a long, sprawling city whose houses are almost hidden by trees. Only a few taller buildings emerge from this greenery: the ornamental tower of the textile mill in the northwestern district, the dome of a former mosque, and, in the center, the thin, gilt tower of the Republic's party headquarters.

We can start our exploration on Svoboda Prospekt, the longest and widest thoroughfare, which is around four and a half miles long and lined by acacia, plantain and poplar trees. Small, open irrigation ditches run on both sides—called *aryks,* they are a regular feature of all Central Asian cities.

The eastern section of Svoboda Prospekt leads to a brewery and to metal and glass factories. We pass the Pioneer Palace and the Fine Arts Museum building with its oriental windows and smooth pillars. The Museum contains works by mainly Russian, Italian and French masters, but young Turkmenian painters and sculptors are also represented, and there is a section displaying Turkmenian carpets. The same building houses the Museum of Local History and Ethnography with zoological, botanical and industrial exhibits.

Near the two theaters on the same main street is the Ashkhabad hotel. Also near here is a huge carpet factory with a small museum displaying samples of its wares.

The race course is on the corner of Svoboda Prospekt and Ostrovsky Street. Races are at least as popular as football matches; the Turkmeni-

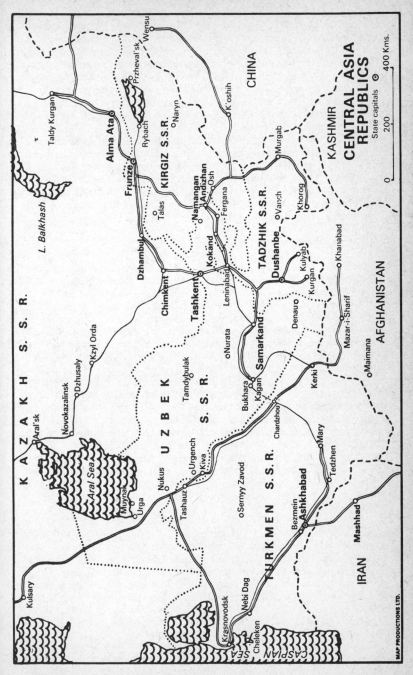

CENTRAL ASIA REPUBLICS

State capitals ◉

400 Kms.

200

0

CHINA

KASHMIR

AFGHANISTAN

IRAN

KAZAKH S. S. R.

UZBEK S. S. R.

TURKMEN S. S. R.

TADZHIK S. S. R.

KIRGIZ S. S. R.

Wensu
Przheval'sk
Taldy Kurgan
Naryn
K'oshih
Alma Ata
Rybach
Frunze
Murgab
Dzhambul
Talas
Namangan
Andizhan
Osh
Fergana
Vanch
Khorog
Chimkent
Kokand
Dushanbe
Khanabad
Tashkent
Leninabad
Kulyab
Kurgan
Kzyl Orda
Nurata
Samarkand
Denau
Mazar-i-Sharif
Dzhusaly
Tamdybulak
Kagan
Kerki
Maimana
Novokazalinsk
Bukhara
Chardzhou
Aral'sk
Urgench
Kiva
Mary
Tedzhen
Mashhad
Nukus
Tashauz
Sernyy Zavod
Muynak
Urga
Ashkhabad
Bezmein
Kulsary
Nebi Dag
Krasnovodsk
Cheleken

L. Balkhash

Aral Sea

CASPIAN SEA

MAP PRODUCTIONS LTD.

ans are justly proud of their fast and beautiful Ahaltekin horses, which were praised by Marco Polo. The Agricultural College is at the western end of Svoboda Prospekt, with the Botanical Garden behind it. More than 900 trees and plants are grown here, with many tropical and subtropical varieties. Turning from Svoboda Prospekt into Gogol Street, we reach the government quarter. At 19 Gogal Street is the not very up-to-date Hotel Turkmenistan, with an Intourist office on the ground floor.

The Ashkhabadians are well provided with city parks. The largest are the Komsomol, on the corner of Svoboda Prospekt and October Street, and the Lenin Park, also central.

Firyuza is the favorite resort of the Ashkhabadians. It is some 20 miles from the city, in the Kopet-Dag mountains, 1,800 feet up, reached by bus or car. The road leads across barren fields and sand, then runs along a deep ravine. After the village of Bagir we find the Golden Spring, after which the fast-flowing Firyuzinka stream leads us to Firyuza. Its parks and chestnut trees make you forget that you are in the middle of hot, desert-like Turkmenistan.

The Kara-Kum Desert

This is the largest desert in the Soviet Union, with an area of over 218,750 square miles. In recent years it has been transformed considerably by the Kara-Kum Canal, which is still under construction and will link the newly-irrigated lands with the city of Krasnovodsk, some 320 miles northwest of Ashkhabad, on the Caspian.

Krasnovodsk was founded in 1869 as a Russian fortress and port. Built at the foot of the Kuva Dag, laid out like an amphitheater, it later became a traffic junction: the Central Asian railway line leading to Tashkent begins here. More recently it has become the center of one of the largest oil-producing areas in the Soviet Union. Lacking water, its development was restricted until the late 1960's when a huge desalination plant (using atomic energy) was built in the nearby town of Shevchenko, supplying nearby oil towns with electricity and drinking water.

East and north of Ashkhabad, via the oases of Tedzhen and Murgab, we reach Chardzhou. This is a river port and textile mill town which stands on the banks of the Amu-Darya, but has little interest for the tourist. Beyond Chardzhou, over the Amu-Darya bridge, Uzbekistan begins.

Uzbekistan

Bukhara and Samarkand, two names that ring in our imagination like those of Istanbul, Isfahan or Shiraz, evoking the poetry of these legendary towns and the glory of Cyrus the Persian, Alexander the Great, the Arabs and the Turks who brought the faith of Islam to this part of the world, the hordes of Genghis Kahn who laid waste to Uzbekistan, and the magnificent reign of Tamerlane (Timur the Lame) who made it the hub of his vast domain. Turkestan—or Central Asia—was conquered by Russia only 100 years ago. Before that, Uzbekistan was divided into three states: the Emirate of Bukhara and the Khanates of Kokand and of Khiva. Feudal in character, these principalities were hotbeds of intrigue and rebellion. Since being taken over by the strong arm of the socialist State, they have undoubtedly gained much in the way of material and social benefits, though some look on the new order with deep misgivings and resent what they see as the cultural straightjacket that has arguably been imposed here as throughout Soviet Central Asia.

Uzbekistan covers a territory of 158,069 square miles, and enjoys a sunny climate of short winters. Its 13,289,000 inhabitants are made up, besides the Uzbeks proper (60 percent), of Russians, Tatars, Kazakhs and Tadzhiks. The Kara-Kalpaks have an independent republic within Uzbekistan. The countryside is rich in varied and colorful landscapes. To the northwest, the sands of the desert of Kyzyl Kum are studded with oases, while the south and east is mountain country, with the ranges of Tien-Shan and Pamir-Alay. The north is bounded by the Aral Sea, beyond the famous plain of Ust Urt. Geologists foretell a booming future for this uninhabited plain. Oil, natural gas, coal, rare metals untainted by iron, copper, marble and sulphates are a few of Uzbekistan's natural riches. Industry and agriculture are fast developing; Uzbek wine—once forbidden by the Koran—is even finding its place on the international market. A top-grade cotton grows on the plain, and the republic's emblem today is an open cotton flower. Uzbekistan provides 70 percent of the total cotton output of the USSR.

Yet the country's artisans still ply the handicrafts passed down from generation to generation: embossed copper, the carpets of Bukhara and of Khiva, the silk tapestry or *suzane,* embroidered headgear. A pity that these artcrafts should be so scarce in the shops. But if you cannot *buy* the folklore, you can enjoy it in the songs and dances of the country. The opera of Tashkent, the Alisher ballet and the Bakhor troupe are worth seeing. There are state schools of music and dance, and 23 theaters. The country's great men are still honored, among them Alisher Nawai (also Navoi), poet-philosopher of the 15th century, and the leading name of classical Uzbek literature.

The plane lands at Tashkent at the foot of Tien-Shan, the "heavenly mountains." From their snow-topped peaks, melted ice runs down to water the cotton plantations, orchards and vineyards of Uzbekistan.

The country awaits you with a legend, that of Farhad the mason and the princess Shirin. The beautiful princess had vowed to marry whoever brought back growing life to the barren steppe, and food for the hungry. Farhad set to work, hollowing a canal through the rock. But the Persian Shah Khosru, thinking to win the princess by trickery, covered the steppe with carpets of grass that shone green as water in the moonlight; and the Shah said to the princess: "Behold my works." The wind brought Farhad, at work in the mountain, the news of Shirin's betrothal; and sorrow turned him into a rock. When daylight revealed Khosru's treachery, the princess opened her arms to her beloved; but it was too late, and she was changed into a flowing river of tears. A hydraulic dam on the Syr Darya now bears the name of Farhad, and two canals begin at the rock that bears his name.

Tashkent

International tourism is an important economic asset to Tashkent. The city is strategically placed: it was in Tashkent that in January 1966, Ayub Khan, the president of Pakistan, and Mr. Shastri, the Prime Minister of India, met to negotiate a peace treaty. It is a refueling stop for planes en route from Moscow to India, Indonesia, Burma and other countries in

Southeast Asia. Although hotel space is still restricted, a number of new large hotels are being built. (The airport is modern and well-equipped and has a pleasant-looking transit hotel.)

Tashkent is, in fact, a mere stopover while waiting for the flight to Samarkand; but you may as well take a guided tour, and get what entertainment and instruction you may from the guide's earnest salesmanship of the socialist state's achievements. Tashkent is the capital of Uzbekistan, an important economic and cultural center, a town of universities, theaters, museums, parks and palaces (of culture). It is also the biggest communications post of the Soviet Orient, and an important industrial zone. With a population of over 1½ million, Tashkent is the fourth largest city in the USSR, and the only city in Central Asia to boast a subway system, opened in 1977. When completed, its length will total over 30 miles.

On the guided tour, you will be taken to the year-round exhibition of Uzbek achievements in Pobeda Park. On the same outing, you will also pass by the Academy of Science, the State University, and many institutes and research laboratories. Of more interest to the layman is the library of Alisher Navoi, containing over two million volumes, among which are ancient illuminated manuscripts. One interesting visit is to the museum of Uzbek art. It has a few old pieces, but also some recent examples of fine workmanship in good taste. You will be proudly shown one recent acquisition, a truly outstanding sample of embroidery. This ornamental panel, unique of its kind, is the handiwork of 40 embroiderers of Bukhara; the design in gold and silver thread, stitched with amazing lightness and intricacy on a background of blue velvet, calls to mind the craft of the old calligraphers.

And the outing continues, along the wide shaded avenues where the *aryks* (artificial streams), the oak, mulberry, hazelnut and plane trees freshen the hot summer air. Largest park is the Komsomol, built by the country's youth for the wellbeing and enjoyment of all. If the town seems too new, remember that it was destroyed not long ago by a succession of earthquakes that did not spare the old monuments; few at any rate remain and they are somewhat disappointing. The 1966 quake was particularly severe, with its epicenter right in the city. More than 75,000 families were made homeless. Extensive rebuilding has, however, transformed Tashkent into a Central Asian showcase.

Sightseeing on Your Own

From the airport, a wide highway lined with trees leads into town. The people of Tashkent are particularly proud of their parks and gardens. Most of the inhabitants wear European clothes, except some women, who stick to oriental garb. Men and women alike wear the *tubeteyka,* the small square or round embroidered cap which provides essential protection against the sun.

The center of Tashkent, where we start our exploration, is the Teatralnaya Square; one of its sides is bordered by Lenin Prospekt, the main thoroughfare. Here we find the Hotel Tashkent, a four-storied, modern building with a roof garden which also houses the Intourist office. Opposite, occupying almost the whole length of the large square, is the Alisher Navoi Opera and Ballet Theater, named after a distinguished writer, scientist and musician of the 15th century. The theater has a repertoire of classical and native Uzbek operas and ballets. Fountains and colorful flowerbeds surround it. To the Opera House's left is Pravda Vostoka Street, beginning in the square, and down which we pass before the Shark Hotel and the State Philharmonia Hall. Another park follows, with the city bell tower, then we reach Kuibyshev Street at the beginning of which stands the Uzbek Historical Museum. Continuing along Kuibyshev Street we come to Gogol Street, where we find the Art Museum, whose treasures are described above.

Our second exploratory walk leads from the Hotel Tashkent north along Lenin Street. We cross Karl Marx Street (with the central department store and the university), then Bratskaya Street and reach one of the finest main streets of Tashkent, Navoi Road, where the Navoi Library is located, leading west. Here the houses are all strongly marked by national, local features—especially by large, loggia-like balconies where people sleep outside in the summer heat.

From here, we walk along Hamza Street and reach the former Old Town. At Chorsu Square (before we reach Hamza Street) the 16th-century Kukeldash Madrasa rises among the small, flat houses. (A *madrasa* is a Moslem seminary, a school for *mullahs*.) Not far away to the north is Barak Khan's Madrasa, also 16th-century. It has been described as the "Vatican of Central Asia," since it is the seat of the *Mufti,* the religious head of the Central Asian and Kazakhstan Moslems. Opposite the madrasa we find a mosque from whose minaret the muezzin calls the faithful to prayer. To visit the mosque is not too difficult for the foreign tourist if he applies to the *mullah;* but permits are usually restricted to men and you are, of course, expected to remove your shoes before entering. Here also you will see the Gumbazi Barak-Khan, the funeral dome of the Samanids of Tashkent, the ancient local dynasty.

The old town market is also close by; here, in the summer and autumn you can buy melons, grapes and pomegranates—and *samsa,* a pie filled with meat and a considerable seasoning of garlic. The *chaikhana* (tea shop) is also an essential element of all Central Asian markets.

The Hunger Steppe lies southwest from Tashkent. Only 30 or so years ago, nomads roamed here, and there was a little cattle-breeding. Now, a large-scale canal system has turned almost one million acres into fertile agricultural land. From Tashkent we can reach it in about two hours by car, passing through the town of Yangi-Yul. The chief produce is cotton, or, as it is called to Uzbekistan, "white gold," which is exported in large quantities.

Samarkand

"Better one look than a hundred stories." This old oriental proverb seems to fit Samarkand (pop. 304,000). The modern town at first sight lacks character, but the old center casts a magic spell as you pass through the glazed tile porches of its ancient monuments. Between these legendary walls, time has come to a standstill. The old city seems barely touched by the stark modern surroundings that enclose it.

The oasis of Samarkand lies in the valley of the Zeravshan River. In Uzbek, Zeravshan means "bestower of gold." Taking its source in a great mountain glacier, the river waters all the plain, fully earning its name. According to legend, Samarkand was founded 5,000 or 6,000 years ago by King Aphrasiab. (Whatever its poets may say, this hardly ranks it with Babylon, Thebes, Rome and Athens.) The first written mention of Maracanda—the ancient name of the city—goes back to 329 BC. In 1971, the town celebrated its 2,300th anniversary.

Passing through on his way to India, Alexander the Great found Samarkand "more beautiful than he had imagined." Tamerlane in the 14th century was the first to make it an imperial capital, and the starting-point of his conquests. He embellished and developed it, and soon it was spoken of by the ancients as "the precious pearl of the world" or "the Eden of the East." It is the monuments of those times that you will visit here.

Under Soviet rule, Samarkand has become an industrial and cultural center, with its university, its chambers of commerce and agriculture, and above all, its karakul breeding research. Uzbekistan being, as we know, the country of astrakhan. Among its many industries (fertilizers, canning, wines, fruit growing and so on), special mention should be made of its silk, worthy of the name of a once-luxurious city.

Group of Shahi Zinda

Placed in the northern suburbs of Samarkand, Shahi Zinda is one of the most remarkable architectural groups of its time. The unequalled craftsmanship of the glazed tiles make of it an outdoor museum of this form of decorative art, peculiar to Islam. The group consists of mosques and tombs built between the thirteenth and fifteenth centuries, a cemetery for the great men of the period, mainly army generals and court favorites of Tamerlane. The crippled conqueror, having chosen Samarkand for his capital, wished to make it the most beautiful city in the world. Between them, artists summoned from everywhere built these marvellous monuments which have survived to this day, partly in ruins but priceless still under their gleaming domes.

Leading to the main entrance there is a narrow little street—more like a corridor—flanked by mausoleums built in the 14th and 15th centuries. The first of these is that of Tuglu-Tekin, the daughter of the Emir Hodzham (built 1375–76); the second belongs to Sirin-Bika-Akad, Timur's sister (1385); on the left, the first is the Emir-Zade (1386) and the second the Sadi-Mulk-Alka (1372), the tomb of Timur's niece. The buildings (there are more than a dozen) are decorated with splendid majolica and terra cotta tiles.

As they appear today, the tombs of Shahi Zinda barely rise above the earth which once engulfed them. The small rampart behind them clearly shows the depth from which they were dug out. As it is now, the site is a garden walk, 65 feet long, bordered by shady arcades dominated by two turquoise-colored domes, with strips of Koranic writing running along the base. The panels of glazed tiles on the façades, though badly damaged, still evoke past splendor, and the colors on the brick walls shine with undimmed brightness. Suddenly, a small pointed vault frames a little courtyard, almost monastic in its calm. You gaze at a bench, the soft green of a tree, you dream and linger. It is hard to take leave of Shahi Zinda.

Mosque of Bibi Khanym

Another architectural splendor of Samarkand, as much for its size, its proportions, the harmony and elegance of its design as for the quality and beauty of its decoration, the great mosque of Samarkand displays the flower patterns of its glazed tiles near the center of town, to the east of Registan Square. It was the biggest mosque in Central Asia and one of the most grandiose and beautiful religious monuments of the Moslem world.

It is called the mosque of Bibi Khanym, whose legend throws a poetic light on the origin of a deeply rooted custom of Islam: the veil worn by Moslem women. Bibi Khanym was a Chinese girl, best beloved of the fierce Tamerlane. In love with her conqueror and ever wishful to please him, she undertook to build a monument of utmost magnificence in his honor while he was away on campaign (1399–1401), and summoned a renowned architect to do her bidding. The master builder fell madly in love with the beautiful Bibi Khanym. The lady turned a deaf ear to his pleadings, but the wily architect threatened to leave his work unfinished unless she granted him a kiss. Faced with this shameless blackmail, Bibi Khanym gave in. But such was the lover's ardor that the guilty kiss left an unmistakable mark, and on his ill-timed return Tamerlane ordered the hapless architect to be put to death. Thereupon, wisely deeming that a woman's beauty was a threat to a man's peace of mind, he ordered all the women in the kingdom to wear veils henceforth.

Of the original minarets, only a few arches remain. The magnificent cupola, though almost in ruins, still shows the gigantic dimensions of the mosque: the entrance to the main room was 140 feet high. In the court-yard there is a huge lectern shaped like an open book, made of marble and richly decorated. Originally it stood inside and the Koran was read from it.

Registan Square and the Gur Emir

Near the mosque of Bibi Khanym, Registan Square marks the center of Samarkand. Framed by the gateways and minarets of three ancient *madrasas* (15th, 16th and 17th centuries), it is, in the midst of the modern town, an evocation of oriental poetry. Renewed and restored, these three madrasas are a fascinating example of ancient city planning.

Building of the Registan began early in the 15th century, during the reign of Ulug-Bek. His madrasa was erected between 1417 and 1420. According to tradition, the learned ruler himself taught in this school. Badly damaged in the fratricidal wars of the 18th century, it has now been largely restored.

The Shir-Dor Madrasa was built on the site of the covered bazaar of the hat makers, which was erected at the turn of the 14th and 15th centuries at the express wish of Tuman-Aka, one of the wives of Timur. The madrasa itself was built between 1619 and 1636, and is a copy of the Ulug-Bek Madrasa, though by no means as perfect.

Yalangtus-Bij, the ruler of Samarkand, was also responsible for the third building on the Registan. The foundations of a projected mosque and madrasa were laid in 1646 on the northern side of the square; later it was named Tillya-Kari (Decorated with Gold). It was finished only after the death of Yalangtus. The elaborate murals are particularly fine, though the building was badly damaged in an earthquake early in the 19th century and its famous colored tiles were never replaced.

From the former main square we can set out to visit the Old Town of Samarkand. High mud walls often hid the houses, with only a TV antenna rising above them. The streets are narrow and traffic is rather heavy with cars, donkey carts and cycles all competing. The artisans work in the open or in half-open huts; bread, meat, textiles are sold from stalls and shoemakers, potters, knife grinders and radio mechanics work cheek by jowl.

You will of course visit the Gur Emir, where lie the Timurid kings: Sultan Mohammed, Ulug-Bek, and the founder of the dynasty, Tamerlane himself, the son of the steppes, whose wish was to be buried in the town which bore witness to his glory. Tamerlane lies under a tombstone of rock jade made to order for him by Ulug-Bek. The Gur Emir is a short walk southeast of the Samarkand Hotel. You can manage on your own by keeping in sight the characteristic fluted dome, outlined from afar against the sky of Samarkand. Over 500 years old, the tomb had suffered rather badly from the ravages of time, but has been carefully restored it to its former splendor, perhaps with overmuch zeal. However, the painstaking restoration bears striking witness to the infinite variety of Central Asian decorative art and the imaginative skills of its artists.

If you still have time, go and have a look at the ancient observatory of Ulug-Bek, grandson of Tamerlane. This is now a museum devoted to the work of 15th-century Uzbek astronomers led by Ulug-Bek himself. The Samarkand school of astronomers had immense influence on contemporary Moslem and Arab science. For hundreds of years, eastern and western astronomers made use of the star charts of this scholarly prince. The memory of Ulug-Bek has been perpetuated at the modern observatory not far from Samarkand which also bears his name.

About 30 miles southeast of Samarkand, the archeological excavations of the ruins of ancient Pendzhikent are also well worth a visit.

Lastly, Samarkand has a museum of history and a museum of Uzbek art, plus an opera house, a bazaar and several lovely parks.

Bukhara

Of the three towns to be visited in Uzbekistan, Bukhara has best retained its exotic charm, with its mud houses and its many religious monuments, madrasas and old mosques. These last, far from having become mere empty shells for sightseeing, have been adapted and are used for a variety of purposes by the locals. The signs of progress are more visible in the television aerials springing from every ancient hovel than in the oil derricks of Bukhara, Khiva, or the drills of Kyzyl Kum that furnish natural gas to Tashkent, Samarkand and Bukhara. And the spirit of progress is more evident in the free and easy ways of the unveiled women: teachers, doctors, agronomists and so on, than in the few modern buildings. As you may have gathered, the first sight of the romantic Bukhara of your bookish dreams is something of a shock: but do not despair. In spite of these changes, you will be gladdened to see a few old men still wearing the traditional *chupan* of Central Asia. Old Bukhara is not lost.

The town was at the height of its glory in the tenth century, under the Samanids. The capital of the country, it was a center of intellectual ferment renowned throughout the East, the town of Rudaki, the "Adam of poets." It still carries on something of this tradition with its music and drama theater, among the oldest in Uzbekistan. You will come across the old and the new as you stroll at random around Bukhara, and the city will reveal its riches as you explore its corners. You will be surprised at the apparent lack of color compared with, say, Samarkand: most of Bukhara's monuments are made of brick—though patterned with great artistry—and there is little faience.

In recent years much has been done to modernize the city which, until the 1930's, did not have even a proper water supply. The traditional handicrafts—gold embroidery, the curing of hides, etc.—have, however, been encouraged and developed. At the end of the 1950's, one of the greatest fields of natural gas in the world was discovered in Gazli, not far away. The gas is now piped to Tashkent, the Urals and other areas.

Bukhara has an extensive educational system. Traditionally, it was a center of religious learning, with almost 100 madrasas in which 5,000 young men studied for the priesthood; but only two percent of the population was literate. Now there is a teachers' academy, 11 general and several specialized high schools, museums, as well as libraries and theaters. Public buses are crowded, though some locals still prefer the donkey.

Bukhara's area is comparatively small; with the exception of one or two monuments which are on the periphery or outside the city, all its sights can be easily reached on foot. However, to visit even the few most famous ones properly, the tourist needs at least two or three days.

One sight that must be seen is the tomb of Ismail Samani, founder of the Samanid dynasty. This light and graceful building is said to be over a thousand years old.

Turning back towards the center of the city from the mausoleum, we see on the left a building with four domes. This is the Chashma-Ayub Mazar. (A *mazar* is a place of miracles, usually the tomb of a Mohammedan saint.) Built in the 12th century, it has four connected chambers, each with a dome. The domes are all of different shapes: one is almost pointed, like a tower.

Not far from this former place of pilgrimage, in the city park, we find the regional Theater of Drama and Music and the 18th-century Bolo-Khauz Mosque. The façade of this delicate edifice rests on 20 tall wooden pillars. This was the "court chapel" of the Emirs of Bukhara, which the extraordinary splendor of the inner decorations. A miniature minaret and a handsome water basin are part of it. The Bolo-Khauz was built opposite the main entrance of the castle—the Emir's winter residence—and when the ruler went to worship, he walked on thick carpets spread between the two.

On the hill in the middle of town is the Ark or citadel, even older than the Samanid tomb. It has an area of some 8 acres and is a walled fortress. Today the Ark houses a museum which displays Bukhara rugs, gold embroidery, ceramics, embossed copper, and silverwork. Other rooms contain gruesome reminders of the horrors and misery of the Middle Ages.

Crossing the large square, which has the statue of Avicenna (an Arab physician and philosopher who lived AD 980–1037) in its center, we reach the main part of the Ark. The entrance is flanked by two towers, linked by a corridor with a terrace which was reserved for the court orchestra and the guard. Once upon a time, a hempen whip, symbol of the Emir's power, hung over the entrance. After entering, we pass through a long, closed corridor; the rooms flanking this dark, sinister passage used to serve as prison cells and torture chambers. The corridor leads to the Dzhuma Mosque (1919). A short street emerges into the court of the Kush-Begi (Prime Minister) and the Charsu Chapel, and then into the Kurinish-Khana—the "Protocol Courtyard," where the emirs were crowned and where foreign ambassadors were received. One of the buildings contains the Museum of Local History; its second department is in the Zindan, an 18th-century former prison, nearby.

Leaving the Ark, we see a Teachers' College. Turning left at its corner into Communards Street, we continue towards the city center, where we find the majority of the historical monuments. On the right of Communards Street stand a huge mosque and a very tall minaret. The first is the Kalyan Mosque (1540–1), one of the most impressive in Central Asia, covering an area of 400 by 250 feet. The large courtyard is surrounded by several rows of galleries. Note especially the portal and the huge dome, decorated in turquoise, rising above the central area.

The Kalyan Minar, built in 1127, was used as a lighthouse for caravans, a watchtower against the enemy, a minaret for the muezzin's call to prayer. Its superbly decorative cut brick is among the finest you can see.

Close to the Kalyan Mosque and minaret there are the two large domes of a madrasa. (The northern one is completely restored, covered by light blue tiles.) This is the Mir-Arab, built in the first decade of the 16th century, and now a Moslem seminary still functioning. Together with the Kalyan Mosque it forms the Bukhara Forum. It was named after the Yemenite Sheikh Abdullah, who was called Mir-Arab by his people.

Continuing along the Street of the Communards, we cross Sovietskaya Street, under a dome called Toki-Zargaron. There were quite a few such domes built in the 16th century over the busiest street crossings for trading purposes. One was where the cap makers sold their wares, others were near the homes of potters and other craftsmen. They provided shade and lessened the congestion of the busy streets. All are different. Under the Toki-Zargaron, jewelers and goldsmiths worked and traded.

Many Madrasas

Close to the Toki Zargaron we see the early 15th-century madrasa of Ulug-Bek, whose sober lines and harmonious proportions served as model for many other buildings throughout Central Asia. In contrast, all the skills of architects and artisans were put to use to embellish the madrasa of Abdul Aziz Khan opposite; it was built in the middle of the 17th century and decorated with squares of shiny glazed tiles, patterns of cut brick, carved wood and dull glaze earthenware. The reckless artist who decorated a vase with a serpent, in defiance of the Koranic law forbidding images of living beings, paid for the blasphemy with his life.

Leaving this striking building, we turn right on Samarkandskaya Street and after a few minutes' walk we see on the corner of Pushkin Street another madrasa, called Kukeldash. It was built in the reign of Abdullah Kahn (1557–98). Its outer walls are distinguished by open balconies or loggias. It used to have 160 cells for the seminary pupils; today it houses the regional archives.

The Kukeldash Madrasa is part of the former merchant center called Liabi-Khauz. Today it is a paved, park-like square with tea-gardens, a favorite place for the Bukharans to sit down and rest. Before walking round the square, let us continue along Pushkin Street and have a look at the Chor-Minor Madrasa, built early in the 19th century. It has a domed, ornamental portal and four tall towers which show the influence of Indian mosque architecture.

The Liabi-Khauz Square was named after the large reservoir in its center, which once provided the Bukharans with water. It was built in 1620. The square is lined with splendid buildings, most of them—except the Kukeldash Madrasa—dating from the 18th century.

On the western side, the square is bordered by the Divan Begi Mosque, on the east by the Divan Begi Madrasa, on the north by the Kukeldash and the Ir-Nazar-Ilchi Madrasas. The last of these was built by a Russian ambassador in Bukhara and largely financed by Catherine the Great. Originally a caravanserai, its façade and first-story arcades are decorated with bird and stag motifs.

Starting from the Liabi-Khauz Square either to the right (towards the Mir-Arab Madrasa) or towards the left, southwards, along Sovietskaya Street, we again pass under the domes of the covered bazaars. On the right, the Toki-Tilpak-Furashon arches above the street where headgear and books were once sold; on the left is the Toki-Saraton, once the home of money-changers.

From Liabi-Khauz Square we can walk along Lenin and Khmelnitsky Streets to Lenin Square.

It is well worth exploring the southeastern and eastern parts of Bukhara and the vicinity of the railway station. From the hotel, follow Shevchenko Street as far as the Sayfuddin Bokharzi Mausoleum, built in the 13th century over the grave of a learned sheikh. The first of its two chambers is the *ziarathana* (prayer room), the second the actual crypt *(gur-hana)*.

The nearby Buyan-Kuh Khan Mausoleum is the final resting place of one of the descendants of Genghis Khan, who was killed in 1358 in Samarkand. This, too, has two chambers; the smaller contains his majolica tomb. The four sides of the building have small ornamental pillars and the walls bear rich terra cotta decorations in light and dark blue, violet and white.

The modern residental quarter of Bukhara are to the south of the two mausoleums.

Finally, an excursion outside Bukhara to see the summer palace of the last Emir, Said-Alim Khan, is strongly recommended. The Sitore-i-Mahi-Hasa Palace is two and a half miles north, and can be reached by car or bus. Near Said-Alim's summer palace we find the palace of his father, Ahid Emir, built in classic Uzbek national style and now used as a hospital.

Khiva

Khiva is in the Kara-Kum Desert, in the oasis of Khorezm, on the left bank of the Amu-Darya River. Excavations show that its history reaches back to the seventh century. From the middle of the 16th century until 1920, this was the capital of the Khivan Khanate. Its character has changed little since the Middle Ages, and it has only recently been included in Intourist itineraries. There are no acceptable hotels and services as far as we know. Khiva lies some distance from the Chardzhou-Kungrad railway line and is best reached by plane from Tashkent via Samarkand to Urgench, the nearest airport. From here, Khiva can be visited only as a one-day excursion by hired car with guide. This means one or two nights in Urgench, which is 50 km. away. Alternatively, a day-trip can be made by air from Bukhara, but this is more difficult to arrange.

An asphalted road runs through the cotton and alfalfa fields, "cuts" through a thick clay wall—and you come upon the enchanting panorama of ancient Khiva, its tall minarets glittering in the sun and a multitude of cupolas topping thousand-year-old mosques and madrasas.

Khiva's streets are a museum of wood carving (almost every home is adorned with fancifully carved doors and columns), painting (the Khiva floral and geometric designs that decorate many minarets and palaces are world famous), and ceramics (majolica tiles of unsurpassed quality which have retained all their original vividness of color).

The ancient city of Khiva looks much as it used to in the olden days, with its narrow streets and roofed bazaars and is a protected area. There are more architectural monuments in Khiva than in Samarkand and Bukhara. Many of them have a remarkable history. The old madrasa of Shirgazi-khan stands in one of the streets, with the mausoleum of the khan himself adjoining it. Right opposite the madrasa there is an arch with a finely carved wooden gate. In the courtyard you will find another door inlaid with ivory and behind it, the mausoleum of Pahlavan Mahmud, a wonderful example of the skill of Khiva architects. The mausoleum, built of kilned bricks, is adorned with glazed tiles bearing the verses and maxims by Pahlavan Mahmud, a philosopher, poet and teacher.

The unfinished Kalta-Minor minaret is in the middle of the town. The Kuk-Minor (Great Minaret) rises 225 feet: a graceful, delicate edifice, it dates from the First World War. The ninth-century Dzhuma Mosque and the Kutli-Murad-Inak Madrasa have been reconstructed from the original plans, as they were burned down some 50 years ago. The castle of Kuna-Ark (12th to 19th centuries), the delicate Tash-Khauli Palace (1830's) and the Madrasa of Allakuli Khan (1835) are in many ways superior even to the Samarkand and Bukhara masterpieces of architecture.

Fergana Basin

This broad, 200-mile-long valley is between the western spurs of the Tien-Shan mountain. Its territory is divided between the Uzbek, Tadzhik and Kirghiz Republics.

The Fergana Basin yields about a quarter of the Soviet Union's cotton. An extensive irrigation system consisting of the Great Fergana Canal, the Southern and Northern Fergana Canals and several others, with a total length of about 600 miles provides water. There is a considerable silkworm breeding industry, plenty of fruit cultivation, and oil, coal and copper ore are also plentiful.

Kokand is a city of 152,000 people along the River Sokh; in the 18th and 19th centuries it was the capital of the Kokand Khanate. Two important Uzbek poets, Mukimi (1851–1903) and Hamza Niazi (1880–

1929) were born here. Among its sights the palace of the last Kokand ruler, Hudoyar Khan, (built in the 1860's) is the most interesting; it now houses the Local History Museum. The palace has remarkable colored woodcarvings and ceramics.

Fergana (previously called Novy Margelan and Skobelev) is a regional center at the foot of the Alay mountains, 1,470 feet above sea level. Founded in 1876, it has an important oil refinery, and factories making fertilizer and artificial silk. Its textile plant was the first in Central Asia. Fergana's park (29 Lenin Street) is also a botanical garden. There are Uzbek and Russian theaters; the Museum of Local History is at 18 Pervogo Maya Street.

Margilan is five miles north of Fergana. An ancient settlement, since the tenth century it has been the center of a flourishing agricultural district. In the 19th century it had several madrasas and about 250 mosques. Today it is the center of the Fergana Basin's silkworm breeding industry.

Andizhan is the largest city in the Fergana area. It owes its importance mostly to the fact that this area is one of the most outstanding cotton-growing territories of the Soviet Union. It is an ancient city, mentioned in tenth-century Arab chronicles. It was also a religious center, with innumerable mosques and madrasas. Among the sights, pride of place belongs to the Dzhami Madrasa (276 October Street), with its Roman-esque, bricked-up windows and two richly carved towers. The museum of local history is at 118 Navoi Prospekt.

Finally, we must mention one of the important, non-Uzbek cities of the Fergana Valley: Leninabad, Tadjikistan's second largest city, lies on the banks of the Sir-Darya, in the southwestern corner of the Fergana basin. For travelers from Tashkent it is the gateway to the whole area. Cotton-growing and silkworm culture have always been the traditional occupations, along with fruit-growing, the mainstay of North Tadjik agriculture.

Tadzhikistan

Tadzhikistan lies in the southeastern part of Central Asia, bordering on Afghanistan and China, separated from Pakistan only by an Afghan corridor of some 20 miles. Its area is 89,438 square miles, its population 3,283,000; the majority are Tadzhiks, with a large number of Uzbeks, Russians, Tatars and Kirghizes. The capital is Dushanbe.

Most of Tadzhikistan is occupied by the Pamir Range. (Only seven percent of the republic's area is either on a plain or has a lower elevation than 3,000 feet.) The valleys in which agriculture is possible lie between the ranges of the Pamir—except in the northern part. In the Eastern Pamir are the highest mountains in the Soviet Union: Communism Peak (22,500 feet) and Lenin Peak (21,400 feet). The principal rivers of Tadzhikistan are the Sir-Darya, the Amu-Darya, the Vakhsh, the Kafirnigan and the Zeravshan.

Tadzhikistan has seven universities or colleges and it is claimed that illiteracy has been nearly eradicated. The incident of typhus, malaria and cholera has been drastically reduced. The highest-developed industries are mining (coal, oil, gold, polymetallic ores), machine tools, cotton milling, silk manufacture and food canneries.

The most important agricultural activites are growing cotton, maize and fruit in the valleys, and sheep-breeding by the seminomadic peoples in the mountains.

For the time being there is little tourism in Tadzhikistan; yet it is interesting, if you have the chance, to visit this thinly-populated mountain republic, whose hospitable people have a culture that stretches back to the ninth century.

Dushanbe

Dushanbe (earlier called Stalinabad) is the capital of the Tadzhik Republic. It lies on the bank of the Dushanbinka River, in the Gissar Valley, 2,475 feet above sea level. The average temperature in July is 30°C (86°F), in January around freezing point.

It is a completely modern city. Until 1922 it was a village called Dush: the building of the railway in 1929 started its rapid growth. The houses are two- or three-storied: taller buildings are avoided because of the danger of earthquakes, though in 1970, some taller apartment houses which are supposed to be "earthquake-proof" were erected on Lenin Prospekt.

Most men wear European clothing and so do the women, but some fabrics have oriental patterns and much silk is worn. The Tadzhiks also like the *tubeteyka,* the flat cap.

The main thoroughfare is Lenin Prospekt, running for five miles, north to south, and on or near it we find the important public buildings. The Prospekt is lined with willows, plane trees, poplars and acacias, with the inevitable *aryks,* the small irrigation ditches instead of gutters. The other main streets—Ordzhonikidze, Rustaveli and Shevchenko—are also shaded by trees.

Lenin Prospekt begins at the railway station. Opposite is the statue of Kuibyshev, one of the commanders of the Red Army in Central Asia during the Civil War. A few yards away, on the left side, is the Hotel Dushanbe with the Intourist office. Here the Lenin Prospekt forms a square, which contains the Historical and Art Museum with its collection of ancient and modern Tadjik art. A short walk and a right turn brings us, between Lenin Prospekt and the parallel Ayni Street, to the municipal market. From here, a fine panorama of the surrounding high mountains opens to the north, east and south—particularly attractive at dusk.

Continuing along Lenin Prospekt we reach the central Moscow Square, with the Ayni Opera and Ballet Theater. On the right side of the square stands the Hotel Vakhsh.

The next section of the Lenin Prospekt contains the Firdausi Library, with its valuable Eastern manuscripts: next to it are the Philharmonia and concert hall. Almost opposite, the Tadzhik Academy of Sciences is housed in a classical building, while the editorial and printing offices of the Republic's newspapers, and the Central Post Office, are next door.

Here the Lenin Prospekt widens once again into a square. On the left, the tall building of Tadzhik Radio, on the right, one of the largest buildings of Dushanbe, monumental Government House, dominate the square.

Farther along Lenin Prospekt we reach Putovsky Street. The central department store is at the crossing and the Russian Drama Theater and the Lakhuti Tadzhik Drama Theater are both close by. If we turn left along Putovsky Street, we soon arrive at the Dushanbinka River, with a bridge leading to the right bank and the newer part of the city.

Returning to Lenin Prospekt, we see on the left the Teachers' college and the Avicenna Medical University. Soon we arrive at a large, well-kept park, also bearing the name of Ayni, the founder of modern Tadzhik literature (1878–1954). There are facilities for both swimming and boating.

Continuing beyond the far end of Lenin Prospekt, we reach a long, picturesque and cool valley. This is the Varzob Resort, with a number of weekend and holiday homes and children's camps, which are fairly crowded from the end of April.

Excursions from Dushanbe

An excursion along the 60-mile valley of the Vakhsh provides a chance to explore the life and agriculture of a Tadzhik village. (The Gissar Valley does the same.) Surrounded by mountains on three sides, the valley is very sheltered. Cultivated since prehistoric times, it was sparsely settled until the early 1930's, when the Termez-Dushanbe railway line and the Dushanbe-Kurgan-Tube Highway were built. In 1933, the Great Vakhsh Canal was completed and many new *kolkhozes* and *sovkhozes* were established in the irrigated areas, while a series of dams was begun on the Vakhsh. From Dushanbe, a good road leads south to the Vakhsh Valley in the direction of the Afghan border, crossing many canals.

The main produce is cotton, but maize is also grown. This has led to the development of pig-breeding on a large scale even though the Moslem Tadzhiks do not eat pork. Much fruit is also grown here, especially melons and grapes. Lemons are grown under glass during the winter (but not in hothouses).

The waters of the Vakhsh are used not only for irrigation but for hydroelectricity. Ten plants are planned of which all but one were in production by 1976.

From Dushanbe the best way to arrive at the upper reaches of the river is to take a car. Traveling southwest, we pass across the plain, past well-tilled fields, through the town of Ordzhonikidzeabad and then begin to climb a long and steep road, with 600–900-foot drops on both sides. Nurek, where the new dam is being built, has no railway; the only access is by road, so it is fairly busy. At Nurek, the Vakhsh is a narrow mountain river, but is some 120 feet deep, and winds between two 900-foot-high mountain ridges. The dam will create a 60-square-mile reservoir, and the hydroelectric plant will provide 10.5 billion kilowatts annually.

East of Nurek are the heights of the Pamir Mountains—the "Roof of the World." The plateau, glaciers and peaks, all well over 12,000 to 15,000 feet high, are for climbers and alpinists. It is only in the last few years that the final "white spots" have disappeared from the maps and the ultimate secrets of this area have been unlocked. Here the hunt still continues for the *yeti,* the mysterious and legendary creature that is supposed to represent the missing link between the anthropoid apes and primeval man. The expeditions of the Soviet Academy of Sciences seem to have decided that the yeti does not exist, at least neither in the

Tien-Shan nor in the Pamir range. Others, more sanguine, still believe that one day he might be found.

At Termez, about 150 miles south-west of Dushanbe, just into Uzbekistan and very close to the Soviet border with Afghanistan, a 2,000-year-old Buddhist temple has been discovered. It is to be excavated and an open-air museum will be set up exhibiting the most interesting finds. At presstime we have no word on whether it is open to foreign tourists—highly unlikely in the present political circumstances. There is a rail link with Dushanbe.

Kirghizia

Kirghizstan is in the northeastern part of Central Asia and is bordered by China. It has a population of 3,219,000, of whom about 40 percent are Kirghizes and the rest Russians, Uzbeks, Kazakhs and Ukrainians. Most of the inhabitants live in the valleys. The greater part of Kirghiz territory is occupied by the Tien-Shan range. Its highest point is the Victory Park (Pik Pobedy), 22,320 feet, but even most part of the valleys and plateaus has an elevation of 6,000 to 9,000 feet. Only the Chu and Fergana valleys lie lower. The principal river of Kirghizia is the Narin, its largest reservoir Lake Issyk-Kul. The capital is Frunze.

Large-scale tourism has not yet come to Kirghizia, though with the development of health resorts around Lake Issyk-Kul, it is bound to increase.

Within the republic there are regular bus lines (roads are built even to the highest settlements) but many towns can be reached only by air—especially in winter. The sights are of the purely geographical variety—spectacular mountain ranges and valleys.

Frunze

Frunze (until 1926 it was called Pshipek, then renamed after Michael Frunze, the Soviet general who was born here) lies in the valley of the Chu River, at the foot of the snow-covered Kirghiz Ala-Tau Ridge, some 2,400 feet above sea level. It has severe winters and hot summers, with a mean temperature of 10.2°C (50°F).

Frunze's airport is an extremely busy place. From the airport, Mir Prospekt leads into the center of the city. We pass the University and other institutions. Crossing the small Ala-Archa River and the railway tracks, we continue along Belinsky Street, in an industrial area.

We can also start from the railway station. Here we find the fairly modern, 250-bed Ala-Too Hotel. Dzerzhinsky Boulevard leads from the station to the center. It is lined with oak, chestnut, birch and elm trees in thick groves, forming a park-like area. Oak (Dubovy) Park is a continuation of this wide thoroughfare. Here we find the Krupskaya Russian Drama Theater. From the parks, a tree-lined road leads eastwards to the Kirghiz State Opera and Ballet Theater, which has an excellent dance company. Near the Opera is the Chernyshevsky Public Library, decorated with busts of famous writers.

To the west, Oak Park merges into the Central Municipal Park. At its edge, we find Government House, with the domed building of the Kirghiz Academy of Sciences facing it. From Central Park, we follow another tree-lined promenade to Panfilov Park. Alongside is the Spartak Stadium.

In the city center, the Art Museum and the Kirghiz Drama Theater, are both on Pervogo Maya Street. On the same street, the birthplace of General Frunze has been turned into a memorial museum. Two modern restaurants are also worth seeing—the *Druzhba* is on the corner of Ivanitsin and Sopokov streets, a two-storied, all-glass building; the *Son-Kul,* on the corner of Dzerzhinsky Boulevard and 22nd Party Congress Street, is like an elegant private villa.

Issyk-Kul Lake

"The Kirghiz Sea" (proper name: Issyk-Kul, or "warm lake") can be reached in three or four hours by car or bus. It lies in a basin, 5,193 feet above sea level, surrounded by 9,000-foot-high mountains. Its length, west to east, is about 110 miles, its width 20 to 30 miles and its maximum depth is over 2,100 feet. Many hot springs rise from its depths; although it warms up slowly, it also retains its pleasant temperature for a long time, reaching 24–26°C (75°–79°F) in the shallow bays.

The Issyk-Kul is said to be the bluest lake in the world. It is very rich in fish, especially carp and perch-pike. Trout weighing over 20 lbs. have also been caught here. Anglers and hunters alike find it a paradise; there are plenty of water fowl, and swans breed freely. Of the 300 miles of coastline, some 200 miles are warm, sandy beaches. On the shore and in the nearby mountains, there are many important medicinal springs. are being developed; Dzheti-Oguz, Ak-Su Koysara and Cholpon-Ata are already well-established, with some 100,000 visitors every year. Apart from these resorts, there are two towns on the lake: Ribachye is a port; Przhevalsk (previously Karakol) was the first Russian settlement in Kirghizia. You can see a mosque resembling a Chinese pagoda, and a church built by the first Russian settlers. Both of them were constructed of wood without the use of a single nail and are decorated with delicate woodcarvings.

Kazakhstan

Kazakhstan lies in the southwestern corner of Soviet Asia. Its area is 1,696,875 square miles, its population over 14 million (second largest after the Russian Federal S.R.); it could accommodate Germany, France, Spain, Great Britain, Norway and Sweden within its frontiers. More than 40 percent of its population are Russians, about 30 percent Kazakhs and the rest Ukrainians, Tatars, Uzbeks, Uigurs, Koreans, Germans, etc. Many of the non-Kazakh inhabitants moved (or were moved) here in the 1950's to help with the industrialization of the vast territory. The capital is Alma-Ata.

Alma-Ata

Alma-Ata (the Father of Apples) lies in the southeastern corner of the Kazakh Republic, at the foot of the Zailisky Ala-Tau ridge of the Tien-Shan mountain range, on the banks of the Bolshaya and Malaya Alma-Atinka rivers, some 2,700 feet above sea level. Its climate is harsh and cold because of this elevation and the resultant exposure to the cold winds from the north. The average temperature in January is −7°C (19°F) while the summer sees a considerable difference between day and night temperatures—sometimes as much as 20°C (34°F).

The city lies in an attractive and romantic valley and is surrounded on three sides by mountains that rise in terraces. On the lower slopes there are irrigated fields, mostly orchards and vineyards. On the higher slopes, up to 5,400 feet, wild apricots and other fruit grow. The next zone is the forest, and above 8,400 feet there are sub-alpine and alpine meadows. In the more distant areas of the Zailisky Ala-Tau, bears, snow leopards and chamois still roam freely. The tops of the mountains are perpetually covered in snow. Avalanches were quite frequent until in October 1966 a protective ring was created above the city by a huge series of explosions. Earthquakes, however, are still a danger and most of the houses are low-slung (though in recent years earthquake-proof, higher buildings have been erected.) There are not many tourists in Alma-Ata yet; the majority come on official delegations and there are few visitors from the West.

From the railway station and the airport, both lie north of the city, Red Guardist Road (Krasnogvardeisky Trakt) takes us into the center; it is a twenty-minute journey by car or express bus. Parallel with the road, along many miles, stretches the Baum Park, named after the agronomist who was the first to organize tree-planting in this dusty city.

Traveling along Kommunist Prospekt we reach the center. The road rises, then reaches Lenin Square, with Government House on one side. On Kommunist Prospekt, in a small park, we find the Kazakh Drama Theater, an attractive building combining modern architecture with national decorative elements. The Hotel Kazakhstan is at No. 49–55 Kommunist Prospekt; opposite, is the Central Department Store, built on primly utilitarian lines.

From Kommunist Prospekt we can turn into Komsomolskaya Street, which crosses Lenin Square. At the corner of the two streets is the all-glass Children's Department Store. Around the square, we find the glass pavilion of the souvenir shop, the Central Post Office and the Hotel Alma-Ata. Continuing, we turn into Kalinin Street. No. 112 is the Abay Opera and Ballet Theater, which presents traditional Kazakh and classical operas and ballets.

Alma-Ata has several fine, tree-lined boulevards running across the city. Lenin Prospekt has the Pushkin Library; nearby, at 22 Sovietskaya Street, is the Shevchenko Gallery with its collection of modern Kasakh artists and Russian paintings and sculpture. On the corner of Sovietskaya and Shevchenko streets is the Kazakh Academy of Sciences.

Abay Prospekt, which runs east to west, cuts across Lenin Street. This thoroughfare leads to the residential quarters, the western and southwestern districts of Alma-Ata. We pass the film studio, the TV studio and the Stadium.

The Kazakh capital has a number of great parks. The Gorky Park covers more than 200 acres; it has a boating lake, tennis courts, a Pioneers' railway, a Ferris Wheel and many other attractions. The park named after the 28 Panfilovist Guards contains the former municipal cathedral, which is claimed to be the second-tallest wooden structure in the world.

The environs of Alma-Ata have many attractions for the tourist. In the valleys and on the slopes of the Zailisky Ala-Tau, there are many chalets for mountaineers. The Medeo winter stadium, some 12 miles from the city, is also in the mountains; several skating records have been made here, apparently helped by the clear mountain air.

Other Cities of Kazakhstan

The other Kazakh cities have little significance for the tourist; most of them are quickly-developing industrial and agricultural centers without historical or architectural importance. Most are also best reached by air.

When our plane takes off from the Alma-Ata airport, the tall sugarloaf of the 15,000 feet Talgar peak of the Ala-Tau mountains remains within sight for a long time. After some 45 minutes' flight, we see a lake: the Balkhash—over 400 miles long, and stretching from east to west. Its western part is fresh water while the eastern section is salt. Almost a quarter of all the carp caught in the Soviet Union come from here.

On the northern shore of the lake, the town of Balkhash is a copper-smelting center. Copper ore was found in the mid-1930's near Kounrad, and the town was built 13 miles from the deposits.

Flying on towards the northwest, we soon see another large city: Karaganda, which is the hub of Central Kazakhstan, a rich coal-mining area. Most of the coal is in the Karaganda Basin. Karaganda also has a number of copper and iron-ore mines (Dzhezkazgan, Atasu, Karsakpay, etc). In the same region there is a small town called Baykonur, which has become famous as the launching point of Soviet cosmonauts.

As we continue northwest from Karaganda, the landscape changes. The gray steppe is replaced by many miles of wheatfields. These are the virgin territories of Kazakhstan. The center is Tselinograd, the former Akmolinsk. Other cities have also been founded: Kustanay and Rudny, where huge iron-ore deposits have been found and the Sokolovo-Sarbay combine has been developed. It is mostly strip-mining, for the ore is only 90 to 120 feet under the surface. The whole area is being intensively exploited and is rapidly developing.

PRACTICAL INFORMATION FOR CENTRAL ASIA

WHEN TO GO. *Not* in the summer, which can be extremely hot. *Not* in the winter, which is often freezingly cold and without the relief of snow in the lowlands. (The air is very dry, however.) Late spring (April-May) or early autumn (September-October) are the pleasantest seasons, though even then you would be well advised to be prepared for extremes in certain spots such as deserts and mountains.

HOW TO GET THERE. Ashkhabad is 4 hours 54 minutes from Moscow by air. The 13 other Turkmenian cities are also linked by air to the capital, while Ashkhabad has direct connections with Baku, the Black Sea resorts, Tashkent and other important centers.

Tashkent can be reached by train from other Central Asian cities and from Moscow (2½ days) or by plane (Moscow-Tashkent, 4½ hours). (Central Asian time is 3 hours later than Moscow time.) The Hunger Steppe, near Tashkent, can be reached in about 2 hours by car from the Uzbek capital. Traveling by train from Moscow to Tashkent is a most rewarding experience, even if a large part of the route is out of bounds to tourists who cannot break their journey at certain stops such as Oranburg and Kazalinsk. But you can travel through to Tashkent without hindrance.

Samarkand can be approached from Tashkent, Bukhara and Dushanbe both by train and plane. (Tashkent-Samarkand takes 35–55 minutes by air.) Bukhara has a direct air link with both Tashkent and Samarkand. There is also a train and long-distance bus connection, but it is 180 miles from Samarkand and 400 miles from Tashkent, with the desert lying between these cities. There is also a train connection from Ashkhabad along the Krasnovodsk-Tashkent line.

The only comfortable way to get to **Khiva** is by air; it is some distance even from the secondary railroad line from Chardzhou to Kungrad. Planes, trains and buses will also take you from Tashkent to the Fergana Valley. The railroad makes a tremendous detour before it gets to Kokand, the center of the western part of the basin, though from Kokand the other towns can be reached easily and quickly by bus. On the new Tashkent-Kokand highway the bus takes 4–5 hours from the Uzbek capital to Kokand.

Frunze, the Kirghiz capital, is also hard to reach by train—there is an enormous detour from Tashkent and Alma-Ata. But by plane it is about 50 minutes from Tashkent and 25 minutes from Alma-Ata. The flight from Moscow takes 6½ hours. Within the Kirghiz Republic there is a regular long-distance bus system, but many places, especially in winter, are closed to all but air traffic. The Issyk-Kul lake is 3–4 hours by bus and car from Frunze.

Alma-Ata is also best reached by plane from Moscow or other points, though it has two railroad stations.

Trains, in short, are not to be recommended for travel in Central Asia. The distances are immense, in summer the heat is hardly bearable and in some districts (for instance Tadzhikistan), the line has to make such detours around the high mountains that 60 miles can easily take half a day. Planes are quicker, more comfortable and not necessarily more expensive.

 WHAT TO SEE. Tashkent, not much antiquity, for the town was destroyed in the 1966 earthquake. You will have to visit the modern town and see what the socialist state has done and also the madrasa of Kukeldash, the tomb of Kafal Shashi, and the madrases of Barak-khan with the Gumbazi Barak-khan, funeral dome of the Samanids of Tashkent.

Samarkand, you will visit first of all the admirable cemetery of Shahi-Zinda where lie buried, the famous men, court favorites and generals, of the time of Tamerlane. You will then go on to admire the mosque of Bibi Khanym, a masterpiece of Timurid architecture. On Registan Square, you will visit the three seventeenth-century madrasas surrounding this grand esplanade. At Gur Emir, you will stop by the tomb of Tamerlane; you will visit the observatory of Ulug Bek, the astronomer prince; and lastly you can make the 30-mile excursion to the Pendzhikent ruins.

Bukhara is a delightful town, which has kept all its oriental character and charm. You will see the ancient monuments of the Samanid dynasty, the tomb of Ismail Samani, and the Ark. Also noteworthy are the Kalyan Minaret (twelfth century), the madrasa of Ulug-Bek (fifteenth century), and the madrasa of Abdul

Aziz Khan (seventeenth century). You will also stroll through the old bazaars of Lyabi-hauz Square, and every street corner will summon up the past of the legendary city.

Ashkhabad: the four local museums; the Botanic Gardens. At nearby Anau, the ruins of the mauseolum of Khan Abul Kazim-Babur; the ruins of Nisaea.

Khiva: the Kuna-Ark, the Dishan-Kala, the Ichan-Kala; the Oasis of Khorezm; the Islam-Khodja Minaret; the Seyid Alauddin Mausoleum; the Djuma Mosque; the Palace of Allakuli-Khan.

Dushanbe: the Firdousi Library.

Frunze: the Oak *Dubovy* Park; the University quarter.

Alma-Ata: the Pushkin Library; the Gorky Park; museums.

 HOTELS. Alma-Ata. *Kazakhstan Hotel,* 500 beds, 307 rooms (some with balcony), is first-class moderate. This 5-story building is at 55 Kommunistichesky Prospekt, definitely best in town.

Next comes *Alma-Ata Hotel,* 119 Panfilov Street, also modern, 8 floors in height, and in the center of town. All rooms with balcony.

Also-ran: *Ala-Tau Hotel,* 142 Kirov Street.

Ashkhabad. Best is *Ashkhabad Hotel,* 74 Svobody Prospekt; *Oktyabrskaya Hotel,* Liberty Avenue; or *Kolkhozchi Hotel,* Engelskaya Street; or *Turkmenistan Hotel,* 117 rooms, an Intourist hotel at 19 Gogol Street, rated moderate or second-class.

Bukhara. Best is *Amu-Darya Hotel.* New Intourist hotel with 378 rooms, central, with foreign currency bar, tea-room, folk-music, barber and beauty shop. Also: *Bukhara Hotel,* 6, 40-Let-Oktyabrya Street, 192 rooms.

Dushanbe. *Dushanbe Intourist Hotel* is best. Located at Ayni Square, it has 313 rooms, is recently opened, and is rated first-class adequate. Also-ran: *Vakhsh Hotel,* 26 Lenin Prospekt. Also, *Hotel Tadzhikistan,* 262 rooms, airconditioned, Kommunisticheskaya Street.

Fergana. *Fergana Hotel,* 27 Kommunistov Street.

Frunze. Best is *Ala-Too,* 1 Dzerzhinsky Prospekt, new and comparatively modern, with 200 beds. Opposite the rail station. Second-best: *Kirghizstan Hotel,* Panfilov Street.

Samarkand. *Samarkand Hotel,* 1, Maxim Gorky Street is best. An Intourist operation, it has 10 floors and 182 rooms (many with balconies), and is first-class moderate. Modern in design, it lacks in room service what it has in architecture, and the toilets leave much to be desired. But, still, it is new and reasonably comfortable. The food is fair. Excellent view from upper floors over the town and the glazed blue domes of the Shahi-Zinda mausoleum and mosque.

Other hotels: *Zeravshan,* 57 Sovietskaya St. Taxi-rank nearby. *Registan:* 36 Lenin St.

Tashkent *Intourist, 50 Lenin Street. Nineteen floors with 262 rooms, quite agreeable and centrally located.*

Shark Hotel, also an Intourist establishment, but with less pretension, is at 16 Pravda Vostoka Street.

Rossia Hotel, Rustaveli Prospekt, is fairly up-to-date.

Uzbekistan Hotel, 45 Karl Marx Street, new, first-class, 479 rooms, airconditioned, Finnish decor, restaurant. Intourist bureau, *Beryozka* shop, Post Office and bank. Swimming pool (?).

Also-rans include: *Zeravshan Hotel,* 15 Akhunbabaev Street; and *Pushkinskaya Hotel,* 18 Pushkin Street.

Urgench. Two modest hotels: *Urgench,* 27, Kommunisticheskaya Street, and *Khorezm,* its annexe, on Turgenev Street.

 RESTAURANTS. Of the five republics in Central Asia, Uzbekistan has the most interesting cuisine. Specialties include skewers of meat grilled over a charcoal fire—*shashliks* (for which either beef or lamb is used, with other ingredients); *tkhumdulma* (a meat croquette encasing a hard-boiled egg); *pakhtakhor salad* (a mixture of chicken, cucumbers, olives, apples, peaches and plums in syrup); soups, such as *lagman* (highly spiced, with meat and noodles), *mstava* (meat soup), *maniar* (another highly-spiced clear soup with pieces of meat, egg and noodles). A special kind of bread is called *obi non.* The wines are excellent and the liqueurs fiery (*Aleatiko* is the best known).

There are few restaurants we can recommend but here are some:

Alma-Ata. *White Swan Restaurant,* amidst the trees by a lovely pond in Gorky Park, is best; then *Aral Restaurant,* also in Gorky Park, or *Issyk Restaurant,* 133 Panfilov Street.

Ashkhabad. *Gulistan Restaurant,* Pervomaiskaya Street.

Bukhara. Try the *Shark Restaurant* in the Intourist Hotel, or the *Bukhara Restaurant,* 1 Frunze Square.

Dushanbe. In town, the *Pamir Restaurant,* Kirov Street. For atmosphere or scenery, the *Dushanbe Restaurant,* at Lake Komsomol, or *Leto Restaurant* (summer only), in the town park.

Fergana. *Fergana Restaurant,* Lenin Street.

Frunze. Try the *Kirghizia Restaurant* on Kirov Street or the *Susamyr Restaurant* on Kirghizia Street.

Khiva. Only place to eat here is the restaurant on Gagarin Street. In summer, another place is open outside the city wall by an artificial lake.

Samarkand. Try the *Shark Restaurant,* Kozhevannaya Street.

Tashkent. Biggest in town (and perhaps best) is *Gulistan Restaurant,* on Kalinin Square. Also: *Bakhor Restaurant,* 15 Kuibyshev Street.

Urgench. Only place: *Urgench Restaurant,* Lenin Street next to the hotel.

THEATER AND CULTURAL ACTIVITIES. The opera houses have performances almost every night: recitals, ballet, opera, singing, dancing, and drumming. Seats can almost always be had up to curtain time, from 80 kopeks to 2 roubles. Or Intourist will reserve for you—at 2 roubles only.

Ashkhabad: Turkmenian Theater and Russian Drama Theater, both on Svoboda Prospekt, Botanical Garden (western end of Svoboda Prospekt).

Tashkent: Alisher Navoi Opera house, 31 Pravda Vostoka Street; Khamza Uzbek Theater, 2 Uigur Street, presenting Uzbek national plays; Maxim Gorky Russian Theater, 28 Karl Marx Street; Uzbek Philharmonic Orchestra, 10 Pravda Vostoka Street; Circus, 46 Lenin Street; Conservatory, 31 Pushkinskaya Street; Navoi Library, 14 Bratskaya Street; Rodina Wide-screen cinema, 34 Navoi Street; Khamza Uzbek Theatre, 5 Khamza Street; Mukimi Music and Drama Theater, 1–87 Almazar Street.

Bukhara: Musical and Drama Theater, in the Town Park.

Dushanbe: Ayni Opera and Ballet Theater, Moscow Square; Firdousi Library, Lenin Prospekt; Philharmonia, Lenin Prospekt (with a concert hall); Russian Drama Theater, Putovsky Street; Tadzhik Drama Theater, Lenin Prospekt.

Frunze: Krupskaya Russian Drama Theater, Dubovy Park; Kirghiz State Opera and Ballet, Dubovy Park; Chernyshevsky Public Library (near the Opera); Kirghiz Drama Theater, Pervogo Maya Street.

Alma Ata: Kazakh Drama Theater, Communist Prospekt; Abay Academic Opera and Ballet Theater, 112 Kalinin Street; Pushkin Library, Lenin Prospekt; Film and Television Studio on Abay Prospekt.

MUSEUMS. Tashkent: *The Exhibition of the Economic Achievements of the Uzbek SSR,* Pobeda Park, open 10–6 exc. Tuesdays. *Art Gallery* (paintings, sculpture), 6 Kuibyshev Street, open 10–6 exc. Tuesdays. *Alisher Navoi Literary Museum,* 35 Alisher Navoi Street, open 10–5 exc. Mondays. *Museum of Applied Art,* 15 Shelkovichnaya Street, open 10–5 exc. Mondays. *State Historical Museum,* 15 Kuibyshev Street, open 10–5 exc. Mondays and Tuesdays. *Textile Factory,* open Mondays, Wednesdays, Fridays 10–1, arrange through Intourist. *Uzbek Art Museum,* Gogol Street.

Samarkand: *Ulug-Bek's Observatory* (at the foot of the Chupan-Ata Hill).

Bukhara: *Local History Museum,* within the Ark (Castle). Another section of the same museum is in the *Zindan,* near the Ark, an 18th-century building, originally a prison. A third section is housed in the *Sitore-i-Mahi-Hasa Palace,* 2½ miles from town.

Dushanbe: *Historical and Art Museum,* Lenin Prospekt.

Frunze: *Art Museum,* Pervogo Maya Street.

Alma-Ata: *Shevchenko Gallery,* 22 Sovietskaya Street.

Ashkhabad: *Museum of Fine Arts* and *Museum of Local History and Ethnography,* 84 Svoboda Prospekt.

SHOPPING. The souvenir and dollar-currency shops in the tourist hotels offer a choice of several items; prices in the tax-free dollar shops are lower. In Samarkand the bazaar by the *Registan* has souvenir and craft items. The most interesting souvenirs in Uzbekistan are the embroidered caps and textiles, often spectacularly colorful and elaborate. Local wines are good too; also enameled silver jewelry. Lacquer ware, carved ivory, ceramics, painted boxes, dolls and pottery are less interesting.

Other best buys in Central Asia are the carpets, and the best place to buy them is in the open air markets you'll see in practically all the cities. Turkmen and Tadzhik skullcaps are also worth purchasing. In Dushanbe, Tadzhik girls do pretty embroidery with gold, silver and silken thread on velvet and other fine cloths.

TOURS. There are special central Asian tours, arranged by Intourist via Moscow or Leningrad. Tours are organized in Ashkhabad, Alma-Ata, Bukhara, Dushanbe, Samarkand and Tashkent and individual tours can be arranged in the vicinity of these centers. A recently opened location is Pendzhikent with its ancient excavations. Can be visited (on day-trip only) from Samarkand.

TRANSPORTATION. Taxis are very few and very expensive. The official rate is 20 kopeks a kilometer. As for public transportation, it is practical and very cheap, but is best avoided at the rush hours. Tashkent is the only city in Central Asia to have a subway (underground).

USEFUL TASHKENT ADDRESSES. *Intourist:* 50 Lenin Street, *Pakhtakor Stadium,* 10 Pakhtakorskaya Street.

SIBERIA

The Wild East

It is only in this decade that Siberia has been opened up to the Western traveler—or, at least, a certain part of it has, for there still are vast areas where the foreigner is not welcome. In 1970 a new short-cut route was inaugurated between Tokyo, Moscow and Paris by way of Siberia for a number of airlines, but bookings, at least from Tokyo to Khabarovsk, are reportedly heavy and waiting lists for seats long. Alaska Airlines were operating charter trips from Anchorage to Khabarovsk in summer, but these appear to have been suspended for the moment, as we go to press. Eastern and Central Siberia have now been put on the tourist map and a whole new world has become accessible to the traveler. Aeroflot is advertising Eastern Siberia and has opened up its immense network covering the vast territory. Information is far from complete as yet and changes in accommodations, travel facilities and so on are frequent; but it will become more and more practicable to enter the Soviet Union by its large backyard if you wish, and after visiting Khabarovsk, Irkutsk and Lake Baikal, to proceed via Central Asia to the Black Sea, Moscow and Leningrad.

Siberia's five million square miles offer fantastic variety. Its meridians pass through the icy wastes of the Arctic, through tundra, *taiga* and the endless steppe. Mountains, high plateaux and plains alternate.

Siberia could easily contain the whole of Western Europe. The Trans-Siberian Railway is the longest in the world, while the potential hydro-electric energy of the Siberian rivers is immeasurable—the Angara alone could provide 70 billion kilowatt hours a year. And yet it is only one of the region's rivers which include the Ob, the Irtysh, the Yenisei, the Lena and the Amur. The largest hydroelectric plant in the world was built at Bratsk on the Angara and some 23 others are being built on the Yenisei.

Siberia's forests are also unimaginably rich. Coal and iron ore deposits are very extensive in some districts of Eastern Siberia and in Western Siberia (Bakchar and Kolpashevo). Siberia contains 90 percent of the USSR's bituminous coal reserves, 75 per cent of the iron ore, 80 percent of the timber. Huge oilfields have been discovered near the ancient town of Tyumen, where the Samotlor field is said to be one of the largest in the world and is producing 50 million tons of oil a year; in 1962 rich oil wells were tapped outside the village of Markovo, on the upper course of the Lena, and a whole new town, Neftelensk, has grown up around them. Siberia is also very rich in gold, silver and precious metals, even diamonds. To develop Siberia's vast potential, the Russians are enlisting Western help and contracts are being or have been negotiated with British, US, French, German, Japanese and Finnish companies experienced in oil, gas and mineral extraction.

Tourism is, of course, less well developed than elsewhere. Many regions are difficult to reach; others are not yet accessible to the tourist. But you can discover the *taiga,* the primeval forest even on the outskirts of major cities. Some *taiga* areas still have tigers and bears—though you're unlikely to meet them near the inhabited settlements! The cities have few art treasures and are not particularly interesting architecturally, as offices, public buildings and administrative centers have largely been built to the same uniform pattern. Nor was the taste of the rich merchants of pre-revolutionary times very distinguished. In Siberian cities at the turn of the century a good many wooden buildings were to be seen and in the less developed settlements and in the northern districts these are still standing. Most of the cities have one or two theaters, and you'll also find local museums, the occasional art gallery, some fine parks and, almost everywhere, a riverside promenade. Many tourists will feel that a visit to a single Siberian city is sufficient—perhaps Irkutsk or Novosibirsk or Khabarovsk.

Exploring Siberia—Irkutsk

Irkutsk is the 300-year-old capital of Irkutsk Territory which has an area larger than that of France, Holland, Belgium, Austria, Switzerland and Denmark put together. It was the final goal of Jules Verne's Michael Strogov—and something of a frontier town. Its University, founded in 1918, was the first institute of higher learning in Eastern Siberia and still has a fine reputation.

Today Irkutsk has quite a few tourists; it is an important junction on the Trans-Siberian railway, and planes land and take off regularly. The flight-time from Moscow is seven hours.

A modern busy city, it has many shady parks; the houses in the center are two-, three- and four-storied, in late 19th-century European neoclassical style. Many of the old-style wooden houses are being knocked down, but some have been scrupulously preserved. Chocolate-brown in color, with richly carved window-frames, portals and gables, they are the most atmospheric sights of Irkutsk.

Though many of the city's old churches are closed, two remain open as places of worship. The 18th-century Church of the Holy Cross has a fine choir. The Church of the Holy Saviour, on the city's outskirts, has an interesting cemetery containing the grave of Gregory Shelekhov, a roving Siberian merchant who founded Russia's first permanent colony in Alaska in 1784.

The Znamensky convent is still open, too, with the Church of the Apparition of Our Lady in its precincts. The main thoroughfare of the modern city is Karl Marx Street.

The Siberian oil-refining center, Angarsk, is close to Irkutsk. A long pipeline brings oil from European Russia; but there are also important oilfields around Irkutsk.

Lake Baikal and Area

From the Central Hotel in Irkutsk the landing stage is only five minutes' walk. From here a hydrofoil will take you to Lake Baikal. (You can also go by car but only as far as Listvennichnaya, a 1½-hour drive.)

The deep-green woods lining the banks of the Angara open like a gate in front of the boat and the horizon widens to reveal a seemingly endless vista. This is the ancient, sacred sea of the Tunguz tribes, Lake Baikal, shining in dazzling blue. Far away on the horizon, snowy peaks rise mistily. Their lines are delicate, and look more like a mirage than reality.

A popular Russian song calls it "majestic ocean, holy Baikal." In the language of the Evenki tribe it is also called *Lama* (Sea) while in the Chinese chronicles it is *Pe Hai,* Northern Ocean.

Lake Baikal is some 400 miles long and has an area of over 12,000 square miles—equal to that of Belgium and the Netherlands together. Its width varies between 18 and 50 miles. According to the latest measurements, it is more than a mile deep in places. It contains one sixth of all the fresh water in the world, and it is also the world's oldest lake. Soviet scientists claim that the depression was formed in the Tertiary era, 25 million years ago. It lies some 1,650 feet above sea level and the mountains around it tower to 9,000 feet. Experts are still arguing about its origins and about how seals and sea cows ever came to be in it—not to mention the *omul,* a white fish of the salmon family which is one of the local culinary specialties. The water is crystal clear; a white sheet thrown into it can be seen clearly at a depth of 90–120 feet. It has hardly any taste, for it contains a negligible proportion of mineral salts. The currents are very slow. It is fed by 336 rivers but has only one outlet, the Angara. The water is cold—even in the hottest summers it never rises above 50–52°F though it rarely freezes before January; then the ice can be 24 or even 36 inches thick. Yet it is a dangerous surface on which to travel for the gases that rise from its depths warm up the water and make the ice unsafe. It is frequently whipped by great storms. The *barguzin,* the northeast wind, blows along its entire length. The other, even more cruel, wind is the 80 m.p.h. *sarma,* the northwest wind, which whips the waves up to considerable heights.

For a shorter excursion, visit Listvyanka, with its Limnological Institute where you can hear a lecture on the extraordinary history and ecology of Baikal. The Russians have created a special scientific discipline they call "baikalology". Experts have identified 1200 different creatures which are unique to Lake Baikal, many of them survivals which have become extinct elsewhere, or so the theories go.

Those who feel inclined to embark on a longer excursion should continue to the station of Bolshiye Koti and explore its neighborhood.

It is best to take food and fishing tackle with you. Lake Baikal provides rich and varied sport for the angler.

Novosibirsk

Novosibirsk is the largest city in Siberia and the eighth in the whole of the Soviet Union. It is the center of the Novosibirsk Territory, an important traffic junction and an industrial center. It is a modern city, laid out on a gridiron plan. The centre of the Inner Town is Red Avenue (Krasny Prospekt), stretching from the banks of the Ob to the air terminal. Along its less wide section are several parks and well-kept squares. Here, almost every 20th-century architectural style has left its trace. There is a large opera house and a Conservatoire which boasts the only organ in Siberia.

Novosibirsk has a separate district called Akademgorodok (Science City), 15 miles beyond on the Ob River. In 1958 a forest of birches and pines was transformed into a university research center equipped with the finest facilities and staffed by some of the best brains in the country. To attract these people, Akademgorodok is well supplied with consumer goods and its accommodations and cultural facilities are certainly superior to those of most other towns. It has a reputation for comparative liberalism. To balance these attractions, however, the weather is inclement, with summer often oppresive at 90°F while winter can mean 50°F below zero, with four feet of snow. Foreign scientists visit Akademgorodok in considerable numbers, but its inhabitants nevertheless do tend to feel isolated in this Siberian fastness.

Khabarovsk

Khabarovsk is a traffic junction and industrial center, the capital of the Khabarovsk Territory. It is reached by plane from Moscow in eight hours.

Built on three hills—called *sopka* locally—each of which is a separate district, Khabarovsk lies on the banks of the Amur where the Ussuri enters the mighty river. The Amur is the second favorite river of the Russians—"Little Father Amur" to "Little Mother Volga." Yet it is a grim river that can smash ships during storms and sweep away villages when it is in flood. The Chinese call it the "Black Dragon." The city as it stands today is only a century old and, because of the damage wrought during the Revolution, architecturally it is even younger.

The main thoroughfare is Karl Marx Street, which links Lenin Square with Komsomol Square on the banks of the Amur. There are a few old redbrick houses intermingled with houses and public buildings designed in the Constructivist style of the 'thirties. Almost all the important institutions are housed here, as well as the largest hotels.

Komsomol Square, at the far end of Karl Marx Street, has the headquarters of the Amur Steamship Company, a fine building of the *belle epoque*. Go on from here to the waterfront and enjoy the view across the river to the treeless steppe, with China in the distance. The river embankment is a favorite walk for the people of Khabarovsk.

Thirty miles from Khabarovsk, in Volochayevka, where the Civil War ended, you'll see a large building topped with a huge statue on the summit of the Iyun-Koran mountain. This is the memorial and museum of the Amur partisans.

Bratsk, Barnaul and Yakutsk

The three cities mentioned so far are the most easily accessible to the tourist. The other Siberian cities are presented only briefly here as you are less likely to visit them.

The site of Bratsk is over 350 years old and was originally a Cossack fort. There are some interesting cave drawings in the vicinity. The modern city sprang up in the 1960s when one of the largest hydroelectric plants in the world was built here. The Bratsk Sea is a huge reservoir; soon after it was completed an aluminum factory and a large timber combine were also erected here. The residential districts are of very recent vintage.

Bratsk is linked to the Trans-Siberian railway by a branch line, which pushes on to Usk Kut and even beyond. There is also a fair road. But the best way of reaching Ust Kut is by plane, from which can be seen the River Angara, which channels the waters of Lake Baikal and the Bratsk Sea into the Yenisei.

Barnaul is the center of the Altaisky Territory. Founded in 1738 when A. Demidov, a merchant, set up a smelting mill on the banks of the Ob River to exploit the silver being mined in the Altai Mountains, it later became an important cultural center. When serfdom was abolished, ending the supply of unpaid labor to the Altai mines, Barnaul began to decline. In more recent years it has begun to flourish again, especially since the opening up of the Virgin Lands. From Barnaul an excursion can be made into the Altai Mountains.

Yakutsk is the capital of the huge Yakutsk Autonomour Republic, an area of over a million square miles. The city was one of the earliest fortresses in Siberia but for a long time only wooden houses were built here. Yakutsk lies in the permafrost zone, where the thermometer can drop to $-70°F$ in January. Large concrete pillars are driven into the soil some 18 feet deep and covered with reinforced concrete in recent construction. They enable quite tall buildings to be erected. The main thoroughfare of Yakutsk, Lenin Street, has many such buildings standing on stilts.

Yakutsk is a major scientific center. Its Frost Research Institute, a branch of the Academy of Sciences, is engaged in essential work for which its location is ideally suited.

Komsomolsk, Krasnoyarsk and Norilsk

Komsomolsk is on the Amur River, some 200 miles from Khabarovsk. Its building began in 1932, partly using forced labor, in the middle of the *taiga,* on swampy soil. It stretches over six square miles and is one of the most important industrial centers of the Soviet Far East.

Krasnoyarsk is the center of the Krasnoyarsk Territory. Lying on the banks of the Yenisei River, it is one of the most important industrial centers in Siberia. The old city is on the left bank, the new town on the right. Founded in 1628, the Cossack fort became a government seat in 1823. Its development was due to the nearby gold mines and to the building of the Trans-Siberian Railway. During Czarist times it was a center for exiles: those sent to Siberia were first taken to Krasnoyarsk and then distributed among the distant settlements. Lenin spent two months here in 1897.

Four miles from Krasnoyarsk are the famous "Pillars", huge (120–270 foot high) columns of rock belonging to outcrops of the Eastern Sayan. They were formed by the combined effect of wind and water. This is a protected area and open to tourists.

Norilsk is one of the major new cities of the Krasnoyarsk Territory in the permafrost region. It has nickel and other metal foundries. Originally a small village, its development gathered pace in the 1950s. Here, too, the buildings are supported on huge pillars driven deep into the ground. Summer brings white nights; in winter, daylight lasts only an hour or two.

Omsk and Tomsk

Omsk, center of Omsk Territory, is situated at the confluence of the Om and Irtysh Rivers. Stretching for more than 20 square miles, it is Siberia's second largest city.

The city was founded in 1716 by a military expedition led by Colonel Bukholts. In 1768 a new fort was built on the site of the previous one, then in 1822 it became the seat of the governor of Western Siberia and from 1839 the residence of the Governor General. It was a place of exile—Dostoyevsky did four years hard labor in its prison. By the early 20th century it had some important industries, mainly textiles and leather; today it is a vast industrial area.

Tomsk, founded in 1604, is one of the oldest cities in Siberia, with a university (established in 1888), a number of colleges and schools and a fine Botanical Garden. Nearby, large-scale excavations have uncovered ancient burial places dating from the Neolithic era, the middle of the first millennium BC.

Ulan-Ude and Vladivostok

Ulan-Ude is the capital of the Buryat Autonomous Republic, on the banks of the Selenga and Uda Rivers. It was founded in 1666 as the winter quarters of Cossack troops. In 1689 a fortress was built here and in 1775 the city was given its municipal charter as Verkhne-Udinsk; (it was renamed Ulan-Ude in 1934). In March 1920 it became the capital of the Far Eastern Territory. With its mixture of old wooden houses and modern apartment blocks, it still has the atmosphere of a remote, frontier town. The main thoroughfare is Lenin Street, where the shops are.

Vladivostok, founded in 1860 on the shores of the Golden Horn Bay on the Pacific, is the center of the Primorsky (Coastal) Territory. An important strategical base, by 1880 it had become a fair-sized city. Many expeditions started from here and it became particularly important as a naval base during the Russo-Japanese War. Today it is the main base for the Soviet Pacific Fleet. It has a large merchant harbor and is also a center for the whaling and fishing fleets.

The Trans-Siberian Railway

The 5,778 miles of railway stretching from the Pacific Coast of Siberia to Moscow is by far the longest continuous track in the world on which through trains are operated. The name "Trans-Siberian Railway" is a purely English invention; to the Russians it is the "Great Siberian". Built between 1880 and 1900 after several decades of debate, it was in its early years a vital and rapid link for Westerners, especially diplomats, who used it to reach the capitals of China and Japan. Today it constitutes the greatest single travel experience a tourist can have, and offers Americans a through route from the Orient to Europe, while Europeans get a fairly cheap and interesting transit to Japan and Hong Kong.

A new "eastern section" of the Trans-Siberian line is at present being built running from the town of Taishet to the city of Komsomolsk on the River Amur. The first several hundred miles of this route (eventually it will be 2,000 miles) are already in full operation and it is planned to be completed by 1984. Known as the Baikal-Amur Railway (initials BAM are becoming well-known) it is a mammoth engineering undertaking which will open up vast new areas of Siberia including the copper deposits in the Udokan area which are said to exceed the combined reserves of the United States, Chile and Zaire. And the new line is some six hundred miles from the Chinese border, closer to which the original Trans-Siberian runs for considerable distances.

For foreigners, the Trans-Siberian doesn't start at Vladivostok, for that is a military port with limited access. The regular ships of the *Soviet Far East Line* come into the port of Nakhodka, about 50 miles to the north, from Hong Kong, Tokyo Bay, and Osaka. A smart boat trains meets the ship (at least twice weekly in summer) and runs for 564 miles to the Soviet Far East city of Khabarovsk. Here passengers must change trains. Eastbound passengers spend a night in Khabarovsk and the next day sightseeing, picking up the boat train in the early evening. Westbound passengers change trains the same day. You can, if you wish, reach Khabarovsk by *Japan Air Lines,* who have weekly flights, but there are reports of long waiting lists on this route.

That first sight of a Russian train at Nakhodka is an encouraging one, for its green-and-cream cars are airconditioned, offering two-berth sleepers with a shower between two compartments an excellent diner, and a powerful electric engine. That first night is an easy one on the train, leaving the port at 8 P.M. with dinner and then a good sleep as the express rolls along through the darkness at about 50 miles an hour. The next morning, lady attendants call passengers with tea from the samovar, typical Russian tea in a glass, and while breakfast is taken in the diner, the Ussuri River may be seen on the left of the train, with wild forest and hill country stretching away on the other. In the forests are the last Siberian tigers.

The boat train is due at Khabarovsk at 11.10 A.M., and westbound passengers go through the city changing trains on the same day. So on Day Two there is a two-hour sightseeing of this big and rather strange Far East city, founded by Erofey Khabarov on his trek to the Siberian Pacific in 1858.

The majority of the route is electrified with the remainder being diesel-operated although you may see steam engines as you cross Siberia.

Electrification is progressing all the while and it should be "under the wires" all the way by the mid-1980s or even sooner.

The train itself is less luxurious than the boat express. There are "soft"- and "hard"-class cars, a diner, a baggage car, and three seating coaches for short-haul passengers. "Soft"-class has two or four berths and "hard"-class four. In addition, the "softs" are made up and have full carpeting and showers between two compartments, while "hard" class passengers must hire their own bedding; there are no showers, only washrooms at both ends of each car. Wide corridors in "soft" are carpeted, with folddown seats, and shaving plugs are placed on the outer walls, so men with electric razors shave in public! Usually one or two of the "SZ" type two-berth sleepers are attached to this train now, a similar type to those on the boat express. The newest "soft" class sleepers have shower units incorporated in their design with two shower units to each coach. It is planned that the entire *Rossia* trains should have these, but they are being introduced only gradually. You may be lucky or you may not.

The Trans-Siberian trains, called *Rossia* and numbered One and Two (No. 1 is westbound) run daily from May to September, four times a week in winter. The basic train sets, in red and cream (marked with brass Cyrillic characters on the side denoting "Moscow-Vladivostok"), were built in 1949, and are *not* airconditioned. The train is sealed in winter, with heating by the train attendants stoking stoves; in summer the dry, burning heat of Siberia with plenty of dust about makes travel conditions unpleasant at times. Light indoor clothing is a *must,* but remember also to take along a heavy coat for stops in winter and spring. Normal garb for Russian passengers is very informal: trousers and shirt, often pyjamas. The four-berth compartments are not divided as to sex and it may happen that three men share with a woman, although for tourists boarding with Intourist at Khabarovsk, using airline-type boarding cards, there is an official attempt to avoid this.

Day Two

The afternoon of Day Two sees the Trans-Siberian train rolling across the mighty Amur River and through dry country with the high hills of China never far away. To get the best out of this journey, travelers MUST have a knowledge of the Cyrillic alphabet (it only takes 48 hours to master), for without it they cannot read the timetable displayed in each car and will not know where they are when the train stops. Even more important, they will not know *how long* the stop is going to be. The train adheres very strictly to schedule—it has to, because the Siberian Railway is extremely busy throughout its length. It is double track and boasts CTC (centralized train control) but passes a fast freight every 30 minutes and a number of passenger trains not going the full length of the line. There are 91 stops from Vladivostok to Moscow, 79 of them affecting those passengers who join at Khabarovsk, and the time at stations ranges from two minutes to a maximum of 22 (at Sverdlovsk). It is normal to get out and walk up and down the platforms, perhaps to buy things from the station "bazaars" (try ice-cream, chocolate and Russian bread), but only one warning blast is given before the train starts away. The "soft" car attendants try to keep an eye on their passengers to prevent their being left behind. Moscow time is kept throughout the train's run, which can vary up to seven hours from local time.

The first stop out of Khabarovsk is at In, a tiny place in the wilds. Ten minutes are allowed. The next stop is at Birobidzhan, capital of the so-called Autonomous Jewish Region, a bleak and swampy area, but this only lasts four minutes. At Obluchye, 135 miles from Khabarovsk, another ten minutes are allowed.

As darkness falls the train is rolling smoothly through the dry, hilly country of the Soviet Far East (they do not regard this region as Siberia proper). The dining car is open all day from nine in the morning until ten at night, and its menus are in six languages. Only those items on the huge and optimistic menus which have pencilled prices against them are available. Being a better "shop" than most in the towns and villages through which it passes, the train's diner is often visited by locals who buy beer and ice cream to take away. This can lead to shortages for passengers, and no replacements are made until Irkutsk is reached. Meals are fairly cheap, foreigners paying by means of Intourist coupons purchased in advance (but taking change in roubles and kopeks). The food is fairly good at times, rump steak fried in breadcrumbs apparently being a stable and consistent favorite and beer, wine and vodka are available. Breakfasts are massive affairs, at least for Russians, who seem to visit the diner for four meals a day. Take a chance with the non-tourist menu, it can be good!

Passengers tend to retire early, soon after ten at night, but the car attendants serve tea at that hour. In the "soft" class you can order tea at any time; in the "hard" it is served twice a day. Hot water can also be obtained for your own tea or coffee. The heavy cars, 56 tons on average, rolling on their wide five-foot gauge, ride easily on excellent track (except that after the spring thaw there may be bad stretches) and sleeping is comfortable. But a lot depends on your traveling companions!

Days Three and Four

As Day Three brightens and the attendants begin their rounds with the inevitable tea, one has settled into the routine of the Trans-Siberian. It is like traveling in a coastal freighter, with tiny cabins, making a lot of stops in small ports. The wide corridors are the promenade decks and the diner is the saloon. There are drinks parties in the "cabins" and you learn a certain amount of Russian!

The scenery is mainly upland forests with rivers and lakes often in sight. The ubiquitous silver birch trees (*beryozka,* a symbol of Russia) are now more in evidence. There is a good exercise stop at 8 A.M. at Skovordino, where 15 minutes are spent changing engines. The train is now 756 miles from Khabarovsk, with 4,500 still to do!

Before noon, the splendid Shilka River comes in sight and the train runs on the right bank of it all day. If one is interested in trees and glimpses of wild life, it is worth sitting on a corridor seat and just watching this little known part of Siberia unfold. Later in the day, the country becomes very dry again as the train enters the fringe areas of the Gobi Desert.

Day Four dawns with a semi-desert aspect, with Manchuria and Mongolia well away to the south. The highlight of the morning is the 15-minute stop at 7.30 A.M. at the city of Chita, junction for the former

Chinese Eastern line to Harbin and Korea. In the early afternoon a transformation takes place as the train begins to climb away from the Gobi region into the Trans-Baikal area, the true Siberia. There is a stop at Yablonovaya, then the great train thrusts upwards on one of the last major climbs left in the world. The range being crossed is the Yablonovy, little known to Western travelers, where summits touch 9,000 feet. The train goes through above 4,000 feet and the temperature in winter plummets like a stone, while in summer it is noticeably cooler. There is a stop at Mogzon, then another stop is made at a station called Petrovsky Zavod. All around are the dense forests, the Siberia of fact and fiction. We stay on the high plateau the rest of the day. At 6 P.M. a stop is made at Ulan Ude, junction for Peking.

Darkness falls as the train nears the fierce Angara River, amid tremendous mountain scenery on the southern side of Lake Baikal. This is the only river to escape from mighty Lake Baikal, into which flow more than 300 rivers.

Days Five and Six

At 2 A.M. there is a 15-minute stop at Irkutsk, where you get a change of linen and towels, and the diner is re-stocked. Its crew, though, goes right through to Moscow, and so does the electric engine up front. The big city glimpsed from the modern station has been called "the Paris of Siberia!"

Thus ends the more romantic section of the great journey; for the rest, there are some highlights, but mostly a great deal of forest. It is ideal for catching up on sleep and reading. There are mountains and lakes as Day Five dawns on the way from Irkutsk, with the train still above 3,000 feet.

Very late on Day Five the train stops at Krasnoyarsk, which means both "red" and "beautiful." These are enormous hydro-electric schemes on the River Yenisei hereabouts. All night the Siberian plain unfolds, with its millions of trees, lakes and streams. Stops are few, only for crew changes, and speed averages 43 m.p.h. At 10.50 A.M. on Day Six we enter highly industrialized Novosibirsk, crossing into the station by the Ob Bridge, longest and most important on the line. Only 20 miles north is Akademgorodok, the Soviet science city.

Days Seven and Eight

Going west you see the famous city of Omsk, on the Irtysh River, where the train stops in the early evening of Day Six. This is the junction for the South Siberian Railway. Contrary to popular belief, the Trans-Siberian doesn't go via Tomsk, but misses it by 100 miles (you change at Taiga Junction).

There is a run of twelve hours across the plain to Sverdlovsk, an important industrial city in the Urals, where there is a 22-minute stop at breakfast time. Soon after leaving it, winding through the comparatively low but rocky Urals, we pass a sign near kilometer post 1,777, about 1,100 miles from Moscow, showing Asia to the east and Europe to the west. It is downhill, gently, most of the way through coniferous forests and wide fields, until the stop at Kirov in mid-evening. This is the last important place short of Moscow, now only 595 miles away.

Day Eight, on the train, dawns with the train amid grain fields and forests as it whirls across North Russia, bearing west southwest towards the capital. This is the morning you get your bills for services rendered by the attendants (all those glasses of tea and cups of cocoa). The price is very modest but they shy at tips although happy to accept a present. At 12.10 A.M., if the train is on time, and it usually is, Moscow's Yaroslavl Station comes in sight and the journey ends amid the bustle of the great Square of the Three Terminals (Komsomol Square).

PRACTICAL INFORMATION FOR SIBERIA

WHEN TO COME. In the summer, unless you like the cold.

HOW TO GET THERE. By rail: from Moscow to Nakhodka, stopping in Novosibirsk, Irkutsk or Khabarovsk. **By air:** from Moscow to Novosibirsk; from Novosibirsk to Irkutsk; from Irkutsk to Khabarovsk; from Khabarovsk to Nakhodka by rail. By air from Niigata (Japan) to Khabarovsk. From Ashkhabad to Novosibirsk via Tashkent, also by air.

There are no authorized automobile routes for foreigners in Siberia.

HOTELS. Bratsk. Best is first-class *Taiga Hotel,* 35 Mir Street, with a good restaurant and foreign currency bar from 9 P.M onward. Sumptuous New Year festivities for foreign tourists.

Irkutsk. *Angara Hotel,* 7 Sukhe Bator Street, a modern, 7-story hotel overlooking gardens and a fountain. All rooms with own toilet and shower. Second-best is *Sibir,* 18 Lenin Street, 250 rooms, first-class moderate.

One hour by rail from Irkutsk, at Listvianka village on Lake Baikal, is the *Baikal Hotel.* Small, but the ideal place from whence to explore Baikal.

Intourist Hotel at Lake Baikal, 64 rooms, many fronting the lake, excellent views. Food better than average.

Khabarovsk. Best, though fairly primitive, is *Amur Hotel,* 49 Lenin Street, with an Intourist Service Bureau. Then *Tsentralnaya,* 52 Pushkin Street, followed by *Dalny Vostok Hotel,* 18 Karl Marx Street, even more primitive. Last in town is *Sever Hotel,* 108 Volochayevskaya Street.

There are also two fairly recent hotels at the *airport,* used especially for those in transit. A new Intourist Hotel was scheduled at presstime, but no information is available yet confirming this.

Nakhodka. Only hotel which can be recommended is the *Vostok,* on Tsentralnaya Square. *Note:* you can only stay in Nakhodka if you are in transit between the USSR and Japan or Hong Kong.

Novosibirsk. Leader is the *Hotel Navosibirsk,* 3 Lenin Street two blocks from Opera House, large and reasonably comfortable. Above average food in the restaurant.

Also-ran: *Sibir Hotel,* 26 Krasny Prospekt.

RESTAURANTS. Unfortunately, there are few restaurants that we can recommend in Siberia, though the region does provide a great variety of splendid raw materials, from reindeer to fish, from beets to pastries. But you are unlikely to experience any gastronomic thrills in the 2,200 miles between Novosibirsk and Vladivostok, in any event! Here are the few:

Irkutsk. Best is the *Artik,* in downtown Irkutsk. Standard food, but amusing atmosphere and a good place to go dancing.

Also: *Almaz Restaurant,* Lenin Street. The *Angara Hotel* dining room often serves "omul", the rare and delicious whitefish from Lake Baikal. You may be treated to midnight festivities including champagne, *bliny* (pancakes), *pelmeny* (Siberian dumplings), caviar and smoked salmon.

Khabarovsk. *Ussuri Restaurant,* 34 Karl Marx Street, shares honors with the *airport* restaurant.

Novosibirsk. Best outside the hotels is *Snezhinka Restaurant,* on Lenin Street. Or try in "Science City".

 CULTURAL ACTIVITIES. Visitors have reported that tours to Siberia don't include enough evening entertainment. It does exist, but you may have to seek it out for yourself. **Irkutsk** has a drama, a musical comedy and a youth theater, a circus, a philharmonic orchestra, Siberia's only planetarium and a fine cycling stadium; **Novosibirsk** is the seat of the Siberian Section of the Soviet Academy of Sciences. There are six theaters: an Opera House, a musical comedy theater, the Red Torch Theater, the Village Theater (with a touring company), a children's Theater and a puppet theatre. Three newspapers and a literary review are published here. Novosibirsk's Science City, *Akademgorodok,* has interesting things going on, if you are allowed to find them.

Khabarovsk has a Pioneer Theater (14 Karl Marx Street), an openair theater in the Pioneer Park (69 Karl Marx Street), a second openair theater in the Town Park. In addition there is a Drama Theater (92 Dzerzhinsky Street) and a Musical Comedy Theater (21 Shevchenko Street).

Krasnoyarsk has two theaters: the Pushkin Theater and a puppet theater. An openair theater has been opened on an island of the Yenisei.

Omsk has a Drama Theater, a Musical Comedy Theater, a Pioneer Theater and a puppet theater, as well as a university and several colleges.

Tomsk possesses a university (founded in 1888), a drama and puppet theater.

Ulan-Ude boasts an opera house, a Russian Drama Theater and a Buryat-Mongol touring theater.

Valdivistok has the Gorky Theater, a Children's Theater, Fleet Theater and a puppet theater.

 MUSEUMS. Irkutsk: *Fine Arts Museum,* the largest in the eastern part of the USSR, with good representation by Siberian artists. *Folklore Museum,* with colorful artifacts of indigenous Siberian tribes, including some superb richly-carved wooden window-frames that adorned early Siberian dwellings.

Listvyanka: *The Institute of Limnology* devoted to scientific research into the fauna and flora of Lake Baikal.

Khabarovsk: *Museum of Local History* 21 Shevchenko Street, founded 1896, exhibits the fauna and flora of the Far East and the *taiga.* Collections built up by famous explorers. *Art Gallery,* 45 Frunze Street. Graphic works by Rembrandt and Rubens, paintings by Monet.

Omsk: *Museum of Local History. Fine Arts Museum.* Tomsk: *Museum of Local History.*

SHOPPING. The best buys in Siberian cities are delicate bonecarvings, jasper and malachite ornaments (if you can find them!) and furs, (sable, marten, kolinsky, ermine, squirrel)—probably no better selection than that available in other Soviet cities, but the salespeople in Siberia may well be more knowledge-able and thus more helpful. Amber is on sale everywhere. Khabarovsk has a new shop called *Souvenirs* which sells artefacts by Far Eastern and Far Northern craftsmen.

TOURS. Intourist tours are arranged to Novosibirsk, Irkutsk and Bratsk, and you can go on if you so wish to Khabarovsk and finally to Nakhodka, the Soviet port on the Sea of Japan. In Irkutsk you can join special sightseeing tours of the city, a tour of the student quarter and of the Geological Museum of the Polytechnic; also tours to four museums—Natural History, Mineralogy, Fine Arts or Nature (each $21); a 3-hour trip to the Irkutsk seed selection station ($27.50); an 8-hour trip to Lake Baikal ($81); a trip to the university campus in Bolshiye Koty; an excursion in the *taiga* (forests) with picnic. Also for an extra fee the Irkutsk Intourist office organizes shooting parties, including bear hunts.

ENGLISH-RUSSIAN VOCABULARY

ENGLISH-RUSSIAN
The Russian Alphabet

Category 1:
Russian Consonants Look
and Sound like English

Category 2:
Russian Consonants Look
Different from Their
English Equivalents

Russian Letter (Capital)	Russian Letter (Small)	English Letter	Russian Letter (Capital)	Russian Letter (Small)	English Letter
Б	б	b	Д	д	d
К	к	k	Ф	ф	f
М	м	m	Г	г	g
Т	т	t	Л	л	l
З	з	z	Н	н	n
			П	п	p
			Р	р	r
			С	с	s
			В	в	v
			Й	й	y

The most important phrase to know (one that may make it unnecessary to know any others) is: "Do you speak English?" — *Gavaree'te lee vy pa anglee'skee?* If the answer is "Nyet," then you may have recourse to the lists below:

EVERYDAY CONVERSATION

Please	Пожа́луйста	pazhah′lsta
Thank you	Спаси́бо	spasee′ba
Good	Хорошо́	kharasho′
Bad	Пло́хо	plo′kha
I	Я	ya
You	Вы	vy
He	Он	on

TOURIST VOCABULARY
Useful Phrases, Words and Signs

Category 3:
Russian Consonants Have
No English Equivalents   **The Russian Vowels**

Russian Letter (Capital)	Russian Letter (Small)	Sound	Russian Letter (Capital)	Russian Letter (Small)	Sound
Ч	ч	ch	А	а	ah
Х	х	kh	Я	я	yah
Ш	ш	sh	Э	э	eh
Щ	щ	shch	Е	е	yeh
Ц	ц	ts	Ы	ы	ih
Ж	ж	zh	И	и	i (ee)
	ь	soft sign	О	о	oh
			Ё	ё	yo
			У	у	u (oo)
			Ю	ю	yu

She	Она́	anah'
We	Мы	my
They	Они́	anee'
Yes	Да	da
No	Нет	nyet
Perhaps	Мо́жет быть	mo'zhet byt
I do not understand	Я не понима́ю	ya ne paneemah'yoo
Straight	Пря́мо	pryah'ma
Forward	Вперёд	fperyo't
Back	Наза́д	nazah't
To (on) the right	Напра́во	naprah'va
To (on) the left	Нале́во	nale'va
Hullo!	Здра́вствуйте!	zdrah'stvooite!

EVERYDAY CONVERSATION (continued)

Good morning!	Доброе утро!	do'braye oo'tra!
Good day (evening)!	Добрый день (вечер)!	do'bree den (ve'cher)!
Pleased to meet you!	Очень рад с вами познакомиться!	o'chen rat s vah'mee paznako'meetsa!
I am from USA (Britain)	Я приехал из США (Англии)	ya preeye'khal eez sshah' (ah'nglee ee)
I speak only English	Я говорю только по-английски.	ya gavaryoo' to'lka pa anglee'skee
Do you speak English?	Говорите ли вы по-английски?	gavaree'te lee vy pa anglee'skee?
Be so kind as to show (explain, translate)	Будьте добры, покажите (объясните, переведите)	boo'te do'bry, pakazhee'te (abyasnee'te, perevedee'te)
Excuse my poor pronunciation	Извините моё плохое произношение.	eezveenee'te mayo'pla-kho'ye praeeznashe'-nye
I beg your pardon	Простите.	prastee'te
I want to post a letter	Мне нужно отправить письмо.	mne noo'zhna atprah'-veet peesmo'
Postcard	Почтовая карточка	pachto'vaya kah'rtach-ka

AT THE HOTEL

What hotel shall we stay at?	В какой гостинице мы остановимся?	f kakoi' gahstee'neetse my astano'veemsya?
Please get me a taxi	Вызовите мне, пожалуйста, такси	vy'zaveete mne, pa-zhah'lsta, taksee'
Please have my bill ready	Приготовьте, пожалуйста, счёт	preegato'fte, pazhah'-lsta, shshot
First (second, third, fourth . . .) floor	Первый (второй, третий, четвёртый . . .) этаж	per'vee (ftaroi', tre'tee, chetvyo'rtee . . .) etah'sh
What do I do about my luggage?	Как поступить с багажом?	kak pastoopee't z baga-zho'm?

DAYS OF THE WEEK

Monday	Понедельник	panede'lneek
Tuesday	Вторник	fto'rneek
Wednesday	Среда	sredah'
Thursday	Четверг	chetve'rk
Friday	Пятница	pyah'tneetsa
Saturday	Суббота	soobo'ta
Sunday	Воскресенье	vaskrese'nye
Holiday, feast	Праздник	prah'zneek
Today	Сегодня	sevo'dnya
Tomorrow	Завтра	zah'ftra
Yesterday	Вчера	vcherah'

IN THE RESTAURANT

Give me the menu, please	Дайте, пожалуйста, меню	dai'te, pazhah'lsta, me-nyoo'
Bring me the bill, please	Дайте, пожалуйста, счёт	dai'te, pazhah'lsta, shshot

IN THE RESTAURANT (continued)

Please give us a	Да́йте, пожа́луйста,	dai'te, pazhah'lsta,
knife	нож	nosh
fork	ви́лку	vee'lkoo
spoon	ло́жку	lo'shkoo
glass	стака́н	stakah'n
plate	ме́лкую таре́лку	me'lkooyoo tare'lkoo

Drinks

cold water	холо́дной воды́	**khalo'dnoi vady'**
mineral water	минера́льной воды́	**meenerah'lnoi vady'**
grape, tomato juice	виногра́дного, тома́тного со́ка	**veenagrah'dnava, tamah'tnava so'ka**
whisky, vodka	ви́ски, во́дка	**vee'skee, vod'ka**
liqueur	ликёр	leekyo'r
lemonade	лимона́д	leemanah't
beer	пи́во	pee'va
tea, coffee, cocoa, milk	чай, ко́фе, кака́о,·молоко́	chai, ko'fe, kakah'o, malako'
fruit juice	со́ки	so'kee

Meat

steak	бифште́кс	beefshte'ks
roast beef	ро́стбиф	ro'stbeef
veal chops	отбивну́ю теля́чью котле́ту	atbeevnoo'yoo telyah'chyoo katle'too
pork chops	свину́ю котле́ту	sveenoo'yoo katle'too
ham	ветчину́	vecheenoo'
sausage	колбасу́	kalbasoo'

Poultry

chicken	цыплёнка	tsyplyo'nka
hazel-grouse	ря́бчика	ryah'pcheeka
partridge	куропа́тку	koorapah'tkoo
duck	у́тку	oo'tkoo

Fish

soft caviar	зерни́стой икры́	**zernee'stoi eekry'**
pressed caviar	па́юсной икры́	**pah'yoosnoi eekry'**
salmon	лососи́ны	**lasasee'ny**
cold sturgeon	холо́дной осетри́ны	**khalo'dnoi asetree'ny**

Vegetables

green peas	зелёный горо́шек	zelyo'nee garo'shek
radishes	реди́ску	redee'skoo
tomatoes	помидо́ры	**pameedo'ry**
potatoes	карто́шка	kar'to'shka

Desserts

cake	пиро́жное	peero'zhnaye
fruit	фру́ктов	froo'ktaf
pears	груш	groosh
mandarines	мандари́нов	mandaree'naf
grapes	виногра́ду	veenagrah'doo
bananas	бана́нов	banah'naf

Miscellaneous

white and rye bread	бе́лый и чёрный хлеб	be'lee ee cho'rnee khlep
butter	ма́сло	mah'sla
cheese	сыр	syr
soft-boiled eggs	яйца всмя́тку	yai'tsa fsmyah'tkoo
hard-boiled eggs	яйца вкруту́ю	yai'tsa fkrootoo'vʌʌ
an omelette	омле́т	amle't

SHOPPING

Description

good	хоро́ший	kharo'shee
bad	плохо́й	plakhoi'
beautiful	краси́вый	krasee'vee
dear	дорого́й	daragoi'
cheap	дешёвый	desho've
old	ста́рый	sta'ree
new	но́вый	no've

Colors

white	бе́лый	be'lee
black	чёрный	chyo'rnee
red	кра́сный	krah'snee
pink	ро́зовый	ro'zavee
orange	ора́нжевый	arah'nzhevee
yellow	жёлтый	zho'ltee
brown	кори́чневый	karee'chnevee
green	зелёный	zelyo'nee
light blue	голубо́й	galooboi'
blue	си́ний	see'nee
violet	фиоле́товый	feeale'tavee
grey	се́рый	se'ree
golden	золото́й	zalatoi'
silver	сере́бряный	sere'bryanee

In the Shop

Baker's	Бу́лочная	**boo'lachnaya**
Confectioner's	Конди́терская	**kandee'terskaya**
Food Store	Гастроно́м	gastrano'm
Grocer's	Бакале́я	bakale'ya
Delivery Counter	Стол зака́зов	stol zakah'zaf
Wine and Spirits	Ви́на — коньяки́	vee'na — kanyakee'
Fruit and Vegetables	Овощи — фру́кты	o'vashshee — froo'kty

NUMBERS

How many?	Ско́лько?	sko'lka?
1	оди́н	adee'n
2	два	dva
3	три	tree
4	четы́ре	chety're
5	пять	pyat
6	шесть	shest
7	семь	sem
8	во́семь	vo'sem
9	де́вять	de'vyat

NUMBERS (continued)

10	де́сять	de'syat
11	оди́ннадцать	adee'natsat
12	двена́дцать	**dvenah'tsat**
13	трина́дцать	**treenah'tsat**
14	четы́рнадцать	chety'rnatsat
15	пятна́дцать	pyatnah'tsat
16	шестна́дцать	shesnah'tsat
17	семна́дцать	semnah'tsat
18	восемна́дцать	vasemnah'tsat
19	девятна́дцать	devyatnah'tsat
20	два́дцать	dvah'tsat
30	три́дцать	tree'tsat
40	со́рок	so'rak
50	пятьдеся́т	pyadesyah't
60	шестьдеся́т	shezdesyah't
70	се́мьдесят	se'mdesyat
80	во́семьдесят	vo'semdesyat
90	девяно́сто	deveno'sta
100	сто	sto
1000	ты́сяча	ty'syacha

INFORMATION SIGNS

Toilet (Gentlemen) (Ladies)	Туале́т (М) (Ж)	tooale't
No Smoking!	Не кури́ть!	ne kooree't!
Taxi rank	Стоя́нка такси́	stayah'nka taksee'
Entrance	Вход	fkhot
Exit	Вы́ход	vy'khat
No exit	Вы́хода нет	vy'khada net
Emergency exit	Запасно́й вы́ход	zapasnoi' vy'khat
Stop!	Стоп!	stop!
Pedestrian crossing	Перехо́д	perekho't
Bus stop	Остано́вка авто́буса	astano'fka afto'boosa
tram	тролле́йбуса	tralei'boosa
trolleybus	трамва́я	tramvah'ya
Underground	Метро́ (М)	metro'
To the Trains	К поезда́м	k payezdah'm
Way Out	Вы́ход в го́род	vy'khat v go'rat
Ticket Machines	Ка́ссы-автома́ты	kah'ssy-aftamah'ty
On, Off	Включён, не включён	fklyoocho'n, ne fklyoo-cho'n
Telephone	Телефо́н	telefo'n
Telegraph Office	Телегра́ф	telegrah'f
Post Office	По́чта	po'chta
Chemist's	Апте́ка	apte'ka
Newspapers, magazines	Газе́ты, журна́лы	gaze'ty, zhoornah'ly
Hairdresser's	Парикма́херская	pareekmah'kherskaya
Café	Кафе́	kafe'
Restaurant	Ресто́ра́н	restarah'n
Dining Room	Столо́вая	stalo'vaya
Snack Bar	Заку́сочная	zakoo'sachnaya
Lift	Лифт	leeft
Booking offices	Ка́ссы	kah'ssy
Inquiry office	Спра́вочное бюро́	sprah'vachnaye byooro'
Waiting room	Зал ожида́ния	zal azheedah'neeya

INDEX

INDEX

In this Index the following code has been used:
(S) after a place name indicates a health resort or spa; E before a page number indicates entertainment – opera, ballet, theater or cinema (except for Moscow and Leningrad where they are given in more detail); M stands for museums and art galleries (except, again, for Moscow and Leningrad); H indicates hotels and R restaurants.

A reference to churches does not necessarily mean that they are used for services; many churches in the U.S.S.R. have been converted into museums. For details of services see the relevant Practical Information sections.

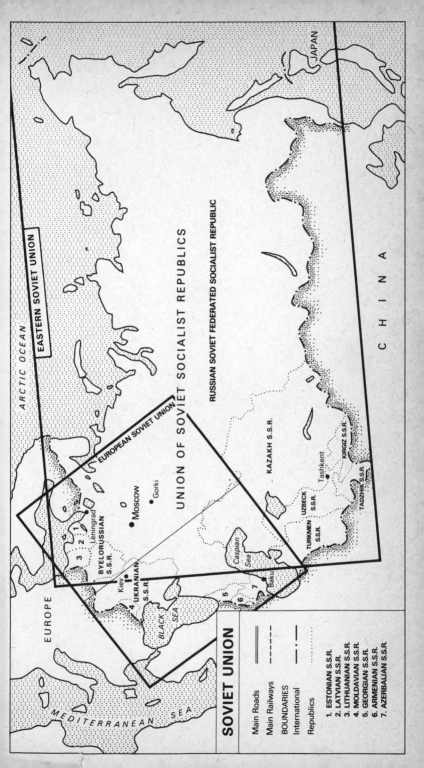

ARCTIC OCEAN

EASTERN SOVIET UNION

JAPAN

EUROPEAN SOVIET UNION

UNION OF SOVIET SOCIALIST REPUBLICS

RUSSIAN SOVIET FEDERATED SOCIALIST REPUBLIC

C H I N A

EUROPE

Leningrad

Moscow

Gorki

BYELORUSSIAN
S.S.R.

KAZAKH S.S.R.

Kiev

UKRANIAN
S.S.R.

Caspian
Sea

Tashkent

UZBECK
S.S.R.

KIRGIZ S.S.R.

TURKMEN
S.S.R.

TADZHIK S.S.R.

Baku

BLACK
SEA

MEDITERRANEAN SEA

SOVIET UNION

Main Roads	———
Main Railways	– – –
BOUNDARIES	
International	–·–·–
Republics	·········

1. ESTONIAN S.S.R.
2. LATVIAN S.S.R.
3. LITHUANIAN S.S.R.
4. MOLDAVIAN S.S.R.
5. GEORGIAN S.S.R.
6. ARMENIAN S.S.R.
7. AZERBAIJAN S.S.R.

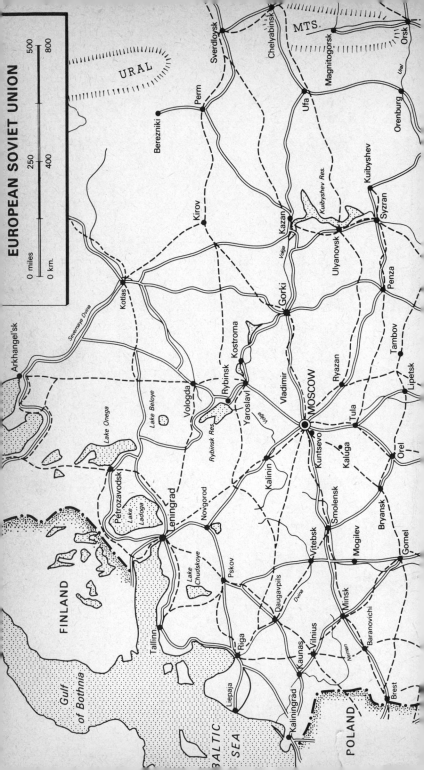

EUROPEAN SOVIET UNION

0 miles 250 500
0 km. 400 800

URAL

MTS.

Arkhangel'sk

Berezniki

Perm

Sverdlovsk

Chelyabinsk

Orsk

Magnitogorsk

Ufa

Orenburg

Kirov

Kazan

Kuibyshev

Kuibyshev Res.

Ulyanovsk

Syzran

Kotlas

Severnaya Dvina

Penza

Lake Onega

Lake Beloye

Vologda

Rybinsk

Kostroma

Gorki

Tambov

Lake Ladoga

Petrozavodsk

Rybinsk Res.

Yaroslavl

Vladimir

Ryazan

Lipetsk

Leningrad

Novgorod

Kalinin

MOSCOW

Kuntsevo

Kaluga

Tula

Orel

FINLAND

Lake Chudskoye

Pskov

Smolensk

Bryansk

Gulf of Bothnia

Tallinn

Riga

Daugavpils

Dvina

Vitebsk

Mogilev

Gomel

BALTIC SEA

Liepaja

Kaunas

Vilnius

Minsk

Baranovichi

Kaliningrad

Neman

Brest

POLAND

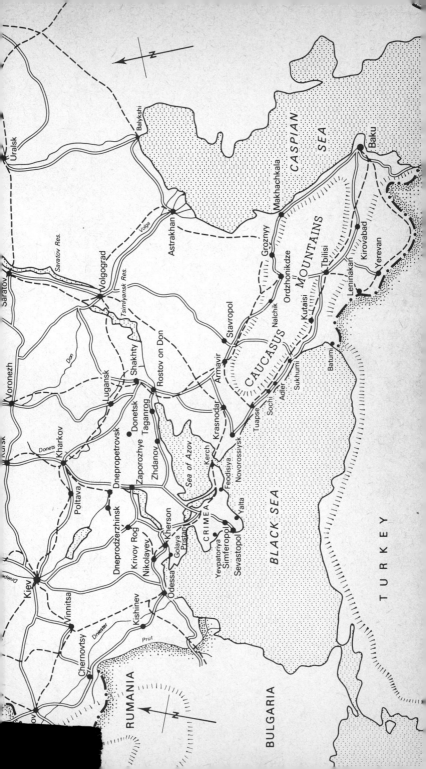

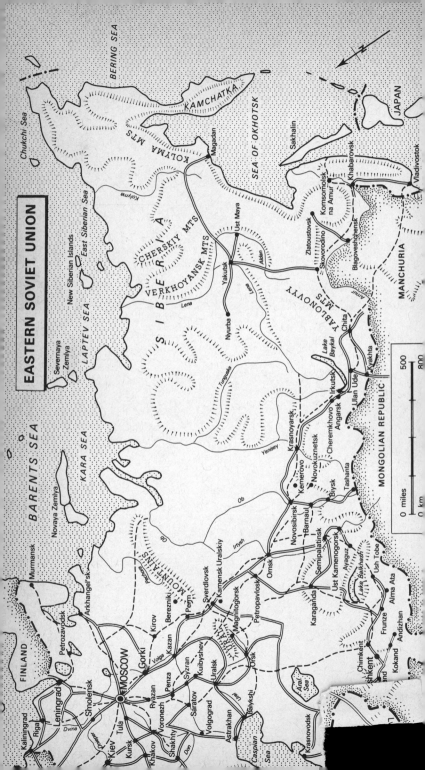